OFF TARGET

OFF TARGET

AMERICA'S GUIDED BOMBS, MISSILES AND DRONES 1917-1950

WILLIAM WOLF

FONTHILL

Fonthill Media Language Policy

Fonthill Media publishes in the international English language market. One language edition is published worldwide. As there are minor differences in spelling and presentation, especially with regard to American English and British English, a policy is necessary to define which form of English to use. The Fonthill Policy is to use the form of English native to the author. William Wolf was born and educated in the United States; therefore American English has been adopted in this publication.

Fonthill Media Limited
Fonthill Media LLC
www.fonthillmedia.com
office@fonthillmedia.com

First published in the United Kingdom and the United States of America 2021

British Library Cataloguing in Publication Data:
A catalogue record for this book is available from the British Library

ISBN 978-1-78155-816-4

Typeset in 10pt on 13pt Sabon
Printed and bound in England

Foreword

Over the years—from the early rudimentary biplane drones concocted by Lawrence and Elmer Sperry and Charles Kettering to today's ultra-sophisticated Unmanned Aerial Vehicles, better known by their acronym UAVs—the development of unmanned drones, guided missiles, and guided bombs has been dependent on the development of accurate control systems. It was not until the last several decades of computer development that the military role of unmanned aircraft systems has progressed at such unprecedented levels that for the first time, by 2012, the USAF trained more UAV pilots than conventional jet fighter pilots. Today, when people think of the drone, it is first as one of the millions sold to civilians who use them several times and ultimately lose interest or wreck them. These remotely piloted military drones execute reconnaissance and attack missions, but are by no means unmanned as they require more men (and women) plus multiple computers and electronics to operate than a conventional military aircraft, but no human, except the enemy, is in harm's way. The American public is mesmerized by the U.S. Air Force's release of the amazing videos transmitted from aboard military drones, showing the remarkably accurate destruction of terrorist leaders in the Middle East,

Of course, it was the well-publicized and well-known World War II German missile programs that laid the groundwork for the post-war guided weapons age. America's role in the development of guided systems and weapons from its 1917 World War I beginnings into post-World War II is largely unknown, yet it paved the way for the country to integrate German R&D and then successfully contest Soviet developments during the Cold War. This book is the first comprehensive examination of the subject.

Acknowledgments

My lifelong hobby has been World War II aerial combat, and over the past forty-five years, I have collected over 27,000 books and magazines, along with nearly 2,000 reels of vintage World War II microfilm. I probably have nearly every book written on World War II aviation and complete collections of every aviation magazine published since 1939. Also included in my collection are thousands of aviation unit histories; intelligence reports; pilot, crew, flight, and training manuals; and technical, structural, and maintenance manuals for aircraft ordnance, armament, engines, and equipment. My extensive microfilm collection includes thousands of intelligence and technical reports; hundreds of USAF, USN, and USMC group and squadron histories and After Combat Reports; complete Japanese Monograph series; U.S. Strategic Bombing Surveys; and USAF Historical Studies.

Individual thanks go to Brett Stolle, NMUSAF Archivist at Wright-Patterson, Ohio, for patiently finding pertinent documents and photos. Andrew Boehly, Archivist at the Pima Air and Space Museum, Tucson, Arizona. A belated thank you goes to Judy Endicott of the Albert F. Simpson Historical Research Center, Maxwell AFB, Alabama; Ms. Endicott was of great help during my ten-day expedition to that facility in the mid-1980s to collect materials and hundreds of photos I have used in this and past books. Thanks also go to the personnel at the Air Force Museum Archives at Wright-Patterson, Dayton, Ohio, and the Library of Congress, National Archives, and the Ferndale Photographic facility, Washington, D.C., which I visited in the 1980s and '90s to copy thousands of photos and documents before Photoshop and digital scanning. Of particular importance to this project were the many previously untapped microfilm Secret and Confidential Guided Missile and Guided Bomb Case Studies and the photos and movie still photos I was able to secure from them (see Bibliography).

The author wishes that every person who contributed photos and materials during the past forty-five years could be specifically mentioned. Over the years, the origin of many of the thousands of photos and materials I have copied at government and military sources and from private individuals have become obscured, and I apologize in advance if some sources are miscredited. The Secret and Confidential nature of the guided missile, bomb, and drone projects described limited the number and quality of available photos used in this book and because of their age and sources, especially many of those photos copied from microfilm, movie stills, and poor paper and print quality of wartime publications.

Caption Credit Abbreviations

AAF:	Army Air force
AFSHRC:	Albert F. Simpson Historical Research Center
LoC:	Library of Congress
NA:	National Archives
NMUSAF:	National Museum of the USAF
PASM:	Pima Air and Space Museum
RAE:	Royal Aircraft Establishment
RCA:	Radio Corporation of America
SNASM:	Smithsonian National Air & Space Museum
USAF:	United States Air Force
USMC:	United States Marine Corps
USN:	United States Navy

Contents

1 Pilotless Weapons: Early Development 1917: Pearl Harbor

Fathers of Remote Control

Remote control is the basis of guided bombs, missiles, or drones, and Serbian-American Nicola Tesla and Brit Archibald Low are considered the Fathers of Remote Control.

Nicola Tesla

A recognized genius and rival of Thomas Edison, Nicola Tesla was an inventor, electrical and mechanical engineer, and pioneer of electrical technology; he is best known for his significant contributions to the design of the modern alternating current (AC) electricity supply system. Among his many achievements was his design and development of a working drone in 1898, which is the original prototype of all modern UAVs and precision-guided weapons. Tesla's drone was a 4-foot-long, remotely-controlled, propeller-driven boat powered by lead-acid batteries and an electric drive motor. The vessel was to be maneuvered alongside its target using commands received from a wireless remote-control transmitter and telegraph keys that shifted electrical contacts on the boat that adjusted settings for the rudder and propeller. Once the boat was in position, a signal would be sent to detonate an explosive charge contained within the boat's forward compartment. Tesla included a secure communications link in the weapons guidance system, between the controller and the boat, to ensure that control could be sustained even in the presence of electronic countermeasures. Tesla introduced his Teleautomaton at Madison Square Garden, and while it certainly impressed the public, the Navy thought it to be too fragile for combat use. In his patent application, Tesla predicted drone warfare by claiming that, by reason of its certain and unlimited destructive power, it will tend to bring about and maintain permanent peace among all nations. Tesla's creation can be considered the birth of robotics and remote control, though he is seldom recognized for this accomplishment because his concept was so advanced for its time that those who observed it could not envisage its practical applications.

Nicola Tesla. (*NA*)

Archibald Low

The genius of twenty-six-year-old Londoner Archibald Low first became evident in May 1914 when he developed an early forerunner of future television, which he called TeleVista. Low was unable to continue this research due to the outbreak of World War I, as during August 1914, he volunteered for the Royal Flying Corps. Soon, Captain Low was named to head the RCFs Experimental Works Unit, which included the elite wireless unit. The unit was assigned to develop a remotely controlled aircraft, proposed both for defense against Zeppelins and to be used as a flying bomb. To disguise its purpose, it was referred to as the Aerial Target (AT). By late 1916, a radio-controlled, pilotless aircraft with an explosive warhead was designed and ready for development for the anti-Zeppelin role, during which it was to be controlled from the ground. While in its flying bomb role, it was to be controlled from an accompanying manned aircraft. The delicate radio equipment, all relays, the receiver, and the key system was installed into a wooden box, suspended on rubber mounts and covered by a glass lid. Low's attempt to build the aircraft from spare parts was unsuccessful; however, Low's concept attracted the renowned Sopwith Company as well as Ruston Proctor & Co. Ltd. During 1916, the Sopwith AT was completed with full servo control but never flew as it was subsequently damaged while in its hangar and abandoned. At Ruston Proctor, Henry Folland, the designer of the S.E.5 fighter, and his assistant, H. E. Preston of the Royal Aircraft Factory, equipped six Ruston Procter ATs with Low's radio-guidance equipment and numerous radio aerials placed vertically down the fuselage sides and across the wing's chord. The AT was a small, 500-pound, shoulder wing (22-foot span) monoplane powered by a two-cylinder

Archibald Low. (*NA*)

AT Rustin Proctor. Inspired by Low's design, the remotely-controlled drone crashed on each of its three testing attempts during July 1917 trials and the project was cancelled. (*NA*)

35-hp. Gnat engine. The first flight, on March 21, 1917, was attended by a large crowd of generals who watched the AT be launched by compressed air from a truck bed and then witnessed Low demonstrate control before the AT's engine failed. During full trials on July 6, 1917, an AT crashed after radio control was briefly in effect, while on July 25, another AT was tested but failed to launch and crashed. Three days later, a third attempt was made and resulted in yet another crash when the engine failed just after take-off. The project was soon abandoned as High Command evaluated it as having limited military value.

Low's inventions during World War I were, generally, too advanced to be appreciated by his own government. However, the Germans did appreciate Low's potential and attempted two assassinations on his life; later, the Nazis improved upon his 1918 rocket-guidance system for their World War II V-1 flying bomb, the first cruise missile.

Sperry Aerial Torpedo/Flying Bomb

On June 18, 1914, fifty-seven specially-equipped aircraft were ready to compete in the French *Concours de la Securité en Aéroplane* (Airplane Safety Competition), held along the Seine River. The last competitor was American Lawrence Sperry, the son of the brilliant Elmer Sperry, the CEO of the Elmer A. Sperry Company, and the holder of more than seventy patents. Elmer Sperry had developed the large gyrocompasses installed on more than thirty American warships, and Lawrence developed a lightweight version of the gyroscope that could be connected to aircraft control surfaces to maintain the flight axes. While most entries highlighted improvements in aircraft technology, Sperry's Automatic Airplane was the only one equipped with a gyroscopic stabilizer device, intended to improve stability and control. Sperry's gyro was mounted on a single-engined Curtiss C-2 biplane with a hydroplane fuselage. Sperry, accompanied by his new French mechanic and assistant, Emil Cachin, flew the Curtiss down the Seine, immediately past the judge's stand. Sperry then engaged his stabilizer device, extricated himself from the shoulder yoke that controlled the C-2s ailerons, and passed with both his arms held high, clearly not handling the controls. The Curtiss continued on its straight and stable flight, but Sperry was not finished demonstrating his gyro. During his second pass, with Sperry's hands still off the controls, Cachin clambered out about 7 feet on the starboard wing. While Cachin moved out on the wing, his weight caused the aircraft to briefly bank, but the gyroscope-equipped stabilizer immediately corrected the attitudinal change, and the Curtiss continued down the river. During Sperry's triumphant third pass over the judge's stand, Cachin was on one wing and Sperry on the other, with the pilot's seat empty, easily garnering Sperry the 50,000 francs ($10,000/nearly $275,000 in 2020) first prize and immediate fame.

Once World War I began, Elmer Sperry, in conjunction with the RAF, linked his gyrostabilizer control system to a bombsight, which maintained the aircraft's steady course while a bomb aimer aligned the target in his sights. During April 1915, Peter

Lawrence Sperry (left), accompanied by his new French mechanic and assistant, Emil Cachin, flew their Curtiss C-2 in the June 1914 French Airplane Safety Competition. (*AFSHRC*)

The Curtiss C-2 biplane with a hydroplane fuselage, equipped with a gyroscopic stabilizer device, intended to improve stability and control. (*AFSHRC*)

Hewitt, an American electrical engineer who had developed the first mercury-vapor lamp in 1901 and early radio related devices, met with Elmer Sperry whose gyro-stabilization work had impressed him. Hewitt proposed his aerial torpedo concept, a pilotless aircraft carrying an explosive charge to a preselected target under automatic control and offered to allocate funds to Sperry to develop the necessary gyro-stabilization equipment. Sperry agreed and after consultation with his board of directors, requested $3,000, which Hewitt provided.

Development of an automatic control device was begun in June, by mounting the 1915-model Aeroplane Stabilizer and a new azimuth gyro in the Sperry Company's Curtiss flying boat. The automatic control equipment was tested while flying from the Bayside Yacht Club to the East River near the Sperry facility. These controls were also installed and tested in a twin-engined Curtiss biplane for test flights from several Long Island, New York, airfields. Sperry kept the purpose of the tests secret; onlookers assumed the aircraft were testing another of Sperry's stabilizers.

The Sperrys and their associates at the Sperry Amityville, New York, facility incorporated a steering gyro with a stabilizer gyro to create one of the world's first automatic pilot systems, which could easily be adapted to a piloted aircraft. That year, Lawrence Sperry filed a patent for an aerial torpedo, including the following features:

1. A gyrostabilizer to maintain the aircraft's level attitude.
2. An automatic steering gyro to maintain the aircraft on a preset heading.
3. A barometer to indicate the cruise altitude, causing the aircraft to level off.
4. A wind-driven electrical generator to provide power for the gyro motors and the servomotors that moved the aerial torpedo's flight control surfaces.
5. An engine revolution counter to determine when the aircraft was to cut power and dive into its target.

These items were to be installed in a pilotless aircraft, which was to be catapulted or flown from the water, and then to climb to a predetermined altitude, fly a preset course, and, after flying a preset distance, drop its bombs or dive into the ground.

During the spring of 1916, Sperry aerial torpedo operations, with Lawrence Sperry as director, were transferred to a more remote location at the Sperry field station at Amityville where a hangar was constructed on the beach of Great South Bay. During flight tests using a flying boat, the azimuth unit, adapted from a torpedo gyro, proved to be inadequate and another, heavier torpedo gyro was exchanged. An automatic altitude control and an air log were assembled and installed to complete the aerial torpedo controls. The altitude control was a sealed bellows apparatus that, preset on the ground, adjusted the aircraft's pitch control in its search for the desired pressure altitude. The air log was a counter that gave an estimate of the distance flown by counting the revolutions of a small propeller. Once equipped with a complete set of controls, the aerial torpedo was ready to take-off on a preset azimuth heading, climb to the chosen altitude, and cruise there until it traveled the correct distance, where it was to dive and explode on the target.

By mid-August 1916, Lawrence Sperry had automatically directed the flying boat off the water about a dozen times and had completed flights of good accuracy up to

Elmer Sperry. (*AFSHRC*)

Peter Hewitt. (*AFSHRC*)

30 miles. When the flying boat approached its preset distance, it automatically went into a steep glide, simulating the final dive of the ultimate, unmanned aerial torpedo, at which time the onboard human pilot then took over before it flew into the water.

The next step was to present the aerial torpedo to the Naval Consulting Board, which had been established on October 7, 1915 to advise the secretary of the Navy on scientific and technical issues. Fortunately, both Hewitt and Sperry were members of the Committee on Aeronautics and Aeronautical Motors of this board, and in this position were able to persuade the Chief of the Bureau of Ordnance, R/Adml. Ralph Earle to order Lt. T. W. Wilkinson of the Bureau of Ordnance to observe and report on a demonstration.

On September 5, Wilkinson and several Sperry observers assembled at the Amityville hangar, but the demonstration had to be postponed for three days due to engine problems. After another postponement, finally, on September 12, 1916, the demonstration took place, although the weather conditions were unfavorable, with a 20-knot wind and choppy water on Great South Bay. Sperry directed the flying boat from the water, placed it under automatic control, after which it climbed to the preset altitude and maintained this altitude until the end of the preset time, after which it dived sharply, the onboard pilot then took control and completed a safe landing.

Wilkinson's report gave a favorable account of the AT in considering its application to naval warfare, as he concluded that it could be developed to be as accurate as gunfire with a better range capability and should have a great moral effect. Nonetheless, he concluded, "It is doubtful that these machines are suitable for the naval service." R/Adml. Earle, then questioned the inability of the craft to change direction after launching, "the assumed target being, of course, moving ships.... It must contend with shell fire as a rival. The manifestly greater speed of the latter would point to the uselessness of this invention for naval purposes as at present developed."

By this time, Hewitt's original $3,000 and $26,000 of Sperry's own funds had been exhausted causing them to appeal to American military services to continue the project. Wilkinson's report had suggested that the AT might be of service to the Army as he concluded that the bomb could not be perfected to the necessary degree of accuracy required for hitting a moving target at sea; he recommended that the development be sponsored by the Army as that service might find it useful against large fixed military targets. Although discouraged by the Navy's negative report, but fortified by the success of the summer tests, Elmer Sperry corresponded with Lt. Col. George Squire of the Army Signal Corps, detailing the aerial torpedo and related the testing successes, but Squire made no commitment. Afterward, several invitations to Signal Corps officers had to be canceled due to mechanical difficulties with the flying boat or its engine. On November 19, Maj. William Mitchell (the future famed air power advocate, Gen. "Billy" Mitchell) was scheduled to attend a demonstration, but he did not appear. Several days later, Lawrence Sperry had an accident in the flying boat, which shut down the AT Program during the winter of 1916–1917.

Then, on April 6, 1917, America entered the Great War, and eight days later, during a New York City meeting, the Naval Consulting Board organized a board consisting of Capt. W. S. Smith, USN, senior member; Naval Constructor Jerome Hunsaker; and USN Lts. G. De Chevalier, W. G. Childs, and T. S. Wilkinson. This board was to determine further action to be taken by the Navy and recommended that the Navy conduct experimental work on automatically controlled aircraft, carrying high explosives, capable of being initially directed and, thereafter, automatically managed.

On May 17, 1917, at a dinner meeting in Navy Secretary Josephus Daniels' home attended by the Naval Consulting Board, Daniels approved the board's recommendation, directing the Bureau of Ordnance to allocate $100,000 and the Bureaus of Construction and Repair and Steam Engineering each to allocate $50,000 in support of the project. Daniels granted final approval for the project on May 22, 1917 and a contract was negotiated with the Sperry Company to develop two types of the weapon: one for wireless control and the other for completely automatic operation. The Navy and Curtiss agreed to provide five Curtiss N-9H seaplanes (later six) with landplane landing equipment. The Sperry Company was to provide testing grounds and new hangers at Copiague, Long Island, along with such technical staff as the Consulting Board might direct, and six sets of the Sperry automatic control apparatus, which were to be built at Copiague.

Above left: Lt. Col. George Squire of the Army Signal Corps. (*AAC*)

Above right: Josephus Daniels, Navy secretary. (*USN*)

Right: R/Adml. Ralph Earle, USN, chief of the Bureau of Ordnance. (*USN*)

On June 15, old hand Cdr. B. B. McCormick, USN, Ret'd (since 1913), was brought back by Adml. Earle and assigned to the Sperry plant as Naval Project Supervisor in full command of the experiments with the intention of completing them rapidly so quantity production could complete 1,000 by March 1918. McCormick would be considered an excellent choice, continuing to be understanding and supportive during the many failures to come.

The Curtiss N-9H was a seaplane version of the famous Curtiss JN-4D Jenny trainer used by the Air Service during the war. To complete the seaplane conversion, a single large central pontoon was mounted below the fuselage, with a small float fitted under each wingtip. These changes required a 10-foot increase in wingspan to compensate for the additional weight. The six Copiague-built Sperry automatic control units were flown by flying boat to Amityville for N-9 installation. The first three N-9s, arriving in June, were to have the older, four-gyro units installed since these aircraft were completed and available at the plant. The remaining three N-9s arrived in July, along with a nine-man Marine security force as the Navy considered the program highly classified.

The previous 1916 tests had been conducted using a four-gyroscope unit for pitch and roll reference, but when new tests took place, they determined that the azimuth gyro to be inadequate. Sperry and Hewitt then decided to return to basics and conducted a series of flight tests using the Washington, D.C., Navy Yard wind tunnel to evaluate the N-9 stabilization system, after which it was abandoned and was to be replaced by a new control unit using a single, heavy torpedo gyro. McCormick requested that Adml. Earle divert three heavy torpedo gyros, awaiting shipment to Newport, Rhode Island, to his program. It is evident that Earle considered Sperry's program of some importance as the request was immediately approved.

When the second N-9 joined the first, tests could be made more frequently, but more difficulties were discovered more quickly. The air log was found to be not repeatable in operation, as for most daily tests, as the distance setting for the second test had to be altered to account for the inaccurate distance of the first test but these alterations only occasionally improved performance. After flying for two months, the N-9s air log mechanisms were finally sent to the Washington Navy Yard wind tunnel for calibration, resulting in a significant reduction in range errors.

The third major difficulty was one of method rather than design. The accepted technique for flight trials was to position the aircraft accurately in azimuth, uncage the gyros, and, with the altitude and range preset in the control unit, begin the take-off run. The automatic controls were then engaged just as the aircraft was leaving the ground. Previously, the onboard pilot was to concentrate on not allowing the aircraft to veer in case the azimuth gyro tumbled. This tumbling occurred more than occasionally, due to turbulence after take-off, after which the pilot usually flew the heading himself and allowed the remainder of the system to perform its functions. When the preset distance was flown, a small marker buoy was dropped to denote the air log's test flight's end as the N-9s were not equipped to dive. So many flights were compromised by the loss of azimuth control on take-off that McCormick requested that Sperry develop an automatic launching apparatus to get the aircraft into the air without disturbing the azimuth gyro. While this request ultimately resulted in catapult launches, they were never used for the daily N-9 flights.

These first N-9 flights were flown toward the Fire Island Lighthouse, Long Island, which was a very short-range journey of about 6 miles. As the equipment was adjusted or modified to produce an improved performance, mainly in azimuth, the range increased from 10 miles in two weeks to 17 miles in three weeks, but it was not until three months that 30 miles was attained, which was still 20 miles less than the intended 50 miles. As the range increased, the course was altered to the eastward to keep it safely over water for its entire journey.

Sperry's trials were being conducted with N-9s, but the aerial torpedo concept could only be achieved with a pilotless craft. Soon after the Navy became involved, Lawrence Sperry wanted to design an aircraft flying 60 mph. faster than the N-9 and to have it built by an outside company. At the end of September 1917, McCormick informed the Navy that Sperry was eager to order two aerial torpedo examples from Curtiss whose practical design was for a very small aircraft with an empty weight of 950 pounds but able to carry a 1,000-pound useful load at a speed of 90 mph. When Adml. Earle visited the Sperry factory and Copiague field on September 29 to assess the program, he witnessed four successful N-9 flights where upon Sperry proposed his new aerial torpedo airframe to Earle as the flying bomb. Earle then decided that this four-month N-9 test phase had been successful enough to warrant the beginning of a new accelerated phase of the program and get it into production.

Earle sanctioned the new project and two days later, Elmer Sperry prepared a memorandum advocating immediate and comprehensive testing of the azimuth gyros in the N-9s to determine whether the design of a new, larger, more powerful component was required for the longer ranges. He also directed overtime on the new control units ultimately intended for the pilotless aircraft.

On October 16, Sperry ordered five Speed Scout-type flying bomb aircraft from Curtiss, three with engines at $10,000 each and two without engines at $7,000 each. The first new airframe was to be delivered within thirty days and the others were to follow immediately. Therefore, it was essential to test these control units in the flying boat before the new pilotless airframes arrived at Amityville for testing. In January 1918, five more airframes, with engines, would be ordered.

The first flying bomb was received at Copiague on November 10, 1917, six days ahead of schedule. By the end of the month, the automatic controls were installed and the flying bomb was ready for launching. However, while the automatic controls had functioned suitably in the large, slow, sluggish N-9 flying boat, their control of the small, fast, responsive flying bomb, which had never been flown, was an unknown before its first test.

A launching system was also required as the design of these early systems of radio control envisioned control of the flying bomb only after it was airborne, which could best be accomplished by catapulting. The flying bomb needed to be robust enough to withstand the required rapid catapult acceleration while having pronounced inherent stability. Moreover, the automatic control system had to function during the rapid launching acceleration. In his design of a new catapult launching system, Sperry

Above: Curtiss N-9H was a seaplane version of the famous Curtiss JN-4D trainer. (*USN*)

Left: Lt. Theodore "Spuds" Ellyson, first Navy officer designated as "Naval Aviator No. 1," was an early test pilot. (*USN*)

Sperry Flying Bomb. (*AFSHRC*)

borrowed from a previous launching device. During 1911, Lt. Theodore "Spuds" Ellyson (the first Navy officer, designated as Naval Aviator No. 1) and John Towers (future admiral and Chief of the Bureau of Aeronautics 1939–1942), while visiting the Hammondsport, New York, Curtiss' Lake Kueka facility, developed a method of launching a seaplane. It was a heavy, inclined cable leading from the top of a pole down to the beach. The underside of the seaplane hull was grooved to ride on the cable and two smaller cables supported the wing tips until the aircraft had adequate speed to maintain lateral equilibrium. On September 7, while Ellyson successfully flew the seaplane off the wire, the catapult was found unsatisfactory for unstable shipboard use and was abandoned until Sperry asked Curtiss to develop and build another catapult for his flying bomb program.

On December 1, the flying bomb, perched on a platform 30 feet above the ground, was fastened to a heavy 400-foot cable attached to the platform with its wings balanced on two auxiliary cables. With its engine running, the flying bomb moved off the platform and began its slide down the cable but tilted to one side, leaned heavily on the wing wire, turned up on its nose, with the cables slicing through the wings, causing the flying bomb to fall to the ground. The damaged airframe was returned to the Curtiss Garden City plant for repair and new wings. Meanwhile, a catapult carriage was devised and was run up and down the cable to perfect the operation and simultaneously Sperry was authorized to design a new launcher using a dropping weight to propel a launching car on a track.

On December 7, the rehabilitated flying bomb was again raised to the upper end of the cable. The catapult functioned successfully, but as the aircraft accelerated down the wire, the upper wing's leading edge crumbled. The aircraft labored into the air, but then fell back to ground and stopped less than 200 feet from the end of the cable. The damaged flying bomb was again returned to Garden City where stronger wings were installed. Meanwhile, the wire launcher was abandoned for a conventional tracked catapult, powered by a dropping weight.

On December 21, the re-rehabbed flying bomb was positioned on the car of the new catapult, ready for its third attempt to fly. The car ran on a 150-foot track and was propelled by a 6,000-pound weight falling about 30 feet, which, with the flying bombs engine running, would produce an expected speed of 50 mph. at the end of the track. With the flying bomb's engine running, the weight was released, but the car slipped out ahead of the aircraft and was hit by the propeller blades. Before the propeller broke, the flying bomb tipped up on its nose and one wing and rolled over, becoming an unrepairable wreck, from which the automatic controls and the engine could be salvaged. The second flying bomb was scheduled to arrive during the next week.

This third failure cast doubts on the catapult's efficacy and the flying proficiency of the flying bomb. As for the catapult problem, McCormick requested that the bureau direct an expert on shipboard catapults to evaluate their equipment and that Curtiss send an engineer to assist in the next test. Despite these failures, the Sperry Company continued its work on the radio control problem, and on December 18, 1917 applied for its first patent in this field that would be issued as U.S. Patent No. 1,792,938.

The second and third flying bombs arrived soon after Christmas. Unlike the first, which had a boat-like hull to expedite recovery after a water landing, these flying bombs were supported on pairs of skids. On January 14, 1918, with the catapult expert and Curtiss engineer attending, the second flying bomb ready for launching. It had no warhead ballast, but the Curtiss engineer recommended that a 40-pound weight be installed in the tail. The engine was started and the car released and the catapult quickly accelerated the flying bomb to flying speed. As it left the car, its elevators were fully deflected downward but it pulled up into a steep climb then swung sharply to the left, stalled, side slipped, and plunged into the ground on its nose and left wing and became a total loss. On January 17, the third flying bomb, with 20 pounds of ballast in its tail and equipped with ice runners on its skids, was to take-off on the ice of Great South Bay off Long Island. An automatically-controlled flight of 200 feet was made, but the elevator appeared to have insufficient movement for adequate control, and at the end of the run, the flying bomb nosed over, breaking its propeller, skids, lower wing, and fuselage. The badly damaged third airframe was sent to Garden City for repairs, where, at McCormick's insistence, temporary controls and a seat were installed in the warhead compartment, so it could also be flown by a pilot.

On February 6, the refurbished flying bomb was flown on a short flight from the ice by pilot Lawrence Sperry, but when the autopilot took control, it rolled the aircraft into the ground, causing slight damage. The next day, again piloted by Sperry and loaded to its designed gross weight, the flying bomb hit a bank of soft snow just as it was lifting into the air. After making two complete somersaults, the Bomb came to a stop, a total loss, with only the engine, radiator, and pilot Lawrence Sperry undamaged.

Auxiliary controls were quickly installed in the fourth flying bomb and piloted flights were resumed with the automatic controls engaged while in the air, and the results recorded to determine any necessary fixes. It was soon determined that the servomotor gear ratios used for the N-9s were inefficient for use in the much more responsive flying bomb, and drums nearly twice as large were installed. The directional and lateral controls were satisfactory, but the flying bomb experienced excessive pitching when the longitudinal control was engaged. Testing continued until two weeks after the manned flights begun, the fourth flying bomb ran into an open water area in the ice during a landing run and turned over in the shallow water.

The next catapult launching was scheduled for March 6 to be a test of the catapult and newly modified airframe rather than the automatic controls. The launching was from an impulse-type catapult powered by a 5,000-pound concrete slab dropping 30 feet and transferring its motion to the catapult car through a system of cables and pulleys. The flying bomb left the catapult car effortlessly and flew off on a straight, steady climb until the engine was throttled by the air log set at 1,000 yards. It then glided, turning slowly to the right, until it struck the surface of the bay, where it settled upright in 3 feet of water, only damaging its wings. At last, a flying bomb flight could be considered a success.

The next launch was made a month later, April 7, carrying a full load of 1,025 pounds. The catapult functioned flawlessly, but when the aircraft left the car at the end of the track, it did not gain any altitude and, after a short distance, hit the ground and was struck off as a total loss.

The persevering McCormick became discouraged by the chronic flying bomb failures and before further tests, requested the assistance of prominent Naval Constructor Cdr. Jerome Hunsaker to help out by offering some intelligent criticism of the Curtiss non-intelligent design. However, Hunsaker was currently unavailable due to obligations to Navy aircraft research and production programs. As an alternative to Hunsaker and the catapult, a Marmon automobile chassis was equipped with a Curtiss OX aircraft engine, giving it a maximum speed of 90 mph., which was to be used to tune the flying bomb's automatic controls, to test its aerodynamics, and to measure its lifting capabilities. The flying bomb's landing gear was replaced with the N-9s sled-type runners and a frame was devised to mount it on top the Marmon, creating an improvised moving outdoor wind tunnel. While speeding along the Long Island Motor Parkway, Sperry adjusted the flight controls to their optimum settings, determined that the fuselage needed to be lengthened by 2 feet and lightened to 950 pounds. Since a reworked catapult would not be available for some time, McCormick decided to use the Marmon chassis to test launch the flying bomb. The Long Island Motor Parkway was not suitable to conduct launching tests, but the Long Island Rail Road's Central Extension offered a straight length of track running southeast from Farmingdale to Babylon. Flanged wheels were installed on the Marmon chassis but during runs in May, the vehicle would not stay on the rails and this launching plan had to be abandoned. As a result, in early June, McCormick expressed his first serious reservations about the project when he stated that he was strongly in favor of closing down these experiments at the earliest possible date, as at that time the schedule for 1,000 completed flying bombs was already three months past fulfilment.

Meanwhile, after the inadequacy of the falling weigh catapult, a new design seemed to be the last hope for launching the flying bomb. In mid-April, Elmer Sperry began investigating the design of this new type catapult using the large stored energy of a flywheel by using it to wind up a cable on a tapered drum. Sperry employed Carl Norden, a brilliant consulting engineer to perform the new catapult's mathematical calculations and design. Norden, who would later achieve fame through his namesake design of a stabilized bombsight, would profoundly affect the direction of the entire flying bomb project. On May 15, 1918, his preliminary report recommended a wheel that, revolving at 2,175 rpm, would accelerate a mass of 1,950 pounds to a final speed of 100 mph over a 150-foot track; nine days later, he was directed to continue with the construction of two flywheel-powered catapults. During July, the new catapult was assembled under Norden's supervision at Copiague, and after several minor adjustments and tests with mock loads, it was set to launch the flying bomb. Its track and car were much like those of its precursor, but its prime mover was totally different. A heavy flywheel was spun at about 2,000 rpm by a 4-hp gasoline engine, while a tapered drum was clutch-engaged to the flywheel to accelerate the car. The combination of the flywheel speed and the taper of the drum determined the launching speed at the end of the track. This Norden Accelerating Catapult was so successful that, after observing a launching, Lt. Cdr. A. J. Stone of the Bureau of Ordnance reported that, in his opinion, the catapult's development was more valuable than the flying bomb. A trial launch of a flying bomb from the new catapult was prepared on August 5, 1918. As the catapult car and Bomb moved a short way down the track, the lifting forces were insufficient to lift the front wheels from the rails, causing the flying bomb to crash into a total wreck. Only two flying bomb airframes were available, although a third was to be assembled from the undamaged parts of earlier wrecks. Nonetheless, the Norden Catapult gave McCormick renewed optimism, and he planned on using one for further tests and the remaining two for a final demonstration.

An early September test failed because the auxiliary batteries that provided electrical power until the wind-driven generator could engage had been run down during ground tests and were unable to drive the servomotors. After a successful launching, the September 23 test failed as, after climbing satisfactorily for about 300 feet, the flying bomb turned sharply to starboard, climbed rapidly, and then corkscrewed down and flattened out just before disastrously hitting the ground. Investigation revealed that fragile wing structure was thought to be responsible, and the wings and fuselage were reinforced. There were plans to initially fly the remaining flying bomb with an onboard pilot, but they never became viable. The September 26 launching was successful, but after climbing along a straight line for about 500 feet, it began to spiral into a crash landing, similar to the previous crash. Flying bomb tests seemingly had come to an end.

Summary of Curtiss-Sperry Aerial Torpedo Flights

Test No.	D/M/Y	Launch Method	Test Result
1	1/12/17	Wire cable slide	Damaged wing on launching cable, damaged
2	7/12/17	Wire cable slide	Plunged into ground at launch; total loss
3	14/1/18	Deadweight catapult	Inverted on nose at launch; badly damaged
4	17/1/18	Deadweight catapult	Stalled and crashed at launch, total loss
5	2/6/18	Manned (L. Sperry)	Autopilot rolled aircraft; recovered safely
6	3/6/18	Manned (L. Sperry)	Somersaulted during taxi on ice; total loss
7	6/3/18	Deadweight catapult	Successful flight; recovered from water
8	7/4/18	Deadweight catapult	Failed to rise, settled to ground, total loss
9	17/5/18	Marmon auto on rails	Lifted auto wheels off rail tracks; test ended
10	5/8/18	Flywheel catapult	Insufficient lifting forces, crash & total loss
11	23/9/18	Flywheel catapult	Erratic 300 foot flight; crash & total loss
12	26/9/18	Flywheel catapult	500 foot flight, spiraled into crash landing

Next McCormick recommended that one of the N-9s be launched from the catapult to conclusively demonstrate Sperry's ability to launch an automatically controlled aircraft satisfactorily. During the entire interlude of flying bomb launchings, the N-9s had been conducting unassisted controlled take-off tests, with an onboard pilot only to monitor the equipment, which showed creditable improvements in operation and accuracy.

Flying Bomb mounted on a Marmon auto chassis set on railway tracks to launch the bomb. The vehicle would not stay on the rails and this launching plan had to be cancelled. (*AFSHRC*)

On October 17, the unmanned N-9 with aerodynamics and stabilization improved and equipped for the catapult launching was ready. Since it was supposed that the previous two launches were unsuccessful due to precession of the vertical gyro during acceleration on the launcher, a caging mechanism was installed in the N-9 gyro, which was to release as the aircraft left the catapult car. Precession is the movement of a gyro spin axis from its initial alignment in space caused by such imperfections as power fluctuation, imbalance of the gyro, friction in gyro gimbal bearings, and acceleration forces. The N-9 was launched from the catapult with its distance gear set at 14,500 yards. It climbed steadily in a flawless straight line within 2 degrees of the intended flight line, showing none of the uncontrollable turning tendencies of the previous two tests. A personnel shortage caused the chase pilot, who was to follow the N-9, to have to assist in the launching. As soon as the N-9 was launched, this pilot scrambled into his N-9 and took off on the pursuit. The pilotless N-9 weighed less and flew faster, quickly opening the distance between it and the chase N-9. However, when it arrived at the target area, the distance gear failed to end the flight and it continued on eastward. The chase plane pilot lost sight of it and an observer at the Bay Shore Air Station reported that it was last seen flying straight and level toward the east. It carried 10 gallons of fuel, sufficient for about 70 miles of flight, and it apparently crashed into the Atlantic. Despite the crash, this launch was a successful catapult launching and had automatically controlled flight up to the target area, which none of the ten flying bombs had achieved.

On October 29, the last, specially-designed flying bomb was launched. It was similar to the Curtiss flying bombs but had larger tail surfaces and ailerons. Its distance gear was set for 12,000 yards, but McCormick was reluctant to chance the accidental loss of another set of classified automatic controls and ordered that the fuel tank be drained of all but 2 gallons of gasoline. However, this decision was to be devastating, as during the catapult acceleration, the fuel ran to the rear of the tank and briefly cut fuel to the engine. Before the flying bomb reached the end of the track, the engine had stalled and left the car but sailed only a short distance, resulting in a total loss of the last flying bomb.

Continued tests of a Sperry autopilot-equipped Curtiss N-9 biplane, controlled to the target by an observer in a nearby aircraft, were satisfactory; however, the aircraft carried a pilot to conduct take-offs and to observe the flight. By November, the autopilot system successfully flew the aircraft, with the hands-off pilot on board, to its intended target where the distance-measuring gear dropped a bag of sand with a reported accuracy of within 2 miles of target.

The Navy requested that Carl Norden evaluate the Sperry components and recommend improvements, but several days later, World War I ended, as did the need for the flying bomb. The Navy then assumed complete control of the program from Sperry and, except for several N-9 flights, the Sperry-Navy aerial torpedo program became inactive. Since Sperry was an international company, it had several foreign scientists working on its radio control system, prompting the Naval Consulting Board to contract Westinghouse, a company without so-called enemy aliens, to develop the system. Despite this lack of support, Sperry continued its radio control development program, and on December 18, 1918, it applied for the first patent. On January 31, 1919, the Navy terminated the inactive Sperry contract and the program officially closed. By the end of May, all Navy material and personnel had been removed from Copiague.

The Legacy of the Sperry-Navy Aerial Torpedo Program

The Sperry-Navy aerial torpedo program, conducted during 1917 and 1918, was the first comprehensive guided missile program conducted in the U.S. or anywhere. The project began with promising initial successes but was followed by developmental problems, which led to a series of discouraging failures. However, these adversities suffered by the aerial torpedo program cannot obscure the fact that they were the true guided missile pioneers. For Sperry, it produced improvements in the aerial torpedo gyros that would affect later company automatic pilots and the development of an adequate directional gyro caused that important component to be added to the Sperry autopilot line. The legacy of the flying bomb program was that the knowledge acquired by both civilian and naval personnel was to be utilized in future aerial torpedo programs. In a time when aircraft and aircraft control devices were in their infancy, this group attempted to accomplish what would not be done for another quarter of a century. Their objectives were realized with greater sophistication in the German V-1 buzz bomb.

Kettering Aerial Torpedo/Bug

During the first three decades of the twentieth century, Charles Kettering, inventor, engineer, and businessman, ranked with the other American giants of engine, automotive, and aircraft science and innovation: Henry Ford, the Sperrys, Glenn Curtiss, and the Wright Brothers. In 1904, Kettering joined the National Cash Register Company, where he met Edward Deeds (its future president), who had devised some prototype electric motors that could be used to power cash registers. Kettering constructed a working production model that transformed the cash register and accounting machine business and established NCR as the leading international manufacturer for years to come. Soon, Kettering and Deeds would form a lifelong friendship and professional association. During 1909, Kettering perfected the first reliable automotive ignition system and electric starter in Deeds' barn, which led the two to form the Dayton Engineering Laboratories Company (Delco). Seven years later, they sold Delco to General Motors (at the time a United Motors Corporation subsidiary) for the then enormous sum of $2.5 million. In the interim, Kettering became one of the few prominent Americans to become interested in flying when he received flying lessons at the Wright Flying School at Dayton, OH. As a result of his new interest, Kettering as vice president, Deeds as president, and four Dayton businessmen formed the Dayton Airplane Company. They retained Orville Wright as consulting engineer, intending to perfect Wright's automatic flight control system and to build private aircraft. But when America entered World War I, the company became the Dayton-Wright Airplane Company and received contracts to license-build 4,000 British de Havilland DH-4 warplanes powered by the new American Liberty engine.

Charles Kettering, inventor and holder of 186 patents and engineer serving as the head of research at General Motors from 1920 to 1947. (*AFSHRC*)

On November 21, 1917, now Maj.-Gen. George Squire and Chief of the Army Signal Corps had observed a Navy demonstration at Amityville of a Navy N-9, which had been converted to an automatically-controlled flying bomb whose purpose was to strike targets beyond artillery range and directed that a similar secret Army program be established.

During December, the Army engaged a committee, which included Kettering from Dayton-Wright, to evaluate the flying bomb concept. The committee's report recommended that the project not be pursued, partially because of the cost of using a full-size aircraft. Kettering believed that a less expensive weapon could be built and was authorized by the Air Service to proceed with all expenses to be charged to Dayton-Wright's contract with the Army for its experimental operations at South Field at Dayton. The report's requirements were that the flying bomb was to cost less than an 8-inch artillery shell, carry about 200 pounds of explosives, and could be assembled in five minutes.

During January 1918, the Army awarded a contract to Kettering and the Dayton-Wright Airplane Company to develop and produce twenty-five Liberty Eagle aerial torpedoes, which were to be less complicated and less expensive than the Sperry design. Kettering's design, formally named the Kettering aerial torpedo, was later more commonly known as the Kettering Bug.

Because the project was very secret, initial design work was begun at the homes of several people connected with the company, rather than at the factory. Besides Edward Deeds and Kettering, who was the project's Chief Engineer, Col. F. E. Harris was placed in charge of developmental work for the Army, Harold Morehouse did much of the drafting, and Orville Wright acted as an aeronautical consultant on the project and contributed his expertise to the development of the airframe. Unfortunately, Kettering was unable to perfect a workable autopilot and was forced to solicit Elmer Sperry, who headed the Navy's aerial torpedo project several months earlier, to develop and adapt the Sperry control and guidance systems to the Bug. While testing his guidance system in the Bug during March 1918, Lawrence Sperry crashed, suffering a broken pelvis that immobilized him for three months; during his recovery, he would design a new and improved parachute.

Kettering listed several requirements for his aerial torpedo (in order):

1. Simplicity
2. Ease of manufacture
3. Ease of field assembly
4. Ease of launching
5. Ease of launching
6. Reliability
7. Load carrying aspects
8. Accuracy

Specifications:

Biplane wings:	Wingspan: 15 feet
	Chord: 30 inches
	Dihedral: 10 degrees
Fuselage:	Length: 12.5 feet
	Height: 7.7 feet
Total weight:	530 pounds
Warhead weight:	180 pounds
Speed:	Take-off: 55 mph/48 knots
	Cruise: 120 mph/105 knots
Range:	50–75 miles/43–65 nautical miles
Control:	
	Altitude: Aneroid Barometer
	Direction: Air valve sensing apparatus on gyroscope
	Distance: Air Log (propeller revolution counter)

Parts for the Bug were fabricated in the northernmost hangar at South Field and the aircraft was assembled in a guarded shed further north, from which launching rails extended southwest. Early versions were rather rudimentary, with the fuselage being constructed of *papier-mâché* and wood laminates (plywood), the wings made of Muslin, brown paper, and dope, and the tail surfaces of paste board (card stock) with metal trim to prevent fraying. The biplane wings were designed on a slightly upward 15-degree dihedral as this shape was the only scheme that provided directional stability. Lateral control was achieved by a dihedral angle tail and rudder developed by Orville Wright. It was powered by a two-stroke, two-cycle, four-cylinder V4, 41-hp Ford De Palma engine designed by Ford's Chief Engineer C. H. Wills, which ultimately cost only $40. The Bug was projected to cost about $575 in large quantities.

The Bug had no wheels and its airframe was placed on a wagon-like launch vehicle, which traveled on a long section of two thin metal portable tracks. The missile's engine was cranked to start at one end of the track, which was aimed directly at the intended

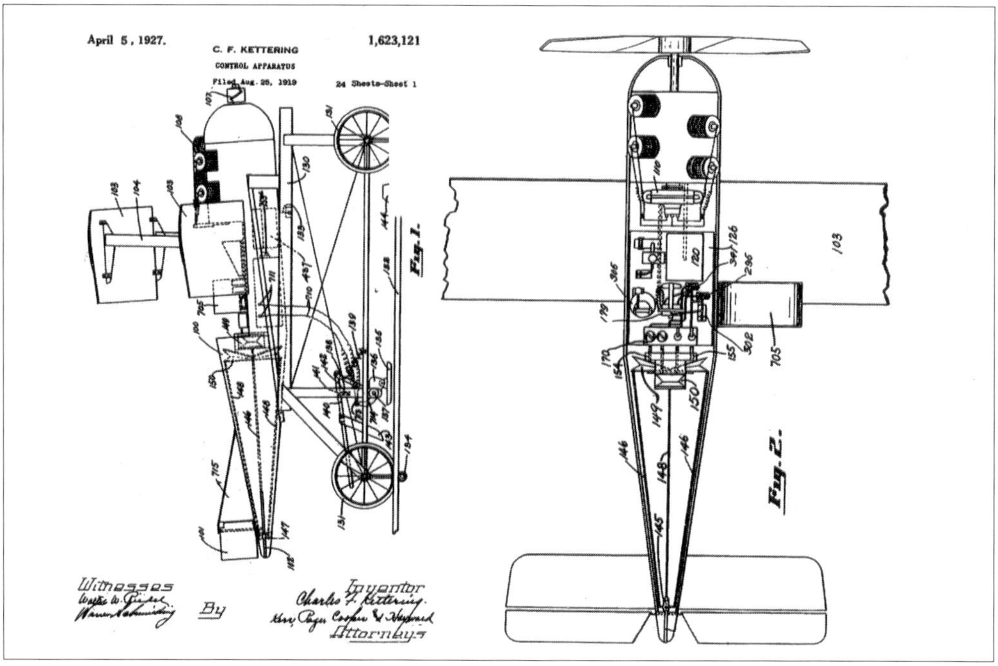

Bug control apparatus patent drawing filed August 25, 1919 and granted April 4, 1927. (*U.S. Patent Office*)

target. When the engine was fully revved, a mechanical counter was engaged and the Bug was released. When it reached flying speed, it lifted off the launch wagon and flew straight ahead toward the target—the direction of the flight was assured by a small gyro. It climbed to a preset altitude that was controlled by a very sensitive aneroid barometer; in fact, so sensitive that moving it from the top of a desk to the floor operated the controls. This barometer sent signals to the elevators of the rudder, which were moved by a system of cranks and a bellows (from a player piano) for altitude control. To ensure the Bug hit its target, a mechanical air log system was devised that would track the aircraft's distance flown to its destination at an air speed of about 120 mph. To calculate the total number of air log propeller revolutions the Bug required to reach its intended target, before take-off, technicians determined the distance to be traveled, considering wind speed and direction along the flight path. The descent altitude was automatically controlled by an aneroid barometer operating a pneumatic mechanism, which controlled the elevator. When revolution counter reached this calculated value, a cam dropped down, which shut off the engine and retracted the bolts attaching the wings, which fell off; the Bug then began a ballistic trajectory into the target, with the impact detonating the 180-pound explosive payload.

On October 2, 1918, the first flight, held at Dayton, was a demonstration for Army and Washington officials. The gyroscope was set for the direction of the flight while the Bug was on a turntable in the tent shelter; it was then launched from the cart after working hours while roads in the rural neighborhood were blocked so the short trials could not be observed by the public. The Bug took off, but instead of maintaining horizontal flight, it climbed sharply to about 600 to 800 feet and then dove abruptly toward the reviewing stand and crash-landed a few hundred feet beyond the scattering dignitaries.

Several days later, a Bug was successfully launched and was scheduled to fly at 50 mph across Ohio farmland, chased by observers in automobiles to the calculated crash site. However, the Bug left its intended path and circled Dayton before crashing an hour later near Xenia. Since the project was secret, there were concerns about security when local farmers found that the crashed aircraft had no pilot, but the farmers were told that he had parachuted before the crash (at the time, the Air Corps had no parachutes). The Bug and its technology would remain secret until World War II. It was noted that propeller torque caused the Bug to fly in wide circles. Three more relatively unsuccessful tests were conducted at Dayton, but nonetheless, the status of the flight tests was such that on October 5, 1918, Gen. Squire in an enthusiastic memorandum to the Chief of Staff wrote:

> The Chief Signal Officer believes that the development of this new weapon, which has now demonstrated its practicability, marks an epoch in the evolution of artillery for war purposes of the first magnitude, and comparable, for instance, with the invention of gunpowder in the fourteenth century. The development is not known to our overseas Forces, nor to the Forces of our allies. It comes as a distinct product of American genius, as applied to our present methods of warfare.

Squire's confidence was buoyed on October 22, 1918, when an aerial torpedo, with the altitude set at 200 feet and the range for 500 yards, impacted almost on target.

The Army had twenty-five aerial torpedoes plus parts in storage at McCook Field, Dayton, Ohio, and transferred flight test operations to the former Navy site at Amityville, Long Island when World War I ended. However, most of the knowledge gained during Dayton testing was not conveyed to the Army test units. Consequently, the Amityville tests led to these recommendations: make improvements in controls, gyroscopes, and engines, develop self-propelled launching cars on a catapult, and develop methods for launching regardless of wind direction. A series of Army flight tests of fourteen aerial torpedoes at Carlstrom Field, Arcadia, Florida, continued to be generally unsatisfactory, with only four considered successes and the aerial torpedo program was closed.

To summarize Flying Torpedo/Bug tests: twenty-four tests were flown with seven considered successful: Dayton, Ohio, two successes in six attempts; Amityville, New York, one success in four attempts; and Carlstrom Field, Florida, four successes in fourteen attempts

Ultimately, these early flying bombs failed because of the limited reliability of vital components, particularly, the engine and automatic pilot, as well as the lack of even rudimentary knowledge of aerodynamics at that time.

Col. Henry Hap Arnold was one of the zealous advocates of the Bug. During 1917, he served as director of Military Aeronautics, and in this role, he recognized the potential of the Bug in combat operations and recommended the immediate manufacture of 100 and future contracts for 10,000 to as many as 100,000. He convinced the Army staff to send him to Europe in October 1918 to persuade Gen. John J. Pershing to use

The Bug on a turntable in the tent shelter before its first flight on October 2, 1918, attended by Army and Washington officials at Dayton. (*AFSHRC*)

On its first flight, the Bug deviated from its planned horizontal flight and climbed sharply and then dove toward the reviewing stand and crashed behind. (*AFSHRC*)

the Bug in the last days of the war. However, Arnold was infected with the Spanish Flu; after recovering, he arrived on Western Front during November, only a few days before the Armistice. The potential of an unmanned weapon would remain in General Arnold's mind over the interwar years.

The war ended before the forty-five to fifty completed Bugs could be tested in combat, but even during testing, there were valid concerns about its reliability while carrying explosives over Allied troops. From April 1917 to termination, the government funded $275,000 to the Bug project.

Although using the World War I surplus of about fifty Bugs in storage was considered during 1942, the idea was finally abandoned; not because of manufacturing problems, a mass production plan existed, but because of its relatively short calculated maximum range of only 200 miles. However, during the fall of 1939, Arnold contacted his old friend Charles Kettering, now vice president of General Motors, wanting to develop the glide bomb to be deployed if war came. Arnold sought an unmanned design that could be used by the hundreds; although American strategic airpower doctrine concentrated on precision, daylight, high-altitude bombing, Arnold was prepared to sacrifice some degree of accuracy in to minimize potential danger to his aircrews to intense German flak, particularly in the last years of the war.

A full-size reproduction of a Bug, built by museum personnel in 1964, is on permanent display at the Air Force Museum in Dayton, Ohio.

Forty-five to fifty Bugs were completed, but despite some success during testing, the war ended before they could be combat tested and they were placed in storage. (*AFSHRC*)

Dr. Henry Walden Almost Develops America's First Guided Missile

During World War I, the military rocket developed to the extent that it was considered as a viable weapon with an inexpensive method of delivering an explosive payload. Its main disadvantage was their lack of control once they were launched, which was the reason they were launched in salvos of many at a time. Dr. Henry W. Walden was a Massachusetts dentist, pioneer aviator (he built and flew America's first monoplane, the *Walden III*, in 1909), and inventor (holder of 100 patents in his lifetime). In 1917, Walden's famous animated electric sign development was used on Times Tower in Times Square and years later, he built Mount Sinai Hospital's first artificial heart. To solve the rocket's inaccuracy problem, Dr. Walden devised a rocket that could be controlled by radio signals from the pilot after it was launched against ground targets. The pilot would visually observe the rocket and prompt its controls through radio signals that operated small servo motors that moved steering vanes on the rocket's tail. Walden's controlled rocket patent was granted, but it never was approved as he never paid the fee, because he received no government or military interest or support. It would not be until World War II that radio-guided rockets would be developed by the Germans.

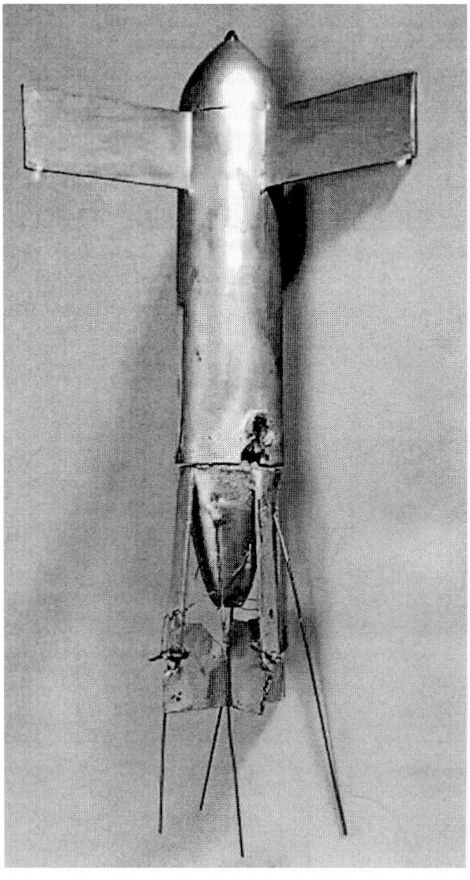

Dr. Henry Walden's first American guided missile 1917. (*Smithsonian*)

Sperry Messenger Aerial Torpedo (MAT)

By 1918, handsome, famous, and recently married to silent film starlet Winifred Allen, Lawrence Sperry, dubbed "Gyro Sperry" by the media, was on top of the world. That year, Lawrence broke with his father, Elmer, to found the Sperry Aircraft Company to enter the post-war small aircraft and aero-instruments business, including developing the new automatic pilot.

After the Navy terminated the aerial torpedo/Kettering Bug contract on January 31, 1919, the AAC remained persuaded that the autopilot could be tested and perfected by installing it in a manned aircraft. On December 30, 1919, the adjutant general directed the Air Service to continue the development of the automatic carriers, and during March 1920, proposals were offered for the development of the flying torpedo concerning three factors:

1. Perfection of the automatic controls.
2. Specification of control methods.
3. Testing of controls in a piloted aircraft as no piloted versions of the Bug were used to test or fine-tune the automatic controls prior to flight testing.

The AAC selected Maj. Guy Gearhart as project manager; he initially led a contract to the Lawrence Sperry Aircraft Company to install autopilots in three Standard Aircraft Corporation, Plainfield, New Jersey, open-cockpit, single-place, E-1 biplane trainers. Later, during April 1920, the AAC allotted Sperry a contract to fabricate automatic controls for six single-seat biplanes and to perform tests under full automatic control. After World War I, Brig. Gen. William "Billy" Mitchell requested the AES McCook Field Engineering Division, led by civilian Alfred Verville, to design an aerial dispatch vehicle able to serve as a liaison between battlefield units replacing motorcycles. The result was a simple single-seat biplane to be used as a messenger aircraft to be built by the Sperry Aircraft Company as the Sperry Messenger. As an aerial torpedo, the Messenger's (MAT) small size, simple construction, and low cost would make it suitable for research and testing in that role.

Piloted flight tests in the Messenger, conducted from September 1920 to April 1921, refined launching and distance control, but the gyroscopes were problematic due to lack of precision bearings, and installation difficulties. In June 1921, Sperry received a second contract for six further Messengers, three to be supplied as aerial torpedoes. By late 1921, Messengers based at Mitchell Field, Long Island, were equipped with advanced gyro-stabilization equipment, which resulted in appreciably improved performance.

Meanwhile, in 1922, Sperry had converted the Messenger into an inexpensive, easy to fly civilian sport plane. Sperry was eager to demonstrate his Messenger and was also upset at the government's unhurried payments on his contracts. He flew to Bolling Field, Washington, D.C., on March 22 to make a statement on both accounts. Circling the Capitol at ground level to disrupt Congress, he landed directly on the plaza in front of the Capitol building and bounced up a few front steps. He got out of the cockpit, contacted the assistant secretary of the Navy, made his point, and taxied to the other end of the Capitol, took off, and circled the Capitol Dome a few times before returning to Bolling Field.

During 1922, remote radio control equipment, developed by Lt. Mark Redman of the Army Engineering Division at McCook Field, Ohio, was installed in the Messenger to counteract variable winds and the inadequacies of current gyros, thus allowing intermittent corrections in heading to be made by an observer following in the two-seat DH-4 mother ship at a maximum distance of 1.5 miles. The new system demonstrated a marked improvement on June 29, 1922, when a MAT, with the usual safety pilot onboard, left Mitchell Field and, after having received a dozen heading corrections by radio during its 30-mile trip, arrived at the target. On the return trip to Mitchell Field, it replicated its accuracy, arriving directly over the field, then being remotely commanded to make a 360-degree turn before the safety pilot resumed control for the landing. Further flights to targets sited at 30 and 60 miles distant were equally successful.

The simultaneous control of multiple aircraft, the logical next developmental stage, was announced by the Engineering Division during January 1923, along with a third contract for Sperry to renovate six more Messengers with remote control equipment. However, on December 23, 1923, Lawrence Sperry left England to cross the fogbound English Channel in his private Messenger and made a forced landing and drowned. Shortly afterward, the Sperry Aircraft Company concluded operations, but the AAC continued the Messenger program, including the development of an apparatus for a

On March 22, 1921, Lawrence Sperry landed his Messenger on the Capitol Plaza and taxied to the Capitol steps. (*AFSHRC*)

Messenger to make the first successful airship hook on and release during December 1924. After new radio control equipment was deemed too heavy for the Messenger, replacement Curtiss JN-6H Jennys were requisitioned, but diminishing Army interest led to the projects termination in March 1926.

U.S. Navy Post-War Witteman-Lewis Flying Bomb

Before the war ended and while associated with the Sperry flying bomb project, Cdr. McCormick requested that the brilliant Carl Norden propose a program for the future development of the flying bomb that would be more successful than the Sperry flying bomb. Norden completed his analysis on October 30, 1918, recommending better-designed aircraft able to accommodate a check pilot during tests and a redesign of the automatic control system so that it could be turned on or off by the check pilot. Applying Norden's recommendations, BuOrd sent new specifications to the Witteman-Lewis Co. of Teterboro, New Jersey, which was awarded a cost-plus-fixed-fee contract to provide five flying-bomb aircraft capable of carrying a check pilot.

The first aircraft was ready for flight tests on February 26, 1919. Meanwhile, Norden designed the recommended automatic control equipment, which could be operated at the discretion of the check pilot. The Ford Instrument Co. built three sets, which Witteman-Lewis purchased under their cost-plus contract to be supplemented by two complete sets of the Sperry automatic control equipment remaining from those previously purchased. Except for the provision of services, the Sperry Co. was virtually excluded from the project, and by late 1918, McCormick endorsed the transfer of the entire project to the Navy. On May 27, 1919, the project moved to the Lower Station, Naval Proving Ground, Dahlgren, Virginia, for more extensive testing under the direction of Capt. T. T. Craven, USN, inspector of Ordnance in Charge.

A catapult had been installed and tested at Dahlgren, and three of the new Witteman-Lewis aircraft had been equipped with Norden equipment and tested under simulated flight conditions only by Witteman-Lewis test pilots until the completion of necessary changes. However, these aircraft were found to be too unsafe to fly as they were tail heavy and the ailerons and tail surfaces were too small. Despite this setback, on October 24, 1919, Norden recommended that the projects be expanded to include the equipping of obsolete aircraft for use as anti-aircraft targets and that radio controls be used in spotting aircraft.

The required modifications to the Witteman-Lewis aircraft was completed during the 1919–20 winter and further tests were approved to begin on April 30, 1920, but no piloted flights were to be launched from the catapult without BuOrd approval. The first catapult launch followed later on August 18, with the aircraft becoming airborne, flying straight for 150 yards, then stalling and nosing over and diving into the Potomac River. Norden determined that the crash was caused by the throttle closing during the acceleration of the aircraft on the catapult and by insufficient electrical power being generated by the windmill generator. Norden's remedy, which was approved by R/Adml. Charles McVay the new Chief of the Bureau of Ordnance, was to have a pilot flight test each aircraft to make appropriate adjustments to the automatic control equipment before it was catapulted without a pilot.

The next catapult test was scheduled for November 18, 1920, only after the aircraft had been flight tested and the automatic controls functioned acceptably. The catapult launch was flawless, the aircraft becoming airborne, climbing slowly, and completing one circle to an altitude of 1,500 feet while flying 5 miles. It then continued circling and climbing to 7,000 feet, where the automatic control deliberately closed the throttle, causing it to go into a spin, with the wings folding at about 300 feet above the water, and then nosediving into the water.

While Norden was actively pioneering the redesign of the Witteman-Lewis project's automatic control system, in which Norden gyroscopes were being tested, he was in contact with Lt. Cdr. Olaf Hustvedt, Chief of the BuOrd Experimental Division, who was responsible for the study of the feasibility of the remote control of aircraft by radio and of flying bombs. Norden appealed to Hustvedt to consider allowing him to proceed with adding gyro-stabilization to a bombsight together with a telescope to better sight the target and a method to provide flight directions to the pilot. Navy funding eventually led to the development of the renowned Norden Mk. XV (or M-9) bombsight in 1932, after which nearly 90,000 of these bombsights were manufactured by the end of World War II.

Continued USN Radio-Controlled Aircraft R&D: 1920–1925

Since the results using Witteman-Lewis aircraft and Norden-designed gyrostabilizers were no better than those achieved by the Sperrys, the Navy's program was reoriented to focus on the research, development, and experimentation with radio-controlled aircraft. On December 30, 1920, Adml. Robert Coontz, Chief of Naval Operations, appointed a board consisting of USN Capts. L. A. Bostwick, W. G. DuBose, A. S. Hepburn, and C. C. Block to investigate and report upon the practicability of the remote control of aircraft by radio. The board recommended that the Navy initiate the project under BuOrd auspices, and on January 20, 1921, Secretary of the Navy Josephus Daniels approved the project.

On April 25, 1921, a test-launched aircraft climbed for a short distance for almost two minutes without any indications of poor stability, but then settled slowly on to the water and turned over. Norden conjectured that the problem was in his initial setting of the horizontal stabilizer. However, BuOrd's Chief, R/Adml. Charles McVay's patience with the project began to diminish as revealed by a letter to Adml. Robert Coontz, Chief of Naval Operations, when he implied his intention to "discontinue further tests unless otherwise directed."

However, the project labored on and it was not until late October 1921 that Lt. Cdr. Olaf Hustvedt, BuOrd, and Radio Aid A. Crossley, BuEng, visited the Dahlgren Naval Proving Ground, Virginia, several times to investigate the inactive flying bomb project and devise procedures for conducting the radio control project. Their recommendations were mostly approved with the responsibility for the design, development, and tests of the radio equipment to be under the Bureau of Engineering. The tests were initially conducted at the Naval Aircraft Radio Laboratory at Anacostia, Washington, D.C., under the direction of Dr. A. Hoyt Taylor. Equipment installation and flight tests were to be held at Dahlgren under BuOrd supervision. By January 17, 1922, the Chief of the Bureau of Engineering informed the Chief of the Bureau of Ordnance that his bureau was ready to proceed. The Bureau of Ordnance then allotted funds, and on January 28, the Aircraft Laboratory was directed to begin the work.

On May 11, 1922, the Bureau of Ordnance directed the Dahlgren Proving Ground to immediately obtain one of the N-9 flying bomb experiment aircraft that had been already equipped with the Norden automatic control system and prepare it for the installation of the radio control system by July 1. The radio control equipment was not available on time and was not installed into the N-9 until July, a year later.

Meanwhile, Cdr. Stanford Hooper, head of the Radio Division, Bureau of Engineering, had engaged Carlos Mirick, a brilliant radio engineer, and assigned him to the laboratory as an assistant to Taylor. Mirick was interested in developing an aircraft radio control system and conducted a comprehensive technology survey in 1922 and then visited several manufacturers to determine which had the most advantageous components available. His visit to the John Hammond Co. was the most productive as that company was redesigning the components of the radio control equipment for the standard Navy torpedo so that it could be assembled in small units that could be installed and serviced through hand holes in the radio control section of the torpedo. By mid-summer, Mirick selected the necessary components for the aircraft radio control system that were readily available; however, suitable relays needed to be developed and tested, which required several months. On September 1, 1923, Mirick submitted a patent application for his Electrical Distance Control System (which was awarded U.S. Patent No. 1,597,416 on August 24, 1926). The patent is credited as being the fundamental concept of the joy stick that, when pushed in a given direction, produced a distinct electronic signal. In his patent application, Mirick states:

> My control system is particularly applicable in maneuvering aircraft without a pilot.... I construct the switch in the form of a joy stick identical with the joy stick provided in aircraft for controlling the machine. An operator at the radio transmitter at a shore station who is an experienced aviator may therefore move the lever in the same-manner in which he is accustomed to operating the joy stick in aircraft and control circuits at a radio receiver, on board an aircraft ... which in turn control the operation of the particular functions necessary in the flight of the aircraft such as operating the elevating planes, the rudder, banking the machine or controlling the engine.

During 1923, Norden further improved the automatic pilot, and the Naval Research Laboratory (NRL) was established during April 1923, with Norden, Mirick, and other key personnel reassigned from Anacostia to the new NRL Radio Division, headed by Dr. Taylor. On April 15, the NRL had proven the radio control equipment in a Curtiss

Carlos Mirick, a brilliant radio engineer and inventor of the joystick. (*NA*)

F-5L patrol plane with a standoff of 10 miles, and considered that radio-controlled take-off and landing was technically viable

On July 21, 1923, Mirick finally completed the integration of the NRL radio control installation in the Curtiss N-9H seaplane at the Dahlgren Naval Proving Ground. Norden's automatic pilot with its supplementary equipment weighed 130 pounds while the radio control equipment weighed 148 pounds. The automatic pilot consisted of a triangular antenna that extended from both wing skid fins to the rudder post; a receiver with a six-stage amplifier; the relays; and the Morkum selector that actuated the proper relay consistent with the signal received. The radio equipment at the control station consisted of a Marconi spark transmitter capable of providing an antenna current. This transmitter was keyed by a pushbutton mechanism, which sent Baudot code (predecessor to the International Telegraph Alphabet).

Lt. John Ballantine, USN, the aviation officer at Dahlgren, flew numerous test flights to evaluate and fine-tune the equipment. The operation of the selector switch, indicated by a blinker light, was monitored over all regions within 2–3 miles of the transmitter station. After successful operation was achieved, several flights under actual radio control were made in which Ballantine rode as a passenger, reportedly with folded arms, as the Curtiss was wholly controlled from the ground.

Between May 18 and November 14, thirty-three test flights were made, all with Ballantine, as safety pilot. Before August 3, Ballantine controlled the N-9 in simple test maneuvers for distances up to 5 miles. The final 1923 test, a successful forty-five-minute flight, using radio control for about twenty-five minutes, was observed by Bureau of

Between May 18 and November 14, 1923, thirty-three remote-control test flights were made in a Curtiss N-9H, all with a safety pilot. (*USN*)

Ordnance officers. The radio control included two down-elevator, three up-elevator, six left and five right turns, as well as several radio signals operating a dummy throttle. Afterward test operations were discontinued until spring before attempting a pilotless flight.

Mirick's NRL team equipped a BuAer Curtiss HS-2 single-engined pusher flying boat, which had the pilot and co-pilot side-by-side in a double cockpit just forward of the wings. The pilot was in the left seat, Mirick with his radio controls sat in the co-pilot's seat, and the control equipment was mounted behind the pilot. The HS-2 was to function as an airborne control station that provided added flexibility in control redundancy, improved situational awareness, and increased operator standoff. With an unmanned flight impending, a backup plan was devised in case radio control was totally lost with the drone and jeopardizing populated areas. Ballantine prepared a plan in which bricks would be dropped into the drone's propeller from a chase plane!

During the 1923–24 winter sojourn, the radio control components were improved and the Curtiss HS-2 was re-equipped. Snap switches were installed in the cockpit to permit the pilot to instantly discontinue the entire radio control system. On July 24, 1924, manned test flights were resumed to test the improved equipment and devise a standard procedure for the use of the airborne control station. On September 15, 1924, the N-9 flew a breakthrough test flight, during which Norden's automatic stabilization and the NRL's radio control systems functioned flawlessly encouraging Ballantine and Mirick to attempt their first unmanned flight later that afternoon. The N-9 was prepared for its first pilotless flight with a sand bag secured to the pilot's seat to compensate for Ballantine's weight. Another HS flying boat took station to assume backup radio control in case of an emergency. The radio and gyro switches were turned on, the engine started, and the wings were physically held level for five minutes to be certain that the gyros came up to speed and settled on course. The rudder gyro was then unlocked, and the on throttle signal was given by the radio control station. The throttle actuator responded to the radio command for full power and the N-9 was released by the ground crew for its take-off run. Once airborne, during the forty minutes from the take-off to the landing, it was controlled through a lengthy sequence of maneuvers, following a triangular flight path ranging in altitude from 200 to 500 feet and within 2–3 miles of the ground controller. Over fifty signals were sent, and all were promptly responded to, except for the right turn signal, which later was easily remedied. For the first time, a pilotless aircraft had been put into the air, controlled through many maneuvers, and landed, notwithstanding, upon landing a pontoon that was damaged so that enough water flooded into it that the aircraft, nosing over into the Potomac.

The radio control equipment salvaged from the N-9 was transferred to one of the two Vought VE-7H two-seat, biplane seaplane trainers provided by the BuOrd for testing. The Vought VE-7 series was the Navy's first fighter and the first USN aircraft to land on a carrier (the *Langley*/October 17 1922). Testing resumed on June 19, 1925, and by September 14, twenty-eight test flights had been performed, with none considered completely successful. At this time, test pilot Ballantine was relieved by Lt. V. H. Schaeffer, USN. On October 28, a successful test was flown with a safety pilot Schaeffer in the Vought cockpit, and from then until the first pilotless test, several successful manned flight tests were made.

On December 11, a pilotless flight was scheduled during a day of idyllic weather conditions. The "throttle on" signal was transmitted and the engine run up to full speed. The aircraft then headed along a seemingly straight take-off course before leaving the water. Just after becoming being airborne, the Vought porpoised, striking the water four times, bouncing higher each time. After the last bounce, the pontoon struts broke and the propeller cut off the nose of the pontoon, causing the aircraft to nose up and submerge. Investigations concluded that the failure was attributed to irregular control responses created by using a teletype selector to interpret single-function Baudot-encoded commands and recommended that no more pilotless flights be attempted until the equipment was modified to supply more graduated and smoother control. Mirick and the Naval Research Laboratory developed a tuned relay system that employed normal pilot controls instead of pushbuttons and provided a much greater level of control and an almost instantaneous aircraft response to the actuation of several controls simultaneously.

By late 1925, the NRL believed that it was possible to control an aircraft by radio beyond the range of vision. Again, interest in this military project in peacetime was beginning to decline and no action was taken on the laboratory's report. Proposals were made to improve the control equipment, but again no action was taken. During the next three years improved radio control apparatus was developed, but no further test flights were attempted, and while the project was not canceled, it remained almost inactive until 1936 when renewed interest was shown for drone aerial targets under Project Dog.

A Curtiss HS-2 was to function as an airborne control station for the first unmanned flight N-9H on September 15, 1924. (*USN*)

Two Vought VE-7H two-seat, biplane seaplane trainers succeeded the N-9H as test aircraft but none of the 1925 manned tests were considered completely successful, with the only unmanned test resulting in a crash. (*USN*)

The British Influence American Unmanned Aircraft Development

RAE Larynx

After Archibald Low's World War I radio-controlled Ruston Proctor AT, Zeppelin Killer program failed, the British continued an insipid radio-controlled, unmanned aircraft development program. During 1920, the Royal Aircraft Establishment (RAE) showed renewed interest in an aerial target. In October 1921, a milestone was reached at RAE Farnborough when a manned Bristol Fighter, equipped with rudimentary gyro rudder control, was controlled automatically in response to radio signals transmitted at ranges up to 8 miles. During mid-1922, attempts to launch and fly the pilotless RAE Target began. The early tests were made without radio control with the prearranged maneuvers being carried out by clockwork programming. Trials began in August 1922 from the Royal Navy carrier *Argus* and were continued by catapult launches from the destroyer HMS *Stronghold*. Unreliable flight performance was corrected by modifications to the gyroscope installation, and in June 1924, it was decided to replace the clockwork programming by radio control. Successful flights were made between September 1924 and February 1925. On September 3, 1924, the first successful radio-controlled flight was completed when the RAE Target was launched from the *Stronghold*. It completed a controlled twelve-minute flight that was only terminated by engine failure. Ensuing flights from the *Stronghold* proved the viability of radio-controlled flight as demonstrated when the tenth RAE Target test flew for thirty-nine minutes, recording forty-three separate commands. The natural progression was to develop a larger and improved aircraft with a larger pay load.

During 1925, the RAE and the Royal Navy collaborated to develop and test the world's first crude cruise missile, the RAE Larynx (Long Range Gun with Lynx Engine), which was to be used as a guided anti-ship weapon, directed by an autopilot. This mid-wing monoplane, with a lightweight metal tubular fuselage, was powered by a 200-hp Armstrong Siddeley Lynx IV engine, enclosed in a low-drag cowling. The aircraft was designed to carry 250 pounds of high explosives over 300 miles and attained a notable speed of over 190 mph, which was faster than most contemporary fighters. Radio control was omitted as the aircraft's predetermined course, altitude, and range were maintained by the compass and aneroid monitors of the air log and autopilot of the type developed by Archibald Low and used previously in the Ruston Proctor AT. To plot the aircraft's track, direction-finding observations were sent by a transmitter on the aircraft. The Larynx was launched from a cordite-fired catapult on the forward deck of the Royal Navy S-class destroyers HMS *Stronghold* and *Thanet*.

Larynx tests: the first test, on July 20, 1927, launched from a cordite-powered catapult on the *Stronghold*, before it crashed into the Bristol Channel; the second test, on September 1, 1927, is thought to have flown 100 miles and then was lost; the third test, on October 15, 1927, underwent a 112-mile flight that impacted 5 miles from the target; there were two launches from the *Thanet*, one in September and another in October 1928, which produced unrecorded results; and there were two land launches during May 1929, with one overflying its target while the other was successful.

The RAE Larynx ("Long Range Gun with Lynx Engine"), the world's first crude cruise missile. (*RAE*)

After testing, subsequent launches and flights were successful. Five Larynx were sent for trials in Iraq during 1929, and although these trials were inconclusive, it is reasonable that, with a very small amount of development, this weapon could have been available to the British Services in the early 1930s.

Fairey Queen

By 1930, at a time when flying targets were typically towed by piloted aircraft, the Royal Navy required a convincing anti-aircraft gunnery target for AA training—one that could take-off, fly back and forth in unpredictable patterns before the gunners, and then be recovered and reused if not destroyed. During October 1930, the RAE was requested to develop a target aircraft based on the Fairey IIIF to be known as the Fairey Queen. The Fairey Queens were a variant of the Fairey III reconnaissance biplane, fitted with floats. To improve lateral stability for remote control, the Fairey Queen had an increased dihedral over the standard Fairey III. Flight trials from HMS *Valiant*. During April 1932, the first two immediately crashed into the sea after launching from the stern of the *Valiant*, after flights of eighteen and twenty-five seconds respectively. The third aircraft was successfully launched in September 1932 and was recovered and hoisted aboard the *Valiant* after its flight. In January 1933, it was successfully launched at Gibraltar and escaped from, undamaged, two hours of Home Fleet AA fire, landing safely. However, in May 1933, HMS *Shropshire* gunners destroyed the last Queen in just twenty minutes at Malta.

Fairey Queen Bee

The Admiralty evaluated the Fairey Queen experience and decided that a full-sized production, returnable and reusable, pilotless target aircraft for anti-aircraft gunnery training was required, and in 1935, the DH.82B Queen Bee, a pilotless, radio-controlled variant of de Havilland Moths was chosen. It used the engine, unslatted wings, undercarriage, and tailplane of a Tiger Moth, but instead of a Tiger Moth fabric-covered metal frame fuselage, it used a spruce and plywood Moth Major fuselage, which was

The Fairey Queen, based on the Fairey IIIF, was developed by the RAE as a target aircraft. (*RAE*)

less expensive and afforded buoyancy during a ditching. It could fly at an altitude of 17,000 feet at speeds of over 100 mph and for up to 300 miles while powered by a 130-hp de Havilland Gipsy Major 1. It had an all-up weight (AUW) of 1,825 pounds, a length of 23 feet, 11 inches, and a wingspan of 29 feet, 4 inches. It was equipped with wheels to operate from runways or floats if shot from steam catapults at sea.

The control panel was operated by a simple rotary telephone-type dial, which the controller could dial in a radio-transmitted command. The commands were represented by numbers on the dial such as #2 turn left, #3 turn right, etc., while other controls operated the ignition and throttle. A similar dial was also mounted in the cockpit to enable the onboard check pilot to test the pilotless function. Compared to the relatively small control panel, the radio transmitter was considerably larger. The front cockpit contained the same controls as the rear, permitting the check pilot to verify the pilotless functions of the aircraft in flight. The radio commands operated a series of pneumatic servos housed in the rear cockpit area. A small four-bladed wooden propeller placed in the engine propeller slipstream on the left fuselage just behind the engine drove a small ram air (wind) turbine (RAT) powered pump mounted on the left side of the fuselage to provide compressed air for the gyro unit and servos. The design did not permit using the ailerons and rudder for coordinated flight; consequently, the ailerons were always locked in the neutral position and controller used only the rudder, elevator, and throttle controls. The aircraft could be remotely operated by a pilot or controller seated in another aircraft, or on a warship, or from a control panel on land. For a remote-controlled landing, an ingenious automatic landing system discerned when the aircraft was near the water's surface and permitted it to land without any human involvement. If

Winston Churchill visiting the DH.82B Queen Bee, a pilotless, radio-controlled variant of de Havilland Moths, on its launching ramp during 1935. (*RAE*)

Ground controllers flying the Queen Bee using a simple rotary telephone-type dial, which the controller could dial in a radio-transmitted command. The *Bee* could be remotely operated by a pilot or controller seated in another aircraft, or on a warship, or from a control panel on land. (*RAE*)

radio control was lost, the Bee would continue to fly until it ran out of fuel, after which it would glide towards the surface and, at the strategic instant, the automatic landing system would assume control go into landing maneuvers.

The Queen Bee was first flown, manned, at Hatfield in 1935 and then remotely-controlled at Farnborough later that year. A total of 412 were built between 1933 and 1943, 360 as float planes operated by the Fleet Air Arm (many on twin floats) and by the Royal Air Force until they were retired from service in 1947. The Fairey Queen and Queen Bee were followed in service by the similarly-named Airspeed Queen Wasp, which never went into series production and Miles M.50 Queen Martinet, of which sixty-five were built and a further seventeen produced through conversion of an M.25. All Queen radio-controlled drones were ultimately replaced by the GAF Jindivik of which 502 were produced between 1952 and 1986.

Aerial Torpedo Resurrected Using Commercial Aircraft

In 1928, Assistant Secretary of War Frederick Davison requested that the aerial torpedo be resurrected, and in October, the Acting Chief of the Engineering Division began to investigate the possibilities of adapting commercial aircraft of various sizes to carry bomb loads of 300, 600, 1,000, and 2,000 pounds, which would facilitate the quick production of aerial torpedoes by commercial aircraft manufacturers in wartime. After testing, one aircraft with the most suitable characteristics was to be selected to carry each bomb weight and be equipped with controls for automatic flight and the data on each successful aircraft could be used for future reference in wartime. The high-wing, enclosed-cabin Curtiss Robin monoplane with increased dihedral and enlarged vertical tail surfaces for improved stability was the first aircraft to be equipped with a Sperry Automatic Pilot superimposed by radio control.

Delivered in October 1929 and designated by the AAC as the XC-10 (serial 29-452) the Robin's 110-hp Warner R-420-1 engine was underpowered, and after accumulating only 100 flight hours, it was replaced by the Stinson Junior, another high-wing, enclosed cabin monoplane powered by a 225-hp Wright Whirlwind J6-7 engine. Because the Stinson used the system whose throttle and landing required pilot control, the ACC judged completely automatic take-off and landing to be economically unachievable in the near future and the project was terminated in mid-May 1932.

The XC-10 was scrapped in March 1935. A C-1 Robin would later be famously flown by Douglas "Wrong Way" Corrigan in 1938 to Ireland. Edward Stinson, the Junior's developer, was killed in the prototype on January 25, 1932 while flying a demonstration flight from Chicago when fuel shortage forced him to attempt a fatal forced landing.

Revival of Radio Control and Aerial Torpedo Development (1939)

During the interwar years, only a few AAC leaders maintained their interest in a pilotless aircraft. Importantly, one of these was the powerful Gen. Henry "Hap"

Arnold who had been associated with the World War I Kettering Bug program and would be an influence for good and bad on America's pilotless bomb programs during World War II. During the 1930s, Arnold had struggled to maintain interest in a radio control and aerial torpedo development, but it was not until August 1938, as America began to rearm, that an interest in the pilotless aircraft program resurfaced.

On August 8, 1938, Chief of the Air Corps Oscar Westover ordered the Chief of the Materiel Division to develop an aerial torpedo ASAP, costing $300–$500 per unit in quantity production with a range of 20 to 30 miles to be controlled by radio. Westover authorized the then large sum of $100,000, of which $10,000 was to be reserved for a design competition. On September 29, specifications for bids were authorized by Gen. Arnold, now Chief of the Air Corps, replacing Westover who had died in the plane crash a week earlier. New specifications mandated a range of 20 to 50 miles, an explosive payload of 200 pounds or a 300-pound bomb, and an accuracy to hit a 2-square-mile target from 20 miles. By late April 1939, the Vega Aircraft Company, Burbank, California, a Lockheed subsidiary formed in 1937, was the only bidder tendering its dubious Model 40 target drone designed by Vega Chief Engineer Jack Wassail, who had once been the project manager for the ill-fated Vega 2 Starliner, an airliner want-to-be. Five Model 40 prototypes were contracted by the AAC, resulting in an 850-pound very basic airframe that did not allow for manned flight. To duplicate flight conditions to assess aircraft control and aerodynamics, the Model 40 was carried by a crane mounted on the bed of a speeding truck. All five Model 40 prototypes were apparently lost during testing without receiving an official AAC Army designation under the initial A-series of radio-controlled targets before the contract was canceled in 1940.

General Motors A-1 (GMA-1, Bug)

A new Bug project was revived by Gen. Arnold's friend, Charles Kettering, who had been the motivating force behind the Army's World War I Bug. On September 7, 1939, Kettering, then the general manager of the General Motors Research Labs, informed Arnold that GM had developed a low-cost 150-hp engine and satisfactory instruments to build a practicable aerial torpedo that would weigh 1,500 pounds and was to cost $1,500 in production quantities. Arnold countered that he desired a $700 weapon that could hit a half-mile-diameter target from 100 miles while carrying 200 pounds of explosive. Kettering quickly replied that an appropriate missile could be built in quantities of 10,000 and could be obtained at a satisfactory, although unstated, price.

In late February 1940, the adjutant general approved the revised military requirements for the new weapon, which now had to be able to hit a half-mile-diameter target at 20 miles, be capable of having its range extended to 100 miles, and be invulnerable to enemy misdirection and/or jamming. The minimum 20-mile range was set as it was also the maximum range of existing ground artillery as the Army believed that the aerial torpedo was essentially long-range artillery. In September 1940, GM made a specific proposal, offering to use one of its established GM X-250 200-hp, two-cycle engines with a 7.33-foot propeller mounted on a Cessna airframe built at the company's Wichita, Kansas, factory. On February 18, 1941, the War Department offered a $500,000 contract to GM for the delivery of fifteen aerial torpedoes. In April 1941, the Army decided to install radio control equipment intended for testing for possible enemy misdirection. On May 21, 1941, as a result of the recommendation of a joint Army/Navy Conference, the Army changed the weapons designation from aerial torpedo to Controlled Bomb, Power Driven. Only six months later, during July, GM unexpectedly quickly delivered the completed Controlled Bomb, Power Driven, now designated as the General Motors Type A-l (GMA-1), which was again nicknamed the Bug.

The GM Bug was successfully tested in Langley's full-scale wind tunnel, and later that year, initial ground and air testing began at the Muroc Bombing Range, Muroc, California. The Bug was to be launched from a dolly pulled by a tow car down a twin-rail track and when 175 pounds of excess lift was attained, a spring mechanism was to automatically release it. After a number of trial runs only down the rails, the first launch attempt from the rails on November 15, 1941 was a debacle as its 91-mph take-off speed was insufficient and the Bug immediately became a total wreck. The second GMA-1was modified so that it was released at the end of a 1,500-foot run when it reached 100 mph. On its December 5 launch attempt, this Bug went into a sharp climbing turn, which the radio controller attempted to correct, but because of insufficient elevator control, the automatic controls were employed, which put the Bug

General Motors A-1 (GMA-1, Bug), pictured in the Langley wind tunnel, was a 1939 revival of a practicable, low-cost aerial torpedo to be managed by Charles Kettering. (*AAF*)

into a steep diving turn and resulted in another devastating crash after two minutes and thirty seconds of flight. The third Bug, with limits placed on the controls, was tested on December 7, 1941, but despite this remedy, it continued to demonstrate over-control characteristics; five minutes after its radio transmitter was accidentally disconnected, this Bug also crashed. The fourth test was conducted the next day, with the controls further limited. The Bug continued to exhibit over-control on both the radio and automatic controls, flying for ninety-five minutes, but because it had neither landing gear nor skids, it necessarily crashed during its landing.

The Bug continued to have such significant control system problems that the altitude and preset controls were sent back to Detroit for further development in late January 1942. Two-axis gyroscopes and spoilers were installed and a new launching system developed while another Bug was sent to Detroit for the installation of television control equipment in February to assist the controller in locating and crashing into a target.

The GMA-1 testing continued at Eglin Field, located in the Florida Panhandle, during March and April 1942. The automatic controls were not yet completed and not installed and all subsequent testing was with radio control equipment. The Bug was mounted atop a Cadillac chassis powered by two engines, geared through a Chevrolet transmission giving the vehicle four-wheel drive. When the driver reached 100 mph, he was to release the GMA-1. On March 10, the initial automobile launch was unsuccessful because of a crosswind and a malfunctioning control connection. On March 19, another GMA-1 took-off and flew for 115 minutes before the controller purposely crashed it after it experienced more control problems. During

The Bug was to be launched from a dolly pulled by a tow car down a twin-rail track, and when excess lift was attained, a spring mechanism was to automatically release it. (*AAF*)

The Bug was mounted atop a four-wheel-drive Cadillac chassis powered by two engines; when the driver reached 100 mph, he was to release the GMA-1. (*AAF*)

Movie still of a Bug in flight. Testing continued into 1943, but the accrual of negative GMA-1 test results caused the project be cancelled on August 24, 1943. (*From AAF movie still*)

the next test on April 2, the Bug flew for 110 minutes before its radio control system failed, possibly due to a malfunctioning generator, and ten minutes later, it crashed. During the flight, it displayed better pitch control but problems with directional control continued. The fifth, sixth, and seventh GMAs were equipped two axis gyro stabilization units, but during tests during March and April, directional stability remained poor; the crashes were uncontrolled and headwinds easily drove them off course. Of the original ten GMA-1s, only three remained at Eglin, with five more being constructed.

On April 16, 1942, General Motors issued a report on the state of its GMA-1 project, relating its concerns about the GMA's range, payload, and control limitations. To increase range and inadequate payload, GM proposed a twin-engined vehicle with a range of 900 to 1,200 miles, a speed of 150 mph, and a 2,000-pound payload. The cost was to be $9,900 for each bomb, $20,000 for the monorail launching gear, $2,000 for the tricycle launching gear, and $1,500 for each tricycle landing gear. A catapult launch was considered impractical and the report recommended a rocket assist along a short track and a GMA-1 with tricycle landing gear for conventional take-offs. Some GMA advocates promoted a 225-mph missile with a 1,500-mile range.

Only a week later, Lt. Col. George Holloman, the Chief of the Engineering Section, raised a number of important questions concerning several GMA problems:

1. Since the General Motors Lab Division was without any manufacturing capacity, to construct and equip a new factory for GMA-1, production would require a year.
2. The existing 500-pound payload was considered too small, but a larger payload would dictate a twin-engined vehicle and a new design, beginning with an entirely new airframe.
3. The method for controlling a GMA-1 directly to the target was not perfected and although in tests the GMA-1 had been controlled to the target by radio from a control aircraft; radio interference limited the number of Bugs controlled to five or ten
4. The training of radio control equipment operators was presenting problems.
5. The report reiterated that launching the GMA-1 remained a critical problem.

Holloman concluded his report stating that he believed that if the GMA-1 could be made operational by late 1943 or early 1944, the project should be continued and the range and payload problems could be confronted in due course.

Note: Lt. Col. George Holloman, a North Carolina State University engineering graduate, achieved celebrity by test-piloting, with Carl Crane, the first automated landing of an aircraft (a Fokker C-14B), via the C-14B automatic landing device at Wright Patterson Air Field on August 23, 1937, for which they were awarded the coveted Mackay Trophy in 1938. He remained involved with AAF drone experiments, including Operation Aphrodite and later would direct the AAF/USN concurrent efforts for RHB (Pelican) and SRB (Bat). Holloman was killed in an air crash on Formosa on March 19, 1946. The Holloman AFB, near Alamogordo, NM (White Sands), is named in his honor for his pioneering work in the development of missiles.

Lt. Col. George Holloman. (*AAF*)

A May 19, 1942 Conference Memo Report recommended the acquisition of five more tricycle landing gear GMA-1as, which could be recovered after tests as well as installing TV guidance and three-axis gyros. In order to facilitate testing, the 500-pound payload was standardized. Concerning launching, the conference recommended launch tests using automobile or monorail launch apparatus and GMA-1a with tricycle landing gear.

On June 16, 1942, GM proposed the pick-a-back air launching of the GMA-1 in order for it to carry a 500-pound bomb and radio and TV control equipment for fifteen minutes at a speed of 185 mph. Land-based tests in July and September continued to be unsuccessful, prompting a conference to be called on October 26, 1942 where conferees decided that the air launching scheme was the original A-1s only practical application "considering the targets against which it can be economically used, the bomb will be useful only as an air-launched weapon due to its short-range and low-weight carrying capacity..." GMA-1 landing gear testing was discontinued because of the new importance assigned to air launching and because the original

A-1 design precluded take-offs with landing gear. Ultimately, three Wright Field wind tunnel tests during 1943 of a GMA-1 mounted on top of a B-25 wooden model was to be the extent that this air launching scheme ever progressed. Also, in December 1942, Arnold approved a new GMA-l development program and authorized the purchase of 100 A-1s with a planned range of 1,000 miles and a payload of 2,000 pounds.

The modified GMA-1s equipped with TV and three-axis gyros showed disappointing results in tests at Eglin during the summer of 1942. On July 17, the eighth so-equipped GMA-1 took off from an automobile top in a steep climb and crashed after being airborne for two minutes when the radio controls became non-responsive due to moisture from the humid Florida air that permeated the control equipment. On September 6, the ninth GMA-1 went out of control while it was taxiing, destroying its wings, while on the 25th, the same GMA-1, with new wings, was destroyed on its final taxi test before launch, possibly because one brake seized. Then, five days later, the tenth A-1 went out of control and was destroyed on a take-off attempt. Despite the lackluster results, Gen. Arnold approved further development and personnel training in a memo of December 18, 1942 to the director of Military Requirements.

GMA-1 tests were transferred to the drier climate at California's Muroc Bombing Range, with land-based launches continuing to be unsuccessful. The final tests of the GMA-l using automobile launching occurred on May 24 and 27, 1943 at Muroc. The GMA-1s were equipped with TV and three axis gyro stabilization with a control aircraft flying about a mile behind the Bug. On the first test, the eleventh GMA-l made an erratic take-off from a car top and became instable in turns and sluggish to control but flew for ninety-five minutes and then, with the aid of TV, the operator purposely crashed the missile within 75 feet of its target. Three days later, the last Bug was launched from an automobile and also was instable in turns and then rolled out of control during a turn and crashed after eighty minutes' flying time. Because of the loss of all available GMAs and continuing problems and the expense of correcting them, it was recommended that future development be restricted to operations with safety pilots onboard.

The accumulation of negative GMA-1 test results caused Col. T. A. Sims, Air Material Command (AMC), Deputy Chief of Staff, to recommend that the project be canceled. On August 24, 1943, a scathing fourteen-page AAF report estimated that it would require 100 tests, $700,000, and eighteen months to successfully develop the GMA-1s control system, but, even so, the weapon would remain of limited value. An alternate plan was to redesign the Bug to accommodate a safety pilot, which would require $200,000 and two years to develop. The elephant in the room remained that even if the GMA-1 could be modified, its limited payload of 500 pounds and range of 200 miles continued to make it a weapon of questionable value. On September 6, 1943, Maj.-Gen. Oliver Echols, Assistant Chief of the Air Staff for Materiel, Maintenance, and Distribution, further damaged the GMA-1's future when he also endorsed terminating the program. Following the successful October Muroc demonstrations of the Interstate and Fleetwings controllable XBQ series of weapons, it was determined that the XBQs promised greater success than the GMA-l and the program was canceled on December 23, 1943. Because of the lack of storage, the remaining GMA-1 airframes and wings were destroyed, the engines reclaimed, and the control equipment and launch car reverted to Wright Field.

The GMA-1 program, despite the large quantity of time, effort, and money spent, was a failure; not only because it did not see combat, but because its development and testing did not advance any new data for future developments and only confirmed that that there were continued problems to be solved in just in putting the weapon into the air and once in the air, the problems of guidance, control, and stability in flight continued. However, the GMA-1 did verify the problems of testing an aircraft without a safety pilot onboard as without him the loss of the weapon was much more probable and, also, without telemetry a reduced amount of information was collected from each test.

2
Guided Bombs

AAF GB Series Glide Bomb

Although unmanned powered bombs such as the Kettering and GM Bugs were the oldest and most developed type of U.S. guided aerial weapon, glide bombs (GB) were deployed in combat before powered bombs by the AAF. Gen. Arnold had been an advocate of guided unmanned weapons for the AAC for several reasons. His primary reason was that they were standoff, allowing the GB to be delivered from outside the range of German anti-aircraft (flak) batteries, which would become increasingly lethal as the war continued. A secondary motivation was, with the exception of the gyro-stabilized GB-1, all GB versions were anticipated to be more accurate than conventional gravity bombs, since their controllers would be able to correct for changes in the winds and the aggregate effects of erroneous calculations of temperature, barometric pressure, and humidity of the air through which the GB was to be navigated, and also to correct for the effects of the typical errors found in contemporary mechanical/analog instrumentation. Lastly, GBs, unlike standard gravity bombs, could be controlled to arrive at the target in a flat trajectory, which improved their probabilities of striking vertical, man-made structures and also to penetrate the weaker sides and doors of reinforced enemy bunkers and submarine pens.

After encouraging pre-war acceptance and initial development, during the months after Pearl Harbor, GB development was briefly placed on hold as America's military required vast quantities of established bombs and ammunition. GB development would be resumed in April 1942 and continue until the project was officially terminated on January 31, 1946, at which time eighteen GB variants would have been developed. However, no matter their complexity, all GB variants would basically be derivatives of the GB-1.

GB-1 Glide Bomb

Brig. Gen. Oliver Echols initiated the glide bomb project on February 19, 1941 with a request to the Intelligence Division to obtain information from the British about their glide bombs and torpedoes. Echols has been given little credit for his very important, but little-known, participation on the Air Production Board and on the Executive Committee of the War Production Board from 1943 to 1945. He represented the AAF in the direction of all production, and the institution of priorities for use of tools, materiel, and manpower within the national war program. Echols was responsible to determine the relative strength of U.S. air *versus* land and sea forces, and also to determine the relative strengths of fighter aircraft to light, medium, and heavy bomber forces. The British Air Commission in Washington, D.C., sent Wg. Cdr. J. D. Brace to Wright Field on February 13, 1941 to discuss the glide bomb. A report on this conference prepared by the Experimental Engineering Section at Wright Field concluded with the statement that effort should be directed to television and/or other equipment, which would permit the changing of direction of the missile while in flight. Since America was not a combatant at the time, no further interaction with the British on their glide bomb project was made.

In a communication to Echols on March 17, Arnold expressed his interest in the glide bomb:

> We are apparently all wet in that we are doing nothing toward producing the simple and effective bomb with a set of wings. I want that started at once. There are many young engineers who can put wings on the bombs and by test and experiment ... (get them ready) ... for mass employment.
>
> Let's get this thing started at once at one of our bombing ranges, probably at Tonopah. Figure on the glide-striking-angle to hit docks, buildings, etc., when a bomb dropped vertically would hit streets, parks and open spaces. The mass of Glide Bomb from a squadron under the law of averages will get hits when Vertical Bombs would make misses.
>
> USAAF, *Case History of the GB-1*
> Maxwell AFB, MF Reel A2082, A2083, and A2051

Wright Field's initial general specification for a GB stated that the weapon was to be a simple winged glider airframe, having control surfaces and gyro and servo mechanisms capable of making small corrections to the bomb's flight controls sufficient to keep the wing's level. The airframe was to be interchangeable for use with the Navy's Mk. XIII torpedo or a standard 2,000-pound M34 bomb. As a result of several Army-Navy conferences during the spring and summer of 1941, the Navy assumed glide-torpedo development while Wright Field concentrated on the GB.

The AAC contacted three aircraft manufacturers to design a suitable GB airframe while the Experimental Engineering Section at Wright Field under Col. Benjamin Chidlaw was to concurrently develop radio-controlled and seeking devices to be installed on the completed airframe. The airframe developed by Aeronca Aircraft Company of Middletown, Ohio, was designated as the GB-1; a design by Bellanca Aircraft Company of New Castle (Wilmington), Delaware, was designated as the GB-2; while Timm Aircraft of Los Angeles designed the GB-3.

Pre-war, Aeronca developed the successful private two-seat Chief and Super Chief, which evolved into the Defender, a tandem trainer. Aeronca was selected to incorporate the GB concepts of the Experimental Engineering Section into a radio-controlled glider design that was more complicated than the original specification.

Initial testing on the basic GB design, code named the "Grapefruit Bomb," began at Muroc Bombing Range on December 8 and 9, 1941, with seven of twelve dropped bombs gliding successfully, one during a flight of 6.5 miles under radio control. These successful tests resulted in a strong endorsement of the GB concept, but after this promising start, the GB project was briefly paused during the first months after Pearl Harbor as America's attention turned to securing conventional bombs and ammunition.

During late 1941, initial tests using a Douglas B-23 twin-engined bomber were conducted to demonstrate that this aircraft was suitable for the project. The B-23 flew at 200 mph carrying the glide bomb below its fuselage between the engine nacelles on specially designed transporting mechanisms. Three B-23 glide bomb squadrons were slated to be formed in Seattle, San Francisco, and Los Angeles by May 1942, but there were not enough B-23s available in tactical quantities. Upon further consideration, Wright Field suggested to Col. Grandison Gardner, newly appointed Commander of the Air Proving Ground Command at Eglin, that the B-17E was the most suitable aircraft; in July 1942, the necessary technical instructions would be issued for B-17E modification kits.

On April 17, 1942, Gen. Arnold, eager for the weapon to reach combat readiness, personally reviewed the work already completed on the project, and recommended that its resumption and that the development of the complex radio control and seeking mechanisms be discontinued until a simple GB with wings and automatic pilot had been perfected and constructed. However, the following day, Echols restated that there was no actual directive eliminating radio control and further emphasized the need to develop all types of control, including radio, television, heat, light, and sound. Echols was supported by Col. Chidlaw who responded that the GB needed to be controlled and stabilized by some method if it was to be as accurate as conventional gravity bombs. Arnold was adamant and on April 20, 1942 sent an immediate and succinct response to Wright Field:

> There appears to be a misunderstanding as to the priorities on development and production of Glide Bomb. In order that all concerned may work to these same objectives I am again listing the order of priorities on these projects:
>
> First Priority: A simple Glide Bomb with stabilization only. This type of bomb will, of course, not have the accuracy of a more complicated type but when used in quantity will accomplish the result desired against vertical area targets. These bombs will be either attached to airplanes for release or be towed by airplanes and released. These will depend upon quantity of projectiles released for effect.

A Douglas B-23 conducted initial glide bomb tests (Nos. 1–11) during late 1941 to demonstrate that this aircraft was suitable for the project, but there were not enough B-23s available in tactical quantities. The photo shows a B-23 testing its carrying capabilities by dropping a 1,000-pound bomb, which was the payload of the GB-1. (*AAF*)

> Second Priority: A Glide Bomb with stabilization plus control, either radio or television, heat, light or what have you. This type of bomb will have the accuracy required for semi-precision work against a particular target.
>
> While work would continue on the radio-controlled versions, clearly the unguided, preset, gyro-stabilized Glide Bomb would receive the bulk of the Air Forces R&D resources at least for the time being.

USAAF, *Case History of the GB-1*
Maxwell AFB, MF Reel A2082, A2083, and A2051

On June 24, 1942, Arnold's gyro-stabilized GB was officially designated as the GB-1 by the Production Engineering Section at Wright Field. The weapon was a 12-foot-long, high-wing monoplane airframe of simple wooden construction with a 12-foot wingspan including two ailerons for turning. Twin, P-38-type booms extended aft from under the main wing and carried B-25-type twin fin tail assembly. This tail unit consisted of a horizontal stabilizer with a movable elevator and had two, square, rudderless vertical fins attached to its ends. The weapon weighed 2,338 pounds including the 2,000-pound M34 bomb warhead. The guidance system, located on a platform just behind the wing between the two booms, was a rudimentary, preset, automatic pilot-type system, gyro-stabilized in azimuth. It was adjusted on the mother aircraft just before release by the bombardier who could, after making his calculations for altitude, airspeed, and wind, adjust the bomb's ailerons, rudder, and stabilizer correspondingly before releasing the bomb. After release, the bomb would then continue on its course without any further input possible from the bombardier. At 15,000 feet, the theoretical accuracy was 700 feet in azimuth and 2,800 feet in range with a glide ratio of six to one (i.e. for every foot of altitude, it could glide 6 feet in distance). However, because of their long flight time, glide bombs were subject to the effect of winds, which significantly influenced their accuracy. The theoretical accuracy and the influence of wind were rationales Gen. Arnold would later use for the GB-1s to be released *en masse* to hit the target.

At Gen. Arnold's request, Brig. Gen. Grandison Gardner investigated the project's status at the Air Material Command. Gardner was advised by AMC Lt. Cols. F. W. Williams and George Holloman that a simple gyro-stabilized GB could probably be design-frozen and mass produced by late summer 1942. Thus, it appears that Arnold was led to believe that the GB-1 was only weeks or a few months away from combat readiness, but when late summer arrived, the Aeronca-built airframe was still in the test stages at Muroc. Gen. Echols recommended to Gen. Arnold: "We might profitably put the glide bomb to immediate use and a directive was issued in October for the necessary procurement to place the GB-1 into combat as soon as possible." The Aeronca design was selected and frozen for production as a controllable GB essentially consisting of a high-wing type of aerodynamic structure with two booms and tail surfaces, equipped with a servo control assembly and attached to a 2,000-pound demolition bomb. The course was to be preset and no control was to be exercised after launch. Designated as Project MX-108, Aeronca was scheduled to provide 4,300 GB-1 airframes at 800 per month by December 1942 and the Hammond Instrument Company was to manufacture the more intricate gyroscopic stabilizers at the same

On June 24, 1942, Arnold's gyro-stabilized glide bomb was officially designated as the GB-1. The 2,338-pound (including the M34 2,000-pound bomb warhead) weapon was a 12-foot-long, high-wing monoplane airframe of simple wooden construction with a 12-foot wingspan, including two ailerons for turning. (*AAF*)

Twin P-38-type booms extended aft from under the main wing and carried B-25-type tail assembly. This tail unit consisted of a horizontal stabilizer with a movable elevator and had two, square, rudderless, vertical fins attached to its ends. (*AAF*)

The guidance system, located on a platform just behind the wing between the two booms, was a rudimentary, preset, automatic pilot-type system, gyro-stabilized in azimuth that was adjusted on the mother aircraft just before release by the bombardier. (*AAF*)

rate by March 1943. Hammond, founded by Lauren Hammond of the electronic organ fame, had manufactured electric clocks in the pre-war. By December, GB-1 production was reduced to 250 per month as Hammond was unable to maintain the required production rate but somehow 2,225 GB-1 assemblies were still scheduled to be delivered by no later than the end of February 1943.

An urgent request was made for a B-17E to be made accessible to Wright Field for ninety days for GB bomb-shackle design and flight testing. There was a delay in procuring a B-17E for testing as officers under Arnold had no interest in the GB, and in July, Arnold finally had to enlighten his subordinates that they had better develop an interest in his project very soon! On July 17, 1942, Brig. Gen. Muir Fairchild, the air staff's director of Military Requirements, noted in a letter to the AMC that a suitable mechanism for attaching glide bombs to B-17s needed to be developed as soon as possible. To facilitate this effort, Fairchild directed the AAF Proving Ground Command "to provide Wright Field engineers with a B-17F plus aircrew, since it was understood that one complete ... installation assembly had been designed and fabricated but had not [yet] been tested due to lack of an airplane."

The Fortress was delivered by July 24 and testing of the bomb shackle began, but General Arnold's impatience with the project was again experienced when he directed that a large-scale test involving the massed, simultaneous drop of twenty glide bombs be conducted at Eglin in the near future. Fairchild sought to expedite this test, directing it initiated not later than August 15, even if other experimental work had to be delayed.

Col. F. O. Carroll, the new Chief of the Experimental Engineering Section, immediately ordered the delivery of ten B-17Fs to the Middletown Air Depot, Pennsylvania, for GB modification by August 18 in time to meet Arnold's order for large scale B-17/GB-1 tests. During the August tests, these ten modified B-17Fs were to drop a total of sixty GB-1s, twenty from each of three selected altitudes, carried on external wing shackles and dropped singly and *en masse*. The results of the tests are incomplete but appears that they were considered successful. When dropped from 5,000 feet, about 70 percent flew straight courses and hit the ground in formation with relatively consistent results; placing them in an equilateral triangle, a mile on each side. Remarkably, the report stated that 100 percent accuracy could be realized in hitting a medium-sized city, similar to nearby Dayton, Ohio, from 30,000 feet! The report continued, maintaining that a smaller target could be accurately hit but from reduced altitude and range, which, of course, exposed the dropping aircraft to increased vulnerability to AA fire, contradicting the project's intention. The report concluded that inaccuracy was a characteristic of the GB-1 design and that it was not planned for precision bombing but were to be dropped *en masse*.

Initial flight-testing using B-17Fs carrying GBs was finally completed at Eglin on August 25, 1942, which, while only ten days after the date initially set by Gen. Fairchild, was four months after Gen. Arnold had demanded that he wanted the GB-1 tested in combat. Ultimately, all these delays would accumulate, and not recognized at the time, GB-1 combat testing would not occur for almost another two years.

The August tests determined many problems that would be influential in delaying the GB-1 program. The GB-1 could not be carried internally so special wing racks and shackles were developed that could be installed in thirty minutes. Underwing hard points had to be retrofitted to provide sufficient structural strength to mount a wing rack unit that was capable of suspending a 2,500-pound GB. Mechanical and electrical connections to the wing racks had to be installed so that the bombardier/controller could activate the GB's stabilizing gyroscopes and program its flight controls before releasing it.

Originally, it was believed that the B-17s could be modified by installing the hard points and wiring for the wing racks and shackles while the bombers were still on the assembly lines. But, on November 6, 1942, the Air Staff Requirements Division reported that the earliest a B-17 could be delivered off the assembly line with all the necessary GB modifications would be on B-17, tail number 1150, due off the assembly line sometime during early February 1943. In the meantime, all B-17s before #1150 delivered to the AAF would have to be modified by the AMC. The externally mounted wing racks produced aerodynamic drag, causing the carrying B-17Fs to experience a substantial reduction in cruising speed, maximum altitude, and range. Consequently, these B-17Fs were internally wired for GB operations before deployment to the U.K., with the bomb shackles and wing racks shipped separately, to be installed on the bombers only when GB missions were scheduled.

		B-17F	
Payload	Max. Speed	at 25,000 feet	Ceiling Range
Internal Bombs	310 mph	28,000 feet	2,300 miles
Glide Bomb	280 mph	26,500 feet	2,150 miles

Bomber aircraft mechanics and ordnance technicians would not only have to commence training to install and uninstall GB equipment, but the GB required considerably more maintenance and upkeep—more than generally given to standard bombs. In October 1942, it was concluded that a minimum of twenty technicians would be required for each bomb group employing glide bombs. The technicians were to maintain the GBs and make certain they were properly mounted and, if not dropped on training or combat missions, dismounted from the bomber. The Plans Division instructed the Individual Training Division to train twenty glide bomb mechanics by December 15, 1942 and 150 by March 1, 1943, using training curricula developed by AMC's Special Weapon Unit. Pilots and bombardiers would also require extensive specialized training, as would the aircraft instrument (avionics) technicians. The training of these GB personnel would require time to establish and proceed. During November and December 1942, there was a shortage of completely modified B-17Fs to fulfill all training and testing obligations and avionics technicians and GB bombardier trainees had to share a single bomber with AAF engineers performing high-altitude glide bombing tests at Eglin. The project's officials agreed that this testing could better conducted at Muroc Lake Field, transferring all GB-1 program avionics and bombardier students and instructors and their single, shared B-17F test bomber there.

In addition to training requirements and B-17 airframe modification issues, the GB-1 itself was also subject to constant demands for modifications as was typical of new aircraft design, which, however, further impeded mass production. On November 6, 1942, the AMC ordered an initial modifications request, which directed that each GB-1 be equipped with a self-destruction charge so that the GB-1's design and construction would not be captured by the enemy if the bomb failed to detonate. The Ordnance Department quickly developed a destruction device using a T-4 detonator/destructor with a modified hand grenade 0.1-second delay fusing for 2.5 pounds of Tetrytol to destroy the GB-1.

On November 19, the Military Requirements Division ordered tests to be performed to determine:

1. The effects of a glide bomb striking a vertical structure with its side versus the nose of the bomb.
2. The effects of nose-on impact on hard surfaces and time delays required to guarantee substantial detonations proportionate with the bomb casing and selected fusing.
3. The vulnerability of externally carried GB-ls to machine gun and cannon fire and also to icing conditions.

The use of 2,000-pound general-purpose bombs for the GB-1 became an issue when the Air War Plans Division Plan 42 (AWPD-42), devised by Gen. Haywood Hansell during August 1942, requested bombs mostly between 300 and 2,000 pounds, which resulted in considerable concern in Air Plans that there would be insufficient 2,000-pound bombs available for the GB program. The 8th Air Force initially projected that each bomb group would require 750 glide bombs per month, with a minimum of four groups trained and competent in deploying them ASAP. This glide bomb prerequisite would denote that 3,000 2,000-pound bomb casings would be required over the normal utilization rate of 10,000 per month.

On September 15, 1942, VIII Bomber Command CO Gen. Ira Eaker wrote an indifferent report on the potential use of GB-1s in the ETO, recommending that, due to their inaccuracy, their use be redirected to targets in Germany to avoid risking unnecessary civilian casualties in occupied countries. He also emphasized that "this method of bombing is contrary to the one we are now practicing," (i.e. high-level point bombing). He then concluded with the halfhearted endorsement, "It is believed that the effort will prove valuable." Spaatz added to Eaker's report that he desired that the full report of the massed glide bombing tests at Eglin be forwarded to him and then suggested that, in addition to the area targets located in Germany, perhaps these bombs could be employed at low-level with A-20 attack bombers or P-38 fighter bombers. He requested Eglin perform these low-altitude tests with guided versions of the bomb with a view to determining their efficiency against precision targets heavily defended by light AA fire.

Between November 20 and 29, 1942, the Equipment Laboratory at Eglin conducted thirteen test drops to collect GB ballistic data, during which only two bombs stalled or tumbled and failed to glide. Tests number 1–11 were single bombs dropped by a B-23, while during tests number 12 and 13, two bombs were dropped simultaneously from a B-17F. The Hammond gyroscopic stabilizers functioned effectively if the bomb was released smoothly and in level flight, which was the standard for the preset glide bombs. The stabilizers held the GB's wings level and corrected for wind gusts and turbulence as necessary. However, small differences in construction caused disparities in the center of gravity, causing several bombs to wobble when they were released. If any movement was too large, the stabilizing gyroscopes were unable to compensate and the GB would tumble. The average miss during these tests was a non-precision quarter mile in azimuth and a half mile in range.

Eglin GB-1 Tests Continue

Reliable ballistic data was critical to resolve any design concerns. It was also essential for training bombardiers to control glide bombs, especially since delivering a GB on target required abilities completely different from those the bombardiers had learned with gravity bombs during their qualification training. So, from December 6–24, 1942, the Wright Field Equipment Laboratory conducted a second series of tests that basically had the same results as the November tests. The GB-1 was established to be a stable glider but was relatively inaccurate and susceptible to stalling and tumbling if the bombardier did not set the rudder and aileron controls correctly before release. The accuracy of the bomb was subject to the bombardier knowing the bomber's exact heading and altitude; the accurate distance to the target before release; and his ability to precisely consider the effect of the winds as they changed from the bomber's altitude to the surface. By December 1942, the GB-1 had proven itself to be a reasonably reliable standoff weapon that, while it lacked the precision of standard gravity bombs, was sufficiently accurate to be used for area or pattern bombing against a target the size of a large city.

Typical of any new weapon, GB-1 mass production had been initially delayed by developmental problems that had compromised previous test data and required modifications and further testing. Consequently, on January 4, 1943, to advance the project, the Equipment Laboratory decided that the GB-1 design was practicable and advocated that its design be frozen. Aeronca was directed to manufacture enough GB-1s for combat use; the B-17F was declared to be suitable to carry and deliver the weapon; and that there were enough trained pilots, bombardiers, mechanics, and technicians to maintain and deploy the GB-1 in combat.

The bottom line continued to be that the GBs were Gen. Arnold's pet project and that he wanted them tested and used in combat, so March 1, 1943 was set for the GB-1s operational debut. Nevertheless, the GB-1 would not become operational for more than another year. The major contributing factor for this delay was that, while GB-1 technical and mechanical testing had been comprehensive, it was not yet complete, as operational concerns employing these weapons had not been completely considered.

On February 20, 1943, Gen. Eugene Eubank of the Air Staff's Bombardment Division forwarded an informative report to Gen. George Stratemeyer, Chief of the Air Staff, which expressed the many concerns threatening the operational use of the GB-1. Eubanks stated that the Tonopah, Nevada, GB-1 ballistic tests would not be completed until the end of February at the earliest, and that at least two to three weeks would then be necessary to convert this data into useable form, which was essential to

GB-1 Glide Bomb Gallery

Above: Fitting the wing on to the GB-1 structure already attached to the M34 2,000-pound bomb warhead. (*AAF*)

Below left: GB-1s line the Eglin runway awaiting placement on carts to be carried to B-17s for tests. (*AAF*)

Below right: Two GB-1s being hoisted from their carts to their special wing racks just outboard the fuselage. GB-1 could not be carried internally so special wing racks and shackles were developed that could be installed in thirty minutes. (*AAF*)

Glide bomb in place. Underwing hard points had to be retrofitted to provide sufficient structural strength to mount a wing rack unit that was capable of suspending a 2,500-pound glide bomb. Mechanical and electrical connections to the wing racks had to be installed so that the bombardier/controller could activate the GB's stabilizing gyroscopes and program its flight controls before releasing it. (*AAF*)

The externally mounted wing racks produced aerodynamic drag, causing the carrying B-17Fs to experience a substantial reduction in cruising speed (30 mph less), maximum altitude (1,500 feet less), and range (150 miles less). (*AAF*)

ensure reliable preparations by operational units. Eubanks also firmly recommended that no glide bomb specialists proceed to 8AF until this data was available. This report very critically emphasized that to date, not one GB-1 had been dropped from combat altitudes of 15,000 feet or higher and that there were continuing problems with the Hammond electric gyros reliability. The gyro's issues would have to be rectified before any GB-ls could be shipped to VIII Bomber Command—a process that would require an estimated six weeks before GB-1 gyro kits were modified and qualified. Eubank reported that sufficient bomb racks and shackles to equip four bomb groups would not be available until March 1 at the earliest. Eubanks then discussed the GB-1's operational limitations. In test drops at Tonopah, the bombs had an extreme net deflection error (i.e. the distance the bomb consistently landed left or right of the target) of between 4,023 and 6,084 feet when the bomb was dropped from an altitude of 9,700 feet (i.e. the error was one-half to two-thirds the altitude of the bomber at the time of release). This deflection error would only increase in combat due to the lack of accurate information on the winds over enemy territory. With a six to one glide ratio, a 10,000-foot release would mean the GB would glide 11.5 miles before hitting the target, and at 25,000 feet, the glide distance would 28-plus miles, which would require perfect visibility (rare in the ETO) and preclude the use of the existing Norden bombsight. When dropping a GB-1 from 25,000 feet, an error of only one degree in the dropping angle would cause a range error of approximately 3 miles, while a one-degree heading error would result in a deflection error of a half mile. The externally-mounted GB slowed the B-17's cruising speed at high altitudes by as much as 30 mph, reducing its maximum combat ceiling by at least 1,500 feet, and adversely affecting the bomber's combat range by as much as 150 miles. Furthermore, the externally-mounted GBs were very unreliable when icing conditions were encountered at any time during the mission. Icing interfered with fuse operation, the bomb release mechanisms, delaying or even preventing the glide bomb's release, and also coated the GB's wings, adversely affecting its aerodynamic characteristics. The report was concluded by General Eubank requesting that the GB-1's combat debut be delayed until at least May 1, 1943. Stratemeyer's February 13 reply approved Eubank's recommendation that the operational use of glide bombs be deferred until approximately May 1, 1943.

This delay would cause immediate problems for Aeronca, which had been under considerable pressure since October 1942 to deliver GB-1 air frames at the maximum rate possible. By late January 1943, Aeronca had accumulated more than 1,500 completed GB-1 assemblies and was quickly filling its storage areas and was anxiously awaiting shipping directives from the Air Materiel Command. Despite the AMCs repeated requests to the 8AF during December, January, and February, no shipping destinations were provided, only because the GB-1 had not yet been approved for operational use from either the technical or the tactical standpoint. General Eubank stipulated that the Operational Plans Division inform the Bombardment Division on how these GB-1s were anticipated to be employed so that some basis or production requirements could be established.

The implications of Eubank's request were wide-ranging, as until then, General Arnold had been demanding that his GB be combat-operational by March 1, 1943, and both the Bombardment Division and AMC had supposed that four bomber groups would be equipped and trained to deploy them. However, only weeks from the GB's projected operational date, there were no tactical requirements for their combat employment, nor had Operational Plans established an operational need for them, except that General Arnold wanted them. Later, it was this lack of tactical development and planning that would frustrate Dr. Vannevar Bush of the Office of Scientific Research and Development (OSRD) and cause him to decline requests for additional research and development for other guided bomb projects in 1944 and 1945.

On March 2, 1943, the Air Materiel Command released a memorandum proposing the termination of GB-1 production, but on the same day, Brig. Gen. Frank Anderson of Operational Plans issued the following recommendations:

1. GB-1 production was to be continued until their worth was definitely determined by actual tactical operations in the ETO.
2. The theater commander was to issue an immediate report affirming a priority for the shipment of glide bombs, together with his combat plans for employing them.
3. The glide bomb offensive was not to be commenced with missions of less than 100 sorties in the ETO.

Two days later, Brig. Gen. George Stratemeyer added a note to this memorandum indicating that Gen. Arnold had seen and approved of these recommendations and GB-1 production was to continue until tested in combat. The Air Materiel Command then took immediate steps to find storage for Aeronca GB-1 airframes. These operational planning problems resulted in the predicted delay of the combat debut of the GB-1 until at least May 1, 1943.

On April 2, the Air Plans Division issued a comprehensive report on the status of the GB-1 to Gen. Arnold that revealed its reluctance to employ this weapon in combat. The report stated that due to the GB-1's large average range and deflection errors, 100 or more GBs needed to be dropped jointly as area bombs from 16,000 feet in clear weather when there was little or no wind over the target area. Because of this inaccuracy and large numbers required, the report also recommended that future GB development concentrate on the precision-guided variants. The report requested that the 8AF promptly evaluate the GB and either reject them or be obligated to use them so that unnecessary production could be halted and avoid accumulating large overstock if the GB-1 was unsuccessful. Concerning future GB development, the report clearly focused on the precision-guided variants of GBs, which demonstrated promise. The report concluded by requesting that the 8AF "promptly assess the value of simple stabilized Glide Bomb ... bearing in mind the lack of precision of the weapon and also its effect on enemy anti-aircraft defenses." The ETO glide bomb requirements and the allocation of shipping priorities for these requirements were also to be promptly evaluated. This report plainly disclosed the Air Staff, Plans Division's lack of enthusiasm about the GB-1's potential usefulness in combat and placed the responsibility on the 8AF to either completely reject them or be obligated to accept them.

The report caused Arnold to visit Eglin to personally investigate his pet project's lack of development. Once there, the general saw the inattention and apathy surrounding his project and launched a tirade and ordered that the unguided GB-1 project be allocated the majority of available funds and personnel. Arnold's dictum would have dire consequences on America's research and development of guided weapons during World War II as the GB-1 was actually a concept weapon that should have ideally been immediately replaced once the basic concept had been proven viable. It could then be adapted to any of the many other guided variations a GB could take. Arnold's insistence on developing and testing the GB-1 and then proving it in combat removed funds and researchers from the more promising and nearly completed guided GB-4 and GB-8 radio-controlled GB-1 versions, delaying their introduction by many months. On May 13, 1943, the 8th Air Force was advised that there were no operational requirements for GBs in the U.K. for that year, thus the GB project continued to be neglected in favor of precision bombing.

Brig. Gen. Ira Eaker, Commander of the 8AF, stated that American bombing doctrine stressed precision bombing of point objectives rather than the inaccurate area bombing demonstrated by the GB-1. Eaker also acknowledged that the GB-1 decreased the speed and payload of the carrying aircraft and increased its vulnerability beyond that of conventional bombing methods and would require fighter escort. When the GB-carrying B-17s flew in formations with conventional bomb-carrying B-17s, the loss of airspeed would open up the tight protective formations as the maximum cruising speed of a B-17F carrying GBs was 280 mph, which was 30 mph less than when carrying conventional bombs internally. The decrease in air speed also meant that the bomber formations equipped with only GBs were over enemy territory 10 percent longer and increased the relative speed advantage of Luftwaffe fighters, which would be more likely to catch and attack the slower GB bomber formation.

Maj. Gen. Barney Giles, Chief of the Air Staff's Operations, Commitments, and Requirements Division (OC&R), subsequently recommended that the procurement of GBs and components was concluded as soon as possible and that permanent storage be arranged for completed units. On June 3, Aeronca was notified that after the initial 4,000 on order were produced and delivered production was to cease. Nonetheless, on May 16, the Materiel Command sent a GB contingent of four pilots and four bombardiers who had received limited GB training—a control technician, an ordnance engineer, and a Boeing factory representative—to England to demonstrate the GB-1 to RAF and AAF personnel, including Brig. Gen. Haywood Hansell and Col. Curtis LeMay. But first, several days were spent locating the glide-bomb kits scattered in U.K. storage depots and warehouses. Once located, they were mounted on a B-17F and demonstrated by two pilots, two bombardiers, and two ordnance officers who were receiving on-the-job training. The AMC report summarized the demonstration, which ended on May 22, by concluding:

1. That GB training in any combat theater would likely be impracticable and detrimental due to the many other activities required in tactical operations in that theater.

2. That complete combat units should be formed, the necessary equipment installed, the personnel trained, all in the United States, and afterward these units be sent, with their equipment, into combat.

General Eaker remained unimpressed with GB-1s as he specified to the AMC representatives at the demonstration that the employment of glide bombs in the ETO was ill-advised because:

1. Present AAF bombing strategy was focused on precision bombing of point objectives.
2. Close formations at high altitudes were necessary for protection against enemy fighters, and the loss of speed of the GB-carrying bombers would cause the formations to open and consequently increase vulnerability.
3. The GB-carrying aircraft had a decreased bomb load.
4. Because of the up-tempo of the ground war in the ETO there was a shortage of shipping space required to transport the necessary GB-1 equipment to the U.K.

After the costly August 17, 1943 Regensburg-Schweinfurt bombing raids (sixty bombers lost and 552 bomber crewmen either killed or captured), an alarmed Gen. Arnold personally flew to Britain to visit Gen. Eaker at 8th Air Force H.Q. to reassess the 8th's operational bombing status and also to evaluate the status of his GB-1 project as an alternative. Arnold ordered the glide bomb program to be immediately instituted in the ETO in early October 1943. On September 11, Arnold directed Eaker to prepare thirty-six B-17s for testing the GB and that 1,000 GB-1 units were to be shipped to the U.K.

One week later, Brig. Gen. Hoyt Vandenberg, AF H.Q. Deputy Chief of Air Staff, informed the AAF School of Applied Tactics (AAFSAT) in Orlando, Florida, for the first time, of the detailed operational and tactical considerations for employing GB-1s in combat:

1. General Arnold directed that the glide bomb program be immediately established in the ETO and that he and Eaker requested that the glide bomb be operational in one month (mid-October) with a minimum of thirty-six B-17s.
2. AAFSAT was directed to conduct tests with a minimum of eighteen bombers at altitudes in excess of 20,000 feet and that these tests were to determine the following:
   a) Determine mandatory tactics to maintain a defensive, mutually supporting formation allowing for the release of bombs from this formation at the same time.
   b) Determine the effect of appropriate evasive action upon the release of glide bombs and the difficulties of employing evasive actions while carrying the bombs.
   c) Determine the problems, due to wake turbulence, encountered by trailing aircraft in flying formation.
   d) Determine the effective range and best indicated airspeed of aircraft carrying glide bombs.

e) Determine the types of targets that would be suitable for the employment of glide bombs and the target identification factors that become apparent due to the distances from the target from which the bombs were released.

Once more, these testing requirements plainly revealed that the operational need for GBs still had not been officially determined, and that the GB-1 existed only because Arnold wanted to use it in combat.

On September 14, the air staff directed Air Materiel Command to ship 500 GB-1s to the 8AF in England ASAP for use in the initial GB missions scheduled to be flown in October. On October 20, 1943, forty U.S. trained crews along with their aircraft arrived in England and were assigned to the 41st Combat Bomb Wing with Capt. James Tillman assigned as the 8AF project officer. Once assigned, the GB crews learned that the supposedly ASAP-shipped GB-1 sets were still in the U.S. and would arrive in about two months, but this delay was beneficial as it would permit the necessary training of the more than eighty ordnance technicians assigned to the project. Also, Brig. Gen. Robert Travis, CG of the 41st Combat Wing, desired additional aircrew training with these weapons before the first mission was flown.

On October 19, 1943, Gen. Arnold wrote Gen. Spaatz:

> At present some doubt is felt that these bombs (GB-1s) in their standardized mass glide version will have sufficient accuracy to attain great effectiveness against specific buildings in submarine pen attacks. From 5,000 feet these bombs can consistently be placed in a one mile square and it is possible that improvements will cut this to a one half mile square. Even this may not be sufficiently accurate for anti-submarine purposes.... Meanwhile we are exerting every effort to make possible the precision version of this Glide Bomb (GB-4s). It now appears possible that this version will be available in the spring and should be a much more valuable weapon than the mass glide type.
>
> USAAF, *Case History of the GB-1*
> Maxwell AFB, MF Reel A2082, A2083, and A2051

Grapefruit Practice GB-1 Missions

By November 19, 115 aircraft and crews were trained, and by December 2, an additional twenty-eight crews in three bomb groups were fully trained to fly operational missions, code named Grapefruit, a designation thought to have been derived from its Florida tests in June 1941. For these practice missions, Col. Maurice Preston of the 379BG delegated pilot Maj. Robert Kittle, navigator Capt. James Edwards, and bombardier Capt. Joseph Glaser to investigate and develop GB bombing tactics. They determined that the minimum speed at bomb release was to be at least 180 IAS (Indicated Air Speed) to put the GB into glide attitude. To acquire

180 to 200 IAS, the bomber had to climb to 2,000 feet above the intended GB release altitude and enter a gentle two-minute descent and release the GBs at the prescribed altitude. After releasing their GB load, the then lighter bombers accelerated to 250 mph to leave the flak in the target area.

The first operational Grapefruit mission was scheduled to be flown on December 12, but it was inexplicably canceled, although twenty-five individual practice missions were flown that day along with one mass-formation drop into the North Sea. The test drops, often in the poor visibility, made it apparent that at least one bomber in each formation would have to be equipped with H2X radar and six navigators were dispatched to receive training on this equipment. Also, special bombardment charts had to be developed to provide data to bombardiers to ensure that they could quickly perform the calculations necessary to accurately predict the GB trajectory, which was much longer than conventional bombs and could continue in flight for as much as six minutes after release.

After December 12, 1943, there was a hiatus in GB activity. The early-arriving winter weather definitely was a major factor as the 8AF was seldom able to assemble large enough formations in good morning weather to achieve the necessary target damage and then return to base before the weather closed in again. Between December 12, 1943 and January 31, 1944, the 8AF was able to fly only ten missions that reached targets in Germany, and most of those required blind bombing using the H2X radar. Because the GB-1s required nearly absolute visibility to be effectively employed, the heavy winter cloud cover prevented GB-1 missions over northern Europe until May 28, 1944, when an actual GB-1 combat mission was flown.

During this winter break, there were many top echelon personnel changes and promotions within the 8AF and U.S. Strategic Air Forces (USSTAF), which also precluded specialized GB-1 missions from being flown. Maj. Gen. James Doolittle assumed command of the 8AF from Maj. Gen. Frederick Anderson on December 22, while in that same month, Maj. Gen. Carl Spaatz returned to the U.K. from commanding the 15AF in the Mediterranean to take command of the USSTAF from Maj. Gen. Ira Eaker. These major command changes unquestionably required weeks for the new commanders and onboard personnel to adapt to each other. Scheduled conventional bombardment missions had priority to be flown as planned, weather permitting, but special GB-1 missions were readily postponed by uninterested operational group and division commanders.

Once the weather cleared, the USSTAF had long-planned to conduct a major, concentrated air campaign against the Luftwaffe and German oil production installations coded as Big Week. These large-scale missions required numerous bombers capable of flying in close formations while reaching and returning from the target ASAP. Bombers slowed by carrying GB-1s could not have been easily integrated into the faster Big Week conventional bomber formations and would have lagged behind, vulnerable to Luftwaffe interceptors. Also, Big Week targets, aircraft factories, airfields, and oil facilities, were pin-point targets unsuitable for the inaccurate GB. So crated GB-1 assemblies remained in ordnance storage depots scattered throughout the U.K. during the winter and early spring of 1944.

Once it appeared that GB operations were possible, GB-1 delivery was delayed as they had been stored for so long that many of the batteries that powered the gyroscope could not hold a charge. The Exide Battery Company was to ship 100 replacement batteries but had ceased production of that type of battery and would have to open a new production line to manufacture them. But to be profitable for Exide, at least, several thousand had to be contracted; once contracted, the batteries would not be available until late spring.

Meanwhile, despite the slower production schedule agreed on with the AMC, Aeronca continued to accumulate stocks of GB-1 assemblies. By April, the Engineering Division was investigating which of the GB-1's equipment could be utilized for use by the radio-controlled GB-8, with the remaining unneeded GB-1 components to be declared as surplus.

Beginning during April 1944, the 15AF had flown missions using the more advanced, guided VB-1 AZON bomb, and so, the 8AF was again being pressured by Gen. Arnold and his staff to get the GB-1 into combat. The first GB mission was scheduled for April 26, 1944 but was recalled because of bad weather. It was not until May 28, 1944 that weather, logistical, and other snafus were remedied so the first GB mission could be dispatched. Three Bomb Groups of the 41st Combat Wing were to drop their GB-1s on Koln Eifeltor (Cologne) marshalling yards.

Fifty-nine aircraft, each carrying two GBs, took off with one 379BG B-17 aborting. After assembly, the lead 303BG (under Col. Kermit Stevens) flew at 19,500 feet, the low 379BG (Col. Maurice Preston) at 19,000 feet, and the high 384BG (Col. Dale Smith) at 21,000 feet. The groups cruised at 140 mph IAS in excellent mission weather with 20-mile downward visibility, encountering no enemy flak or fighters. As the initial point (IP) was reached (about 20 miles from the dropping point, using a north–south road as a reference) each group went into a predetermined dive sequence of 1,000 to 1,500 feet per minute for ninety to 120 seconds to pick up the necessary 195-mph release speed. At 1:06 p.m., the first of 108 bombs were released by the low 379BG at 17,000 feet, followed by the lead 303BG at 17,600 feet and finally by the high 384BG at 19,300 feet. After release, the three groups made a climbing turn, reassembling with the lead group at 19,000 feet. The B-17 ball turret gunners watched as twenty-eight of the bombs went into either nose-down spins or flat spins, while others did acrobatics. As they continued to watch, they saw explosions occur over a large area, with the P-38 recon aircraft recording the debacle. The results were very poor and were described as comparable to the worst kind of indiscriminate area bombing:

GB Bomb Data	303BG (Lead)	379BG (Low)	384BG (High)
Bombs on Target	28	22	31
Bombs Spun In	10	14	4
Late Release	0	2	2
Accidental Release	0	0	2

Of the eighty-one on-target bombs, forty-four bursts were counted within the city as defined by a radius of 3.5 miles from the central cathedral, with seven hitting factories

GB-1 First Mission Gallery

It was not until May 28, 1944, that weather, logistical, and other snafus were remedied so the first glide bomb mission could be dispatched. Three bomb groups of the 41st Combat Wing (303BG, 379BG, and 384BG) were to drop their GB-1s on the Cologne marshalling yards. (*AAF*)

Fifty-nine B-17Gs, each carrying two glide bombs, took off and cruised at 140 mph IAS in excellent mission weather, with 20-mile downward visibility, encountering no enemy flak or fighters. (*AAF*)

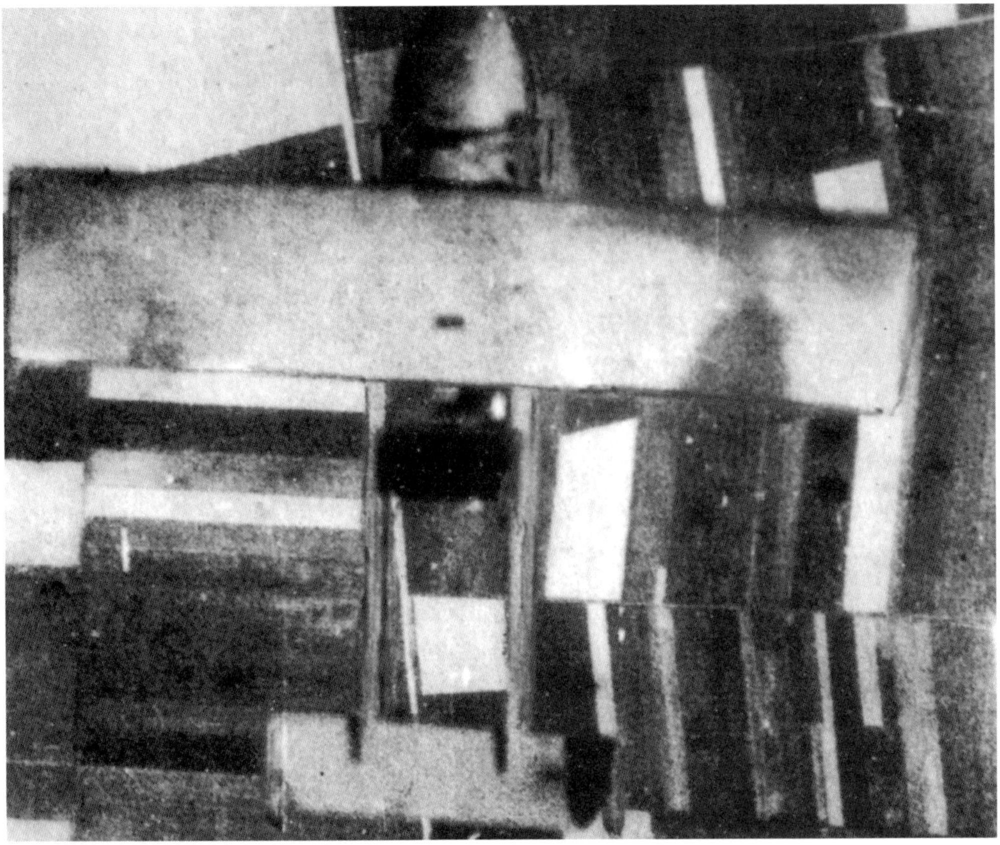

Above: The three groups, staggered in altitude, released 108 bombs. After release, they made a climbing turn, reassembling with the lead group at 19,000 feet. (*AAF*)

Right: The results were very poor and were described as "comparable to the worst kind of indiscriminate area bombing." After the GB-1's debut fiasco and subsequent quality control issues, interest in the program quickly subsided. (*AAF*)

and railroad yards; six hitting residential areas throughout the city; six hitting previously bombed out areas in the central city; and at least twenty-five hitting parks, rivers, and other open areas within the city. However, fifteen bursts were seen in open fields located 17 miles to the southwest of the city center, while another hit an open field 15 miles to the west of the city. There were three effective hits, which were probably accidental: one hit was recorded on the Shagen-Hagen submarine battery factory, another on a siding of a railroad marshalling yard, and a third hit on a small warehouse on the at the river wharf northeast of the city. The bombs arrived before German air raid sirens sounded and the Germans reported that eighty-two civilians were killed and at least 1,500 injured in what Nazi radio propagandist, William "Lord Haw Haw" Joyce described as a terror raid, which perhaps it was considering the weapon's gross inaccuracy and lack of civilian warning.

On May 28, a post-mission investigation concluded that the Mutual Furniture Co., an Aeronca subcontractor, was found to be responsible for faulty workmanship in airframe fabrication, particularly in the gluing of joints and skins. The preset automatic pilot data was extremely sensitive to inaccuracies in construction, especially on the forward ends of the booms. Also, it was concluded that the large number of times the bombs were loaded and unloaded on to their B-17s, waiting for good weather, also affected settings. Prop wash and imperfect adjustment were determined to cause twenty-eight of the bombs to spin-in.

A memorandum from Brig. Gen. Robert Williams of the 1BG assessed the mission and made the following recommendations:

> This type of bombing while it avoids flak, subjects the airplanes to greater fighter hazard, and results in the worst type of area bombing. It is the opinion of this headquarters that for an enemy installation in this theatre much better results can be accomplished at very little extra cost by utilization of conventional type, high altitude precision bombing. It therefore recommended that a review be rendered on this project and its use be discontinued in this theater.
>
> USAAF, *Case History of the GB-1*
> Maxwell AFB, MF Reel A2082, A2083, and A2051

Another, later report weighed the operational advantages and disadvantage of GB-1 deployment:

Advantages:

1. Safety of release away from anti-aircraft defenses.
2. The weapon's flat trajectory increased the percentage of hits on built up areas as compared to conventionally dropped bombs.
3. The GB had a very large skip on impact, up to one mile on land and one-third mile on water with a 40- to 50-foot-high bounce. This gave the GB a good chance to hit some obstacle in its path.

Disadvantages:

1. The wind affected ballistics.

2. The 6 to 1 glide angle required a release of 20 to 25 miles from the target and therefore the visibility needed to be excellent.
3. At 25,000 feet, a one-degree error in the drop angle caused a 3-mile range error. A one-degree error in heading caused a half-mile deflection error.
4. The external mounting of the GB-1 precluded its use in any weather condition where icing threatened, as ice would coat the missile's fuselage and wings and often clog the release mechanism.
5. Also, the external mounting of two GB-1s slowed the B-17 mother aircraft by 30 mph at high altitudes, decreased the service ceiling by 1,500 feet, and decreased its range. The bombers lift was decreased and its stalling speed decreased by nine mph.
6. Since the release speed was 195 mph, the maximum formation altitude was only 20,000 feet, making the mother bomber more vulnerable to AA and enemy interceptors.
7. GB-1 release speed was critical. If the release speed exceeded that for the control settings on the missile, the GB-1 could fly up into the mother aircraft, and if the release speed was too low, then the GB-1 would go into a spin.
8. The GB-1 when used as an area bombardment weapon had a better chance of hitting vertical targets such as buildings than a conventional bomb. The GB, however, was not as destructive, as it would hit the upper one-third of a building on its glide-in or bounce rather than hit the buildings base, which often destroyed the entire structure. Also, the destruction of utilities and blockage of streets was not as great.

Furthermore, the conduct of a major GB offensive would require a large amount of precious shipping space transiting from America to England. At this time, the upcoming Allied invasion of France required vast amounts of supplies and cargo space was at a premium

Two days after the Cologne GB mission, Reich Minister for Air Albert Speer warned Nazi civil and military authorities of their danger to the population, reporting that enemy bombers using GBs turned away before reaching their targets and that these new bombs could suddenly impact an area even if no enemy aircraft are seen or heard. Moreover, danger to exposed personnel and equipment was considered greater than with conventional vertical bombs because the flat trajectory of these GBs caused them to often skip off the ground and explode in the air, increasing the radius of damage.

After the GB-1's May 28 debut fiasco and subsequent quality control issues, interest in the program quickly subsided. On June 23, the Production Engineering Section notified the Equipment Section that all GB-1 parts and subassemblies were to be examined and those that were considered to be of poor quality were to be written-off. On August 4, the Air Materiel Command was directed to inventory all GB-1s stored in the Continental U.S. so that a plan could be instituted to dispose of them. On September 15, 1944, the GB-1 program was officially terminated by finance report #405710, which stated that the program had cost $2,223,261 (almost $33 million U.S. 2020) and the cost of its termination was $275,112.

Despite Gen. Chidlaw's exasperation at having to support the simple, unguided, grossly inaccurate GB-1 program, it undoubtedly was Gen. Arnold's unflagging sponsorship of developing the GB-1 program first that retarded more promising radio-controlled GBs that were already being tested. Ultimately, the GB-1 can be recognized as being the archetype for all other U.S. glide bomb employed in the war. While the GB-1 was no longer considered a viable weapon, its airframe would be used for the GT-1, air-dropped Mk. 13 naval torpedo.

GT-1 Glide Pattern Torpedo

During March 1941, while the British were working on their glide torpedo project, Gen. Arnold ordered Maj. Gen. Oliver Echols, CO of Wright Field's Air Materiel Division, to assemble the necessary personnel to develop an American glide bomb and glide torpedo, the latter to be patterned after a British design.

Before work could be initiated on the glide torpedo, several Army-Navy conferences became necessary during the spring of 1941 as the Navy believed that the torpedo was in their sphere of influence. Working in cooperation with the Joint Air Advisory Committee, the Army and Navy had to establish the difference between the terms glide torpedo and glide bomb. On April 16, they determined that a torpedo was a weapon that was intended to travel horizontally under water to affect its final contact with its target while the glide bomb was any explosive delivered from an aircraft intended to be controllable in flight beyond the usual gravity or parachute types. The conference established that the Navy would develop the glide torpedo and the Army the glide bomb. However, the AAC did not concur with this definition and continued to lobby, and finally, after much inter-service bickering, it was allowed to continue both projects. Some sources state that the AAC, in deference to the Navy, changed the glide torpedo designation to Hydrobomb, but the Hydrobomb was a distinct project utilizing an uncontrolled bomb that was propelled underwater by a solid fuel.

After Pearl Harbor, there was a renewed Air Corps interest in air-dropped torpedoes by land-based medium bombers. As early as December 1941, AMC's Wright Field Equipment Laboratory recognized the possibility of combining a modified GB-1 airframe to a standard Navy Mk. 13, Model 2 Torpedo. The Navy Mk. 13 was to be used by the AAC, as any effort to design its own torpedo breached the earlier Army-Navy agreement and the Air Corps quickly yielded following persistent Navy opposition in March 1943. Besides, the AAC found that the problem in developing an aerial torpedo to be released from medium altitudes at high speeds would greatly slow their torpedo project.

During January 1942, the AAC requisitioned 5,000 Mk. 13 Torpedoes, but the Navy was able to transfer only 114 torpedoes due to their own combat commitments and also due to production problems and shortages. Despite the prospect of not receiving any more torpedoes from the Navy during the next year, during February 1942, the AAC set specifications to attach a standard Mk. 13 Naval aerial torpedo to a slightly modified GB-1 glide bomb twin-boom airframe. The Office of the Assistant

After Pearl Harbor, there was a renewed Air Corps interest in air-dropped torpedoes by land-based medium bombers. As early as December 1941, AMC's Wright Field Equipment Laboratory recognized the possibility of combining a modified GB-1 airframe to a standard Navy Mk. 13, Model 2 Torpedo. However, serious development on the GT-1 design did not begin until the summer of 1943, as the GT-1/ Mk. 13 "standoff" weapon. (*AAF*)

The GT-1 airframe was the same gyro-stabilized wing and boom assembly used with the GB-1, although the booms were somewhat longer than those of the GB-1 to correctly position the tail for the longer torpedo. The GT-1 weighed 2,455 pounds, of which 2,120 pounds was the Mk. 13, Model 2 Torpedo that measured 13 feet long and was 22.4 inches in diameter. Engineering trials established that the GT-1 could most readily be attached to the underside of the B-25J medium bomber, although only one GT-1 could be carried at a time. (*AAF*)

Chief of Air Staff, Operations, Commitments, and Requirements (OC&R) of the Special Weapons Branch at Wright Field, directed that facilities and personnel be made available to develop an airborne glider torpedo.

However, serious development on the GT-1 design did not begin until the summer of 1943, after representatives from Lt. Gen. George Kenney's 5AF Staff arrived from the Southwest Pacific to investigate new and better methods to make land-based bombers into more potent and less vulnerable to anti-shipping weapons. The 5AF had found that the problem with conventional aerial torpedo attacks was that the attacking aircraft had to approach the target in a low, straight, and level run before releasing the torpedo, making it vulnerable to enemy defensive AA fire. The GT-1/Mk. 13 standoff weapon was to be considered as a possible solution. However, after both the British and U.S. Navy had previously abandoned the weapon in tests against moving targets, Wright engineers believed that the GT-1 would be only effective against stationary maritime targets.

The GT-1 airframe was the same gyro-stabilized wing and boom assembly used for the GB-1, although the booms were somewhat longer than those of the GB-1 to correctly position the tail for the longer torpedo. The GT-1 weighed 2,455 pounds, of which 2,120 pounds was of the Mk. 13, Model 2 Torpedo that measured 13 feet long and was 22.4 inches in diameter. The GT-1 had a glide ratio of 6:1 and was dropped from 5,000 to 6,000 feet that would make the launching aircraft only safe from light-caliber AA. The proposed accuracy of the GT was comparable to placing a dropped bomb into a 1,000-foot circle from 5,000 feet. The range of the Mk. 13 Torpedo was 19,500 feet and could be used with any run pattern. The GT-1 controls were to be preset and a paravane was to fire explosive bolts, which released the airframe when the torpedo was at the correct altitude above the water for normal launch. The release of the torpedo from the glider would be much more complicated than just releasing a glider transporting a bomb from an aircraft. The weapon was intended for use against slow, massed convoys or in congested harbors such as at the Japanese bastions at Truk and Rabaul, where forty to fifty ships were often concentrated. Also, the GT, running in a spiraling underwater pattern, was a choice weapon for night attacks. Conventional torpedoes had to be very precisely aimed at night at a close-in low altitude that would expose the torpedo bombers to search lights and AA fire. In the face of these problems, it was fortunate that the GT program had some zealous supporters—of course, Gen. Hap Arnold, and Maj. Gen. Barney Giles and Col. George Younger, who were Arnold's movers and shakers.

Col. George Holloman, Chief of Special Weapons, organized the tests at Eglin under Maj. Maryrath, Capt. Pierce, and Lt. Moorman, who all had extensive experience with the GB. At Eglin, Maj. James Muri, CO of the First Proving Ground Torpedo Squadron, was assigned to the project. (Muri had participated in the AAF's only conventional bomber torpedo attack of the war while flying a B-26 at the Battle of Midway.) The unit was supplied with GB-1 glide bomb airframes, a B-17 equipped with standard GB wing racks and the associated electrical release mechanisms, and Mk. 13 Torpedoes procured from the Navy. From August 25 to September 12, 1943,

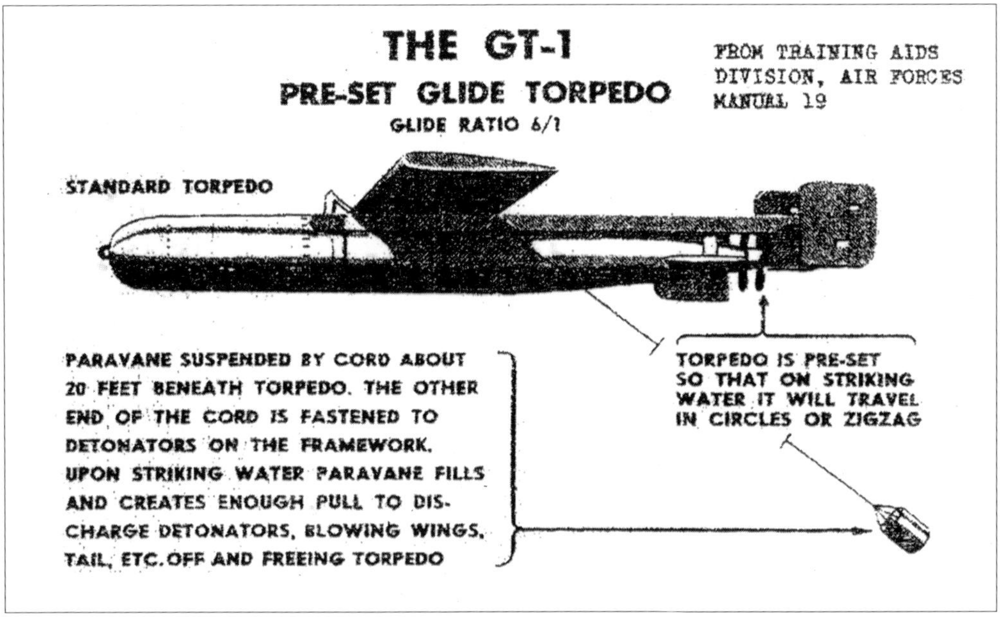

The GT-1 was dropped from 5,000 to 6,000 feet that would make the dropping aircraft safe from light-caliber enemy AA. The proposed accuracy of the glide torpedo was comparable to placing a dropped bomb into a 1,000-foot circle from 5,000 feet. The range of the Mk. 13 Torpedo was 19,500 feet and could be used with any run pattern. (*AAF*)

nineteen of twenty-two GT-1 GBs released from B-17s at the Eglin were successfully guided to their targets. However, these drop tests revealed several basic problems that needed to be resolved before the GT-1 could become operational. The torpedo had to separate from the glider airframe before it entered the water at the proper angle to be able to dive to the correct depth and remain on course. If the angle of entry were too steep, the torpedo tumbled, damaging the control surfaces, and could even cause it to fracture. If the torpedo entered the water at too flat an angle, it could skip, probably damaging the control surfaces, fracturing the propeller shafts, or damaging the internal machinery, including the main turbine bearings, all rendering the torpedo inoperable. For aircraft drops of conventional torpedoes, the Navy had previously determined the correct angle of entry to be between 18 degrees and 33 degrees but for glider drops the proper angle had not yet been determined. A conventional torpedo was dropped directly from an aircraft from about 300 feet whereas a torpedo was released from the glider when it and the airframe hit the water. To achieve the correct angle, the torpedo was mounted on the GB airframe at a 10-degree nose-down attitude when it hit the water attached to the glider. Tests disclosed that, at this setting, the torpedo/GB airframe would not continue to glide into the water but immediately spun and crashed into the water. During the November 1943 drop tests, to achieve the correct diving characteristics, the torpedo was mounted on the glider with its longitudinal axis parallel with the glider's twin booms. However, in this configuration, the torpedo/GB airframe hit the water flat and skipped off the surface.

Engineering Division designers reasoned that this upward movement of the GT-1 assembly could be controlled by pulling the tail of the torpedo up to cause its nose to hit the water first. Their solution was for the glider to be released from the mother aircraft and while in the glide, a small paravane was released from the glider, which permitted the torpedo to fall free, allowing it to attain the proper entrance angle during its free fall. The paravane resembled a bucket suspended below and behind the torpedo on the end of a 20- to 30-foot cable. When the paravane bucket struck the water and it filled, the weight of the water exerted enough pressure to close an electric circuit, which actuated an electric firing mechanism that detonated the retaining pins; this contained an explosive charge that released retaining bands, which held the torpedo to the glider.

The Eglin tests were considered satisfactory enough to prompt the Air Materiel Command to immediately order 700 followed by 250 more, with a production rate of about seventy-five per week, and then to place further orders in November, with more in February and March 1944. On April 6, 1944, 290 GT-1s were available, with ninety delivered to Eglin for testing and the remaining 200 to be delivered to the Pacific for combat use in a priority project.

The AAF still had to determine which bomber was to carry the weapon operationally. Engineering trials established that only one GT-1 could most readily be attached to the belly of the B-25J medium bomber. Operational testing using the B-25/GT-1 combination began in February 1944, during which the Mitchell demonstrated it could transport and successfully drop the GT-1, but with some accuracy problems. As was seen during the earlier conversion of B-17Fs to carry the GB-1, modifying large numbers of B-25Js to carry the GT-1 was much more difficult than making modifications to a single B-25J for test purposes.

A minor setback occurred during March 1944, when the Hammond Instrument Company reported that it would be unable to meet mass production requirements for the specified electrical switching equipment for the B-25J to carry the GT-1 until late spring 1944, at the earliest. During early April 1944, eighteen B-25J-1s (43-3905, 3906, 3907, 3955, 3957, 3959, 3963, 3971, 3973, 3975, 3976, 3977, 3978, 3979, 3980, 3981, 3982, and 3983) were modified by Hammond Instrument and equipped to transport the GT-1.

Crews were trained in GT-1 use at Hunter Field, Georgia, and during December 1943, final launch tests were conducted with both dummy and live torpedoes. These tests demonstrated that the Norden bombsight was less accurate than the pilot's standard NC-3 gunsight for delivering the GT-1, but neither was accurate enough to hit the water within a circular error of 1,600 feet, while 75 percent launched at 5,000 feet would hit within a half-mile of the aiming point. The Joint New Weapons Committee concluded that the GT-1 proved to be an area weapon that would have to be released in large quantities to be effective. Corresponding to a B-17 carrying the GB-1, the smaller B-25 also suffered reduced air speed and even greater loss of range when carrying the GT-1; so much so that 5AF and 7AF commanders resolved that the GT-1 program was not practicable and should be abandoned. Air Staff Requirements agreed, appending that the GB-1 and GT-1 airframes were comparatively primitive,

The Eglin B-25 tests were concluded on October 11, 1943, and the results prompted the Air Materiel Command to immediately order 500 and to place further orders in November with then more in February and March 1944. (*AAF*)

having been superseded by newer lifting bodies. So, by January 1945, both assessments seemed to doom the GT-1 program to cancellation.

However, the GT-1 program again received a reprieve, probably because of Gen. Arnold's unwillingness to abandon his GB without an operational test. Arnold assigned the Air Technical Service, abetted by the 594th Air Materiel Squadron Command, to voyage to Central Pacific to prepare the GT-1 for combat in May 1945. The First Provisional Glide Torpedo Squadron (1PGTS) was formed and trained for a month on operational tactics. Its aircraft and crews then proceeded to McClellan Field, Sacramento; then to Fairfield-Suisun (Travis AFB today), California; and on May 1, departed for Hickam Field, Hawaii, for assignment with the Seventh Bomber Command Training Detachment.

To test the GB-1 in actual combat the First Provisional Glide Torpedo Squadron was assigned to the 41BG/47BS of the VII Bomber Command of the 7AF. This unit, consisting of eighteen crews, was issued fourteen B-25J-1s that were equipped with specially modified bomb racks to carry the GT under the fuselage. The initial testing was completed in Hawaii when the 1PGTS arrived with four officers: Lt. Col. George Younger of the Bombardment Office of the Chief of the Air Force; Capt. Atwood, Operations Officer of the Torpedo Training Command at Eglin; Lt. Moorman, a torpedo engineer from Wright; and Lt.(jg) Hoover, the USN Torpedo Ordnance Representative. In Hawaii, the crews not only completed their GT torpedo training but also their combat training as they were also to fly conventional missions. Tests found that to make the GT-1 more effective, once its torpedo was in the water was to mount a tail mechanism that was preset to enable the torpedo to travel in a spiral pattern that threatened shipping in a large circular area and helped it to avoid detection. The tail mechanism automatically placed the torpedo into an ever-increasing circular pattern that would reach a 2,000-foot-diameter limit and then return into an ever-decreasing circular pattern that would be reversed when the rudder reached its original position. During a demonstration off Molokai Island the crews made perfect drops with the torpedoes entering the water successfully and then functioned perfectly in their spiral patterns.

After about twenty hours of training, the First Glide Torpedo Squadron rejoined the 41BG stationed at Okinawa and the glide torpedo was scheduled for combat for the first time on July 28, 1945, but the mission was scrubbed when its fighter escort failed to rendezvous. The following day, nine B-25Js took-off to attack two Japanese fleet carriers (CVs) and one light (CVL) carrier, which were discovered by aerial reconnaissance in Sasebo Harbor, Kyushu, Japan. The fighter escort arrived late and the carriers could not be attacked as the fighters would have run out of fuel while continuing the escort. Instead, secondary targets were attacked. Six Mitchells hit merchant shipping in Makurazaki Harbor while the other three attacked shipping at Kagoshima. The results of the attack were difficult to determine as many torpedoes were dropped far from the target and the paths of the torpedoes could not be observed to their spiraling termination due to the necessary, preplanned evasive action and break away of the carrying aircraft soon after the drop to avoid the moderately heavy AA fire in the area. Another mission on July 30 was again aborted when the fighter escort did not appear.

On the 31st, thirteen B-25s attacked the enemy carriers at Sasebo and all thirteen GT-1s were dropped from 7,500 feet. One failed to glide and spun in and another suffered a direct AA hit after leaving the aircraft and exploded in midair. The remaining eleven torpedoes made their entrance into the water normally and then circled around the harbor. Two GT-1s hit the shore, two were lost from observation, and the remaining seven entered the area where the carriers were moored. Again, the results of the attack were difficult to determine as many torpedoes were dropped far from the target and the paths of the torpedoes could not be followed to their circling termination, again due to the evasive action and break away of the carrying aircraft

To test the GT-1 concept in combat the First Provisional Glide Torpedo Squadron was assigned to the 47BS of the 7AF, which conducted several combat missions in the Pacific. However, the war in the Pacific ended before any further glide torpedo missions could be conducted, but these wartime tests eventually led to an entirely new family of postwar anti-shipping weapons. (*AAF*)

soon after the drop to evade the moderately heavy AA fire in the area. Post-strike photos did indicate that hits could have been made on the enemy carriers *Haystake* and *Kasegi*, or their surrounding torpedo nets. Two B-25s returned to base with AA damage.

The final GT-1 attack was made on August 1 by nine B-25s against shipping targets in Nagasaki harbor. On their arrival, a haze was encountered, restricting vision to 4–7 miles near the harbor, as a portion of the city was on fire from an attack on the previous day by carrier aircraft from Adml. Halsey's Task Force 38, which further obscured the harbor targets. Nine GT-1s were dropped with one spinning in on the drop. Three were seen to hit the water but five just disappeared into the haze heading normally toward the targets. The results were not observed due to the narrowness of the harbor, the evasive action of the retreating bombers, and heavy AA fire. Eight days later, Nagasaki would suffer a fate worse than eight GBs as the B-29 *Bocks Car* would drop its A-bomb on the city.

These operational tests concluded that in the future, it would be necessary for reconnaissance aircraft to accompany the B-25s on these missions to determine their effectiveness. However, the war in the Pacific ended before any further GT missions could be conducted, but these tests eventually led to an entirely new family of postwar anti-shipping weapons.

Both the gyro-stabilized GB-1 glide bomb and its GT-1 glide torpedo offspring were abruptly removed from AAF inventory as glide weapons as, at best, they were only an option to strategic bombing. Both weapons, but especially the GB-1, suffered from the apathy of operational commanders, while their designers often worked at cross-purposes. They were satisfactory as proof of concept vehicles, but as combat weapons, they disappointed; although the Navy continued to show some interest in glide torpedoes after the war. These glide bombs proved it was possible to develop a standoff weapon that could be successfully launched against targets that were heavily defended by AA.

GB-2 and GB-3 Glide Bomb

Both the GB-2 and GB-3 were armed with 2,000-pound AN-M66 bombs. The Bellanca GB-2 was 11.75 feet long, had a span of 12 feet, glided at a speed 309 mph, and used the same preset glide path principle as the GB-1. However, compared to the latter, the GB-2 had more adverse effects on the carrying bomber and the control equipment was more difficult to install. The Timm GB-3 was 14.1 feet long, had a span of 12 feet, glided at 168 mph, and had similar disadvantages as the GB-2. Consequently, both the GB-2 and GB-3 were canceled in early 1942 after their unimpressive initial test flight phases and once the GB-1 was selected for mass production.

GB-2. (*AAF*)

GB-3. (*AAF*)

GB-4 Television Controlled Bomb

During July 1942, the AAF's Wright Field Equipment Laboratory began the development of the GB-4-guided GB under Project MX-108, which was later continued as MX-618. The GB-4 program used a modified GB-1 Aeronca airframe designated as the Pomykata Glider named after Maj. J. M. Pomykata of the Technical Service Command. The Pomykata version, built by the Klassen Company of Los Angeles, had the same general dimensions as the Aeronca type (12-foot wingspan and length including the bomb), but the twin tail boom assembly was replaced by a cylinder, which was bolted to the bomb itself. Design changes were to make the GB-4 more aerodynamic and thus more expensive.

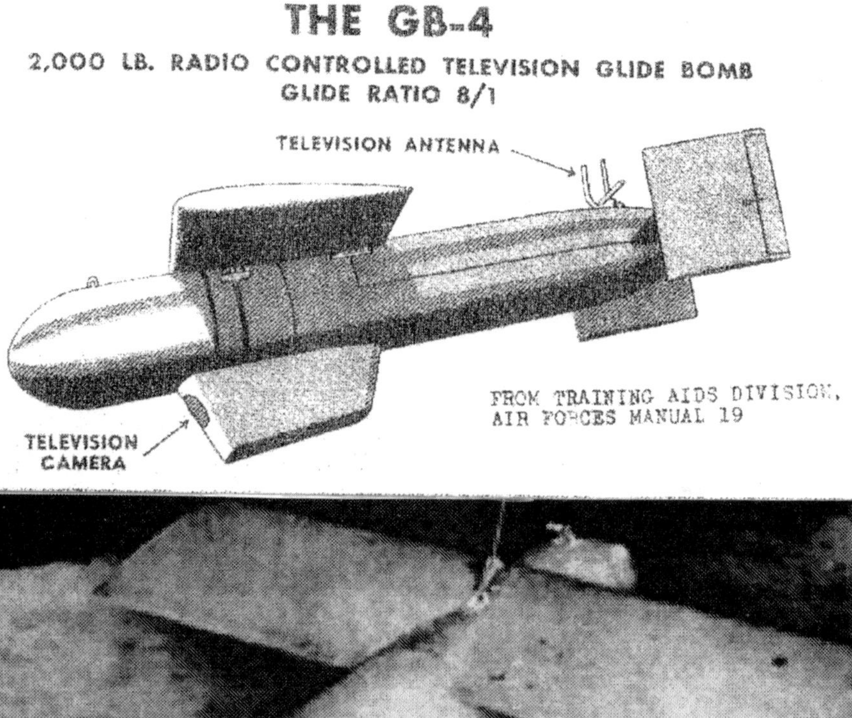

The GB-4 was a gyro-stabilized GB, utilizing radio signals to control range and azimuth by the bombardier who was provided with a small TV image for position determination. The flight-servo, radio control, and television transmitting equipment were housed in the body of the airframe, while the camera was mounted inside a streamlined nacelle beneath the bomb. Two seven-cell storage batteries connected in series provided the voltage for the SCR-549-T3 equipment. The television transmitting antenna was mounted on top of the bomb toward the rear, with the reflector in the forward position. The GB-4, like the GB-1, carried a 2,000-pound bomb attached to its 500-pound wing and boom airframe assembly. Two GB-4s were to be mounted on external wing racks on the B-17, decreasing the bomber's speed by only 8 mph due to the better aerodynamics of the missile and carrying racks. For use in the Pacific, design provisions were made on a B-25 to carry one GB-4. The missile had a 6:1 glide ratio, which could be extended to more than 8:1 under the bombardier's control. It traveled at 230–240 mph, with this speed increased by putting the mother aircraft into a dive before release. The 8AF strategists were opposed to the area bombing characteristics of the GB-1 because it contradicted their precision bombing doctrine; however, they accepted the GB-4 and its development because it employed a guidance system intended to provide very high precision to allow the bombardier to strike individual targets, such as bridges, dams, docks, tunnels, and easily identifiable buildings. Another validation for the GB-4 was that after launching, the carrying bomber could by changing course or seek cloud cover while the GB-4 continued being directed toward its target via its remote television receiver.

GB-4 Production and Hammond Control Boxes

There were 2,000 GB-4s ordered from the Klassen Company with an initial experimental order for 200 for delivery on April 15, 1944, 300 in May and June, and 300 per month until the contracted 2,000 was completed. However, there were no Hammond control boxes available in April, with 100 due on May 8, 250 to 300 in June, and 350 to 400 per month until the contract with Hammond was completed. The Aircraft Radio Laboratory had only 300 television sets immediately available with no more available until August.

CTI-811 and the GB-4

On October 19, 1942, Air Materiel Command circulated CTI-811, which permitted the procurement of radio-controlled and television-guided GBs. CTI-811 did not mention any specifications for the GB-4's components or capabilities, which would be central for design engineers. These GB specifications were to be furnished to the AMC by Air Staff's Directorate of Operations, Commitments, and Requirements (OC&R), which was to obtain the general specifications from the end users. The OC&R did not or could not furnish them, either because of Gen. Arnold's attention on the GB-1 or because the OC&R was just too preoccupied consolidating the massive early expansion of the AAC after Pearl Harbor. Nonetheless, AMC design engineers at the Air Radio Laboratory (ARL) had to develop the new weapon without explicit end user specifications and were then to let design contracts to civilian manufacturers to construct a prototype.

On February 9, 1943, four months after CTI-811 was issued, the ARL as yet did not have any approved specifications and was unable to delineate requirements, propose modifications, or elucidate performance limits for civilian companies wishing to construct GB-4 television equipment. To advance the GB-4 project the ARL drafted and tendered a list of minimum requirements to the AMC, which its Engineering Division should provide such as detailed drawings, allowable weights, service range, the desired operating life with fully charged batteries, and that the designed equipment was to be compatible with an SCR-550-T3 receiver. Meanwhile, the NDRC and civilian industry researchers continued to be left in design limbo with only a modicum of GB-4 research and development continuing.

During early 1942, RCA received developmental contracts for a large order for 1,000 (500 each for the AAF and USN) of the new 300 mc BLOCK III system television sets for GB installation. The BLOCK III sets were not standardized and were relatively untested, and because of the lack of specifications, they were found to be too large and heavy for use in GBs. By March 1943, it became apparent that the entire GB program completely lacked integrated administration, direction, and coordination and, most significantly, did not have the priority of other programs. Because of the delays in the GB-1 program and Arnold's persistence on continuing its priority, advanced GB programs were again neglected for the balance of the year.

GB-4 Television Installation and Testing

The first AAF BLOCK III models, SCR-549-T3 Transmitting equipment, and SCR-550-T3 Receiving equipment were delivered during June 1943 and were being tested in small pilotless target aircraft at Muroc when a small number of GB-4 airframes became available to test the performance of the improved SCR-549-T3 TV system. The T2 and T3 versions were essentially similar, except the T3 operated, for technical reasons, at 300 mc instead of 100 mc, and in the T3, the camera and transmitter were separate units that increased the unit weight to 90 pounds. The servo control mechanism, radio control equipment, and television transmitter were located in the airframe body, while the camera was housed in a faired nacelle under the GB-4.

The first installation of the BLOCK III transmitting equipment in the GB-4s was completed in July, and preliminary flights at Eglin Field were conducted without releasing the GB-4 from the control aircraft and seemed to indicate satisfactory operation. (It was typical to test the expensive television equipment in this manner before it was to be demolished in its combat dive into the target). When flight-testing the 88-pound television equipment in expendable GB-4s, permanent, visual records of the results were required, both in the air and on the ground, especially for very short flights. The development of portable motion picture equipment for making movies of the missile's receiver screen was initiated. The television receiver and the movie camera had to be mounted on a common base plate to minimize the effect of different vibration phases of the two units. Heavy-duty batteries supplied 110-volts to operate the camera motor to take 10,000 feet of film before replacement was needed. An AAC trailer was completely equipped to receive and photograph the television pictures.

Five GB-4s were launched at Eglin Field, during August 1943, to determine the feasibility of striking a small pyramidal target constructed for the tests. The results of actual launches were not encouraging as numerous problems appeared on the controlling aircraft receiver screen during flight and other problems were also seen on the receiver at the ground station. Extensive post-test evaluations were performed to determine and resolve the very poor TV picture resolution. The horizontal line disturbances were traced to camera/transmitter acoustic pickup problems generated by the glued plywood body of the airframe. They were solved by placing the camera in a sound-proof box and by also sound-proofing the inside of the airframe by coating it with automobile-body silencing (undercoating) compound and a thick layer of felt. Vibration problems and heavy streaking in the picture were caused by the loose glue bonding of the plywood airframe body and was solved by more careful bonding at the factory. The iconoscope (TV camera) could be saturated by bright light levels, while haze caused low contrast, both of which were resolved by placing a yellow filter over the camera lens. A heater was installed to reduce lens fogging. A change in the picture shading was caused by the influence of the earth's magnetic field on the iconoscope and was solved by shielding the entire iconoscope. Tests and initial tactical hypotheticals disclosed that the GB-4's 12- to 20-mile range would have to be increased to take full combat advantage of the system. A directional antenna in the receiving aircraft linked to a gyro-stabilized antenna mount resulted in an increase in range to 50 to 80 miles.

Flight tests in early 1942 using 100 megacycle equipment in a Douglas B-23 bomber, showing that lightweight television equipment was feasible but had a number of inherent limitations for military use and that new performance and operational standards needed to be formulated. The photo shows a TV camera installed in the side fuselage door. (*AAF*)

GB-4 TV controller looking into a BLOCK 7-inch CRV-60AAR monitor during GB-4 tests during August 1943. (*AAF still from training film*)

GB-4 gliding into a target at Eglin during the August 1943 tests. (*AAF still from training film*)

Finally, in November 1943, several GB-4s equipped with Block III television transmitters, incorporating the required improvements, had been successfully released at Eglin Field and controlled from both B-17s and B-25s with satisfactory reception of television images at ranges up to 80 miles and with the bomber flying 180 degrees away from the missile as it was being guided toward the target area. Although the AMC Engineering Division firmly recommended that further testing was required before GB-4 standardization and production. Nonetheless, the GB-4 standardization and production schedule was accelerated to January 15, 1944 and aircrew training was to begin as soon as possible.

Unfortunately, as the AMC Engineering Division had warned, GB-4 television guidance development was not as advanced as the November tests had indicated as there was a great difference between successfully controlling a GB in flight only toward a target and controlling it to accurately hit a precision target. Therefore, the decision was made to prioritize and build the radio-controlled GB-8 to get it operational, which diverted funds and personnel from the GB-4 project that no longer could meet the January 1944 objectives.

However, by late December 1943, the inherent inaccuracy and lagging development of the GB-8 was apparent and the compelling promise of the GB-4's TV system left little doubt with further modifications and testing that it would soon once more be the primary radio-controlled version of the GB. The AMC then redirected the Hammond Corporation to halt the manufacture of GB-8 radio transmitters and resume the manufacture of the GB-4 compatible sets beginning with fifty GB-4 radio transmitters to be available within two weeks so that accelerated GB-4 testing could begin again in January 1944. Also, if the January GB-4 tests were successful, the AMC, foreseeing the possibility of an early combat debut, contracted Hammond and RCA for an initial production run of 250 television and radio units. GB-4 compatible B-17s would be required, and the B-17Fs that were already wired for the GB-1 were found to be most easily modified for GB-4 deployment; it was recommended that these conversions be more expeditiously completed in the U.K. Operationally, the GB-4 unit would require nine B-17s, plus six spares to cover maintenance requirements and combat attrition. Another requirement was to accelerate the GB-4 training of bombardiers as well as radio and ordnance technicians.

The operation of the GB-4 required two bombardiers—one located in the bombardier's usual position in the bomber's nose to preset the GB-4's controls and conduct the bomb run up until release and the other bombardier located in the navigator's position, using the television screen and control equipment to guide the bomb after release. The television bombardier guided the GB-4 with a joystick while watching its flight on a 5-inch cathode ray television screen. The complexity of the unit required the bombardier to receive twelve to fifteen additional weeks' training to learn to use it correctly, which meant taking vital bombardiers already proficient in conventional bombing away from their combat units.

To expedite personnel training, bomber modifications, and the accelerated production that GB-4 combat operations would involve, the Air Communication's Special Projects Section was assigned to act as the central coordinating authority. A meeting was scheduled for January 28 to include the Air Communications Officer (ACO), Aircraft Radio Laboratory (ARL), and the Hammond Instrument Company to determine potential problems and to expedite production as necessary. Finally, consolidated management and direction, which had been absent since the beginning of the guided bomb program, was being established.

After the GB-4 was standardized, the tests beginning on January 17, 1944 were the first to attempt to hit a precision target using television guidance. Two of the first six tests did not use television guidance as they only tested the radio control from the B-17F control bomber. All four other GB-4 tests failed to hit the target either due to television or radio malfunctions, or because, in one case, the test was flown in the late afternoon and there was insufficient daylight to determine the target on the small television screen.

Additional tests were required and between March 18 and April 13, which revealed more frustrating problems, particularly concerning the malfunctioning of the GB radio receiver, television transmitter, and the mass-produced gyroscope. Poor-quality vacuum tubes were the biggest cause of the failures, but the control boxes needed to be built under better quality control and standardized before operational use. The bombardiers often had significant difficulties in distinguishing the target on the small television screen due to the lack of ambient light, too little contrast between the target and its surroundings, or simply poor picture quality that was too grainy or distorted. However, there were some impressive successes; for example, the March 31, 1944 test made a direct hit on the blockhouse target. Overall, the test results were inconsistent with encouraging successes and discouraging failures, often due to bombardier errors that could have been prevented with additional and better training.

While improved training did increase controller proficiency, further testing uncovered and resolved technical problems. The March–April tests revealed that low-quality vacuum tubes and control boxes continued to be the main causes of failure. Tests in May revealed the deficiencies of the television equipment for target identification and then guiding the GB-4 to a distinct target. Continued testing isolated and resolved technical concerns, but once production began, new issues arose. Before they could become operational, most of the available GB-4 airframes, which had been built before the March–April tests, had significant problems that required modifications. The 500 available radio control receivers and television transmitters also required modifications at the ARL. A high demand for BLOCK III television equipment developed in the spring of 1944 as it was also earmarked for use in other priority projects, such as the AAFs Project Castor involving war-weary B-17 guided drones and for the Navy's Campbell Project (radio-controlled, television-guided boats).

Eventually, as the GB-1 development progressed, funds and personnel became available and were released for the GB-4 and GB-8 programs. Slowly, GB-4 problems were eliminated, and satisfactory television pictures were finally transmitted allowing a procurement order for 2,000 GB-4s equipped with SCR-549-T3 BLOCK transmitting units to be manufactured. During January 1944, letters of intent to contractors were issued for airframes and controls, and the Signal Corps was instructed to produce the television guidance system. By the spring of 1944, Wright Field received the first units and stated that while the bomb itself functioned with excellent reliability, the degree of skill required to hit a target with desired accuracy was more than was anticipated.

After additional testing, the AAF Board released a report on August 5, 1944 that declared that the GB-4 was not ready to be deployed for combat except in special circumstances and that technical and tactical development was to be continued. The board's report determined that the proper GB-4 targets were those that could be easily penetrated by large bombs at low terminal velocity; those easily identified by television by their distinctive features and landmarks; and those that were small in area. Nevertheless, only two weeks after the AAF Board had recommended the GB-4 not be deployed in combat, they were engaged in operational testing in the ETO despite obvious significant operational vulnerabilities.

The GB-4 was only operational between the AA vulnerable altitudes of 4,000 and 15,000 feet and only in excellent weather conditions. The B-17s carrying the GB-4 externally were unable to implement evasive maneuvers and had a reduction in combat radius, restricting them to areas with limited enemy fighter defenses. However, limited enemy fighter defenses were only found on the fringes of enemy territory, where so-called vital centers were unlikely to be situated as targets.

The GB-4 in Combat: Batty Missions

The testing of the GB-4 under operational, combat conditions, called Batty Missions, was conducted by a small, secretive unit of GB specialists from the Air Technical Service Command at the 388th Bomb Group based at Fersfield, England. The unit was led by Maj. J. M. Pomykata, who directed the modifications on the carrying B-17s and personnel training for the GB-4 combat tests. The 388th Bomb Group History, published in 1946, recorded this about the "strange things" going on at the Fersfield Base (U.K.): "Two or three complete crews were transferred to Fersfield and such transfers were made orally as no paper was kept.... Not too much was told of the activity at Fersfield but that was the proving ground for robot planes or radio-controlled planes..."

At the end of June 1944, seven GB-4s and seven GB-8s were shipped to Fersfield, along with two veteran B-17Gs (42-97518 and 42-40043) and Batty personnel. All GB-4 and GB-8s were assembled and ready for use in one week. Both aging B-17s were in very poor mechanical condition and 42-97518 required two weeks to arrive due to mechanical problems during the entire flight from the U.S. On its arrival, 42-40043 was assigned to the Aphrodite/Castor expendable, war-weary drone project. Once 42-97518 arrived, it was repaired, but unfortunately this B-17 crashed and burned on July 29, leaving Batty without a mother aircraft. At the time, Third Division H.Q. decided that the GB-4 (radio/television) GB would be used first and the GB-8 (radio/flare) GB afterwards (but eventually not at all). This decision came at a time when no targets had yet been selected for the GB-4. On August 6, the original B-17 (42-40043) was returned by the Aphrodite/Castor project and restored to serviceable condition and finally all was ready for GB-4 tests and deployment. Only one GB-4-equipped B-17 would be flown at a time, rather than the nine bombers originally advocated by the School of Applied Tactics. Each GB-4 test mission was provided the special sortie designator, the code name Batty, and was considered a sub-element of the Aphrodite Program governing television-guided weapons and aircraft employed by 8AF. Castor was also to use a TV guidance system. (Aphrodite and Castor will be discussed in detail later.)

Five personnel were used on all the missions flown: Maj. J. N. Hall (pilot); Maj. J. M. Pomykata (radio/TV control operator); 1Lt. L. Kata (TV operator); 1Lt. R. J. Norris (bombardier); and T/Sgt. F. L. Wallis (radio operator).

Initially Noball V-weapon sites were scheduled to be attacked by the GB-4s, but the compactness of the target and the nature of the surrounding area made TV picture resolution poor for identifying these targets. It was then decided that the GB-4's first mission, scheduled on August 7, were to be directed against E-Boat pens at the German-occupied port of Le Havre, located on the English Channel on the northern coast of France. However, due to poor weather conditions, no missions were flown until August 13.

The first Batty mission (also known as Aphrodite Mission #4) was flown on August 13, 1944 against the Le Havre E-Boat (patrol boat) pens. A single B-17 carrying two GB-4s, escorted by a P-38 observer/pathfinder, a Mosquito photo reconnaissance aircraft, and a B-17 observer carrying another TV receiver, took off for Le Havre. The observer B-17 remained over the English Channel about 20 miles northeast of the target. There was neither flak nor enemy fighters, and the visibility was considered excellent. The first bomb run was made from south to north in good visibility with scattered clouds. The first GB-4 was released at 4:43 p.m. from 15,000 feet at 170 mph at the standard 80-degree bombing angle, 13 miles from the target. After the release, the mothership followed the normal procedure of turning 180 degrees and flying in the opposite direction. The second GB was dropped at the same release point as the first at 5:08 p.m. from 14,700 feet and 175 mph. The TV picture in the mother B-17 on both drops was of poor quality and unusable for control. Consequently, the first bomb landed in the Seine River Estuary, a mile short of the target, while the second exploded on a mudflat a mile east. Both bombs were found to respond (too late) to radio control from the other observer B-17, which had good reception from the GB-4s TV camera, and it was determined that the GB's TV unit functioned satisfactorily. After the mission, the poor quality of the TV picture was determined to be due to interference from the bomber's radio equipment. Unfortunately, the Mosquito photo aircraft crashed when it evidently was damaged by the explosion of the second GB-4, which the Mosquito had followed down to about 200 feet above the mudflat.

First Batty Mission

On August 17, the second Batty GB-4 mission took off at 2:45 p.m. to attack the U-Boat pens at La Pallice on the Bay of Biscay. The formation consisted of twelve escorting P-51s, one P-38 photo recon aircraft, the B-17 observer/TV aircraft, and

Movie still of a B-17 drone preparing for the first Batty mission, which was also Aphrodite Mission No. 4, on August 13, 1944 against E-Boat pens in the German-occupied port of Le Havre, located on the English Channel. (*From AAF movie still*)

Once the glitches in the BLOCK TV system were corrected, the tactical deployment of the GB-4, codenamed Batty, was initiated. Pictured is a Batty control/mother B-17 of the 388th Bombardment Group based at Fersfield, England, carrying two GB-4s on the first mission. (*AAF*)

The first mission was flown by a single B-17 carrying two GB-4s escorted by a P-38 observer/pathfinder and a Mosquito photo reconnaissance aircraft that crashed when it evidently was damaged by the explosion of the second GB-4, which the Mosquito had followed down to about 200 feet. The mission was also a failure as each of the GB-4s exploded over a mile from their target. (*From AAF movie still*)

the mother B-17 equipped with two GB-4s. The briefed dropping altitude was to be 20,000 feet but due to the poor mechanical condition of the mother B-17, it was not possible for it to climb above 17,000 feet while carrying two GB-4s, even after two hours and thirty minutes of climbing. In excellent weather and visibility, the first bomb run was made over water at 5:59 p.m., at 17,000 feet, 165 mph, and initiated at 25 miles from the target. The shutter on the bomb's TV camera failed to open and the bomb was quickly lost from the screen and was not seen to hit. However, visual observation confirmed that the bomb responded to radio control. Seven minutes later, the second bomb was released at 17,000 feet and 175 mph. TV reception was again unusable due to sunlight reflections off the water, but this bomb responded to radio control during its five-minute and thirty-second flight. It exploded in the city to the right of the target and was out of control for the last few seconds of its flight. No enemy fighters and only meager, but accurate flak were reported on both bomb runs. Despite extensive preflight checks, the mother's TV unit malfunctioned, but the observer B-17 again had good reception. After this mission, the mother's TV unit was again intensively tested. The original receiver with a gyro-stabilized antenna was adjusted and remained and a second receiver with a fixed antenna was installed on the B-17's left horizontal stabilizer. This new arrangement provided a better picture and in future operations both receivers were to be used simultaneously. In order to achieve the desired 20,000-foot altitude, only one GB was to be carried. Also, due to the reflection of sunlight on the water, it was recommended that future attacks against coastal targets be made from an overland approach.

On August 26, the third Batty mission, consisting of seven P-47 escorts, one P-38 photo recon aircraft, the B-17 observer, and the mother B-17 carrying only one GB-4, took off to attack a railroad bridge at Ravenstein, Holland. As the pilot approached the target, it was shrouded by clouds and the mission was aborted and the GB was brought back to base.

No missions were flown between August 27 and September 10 due to poor weather conditions. On September 10, nine P-38 escorts, one P-38 photo recon aircraft, and the mother B-17 carrying one GB-4 (so the mother B-17 could climb to 20,000 feet) attacked a steel factory transformer switching station at Duren, Germany. At 4:14 p.m., the bomb run was made from 20,000 feet, 25 miles from the target in 6–8/10th cloud cover, which obscured the GB until it broke out of the clouds at 3,000 feet, which, by that time, had passed over the target. Since no suitable alternative target could be located, the bomb was directed toward a tree in an open space about 3 miles from the target. The TV picture on the new fixed antenna installation was very good, while the old unit again produced a useless picture.

The next day, a Batty mission took off to attack a railroad bridge and locks at Münster, Germany. Upon climbing to altitude, a short circuit developed in the GB's TV unit, making it necessary to abort the mission. The mission scheduled for September 12 was canceled due to lack of escort fighter cover.

On September 13, the final Batty mission was flown against an oil refinery at Salzbergen, Germany. The mission consisted of the B-17 mother equipped with one GB escorted by eighteen P-47 fighters and a Mosquito photo ship. There were no clouds over the target, but a ground haze made target identification difficult. During the first two bombing runs, the bombardier made an error in locating the target due to the haze. At 5:09 p.m., the GB-4 was released at 20,200 feet towards Ensburen, located 6 miles northwest of Salzbergen. Maj. Pomykata, the TV operator, chose the largest building in Ensburen as a target of opportunity and directed the bomb towards it. After the bomb passed through the haze, the TV picture became clearer, and it appeared the target might be a church. The operator attempted to change the missile's course, but it was moving too fast, and due to the response lag experienced with radio-controlled GB, it was too close to miss. Post-mission strike photos confirmed a direct hit, totally demolishing the building, which no longer was identifiable as a church or not. Again, the radio control and the new fixed antenna functioned very satisfactorily, but the TV unit was again useless.

From September 14–30, there were no GB-4 missions as fighter escort could not be provided due to other operational obligations. So, after six GB-4s were dropped in five missions, resulting in the destruction of an enemy tree, a church (?), and one Allied Mosquito photo reconnaissance aircraft, orders were cut to give the British the remaining GB-4 and the seven GB-8s. All Wright Field personnel were returned to the U.S. on October 2.

On February 15, 1945, the GB-4 program was re-evaluated by the AMC and was found "unsatisfactory in its present state." The following conclusions were made:

1. Carrying the GB-4 externally limited the aircraft's speed, range, altitude, and maneuverability.
2. The adverse weather conditions prevalent in the ETO precluded the missiles use throughout most of the year.
3. The GB-4 could only be used effectively on targets, which could be easily distinguished from their surroundings on the TV monitor.
4. No GB-4 unit was to be sent into operations unless it could operate independently without depending on other organizations (obviously the 8AF was less than cooperative with the GB-4 mission as shown by their reluctance to provide fighter escort.)
5. Only new and fully equipped mother aircraft were to be used in future operations.

That same day the AMC sent Gen. Arnold a memorandum, stating:

> ... considerable technical difficulties which were not previously encountered have caused an extensive delay in the program ... and that the principal issue in these failures devolved from the poor television image quality, which was unlikely to be improved in the near future.
>
> USAAF, *Case History of the GB-1*
> Maxwell AFB, MF Reel A2082, A2083, and A2051

On February 19, Gen. Arnold notified the Air Technical Section that all future production of the GB-4 (after 1,200 were manufactured) was to be canceled. However, despite the poor operational results, the GB-4 showed sufficient promise for continued testing and further development for use against Japanese caves and fortresses, but on a very low, 3A, priority basis as part of the Hermit, Willie/Abusive TV-controlled drone project. It was decided that war-weary bombers, equipped with GB-4 TV and control equipment, could more effectively perform the GB-4 function. Thus, the GB-4 glide bomb project was abandoned. A resurrected GB project, designated as the GB-15, that used APW-5 radar and TV control, will be discussed later.

Conclusions

Generally, the radio-controlled GB was as ineffective as the gyro-stabilized, unguided GB-1. When the radio control was supplemented by television guidance, the GB-4 bombs were not any more accurate than conventional bombs. A major reason for their use was to decrease the carrying aircraft's vulnerability by being used as a standoff weapon away from enemy AA fire. But, in fact, the drag-inducing GB-4 increased the vulnerability of the bombing aircraft to enemy fighters without a related increase in offensive capabilities. The television guidance was expected to increase accuracy as the images transmitted from the GB should have allowed the bombardier to direct the path of the bomb into the target. In reality, the television images were so poor from the distant launching ranges and the speed of the bomb was so fast that the bombardier was unable to determine the target to guide the bomb into it. The mothership had to decelerate upon bomb release, so momentum would carry the bomb in front of the aircraft where the bombardier could see and guide it. This deceleration was achieved by making a steep climb and then level out. The bombardier could make a maximum correction of 1,600 feet in range and 1,100 feet in bearing.

The bottom line does not seem to indicate a deficiency in GB-4/-8 technology but denotes the AAFs inflexible airpower doctrine of high-altitude, daylight, strategic precision bombardment from heavy bombers flying above 20,000 feet. When using the GB-4 or -8 as a standoff weapon, the AAF should have followed the Luftwaffe's SD-1400 Fritz X example and deployed these weapons against more appropriate (easier to distinguish) tactical objectives (particularly maritime targets), using a smaller mother aircraft (medium bombers, such as the Luftwaffe Do 217/Fritz X). The Germans used the Fritz X to maximize the potential for a hit, sneaking in at short ranges, attacking at medium altitudes, below 8,000 feet, and launching the bomb within 2 miles of its target.

Advanced Guidance GBs

The AAF had several advanced guidance systems for use in their GB glide bomb series during the war, and despite very promising results during experimental testing for some of them, none were ever employed in combat during the war. These systems utilized their special sensors to detect and track the target, using this data to adjust their glide paths, improving their prospects of hitting the target. On October 29, 1942, the newly created Subcommittee on Controlled Missiles issued its initial report stating that missile control research should not only consider radar, but also utilize the energy from visible light, infrared, and sound to control guided missiles. The Navy's extensive research on sound detectors led to the very effective guidance of underwater torpedoes but would have little usefulness in guiding aerial missiles. Radar, infrared, and visible light would all indicate potential, but of these, light would be the most reliable method to detect a target.

Light-Seeking GBs

The photosensitive, light-seeking sensors used on guided bombs during World War II were among the most successful employed. They were deployed on variants of the GB-12 and GB-13 glide bomb, with the two most important seekers being the maritime light contrast- seeker and the flare-seeker.

Although Col. Benjamin Chidlaw of the Experimental Engineering Section at Wright Field initially requested that NDRC's research assistance to be for a radar-controlled missile, the September 17, 1942 Summary Report of the Joint New Weapons Committee (JNWC) found that, at this time, the most advanced guidance seeker probably was the photo-electric cell as developed by Hammond Electric Company. Since the NDRC's original commission was to provide improved weapon systems that were not readily understood or appreciated by military officers and because the objective of the JNWC was to develop weapons having greater utility than existing weapons, the joint decision of both organizations was to supersede Col. Chidlaw and place the light-contrast sensor on an equal priority with the radar sensor. As was foreseen by NDRC scientists, development of the seeker progressed satisfactorily and relatively quickly. The seekers designed and produced by the Fairchild Corporation were deemed sufficiently simple in construction that they could be produced quickly in comparison to other more complicated Hammond seekers.

Considering the research and development aspect, the higher priority for light-seekers was the correct decision, but as a weapon that was preferred by the AAF, this decision was doubtful. While the Navy expressed some interest in the GB light-seekers, it was eager to develop a radar-guided system that could be used in any light and most weather conditions and was more suited to attacking maritime targets. The AAF just was not interested in a weapon that was primarily designed to attack maritime targets and was plainly pursuing a weapon to attack land-based targets. Furthermore, while the light-seeker concept had been proven reliable under the suitable conditions, using light contrast to locate and hit a target while the sensor was attached to a GB needed to tested and proven.

GB-5A Photo-Electric Target-Seeker

The GB-5A was a 2,000-pound GB-1 Aeronca airframe equipped with a Fairchild photo-electric marine target-seeker that homed on the light contrast between a ship and the water surrounding it. The Fairchild homing unit was a small 10.5-inch-diameter by 11-inch-long cylinder with an 18- by 12- by 2-inch relay box connected to a 12-volt battery. Testing began during November and December 1943 but met with many weather delays. While the seeker was able to detect the target, if and when the weather cooperated, its ability to control the bomb was questionable. During testing in good weather, the seeker realized sensor acquisition of the target at ranges of 5 to 25 miles, depending upon the light conditions and position of the sun. However, the system required too much time to acquire control of the bomb after release as the falling bomb oscillated for over 4,000 feet before the internal guidance stabilized it and meanwhile lost 1,000 feet of altitude in fifteen seconds over a 3–5-mile range. Often during testing, these oscillations were so large that the seeker lost the target and would guide on any contrasting structure that came into its range. The Engineering Division determined that redesign and more testing became necessary but proceeded slowly, and nine months later, the GB-5A development priority had been reduced to a lowly 3A. At the time, the LAB (low-altitude bombsight) was successfully integrated into several combat units and the additional training and problems that would be met in introducing the GB-5A into combat could not be justified. The GB-5B equipped with a Hammond flare-seeker was considered obsolete during its design stages and was abandoned. While work on light contrast-seekers continued until the end of the war, it was apparent the development was for research only rather than to develop a tactical weapon. GBs that briefly were given a much higher priority were the GB-5C light seeker and the flare-seeking GB-5D, which were redesignated as the GB-12 and GB-13 respectively and will be discussed as such.

GB-5A photoelectric target-seeker bomb. (*From AAF movie still*)

GB-12/GB-5C Photo-Electric Light-Seeking Bomb

The GB-12, renamed from the GB-5C and developed under Project MX-615, was considered by the Air Material Command as the most promising marine-seeker. The Hammond (developer)/Crosley (manufacturer) unit was a marine-type photocell contrast light-seeker, using the standard GB airframe housing the B-1 light contrast-seeker in its faired nose. The amplifier and control system directed the missile on a collision course against shipping that offered a contrast against the water. Some 7 to 10 miles was considered the operational range due to target identification difficulties, but the missile could be dropped at longer ranges as the preset photocell eyes opened automatically at the operational range. This GB was also tested as an air-to-air missile to detect aircraft up to 2 miles away. The seeker needed to be pointed upward, away from the distracting horizon, and the background needed to be uniform—either all cloudy or entirely clear. Initially, twenty-five were procured, with five used in preliminary tests in May 1944 at Tonopah before the project was abandoned.

GB-12/GB-5C photoelectric light-seeking bomb. (*AAF*)

GB-13/GB-5D Photocell Flare-Seeking Bomb

While the development of light contrast-seekers would continue until the end of the war, it was evident this was for scientific research purposes only, rather than to develop a weapon having any tactical utility or possibility of being used in World War II. However, a photo-sensitive seeker that briefly enjoyed a higher priority and some developmental success was the flare-seeking GB-5D.

The GB-13 (Project MX-619) was originally developed as the GB-5D, a weapon to be used against pinpoint enemy land targets such as searchlights. The GB-13 used a standard GB airframe with a 2,000-pound bomb and a faired nose containing a Fairchild B-3 photocell flare-seeker, which fit into an 8-inch-diameter by 10-inch-long cylinder and had a homing cone of 70 degrees. The carrying aircraft would release the GB-13 at 6 miles on a preset automatic pilot course, which was overridden when reaching the Fairchild's operational range. The Fairchild unit was adapted for use against burning targets or flare-illuminated targets such as specific point targets such as blockhouses, power plants, etc. Because of its flat trajectory, the bomb would skid into the target. The flare could be planted in front of the target by fast, low-flying aircraft or by ground-based mortars or rockets. The flares, dropped by parachute by low-flying target marking aircraft, were 3 feet long, 7 inches in diameter, weighed 80 pounds, and burned at a million candlepower for three minutes.

An interesting plan to use the GB-13 against enemy dams was proposed as these targets were usually heavily defended by anti-aircraft fire and were resistant to conventional bombing tactics and ordnance. The suggested scheme was to drop flares at night into the dam's reservoir and have them float with the current to the lip of the dam where they would remain. The light-seeking homing device on the GB would guide it to strike the face of the dam at a preset level below the flare to explode.

Twelve GB-13s were produced for tests conducted between December 13, 1944 and January 9, 1945. During these tests, three of six GB-13s missed the target by only 10 feet, and on December 21, one hit the flare directly. Tests proved the seeker to be very reliable and fifty GB-13s were ordered for the next stage of testing. However, these fifty GB-13s were never delivered and the next tests were conducted with the remaining GB-13s. The results of these tests are undocumented and testing of the GB-13 ended in the late spring of 1945, but low-priority research and development on the light-contrast and flare-seeking systems continued until the end of the war.

GB-6 Infrared-Seeking Bombs

The Aeronca GB-6, which was developed as part of Project MX-612, was based on the GB-1 using an Offner heat-seeking device to home on targets. This infrared (IR) carrying GB began its development in the spring of 1942 by the Offner Electronics Corporation of New York City under NDRC direction. The GB-6 was basically an Aeronca GB-8 airframe carrying the usual 2,000-pound bomb, and when assembled with its IR-seeker, it had a considerable resemblance to the GB-13 flare-seeker. The GB-6 included the standard Hammond Corporation gyroscopic stabilization equipment and a faired nose housing containing an Offner thermopile heat-seeker and amplifier unit. The thermopile converted thermal energy into electrical energy by measuring the temperature differential from their junction point to the point in which the thermocouple output voltage was measured. The GB-6 traveled on a preset course with the thermopile-seeker taking over control when in range of targets that radiated more heat than their surroundings, such as shipping, refineries, steel mills, blast furnaces, and power plants.

The Offner-seeker had an effective detection range of 7 to 10 miles under perfect conditions and was considered as a promising heat-seeker if the target was sufficiently isolated. Initial Offner IR-seeker unit tests were conducted on July 7 and 8, 1943 by Offner at its New York City offices. The IR-seeker was installed on a tripod on the thirty-fifth floor of the Offner building, where it was to detect and track ships moving on the Hudson River. It was quickly discovered that good results could be expected as long as the sun or its reflection off the water did not enter the IR-detector. The Experimental Engineering Section representatives were sufficiently impressed and approved air testing. Although the Bemis Corporation had developed a more effective IR-seeker, it was allocated for use on the VB-6 Felix bomb so the GB-6 retained the Offner system

The initial AAF aerial tests were conducted at the Eglin throughout 1943 and into 1944 to determine if there were a way to improve its ability to discern ground targets that interested the AAF more than maritime targets. Although the test results were generally considered to be poor, it was shown that the IR-seeker was much more effective against isolated heat sources such as shipping than against ground targets that had more radiant heat surrounding them. During a test in the late afternoon of February 27, 1944, a GB-6 was directed to a beacon fire, but the bomb quickly lost

GB-6A infrared-seeking bomb. (*AAF*)

the target and crashed into the ground. Investigation found that the Florida humidity and ambient background heat radiation greatly affected GB-6 performance causing the project to be was relocated on June 22 to less humid Wendover Field in Utah. During the summer and early fall of 1944, tests at Wendover showed that the optimum detection range over land was 3 miles when the test drops were made in the very early morning when background IR interference was minimal. Testing against actual industrial targets was impractical but attempts were made to duplicate them for test purposes. A scheme using 3,000 square feet of metal sheeting, warmed by orchard heaters, was tried with some success. By late September 1944, only three of the fourteen bombs dropped on the 3,000-square-foot sheet metal target either struck or missed it by a few feet (the remainder were wide misses) as weather, haze, dust, humidity, and mostly the variations and gradations in ambient IR energy that surrounded the target continued to interfere with GB-6 accuracy. A relay malfunction was determined to be the cause of two poor results. It was also found that the slower speed of the B-17 at release made the GB much more difficult to control during descent than when it was released from the faster B-25 Mitchell medium bomber. Humidity and haze could seriously affect both detection ranges and the ability of the bomb to stay on target once released. When the Wendover relative humidity reached 70 percent between October and March, continued testing became virtually impossible, even against large land targets.

Unless the weather, haze, humidity, and dust limitations could be resolved, the value of the GB-6 against land targets in the climate over northern Europe or the Japanese Home Islands would be seriously reduced. The project remained on a very low priority throughout its existence and never progressed beyond the testing stage. Once the VB-6

Felix Bemis IR system, which could be carried internally by a B-17, was proven to be a better and more reliable weapon, the GB-6 quickly lost what little support it had in the AAF, and in February 1945, the GB-6 project was canceled. The 150 GB-6s (145 for the AAF and five to the USN) on the August 1, 1944 order were expended during testing.

Radar-Seeking GBs

Already well-established at the time, radar technology was deemed to be superior target-seeker than light, infrared, or television as it could function in darkness or bad weather. During April 1942, Col. Benjamin Chidlaw requested that the NDRC develop a radar system and equipment for controlling GBs, which resulted in three radar-directed GB projects being developed concurrently: the GB-7, -7B, and -7C. The Dryden 2,000-pound vehicle with a 12-foot wingspan was intended to be the vehicle, but the Aeronca 2,000-pound target-seeking vehicle was available and considered better. The Navy Moth (described later) was a radar homing glider bomb developed simultaneously but was canceled.

GB-7A

The GB-7A (Project MX-613) was designated as radar-homing bomb (RHB) because its seeker homed in on the radar energy that bounced off the target. In today's radar idiom, this is known as semi-active homing, in which the missile's seeker is merely a passive receiver of the radar energy, which must be provided by another source, such as a radar transmitter located on the launching aircraft. This GB used Hammond gyro control and an accelerometer for pitch control. Two rates of turn control were employed: a slow rate during the early portion of the flight and a much higher rate during the final portion. The unit was built around a 2,000-pound Aeronca target-seeking vehicle, which had a similar airframe to the GB-8 but used special plywood nose and a different control box. The nose section was mounted forward of the bomb and a metal plate in four quadrants was mounted in the nose, while the batteries, stabilizing equipment, servo mechanisms for the operation of the control surfaces, and the control relays that were connected to radar receiver were located in the mechanism housing. The radar homing device homed on radar pulses transmitted by a radar transmitter in the control aircraft and reflected from the target. In operation, the target was radar illuminated from the GB-7 and the return signal differentials between the target and the background were received by the radar receiver to give up, down, right, and left signals in accordance with the targets location. These signals were used to operate the control relays to transmit the correct control through the stabilizing equipment to the servo mechanisms and then to the airframe control surfaces so that the GB would be guided to the target. The GB-7A was planned for use against lone marine targets or isolated large buildings as the target had to be sufficiently isolated (at least by 500 feet) to prevent distraction from other sources of reflection that would be within the range of the bombs receiver.

GB-7A radar-homing bomb (RHB). (*AAF*)

GB-7B Radar Send-Receive-Bomb (SRB)

The more complicated and technically challenging GB-7B (Project MX-616 and later redesignated as the GB-14) system had its radar transmitter and receiver contained in the weapon itself. It carried its own AN/APG7 radar transmitter (500 ordered from the Navy) to illuminate the target. Using its RC 171 radar receiver, it rode the returned echo to its source, making it independent and self-contained; it did not require the mother aircraft for control. Today, this is known as active homing, since the missile performs both the transmitting and the receiving of radar energy after it is released from the bomber.

GB-14 Radar Send-Receive-Bomb (SRB)

The GB-14 was intended to be used against naval targets. Production was scheduled to begin in September 1943 with 200 units to be finished by January 1, 1944 and then at fifty per month afterward. The program was canceled after only one test.

GB-7C

The GB-7C, called the Hairy Butterfly, was an end-of-the-war design employing an AN/APQ-14 radar-seeker for homing on enemy early-warning and fire-control radar signals by adjusting to enemy frequencies so that it would home on their transmitting antennas.

GB-7B radar send-receive-bomb (SRB). (*AAF*)

GB-14 radar send-receive-bomb (SRB). (*AAF*)

The Aircraft Radio Laboratory ordered twenty-five for experimental use, and the NDRC hand-built five, which were test-dropped; however, the developmental and technical problems were too overwhelming, and it wasn't until the 1960s before the AAF developed the successful Wild Weasel against enemy radars during the Vietnam War.

Radar-Homing Bomb (RHB) and Send-Receive-Bomb (SRB) Radar Development

Since the AMC assumed that the less complex radar-homing bomb (RHB) would be finalized and enter operations first, it was decided to develop the tactically more desirable send-receive-bomb (SRB) simultaneously. This was to be the first of several poor decisions that would unnecessarily muddle radar-controlled bomb research and design efforts during the war and one that unquestionably impacted their delay in becoming operational.

The SRB was tactically more desirable because it was a so-called fire-and-forget weapons system. After launching, the SRB bomb was self-guiding, allowing the mothership to turn immediately away from the target to safety or execute any necessary evasive maneuvers. The less sophisticated RHB was a semi-active system that required the mother aircraft to illuminate the target with radar energy, which the RHB then guided on. This procedure required the illuminating aircraft to continue to fly towards the target without taking any evasive actions until the bomb struck, which greatly increased its vulnerability, sometimes for several minutes.

With the support of the NDRC, some encouraging preliminary laboratory tests were conducted at the MIT Radiation Laboratory, which was the main center for the crucial developmental radar effort to prove the theoretical capabilities of semi-active homing. The Radiation Laboratory Lab, also known as the RadLab, was created in October 1940 under the innocuous *nom de guerre* Department of Industrial Cooperation (DIC), a subterfuge name to thwart enemy espionage attention.

Alfred Loomis was central figure in forming the RadLab as an epicenter for scientific experts to quickly develop newly emerging technologies during the war and directly transition these discoveries into production for the war effort. The influential and multi-talented Loomis, an investment banker, scientist, and physicist, had previously established the Loomis Laboratory in Tuxedo Park, New York; Loomis had money, an influence with OSRD Head, Vannevar Bush, and an enthusiasm for science, as well as personal relationships with top scientists of the era. He was committed to the war effort and did not waste any time establishing a site for new radar technology. Loomis, who headed the NDRC Microwave Committee, was central in establishing the Radiation Laboratory as a joint Anglo-American effort for general microwave and radar research and system development using the new top-secret cavity magnetron developed by Britain. His role in the development of radar and the atomic bomb contributed much to the Allied victory. At its peak, the RadLab employed 4,000 and is credited for designing half of all the radar systems used during the war and was influential in the research and development of the critical radar-seeker.

Wall Street financier Alfred Loomis was central in establishing the RadLab as an epicenter for scientific experts to quickly develop newly emerging technologies during the war. (NA)

While RHB was in the laboratory test stage, the AAF considered the results sufficiently promising, and on October 7, 1942, the AAF requested RHB aerial testing. Due to the large size and weight of the radar-homing device, initial testing was performed using a twin-engined Beech AT-11. The aerial test results were generally considered inconclusive, but on October 28, as testing was being concluded, the AT-11 successfully homed on an anchored 125-foot lightship that was illuminated by ground-based radar positioned on a nearby island. This test was sufficiently promising that further testing was ordered to begin immediately. These new tests were conducted from November 9–12, 1943 to establish the maximum and minimum operational range; to determine if the RHB equipment functioned when the radar energy was provided by an airborne set operating from another aircraft; and to determine the RHB's ability to pick out the largest target when it was surrounded by smaller vessels. The results of these tests were disappointing as, for example, it was determined that the RHB could not distinguish the largest vessel situated near several smaller ones, but instead would aim for the center of the largest collective mass of returned radar energy. There also were frequent equipment malfunctions, but, nonetheless, the AMC again requested that the testing continue as some useful and promising data was acquired.

On January 1, 1943, Col. Chidlaw requested that NDRC Division 14 begin development of the SRB system (Project AC-51) to be installed on both powered vehicles and GBs while tests were to be continued on the RHB system by the Radiation Laboratory. Both projects were successfully tested into the late spring of 1943 and both were standardized on the same day, June 12, 1943, with the radar receiver to be installed on a controllable missile to guide the bomb. The RHB was to use energy from a distant source while the SRB was to provide its own radar signal that was to be powerful enough to illuminate the target and receive reflections from it.

Meanwhile, the Navy BuOrd and the MIT Radiation Laboratory had been occupied with the development of a larger semi-active RHB system for an anti-shipping adaptation, which was to guide either towed gliders or powered bombs equipped with a warhead large enough to sink a capital warship. At this time, slowing all radar-seeker development, there was an apparent duplication of effort concerning the development of both at the larger Navy/MIT RHB and the smaller AAF/Wright Field Equipment Laboratory RHB (the GB-7A). If these weapons were to have any possibility of being completed in time to become operational in the war, some prioritization would have to intervene, ideally placing responsibility for all RHB research with one organization and all SRB with another.

On June 14, Dr. Louis Ridenour, director of the Radiation Laboratories, proposed that the AAFs GB-7A, which was also being developed by the Radiation Laboratories, should be transferred to the NDRC's Division 5 due to its small size. Ridenour then also suggested that to preclude unnecessary duplication that all SRB development be transferred from MIT to Bell Telephone Laboratories, which had been contracted to develop SRB components for the AAF. Unfortunately, only Dr. Ridenour's suggestion to move the development of the GB-7A airframe, its automatic controls, and the radar to NDRC's over-worked and unqualified NDRC Division 5 was taken.

This decision placed the responsibility on Division 5 Chief Harold Richmond and his researchers, not only for the design of the airframe and its automatic controls but also now gave them responsibility for designing the GB-7A radar. On July 12, Richmond sent a letter to the air staff objecting that RHB research had not progressed sufficiently that it could not successfully direct a GB to hit a target and suggested that it had been a hasty and unreasonable decision to expect Division 5 to undertake this project. Richmond also noted that "Just as soon as we know that RHB is a reality then tests can be made on all (Army and Navy) vehicles." Nevertheless, despite Richmond's objections, Division 5 was required to continue to have the main part of the RHB design responsibilities for the GB-7A program.

During the spring of 1943, MIT's Radiation Laboratory, the Bell Telephone Laboratory, NDRC's Division 14, AMC's Engineering Division, and the Navy's BuOrd were all involved in SRB development with each having authority over some aspect of SRB research and design. The resultant bureaucracy not only disrupted SBR R&D but threatened the development of the entire radar-guided GB program. During May 1943, after the NDRC had developed the first satisfactory SRB unit, it did not have the facilities to develop the service test models so the Aircraft Radio Laboratory (ARL) was assigned to place contracts with companies in the field with General Electric and Zenith being recommended. The ARL, as the primary organization concerned with SRB research, was to be assigned the necessary authority to fulfill any requirements for any equipment in quantities required for continued experimental work, but this recommendation somehow vanished in bureaucratic battling. Despite several conferences to remedy the SRB situation, the unrelenting wrangling continued into late September without any headway. However, in October 1943, not only the SRB program, but the entire guided weapon program appeared to have new expectations of resolution when Brig. Gen. H. M. McClelland, the Air Communications Officer (ACO), had been assigned the inclusive responsibility for guided aerial weapons research, design, and development, particularly for bombs having integral electronic components. However, McClelland had little expertise outside the field of communications and had no authority within the AAF. As a consequence, the ACO was ineffectual and any results were marginal for guided bombs in general and radar-guided GBs in particular. The SRB and RHB programs then stagnated under the weight of duplication of effort and bureaucracy. The radar-seeker programs were stymied at every level, from the design unit to the upper echelons of military and civil administration.

Meanwhile the SRB program continued to decline as it was condemned to twenty-sixth place on the joint Army-Navy Radar Research and Development Precedence List. On November 17, 1943, MIT's Radiation Laboratory unexpectedly announced it was withdrawing from all RHB research because the project was considered only an interim weapon for the AAF before the SRB was perfected, and their research organization transferred to more urgent and meaningful projects. The NDRC allowed RadLab's departure, but more gradually in order to consolidate research results. Meanwhile, the SRB continued to languish, and on November 18, 1943, Brig. Gen. Chidlaw recommended that the SRB situation be changed quickly if there was to be any chance of the SRB becoming a reality in the war, but the situation was not quickly changed.

On May 11, 1944, Maj. Gen. R. B. Colton, Chief of Engineering and Technical Service, suggested the cancellation of the AAFs SRB program in favor of the Navy's Bat project, which was considered to have more potential. (The Navy used the Bat operationally against Japanese late in the war, which is discussed later.) On May 18, ACO McClelland agreed with Colton's recommendation and the NDRC closed out its research on the SRB system formally on June 6, 1944. Certain elements of the GB-7B/GB-14 research performed to date would eventually be applied to the GB-7A, but otherwise, the AAF's SRB project was shelved until after the war.

GB-7A Continued Testing

Because it was so similar to the Navy's Bat project, GB-7A/GB-14 tests were held in abeyance until Bat tests were completed. Once resumed, GB-7A tests were performed in conjunction with the Navy's tests on their Pelican system. While the GB-7A had a 2,000-pound bomb attached to a GB-8 airframe, the Pelican initially used a 500-pound bomb, which was later increased to 1,000 pounds when carried by Dryden glider airframe. During tests in the summer of 1944, the Pelican was shown to be very accurate as out of sixteen test drops from 6,000 feet and 6 miles distance, six direct hits were recorded on a stationary Liberty ship. (The Pelican is discussed in more detail later.)

During the renewed testing, the GB-7A's technical problems were basically the same as those encountered by the IR-guided GB-6. The GB-7's radar was able to detect isolated marine targets but had almost no capability to distinguish point targets on land, particularly in built up areas, so would be ineffective against strategic targets such as factories, oil refineries, and like targets considered to have strategic worth in the late war. Thus, the AAF lost interest in the GB-7A for the same reasons it lost interest in the GB-6, and when there was little demonstrable progress made by November 1944, the GB-7A program was reduced to a 3-A priority. GB-7A development was discontinued in August 1945, as the Navy's attempts to use the Bat against Japanese caves on Okinawa ended with poor results and in need of further development.

While television and heat-seeking guidance would be devoted to powered and vertical bombs, radar guidance remained solely the province of GB during the war. As GBs plummeted into continued disfavor with the AAF operational ranks, radar guidance also became more discredited as while radar was excellent at seeing from the ground up, it had great difficulty seeing from the air to the ground. Subsequently, it became evident that the GB-7A radar would never have sufficient accuracy against a precision land target. Even if the GB-7 had not experienced the delays due to an overly complicated research and design process and bureaucracy, it nevertheless would have been considered an unwanted weapon, to be employed only with great reluctance by the AAF's mainstream operational bombardment echelons.

GB-8 Radio-Controlled Bomb

During the development of the GB-4 (as Project MX-645), television transmitters and receivers continued to cause numerous technical problems; by late 1943, it was decided to eliminate television guidance and to concentrate again on a radio-controlled only GB. The bomb was designated as the GB-8 and resembled the successful radio-controlled German FX-1400 Fritz X winged bomb. This German missile had sunk the Italian Navy flagship, the battleship *Roma*, on September 9, 1943, and two days later, during the air-sea battle off Salerno, hit the USN light cruisers *Savannah* and *Philadelphia*; on the 13th, the missile hit the Royal Navy's light cruiser *Uganda*, then several merchant ships, and finally the RN battleship *Warspite* on September 16. The GB-8 used the same radio controls for azimuth and range as the GB-4, but instead of TV control, a smoke flare was installed in its tail, which was used by the bombardier to visually guide the GB-8. This GB, like other GB projects, used surplus GB-1 airframes modified to the GB-4 non-twin tail boom design. Because the GB-8 used a modified GB-1 airframe, which was somewhat smaller than the one designed for the more complex GB-4, the GB-8's radio equipment component that was designed for use with the GB-4 had to be redesigned to fit the GB-8 Aeronca airframe. There were 2,000 GB-8s on the production order, with 130 scheduled to be delivered during April 1944 (with 100 Hammond control units) and then 500 per month thereafter (with 300–400 Hammond control units).

The GB-8 had a glide ratio ranging from 5:2 to 6:1 and its speed on this glide path was approximately 250 mph, which could be increased by diving. The GB-8 was guided by the bombardier who operated a small joystick located on top of the radio control box. As the bombardier had to observe the GB-8 the entire way to the

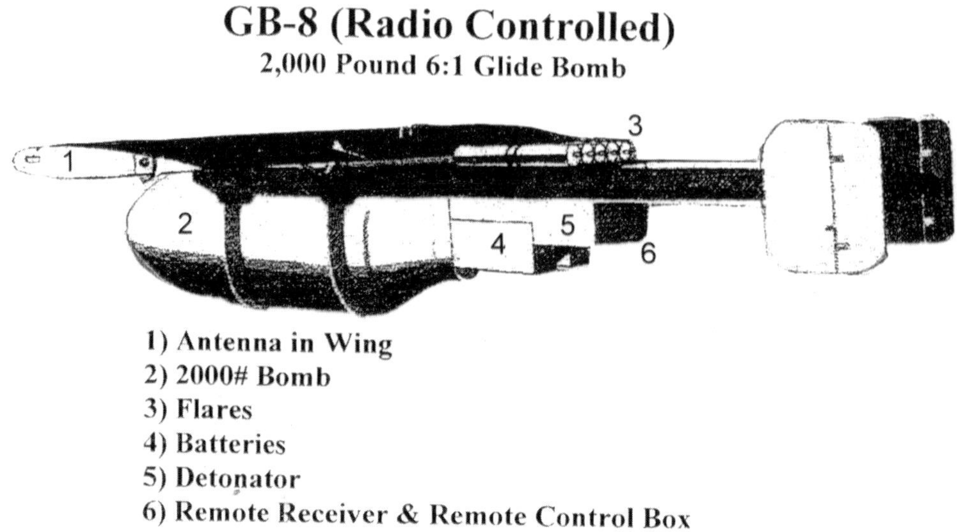

In late 1943, the AAF decided to eliminate television guidance and to concentrate on the GB-8 radio-controlled glide bomb using a modified GB-1 airframe. The GB-8 used the same radio-controls for azimuth and range as the GB-4, but instead of TV control, a smoke flare was fitted to the airframe, which was guided visually by the bombardier. (*AAF*)

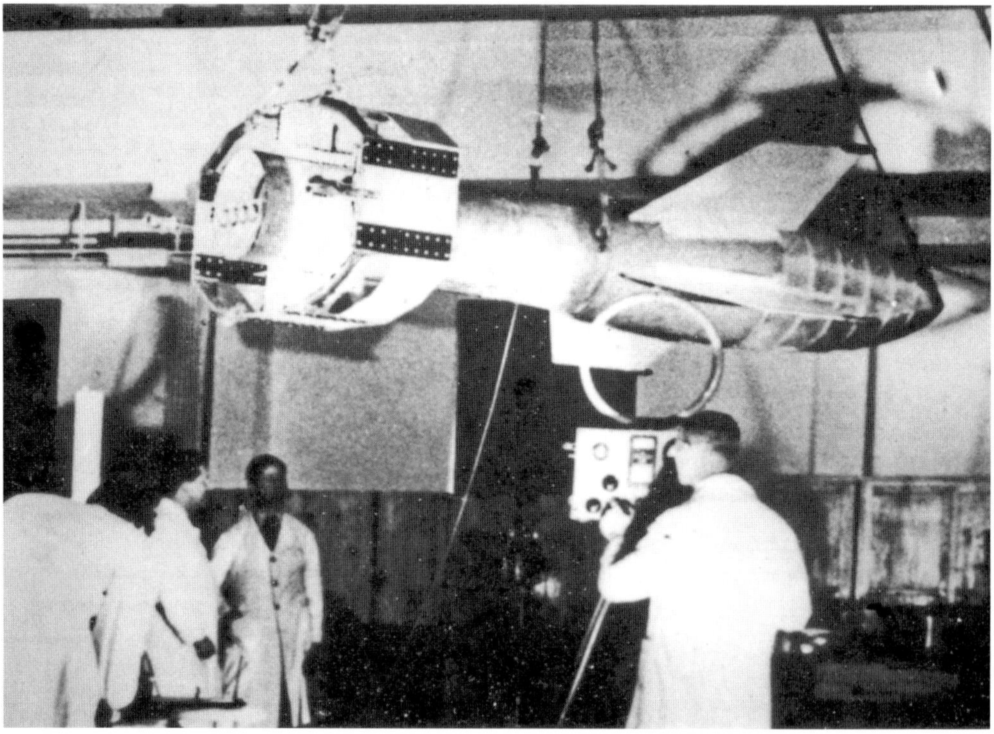

The German *Fritz X* was the world's first precision-guided weapon deployed in combat and the first to sink a ship in combat. (*Author*)

The GB-8's lack of precision at the long ranges and high altitudes during testing caused its cancellation in the summer of 1944. (*AAF*)

target, the mother B-17s had to fly a curved path after releasing the bomb and could not immediately turn away from the target, as could be done upon releasing the GB-1. The bombardier had the difficult task of estimating angles, distances, relative movement, and rates of closure from long distances and at difficult perspectives. The average release point from the target was 8 miles, so to hit the target, the bombardier had to eclipse or visually cover the target with the moving bomb, which was only 15 degrees below the horizon and flying at about 300 mph just before impact. The bomb could only be corrected at a rate of 3 degrees per second, but there was a sizeable time lag between applying controls and the bomb responding. The bomb's wingspan was only 12 feet, and when viewed against surface objects surrounding the target at such long distances, it was impossible for the human eye to distinguish the bomb's rate of descent or if the wings were level. Bombardiers were given an additional ten weeks of GB-8 training, but nonetheless, they were unable to make it a precision weapon.

A problem that affected not only the GB-8 but all other radio-controlled guided bombs—glide, vertical, or powered—was the limited number that could be deployed at one time. Each guided bomb required as many as five separate radio channels to control it: one each for commands to climb, dive, turn left, turn right, and for powered bombs to increase or decrease the throttle. Radio frequency could be partially modulated allowing more bombs to be controlled simultaneously in the same radio bandwidth. However, it became obvious that there were too few available radio channels to allow more than a few bombs to be controlled in flight, and those available channels could be easily jammed.

During early 1943, the 8AF considered the combat box containing sixty-three bombers to be the smallest bomber formation to have satisfactory defensive armament for operations over Germany. B-17s carrying externally mounted GBs did not have the sufficient speed, range, or ceiling to be added into conventional bombing formations and needed to fly independently. The AAF School of Applied Tactics recommended that the optimal formation for GB-4, GB-8, and all other radio-controlled bombs was to be nine B-17s in elements of three aircraft each. The bombardiers in the nine B-17s in GB formations could deploy only one weapon at a time and were very vulnerable to enemy fighters—a system that just did not fit in the scheme of AAF strategic bombing tactics. During May 1944, because GB-4 development was lagging, a higher priority was given to the GB-8 and recommendations were made to have it become operational as soon as possible. Seven GB-8s were sent to England as part of the Batty GB-4 operational testing program but none were employed.

The GB-8's lack of precision at the AAF-mandated long ranges and high altitudes during testing would eventually cause its cancellation in the summer of 1944, after less than half of the 2,000 ordered from Aeronca for the GB programs were delivered and the remaining GBs on order were canceled. After the GB-8 project was halted, GB-8 airframes were transferred for further development and testing and to other GB programs. Nevertheless, GB-8 testing did produce some constructive results and lessons learned that were utilized to improve the GB-4 and later GBs. All the GB-8 radio technicians could be quickly diverted to reinforce any other radio-controlled glide-bomb project. Also GB-8 testing established the basic flight characteristics, glide ratios, and airspeeds for all similar radio-controlled GBs. Lastly, GB-8 research and testing at least allowed the radio control feature of the GB-4 design and development to continue until the television guidance issues were resolved.

During its development, several new operational uses were suggested for the GB-8. The flare-carrying GB-8 was intended for tactical use to lead conventional night bombing missions to illuminate the target area. The standard glider frame and GB-8 control box were used, but instead of carrying a bomb, it was equipped with a streamlined wooden box containing ninety parachute flares with a mechanism to release the flares at one second intervals by radio control. The first bomber in a large formation would drop its gliders over the target area and steer it by observing an electric light mounted on top of the glider, which could only be seen from above. When the glider reached a low altitude over the target the glider controller would hold down a release button that would drop flares 200 feet apart with the ninety flares lighting an area about 3 miles long. Several gliders launched in parallel simultaneously could light up a large section of the target. Since American bombing strategy was directed toward daylight bombing, this flare-carrying GB-8 never saw fruition.

The anti-personnel GN-8 used the standard glider, control box, and flare panel unit, but in place of the bomb, a streamlined wooden box (similar to the flare-carrying GB-8 box) was employed. Instead of flares, eighteen 100-pound anti-personnel bombs (or a larger number of smaller bombs) were carried and released individually or in train during attacks on roads carrying enemy personnel and vehicles.

In order to determine if the GB-8 could be used as a close-support weapon for ground troops, a series of tests were conducted to determine whether reliable control could be obtained with a ground control transmitter, which was to allow azimuth control of the GB from one station and elevation or range control from another. During tests to compare control surface responses to radio control signals, fifteen GBs were tested; this consisted of eleven standard GB-8s (with rudder only/azimuth control) with Hammond radio control, two with ARL radio control, and two GB-6 airframes (with rudder and aileron control) with Hammond radio control. In these tests, the Hammond system was determined to be satisfactory, but the rudder and aileron controls of the GB-6 airframe responded better to radio control. The accuracy of the ground control was dependent on the controller's skill to judge the amount of turn required to bring the bomb on course and to apply the correct amount of control to make this turn. The relatively slow and variable response of the standard GB-8 to azimuth control signals made accurate control very difficult for even the most experienced controller. It was essential that the azimuth controller place the GB on course early in the flight because the flight path as observed from the range station would be distorted and accurate range control would then be impossible. Development and testing continued until September 1945 when this facet of GB development was terminated.

The Quest for Better and More Exotic Guidance Systems

After Gen. Arnold's April 1942 resolve that the simpler GB-1, gyro-stabilized GB be developed first, the AAF was forced to neglect the research and development of the technically superior radio-controlled and more exotic control techniques, especially since the AAF's AMC Engineering Division was compelled to divert its efforts from radio-controlled projects to support in GB-1 development. Despite Arnold's GB-1 penchant, the American civilian scientific coalition would voice its case for more accurate advanced control systems. During June 1942, the NDRC's Division D (Detection, Controls, and Instruments) proposed target-seeking bombs, equipped with television, infrared, or radar, to acquire and track a target and that aircraft suitable for experimental purposes be obtained ASAP. Importantly, the NDRC acknowledged the Navy's BuOrd and the NDRC's Joint New Weapons Committee as influential patrons for the research and development of advanced GB. During September 1942, the Joint New Weapons Committee was assigned to investigate and develop radio control, target-viewing and target-seeking systems, sighting and navigational aids, aerodynamic design, and the development of countermeasures for electronic control and targeting systems. Meanwhile, the AAF attempted to support advanced glide bomb research by assigning several AMC Engineering Division electrical and aeronautical engineers who could be spared from the GB-1 program to the GB-4 television-controlled bomb, which led to several television-controlled guided weapons. Therefore, before describing these GBs, a brief history of development and types of TV systems for the military needs to be undertaken.

The Development of Television-Controlled Military Applications

During 1927, inventor Philo Farnsworth developed and patented the dissector tube, which was the basis of all current electronic televisions. Many inventors had developed electromechanical television systems before Farnsworth's ground-breaking scheme, but he designed and built the world's first working all-electronic television system, employing electronic scanning in both the pickup and display devices, which he first demonstrated on September 3, 1928. In 1931, RCA President David Sarnoff offered to buy Farnsworth's patents for the large (for the time) sum of $100,000, but also specified that he had to become an RCA employee, but Farnsworth refused and joined Philco. RCA filed lawsuits against Farnsworth, claiming RCA head researcher Vladimir Zworykin's 1923 patent had priority over Farnsworth's design. In 1934, the U.S. Patent Office awarded Farnsworth priority of his image dissector invention. RCA lost a subsequent appeal, but litigation over an assortment of issues continued and failed. Meanwhile, Farnsworth had severed his relationship with Philco and spent years attempting to sell his dissector tube to pay his ongoing RCA legal bills. In 1938, he set up his own firm, the Farnsworth Television and Radio Corporation, in Fort Wayne, Indiana. During 1939, Sarnoff finally agreed to a multi-year licensing agreement with Farnsworth for $1 million, allowing RCA to sell television cameras. The RCA litigation finally took its toll on Farnsworth, who moved to Maine to recover after a nervous breakdown in 1939 where he founded the Farnsworth Wood Products Company. Without Farnsworth, Farnsworth Television and Radio profited on defense contracts during the war, and appeared to be well-positioned to capitalize on the promising post-war consumer market for television receivers. During 1947, Farnsworth returned to his company, which had just produced its first television set, but found that mismanagement caused the company to falter just as the consumer television market began to boom. The company was sold to International Telephone and Telegraph in 1949 and reorganized as Capehart-Farnsworth, a minor factor in the TV market compared to RCA. Farnsworth was retained as vice president of research, developing the PPI Projector that would be the forerunner of today's air traffic control system. He continued to work, unsuccessfully, on the Fusor, a fusion reactor, until 1967. He passed away on March 11, 1971.

After spending seven unsuccessful years at Westinghouse, Pittsburgh, attempting to develop an all-electronic television system, Vladimir Zworykin was recruited by RCA in 1930 to head its Television Development Department at its Camden, New Jersey, laboratories. Zworykin and his RCA team began TV camera development during April 1931 and exhibited the iconoscope camera in a press conference in June 1933. The Zworykin iconoscope was much more sensitive than the Farnsworth image dissector, displaying a very clear image, and was also easier to manufacture. Zworykin continued to refine his iconoscope and Telefunken, a German company, purchased the rights from RCA and used its iconoscope camera for the historic TV transmission of the 1936 Berlin Summer Olympics. The iconoscope was replaced in Europe soon afterward by a more sensitive camera, while in America, the iconoscope was the principal camera tube used for broadcasting from 1936

Inventor Philo Farnsworth developed and patented the dissector tube, which was the basis of all current electronic televisions. (*NA*)

Vladimir Zworykin, RCA head researcher and Farnsworth rival. (*RCA*)

until 1946, when it was replaced in public broadcasting by the image orthicon tube.

Prior to 1935, television equipment was too heavy and bulky to be used in an aircraft, but that year, RCA, on its own initiative, directed Raymond Kell to begin the development of an aerial torpedo with an electric eye based on an April 25, 1934 proposal submitted by Zworykin to RCA. Zworykin's proposition basically delineated a plan for television control of a guided missile. Influential RCA President David Sarnoff arranged a meeting for Zworykin, Army Generals Oscar Westover and William Tschappat (Chief of Ordnance), and Navy Admirals Ernest King (Chief of BuAer) and Harold Stark (Chief of BuOrd). The meeting resulted with the four assuring financial support for the project's development.

With this financial reassurance, during 1935, Kell and assistants, Waldamar Poch and Henry Kasanowski, began the development of a lightweight aerial reconnaissance television unit using a Model 1850 Iconoscope, which they first demonstrated in 1937, mounted in a Ford Tri-motor. On April 30, 1939, NBC began regularly scheduled broadcasts in New York with a broadcast from the World's Fair using RCA TV equipment. On March 6, 1940, the aerial unit was finalized and was demonstrated to the public by RCA and NBC. The small camera and transmitter were installed in an American Airlines' Boeing 247 Mainliner. After leaving LaGuardia Field, the aircraft circled New York City for forty-five minutes at 2,000 feet with the TV camera successfully transmitting well-defined pictures of New York City to a battery of receivers installed at Radio City. This demonstration was witnessed by Army and Navy officials, and the Zworykin design was approved for further development, with the military applications in mind.

Encouraged by the military's interest, RCA began its development program on a more compact, lightweight airborne TV equipment under engineering groups headed by M. A. Trainer and Waldamar Poch of RCA Victor, and Raymond Kell of RCA Laboratories. Reduced weight was paramount, so Trainer and Poch, with some sacrifice in picture quality, redesigned their portable iconoscope equipment, and in 1940 produced a 100-mc, 15-watt airborne camera-transmitter. Kell continued the development of a smaller and lighter television unit for use in the smaller aircraft that could be used as guided missiles. This unit, the 1848 Iconoscope, was developed from RCA's commercial systems, and in 1940 led to the smaller 340-pound Jeep (and Jeepette) system, which displayed 640 lines at twenty frames per second and would lead to the BLOCK I system, two years later.

Flight tests using this set demonstrated that compact, lightweight television equipment could be developed and used in bomber-size aircraft; albeit, the received picture was at somewhat lower than broadcast quality but seemed to be adequate for military purposes. Fluctuating voltages and multi-path reception, always disruptive in television transmission, as well as humidity and temperature changes in the aircraft were problems that required resolution.

During August 1940, with war raging in Europe, RCA, buoyed by the success of its television/radio control unit, discussed the development of the aerial torpedo with Richard Tolman, vice chairman of the NDRC. The influential Tolman was in charge of the coordination of the enormous scientific component of the American war effort and later was appointed as Chief Scientific Adviser to Gen. Leslie Groves on the Manhattan Project and the development of the atomic bomb. RCA proposed the initial use of radio-controlled GBs, combined with television guidance. RCA's basic scheme was to have a bombardier/controller guide the bomb by remote radio control while watching a televised image from a camera mounted in the bomb's nose. Since a guided missile was much smaller than a bomber, consideration was given to the camera/transmitter unit's size, weight, reliability/durability, and power demand along with picture quality and sensitivity. Whenever feasible, broadcast TV standards and equipment were to be used. However, early television transmission and receiving equipment was reliant on vacuum tube technology, and consequently was very large, heavy, and also very fragile.

During January 1941, RCA collaborated with Dr. Hugh Dryden at the Aerodynamics Section of the National Bureau of Standards (NBS) to commence the development of television control. Today, the NBS is known as the National Institute of Standards and Technology (NIST). During the war, the NBS was one of America's principal agencies concerning scientific issues. Between August 1941 and September 1942, the RCA Princeton, New Jersey, Research Laboratories were consolidated into the world's largest radio laboratory. Otto Schairer was its general manager and vice president;

Above left: Dr. Richard Tolman, vice chairman of the NDRC. (*NA*)

Above right: Dr. Hugh Dryden, head of the Aerodynamics Section of the National Bureau of Standards; he later served on numerous government and military advisory committees. (*NA*)

Albert Rose, Paul Weimer, and Harold Law were the main RCA researchers into the Orthicon tube, a key advance in the television field. (*RCA*)

Ralph Beal was its director of research and development; C. B. Jolliffe was Chief Engineer of the frequency bureau; and Elmer Engstrom was overall director assisted by Browder Thompson and Zworykin.

The Orthicon tube, a key advance in the television field, was developed at RCA by Albert Rose and Harley Iams in 1937 and was the camera tube used in RCA's introduction of television at the 1939 New York World's Fair. In 1942, when RCA Laboratories was established, Rose transferred there, bringing with him a completed model of what later became the Image Orthicon, which was a combination of the image dissector and the Orthicon technologies. At the RCA Laboratories, he was joined by Paul Weimer and Harold Law, who had previously developed what was basically an electrostatic equivalent of Rose's tube. The National Defense Research Committee entered into a contract with RCA after which the NDRC financed its further development. The three scientists collaborated to perfect a new pickup tube, the Image Orthicon, which had increased sensitivity, greater contrast, improved picture quality, and decreased size and weight. In 1943, RCA and entered into a production contract with the Navy, the first tubes being delivered in January 1944 for use in guided missiles. RCA began production of image orthicons for civilian broadcasting in the spring of 1946, and during the post-war until 1968, it was the main camera tube for television broadcasts throughout the world.

RCA BLOCK TV Equipment

RCA 100-mc BLOCK I TV Equipment

The RCA equipment, later designated as BLOCK for security reasons, interested military officials, and during April 1941, the first compact BLOCK set was flight-tested in an AAC B-23 at Wright Field. Three months later, it was installed in a Naval Aircraft Factory TG biplane, which were a series of prototype seaplanes used for gunnery training. As a result of these tests, development and production contracts were instituted between RCA Victor and the Army, Navy, and the National Defense Research Committee.

Prior to Pearl Harbor, RCA had finalized their lightweight airborne television transmitter, monitor, and receiver, which were specifically designed for use in guiding pilotless aircraft and GBs to their targets. The New Image Orthicon, a small, lightweight, compact iconoscope represented some of the best miniaturized technology of the time. It weighed only 33 pounds and measured only 20 inches long, 9 inches wide, and 10 inches high and contained seventeen vacuum tubes, including the iconoscope tube. It had been simplified, particularly with the reduction in the number of scanning lines (350 lines and forty frames per second, sequential scanning), resulting in in an adequate picture for the purpose. The CRV-59 cameras used in the BLOCK series were part of the ATJ/ATK (transmitter) ARK (receiver) system. The 22-pound, 7-inch, RCA Kinescope monitor, used for pre-flight adjustment of the transmitter, was frequently taken onboard the control aircraft with the receiver and used as an auxiliary method for viewing the picture. The receiving equipment could not be abridged too much, as it needed the utmost sensitivity to balance the lower power output of the transmitter.

The ATE, ATF, ATG, ATH television camera/transmitters series (contracted in 1942) was known as BLOCK I and were housed in a single case. The sets consisted of four fixed frequencies, 78, 90, 102 and 114 MHz with the channels 9-mc wide due to the use of double sideband transmission. The pickup tube was an iconoscope and the output tube was an 829. The input voltage was 12.5 VDC (volts direct current) and the RF power (radio frequency power) was 15 watts. The components to the system were the CRV-59AAA to AAD camera transmitter, CRV-21ABY dynamotor, CRV-66ACS to ACV antenna, and CRV-60AAR monitor.

Note: A mc was a unit of frequency, equal to 1 million cycles per second, which has been replaced by megahertz (MHz) today. A kc was a unit equal to 1,000 cycles per second, which has been replaced by kilohertz (kHz).

The ARE, ARF, ARG, ARH sets were the corresponding receiver/displays for the accompanying camera/transmitters. The receivers were fixed frequency, complements to the transmitter, with a self-contained dynamotor and 7-inch green phosphor CRT (Cathode Ray Tube). The input voltage was 25 VDC. The components to the set were the CRV-46ABP to ABS receiver, CRV-23ACR voltage control unit, CRV-66ACO to ACR, and ADV to ADY antenna.

The Signal Corps' version of the camera/transmitter was the SCR-549-T1 and T2. The receiver was the SCR-550-T1 and T2. The AAF sets were similar to the Navy

The small, light, compact TV Camera (CRV-59) iconoscope, "New Image Orthicon," represented some of the best miniaturized technology of the time. (*RCA*)

The ARE/F/G/H receivers (Signal Corps SCR-550-T1) were the corresponding receiver/displays for the accompanying camera/transmitters. The 7-inch green phosphor CRT (cathode-ray tube) is seen on front of the set. (*RCA*)

sets except for slight modifications of design. BLOCK I was flight tested in a B-18 in April 1941 at Wright Field.

Between 1941 and 1942, RCA manufactured over 500 of these early BLOCK I units in their Camden plant and supplied them to the AAF, USN, and NDRC. The Navy was concentrating on the use of BLOCK I units their TDR powered drone as a carrier aircraft and experimenting with a glider GLOMB, which in later tests were found to be very satisfactory. The AAF's main interest was for BLOCK's use in the GB-4 glide bomb and in war-weary bombers that could be expended in carrying up to 14 tons of explosives into a target.

The requirement to produce a small and lightweight unit compromised the BLOCK I sets for highest picture quality, although commercial or broadcast standards were observed as faithfully as possible. Provisional standards were approved for the first military TV equipment, after consideration had been given to picture quality *versus* power demand and circuit complexity. These standards would provide the general basis for the design of all the ensuing *BLOCK* equipment:

1. 350 lines, sequentially scanned.
2. 40 frames per second.
3. 4.5 mc video bandwidth, double-sideband transmission.
4. Horizontal and vertical synchronizing pulses different than RCA standards.
5. No DC transmission.
6. Vertical polarization of the radiated signal.

BLOCK I transmitting equipment consisted of three units: the camera-transmitter unit, housing the R-F transmitter, modulator, picture amplifier, iconoscope and deflection circuits; a dynamotor power supply; and the transmitting antenna. The operating frequencies ranged from 78 to 114 mc.

The AAF conducted numerous BLOCK I television flight tests at Eglin and Wright Fields, which demonstrated that airborne television was practical. The design of the first small SCR-549-T1 television system to new military standards created a 60-pound transmitting set with a power output of 15 watts at 100 mc. The monitor weighed an additional 20 pounds while the 14-volt, seven-cell storage battery (that delivered 32 amps at 13 volts) weighed 37 pounds. The SCR-550-T-2 receiver could not be abridged because the maximum possible sensitivity was required in order to complement the relatively low power output of the transmitter. A small 40-pound receiver, delivering 9 amps at 25 volts, was ingeniously designed by placing the components, including the dynamotor power supply in one case. A monitor unit was designed for adjusting the performance of the camera/transmitter and for providing an additional picture at the receiving point.

Flight tests in early 1942 using this 100-mc equipment in a Douglas B-23 bomber showed that lightweight television equipment was feasible but had a number of inherent limitations for military use requiring new performance and operational standards to be formulated. Among the new requirements were the following:

1. Change the input voltage requirements from 12.5-volts to 28-volts DC.
2. The necessity for simultaneous operation of several television channels.
3. The benefit of separating the camera and transmitter into two units.
4. The necessity of a smaller antenna.
5. The need for the equipment to operate at low temperatures and high altitudes.

During May 1943, the 100 mc transmitting unit and camera were placed in a small Culver PQ-8 radio-controlled target aircraft at Muroc Dry Lake. The PQ-8 carried the television camera/transmitter guidance unit housed in a streamlined ventral nacelle while the dorsally mounted antenna and radio control and flight servo equipment was placed inside its fuselage. The receiving equipment was installed in a B-23 bomber. The PQ-8 was one of the first aircraft to be flown only with a television camera assisting in steering it into a collision course. (See PQ-8.) While the 120-line picture resolution was considered satisfactory by AAF personnel, the NDRC was disappointed as it was not possible to identify a small building from 9,000 feet. Continued testing and failures and modifications finally led to a successful TV guidance and radio control system.

Other BLOCK 1 tests were conducted at Muroc, using a General Motors A-1 (GMA-1) Bug as a guided missile. A BLOCK 1 Camera-transmitter, SCR-549-T2, was installed in the Bug, and a BLOCK I Receiver, SCR-550-T-2, was installed in the B-23 control aircraft. For this installation, the television camera-transmitter unit, housed in a streamlined nacelle, was suspended under the Bug's fuselage while the antenna was mounted on top of the Bug. The radio control and flight equipment were installed in the fuselage interior. Due to the camera's location, much of the viewed scene was intersected by the propeller, resulting in the generation of low-frequency interference that would be adjusted and reduced. The Bug was test-launched once all the required ground checks had been completed. After being guided by a satisfactory picture during the entire flight, the Bug was lastly dived into a target by radio control, using the television picture for guidance. (See General Motors A-1 (GMA-1) Bug.)

Other successful tests were conducted at Muroc, using different types of aircraft. For one test, BLOCK I camera/transmitter equipment was installed in AAF YPQ-12A target aircraft to be used as power-driven bombs. Because the YPQ-12A was a single-engined aircraft, it was necessary to locate the television camera so that its line of vision would be outside the propeller arc. A nacelle for holding the camera-transmitter was mounted under the YPQ-12As right wing, just outside the propeller arc. To compensate for the weight of the camera transmitter nacelle, a lead weight was mounted on the left wing. Although the camera was shock-mounted and acoustically-shielded, the noises from the exhaust, propeller, and wind were so great that the low-frequency response of the picture amplifier had to be modified. Also, the operation of a television transmitter and radio control receiver near the missile made special protection of the radio control receiver imperative. There were approximately ten hours of preliminary BLOCK I flight tests, during which an YPQ-12A was under radio control, the television picture being the only source of information for the B-23 control aircraft pilot. For the final test, a 500-pound bomb was placed in the YPQ-12A target plane's safety-pilot's cockpit, which had a hatch to cover that compartment. The television picture was adequate, and complete control over the target aircraft was sustained during its flight. Ultimately, it was maneuvered 75 feet behind a radio-controlled PQ-8, and was exploded by radio control. (See Fleetwings PQ-12.)

NBC made several tests with BLOCK I equipment for both the Navy and the National Defense Research Committee. Under the NDRC contract awarded to RCA for the development of airborne television equipment, field service was provided completely by NBC technical personnel. Assistance was given during a demonstration of BLOCK I equipment at Anacostia in October 1942 to determine the practicality of the equipment for aerial reconnaissance. Other flight tests were conducted at Wings Field, Ambler, Pennsylvania, and at the Naval Aircraft Factory, Philadelphia.

Overall, these tests disclosed that satisfactory picture transmission from aircraft required the precise operating characteristics of the television equipment. After the pilotless, transmitting aircraft took off, the readjustment of any of the camera-transmitter controls was impossible. Poor picture quality and loss of synchronization frequently resulted from variations in power supply voltage, changes in light-intensity at the camera, and in signal strength at the receiver. Acoustic vibration of the transmitter components was mostly responsible for the loss of picture definition.

Under the Army and Navy contracts, upgrades were to be completed on all BLOCK components: cameras, transmitters, receivers, power supplies, and antennas. More efficient optical systems were developed, pickup tubes with greater sensitivity were designed and built, and several circuits were developed to make the receivers resistant to jamming.

During the continued military TV research, size, weight, power requirement, circuit complexity, resolution, and linearity interrelationships had to be determined before

BLOCK I camera/transmitter equipment was installed in AAF YPQ-12A target aircraft to be used as power-driven bombs. (*AAF*)

Early RCA television camera being installed in a Beech AT-11 Kansan for testing. (*AAF*)

new standards could be established for military TV use. A powerful transmitter small enough to be installed on a GB was required but was considered too technically involved to develop. Consequently, in February 1941, the development of television guidance was abandoned until additional basic research could be conducted at a more theoretical and elementary level, to be led by the NDRC, in cooperation with RCA, the Farnsworth Corporation, and the Aircraft Radio Laboratory (ARL). Meanwhile, prioritized radio-controlled only GBs continued to be refined and developed under NDRC patronage in cooperation with the ARL at an accelerated pace geared to enter operations ASAP.

RCA 300-mc BLOCK III TV Equipment

The more compact and efficient 300-mc BLOCK III television unit, with its small, lightweight TV cameras, now constructed as individual units, was a result of the 100-mc BLOCK I tests and its further development. During early 1942, RCA Television received a very large developmental contract comprising of 1,000 BLOCK III 300-mc sets—500 each for AAF and USN. The BLOCK III would be found to be so effective that RCA eventually provided more than 4,000 BLOCK III units under Army and Navy contracts.

There were two versions of the higher-frequency BLOCK III equipment: BLOCK III-A and BLOCK III-B. The BLOCK III-B was tunable over ten channels in the frequency range from 264 to 372 mc, while the BLOCK III-A covered only five channels, from 264 to *312* mc. The significant improvements in the BLOCK III-B receivers were concluded in a BLOCK III-BB receiver. BLOCK III transmitters were developed through four models: BLOCK III-A, III-AB, III-B, and III-BB. The succession of models was partially due to the unwanted frequency-modulation that occurred in early models, and partly because simplification of transmitter controls later became required. The camera and the transmitter were constructed into two separate units.

The camera circuits of the earliest 300-mc BLOCK III television sets were similar to those of the 100-mc BLOCK I equipment. The camera, or conversion unit as it was sometimes called, contained the RCA 1S46 Iconoscope, optical lens, picture amplifiers, synchronizing and blanking circuits (prevents the transmission of brightness variations) and the deflection circuits (controls vertical and horizontal). There were two electrical outputs: a picture and blanking output delivering 0.5 volts peak-to-peak and a synchronizing output delivering 3.5 volts peak-to-peak. These two signals were not mixed because, as in the BLOCK I equipment, the transmitter was grid-modulated by the picture signal and plate-modulated by the synchronizing signal.

The new 300-mc SCR-549-T3 and SCR-550-T3 equipment avoided the limitations of the 100-mc equipment with several improvements incorporated. The operation of the 300-mc set was similar to the 100-mc set and differed only in details. The camera/transmitter was separated into two units and the total weight was increased to 90 pounds. Because of the lower efficiency of the 300-mc system operation, the input power was raised to 29 amps at 26 volts. The monitor was of the direct-driven (slave-sweep) type and could be used either for observing the output of the camera and to provide an additional picture at the receiving location when driven from the output of the receiver.

By June 1943, a small number of GB-4 glide bombs became available to test the BLOCK III 300-mc equipment. After initial problems were solved, the 300-mc equipment was used in the GB-4 and Castor war-weary bomber guided missiles. A more detailed description of GB-4 television control is discussed with that missile.

During August 1943, the 300-mc radio control and television guidance systems had been sufficiently developed prompting the demonstration of their military potential to be scheduled at Muroc. For the demonstration, a SCR-549-T2 transmitter was installed under the right wing of an unmanned Fleetwing YPG-12A single-engined target aircraft that had a 500-pound bomb placed in the former pilot's cockpit for the final test. During the trials, the television picture was adequate so that the YPG-12A was always under radio control and was controlled to crash into the target on its final self-destructive run.

The BLOCK TV was used over Europe during 1944 as part of the Aphrodite and Castor projects and over the Northern Solomons in the Southwest pacific as part of the TDR drone projects. Both projects are discussed in detail later.

Later Television Systems Used During World War II

Three basic television systems were developed for the military during the war: the initial BLOCK system, and later RING and MIMO systems.

RING System

The RING system, contracted in 1944 as a joint development between NBC and RCA, has a receiver and monitor that was similar to the BLOCK equipment, but it was a more sophisticated high-resolution system developed for long-range, high-altitude reconnaissance, not guidance. This non-expendable equipment was designed for operation by cameramen who operated two or more cameras installed in the nose and waist positions. Weight and complexity considerations were secondary to the production of high-definition television pictures. It operated at 567 lines interlaced at twenty frames per second at 8 MHz bandwidth. Two cameras were developed using image orthicons, PH-536/AXS-1 and PH-537/AXS-1, the AN/AXT-5 transmitter, R-90/UXR-2 receiver, and ID-86/UXR-2 monitor. The transmitter operated on 90 to 102 mc, emitting a peak power of 1,400 watts via a non-directive antenna mounted under the fuselage over a 200-mile range at 22,500 feet.

MIMO System

During the war, advances in tube miniaturization made MIMO (Miniature Image Orthicon) system possible. While it was comparable to the BLOCK system, it was lighter and more compact, weighing only 50 pounds. The MIMO system, contracted in early 1945, was to consist of a small cylindrical camera unit placed in the nose of the missile, along with a small transmitter, power supply, and a dipole antenna. The transmitter was a 325-line, forty-frame-per-second sequential type that sent a TV picture back to the controller. The pick-up tube in the transmitter was stabilized and the lens iris was controlled by the video signal to give constant average signal intensity. The complete system had a power of 8 watts in the 264- to 372-mc range. The MIMO system, designated as the AN/AXT-7, was to be installed into the AAF Douglas-built ROC medium-angle guided bomb for which it was specifically designed. Flight testing occurred with the ROC between December 1944 and August 1945 at Santa Monica and Inyokern, California, and Wendover, Utah. (The ROC is discussed later in detail.)

GB-9 Barometric-Seeking Bomb

Developed under Project MX-494, the GB-9 or ground-skimming bomb resembled the GB-8 design once more using surplus Aeronca GB-1 airframes. The GB-9 employed pull-out stabilizers and radio altimeter control or aneroid (barometric) control. The radio altimeter unit maintained the bomb at a constant level above the ground irrespective of altitude above sea level, but the unit was easily jammed. The aneroid (barometric) unit maintained the missile at a constant pressure (altitude above sea level) but, inevitably, this method met problems when flying over mountainous terrain; however, it could not be jammed and was simpler and less expensive to produce. The GB-9 was released at a steep 45-degree dive, building up speed, and was leveled out at a pre-determined 1,000-foot altitude and 400 mph by the APN-1 radio altimeter or aneroid unit controlling the pullout stabilizers. During that glide phase at a constant altitude for 3–5 miles, the bombardier could track the bomb visualizing a flare or smoke trail and send commands via a radio control link to guide the missile for azimuth and range accuracy. Once over the target, the operator would dive the GB-9 abruptly on to the target, which were primarily intended to be targets that were relatively immune from attacks from above, such as submarine pens. The GB-9 project began in January 1944, and by November, a successful test flight resulted. By V-J Day, the project remained undeveloped but later versions were projected to be jet-propelled to extend the range of level flight to 10 miles but were not selected for mass production and operational service.

GB-10 Television Glide Bomb

The GB-10 was a GB-4 equipped with television equipment located in a plywood nose instead of being suspended under the fuselage as with the GB-4. The TV apparatus was Farnsworth or modified BLOCK III with image orthicon. The TV incorporated a built-in attitude adjustment to compensate for variable angles of attack. It was to be flown on a glide path or on the GB-9 leveling out system, until the operator could take over control. The GB-10 project was put on low priority and canceled in an undeveloped stage at the war's end.

GB-11 Chemical-Carrying Guided Bomb

The GB-11, developed under Project MX-614, was a GB-1 derivative designed to be used for chemical warfare attacks. The GB-11 used the basic GB airframe with a 12-foot wingspan but instead of the 2,000-pound GP bomb, it was equipped with a M33A smoke tank to be filled with a chemical agent, and an M-2 discharge tube. After launching from 10,000 feet, the GB-11 was to go into a dive to gain speed (350 mph),

GB-11 chemical-carrying guided bomb. (*AAF*)

and then continue to glide to a predetermined altitude (200 to 300 feet) where it would level out for about 2 miles while dispersing its chemical. The GB-11 had only a simple gyro-stabilization system and could not be guided after it had left its parent aircraft. The program was still in the experimental phase, when it was canceled at the end of the war

GB-15 Radar/TV Seeking Bomb

During June 1945, the Air Technical Service Command directed the Engineering Division to continue its efforts to find a method to employ APW-5 radar in the radar/TV-controlled GB-15 project, developed under Project MX-717. The initial radar tracking permitted the bombardier to establish the location of the bomb relative to the target through most of its flight. Once the bomb was close to the target the television image could provide the final guidance to the target. However, the final the ATSC report on the ETO operations concluded that the present TV control was too primitive to reach effective operational development in the near future and the TV control phase of the GB-15 project was canceled in February 1945. The radar-only GB project was presented to Gen. Curtis LeMay, Commander of the XXI Bomber Command, for use against Japanese targets. LeMay responded that due to a shortage of combat crews in his theater he could not allocate any for GB training. LeMay also believed that the GB-4 could not be justified as its 2,000-pound bomb load was not commensurate to the B-29's 12,000-pound bomb load over 1,600 miles at medium altitudes.

So, because of the Lemay's lack of interest and the technical problems associated with the APW-5 radar system, the GB-15 was effectively, though not officially, canceled when Air Technical Service Command recommended no further development on the GB-4 be pursued until the radar could be perfected which was projected not to be until March 1946. These delays in the development of the radar equipment until then caused the project to be canceled by the Wright Aircraft Projects Section and further work on radar control was transferred to other projects.

GB-15 radar/TV-seeking bomb. (*AAF*)

XBG Series

The last of the AAFs GB series was not of the GB series designation but was designated as the XBG. It was a towed bomb similar in design to the GB series and is discussed with the GLOMB, glider bombs as the BG gliders were more similar in concept to the Navy's GLOMB.

Conclusions: The Failure of the American Glide Bomb Series

Generally, it seems that the Air Force was uninterested in the GB as a tactical weapon assigning the program with low priorities and providing few funds. It was the enthusiastic personnel at Wright Field, looking for advanced ideas from the NDRC and private industry which pushed these projects as far as possible under the circumstances. Also, when a project, such as the GB-1 and GB-4, roused the imagination of Gen. Arnold, they were given high priorities in order to reach combat as soon as possible, but this was done so in a hurried and haphazard manner, which ultimately was deleterious to the project. Little cooperation was given these projects by upper echelon operational officers who were steeped in conventional tactics and weapons. This anti-GB-1 and GB-4 cadre pointed to these missile's often prolonged and troubled developmental history and poor operational results to demonstrate the correctness of their allegations. Later, other promising homing systems, which basically, though not intentionally, used GB airframes as test beds, received the same treatment resulting in deliberate development and slow, often incomplete testing.

By 1945, AAF precision daylight bombardment doctrine required that bombers penetrate enemy airspace by the use of massed aerial formations that could deliver massed pattern or area bombing. GBs, no matter how precise, plainly did not conform to the tactics imposed by massed raids over Germany and the massed fire-bombing missions over Japan. The June 1946 AMC study *The Development of Guided Missiles* stated that, after February 1945, all GBs were assigned a very low priority because the prevailing attitude was that they had no military usefulness so long as they had to be carried externally by the bomber. These early GB seeking systems did have merit as many were resurrected in the post-war missile-oriented environment and led to seeking systems that were effective in combat.

Pigeon Bombs: First Touchscreen TV

During the late 1930s, Burrhus Frederic "B. F." Skinner, a behavioral psychologist at Harvard University, developed the concept of operant conditioning, which simply was the theory that the reinforcement of a repeated negative stimulus (punishment) or positive stimulus (reward) formed the basis for learned behavior. For his studies, Skinner identified the "significance of constancy of conditions" in his experiments and developed the instrumental conditioning chamber better known as the Skinner

Box, which typically contained one or more levers that an animal could press, one or more stimulus lights, and one or more places in which positive or negative reinforcers would be provided. The rats' or pigeons' pushes on the levers were sensed and recorded and a contingency between these pushes, the state of the stimulus lights, and the delivery of reinforcement was set up automatically. To teach the desired response, Skinner developed the idea of "shaping" which was the "method of successive approximations." Shaping was initiated by reinforcing a behavior that was somewhat like the desired behavior. Once that behavior was established, when variations occurred that were closer to the desired behavior, those were rewarded until the desired behavior was being carried out. The pigeons in Skinner's early trials could dance, spin, and play ping pong.

Once World War II in Europe began, Skinner contemplated using pigeons to navigate bombs dropped from aircraft so they would hit their targets accurately. Pigeons had better vision than humans, had quicker movements and reactions, could distinguish colors, did not get airsick, and were more easily managed than many other animals. Using his operant conditioning and shaping techniques, Skinner taught the birds to earn kernels of grain by pecking at a specific target image on a screen. The birds had to be specially harnessed in a sock with its head and neck protruding through a hole in the big toe area and its wings and legs bound lightly in the sock by a shoestring. The bound pigeon was strapped to a wooden block and placed into the modified Skinner Box. The pigeon's eyes would select a target, the movement of its neck would then generate signals to steer the missile while its head and neck combined to pick up pieces

Burrhus Frederic "B. F." Skinner, a behavioral psychologist at Harvard University who trained pigeons to guide missiles. (*Author*)

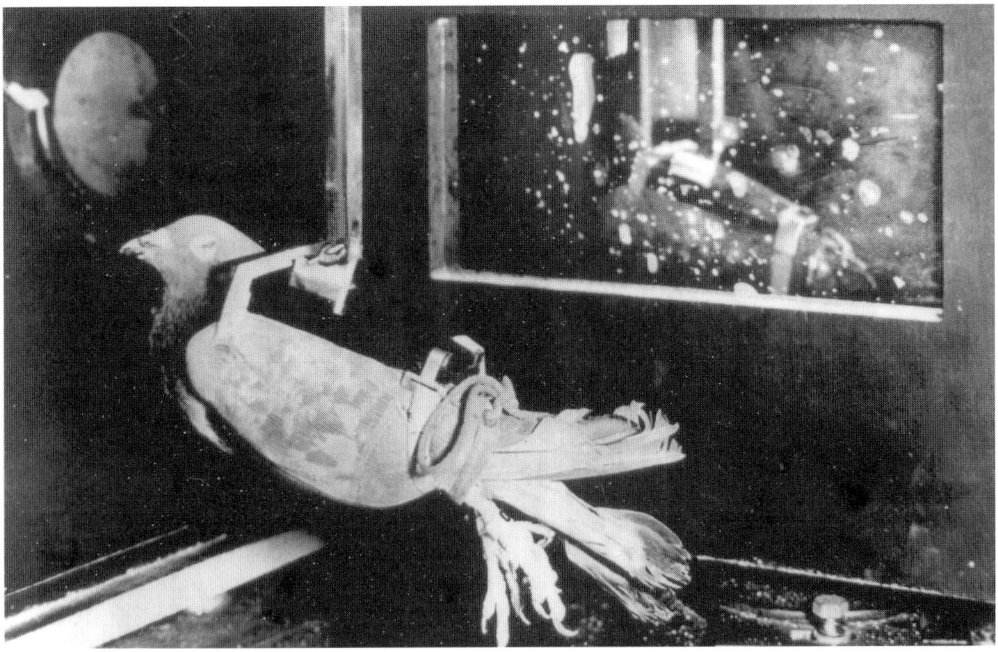

The bound pigeon training in the Skinner box. The pigeon's eyes would pick out a target, movement of its neck would then generate signals to steer the missile, and its head and neck together would pick up grain as a reinforcement. (*Author*)

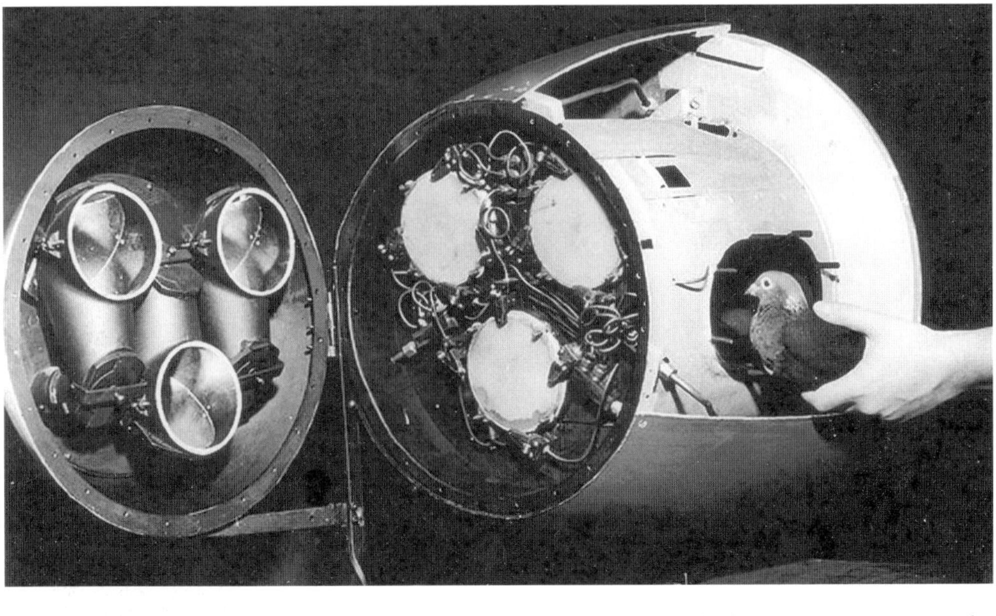

During the development of the SWOD Mk. 7 Pelican, a trained Skinner pigeon was to be harnessed inside the nose cone and navigate the guided bomb using aerial photographs of the target; if it kept the crosshairs on the target, the pigeon was rewarded by grain deposited in a tray in front of it. (*Author*)

of grain as a reinforcement. The pigeon steered by moving pairs of lightweight rods placed around its neck. When the pigeon lifted or lowered its head or moved it from side to side, it closed electrical contacts that operated a motorized hoist that moved back and forth on an overhead track.

Skinner placed a bull's-eye on a far wall of the room and placed a few grains of bird food in a small cup in the center. The bird was pushed toward it, and by moving its head up or down and from side to side, the pigeon could move toward the wall to a position to reach and eat the grain. On successive runs, the pigeons were moved more and more quickly toward the target and soon operated the hoist as fast as the hoist motors permitted. Next, Skinner devised a method that recorded pigeon pecks as an electronic signal that was transferred to a control system. If the image moved off center, the pigeon would peck quickly to bring the device back on track, and the resulting signals would operate the simulated missile control system to center the device on the target. With training, the birds could easily differentiate one target from another and were able to hit the target almost flawlessly.

During mid-1941, Skinner submitted a proposal for his guidance system to both the National Inventor's Council and the NDRC, but it was rejected. Once America entered the war, Skinner resumed the project and sent a film of his pigeons in action to the NDRC, which showed only slight interest. A. D. Hyde, head of the Mechanical Division of General Mills, became interested in the project and was able to persuade company headquarters to support the project with technical assistance until it could be transferred to the government. With General Mills' support, Skinner was able to improve his system. The previous bird harness was discarded for a more practical lens and screen grid with a special servo-control mechanism. The force of the pigeon's pecking motion was increased by running a bomb's gyro and controls in a vacuum and by placing valves behind the top, bottom, and sides of the flexible screen. When the pigeon tapped one of these valves, it opened, permitting air pressure to build up in the system and operate the fins on the bomb. When the target image was at dead center and the pigeon pecked at dead center, all the valves opened an equal amount and the setting was unchanged towards the target.

By June 1943, the project had shown enough potential that the newly formed Office of Scientific Research and Development (OSRD) awarded Skinner a contract for a homing device designated as Project Pigeon. Skinner gathered forty homing and twenty-four ordinary pigeons and began their training. The target for the Florida bombing trials was a white pyramid on a green field, so Skinner placed white triangles on a lightweight sheet of green paper in the bird's cage. Eventually, the bird learned that pecking the white pyramids would produce a few kernels of grain and became conditioned to expect to be fed when it saw them. As soon as the bird had learned to break through the paper, heavier sheets were substituted until the bird would peck very forcefully.

After this primary training phase, the pigeon was placed in a lightproof box mounted over a projection screen, which had a moving picture of a ground target projected on it. Whenever the pigeon pecked the target on the screen, an electrical contact closed, and a small drawer opened containing kernels of grain. Soon, the pigeons learned they could get the grain no matter where they pecked the screen and began to disregard the target. Skinner outwitted the pigeons by crossing two beams of light at right angles in front of the image, causing the pigeons to peck the target image directly in order to break both beams of light and actuate a photoelectric relay to release the food. Skinner then fed the birds at regular intervals or after a defined number of pecks. Eventually, the pigeons learned to peck as fast as four pecks a second for more than two minutes without stopping, working industriously to prevent the target image from moving from being centered. One diligent pigeon pecked at the screen image 10,000 times in forty-five minutes. All sixty-four pigeons in the tests performed successfully and tests continued to subject the pigeons to battle conditions. Skinner placed the pigeons in a pressure chamber set at 10,000 feet and they were whirled around in a centrifuge, subjecting them to large G-forces. Pistols were fired close by and exposure to excessive vibration and bright flashes that simulated shell bursts did not cause them to miss a peck or even look up. Skinner found that the pigeons were less easily disturbed under confusing circumstances if they were fed hemp (marijuana) seeds rather than grains.

Once trained, Skinner's pigeons were ready to navigate guided bombs dropped from aircraft. The NDRC was developing its SWOD Mk. 7 Pelican guided missile (as described elsewhere) and interest was shown in Skinner's Project Pigeon guidance project. While harnessed inside the nose cone of a guided bomb, the pigeons were trained with slides of aerial photographs of the target, and if they kept the crosshairs on the target, they were rewarded by a grain of food deposited in a tray in front of them. Skinner's control system used a lens in the nose of the bomb to project an image of the approaching target on a ground glass screen. If the target's image moved off center, the pigeon's pecking tilted the screen, which moved the bomb's tail surfaces and corrected the bombs course.

After the successful completion of those experiments, Skinner placed pigeons in three, five, and even seven tandem positions to control the bombs direction by majority rule. If one or more birds became stubborn, lazy, or distracted, the majority could override any incorrect signals and keep the missile on course. In a very large percentage of cases, they pecked away at the target as hunger overcame any other needs.

Skinner sent the results to OSRD for evaluation, and eventually, he was asked to demonstrate a pigeon working in a box with the target screen. The demonstration was eminently successful as it exhibited the extraordinary predictability of the pigeon's behavior, its acute vision, the accuracy of its responses, and its freedom from distraction. Nonetheless, on October 8, 1944, Skinner was informed by the OSRD that further action on his project would seriously delay others that the division considered to have more immediate promise of combat application. So Project Pigeon, like the bats carrying tiny incendiary bombs into Japanese building's attics, quietly came to an end as an intriguing footnote, which was classified until 1959.

After World War II, the U.S. Navy became interested in using missiles against surface ships; in 1948, it reopened the classified Project Pigeon and redesignated it as Project Orcon (for organic control) under the Naval Research Laboratory. Tests were conducted over the next five years, using a sophisticated trainer that simulated a missile. The tests repeatedly showed that the pigeons could guide missiles satisfactorily to score hits under ideal conditions, although clouds, waves, and shadows could cause them to deviate from course. Project Orcon was canceled in 1953, when electronic guidance systems for missiles were considered more reliable.

AAF VB Series Vertical Bomb

VB-1: AZON Guided Vertical Bomb

During September 1940, a group of scientists visited Wright Field to study target-seeking controls for the AAC GB. Among their considerations was the possibility of controlling and correcting high-angle bombing errors. It was the group's initial consensus that the conventional high-angle bomb fell so rapidly that any manual guidance would be inadequate to improve accuracy. As the European war escalated and America moved closer to war, the control of vertical bombs was reconsidered leading to the AZON guided vertical bomb (VB-1), which was to be America's most successful guided aerial weapon of the war. A major reason for its success was that, unlike the GB, the National Defense Research Committee was mainly responsible for its research and development. The NDRC, being a prominent civilian scientific establishment, meant that General Arnold and the military had less oversight on the vertical bomb's design and testing, and was not constrained by the numerous delays and diversion of manpower and funds to less important projects as did the GB projects. Consequently, the VB-1 was combat tested over a month before the GB-1 and functioned so satisfactorily in this and succeeding combat trials that it eventually became America's only fully operational guided bomb.

As part of Project MX-225, the NDRC originally designated the remotely-controlled vertical bomb as the AZ-1, but the AAC designated it as Project AC-1, with the purpose of determining the means and methods of precision bombing while flying above or in overcast. This designation was changed to AC-36 on December 30, 1941

U.S. vertical bomb. VB-1 AZON. (*AAF*)

when Lt. Col. Bernard Chidlaw, the AAC representative to the NDRC, asked them to undertake development of controlled trajectory bombs. The specification stipulated that the bomb be controlled in flight by a bombardier. Azimuth control was essential and both azimuth and range control highly desirable. Before February 1944, the bomb was usually referred to by the VB-1 designation but in press releases the VB-1 was usually referred to by its acronym AZON for AZimuth ONly.

AZON: General Description

AZON was essentially a 1,000-pound, GP/HE, AN-M65 bomb equipped with a special radio-controlled cruciform/quadrilateral four-fin tail design, which provided guidance by adjusting the vertical trajectory in the yaw axis, giving the AZON unit a lateral (only left and right) steering capability but could not change its pitch (rate of fall). The AZON tail package was bolted on to the standard iron bomb warhead, in place of the usual sheet-metal fixed fins. The guidance and control units were separate pieces that attached to the tail and/or nose of a standard bomb, converting it into a guided weapon. The central compartment of the tail package contained the radio receiver, gyroscopes, and actuators. The gyroscopes autonomously stabilized it in the roll axis by operating a pair of ailerons, while a radio control system operated the proportional-control rudders to directly control the bomb's direction of lateral aim, with the antennas for the tail-mounted receiver unit built into the diagonal support struts of the tail surface assembly. The bomb's receiver and control system were

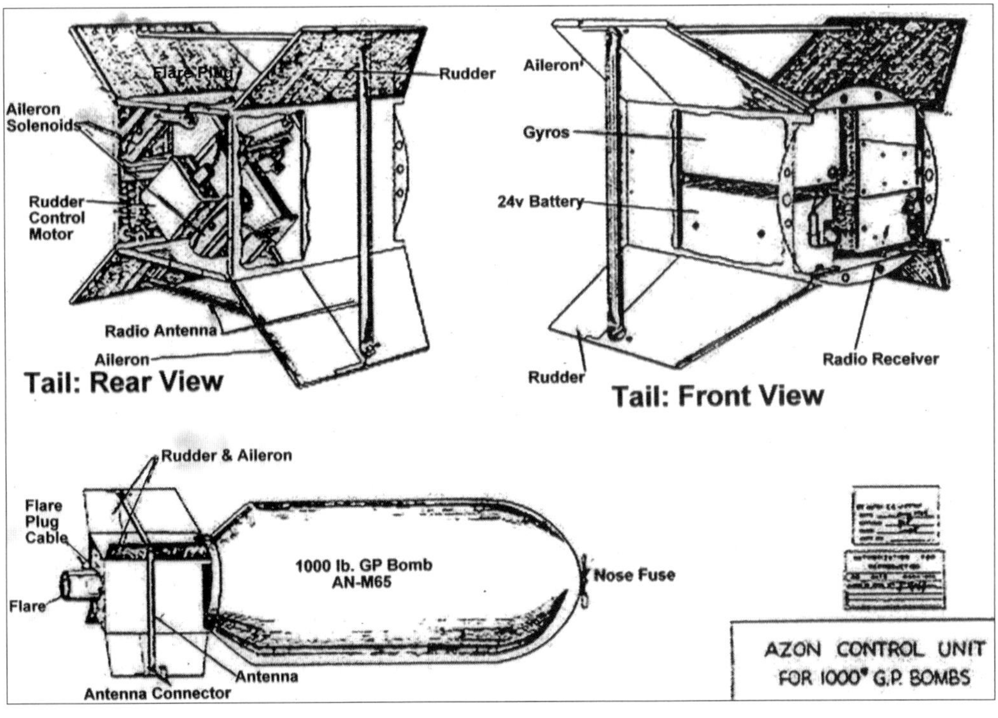

AZON control unit. (*AAF*)

powered by a three minutes of battery life. The tail package system was sufficient to guide the weapon from a 5,000-foot release altitude to the target. A 600,000-candlepower pyrotechnic flare was installed externally, which also left behind a noticeable smoke trail for fifty seconds to enable the bombardier to observe and control it from the control aircraft. Tail fusing was deleted for lack of space and all AZON bombs were nose-fused to burst on impact.

Advantages of the AZON over the Glide Bomb

The major advantage vertical bombs had over the externally mounted GBs was that, having no wings, they were smaller and could be carried inside the bomb bay of both heavy and medium bombers, which would consequently experience no loss of range, altitude, or speed. Also, because the VBs were carried internally, they were not exposed to the weather *en route* to the target, which permitted pilots to fly through icing conditions.

Flight Testing and Development

Flight testing was conducted at Eglin Field, Florida during April 19–23, 1942, where it was verified that the normal trajectory of a bomb could be controlled after its release. Projectiles tended to rotate when they fell which was desirable and even enhanced by tail fins in conventional bombs. Comparable to the rifling in a gun barrel, spin made bombs more accurate and caused less dispersion. However, spin made the remote control of a bomb difficult. Early attempts to reduce or eliminate this rotation were to add an aerodynamic structure to the bomb casing but made the bomb so large as to be impracticable. The addition of a small tab or rudder on the tail fin controlled by radio signal caused the tail to oscillate in a wider circle than the nose, lessening, but not eliminating, the spin. During design and testing at Aberdeen Proving Ground (APG), Maryland, Dr. L. O. Grondahl's NDRC unit concluded that gyro-stabilization was the solution to the rotation issue. Like those mounted in GBs, two gyroscopes were installed in the AZON: the free or directional gyro was used to prevent yaw by returning the bomb from any position at which the rudders were not vertical while the rate gyro was used to keep the speed of rotation of the bomb below a specific value. The directional gyro alone would return the bomb to its normal position with such high angular velocity that it would overshoot its course and go into violent oscillations. With the rate gyro collaborating, it did not overshoot by more than about 3 degrees and quickly returned to stable flight. Compressed air kept the gyros spinning during their time of fall.

By early 1943, it was understood that it would not be realistic or timely to develop all the types of guided bombs that were in progress, and it became necessary for the NDRC to choose the course that the American guided bomb program should follow. A meeting of NDRC Division 5 and Section 5.2, also attended by a large number of armed forces representatives and other involved organizations, was organized, during which the section chief elucidated the guided bomb situation and recommended the development of direct-vision bombs.

The aerodynamics of high-angle controlled bombing presented new problems that required resolution by a series of wind tunnel tests at MIT and model bomb drops at the Aberdeen Proving Ground. The earliest tests using small models in the MIT wind tunnels indicated that the proposed controls would be adequate. To verify the results and the very large extrapolations that were necessary, 100-pound practice bombs were moved to the Aberdeen Proving Ground and tested to determine their performance in the air. By direct observations from the mother aircraft and from the ground, it was determined that most of the bombs rotated so rapidly that it was very difficult to even determine an estimate of the effects of the rudder surfaces. These tests determined that control by rudders was feasible, that gyro-stabilization was necessary, and that a tail flare was required to adequately view the falling bombs to control them.

During preliminary testing, it was determined that it was imperative that all test bombs be equipped with a simple pyrotechnic flare attached to the tail that kept the bomb visible to the controller in the mother aircraft until impact. Reliable ignition of the flare created initial problems that were solved by using electric ignition of a time-delay powder train, which sequentially fired the flare eight seconds after the ignition circuit was energized by the bomb release. The flare-energizing circuit was to be closed by a contact on the tail fuse, which was contingent on travel for several hundred feet through the air for arming. This solution did cause problems as one bomber was destroyed by fire when a flare-equipped bomb dropped on the taxi strip before take-off, while another bomber suffered a serious fire in the air when a live bomb with its flare flaring hung up in the bomb bay. The use of colored flares and selective filters on the Crab bombsights for mass attacks was studied in cooperation with Divisions 11 and 16. Division 11 contracted Wesleyan University to experiment with various flare colors with unproductive results as most pyrotechnic colors and filters were subtractive. For example, a bombardier using a red filter was unable to distinguish between a white flare and a red one. It was then decided that all flares were to be white as a bombardier had no problems concentrating on his own bomb even in tight formations.

These drops revealed the relative simplicity of right-left control as compared with up-down control, but it was believed by most testers that the bomb's problems could be resolved in time. However, against zealous opposition, Grondahl asserted that azimuth (right-left) control was more advantageous and could place AZONs into combat long before the two co-ordinates (left-right and up-down) RAZON bomb.

However, the VB program would suffer a major setback when Gen. Arnold's April 1942 memorandum gave his GB-1 priority for guided bomb development, relegating the VB-1 to continue only at the basic level of research, with the AMC transferring many of its personnel from vertical bomb research and design to his GB program for the remainder of 1942.

At about this time, the VB-1 prototypes were nearing completion to conduct field trials and the NDRC contracted the Gulf Research and Development Company of Pittsburgh to join the project with primary responsibility for the entire program, but MIT was to continue to supply wind-tunnel data and to assist in design. Gulf's experience and facilities were considered optimal for the operation of a central laboratory and the company's original TV study contract was augmented with a six-month $2 million allocation. Ralph Wyckoff was selected to direct the Gulf program, with J. P. Molnar as his assistant to solve the rotation problem and to establish methods of control. After the war, Wyckoff was instrumental in developing the revolutionary Gulf geophysical prospecting airborne magnetometer, which would discover millions of barrels of oil. Dr. Grondahl, the project chief, was to develop control by direct visual sighting as he believed it was the most feasible VB control method, and that by using it, the VB could be introduced into combat in the shortest time.

Because of the new, widespread, now wartime interest in various guided weapons, the necessity arose to review and coordinate America's guided missile programs and to propose a comprehensive research and development program. In response, on June 5, 1942, Joint New Weapons Committee (JNWC) established a temporary subcommittee consisting of Ralph Booth, Capt. Oscar Smith, (USN), and Col. John Murtha (AAF). The JNWC had been recently created by the Joint Chiefs of Staff to evaluate new weapons and equipment, and to investigate methods of using guided missiles and other strategic weapons.

On September 17, 1942, after an all-embracing analysis, the JNWC subcommittee presented a summary report which was expanded on October 29. Their conclusions were as follows:

1. Controlled missiles showed merit.
2. Three fundamental problems remained unsolved: control at velocities close to the sonic regions, stability, and an adequate available control method.
3. Failure to consider the cost-result ratio had led to the funding of some programs of doubtful value.
4. In order to coordinate and accelerate the present programs, a central control agency should be created.
5. Tactical soundness was an aspect that had been ignored.

On November 28, 1942, the Radar Research and Development JNWC subcommittee, reported that the further development and test of the high-angle bomb should be "vigorously prosecuted and that the television bomb required development, but the direct-sight weapon continued to be promising."

During October, Dr. Vannevar Bush of the Office of Scientific Research and Development (OSRD) had appointed H. B. Richmond as chairman of a special committee to co-ordinate the NDRC guided-missile program. However, the reorganization of the NDRC during December 1942 caused Richmond's special committee, with the addition of J. C. Boyce, to become Division 5. In his report to the JNWC, Richmond gave the high-angle bomb a very low priority, stating that the project had been active for thirty months, and although adequate control surfaces had been designed and tested, more tangible results were necessary to confirm that accuracy could be improved and that roll stabilization was possible.

The project was placed under Division 5's Section 5.2, whose AZON advocates then conducted an intensive study providing more aerodynamic data, collected from both wind tunnel and drop tests. As the aerodynamic study proceeded, it became apparent that its cruciform tail fin design exacerbated the bomb's roll stability problem, which resulted from the simultaneous application of pitch and yaw controls on the bomb's cruciform tail. To eliminate these powerful roll torques, Gulf investigated developing a fin structure from MIT designs having circular symmetry, which was virtually free from roll torque. It could be steered by a tiltable auxiliary cylinder and testing demonstrated it to be much more satisfactory from the aerodynamic standpoint. Gulf easily modified this tail structure to eliminate these difficulties by initially building six bombs having a cylindrical lift shroud surrounding the bomb at its center of gravity, and an octagonal tail for stabilization and steering. Movable flaps on the trailing edge of the tail surfaces served as elevators and rudders for steering. Gulf also began a substantial field test program of the complete AZON instrumentation which would later be very successful.

As in the GB-8 project, direct visual line-of-sight control of the VB-1 required bombardiers to rely upon visual acuity and eye-to-hand coordination to manually use a joy stick to guide the bomb and initially bombardiers collectively rejected the system. The majority reported that it was almost impossible to judge where the bomb was headed and many times the bomb appeared to be accurately aimed on the target and then missed. However, gradually, with practice, bombardiers, like today's X-Box gamers, were able to accurately guide the VB-1 for 1–2 miles *versus* the 8 miles for the GB-8.

The VB-1 was easier to guide than the GB-8, not only because of the shorter distances to the target, but also because the bombardier did not have to fly vertical bombs as he did the radio-controlled glide bomb. GB glide bombs were small gliders that had to be flown in three simultaneous axes: yaw (using the rudder to point the nose on the horizontal plane), roll (using ailerons to keep the wings level), and pitch (using the elevator to point the nose up or down on the vertical plane) so that they would not stall and spin out of control. The bombardier did not fly the vertical bomb, but only changed its trajectory as it fell, and it was virtually impossible to create a stall large enough to cause the bomb to go out of control. To control VB trajectory, the bombardier needed only to use rudder control as AZON bombs moved only in azimuth, requiring a left or right correction, which was relatively easy to judge, when viewing the bomb from above as it moved toward the target.

During February 1943, NDRC designers demonstrated ten VB-1s to the AMC at Eglin, with very much less than mediocre results. Nine bombs were failures, with five bombs becoming uncontrollable and spinning in; one had a flare failure and was quickly lost from sight; two had obvious radio control problems; and one bomb was lost due to a miscommunication between the bombardier and radio control operator. There was only one test with excellent control, and somehow this success gave hope that the AZON project was headed in the right direction and further design and testing was authorized.

On June 1, 1943, to facilitate further design, Brig. Gen. Benjamin Chidlaw, Chief of Materiel Division of the Air Staff's Materiel, Maintenance, and Distribution (MM&D) Directorate, circulated the military requirements for the VB-1: control in azimuth; good ballistic characteristics; suitable radio control apparatus; a method to visually follow the bomb in flight; and the trouble-free, uncomplicated, and most durable components possible were to be used. Chidlaw went on to emphasize that VB-1 design and testing should in no way interfere with the further development of radar- or television-controlled versions having control on two axes (i.e. RAZON). On June 5, 1943, the design and procurement of the VB-1 was officially requested by the Air Materiel Command.

A second key series of VB-1 tests were conducted at Eglin from June 23 to July 7, 1943 to determine if the roll stabilization problem had been solved, which it had. During August 1943, AZON bombs were included as part of a guided missile demonstration for VIPs at Muroc Lake. During these demonstrations, bombardiers were directed to aim at a cross-shaped target with the long arm being 4,000 feet in length to aid in determining azimuth control. A B-25 flew all test drops using two bombardiers, one in the nose, to complete the bomb run emphasizing range and the second, located in the rear of the aircraft, to radio control the bomb in flight, with an emphasis on azimuth. Of the twenty-four test drops, twelve were released and accurately controlled, but nine had radio malfunctions and three had inoperative tail guidance flares. For some unknown cause, two of the flare failures occurred during the only two drops from 22,000 feet; all other drops were made from 17,000 feet. Of the twelve VB-1s that were accurately controlled, the mean deflection error was 35 feet, while mean range error was 427 feet. Despite the 50 percent failure rate and large range errors, the AZON concept was beginning to show potential for the degree of accuracy necessary for pinpoint bombing.

The NDRC showed movies of these successful direct-sight control tests to the Special Weapons Branch of the Air Technical Service Command (ATSC) under Project Officer Maj. J. H. Evans. The Special Weapons Branch realized that the AZON would be a very effective weapon against difficult to destroy long targets such roads and bridges and directed that all subsequent undertaking was to be limited to direct-sight controls and that AZON development be completed ASAP followed by immediate production.

The ATSC followed this success to further comparison testing by of sixteen test AZONs that had an average error of 42 feet, which compared extremely favorably to the average error of 1,215 feet by eight uncontrolled conventional comparison bombs. The result of these tests was the restoration to top priority of direct-sighted AZON bombs followed by the RAZON (Range and AZimuth ONly) bombs while television guidance and target-seeker development was deferred.

However, there were necessary changes to be made from the experimental AZON before production and before operational use. Among the main changes:

1. The body of the tail structure was to be changed from a round section to a square section of a welded construction integral with the fins. The whole structure was equipped with the standard sleeves of the 1,000-pound GP bomb.
2. In order to provide more sufficient torque and easier detachment from the carrying aircraft, the gyroscopes were changed from air-driven, vacuum-operated to electric drive.

3. The 12-volt battery was changed to a smaller 24-volt battery, which made it convenient to warm up the equipment in the aircraft.
4. The solenoids were changed to reduce mechanical linkage and to reduce the power requirement.
5. A super-regenerative radio receiver was used. The selection of functions was changed from the long and short pulse code to audio frequency modulations. Later, the radio was changed to a super-heterodyne.
6. The experimental antenna was a wire supported outside the normal over-all dimensions of the tail. In the production model the struts, which were installed to stiffen the fins were also used as antennas, being streamlined and placed inside the circumscribed square.
7. The servo motors were changed to 24 volts with higher speed and more complete noise suppression.
8. The circuits were modified by adding a switch and a coupling, which enabled the equipment to be operated from the aircraft's power while in flight and to be transferred easily to the battery when the bomb was released. A protective relay was added to prevent the ignition of the flare until the bombardier had operated a switch after take-off. An electric gyro release was added.
9. The flare ignition was changed to an electric squib (a miniature explosive device) and Army Ordnance was able to reduce the over-all dimensions of the flare and made its chemical operation more reliable.
10. The installation of the apparatus in the tail structure was changed so that each part could easily accessed for removal.

Production, Tactical Testing, and Teething Problems

On August 24, 1943, Col. R. C. Wilson, Chief of the Development Engineering Branch of the AMC, was appointed to expedite the AZON Project. The promising August tests warranted the procurement of a pre-production lot of 200 AZONs, and on October 13, Gen. F. O. Carroll released the bomb for final ballistic and evaluation testing and for possible training purposes to a tactical group. There were 150 of these modified AZONs manufactured on a pilot production order by MIT. On November 25, 1943, the first few were delivered to Eglin and were immediately tested.

Once the weapon appeared to be ready for production, it was realized that MIT would be unable to manufacture them in large production quantities, and during early September 1943, the NDRC, in collaboration with the Union Switch and Signal Company of Swissdale, Pennsylvania, had the standardized machineries for the mass production of VB-1 assemblies. Union Switch subcontracted Schwien Engineering, Los Angeles, for gyros; Willard Battery, Cleveland, for 6-volt batteries; and White Rogers Motor Company, St. Louis, for servo motors. On October 23, 1943, Col. Wilson directed the AMC to contract Union Switch and Signal for an initial production run of 10,600 VB-1 tail and flare assemblies for $10,600,000 ($1,000 per unit): 10,000 for the AAF and 600 for the USN (as well as a possible fifty for the RAF). The first lot of

600 was scheduled for January 1944 production, then 1,200 for February, 1,800 for March, and followed by 2,200 in May, and 2,400 in June. This production schedule was modified to 500 for March delivery, at least 1,000 for April, 2,000–2,500 in May, and 3,000 per month thereafter for a total of 20,600 AZONs, but with the admonition that radio shortages could prove to be a bottleneck to production. In June 1944, the production schedule was again amended to greatly increase AZON production from 20,600 to 50,600 in 1944 and 60,000 for 1945, again with the admonition that availability of radios and other subassemblies could pose a problem. Another yet to be named manufacturer was to supply 15,000 AZONs (1,000 in September, 4,000 in October, and 5,000 each in November and December) for 1944. Union Switch was to supply 3,000 in June, 4,500 in July, and 5,000 per month for the rest of the year. A realistic estimate dated August 25, 1944 decreased the 1944 total from 50,600 to 37,967, but with 110,600 planned to be completed by August 1945 with a production of 10,000 per month to begin in December 1944. After technical testing was completed and production contracts awarded, Gen. Arnold increased his demands to deploy the VB-1 operationally. To provide for training, the AAF Board Project 13 (T-1) was created. Technical training was to be performed at Ft. Dix, New Jersey, while practical bombing was conducted at Eglin.

Since the pre-war, the organization of the AAF's R&D establishment had been in disorder, and finally, to correct the situation, Arnold attempted to appoint a single, flag-rank officer in control of all AAF guided-bomb R&D during the war. Brig. Gen. H. M. McClelland was selected as the ACO of the Development Engineering Branch of the AMC. The position of ACO was the most important in the guided bomb program as this senior officer had the authority to prepare design plans and policies for all guided bomb development. Like Gen. Arnold, the ACO needed to have a dominant and influential personality; be a staunch advocate of the program; to understand its complexities; and be able to drive it through its development, from research, to design, to procurement, and, finally, to AAF acceptance for testing and deployment in combat. However, McClelland was to prove a poor choice for ACO as his understanding of guided bombs and their development was inadequate, his personal influence in the AAF hierarchy was limited, and he was also burdened with other responsibilities that precluded his full attention to the new and complex guided bomb programs. As the ACO, McClelland was understaffed and reluctant to exercise or not authorized full authority to execute the duties of the position. When Arnold finally relieved McClelland in November 1944, he did not name a capable replacement and, consequently, the AAF guided bomb R&D program remained virtually leaderless for the entire war, resulting in a failure to properly prioritize guided-bomb projects or correctly coordinate them with the civilian R&D organizations. By December 1944, Dr. Vannevar Bush, OSRD president, had become totally frustrated with the poorly disjointed and badly managed AAF guided bomb research and development structure and officially declined any future AAF guided-bomb R&D requests until the Arnold and the AAF rectified the situation, which never really happened.

The Special Projects Section was pressed to begin tactical VB-1 testing as soon as possible. Six B-17Gs and aircrews were provided by the Operations, Commitments, and Requirements to begin VB-1 training at the School of Applied Tactics in Orlando by February 7, 1944 with the goal of deploying to 8th Air Force for combat trials not later than March 1, 1944.

During tactical tests at Eglin during February 1944, teething problems appeared with these first AZONs, which delayed the production schedule. It was found that the amount of azimuth control applied to the bomb significantly decreased the bomb's range as every azimuth correction increased the aerodynamic drag when the bomb changed directions. A VB-1 with no azimuth corrections had a range of 10,573 feet when dropped from an altitude of 15,000 feet with the bomber flying at 250 mph ground speed. When the same bomb under the same parameters was adjusted by the bombardier to the average azimuth correction, the range only decreased 32 feet. But if the bombardier made nearly continuous azimuth corrections, the generated drag reduced the range by 607 feet to 9,966 feet. Also, range differences increased as the bomber's airspeed and altitudes increased. In addition to the experience they received during testing, the bombardiers were assigned to receive further extensive training in target recognition and AZON technique. The tactical use of the AZON for precision bombing was now being questioned and it was suggested that perhaps the AZON was better suited to strip target bombing.

During tactical testing at Eglin, problems occurred when the VB-1 was equipped with the standard 1,000-pound bomb nose and tail fuses. Most standard 1,000-pound bombs included nose and tail fuses to increase the chance of the bomb exploding. Bombs were designed to hit the target nose first, but nose fuses could be easily damaged on impact and not ignite the bomb's explosive charge, while the better protected tail fuse was more likely to detonate the bomb. These fuses were armed by wind vanes driven by the wind stream after the bomb was released. An arming wire, which was withdrawn on release of the bomb, pinned the wind vanes and prevented their rotation from drafts in the bomb bay. The standard nose fuse could be easily installed in the AZON, but the tail fuse posed a difficult problem since the AZON mechanisms in the tail prevented the use of wind stream arming. Electric arming motors were suggested but possible circuit failures could cause the bombs to arm before they were released, and this unsafe system was abandoned. Due to lack of space, the AMC decided to delete the tail fuse despite the dependence only on a nose fuse could increase the probability of duds.

The problem of providing a suitable radio link for the remote control of missiles was a major undertaking of the division. The initial work on the AZON-RAZON program used a radio having two RF (radio frequency) carriers that were pulsed by a commutator keying circuit. The ratio of time-on to time-off of the pulse on one carrier was determined by the position of a rudder-control stick. An integrating circuit following the detector in the receiver instigated the servo link to cause the rudders to assume a position corresponding to that of the rudder control stick. A similar system produced proportional control of the elevators. Field tests at Eglin during April 1943 showed that although proportional control was available, it was not used; specifically, the controlling bombardier put the rudders hard over, adjusting the amount of error correction by the timing of full rudder commands. Consequently, the standard RC-186

Transmitter, having six audio tones, was employed on all further work with an on-off modulation: two tones with AZON, four tones with RAZON.

The RF section of the receivers was super-regenerative for compactness, and the gain was adjusted so that the final stage saturated with the lowest expected signal. The super regenerative radio receiver was able to provide significant improvements in performance over the previous tuned radio frequency receiver and the regenerative radio. A super regenerative receiver with a resistance-capacitance filter in the audio end of the circuit operated two relays giving right and left signals to the rudders. However, the poor quality of construction and workmanship of the VB-1s tail assemblies, particularly concerning the super-regenerative radio control receivers and flares, became apparent. While this radio receiver was sufficient for the original testing program, it was found to be wanting in selectivity and stability for operational use. During pre-flight preparations, 30 percent of these receivers were rejected for testing, and of those accepted, an astonishing 71 percent failed during flight testing. The super-regenerative receiver was considered deficient in selectivity and stability and was suspected of being subject to false operation from microphonics (the transmittance of mechanical vibrations through an electrical component as an undesired electrical signal noise) occurring in the AZON tail. MIT, in cooperation with Harvey Radio Laboratories, Brookline, Massachusetts, developed the crystal-control super-heterodyne receiver. Although this receiver was more complicated, it offered many advantages regarding performance, particularly its sensitivity, stability, and selectivity; it was also able to remove unwanted signals more effectively than the previous tuned radio frequency sets and regenerative and super regenerative radios. The precise tuning of this unit allowed more control frequencies within the operating band, which permitted more individual bombs to be controlled simultaneously. Enemy jamming was of some concern, although it was assumed that the enemy could not acquire complete control of the AZON because it would be too difficult to quickly determine the modulation and frequency combination used for control during the short time the AZON was in the air. However, by transmitting enough energy over a broadband, the enemy could interfere with the bombardier's control signal. The superheterodyne unit made jamming much more difficult due to its fine-tuning feature.

However, once the AZON's radio receiver problems were remedied, there was a bottleneck in their production. Problems continued when the Picatinny Arsenal, New Jersey, and Wesleyan University, Middletown, Connecticut, investigated problems with the tail flare and found that they were not suitably sealed against humidity and would fail to light or continue burning, if they ignited at all. Although the flare situation improved, flare malfunctions continued throughout the war. Other testing problems occurred as the AZONs rolled and the ailerons had to be connected mechanically and the storage battery had to be redesigned by the Willard Battery Company. Finally, the AZONs were considered to be acceptable for operational use.

The Operational AZON

Once the testing problems were finally remedied, the VB-1 was declared as operational. The operation AZON consisted of remote-controlled movable fins attached to the special tail fixed to a standard AN-M-65 1,000-pound high-explosive GP bomb. The AZON was adapted for guidance in azimuth (right or left control), but not for range, by the bombardier who altered the bomb's trajectory in flight with radio signals, which moved the fins. Also, a collar was added to its mid-section for additional control by attached elevators, which were similar to preset trim tabs on control surfaces of an aircraft. The elevators created a stabilizing effect on the falling bomb, allowing the AZON to be more easily controlled in azimuth.

AZON Control: Television *versus* Directly Viewed Control

After it had been demonstrated that the controlled bomb was feasible, its method of control needed to be determined. Three control systems were proposed for the project:

1. Installation of a television camera and transmitter to show the operator the deviation from the true course of the bomb and the application of course corrections by the radio link.
2. A target-seeking device that would independently and automatically direct the bomb.
3. Direct-sighting of the bomb from the controlling aircraft by the operator who would manually steer the bomb via radio link.

AZON Television Control

In their initial investigation of television control for vertical bombs, L. O. Grondahl and J. P. Molnar of NDRC's Section D-3 visited Hazeltine Electronics Corporation Laboratories of Little Neck, New York, where they observed a television camera and receiver, which Hazeltine had developed for use in falling bombs. After a convincing laboratory demonstration, the section presented the NDRC with a proposal for development of the television and the radio control, and an aerodynamic study of the bomb. The OSRD director approved the $45,000 project even though there was an analogous RCA program. This seemingly innocuous Section D-3 project was significant as it was the first directed toward elimination of all bomb dispersion factors by correcting the trajectory of a high-angle bomb during its flight. Previous work was directed toward the perfection of the Norden bombsight and the calculation of the dispersion factors concerning the aerodynamic characteristics of the bomb and atmospheric conditions during the bombs flight, not its direct control.

Hazeltine's A. V. Loughren and D. E. Harnett supervised the development of lightweight television equipment, while Molnar designed controls for the bomb. These designers were under two basic design limitations: rudder control had to be sufficient to guide the bomb to a predetermined target and the bomb's shape was to differ as little as possible from the standard American 1,000-pound GP Bomb. This latter limitation required that full use be made of the bombsight with the rudders used only to the small degree necessary to guide the bomb into the target. At the time, D-3 very mistakenly believed that roll stabilization would be unnecessary.

The first demonstration of Hazeltine's television equipment in flight was considered unexceptional at best. The picture resolution (120 lines), while considered satisfactory by the AAC representatives, was unacceptable to the NDRC as it was impossible, as reports stated, to identify a small house from 9,000 feet. Development would slowly continue with steady but usually promising results, but there remained skepticism as to the possibility of any successful control even with a suitable television system. To resolve this control uncertainty, the section engaged E. A. Eckhardt of the Gulf Research and Development Company Laboratories to install a forward-looking motion picture camera into a standard-size bomb casing. The camera-carrying bombs were built during the summer and fall of 1941. The scene was photographed at sixty-four frames per second by a 16-mm camera, having a mirror positioned to superpose on the field of view illuminated cross hairs and the time indication from a stopwatch. The moving pictures analyzed the bomb's trajectory, how the bomb responded to aileron control, how much yaw or pitch was involved in the application of the controls, the period of oscillation of the bomb in yaw or pitch and in rotation, the rate at which the bomb responded to control, and many other aspects. To preserve the cameras, the bomb was equipped with a parachute that would open at about 2,000 feet, which, unfortunately, prevented any observation of the final, and vital, part of the flight—its closure on the target.

During tests, it became immediately obvious that when the television camera was rigidly mounted along the bomb axis, the bomb could not be satisfactorily steered. Following a free-fall trajectory, a perfectly dropped bomb would gradually nose over, the target first appearing on the bottom of the screen and reaching the center only in the last few seconds. It was determined that the television eye had to face in the direction of travel (along the tangent to the trajectory) by using vanes projecting into the wind stream.

Meanwhile, RCA had also been working on a television-equipped controlled aerial torpedo, under the direction of Section A-E. In April 1941, Section D-3 saw a demonstration of a RCA television unit that was to be used in the high-angle bomb. Although it was too large, its performance was clearly superior to that of the Hazeltine unit, which was particularly troubled by shading and by lack of contrast. As the war in Europe intensified, the NDRC decided against RCA/Hazeltine duplication of effort and authorized a contract with RCA to develop small size, high sensitivity, and reliable television equipment.

By August 1941, with promising preliminary results, MIT was authorized to build radio-controlled bombs suitable for dropping with television equipment. For television use, the control of these bombs was to be restricted to a rate of one-half revolution per second. There was only one set of control surfaces, installed in a plane normal to that of the steering surfaces, for steering with the ailerons to control roll. For steering, the bomb was rolled so that a plane normal to that of the rudder contained the target, the bomb, and the aircraft. The action of the rudder then gave the bomb an angle of attack to produce lift, and consequently an acceleration in the intended direction. If a right turn was to be made, the bomb was rolled until the rudder was vertical, and then the bomb was yawed. For a dive, the bomb was rolled until the rudder assumed the position of conventional elevators and then the bomb was pitched. However, control of a rolling bomb proved to be too difficult for even experienced operators. The appeal of this system was that the rate gyro could be easily installed to restrict the roll velocity to the desired value due to the lack of the requirement of absolute roll stability. Conversely, control in normal Cartesian co-ordinates (two perpendicular axes that cross at a central point called the origin) required absolute roll stabilization, which necessitated the use of the more complex combination of free and rate gyros that reduced target overshooting; eventually, all Division-3 missiles were to be roll-stabilized and controlled in the more reliable Cartesian co-ordinates system.

In the meantime, the television program continued. After the results of the Hazeltine equipment had been unexceptional, two drops using the RCA television transmitter and receiver gave very good pictures. However, on one test drop, the engineer on the ground, watching the picture on the monitor scope, was appalled to very clearly view his position on the screen, designating him as the bomb's target. Fortunately for the engineer, the bomb hit a short distance away with no explosive effect as a very major flaw in the television program was that the television-guided bomb had virtually no room for explosive.

However, many aerodynamics experts continued to believe that for homing on a target, target-seeking units and a television guidance system were the most practical. Their premise was accepted when NDRC researchers moved VB-1 testing to the Aberdeen Proving Grounds where they worked with Gulf Research and Development. At Aberdeen, the NDRC and Gulf designers wasted time and funding to develop a TV unit very similar to the one that would be used on the GB-4. When their efforts failed to perform satisfactorily in tests in August 1942, their television guidance scheme was discarded, and the control of the bomb reverted to Grondahl's direct visual sighting proposal.

Meanwhile, Remington-Rand President James H. Rand had also conducted some preliminary studies in the application of television to torpedoes and GBs. When Rand Chief Electronic Engineer J. J. Lamb presented his proposal to Wright Field, no noticeable enthusiasm was roused. The NDRC proved more open to the idea and a contract was agreed upon. Remington-Rand was to investigate the reduction of the size and weight of the orthicon tube (as distinguished from the iconoscope favored by RCA and Hazeltine) to adapt it to the vertical bomb. By that time, television bombs had given way to the directly-controlled AZON concept as functioning television equipment with a usable picture was proving problematic.

Meanwhile, other more exotic and complex independent and automatic bomb control systems were under investigation and early development. Fairchild Camera Corporation engineers Henry Blackstone and Curtis Hillyer worked on photoelectric homing controls; Laurens Hammond on homing controls; and the MIT Radiation Laboratory on radar-control. However, the most uncomplicated solution seemed to be direct-sighting of the bomb from the controlling aircraft by the operator who would manually steer the bomb via radio link.

Direct-Sighting AZON Control

During October 1940, Section D-3 of the NDRC was overseeing a few contracts and was actively pursuing more. On September 16, 1940, all D-3 members, led by Capt. George Holloman, visited Wright Field to reply to the AACs request that they investigate a target-seeking controls for the Army GBs. Included in the discussion was the control of a conventional high-angle bomb, but the subject received little consideration as it was the consensus that a high-angle bomb fell so swiftly that there was little expectation of improving its accuracy by any manual guiding.

Very little investigation had been performed considering the exact characteristics of the bomb itself in regard to control. Russian-born French scientist Constantin Chilowsky had conducted rudimentary wind-tunnel experiments using a small guided aerial torpedo model prior to the fall of France. Prior to immigrating to America, Chilowsky was the co-inventor with Paul Langevin of the sonar principle in 1917, which led to the eventual development of medical ultrasonic systems. During 1940, Chilowsky met with NDRC's D-3's J. P. Molnar to discuss his general idea of a GB or a torpedo controlled either by radio link or an attached thin-wire cable and guided by direct sight. D-3 would borrow some of Chilowsky's ideas to transform them in to a workable control mechanism.

During 1927, Dr. Hugh Dryden of the National Bureau of Standards had published the benchmark account on the *Aerodynamics of Aircraft Bombs*, which had tabulated all the available data based upon the standard bomb without control surfaces. In considering the control of the standard vertical bomb, Molnar was faced with the questions of could adequate controls and control surfaces be mounted into the limited space available in a bomb and then would a controlled bomb be aerodynamically stable? Molnar used Dryden's mostly valid data to calculate the allowable control surface dimensions that would give sufficient maneuverability to deviate the bomb's course.

In early design stages, the vertical bomb models were directed with rudders to control azimuth and elevators to control range. It was obvious that this method of control required that the bomb could not rotate as the rudders always had to remain vertical and the elevators horizontal to achieve the correct control response. However, as sophisticated bomb control development proceeded, it became obvious that the information on bomb aerodynamics regarding control was more deficient than was realized. As a result, television equipment development and control were badly lagging and direct-sighted bombs would be available for testing before television-controlled bombs. Within the next few months, D-3 conducted field tests and their experience validated their decision that the quickest and easiest method of control was by direct-sighted steering and that radio control was the only practical link between the controlling mother aircraft and the bomb.

B. E. Warren was assigned to head an expanded MIT group, which was to increase its activity in developing and building test bombs in the MIT shop. Dr. L. O. Grondahl, head of NDRC's Section 5.2 at MIT on the AZON project, began an analysis to solve the problems of high-angle bombing. Grondahl soon realized that it was necessary to control both the bomb's range and direction, and it was decided to base control on a rectangular coordinate system moving with the bomb, thereby controlling the flight of the bomb in azimuth by rudders and the range by elevators. This method of control required that the bomb could not be allowed to rotate about its own axis during flight. The rudders were always to be kept vertical and the elevators horizontal to obtain the correct response when controls were applied. It was decided that radio was the only practical linkage between the mother aircraft and the bomb. Grondahl discovered with the direct-sighting, range control was very difficult. To control range and azimuth without the development of additional equipment, it was necessary to maneuver the aircraft so that the bomb was silhouetted ("coincidence") directly over the target. In normal flight, the bomb, as seen from the controlling aircraft, continually appeared to be well behind the target. The bomb/target coincidence could only be obtained by the prompt reduction of the aircraft's speed during the first ten seconds or so after the bomb was released. The aircraft's speed could be decreased from 220 to 120 mph by placing the aircraft into a very steep climb with the throttle retarded. After the aircraft continued at its reduced speed in the direction of the original bombing run, it was then possible to hold the bomb on the straight line connecting the aircraft and the target. This maneuver was very difficult and later instruments were developed that made it unnecessary.

AZON Direct Guidance: AN/ARW-38 VB-1 (and VB-3) Guidance

The Radio Transmitting Set AN/ARW-38 was the transmitting equipment designed for the remote control of free-falling bombs. When used in conjunction with radio receiving set AN/CRW-7, it provided RAZON (range and azimuth) control of the VB-3 free-falling bomb or AZON (azimuth only) control of the VB-1 or VB-2 free-falling bombs. Used in conjunction with radio receiving set AN/CRW-2, it provided AZON control of the VB-1 or VB-2 free-falling bombs.

The AN/ARW-38 unit contained all the major components of radio transmitting equipment RC-186, plus an additional control box (BC-1156-A) and two relay units (RE-52/ARW-38), which increased the utility of this equipment for this type of use. The two control boxes (BC-1156-A) were provided with the AN/ARW-38 for control of VB-3 free-falling bombs. One was used by the bombardier, with the aid of the bombsight, to control flight of the missile in range (up or down), and the other by a second operator (usually located in the aircraft's rear) to control flight of the missile in azimuth (right or left). The unit's range was the maximum visual range, but high-intensity flares, attached to tail of the bomb, extended the normal visual tracking range. The unit weighed 50 pounds, of which 32 pounds included the radio modulator and transmitter, but its modification to the B-24 Liberator added an additional 25 pounds. Each aircraft had three antennas mounted beneath its tail section for control purposes. One transmitted a signal on 475 cycles for left deflection, the second on 3,000 cycles for right deflection, and the third at thirty to forty cycles to activate the flare. All three frequencies were changed periodically to prevent jamming by enemy radio monitoring crews.

Relay Unit RE-52/ARW-38 controlled a circuit that supplied correcting voltages to the bombsight to compensate for the delay in descent of the bomb as a result of the controlling action. In addition, actuating voltages were supplied to special light circuits within the camera equipment that recorded the bombs descent to provide a permanent record of the control of the missile during flight.

Radio modulator and crystal-controlled Transmitter BC-1158 could be set to any one of fifty-seven pre-determined frequencies within range of 53 to 95 Mc. The modulator portion contained six different audio-oscillator channels, any one of which, or one of four two-tone combinations, could be used to tone-modulate the transmitter carrier frequency.

Remote control of the VB-1 could be achieved within visual range by manipulation of the two BC-1156-A control boxes, which resulted in the tone modulation of the carrier and transmission of certain tones for each control movement or function that could be chosen (right, left, up, down, right-up, left-up, right-down, left-down). Reception of these tones at the missile resulted in application of actuating voltages to the proper flight control mechanisms after discrimination by the audio-filter selective circuit. AZON operation required the use of only two-tone channels while RAZON operation required the use of only four-tone channels.

Probably the most limiting technical issue for radio-controlled was that their use was restricted by the number of radio channels available. A B-17 bomber flying in a conventional formation, armed with conventional bombs, could drop as many as six 1,000-pound bombs in a single run. Flying Fortresses carrying radio-controlled vertical bombs could control only one bomb at a time, with no more than nine AZONs being controlled simultaneously from a bomber formation seeded with nine AZON bombers. These nine AZON bombers could have been armed with thirty-six to fifty-four conventional bombs. Tests dropping and controlling more than one radio-controlled vertical bomb per aircraft per bomb run showed that each bomb under supposed control responded individually to the guidance signals, resulting in all but the single bomb upon which the bombardier was individually directing to miss their target by more than if they were standard conventional bombs.

AZON Control Equipment Gallery

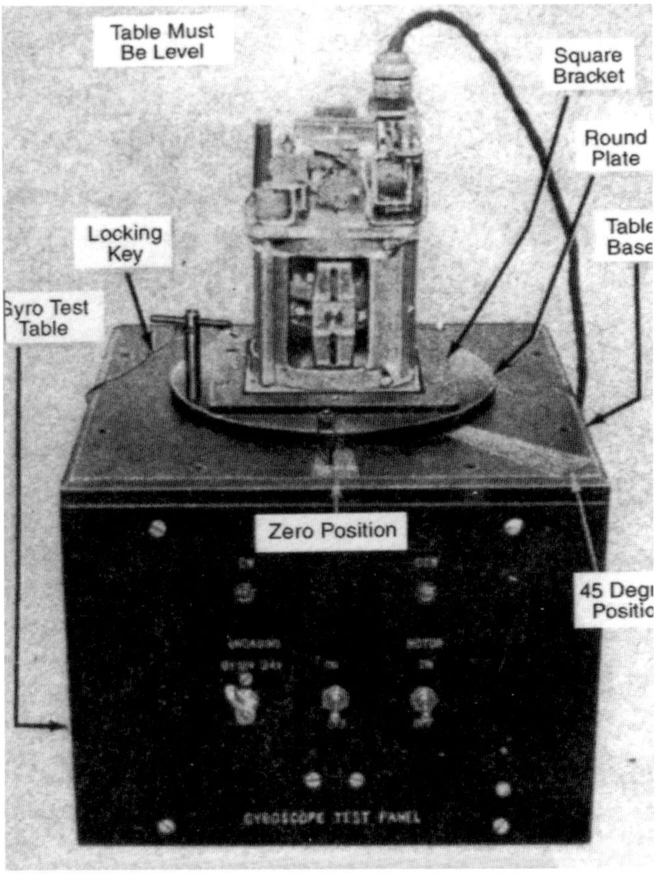

Above: AZON control equipment. (*AAF*)

Right: Gyro. (*AAF AZON Manual*)

Radio receiver (CRW-7). (*AAF AZON Manual*)

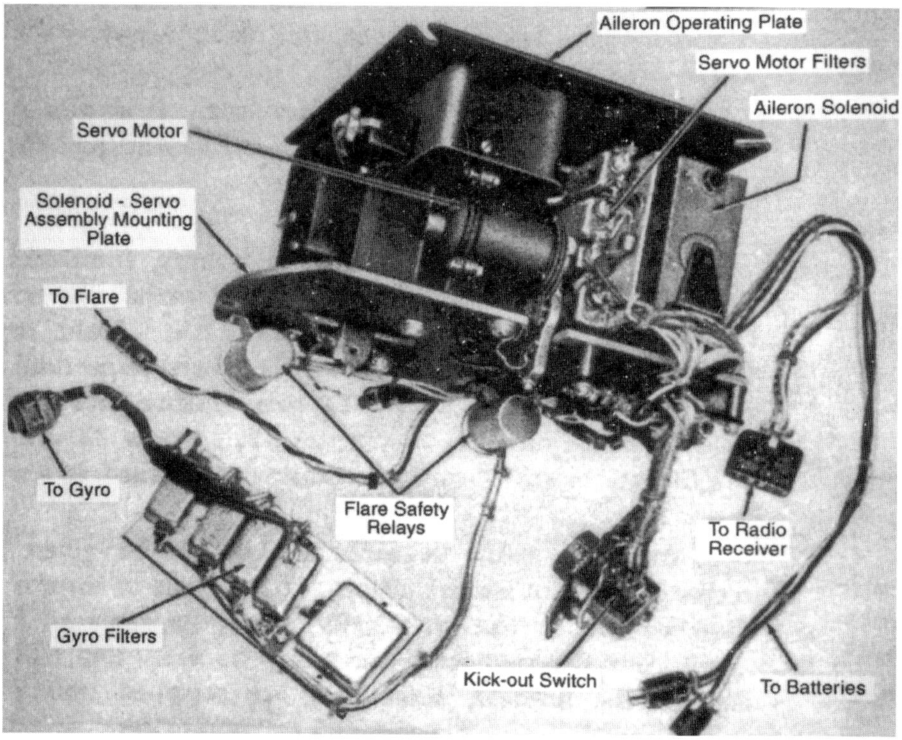

Servo. (*AAF AZON Manual*)

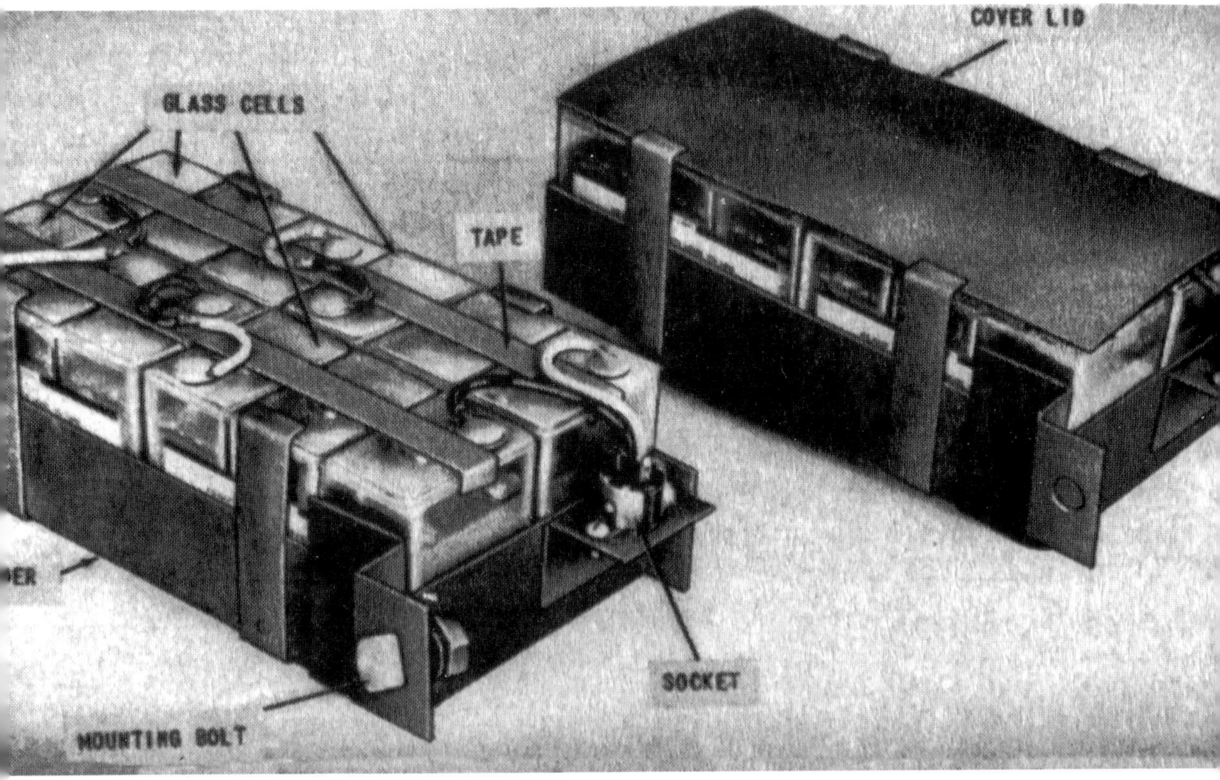

Battery. (*AAF AZON Manual*)

Antennas. (*AAF*)

Preparing the AZON for Operations

Generally, it required about five hours for an AZON to be readied for operations. During the unpacking of the AZON tail units from their shipping crates, the tail units in each crate had to be separated to those with the Emerson and those with the government issue (GI) CRW-7 receivers. Due the differences in their function, maintenance, and adjustment, the GI assemblies were favored and the Emerson receivers were placed in reserve. Once the tail was unpacked, the collar, gyro, and receiver was removed from the tail. The fins, controls, and general framework of the tail were examined with particular attention paid to the wiring, the servo mechanism, and mechanical coupling of the moving parts. The receivers were tuned to the bands transmitted by the equipment mounted in the bombers. If the Emerson receiver was to be used all sets required major maintenance of the wiring to increase their sensitivity. Once the receiver had been checked and any necessary adjustments made, it was remounted in the tail assembly and checked again. It was found that about two-thirds of the sets lost sensitivity after being mounted and required a change in grounding of the tail antenna. After unpacking, each gyro was tested for balance, precession, and uncaging, and that it would rotate properly through a 45-degree rotation of axis of the bomb after it fell free of the bomb racks. After testing, the gyro was installed in the tail. Once the flare was unpacked, its socket contacts were scraped clean of the shipping wax, which was used to prevent corrosion during shipment and storage. The flare was then installed in the tail assembly. The batteries were filled and charged to the proper potential a few hours before their installation in the tail.

The AZON-carrying bombers underwent several routine checks of the transmitting equipment usually requiring an hour. The transmitter frequencies were measured by a signal generator, and these values were applied to tune the receivers. The warm up circuit wiring on each bomb station was checked and the antenna was cleaned to achieve optimal control.

Adding the AZON Unit to the M-65 Bomb

The normal fixed tail of the AN-M-65 bomb was removed and replaced with a special AZON tail assembly or shroud, which was cruciform and had movable flaps on each side of the four fins. Two of these flaps were installed on opposing fins to function as ailerons. The other pair of opposing fins functioned together as rudders to steer the AZON to the right or left of the plane of its trajectory. The rudders were powered by an electric motor, responding to simple on/off radio signals received from the remote controller.

The AZON tail contained a central compartment that housed the gyroscopes/solenoid, radio receiver, battery, and servos. The gyroscope and solenoid changed the pitch of the ailerons to prevent rolling as the bomb fell and various corrections were made. The gyros were kept spinning by compressed air during the time of fall. The radio system was powered by a dry cell battery whose life was about three minutes, which was ample for the AZON to strike a target. To mark the bomb's flight path a 600,000 candle

The exterior AZON tail unit contained the guiding flare (A), radio antenna (B), rudders (C), and ailerons (D). (*AAF*)

The interior AZON tail unit was comprised of the rudder control motor (A), aileron actuating solenoid (B), radio interference suppressor (C), the radio receiver (D), 24-volt battery (E), and gyros (not visible). (*AAF*)

power* pyrotechnic flare, which burned for fifty seconds, was positioned centrally and behind the shroud. It produced a streamer of red, white, or green smoke (yellow was added later) to distinguish between individual bombs being controlled. Later, it was decided that all flares were to be white as a bombardier had no difficulty concentrating on his own bomb even in tight formations. (*candle power is an obsolete unit of the measurement of luminous intensity. Today's term is candela as one wax candle equals approximately one candela and one candle power equals 0.98 candelas.)

Due to the lack of space, tail fusing was omitted, but the impact nose fuse remained set for instantaneous detonation. Difficulty had been encountered early in the nose fuse development stages as when using as little as a one-second delay, there were almost as many duds as explosive bombs. This created disadvantages in some types of targets where a delay fuse would have more destructive force as in the armor-like surface of bridge spans or concrete construction. But it did add a security factor, deemed necessary, in that the secret weapon would more likely be destroyed on contact rather than fall into enemy hands intact.

The weight and size of the AZON tail units was approximately 75 pounds and consisted of the following: RC 106 transmitter, (9 by 19 by 17 inches) 32 pounds (with batteries); dynamotor, (8 by 7 by 9.5 inches), 16.25 pounds; control box, (7 by 5.75 by 5 inches) 2.125 pounds; and wiring and antenna, 25 pounds.

Loading the AZON into the Bomber

Initially, it required about an hour per bomb to load the aircraft, but eventually, the total time decreased to an hour for all bombs. The bomb without the tail assembly and without fusing was hung on the rack by the armorers. The tail collar was mounted on each bomb after it was slung from the racks and then trued so that the two studs used in aligning of the tail assembly were vertically one above the other. The tail assembly was mounted on the collar so that it was level. The armorers then rechecked that all parts were in place and then completed another inspection after the bomb was mounted.

Checking the AZON after Loading

The AZON bombs that were checked on the ground were rechecked after loading into the aircraft. The main line switch, battery switches, AZON warm-up switch, and filament switch on the control transmitter were all turned on. No engines, generators, or auxiliary power units (APU) were to be operating, then the control transmitter was to be switched to high power, but if the generators were charging the bomber's batteries and the APU was running, then the control transmitter was to be switched to low power. The kick-out plug on the first AZON was connected, and after sufficient warm up time (thirty to sixty seconds), the bombardier was to turn the carrier switch on and give right, center, and left rudder signals of at least five seconds each. The radio operator or another crewman was to observe the movement of the AZON rudder for proper functioning. The first bomb was then to be unplugged and the kick-out plug was placed into the second AZON and the procedure repeated for all AZON bombs loaded onto the aircraft. When the check was completed on all loaded bombs, the kick-out plugs were placed into each bomb. The arming wire was to be inserted through the kick-out plug, passing through the bomb lugs, and it was to extend no more than 4 inches without too much slack and was to be secured by a Fahnstock clip (an early type of spring clamp electrical terminal for connections to bare wires). The bombs were to be checked for correct fusing, correct delay, and that the arming wire and Fahnstock were properly installed. Once all units were thoroughly checked, the bombardier turned all switches off and reported to the project officer or his assistant.

Checking the AZON in Flight

The AZON bombs were checked in flight by the following procedure. The bombardier was to turn the AZON warm up switch on immediately after take-off, which caused the batteries in each AZON to be charged by the bomber's generators. The bombardier then entered the bomb bay to connect the flare plug on each AZON, remove the kick-out plug pin (after inspecting the arming wire), and remove the safety cotter pin on the nose fuse.

Dropping and Controlling the AZON

When each AZON was checked and ready to be dropped, the bomb bay doors were opened and the bombardier turned on both the flare arm switch and the carrier switch on his control-stick box. After all the AZONs were dropped, both the above-mentioned switches were turned off. Control of the AZONs was not to be applied until two-thirds of the time of fall had elapsed. If the aircraft returned with unused AZONs, the bombardier was to insert safety pins in the nose fuse and kick-out plug and pull out the flare plug.

Initially, the bombardier in the mother aircraft aimed the bomb using the conventional Norden bombsight procedure. The only change from normal bombing was the setting of a larger trail angle to compensate for drag due to the use of the AZON shroud for the application of control. Prior to release, the bomb's gyros were run up using electrical power from the mother aircraft. Upon release, power was transferred to the AZON's battery. Six to nine seconds after release, the flare automatically ignited at 8,000 to 10,000 feet. The bombardier tracked the falling AZON flare directly without any telescope or other optical aid. The AZON's flare was seen a bright circle of light against the ground and the bombardier guided it right, zero, or left to keep it on line. Within the limits of not impairing the bombardier's view, it was not necessary for the controlling aircraft to maintain straight and level flight or constant speed.

The cruciform tail had moveable flaps on each of the four fins; two acted as ailerons to stabilize the bomb so that it did not roll as it fell, while the other pair acted together as a rudder steering the bomb to right or to left of the plane of its trajectory. An electric motor powered the rudder in reaction to received commands, but if there were no commands, the rudder returned to center. Full rudder travel was 15 degrees each

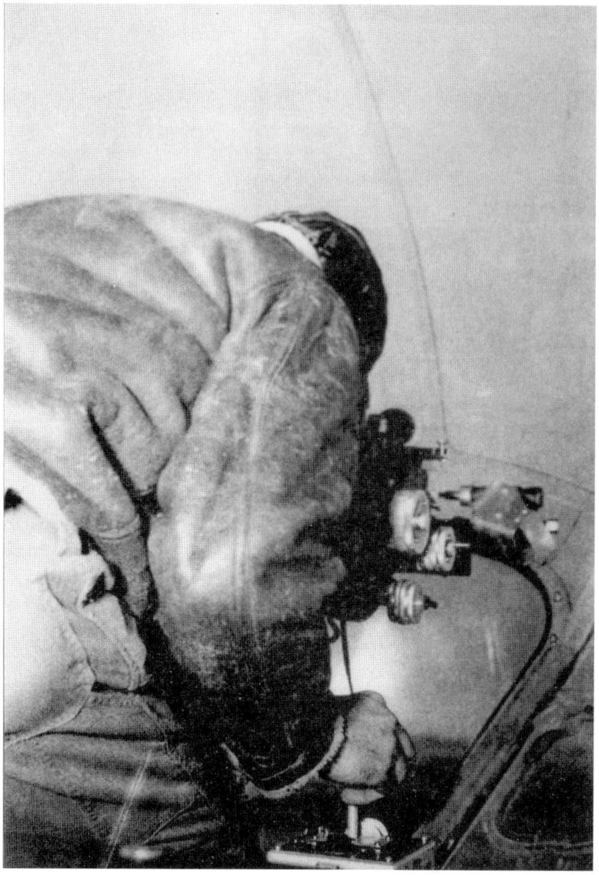

Left: Initially, the bombardier/controller in the mother aircraft aimed the bomb using the conventional Norden bombsight procedure. Six to nine seconds after release, the flare automatically ignited at 8,000 to 10,000 feet. The bombardier tracked the falling AZON flare visually without an optical aid. Accuracy was wholly the consequence of the bombardier's individual skill in using the joystick, much like playing today's computer games. (*From AAF training movie still*)

Below: AZON control stick. A simple three position (left-center-right) joystick unit was used to signal commands to the falling AZON. (*From AAF training movie still*)

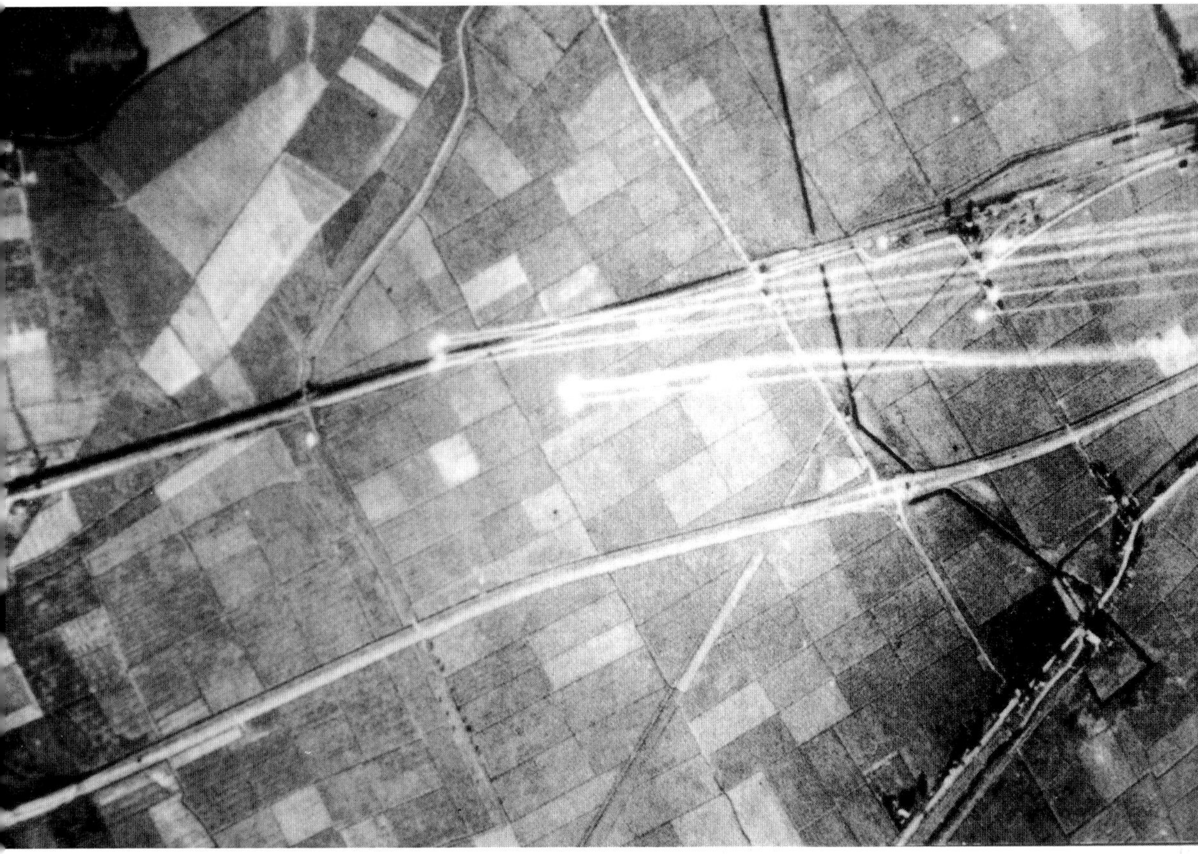

Flare. (*From AAF movie still*)

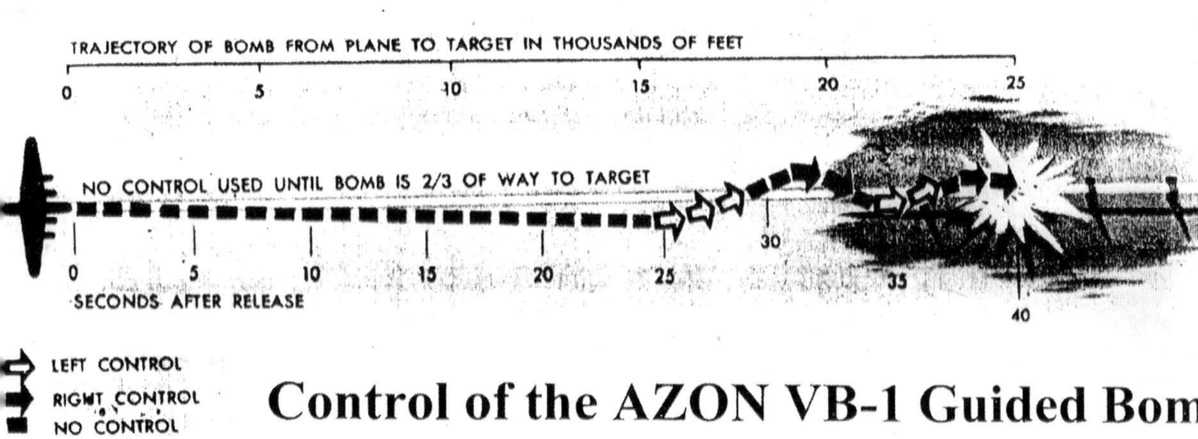

way and was attained in 0.7 seconds. The bomb responded by yawing to a steady angle of about 12 degrees while the period of oscillation in yaw was from 0.5 to 1.0 seconds, depending on speed. The bomb responded to command by accelerating sideways after a time delay of about 0.9 seconds.

The transmitter had six frequencies to permit simultaneous drop of six AZONs. At 1,500 feet, it was possible for the bombardier to detect azimuth errors of 5 to 10 feet as the bomb reached a speed of 850 feet per second (580 mph). The AZON control system was designed to correct deflection errors, which testing indicated could be potentially reduced to zero but would not improve range errors. Accuracy was solely the consequence of the bombardier's individual skill in using the simple three-position control stick (left-center-right) for signaling his commands, much like playing today's computer games. An experienced bombardier could master AZON technique within a week after six to eight practice drops; however, in the field, many bombardiers were shown to be somewhat haphazard in solving range problems. Some were able to shorten an AZON bomb's flight, but few, if any, were able to extend one's range.

AZON Aircraft

Typically, an AZON could be carried by any aircraft having a 1,000-pound bomb bay station, and therefore, any aircraft could carry more AZON bombs than GBs. The only requirement was that the inclusion of the AZON equipment did not in any way hinder the aircraft from performing its regular bombing function. Aircraft scheduled to carry the AZON were the B-17 (six AZONS), B-24 (eight), B-25 (two to three), B-26 (four), B-29 (sixteen), and P-38 (two). Additionally, a bomber could carry a mixture of VB and conventional bombs. These bombers required very few modifications to carry and deploy vertical bombs. The major structural change to the bomber was the installation of a bomb rack inside the bomb bay that could accommodate the somewhat larger

Aircraft scheduled to carry the AZON were the B-17 (siz AZONS), B-24 (eight), B-25 (two to three), B-26 (four), B-29 (sixteen), and P-38 (two). Pictured is B-24J, *Double Trouble*, which flew AZON missions in the CBI with the 7BG/483BS/10AF. Its AZON antenna can be seen under the rear fuselage. (*AAF*)

tail assembly of the vertical bomb. Also required were minor structural and electrical system changes, such as installing the proper radio control gear or cutting observation ports in the nose or side of the bomber.

The only practical AZON targets were long, straight, and narrow, such as rail lines, highways, long bridges, and railway marshalling yards, which were classified as interdiction targets that were the province of low-altitude medium bombers such as the B-25 or B-26 rather than the B-17 or B-24. However, this seemingly valid concept of dropping the AZON from medium bombers was never embraced until testing at the end of the war. The initial combat tests were implemented by B-17s, and most VB-1 combat missions were flown by heavy bombers.

Tethered AZONS

In June 1944, it was thought that the AZON's one bomb at a time and dispersion problem could be minimized by fastening two bombs together. The tethered method was tried in a practice mission on June 10, 1944 against a target on Pianosa Island in the Adriatic Sea. In the test, two VB-ls were tethered with a 25-foot length of wire with only one of the bombs controlled. The tests showed that the bombs could be tethered without separating and tethering did not interfere with guidance or negatively affect ballistics and would ensure that the two bombs would land within 25 feet of each other. However, the basic AZON ballistics problem remained and to effectively drop and control three or four pairs of tethered AZONs on a single bombing run; every controlled bomb would have to respond exactly the same way, every time, which they did not and could not.

Movie still of two tethered AZONs that were connected by a 25-foot length of wire, with only one of the bombs controlled. (*From AAF movie still*)

AZON Operational Use in the MTO

After having discovered the threat of the German V-1 buzz bomb launching sites on the French Channel Coast during the spring of 1944, a brief informational film introducing the AZON was shown to 8AF Brass in England. An initial order for 100 AZONs was requested to attack the German missile sites, but further target analysis determined that their small size prohibited AZON use and the 15AF in Italy inherited the bombs.

On March 25, 1944, four weeks behind schedule, the first experimental AZON Squadron furnished with six AZON-equipped B-17Gs was sent to conduct operations with the 419th Bomb Squadron of the 301st Heavy Bomb Group of the 15AF, based in Italy. Lt. Col. F. F. Helmick was the AZON project officer and Abner Wollan served as technical observer. The unit was preceded by 100 VB-1 tail assemblies airlifted to Caserta, near Foggia, with an additional 400 being shipped by sea. Special storage facilities and workshops were constructed next to the bomber's hardstands where the VB-1 tail and flare assemblies could be stored, maintained, and assembled. By April 9, the aircrews and aircraft had arrived from North Africa.

Wollan directed the unpacking, assembly, and testing of each VB-1 before it was ready for combat. Each of the six B-17s was allocated a separate flare color, and all assembled individual VB-ls and their radio equipment were marked with that color. Once assembled and loaded into a bomb bay, the VB-1 control mechanism deteriorated quickly. The flare/moisture problem continued but the most serious problem was the ability of the batteries in each VB-1 tail assembly to hold an adequate charge to be able to control the bomb. After five days stored in the bomb bay, the battery charge often fell below the minimum optimal 20-volt level. The B-17's onboard generators could recharge these batteries, but often, the tail assemblies of bombs containing weak batteries had to be removed and new batteries had to be reinstalled, which could be a very time-consuming procedure depending on the location of the AZON in the bomb bay.

On April 17, 1944, the 419BS flew the first AZON mission against railway lines between Rimini and Ancona in central Italy, but soon after take-off, heavier-than-expected cloud cover caused the three bombers to become lost and unable to rendezvous with the sixteen P-38s of their fighter escort. The three lost B-17s were intercepted by twenty to thirty-five Luftwaffe Fw 190 and Me 110 fighters that badly damaged one B-17, whose AZON transmitter was heavily damaged and its operator was slightly wounded. A second Fortress suffered minor damage, but all the bombers and their valuable AZONs were able to return to their base.

On April 24, thirty AZONs were released by five 301BG B-17s, escorted by eighteen P-38s against lines of rail track and four railway bridges between Rimini and Ancona. Nineteen AZONs were dropped from 19,000 feet and were followed to their targets. On strike photographs, no bridges were hit, but the rail line was reported to have been cut in three places and one bomb made an incidental hit on a warehouse near the Cesano River Bridge. Three AZONs suffered flare failures and two were accidentally dropped, falling into the Adriatic Sea north of Rimini. The average deflection error (right/left of target) was 700 feet that compared very favorably to the 1,250–1,500 feet deflection of conventional bombs. However, range errors tended to be greater averaging 1,900 feet, which was approximately equal in magnitude to conventional bombing results. At the debriefing, the bombardiers reported that they seemed to lack control of the remaining fourteen VB-1s during the last portion of their flight, which was thought to be due to low battery charges.

On April 29, the third AZON mission was flown by five B-17Gs that dropped twenty-four VB-1s on three railroad bridges on the Rimini–Ancona rail line from 5,000 feet. One AZON was reported to strike the Fano Bridge over the Metauro River, one of three bombs dropped apparently hit the Senegalila RR Bridge and one hit the highway at Pasaro. Four bombs could not be controlled due to flare failure, but the accurate assessment of the mission could not be analyzed due to poor strike photography and bad weather.

The next AZON mission was flown on April 30, once more against the same railway bridges as the previous missions. Five B-24s attacked in column, stacked down, with each bomber carrying two AZONs. Experienced group bombardiers made the drops and controlled the missiles. Despite only one bomb having reported control problems, only one bomb of thirty hit its target; this happened to be the Fano Bridge, which was being repaired from the previous day's damage.

After four missions that could claim only two hits scored out of seventy-three bombs dropped, there was a hiatus in the program while the test unit evaluated the AZON's huge decline in accuracy compared to its Eglin test results. The test report on these four AZON missions noted that they had been assigned to attack rail bridges and were flown in heavy clouds and poor weather by no more than five AZON bombers rather than large formations. Technical failures such as weak batteries, radio receivers with bad vacuum tubes, gyros damaged by rough field take-offs, and nose fuse damage on impact were blamed as contributing factors in bomb failures. The most important finding of the report was that the bombardiers had problems accurately dropping the bomb and then controlling it, particularly when the bombers arrived over targets in rapid succession. The training and use of the radioman, navigator, or other regular crew member to be control the bomb was decided to be ill-advised as these crewmen could be needed to operate machine guns against enemy fighters. The report suggested that the regular bombardier drop the bombs and then have a specially-trained AZON bombardier control them.

After another two AZON missions had been flown, the AAF Board prepared another evaluation report on May 8, 1944 that ambiguously stated that the VB-1 had performed well, with fifty-eight of the 108 bombs dropped operating successfully, but that the AZON required better weather than ordinary bombs. The low success rate (compared to Eglin test drops, not to conventional bombs) was attributed to the use of the last of an experimental lot of bombs, and that the new standardized operational AZONs would function much better. The report went on to specify that the control of the bomb was "positive, adequate, and satisfactory," and that while the cost of the AZON was about four times more than a conventional bomb, its accuracy justified this additional cost.

The report recommended that the bombardier was not to begin to control the bomb until it had fallen two-thirds of the elapsed fall time, which would positively affect range calculations since the induced drag due to changing the trajectory would be minimized. As the bomb neared the end of its fall, it approached terminal velocity, which made it more responsive to its controls, thereby requiring shorter commands to initiate trajectory changes. Also recommended was saving battery power until the most critical, last stage of the guidance sequence. The report noted AZON-carrying bombers could not take evasive action against enemy AA fire and fighters until the bombardiers completed control and the bombs impacted. Thus the AZONs could not be used against the well-defended targets specified by the AAF daylight, precision, strategic bombardment policy. Since the number of existing radio channels restricted the number of AZON bombers that could be employed at any given time, the report suggested that the AZON bombers be added to formations carrying conventional bombs. However, in order to maintain formation integrity, this procedure would expose the ordinary bombers to AA fire for an additional length of time while the AZON operators controlled their bombs.

On May 13, the Avisio Viaduct, located about 10 miles north of Trento in northern Italy on the Brenner Pass rail line, was attacked by AZON bombers that were dispersed into conventional formations. Due to the effort of the 1st Combat Camera Unit, this raid was significant as it was the first to successfully evaluate an operational AZON sortie. The 3,500-foot viaduct was located on the left bank of the Adige River and crossed the gorge at the confluence of the Adige and Avisio Rivers. The Germans had many 88-mm AA guns sited along the gorge and could call on fighter defenses, which 15AF Intelligence had considered as moderate. The viaduct was curved, making it a poor AZON target with the most suitable bombing approach being from the south, following along the railway tracks to give the AZONs full right deflection to follow the curve of the viaduct. Since the four AZON bombers were only a small part of the total 301BG's attacking B-17s, the mission approached from the north giving the AZON bombardiers no guide line to lead them into the viaduct's long axis. The initial reports of this mission highly praised the AZONs, crediting them with scoring four direct hits (of twenty-one bombs released) on the viaduct, which blocked the pass to all rail traffic and made repairs very difficult. This encouraging report influenced senior AAF officers to continue use of the AZONs.

However, it was not until five months later, on October 2, 1944, that 15AF's Operational Analysis Section thoroughly examined the strike and post-mission photos. They found that the AZON bomb dispersion had been too great, and that although the initial report had indicated four AZON hits, the damaging hits were from regular bombs. They discovered that some AZONs missed their target by so much that they could not be accounted for on the post-strike photos, and the others on the photos had impacted a considerable distance from the viaduct. The raid was also a technical failure for the AZONs as the strike photography showed very little indication of control and no sign of any last-second corrections to bring the bombs on the target. Only one of the four AZON bombardiers had a good view of his bombs and, therefore, the others were unable to gain effective control of their bombs until they could see them in the proximity of the curving railway lines during the last eight or nine seconds of fall. The AZONs were dropped in clusters of six, with each controller transmitting the same command to all six bombs in the cluster, which invariably led to a wide dispersion of all the bombs in the cluster except the one selected as the guide bomb. Several possibilities were suggested for this lack of control but probably the most likely reason was the danger of the mission itself, which encountered heavy AA fire and unexpected substantial fighter interception. Confronting a heavily defended target, the AZON crews did not relish continuing a less than a choice bomb run while controlling bombs until they impacted. Strike photos indicated that the bombardiers chose their best bombs from the cluster and gave them one or two long controlling maneuvers to line them up during the early part of the bomb's fall. The bombardiers would then abandon control of the bombs to allow the pilot to take evasive action before the AZONs impacted. The report concluded that ideally an AZON bomber accurately dropped only one of its six 1,000-pound VB-1s at a time. With six AZON bombers seeded in each formation, only 6,000 total pounds of guided bombs, albeit each having a much greater probability of attaining a hit on the target, was pitted against a conventional B-17 that could drop strings of six 1,000-pound bombs at once but with much less accuracy on their standard single bomb run. This one ideal AZON 1,000-pound bomb per heavy bomber bomb run did not conform to AAF operational doctrine, and it was decided that each AZON bomber was to continue to release strings of three to six AZONs simultaneously during the formation's conventional bomb drop. Each AZON bomber was directed to drop multiple VB-1s in rapid succession and then control all of them by guiding the center bomb only. Six AZON bombers were then able to release up to thirty-six VB-1s in a single bombing run, ideally responding as a single, compactly controlled cluster while being carefully guided to the target by six bombardiers. The logical progression of this idea was to have one bombardier control all AZONs, up to thirty-six bombs, simultaneously released by six AZON B-17s.

During the June 2 raid on the marshalling yards at Oradea, Romania, a solitary AZON bombardier attempted to control twelve VB-ls dropped by six B-17s in a single bombing run. Because the target was a large area, the radio receivers of the twelve AZON bombs were tuned to the same frequency and all were controlled by the lead aircraft from 22,400 feet. The bombardier directly guided one bomb with reasonable accuracy, but the other eleven indirectly controlled bombs finished their run dispersed over a very wide area. The cause for this extreme dispersion of the indirectly guided bombs was that casing of each bomb had small exterior flaws and when the bomb was spinning the effect of these flaws was nominal. But because the AZON bomb did not spin, a flaw on one side could deflect the bomb in that direction. If the bombardier was guiding a bomb with a casing flaw, he could appreciably offset its effect. But when the bombardier was guiding several bombs at once, a signal to turn the guide bomb would move it in the correct direction but the same signal to the other bombs with casing flaws would cause them to deviate from their original trajectories. Also, each bomb had slightly different control characteristics and along with flawed casings the result was widely scattered bombs that had a much greater dispersion error than conventional bombs. After the June 2 Oradea mission AZON dispersion setback, it was decided that only one AZON was to be controlled at a time from the mother B-17.

During June, the 301BG flew two missions against locks on the Danube River Gorge near the Iron Gate, and although the unofficial news release stated the locks were successfully attacked, the AZON results were inconclusive due to the raid seeding only a few one bomb at a time AZON bombers with many conventional bomb-carrying B-17s in the same formation, which could claim credit for any damage. The 301st suffered the loss of its first AZON bomber in an attack against a railroad bridge in Szolnok, Hungary, on July 2, 1944. But the decision to drop one controlled AZON at a time ended the AZON's possible role as a strategic bombardment weapon, and the 15AF had had enough of the AZON experiments, which it considered a nuisance and superfluous in the context of its overall mission. On July 13, the 15AF notified the CG of the Mediterranean Allied Air Forces (MAAF) that the five remaining AZON bombers were to be restored to their regular heavy bombardment duties as they had flown only an average of one sortie every twenty-one days, carrying a lower weight of explosives that "had accomplished little" and had served their purpose as "a successful" experiment! It was proposed that the MAAF AZON equipment be installed on 12th Air Force MATAF B-25s.

The following is a summary of 15AF AZONs sent by Gen. Ira Eaker to Gen. Carl Spaatz (Message M27820 August 11, 1944: Eaker to Spaatz):

AZON project discontinued by 15TAF and is now in hands of MATAF (B-25s)

1) Total combat missions flown: 14
2) Total AZON bombs released: 316 (three missions were ineffective)
3) Release of bombs was first done with each aircraft releasing independently (three missions) with bombs individually controlled.
4) On two missions bombs were released in salvo and each aircraft controlled its own pattern.
5) On six missions bombs were salvoed from a three ship element with center bomb as guide. The entire pattern was controlled.
6) Average altitude of release was 15,000.
7) On the earlier missions the aircraft attacked the target singly in line astern. For pattern release and control the aircraft flew in a three-ship element and in two element line astern.
8) Under individual release and control a deflection correction of 1,340 feet was obtained. Average deflection error for 63 bombs was 605 feet and average range error was 1,600 feet. These figures compare with average errors for normal bombing (15,000 feet altitude) of 780 feet deflection and 950 feet range.
9) In salvo release and control the average deflection error was 702 feet and average range error was 1,400 feet.

Report 8: The Accuracy of AZON Bombs as Affected by Battle Conditions in World War II explained the reason for the large degradation of combat compared to proving ground AZON results was due to the almost complete failure of the AZON control, beginning with the basic aiming of the AZON prior to release. The AZON had ample steering power to eliminate the azimuth errors latent at release and evidently this was hardly used at all. The AZON project was discontinued by 15AF B-24 heavy bombers and was transferred to MATAF B-25 Mitchell medium bombers.

AZON Operational Use by Medium Bombers in the MTO

Several weeks after the 301BG gave up on the AZON, it transferred the equipment, six specially-trained AZON crews, and remaining VB-1 tail assemblies to the 446th Bomb Squadron of the 321st Bomb Group based on Corsica, which began AZON training during the first week of August. The squadron flew the B-25 that could carry two VB-1s. By the end of September, the squadron had flown only two unsuccessful AZON missions against steel bridges and trestles as the bombs missed or passed through the steel structure before detonating. Previously, Gen. Alexander Patch's Seventh Army had invaded Southern France on August 15, 1944 and was quickly driving north to link up with Patton's Third Army, advancing from the north. Both Patton and Patch wanted bridges to remain undamaged so that the rapidly advancing Allied forces could use them and for most of August and September AZON missions against bridges in South France were prohibited. Besides, the group experienced a shortage of crews and found it impossible to conduct both AZON and conventional missions. There were 183 AZONs on hand in Corsica and another 1,112 ready for shipment in Naples, which amounted to a three months' supply with missions flown every day. The crews of the 321st continued to fly their conventional missions and became more and more disinterested in flying AZON missions. Finally, when the group's request for an additional six specially-trained AZON crews was ignored and with approaching poor winter weather conditions; the 321st would fly no further AZON missions during the war.

B-26 Marauder medium bombers equipped to carry four VB-1s were assigned to the 397th Bomb Group of the 9AF. On August 4, 1944, the unit flew its first and only AZON mission of the war when five B-26s armed with ten VB-1s attacked bridges near Chartres, France, to prevent the Germans from counterattacking Patton's breakthrough at Avranches. The B-26s attacked a series of three bridges in quick succession from 11,500 feet, but the lead bomber flew too close to the concentrated German AA batteries causing three B-26s to be hit. One Marauder immediately burst into flames and crashed, but most of the crew baled out; the second was so severely damaged that it could not continue on its bombing run; while the third returned to base so badly damaged that it was written-off. The two undamaged B-26s failed to hit the bridges although one VB-1 cut the rail tracks just short of the first bridge. The 397th's operational report concluded that unquestionably enemy AA fire was effective against the AZON Marauders at their 10,000 to 12,000-foot operational altitude and that against defended targets the thirty seconds longer bombing run required to control the AZON was a "deterring factor" in AZON operations and some new tactic was required to counteract it.

AZON Operational Use in the ETO

The second group of AZON trainees were assigned to the 753rd Bombardment Squadron under Maj. Robert Holbrook and his assistant, Lt. David Baltics, with Maj. J. Henry Rand, AZON designer, serving as the technical liaison. Ten B-24J-155-CO Liberators that had been especially AZON-modified in the U.S. and loaded with AZON tail (guidance) units left Florida's Pine Castle Field on May 2, 1944, for bridge-busting operations in Burma. With the invasion of France imminent, Gen. Carl Spaatz, Commander of the U.S. Strategic Air Forces, believed the AZONs could be useful against bridges in Northern France to prevent German armor and supplies from reaching the Normandy beachhead. On May 8, 1944, a request for AZON crews and bombers to be sent to the ETO was issued and the Burma-bound Liberators, which were crossing Africa *en route* to Burma were diverted to the 8AF. The Liberators arrived at the 458th Bombardment Group Station at Horsham St. Faith, Norfolk, U.K., on May 16 to conduct AZON ETO sorties under the Project Code 90653-R.

The 753rd Bomb Squadron was assigned to establish an AZON operational procedure, which mandated that upon approaching the target area, the AZON B-24s break formation and assume an in-trail position at the initial point (IP) to attack individually at between 10,000 and 20,000 feet, as at higher altitudes, the AZONs became uncontrollable at terminal velocity. The bombardier in the nose of the B-24 operated the standard Norden sight and used normal procedures to sight for range and release of the AZONs. At the bomb's release, the bombardier moved to a separate observation window in the fuselage floor aft of the bombsight that enabled him to see the AZON fall and the flare ignite in the bomb's tail. The bombardier used a simple left-right toggle switch to alter the direction of the bomb as it descended towards the target. Fifteen different radio frequencies were sent by the 25-watt AN/ARW-9 transmitters installed on the flight deck. This equipment weighed 33 pounds, and modifications to the B-24, for accommodating it, amounted to an additional 25 pounds. It was linked to three mast aerials attached under the rear fuselage: one antenna transmitted signals on 475 cycles for left deflection; one on 3,000 cycles for right deflection; and the third thirty to forty cycles to activate the flare. All three frequencies were changed intermittently to prevent enemy jamming. The transmissions adjusted the two movable tail rudders on the bomb, which was prevented from rolling by the automatic action of two gyro-stabilizers. The azimuth control allowed approximately 2,000-foot deflection on either side of what would have been the normal impact point but the forward trajectory (range) of the bomb could not be altered. After all aircraft had made their runs, formation was resumed for the flight home.

The original AZON B-24Js and their pilots assigned to the 753BS were:

44-40264	*Kiss Me Baby* (2Lt. John Lansing)
44-40273	*Howling Banshee* (F/O Arnold Piskin)
44-40275	*Shack Time* (1Lt. John Jones)
44-40277	*Miss Used* (1Lt. Gerald Matze)

44-40281 *A Dogs Life* (2Lt. John Lamed)
44-40283 *Lassie Come Home* (F/O John Tracy)
44-40285 *Table Stuff* (Capt. Maurice Speer)
44-40287 *Bachelors Bedlam* (2Lt. Patrick McCormick)
44-40288 *Bad Girl* (2Lt. Frank Fuson)
44-40291 *Royal Flush* (1Lt. Robert Morford)

(Notes: Later pilots were Lt. Col. Frederick O'Neill, Lts. Charles Shaw, Frederick DeNeffe, ? Griffith, John Lansing, John Larned, and Wilfred Tooman, who flew the operational missions; nine additional B-24H and Js of the squadron were to be eventually modified in England; and *Royal Flush* crashed on take-off on February 30, 1944, but all crew escaped without injury.)

By May 26, nearly 3,000 AZONs were ready for combat use in the ETO. As the 458th was eager to combat test the AZONs and because the 753rd had not completed its move to Horsham St. Faith, it was decided to use a single B-24 (41-29300), *Lorelei*, which was not among the original ten AZON-trained crews. An unofficial trial mission on May 23 was escorted by eight P-51 Mustangs and was led by Lt. Col. Frederick O'Neal, the 753rd Squadron's CO, and Capt. Frederick DeNeffe over Northern France where four bridges were claimed to be damaged or destroyed by four AZONs. A total of thirteen AZONs missions were flown between May 31 and September 13, 1944 in the ETO.

Originally intended for duty in the China-Burma-India (CBI) Theater, *Howling Banshee* was one of the original ten specially trained AZON crews flying B-24Js assigned to the 753BS of the 458BG for the initial operational use of AZONs in the spring of 1944. (*AAF*)

Mission #1: May 31, 1944

The first official and large-scale AZON mission took place on May 31 with five B-24s, carrying five AZONs each. The mission was escorted by five specially-briefed Mustang groups (forty-eight aircraft), which upon making rendezvous eight P-51s were assigned to each bomber with the last eight of the forty-eight to fly general support top cover. Second Lieutenant John Lansing was the AZON lead pilot with Shaw, DeNeffe, Larned, and Tooman piloting the four following AZON Liberators. Lt. Col. Frederick O'Neill was the command pilot for the mission, accompanying Tooman. The bombing was to be by individual bombers in trail, stepped up 200 feet each from an altitude of 17,000 to 17,500 feet. Only four of the five bombers attacked their target as one (Shaw) aborted due to mechanical problems.

Five bridges in the Paris area were attacked in 5/10ths total cloud around all targets with 10-mile visibility above. A summary of the attack on these bridges was as follows (in the order they were made):

No. 1: Melun Bridge embankment (5,300 feet long)
Four AZONs dropped by three aircraft:
1 fell in the river near the bridge
1 fell near the entrance to the bridge
1 hit 100 feet from the bridge
1 hit the far side tracks
Strike Attack Vertical (SAV) photos were taken of two bombs.
No. 2 Verberie Bridge (300 feet long)
The mission was scrubbed prior to briefing as clouds obscured the three assigned targets.
No. 3 Precy Suspension Bridge (350 feet long)
Two AZONs dropped by two aircraft:
1 fell 300 feet from the target
1 fell short
Determined by crew interrogation. No Strike Attack Vertical (SAV) photos were taken.
No. 4 Beaumont-sur-Aire Bridge (300 feet long)
Four AZONs dropped by four aircraft:
1 hit the end of the bridge
1 hit just over the end
1 hit 100 feet over the end
1 hit 300 feet over the end
No. 5 Mantes-Gassicourt Paris RR Bridge (250 feet long)
Three AZONs dropped by three aircraft and SAV photos showed:
1 hit an island in middle of river
1 hit the RR tracks just short of the bridge
1 hit the RR tracks at end of bridge

A target of opportunity, the bridge at Meuhlan was attacked by one bomber with poor results.

A total of thirteen AZONs were dropped with each being controlled individually and the seven unused bombs were returned to base. The group reported only meager inaccurate flak and no enemy aircraft encountered.

Mission #2: June 1, 1944

The mission was scrubbed prior to briefing as the three tactical targets were reported as obscured by reconnaissance.

Mission #3: June 4, 1944

On June 4, the Melun railway flyover and double line junction and the 5,300-foot-long Melun Bridge and embankment over the Seine River were attacked with thirteen AZONs carried by six B-24s piloted by Shaw, DeNeffe, Larned, and Tooman, Griffin, and Lansing. The mission was led by Lt. Col. Frederick O'Neill riding in DeNeffe's bomber. Some 15 miles inside enemy territory, Griffin's B-24 *Bad Girl* returned to base when a hydraulic line was cut by flak before arriving at the target, and five B-24s continued to their targets. Just prior to reaching the target, Larned's Liberator had a bomb rack malfunction causing three bombs to be released over the French countryside. The remaining four aircraft attacked the Melun line junction, dropping one AZON each, all falling within 200 to 1,000 feet from the target. The four bombers continued to the Melun Bridge, with three dropping one bomb each and the fourth dropping three bombs. The visibility was 10 miles—hazy with a 2/10ths cloud cover. Near misses were reported with most bombs off in azimuth, but no conclusive results were assessed as there were no SAV photos taken. Flak was reported as moderate and accurate and enemy aircraft opposition was nil.

Mission #4 and #5: June 8, 1944

Fifteen 458BG Liberators, with no fighter escort, flew to the Melun Bridge embankment and found the target was covered by undercast; they circled three times to obtain a sighting before returning to base at 8:45 a.m. without dropping their AZONs. A second mission was attempted that afternoon and also returned.

Mission #6: June 14, 1944

There was a change of tactics for this mission, forced by the vulnerability to flak of individual aircraft remaining in the target area for too long. On this mission and on all subsequent missions, the AZON Liberator force bombed in flights of five, the lead aircraft performing normal sighting while the four other aircraft individually controlled their AZONs for range only. On this mission, fifteen bombers in sections of five each took off to attack six French bridges: Corbie Bridge (180 feet long), Perrone Bridge (150 feet), Honsur-Somme Bridge (170 feet), Estaples Bridge (1,004 feet), Frevent Bridge (2,460), and Doullens Bridge (150 feet). All bridges except Target 2 (Perrone Bridge) were obscured by cloud, and B-24 sections No. 1 and No. 2 remained together to attack that clear target while section No. 3 flew unaccompanied to a target of opportunity. Ten bombers approached Target 2 but two had AZON equipment malfunctions and one was too far off course to bomb effectively. The seven attacking bombers recorded no results. The five bombers of Section No. 3 became lost and attacked an unidentified target of opportunity with no results seen or recorded before returning to base, exiting enemy territory at Calais. Of the thirteen AZONs dropped, only one was considered to have caused damage, hitting 200 yards short of the Harim Bridge center, exploding on the tracks.

Mission #7: June 15, 1944

Fourteen bombers, carrying twenty-seven AZONs, attacked the RR bridges at Estaples, Perrone, and Doullens. Twenty AZONs were controlled from 21,000 feet (considered too high for AZON operations as the bombardier was required to maintain visual contact with the disappearing AZON to the target) controlled in 4/10ths cloud and 5 miles, hazy visibility. The results were good with Perrone being destroyed by direct hits, and Estaples and Doullens severely damaged by near misses. No enemy aircraft were encountered and generally the flak over the targets was light and inaccurate, but that over Caen was very accurate with six aircraft receiving minor damage, but *Bachelors Bedlam* received major damage in which the nose gunner, Sgt. Raymond Tomlinson, was killed.

Mission #8: June 18, 1944

Mission scrubbed.

Mission #9: June 22, 1944

Railway bridges over the Loire River were attacked by nine B-24s (one aborted due to mechanical problems) in 2/10ths cloud and unlimited visibility. The Saumur RR Bridge (3,600 feet) was attacked with eighteen AZONs, of which nine were controlled with three hitting close enough to damage the bridge. Another eighteen AZONs, nine controlled, were dropped on the Tours le Riche RR Bridge, spanning 1,120 feet, reportedly damaging it. Enemy flak was heavy, and most Liberators suffered some degree of damage.

During the first series of completed missions, there were changes made in AZON sighting and controlling tactics:

Missions #1 and #2: Aircraft flown in trail with bombardier sighting and controlling individually.

Missions #3, #4, and #5: Lead aircraft made a regular sighting, the wing aircraft sighting for range only and each controlling individually.

Missions #6 (through #13): All aircraft dropped on lead aircraft and controlled individually.

ETO AZON Missions Paused

Despite the good AZON results on June 15, Gen. Doolittle, who had never been particularly impressed with the AZON, believed that with the current pressure on 8AF pre-invasion resources, it would be beneficial to postpone further AZON tests until more forces were available and there would be less chance of the weapon falling into enemy hands at an early date. Postponement of the project followed but not before the successful June 22 mission. Subsequently, the 753rd returned to normal operations, although its AZON aircraft with their secret equipment could not be used; B-24s had to be borrowed from other squadrons so its AZON pilots could fly regular missions. Three of the AZON B-24s and crews were detached to the Aphrodite project and would not return to the 753rd.

During July, the 753rd's AZON Liberators were being held in reserve for tactical missions suited for AZON operations and participated in only seventy-one of the group's 387 normal bombing sorties, although several AZON non-combat practice missions were flown. AZON pilot Lt. John Jones and crew were lost while flying other combat missions.

During August, the 753rd participated in the constant aerial assault on German targets in the post D-Day advance from the beachhead, flying eighteen missions in the first eighteen days of the month. During mid-month, a further phase of experimentation with the AZON was ordered. The 753BS then had eighteen aircraft with transmitting equipment available with three different pilots serving as AZON command pilots: Squadron CO Maj. John Hensler; Squadron Operations Officer Capt. Frank Wright; and pilot Capt. Maurice Speer.

Between the two operational periods for AZON, May 31 to June 22 and August 17 to September 13, three aircraft—44-40066, 44-40277, and 44-40283—were detached to operate with the Aphrodite Double-AZON guided drones. Although these aircraft returned to the 753rd in August, their crews were transferred to the Aphrodite project.

ETO AZON Missions Resumed

Mission #10: August 17, 1944

In the resumption of the AZON project, a mission on an unidentified RR bridge near Les Fallons was aborted as clouds obscured the target.

Mission #11: August 25, 1944

The 340-foot Moerdijk RR Bridge in Holland was attacked by sixteen AZONs dropped in clusters, with all bombs under one set of commands. This method was used to increase the mission's effectiveness in a single run over the target rather than expose the bombers to anti-aircraft fire and enemy fighters during the repeated runs for individually controlled drops. The dispersion of the AZONs was very large except for the control bombs near the center of the cluster, one of which scored an apparent direct hit on the bridge. That same day, the Tours le Riche Bridge (1,100 feet) was attacked with sixteen AZONs, ten controlled, with at least one hit seen on post-mission recon photos. The visibility was 20 miles with no clouds on both attacks.

On August 25, 1944, the 1,100-foot Tours le Riche Bridge was attacked with sixteen AZONs, ten controlled, with at least one hit seen on post-mission recon photos. The photo shows three AZONs as bright circles (arrows) heading for the target. (*From AAF Strike Photo*)

Mission #12: August 26, 1944

This mission to the Moerdijk Bridge was scrubbed due to heavy cloud cover obscuring the target. However, AA fire during the mission caused slight damage to six aircraft and major damage to one.

Mission #13: September 1, 1944

The Ravenstein RR Bridge, Holland, was the scheduled primary target, but the secondary target, an ammunition depot near Kropp, Germany, was attacked by six AZON bombers that dropped twelve AZONs in clusters, ten controlled, with a few near misses and fires recorded. The cloud was 7/10ths and the visibility unlimited. No enemy aircraft or flak were encountered.

Mission #14: September 5, 1944

A mission to an unidentified RR bridge near Mulheim, Germany, was recalled near the English coast due to bad weather.

Mission #15: September 13, 1944

A mixed formation of eleven aircraft with were dispatched to attack an oil refinery at Hemmingstadt, Germany, but due to last-minute cloud cover that interfered with sighting, five non-AZON Liberators dropped their twenty-five 1,000-pound GP bombs on this target. Six AZON Liberators then diverted to the secondary target—a large ammunition dump at Kropp—and guided twenty-five AZONs from 16,000 feet with some hits being made and fires started, but most of the AZONs fell short. The cloud was 4/10ths and the visibility was unlimited. There was no battle damage or casualties.

ETO AZON Missions End

After fifteen missions, the 753rd would abandon AZON missions with the special equipment removed from all Liberators, which were returned to full participation on normal daylight bombing operations within 458BG missions. The ETO was found not to be conducive to AZON operations for the several reasons. Poor weather conditions were prevalent in this theater, especially during the time the 458th was to fly its AZON missions. Any cloud conditions over 3/10ths interfered or precluded AZON use; for example, on D-Day alone, the group was alerted three times but flew no missions. During this period, the 458th remained in a constant state of alert, which was necessary to take advantage of any break in the weather. However, this alert, with few missions flown, and five missions recalled over the target, caused a morale problem. Targets had to be limited to objectives not heavily defended by AA guns or interceptors. While flying at higher altitudes gave the bombers more protection against flak, guiding the bomb from 20,000 feet was much more difficult than from 10,000 feet because high-altitude drops made visual tracking of the tail flare difficult due to the chronic smoke and haze over the targets. It was found that flak turbulence, evasive action, or even simple weaving upset the bombardier's aim and perhaps composure. The threat of enemy fighter interception made the use of small groups of AZON-only bombers hazardous and Allied fighter escort was in short supply and could not be delegated to small AZON raids. Thus, the AZON bombers were included as only a small fraction of a larger formation of conventional bombers. Consequently, AZON operational plans were formulated to suit the larger formation. At that time, Air Force bombing evaluation was based on tonnage of bombs dropped (quantitative) rather than damage done (qualitative) and ordered their resources and tactics in that direction.

If the AZONs were utilized as recommended, one dropped and controlled per aircraft per bombing run, the total bomb released tonnage decreased. Only one AZON bombing run could be made as the conventional bombers would be jeopardized by waiting for AZON bombers to make individual attacks in the face of enemy AA fire and interceptors. Therefore, all AZONs were dropped at once in salvo with the one bomb being used as a control. This method resulted in a wide dispersion of hits even though all bombs from each aircraft were under single-simultaneous control. As previously discussed, the reason for this dispersion was that each AZON had slightly different aerodynamics due to manufacturing inaccuracies and each also had slightly different control characteristics.

A *Report on AZON Operations* dated October 31, 1944, from H.Q. 8AF: Office of the Commanding General for the Commanding General, concluded:

> AZON equipment was found to be satisfactory and proved that this type of weapon properly employed would be effective. It is believed that, for the successful

employment of AZON, target weather must be clear. Cloud conditions of more than two to four-tenths (2 to 4/10th) stratus or strata-cumulus preclude the use of this weapon, because any cloud coming between control airplane and the bomb prevents proper, guidance of the missile. It is here pointed out that clear weather is rare in this theater. During the period of these operations a constant state of alert, with very few resulting missions, caused an unfavorable state of morale amongst crews. This state of alert was necessary in order to take advantage of any breaks in weather which might occur. The limit of availability of control stabilizers made practice missions negligible. Consequently, the AZON equipped aircraft, the crew technical specialists and other highly trained personnel could not be utilized to the best advantage of the war effort. It has been proven in the course of these experiments that regular strategic precision pattern bombing could do any tasks so far assigned to the AZON squadron. It was necessary before the above operations commenced to train crews in the handling and operation of this weapon. At the beginning of the AZON experiments the squadron assigned this project had three (3) crews in category A trained as lead crews, who were proven in combat and had led the group, (3) crews in category B and all other crews of the squadron were regular combat crews. Ten (10) new crews of the squadron were received from the United States who had been especially trained for AZON bombing. The bombardiers were proficient in target recognition and map reading, and no difficulty was experienced in this respect. Every effort was made to develop teamwork between the pilot, navigator and bombardier. Pilots and navigators were assigned permanently to the lead crews. When the ten special AZON crews were received from the United States, the pilots were flown as co-pilots with the lead crews, and the AZON bombardiers were used on the lead ships. Later the special AZON crews were reassembled as lead crews after having gained some experience flying with the proven lead crews. An attempt was made to splice the AZON bombs together with wire and cable, but in most cases they broke apart before reaching the target. Heavier cable could not be used because it was necessary to tie the cable to the nose fuses. It is believed that the weather expectancies in this theater and bombing results obtained on these experimental missions justify the following recommendations: The AZON bombing project be discontinued in this theater. AZON equipment now assigned to the group which has been conducting these experiments be released to that unit to be utilized as radio bomb release equipment.

USAAF, *Case History of Vertical Bombs: AZON, SPAZON, RAZON, Felix, ROC*
Maxwell AFB, MF Reel A2082, A2083, and A2051

AZON Operational Use in the CBI

On April 5, 1944, ten B-24J bombers, which were destined for service with 10AF in the CBI, arrived at the School of Applied Tactics, Orlando, Florida, to begin their transitional VB-1 training. Soon, all ten bombers were equipped with special new AZON radio transmitters and antennae. Also, further modifications were necessary to give the bombardiers adequate visibility to acquire and track the bomb as it fell, so a small, 6-inch-diameter hole was cut in the forward right corner of the floor in the bombardier's compartment and covered with a Plexiglas window.

Training began at once as ten B-24 bombardiers controlled 103 test VB-1s, but of the first forty drops, nineteen failed. These malfunctions were due to problems with the bomb rack, gyros, radio transmitter or radio control box, and, as was too common, with the flares. The AZON technical representative quickly determined that the radio transmitter problems were caused by frequency drift in the radio tuners. In contrast to today's aviation radios, which can lock on to and track a specific frequency, those of the World War II era had to be constantly monitored to ensure reception and transmission remained identical to those originally dialed in. These radios could drift off frequency and the signal to become garbled or lost altogether due to vibration, changing antenna angles as the aircraft or bomb maneuvered, and atmospheric conditions. Radio technicians were dispatched to set up new radio tuning procedures, after which not one radio failure occurred during the following sixty VB-1 practice drops. After the bombardiers had dropped and controlled four or five VB-1s each, azimuth errors of zero feet were the norm for any bomb not having a malfunction. Of the last fifty-three VB-1s dropped, forty-three had a zero azimuth error and twelve also had a zero range error. The B-24 crews completed their U.S. training and departed for the CBI, and the 10AF on April 29, 1944 as part of the 7th Bomb Group (H), hoping that the AZON accuracy achievable over practice ranges in the U.S. were as easily to reproduce under combat conditions

In late September, the B-24s and crews of the 493rd Bomb Squadron reported to the 7th Bombardment Group of the 10AF under Col. Harvey Alness stationed at Pandaveswar, India. Because the negative reports of the AZON experience of 15AF and 8AF in the ETO had preceded them, these recently trained crews were greeted unenthusiastically upon their arrival. Since the CBI was a low-priority theatre of operations, there was a chronic shortage of aircraft, which were vitally needed for purposes other than experimental bombing. Consequently, the AZON tails and transmitters were removed from their B-24s and stored in warehouses and the valuable, now AZON-less B-24s were allotted to the four squadrons of the 7BG for conventional operations. Also, the AZON maintenance officer who had arrived a few weeks earlier had difficulty obtaining the other AZON tails stored at Calcutta, India, and vital AZON testing equipment was not shipped from the U.S. and had to be reissued from there. Meanwhile, two of the AZON B-24s were lost in conventional bombing raids and five were consigned to the Hump Airline, ferrying gasoline to the B-29s then based in China.

Administratively, the 7BG was part of the 10AF but was under the operational control of the Strategic Air Force within the theater. At the time, with no ordinary strategic targets to attack in their theater, such as industry and cities, the Strategic Air Force attacked supply lines as high-priority targets to cut Burma off from supplies coming from Thailand and Malaya. Railways and particularly their bridges and trestles were the priority targets assigned to the AZON bombers. The Burma Railway, also known as the Death Railway, was a 258-mile railway built by Japan, connecting Bangkok, Thailand, and Rangoon, Burma, and was finished during October 1943 to support its operations in the Burma. The railway, made infamous by the film *The Bridge over the*

River Kwai, was built by the forced labor of between 180,000 and 250,000 Southeast Asian civilian laborers and about 61,000 Allied POWs, of which 90,000 civilian laborers and more than 12,000 Allied prisoners died. The 10AF would carry out continual attacks against these railway bridges during late 1943 and throughout 1944 with ordinary GP bombs, but then, beginning in December 1944, mainly with AZON bombs. Once the railway's river bridges were destroyed, the Japanese throughout Burma were forced to unload many railway cars on one side of a destroyed river bridge into ferry and barge transport and then reload it back into railroad cars on the other side. As a footnote, some sources have stated that AZON bombs destroyed the infamous bridge over the River Kwai on January 23, 1945, but bad weather prompted the cancellation of that mission and the AZON was never deployed against the bridge.

All AZON bombers were retained in the 493rd Squadron that was to function as a conventional bomb squadron with the other three 7th Bomb Group squadrons except when assigned to AZON missions. By retaining the AZON B-24s in one squadron, all special equipment and maintenance crewmen and equipment was concentrated and operational briefings, procedures, and training were greatly simplified.

On December 10, NDRC official Maj. William Donics and technical advisor Dr. T. J. O'Donnell arrived in India to act as AZON liaison to H.Q. 10AF. The data and films they brought with them sufficiently demonstrated the bomb's merits to regain the commandeered five AZON B-24s used for Hump gasoline hauling operations. The necessary instruments and equipment were reinstalled in the B-24s, so that by late December, three were available for the first AZON sortie in the CBI.

On December 27, 1944, these three Liberators took-off carrying eight bombs, four AZONs and four standard 1,000-pound M65 bombs, to attack the Pyinmana Railroad Bridge located between Rangoon and Mandalay. The bridge had withstood conventional aerial attack for nearly two years and was a perfect AZON target, having a straight bombing approach and was long enough at 380 feet in three spans to permit the predicted range errors to destroy the target. Two bombardiers were used with the first bombardier positioned in the standard nose station to initially aim the AZON using the Norden bombsight. He was to aim the AZON as close to the target as possible, thus reducing range errors. The second bombardier was located in the tail of the dropping Liberator giving him an unobstructed downward view of the falling bomb, which he was to guide towards the target. Each bombardier was given one practice bomb run on railway lines on the way to the target. Three passes were made on the target by each Liberator, with one AZON and one standard bomb dropped on each pass, all from 9,300 feet without anti-aircraft fire or enemy fighter opposition. Three hits were made on the bridge with the center span destroyed and another span damaged by AZONs as all standard bombs missed.

On December 30, four B-24s armed with twenty-eight AZONs were to attack one bridge with two alternatives from 10,000 feet; all bridges supplied the Japanese offensive on the Arakan Front. The 225-foot steel road bridge on the Prometaugup Road and 400-foot concrete bridge at Tausgup were destroyed with sixteen bombs. Having twelve unused bombs, the B-24s attacked the 200-foot Okshitpin Bridge, destroying it with eight bombs, leaving four unused bombs. An unscheduled 75-foot wooden bridge was located and destroyed by three of the four bombs.

On December 30, 1944, the 400-foot Tausgup concrete bridge at was destroyed with sixteen AZONs. (*From AAF Strike Photo*)

Four B-24s, each carrying four AZONs flew the third mission on January 1, 1945, attacking three bridges at 10,500 feet with poor mixed 4/10ths to 10/10ths cloud cover. One bridge was confirmed destroyed, but two others were rated as possible but doubtful.

The fourth mission on January 3 dispatched three bombers carrying six AZONs each at 8,000 feet. Two bridges and a section of track were attacked with one bridge destroyed, two probably damaged, and three direct hits were made on the tracks.

On the fifth mission, January 8, six bombers carrying six AZONs each attacked four bridges from 10,000 feet with three bridges destroyed but the fourth was undamaged.

On the sixth mission on January 9, three bridges were attacked from 10,500 feet by three bombers carrying four AZONs each resulting in two bridges destroyed and the third undamaged.

The seventh mission on January 11 had two bridges attacked by five bombers carrying five AZONs each at 10,500 feet. Both bridges were destroyed and for the first time insignificant, inaccurate AA fire was encountered, doing no damage.

The 493BS squadron had flown seven missions in fifteen days before expending their AZON bomb supply. A total of 154 bombs were released, with thirty-four hits being scored to destroy fourteen bridges and damaging three more. Of the 154 bombs, about thirty-five were considered to be wasted for various reasons with the majority being salvoed because of engine problems, a few being released late because of rack malfunctions, and a few because of personnel failure. A memorandum of March 1, 1945 from Division H.Q. stated:

> The overall economy of AZON bombing on those seven missions is somewhat startling. At least 35 of the AZONs were either direct hits or close enough to damage the targets.... Conservatively, we can say that one out of five AZONs gave a damaging hit ... (when) one damaging hit of 50 bombs would be an over-optimistic guess.... On this basis AZON is ten times as effective against bridges as standard bombing or one AZON Squadron is equivalent to two and a half standard bomb Groups.
>
> USAAF, *Case History of Vertical Bombs: AZON, SPAZON, RAZON, Felix, ROC* Maxwell AFB, MF Reel A2082, A2083, and A2051

During these seven missions, the most efficient AZON bombing technique was determined. The best bombing altitudes were to be at 8,000 to 10,000 feet, which allowed enough time for the bombardiers to determine and enter corrections but was not too high that the range error would be too great due to human error and individual ballistic error due to bombs not spinning. Individual AZON release rather than train release was employed as each AZON bomb required a different amount of control and the bombardier had to concentrate on controlling one at a time to hit a target as narrow as a bridge. It was particularly important that experienced lead bombardiers be used as it was necessary that the bomber be correctly lined up on the bridge.

On these initial missions, AA fire and enemy fighter interception was absent, as was typical of Japanese target defense at this stage of the war in the CBI. The Japanese attempted to defend their bridges but lacked supplies of heavy anti-aircraft ammunition and primarily relied on light cannon, machine guns, and small arms, each only effective against low-flying fighter bombers. AZON bombers flying at 9,000 feet were out of AA range, and, with little chance of meeting Japanese interceptors, the AZON crews could concentrate on the mission as if it were a training mission.

On missions where there was little chance of enemy fighter interception, the first IP (initial point) was chosen, and upon arrival there, each bomber flew in trail at thirty-second intervals. At the second IP, each bomber turned in on its bombing run. A pattern was made around the target, with each bomber sighting for its own range and deflection, dropping one bomb on each run.

On missions during which enemy fighter interception was probable, a formation of six bombers in two three aircraft elements was flown javelin down (a basic formation consisting of high, middle, and low two-plane elements stepped diagonally downward toward the sun). This bomber formation made a pattern around the target, each bomber dropping one AZON on each run.

If AA fire was expected, then fighter bombers from other squadrons were sometimes assigned to attack the gun emplacements with 20-pound cluster fragmentation bombs to neutralize the gun positions at least long enough for the AZON bombers to complete their bombing runs. If there were no fighter bomber support on missions where AA fire could interfere with the completion of six AZON bombing runs, the bombers were loaded with three AZON and three standard 1,000-pound bombs. Each bomber made three runs, dropping one AZON and one standard bomb on each run.

Most mission failures were caused by undercasts of 3/10ths or more in which the path of AZONs could not be followed closely enough for proper control. Missions under these conditions were either canceled or aborted over the target. Equipment failure occurred about 3 percent of the time, with half due to flare failure and the remainder due to bomb control failure right or left.

Maintenance was considered the most significant factor for effective operational AZON use. Included in the 493BS were ten enlisted men and one officer in charge of AZON maintenance and testing who performed exceptionally, in view of twenty-five men being considered optimal.

The group considered themselves so successful that they put up a sign stating "Dentists Office: Bridgework: Our Specialty." The missions were so successful that Hugh Spencer, Chief of Division 5/NDRC, and Maj. William Donics requested the expedited shipment of kits to modify fifty more B-24s for AZON use before the monsoon season that was expected to begin in May. They also requested a monthly shipment of 700 VB-1s and 300 VB-2s to the CBI.

Once the new supplies of the bomb arrived, the good results continued as the group's official report for the period December 27, 1944 to March 5, 1945 stated that the 7BG had released 459 AZONs that destroyed twenty-seven bridges averaging 250 feet in length while maintaining an average range error of 201 feet and an average deflection error of 131 feet. Some ten to 15 percent of the AZONs dropped were direct hits, which did not include AZONs dropped as standard bombs, nor malfunctions or significant errors due to heavy overcast.

The following table demonstrates the effectiveness of the AZON compared to the conventional 1,000-pound general-purpose bomb:

Bomb Type	Effectiveness Ratio
6 × 1,000-lb. GP bombs	1.0 (as a standard)
1 × AZON	4.0 to 8.0
1 × AZON plus 5 × 1,000-lb. GP bombs	4.7 to 8.7
6 × AZONs (in salvo)	5.2 to 9.2

As can be seen, one AZON dropped on the same target was four to eight times more effective than six 1,000-pound GP bombs, and any use of the AZON was more effective than conventional bombing techniques.

Unlike the MTO and ETO, in the CBI there was a significant improvement in the accuracy of the unguided bombing after the beginning of the AZON missions—often better than proving ground test results. The improvement was due to two factors. The primary factor was declining enemy AA and fighter opposition, which enabled AZON bombardiers to carefully and confidently control one bomb per run at low altitudes and then make several more controlled attacks. After their successes, the AZON crews became very self-satisfied, leading to rivalries between crews in squadrons and between the other three squadrons in the group. The military situation in the CBI was less strident and more relaxed during the period of AZON operations as the CBI Campaign was virtually concluded.

AZON CBI Summary

The following table is from the actual summary of operations by the 493BS between December 27, 1944 and March 5, 1945. This table denotes a variance in AZON/ conventional bomb effectiveness from the preceding table. The unguided bomb figures in the table are outstanding due to the two factors mentioned above.

Summary of Operations by 493rd *AZON* Squadron/7th Bomb Group
November 1944-March 1945

Date	Target	Size (ft)	No. of Bombs GP	No. of Bombs AZON	Hits GP	Hits AZON	Bombs per hit GP	Bombs per hit AZON
1 Nov	RR Br.	780 x 18	6	-	1 poss.	-	6	-
5 Nov	Tunnels		10	-	0	-	10	-
23 Nov	RR Br.	500	72	-	0	-	72	-
26 Nov	RR Br.	320	35	-	1	-	35	-
26 Nov	RR Br.	770	54	-	0	-	54	-
27 Dec	RR Br.	380 x 14	21	9	0	3	3	3
30 Dec	Road Br.	75 - 400		28		4		7
1 Jan	2 RR Br.	200 x 15 210 x 14	10	16	0	0	10 above	16
3 Jan	RR Br.	11400 x 14	6	11	0	1 ?	6+	11 ?
3 Jan	2 RR Br.	-	2	5	0	0	2 above	5
8 Jan	RR Br.	-	0	17	-	2	-	8.5
8 Jan	RR Br.	-	0	9	-	3	-	3
8 Jan	RR Br.	-	0	3	-	0	- above	3
8 Jan	RR Br.	-	0	1	-	0	- "	1
9 Jan	RR Br.	-	6	6	2	2	3	3
9 Jan	RR Br.	-	4	5	1	2	4	2.5
9 Jan	RR Br.	-	2	1	0	0	3	(salvo)
11 Jan	RR Br.	450	1	9	1	8	1	1.12
11 Jan	RR Br.	-	13	15	2	8	7.5	1.19
13 Jan	Jetty	1350 x 450	0	15	-	1	-	15
27 Jan	RR Br.	430	0	18	-	6	-	3
27 Jan	RR Br.		0	18	-	3	-	6
3 Feb	RR Br.	360 x 15	0	16	-	3	-	5.3
5 Feb	RR Br.	360 x 15	0	12	-	1	-	12
7 Feb	RR Br.	740 x 16	24	24	Multiple		Few	Few
9 Feb	RR Viaduct	1230	24	18	2 Caps		Indeterminate	
11 Feb	RR Br.	500	0	18	-	4	-	4.5
11 Feb	RR Br.	150	6	9	0	-	6	-
15 Feb	RR Br.	260 x 15	12	24	0	2	12	12
21 Feb	RR Br.	500 x 16	11	21	0	3	11	7
23 Feb	RR Br.	300 x 15	0	6	-	2	-	3
25 Feb	RR Br.	400	48	0	6 or 8	-	7	-
27 Feb	RR Br.	430	0	18	-	4	-	4.5
3 Mar	RR Br.	800 x 16	0	24	-	1	-	24
3 Mar	RR Br.	740 x 16	48	0	2	-	24	-
5 Mar	RR Br.	280	36	36	Damage	7	36	5.1
Totals	30 Bridges	-	226	361	18 approx.	50 approx.	12.5	7.2

The 10th Air Force's outstanding AZON results, as opposed to those in Europe, can be attributed to the considerably lighter AA defenses in the CBI, which permitted repeated passes by AZON-equipped B-24s, allowing them the luxury of dropping one guided bomb per bomb run. To deal with targets having heavier than normal AA defenses, however, 10AF routinely flew fighter bombers loaded with twenty fragmentation cluster bombs to deliberately attack AA batteries a few minutes before the B-24s carrying VB-1s arrived. However, 10AF operational planners did recognize and clearly state that in theaters having heavier air defenses, repeated passes with the VB-1 would have been impossible. By March 5, Japanese resistance in Burma was limited to pockets without outside supplies, and the arrival of the 1945 summer monsoon season sidelined the VB-1 in the 10AF once again. By the time the weather had cleared in August 1945, the war was over.

On April 21, 1945, AZON equipment was standardized and design frozen, and by May 5, the project was closed except for manufacture. A total of 15,271 AZONs were built and an additional order for 10,000 was canceled after V-J Day.

VB-2 SPAZON Bombs

The object of the SPAZON (SPin AZimuth ONly) or spinning AZON's program was to determine the dispersion between two VB-2 bombs released simultaneously. The only method that finally solved the AZON ballistics' problem was to allow the bomb to spin but still have some control over it. The advantages of the SPAZON bomb were to increase the bomb's performance probability, as one in five or six AZONS failed in some way to operate as anticipated. Therefore, if two bombs were dropped simultaneously, the probability of at least one performing correctly would be much better. Also, if enemy AA fire prevented more than one pass at the target, two bombs would be more likely to hit the target than just one. Work on anti-dispersion modifications by the Development Engineering Branch at Wright Field and Gulf Research and Development permitted the VB-1 to rotate for the first half of its fall, then become stabilized, and then be guided as before. There was an initial fifteen-second preset period of spin through 15,000 feet after which there was a three-second interval for stabilization with 1,200–1,500 feet left for azimuth control by the bombardier toward the target. Because of this spinning, the innate dispersion introduced by the asymmetric properties of the bomb were partially canceled and the dispersion pattern was substantially reduced. Basically, the VB-2 was a 2,000-pound version of the VB-1 using the identical gyros, radio, and battery as the VB-1. It differed in that it was larger, required a shorter flares, and stronger solenoids. It could be carried by any bomber equipped with 2,000-pound bomb racks.

There were two SPAZON programs, which varied considerably in content: one conducted by the Gulf Research and Development Company working under an NDRC contract, and called the Gulf Approach, and one by the AAF's Development Engineering Branch at Wright Field. Gulf's SPAZON development used RAZON bomb testing but never fully implemented or tested these on real bombs, whereas the

VB-2 SPAZON bomb. (*AAF*)

AAF used the AZON.

Gulf's RAZON testing placed a spin on the bombs after release then, after a time, applied control. Spinning tended to keep the bombs closer together immediately after release, after which cluster control (i.e. control the mean value of control on the bombs after the spinning action) was to be applied. However, Gulf did not continue work on this technique for SPAZON bombs as the company was engaged in other higher-priority projects.

Wright Field sent twenty VB-2s to Tonopah, Nevada, for tests during June 1944, with twelve long-flare SPAZONS being dropped from external racks on a B-17 as the short flares (which fit into the B-17 bomb bay) were unavailable and the VB-2s with long flares were too lengthy to be carried internally. The bombs were dropped together because a better estimate of control could be obtained by observing and photographing the parallel flight paths of the two bombs. Of the twelve bombs dropped in the test, eight performed satisfactorily for the full flight. The VB-2 successful anti-dispersion method required a time switch and linkage within the gyro case. At the end of the month, the Development Engineering Branch requested increased funding and that the project to be accelerated.

During February 6–16, 1945, twelve VB-2s were dropped as tests continued at Pinecastle AAB, Orlando, Florida. These tests also revealed the VB-2's potential and it was suggested that the anti-dispersion modification be incorporated into the VB design. However, making modifications after the bombs left the factory assembly lines would require retooling and retraining of workers to add the new components on the assembly line would cause delays in production and additional resources. The AMC found both solutions to be unsatisfactory, and the next 30,000 tail assemblies were to be produced without the anti-dispersion modification and the bomb remained an AZON type.

These test results concluded that the dispersion of the multiple release of two controlled bombs would not be very great, particularly in azimuth. However, if dual controls were applied, as would occur with RAZON bombs, the dispersion could increase. Therefore, it was recommended if the SPAZON project were to continue that tests be conducted with the RAZON bomb and to guide each bomb separately. The AAF AZON tests on the SPAZON project were the last to be performed and the project was closed out. Only 132 SPAZONs were produced, and although research continued through the end of the war, none were deployed in combat trials.

RAAZ

The Air Corps requested that the National Defense Research Committee undertake the development of controlled trajectory bombs at the end of December 1941. This very complex and multifaceted project was to be conducted under the sponsorships of the H.Q. Army Air Forces, Weapons Branch, Air Technical Service Command with MIT serving as project engineer of Controlled Bombs for the NDRC under contract with the Office of Scientific Research and Development. Gulf Research and Development Company was the Project Development Contractor.

The ACC specification requested that "the bomb be controlled in flight by a bombardier. Azimuth control was essential and ... range control highly desirable." In April 1942, the RAAZ (RAnge and AZimuth) bomb project was initiated, but several considerations caused the de-emphasis of the RAAZ with two co-ordinate control in favor of the one co-ordinate control AZON.

The early RAAZ developmental phase experiments utilized sand-filled 1,000-pound bomb casings attached to the square/cruciform AZON-type tail assembly that had controls on both axes, during which the bomb was to be controlled on the vertical and horizontal axes simultaneously. The rear shroud, termed the control shroud, had moveable surfaces that responded to control inputs for pitch and yaw or up-down and right-left. The displacement of these surfaces in flight produced aerodynamic forces on the bomb causing it to rotate from the reference provided by the directional gyro. Forward of the control shroud was the lift shroud that had been added to furnish a forward force when increased range was needed. The lift shroud would have been more effective if it were located nearer to the center of gravity (C.G.), but other factors caused it to be an added as an approximately 185-pound part of the tail assembly. These tests were to determine the response to control signals and oscillations, emphasizing the amount of intentional yaw, as well as to determine the amount free fall trajectory that could be deviated from using the control assembly. The primary purpose of these experimental tests was not for accuracy but to investigate the theory and mathematical data compared to the performance during the controlled portion of flight.

Following these initial tests, Ralph Wyckoff, project director, believed that the problem of roll stabilization by ailerons to be insurmountable when simultaneous pitch (range) and yaw (azimuth) control was utilized—the crux of RAAZ viability.

However, Gulf Research & Development found roll could easily be prevented if only either range or azimuth control were used. If there was a choice to be made, experts felt that azimuth (AZON) control was to be used as its design and development was simpler and it could be of more tactical use than a range-only bomb. A last consideration was that the AZON was easier to steer than the RAAZ, which was plagued with the problem of parallax. Because the eyes are in different positions on the head, each presents a different view simultaneously to gain depth perception and estimate distances to objects but can result in horizontal disparities in the apparent position of an object when viewed along two different lines of sight (i.e. looking at the positions of the hands of a clock from directly in front or from the side). This problem meant that the bombardier could not look along the bomb's trajectory and decide the probable point of impact. This occurred because the RAAZ fell virtually in the same forward motion as the aircraft, so the bombardier viewed the RAAZ as moving at an increasing distance almost directly below him. As the bombardier did not know the remaining distance the RAAZ had to fall at any given time in its trajectory, he had no direct method of determining the projected point of impact in the range co-ordinate. Parallax would be a continuing problem for the VB bomb series.

Gulf built six bombs controllable in both range and azimuth for AAF demonstrations at Muroc between June 23 and July 7, 1943. These bombs were controlled as AZONs and had fixed range control that relatively easily moved the bomb from right to left (azimuth) and paradoxically would demonstrate that the AZON was the viable weapon and so the AZON project was given priority, but the RAZON (Range and AZimuth ONly) design, known to the AAF as the VB-3, would be resurrected and assigned to Gulf Research & Development in favor of the RAAZ version.

RAZON

VB-3 and VB-4 RAZON

Generally, the RAZON consisted of a radio control package coupled to a standard AN-M65 1,000-pound bomb that was controlled manually by the bombardier who tracked the bomb visually with the aid of a flare in the bomb's tail. RAZON was similar to the AZON bomb, but instead of using the AZON cruciform type fins, either one or two octagon-shaped fins were used, and were adaptable to any standard bomb and could be installed similarly as the standard fins. The RAZON assembly had two gyros that controlled stabilization in flight, one in azimuth and one for range. Control was directed by a five-channel radio receiver (only four channels were used), which received a signal from the four-channel transmitter located in the mother aircraft, operating on a high-frequency carrier wave upon which was impressed audio frequencies. The four bands of the receiver were tuned to receive signals from corresponding bands of the transmitter. To provide the correct signal for control of the bomb, a control box with a stick similar to the control stick in the pilot's compartment was installed so that it was close to and convenient for the bombardier.

The results of the initial field tests were decidedly successful. The range control added to the azimuth control made it possible to hit short-length targets with a much greater accuracy than was possible with the AZON. The additional drag resulting from the controls was compensated for and further reduced the average error from 15,000 feet to approximately 45 feet, while the azimuth error from this altitude was generally less than 15 feet.

After these initial tests, RAZON was granted a high priority and Gulf continued to develop it into a number of separate models.

Mark I: Single rear-mounted shroud with an 11.5-inch-diameter central cylinder that contained the radio, gyro, and battery mounted in the forward half of the cylinder. The rudder and elevator surfaces were 2.5 × 12 inches and had a travel of 20 degrees in 0.5 seconds. There was an individual linkage to the ailerons from the solenoids. The servo motors moved at 6 rpm. It had no tail fuse cavity.

Mark Ia: Single rear-mounted shroud with a 12-inch-diameter central cylinder that contained the radio, gyro, and battery mounted in the forward half of the cylinder. The rudder and elevator surfaces were 3 × 12 inches and had a travel of 15 degrees in 0.5 seconds. There was a disc linkage common to all four ailerons. The servo motors moved at four rpm. It had a tail fuse cavity.

Mark II: Single shroud mounted near the front with a 12-inch-diameter central cylinder that contained the radio, gyro, and battery mounted in the rear half of the cylinder. The rudder and elevator surfaces were 3 × 12 inches and had a travel of 20 degrees in 0.7 seconds. The servo motors moved at four rpm. It had a tail fuse cavity.

Mark IIa: Same as the Mk. II except that the shroud was moved aft 2.125 inches. This model was tested and found to have low stability.

Mark III: Double shroud with the leading edge of the forward shroud extending beyond the forward end of the 12-inch central cylinder and with the trailing edge of the rear shroud extending beyond the rear end of the central cylinder. The rudder and elevator surfaces were 3 × 12 inches and had a travel of 20 degrees in 0.7 seconds. The radio, gyro, and battery were mounted in the forward half of the central cylinder. The servo motors moved at four rpm. It had a tail fuse cavity. This design never went beyond the design stage.

Mark IV: Double shroud with the trailing edge of the rear shroud flush with the rear end of the central cylinder and with an octagonal forward lift shroud and a 12-inch central cylinder. The radio, gyro, and battery were mounted in the forward half of the central cylinder. The rudder and elevator surfaces were 3 × 12 inches and had a travel of 15 degrees in 0.5 seconds. The servo motors moved at 4 rpm. It had a tail fuse cavity.

The models with a central lift cylinder and an octagonal tail shroud prevented the loading of the RAZON on to standard 1,000-pound bomb bay racks. Gulf then redesigned the VB-3, making the central lift cylinder part of the tail while continuing to maintain adequate stability and maneuverability. This redesigned tail shroud consisted of three sections: the tail section or control shroud had flaps in the horizontal and vertical surfaces of the octagon itself which acted as elevators and rudders, respectively to steer the bomb. Ailerons, called the lift shroud, were located

The single shroud tail appeared on the Mk. I, II, and IIa RAZON models. (*AAF*)

The double shroud tail appeared on the Mk. III and IV RAZON models. (*AAF*)

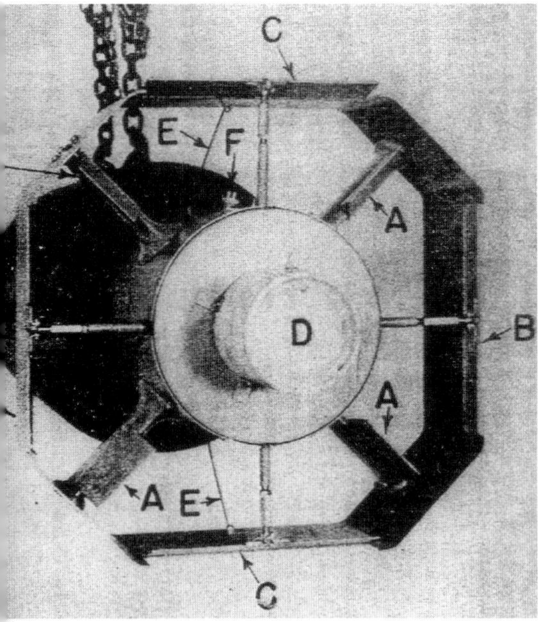

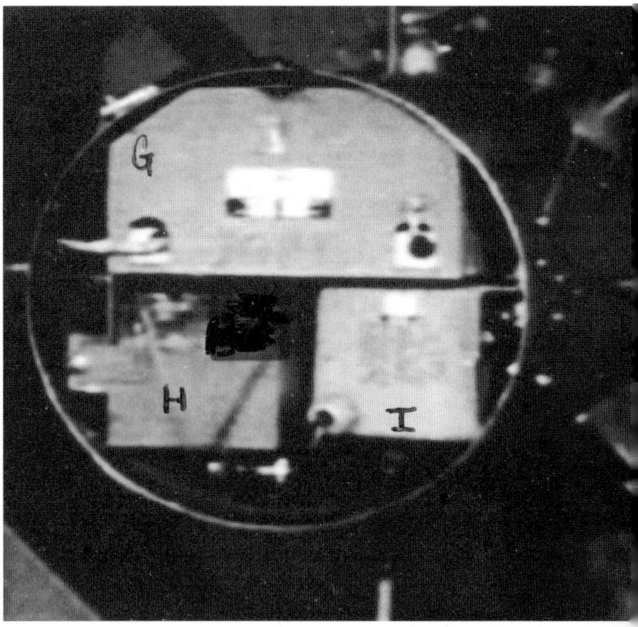

RAZON VB-3 Tail Assembly Legend:
A) Ailerons
B) Rudders
C) Elevators
D) Flare
E) Antenna
F) Arming Plug
G) Radio Receiver
H) 24-volt Battery
I) Gyroscope

on the 45-degree struts attaching the octagon to the bomb and were gyro-controlled to prevent rolling. The third component was the cylindrical section.

Neither the AZON nor the RAZON-guided weapons received much attention until the Luftwaffe successfully deployed the FX-1400 Fritz X vertical bomb (July 1943) and the Hs 293 glider bomb (August 1943) in combat. With the Fritz X, the Germans had overcome the chronic parallax problem that plagued guided weapon systems by having the bombardier first sail and then dive the bomb, while the controlling medium bomber went into a steep climb to its decrease speed. By using these maneuvers, the bombardier could direct the bomb so that it could eclipse the target during the last several seconds of its fall. Gulf tried several adaptations of the Luftwaffe method but decided that the AAF mother heavy bombers could not climb steeply enough to reduce speed without stalling.

The parallax problem made it exceedingly difficult for the bombardier to distinguish the bombs height above the ground when looking down on it from the mother aircraft. It was almost impossible for the bombardier to determine if the falling VB-3 was going to travel too long or too short and when to apply the proper downward or upward control. During February 1944, testing was conducted to remedy the parallax problem by using a second bomber positioned to the side of the dropped bomb to better observe its height and control the vertical axis. This method was quickly rejected by operational commanders, who already had to tolerate having one of their heavy bombers used deliver only one 1,000-pound VB-1 during a bomb run and would now have another bomber used to observe the delivery of that single RAZON.

At the time, renowned bombsight designer Carl Norden had the solution to the parallax problem, which was then developed into the Crab I bombsight by H. A. Van Dyke, first at the Franklin Institute, Philadelphia, and later at L. N. Schwien Engineering Company, Los Angeles, after he transferred there. The Crab I/Norden bombsight consisted of a small stationary silvered mirror that was inserted between the telescope objective lens and the target mirror to intercept a portion of the light from the target normally entering the telescope and to substitute for this portion was the light coming from the flare of the controllable bomb. To follow the trajectory of the bomb to its target, the RAZON used the standard AZON flares. In the Tonopah bombing range tests, red flares were considered very satisfactory, while at Wendover white flares were considered satisfactory. The Crab I allowed the bombardier to view and track both the target and the falling bomb simultaneously. Simultaneous tracking was essential since the bomb's horizontal speed fell off quickly after it was released from bomber, causing the bomb's trajectory to trail behind the bomber. The amount of trail was a dynamic of the bomber's groundspeed and altitude when the bomb was released and how long the bomb had been falling (i.e. the higher and faster the bomber flew, the more distance behind the bombers the bombs were when they struck the target). As a result, when the target was in front of the bomber, the falling bomb would be slightly behind. When dropping conventional bombs, once the bombardier had considered lateral drift due to winds, he could then more easily drop the bombs based upon time of fall calculations, but once the bombs were dropped, he was unable to further influence the bombs. When guiding the VB-3, the bombardier had to continuously measure the difference between the target's position and the relative position of the falling RAZON and apply corrections accordingly, which only could be achieved if the bombardier could see both at the same time.

When using the Crab attachment, the bombsight lens was calibrated to move to keep the crosshairs on the target as the bomber passed over it while the Crab mirror was fixed on the proper ballistic trajectory of the falling VB-3. Initially, the bombardier would see two widely separated images, which would gradually converge as the bomb fell and the bomber flew over the target. If the bombardier kept the falling bomb in the center of the mirrored reflection, the VB-3 would hypothetically hit the target. When the VB-3 struck the target, the bombsight lens would have rotated so that both the target and bomb images were one.

Studies by Gulf demonstrated that time of bomb fall (and range error) varied by as much as three seconds due to the amount of control required during the fall. To inform the bombardier of this error and to eliminate the necessity for using an average time of fall, a device known as JAG (Just Another Gadget) was designed, one by Gulf and the other by the Union Switch Company, with both being nearly identical. JAG, attached to the Crab I, was a small silvered mirror that projected the image of the falling RAZON's tail flare onto the bombsight's field of view. JAG caused a small rotation of the range rate synchronizing knob, up, right, or left control when applied to the bomb. The effect of this rotation was to delay the predicted time of coincidence of

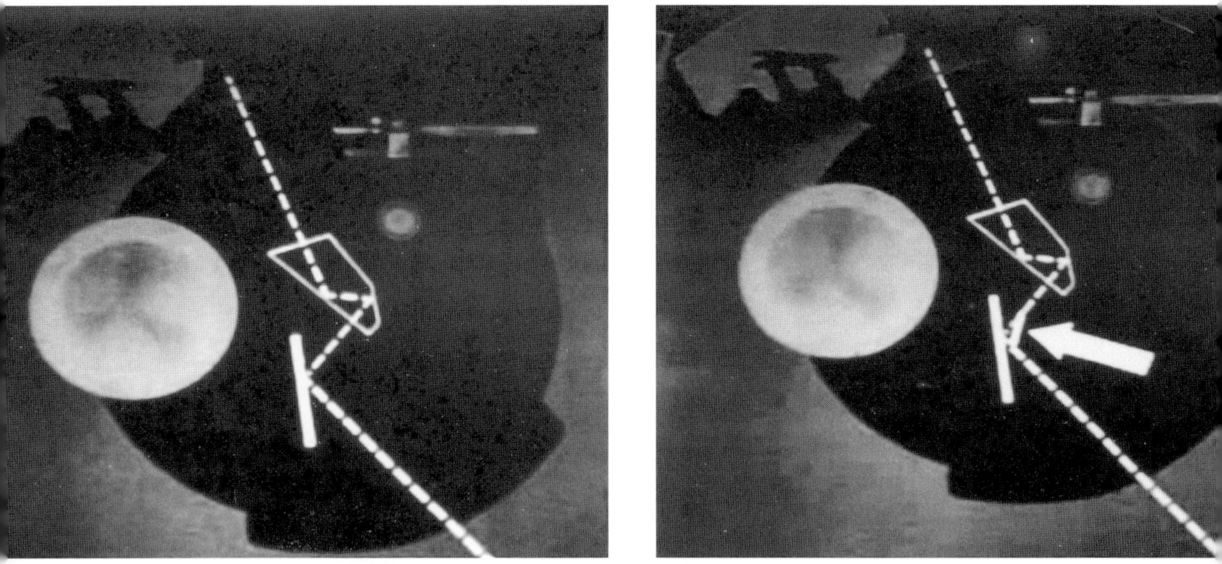

The Crab I Norden bombsight (right) solved the parallax problem in sighting the moving RAZON. It consisted of a second small stationary mirror that was inserted between the telescope objective lens and the target mirror (see the left standard Norden drawing) so as to intercept a portion of the light from the target normally entering the telescope and to substitute, for this portion, light coming from the flare of the RAZON. (*From AAF movie still*)

the target-tracking and Crab mirror angles. The operator would control the RAZON, keeping it lined up in the sight at the point where the bomb should strike and no further control would be necessary. Later the control mechanism was integrated into a one operator unit.

Feasibility tests at Eglin during February 1944 proved the RAZON idea to be too complicated as the system required separate frequencies for each tail assembly and the control surfaces were found to respond much differently in the vertical plane as opposed to the horizontal plane. Whenever either range or azimuth control was used, the falling bomb went into a spin, losing control. To solve this problem, Gulf attached two AZON VB-1s together by their tail assemblies at 90-degree angles, by which a left correction signal on the horizontal tail assembly would register as a LEFT whereas it would register as an UP on the tail assembly turned on its side. Significantly, the center of gravity of two bombs attached to each other varied so greatly between each different pair that no two responded the same way to radio control and bombardiers consistently over-controlled these bombs, causing them to roll into a spin or to tumble.

MIT submitted several anti-roll fin designs to Gulf's R&D Department to eliminate roll during simultaneous range and azimuth control. These new fin designs removed the square/cruciform AZON tail and added tail configurations that had circular symmetry, which were almost free of roll torque and could be steered by an auxiliary tiltable cylinder. These circular structures afforded much larger and far more responsive control surfaces than were available with the AZON tail. While the design was aerodynamically superior, it was larger and the tiltable control cylinder used excessive power for control.

Gulf modified the design by surrounding the bomb at its center of gravity with a cylindrical lifting shroud and installed an octagonal tail for steering and stabilization. Movable flaps serving alternately as elevators and rudders were placed on the tail surfaces. The downside to this change to the tail assembly was that it made the VB-3 considerably larger than the VB-1, resulting in fewer VB-3s that could be loaded inside a bomb bay. The B-17 could carry up to six VB-1s but could carry only two VB-3s; the B-24 was able to carry eight VB-1s but only four VB-3s; while the large B-29 could only carry eight VB-3s *versus* twelve VB-1s. But the fewer VB-3s carried would be acceptable if the VB-3 was found to be more accurate than the VB-1.

Until June 1944, the NDRC had directed most of the experimental effort on guided missiles, but at that time, the AMC was authorized to assist the NDRC in conducting tests. Capt. J. H. Evans was appointed the project engineer for the VB-3 and VB-4. In tests at Wendover during July 1944, two of six VB-3s landed within 45 feet of the target using the Crab 1 attachment and during tests between August 4 and September 9 at Tonopah, the Crab 1 further improved VB-3 accuracy. Although during these tests eight of nineteen VB-3s failed to guide due to radio and other malfunctions, the other eleven had an impressive mean impact of 3 feet to the right and 17 feet over in range when dropped from 15,000 feet. Capt. Evans stated that the VB-3 showed promise of becoming an invaluable weapon against special targets but was not yet ready for combat use. Evans recommended that changes necessary for mass production should be made so that adequate bombs could be available for final acceptance tests.

Drop tests of ninety-three VB-3s from a B-17 were conducted at Wendover from November 1944 to September 1945 to determine operational data on the Crab and JAG bombsight attachments. Twenty-five tail assemblies built by Gulf had aluminum shrouds, giving the tail assembly a total weight of 166 pounds. The remaining sixty-eight tail assemblies were built with steel shrouds as production models by Union Switch and Signal with a weight of 184 pounds. The anemometer fuse and flare arming device were also tested during these drop tests. Operational data on the JAG attachment obtained on these tests proved that it would considerably increase the overall accuracy of the VB-3 as it permitted the added time of fall of the bomb due to its maneuvering to alter bombsight settings and thus synchronized the computed time with the real time. This was not a critical factor for azimuth control, but for range, it had to be considered.

At the end of October 1944, the NDRC, at the urging of the Air Technical Service Command and the Navy BuOrd, placed a tooling contract for 150 RAZON assemblies with Union Switch and Signal for delivery by the end of January 1945, with fifty each to the AAF and Navy, while the remaining fifty would be used by the NDRC for continued testing. Meanwhile, Gulf was to supply twenty VB-3s for tests in November 1944. On October 28, Brig. Gen. H. M. McClelland, ACO, authorized Maj. Gen. Oliver Echols, Chief of Air Staff, Materiels and Services, to produce 3,000 RAZONs for the 20AF to ensure sufficient numbers were on hand for both future testing and initial operational needs. However, no quantity production had yet been authorized, although the ATSC had been directed to fund no more than $1 million for the first 1,000 RAZON tails and then produce 2,000 more. Although the service tests scheduled for November 1944, RAZON development were incomplete as the optimal shroud type, double or single; fusing; arming devices; and antennae had not yet been determined and modified designs were prepared.

The recommended design change to add a second shroud to increase the VB-3s maneuverability would cause unforeseen issues that caused critical delays in the VB-3 becoming operational. By appending a second octagonal shroud to the tail, the maximum azimuth correction range was increased from 1,600 feet to 2,660 feet when dropped from 15,000 feet. This was a substantial upgrade in guidance performance, offering the bombardier a 60 percent increase in azimuth correction capability. Unfortunately, this design change required redesign of many of the VB-3's other components, including the radio receiver and repositioning of the gyros, which all required additional time. While all these changes did increase range correction, they also made the VB-3 much less stable aerodynamically and more difficult to steer. This instability became so obvious in the test drops from November 6 to December 8, 1944 that the AMC recommended that the NDRC return to the original, single-shroud design.

On January 19, 1945, a military and civilian conference was formed to discuss the future of the RAZON program. The surplus AZON components were anticipated to be used for the continuation of the RAZON program but the radio receivers from the Signal Corps were delayed and the RAZON tails would not be ready before April 1945. Union Switch began retooling but the final design would not be available before mid-February, with an anticipated monthly total of 2,000 to 3,000 thereafter. However, Union Switch soon modified that optimistic estimate to 150 in July, 500 in August, and 1,000 per month thereafter.

Later tests of the Mk. Ia and Mk. IV RAZONs at Wendover proved both types to be satisfactory, although the Mk. IV with the improved double octagonal shroud was preferred because of its greater maneuverability. Additional tests of eighteen VB-3s in April were very satisfactory and determined that one RAZON-equipped bomber had the same operational effect as two bombers dropping less accurate conventional bombs. The RAZON's mean error was 150 feet in range and only 16 feet in azimuth, which was considerably better than the 580- and 384-foot errors when using standard 1,000-pound bombs dropped at the same time.

During May 1945, the Physical Vulnerability Section of the Joint Targeting Group listed targets considered most appropriate for the RAZON. Since only one RAZON could be guided per bombing run, certain targets were more suited to RAZON attacks. Generally, the targets were those that could be delineated by a square 200 feet on each side:

1. Any AZON target (e.g. bridges, causeways, roads, railway lines) but improvement over AZON was considered minimal except for short bridges or overpasses.
2. Power plants.
3. Industrial facilities such as steel mills, coke ovens, power houses, boiler houses, aluminum industry rectifier buildings.
4. Ships.
5. Gun positions.

Interestingly, the Joint Targeting Group study emphasized that if a bomber could carry eight 1,000-pound conventional bombs, the accuracy of RAZON against a given target must be at least eight times that of standard bombs before there was any advantage to the RAZON before it could be recommended and that the RAZON should be used only against those targets on which the percentage of RAZON hits was expected to be fifteen to twenty times the percentage of hits with standard bombs.

By early 1945, Union Switch and Signal was unable to meet its contracted quantity production because of all the VB-3 design changes. While these technical design issues were being resolved, the need for and interest in VB-3 guided weapons began to wane, particularly in the ETO, as after March 1945, bombing operations against a defeated and badly damaged Germany began to decrease. In the Pacific, the Tactical Air Forces showed little interest as their operations were quite successful using more conventional weapons. In the CBI, both the 10AF in Burma and the 14AF in China were definitely interested, but the summer monsoon season would be in progress before the VB-3 would be available for combat testing. The strategic 20AF using B-29s found that the previously unknown jet stream over Japan precluded the use of the VB-3 as it was virtually impossible for the bombardiers to calculate the effects of these high winds on the trajectory of the bombs as they fell. Also, the nature of Japanese targets, which, unlike the large, concentrated European industrial targets, were smaller and interspersed throughout built up areas in major cities, were very susceptible to the devastation of low-altitude incendiary bombs.

The heavy deck armor of capital ships rendered them almost invulnerable against attack with 1,000-pound GP bombs, while the weight of the armor piercing or semi-armor-piercing bombs made them difficult for RAZON control. Moreover, the pitching and yawing required for controlling the RAZON would reduce its striking velocity, which was the missile's anti-shipping strength; also, there was the high likelihood that the bomb would strike the ship obliquely, losing its armor-piercing power. The division requested Division 8, Explosives, to explore using the Munroe effect of a shaped charge (i.e. the reinforcement of shock waves in a concave, hollow end of a shaped charge, producing a resultant wave and concentrating the explosion along the axis of the charge) in a 1,000-pound GP bomb casing. This study and scale-model tests indicated that this bomb configuration could penetrate 11 inches of armor without loss of blast effect, which was confirmed during full-scale firing tests conducted at Dahlgren Naval Ordnance Station on April 1, 1945. The bomb was statically fired against the target, which consisted of one 11-inch and one 4-inch armor plate and three-quarter-inch mild-steel plates with each plate separated from the next by an 8-foot air space. Some unfused 100-pound bombs were stacked between the second and third mild steel plates. The jet from the bomb blast penetrated all the plates of the target and detonated several of the 100-pound bombs. Consideration was given to the design of a composite bomb having a shaped charge with a follow-through explosive charge. The problem of preventing detonation of the follow-through when the shaped charge was complex, and no solution was found before the end of the war.

Technical testing of the VB-3 continued through May 1945, when the development of the prototype was sufficient to freeze the design for standardization for tooling and production. In tests, the VB-3 production model had realized consistent impact errors of 150 feet in range and 16 feet in azimuth from combat altitudes of 22,000 feet. These figures were projected to improve as bombardiers became more experienced. On May 10, 1945, the NDRC recommended that the AAF Board begin tactical evaluations of the VB-3 and, if successful, an initial order of 3,000 was to be made and due in July. At V-J Day, 3,150 VB-3s were completed for shipment to the Pacific for tactical testing but were never used.

During the autumn of 1950, an Air Proving Ground Command technical team worked with the B-29-equipped 19BG based on Okinawa in testing 1,000-pound RAZON bombs against bridges during the Korean War. These RAZONs had been stored in crates somewhere in the CBI Theater since the end of the war and, consequently, were in poor condition, especially the tail assemblies, and had to be sorted the good from the bad and then refurbished and tested before operational use. During September through November 1950, only thirty RAZONs had been reconditioned for test drops, which were mostly unreliable but did show a 50 percent accuracy rate when functioning correctly. When the RAZON team returned to Wright Field to report these results to Gen. Chidlaw, he was disappointed in the condition of the remaining RAZONs and the effort required to restore them into operational condition and decided to terminate the project.

Advanced RAZON Bombs

The VB-5 through VB-8 VB-series were true RAZON vertical bombs, while the VB-9 through VB-12 were medium-angle ROC system bombs. Of these, only the infrared-seeking VB-6 reached the prototype stage before the war ended.

VB-5

The VB-5 was essentially a VB-3 equipped with a light-seeking homing device, which was small was enough to be installed in the nose of the VB-5 and could direct the bomb to a flare previously dropped on the intended target by a pathfinding aircraft. The VB-5 used the same simple, rugged, easily-produced light contrast seeker that was used on the GB-5 glide bomb. Like the GB-5, the VB-5 was ineffective against strategic targets, but under specific circumstances, it could have been used against targets that were in complete contrast with their background such dams, large bridges, and maritime targets against the surrounding sea. Since the VB-5 was only marginally effective against industrial targets, it did not interest AAF operational commanders. Difficulties with the light-seeking device and low priorities kept its development in the experimental stage and the VB-5 project was canceled in June 1944, at the same time as the VB-7 and VB-8 projects.

In October 1944, the VB-5 project was briefly re-evaluated when the possibility of using light-seeking VB-5s to track and follow the flare of radio-controlled VB-1s or VB-3s was considered. This would allow a bomber to drop one radio-controlled VB-1 or VB-3 bomb that would be followed by a string of 1,000-pound, self-guiding

VB-5s. However, this technique was impracticable at the time due to the ballistics of falling bombs. If the VB-5 was to track the flare of the radio-controlled bomb released earlier, its light-seeker would have had to look down and aft, which was beyond contemporary technology; the project was shelved.

VB-6 Felix

Soon after the formation of the NDRC in late June 1940, Dr. Karl Compton, prominent physicist and president of MIT (1930–1948), became head of Division D, which was responsible for gathering a group of academic and industrial engineers and scientists that would mainly investigate radar, fire control, and thermal radiation. Compton appointed Dr. Alan Bemis of MIT as chairman of the newly created NDRC Section D-4 to examine the many proposals of target detecting devices submitted by inventors and decide which could be beneficial and could be made operable. During the D-4's first meeting in December 1940, there was discussion of installing a homing device in the high-angle bomb but other more demanding projects required attention.

It would not be until the end of 1942, after Division 5 was organized, that more attention could finally be devoted to a vertical bomb with a homing device to be designated as the VB-6 Felix. Because Felix relied on infrared to detect and home on targets at night, it was this cat-like ability to see in the dark that gave the weapon its name, after the then popular Felix the Cat cartoon character.

Division 5 discovered through experience that a guided missile was a complex mechanism comprised of many interrelated parts and that the design of any one component affected and was affected by the design of any other. Only those missiles that were designed as a unit rather than assembled from separate components were ever successful in the field. Nevertheless, components that showed promise and possibility of utilization in combat required investigation. The exploration of several similar lines was necessary before a decision could be made to determine which should be continued and which abandoned. Section 5.5 was the sponsor for the subsidiary projects on components.

The Felix consisted of a standard 1,000-pound AN-M65 bomb or M-44 GP bomb with a metallic bolometer (an instrument for detecting and measuring radiation such as visible light, and infrared and ultraviolet radiation) heat-seeker located in the nose compartment and a gyro stabilization control servo mechanism operating the control surfaces in both range and azimuth located in the tail compartment.

A false nose was attached to the Felix's front end by the nose-fuse thread. It contained a scanning system to detect thermal targets and to transform the heat signal to an amplified electric signal.

Felix Nose Assembly Component: Manufacturer
Commutator and Speed Regulator: Harvey Radio Laboratory
Six-Volt Battery: Willard Storage Battery
Bolometer and Tubes: Cambridge Thermionic and Eppley Laboratories
Mirrors: Polaroid
Scanning Motors: Electric Motor Corporation

"Felix" VB-6 heat-seeking bomb. (*NMUSAF*)

A false tail, mounted by a fin-lock thread, housed servomotors that operated the elevators and rudders in response to the electric signals developed in the nose. In addition, the tail contained a twin gyro unit, one free and one rate gyro, which controlled the ailerons to maintain the fixed position of the missile with respect to the roll axis.

Felix Tail Assembly Component: Manufacturer
Servo Motors: White-Rodgers
Gyroscopes: Schwien Engineering
24-volt Batteries: Willard Storage Battery
Kickoff Switches and Plugs: Union Switch and Signal

Of the two types of tails developed for the VB-6, the cruciform was preferred, although tests seemed to indicate the octagonal shroud could be controlled most successfully. The accuracy of aim and the short interval of fall compensated for the missile's lack of maneuverability due to its small aerodynamic surfaces. Felix had an estimated range of 10,000 to 15,000 feet with a minimum extent of control of 2,000 feet during a 15,000-foot drop.

After collaborating closely with Section D-3 on the high-angle bomb, Section D-4 was to be responsible for the detector. Shortly after the reorganization of NDRC in December 1942, the Felix contract was assigned to Section 5.5 while Gulf Research was to be supervised by Section 5.2. Fortunately, John Strong at the California Institute of Technology (CIT) and later Harvard had studied target discrimination and guided Dr. Bemis and his colleagues in the basic precepts of high-angle bomb homing guidance that had been established for the Felix high-angle bomb.

Of the two types of tails developed for the VB-6, the cruciform tail was preferred, although tests seemed to indicate the octagonal shroud could be controlled most successfully. (*NMUSAF*)

The scanning system, generally, consisted of an optical bolometric assembly, which scanned the terrain in a field of 10-degree radius approximately centered on the point where the bomb would fall with no further control added. The received heat measured by the bolometer while scanning opposite half-fields was compared, and the missile was directed toward the half-field radiating the greater heat. Two channels provided one pair of half fields in the range sense and another pair in the azimuth sense. The bolometer requirements for the thermosensitive element in the Felix system were to be high-sensitivity, freed from microphonics, and low time constant. Thermopiles* were tested but found to be inferior to bolometers, although General Motors, in an investigation sponsored by the AAF, was reported to have had some success with infrared detectors of this type. Many bolometer types were tested and the pure-metal nickel or gold type were most suitable. The gold bolometers functioned effectively in drop tests but were less well-suited to manufacture than the nickel strip bolometers developed at MIT. (*A thermopile is an electronic device that converts thermal energy into electrical energy. It is composed of several thermocouples connected usually in series.)

In the instant after the bomb cleared the bomb bay, its flight was horizontal, moving toward the horizon. It was only after several seconds before the bomb nosed over enough for the bomb's roll axis to point toward the target. The bomb's control mechanism included a time switch that kept the elevators and rudders locked in neutral until the bomb had descended to a point where the axis of scan intersected the ground near the target, which, for a drop from 15,000 feet, would be at about

The Bemis infrared heat-seeking bolometer head manufactured by Cambridge Thermionic and Eppley Laboratories was installed in the VB-6 nose. (*AAF*)

10,000 feet. Transverse lift was provided by the missile body itself by the same method as the AZON and RAZON. However, the missile body was not an ideal airfoil and a substantial angle of attack had to be applied to develop sufficient transverse acceleration to correct errors of aim or to follow the maneuvers of an evasive target. To accomplish this, the scanning system was mounted on gimbals and connected by cables with the rudders and elevators to align the axis of scan more nearly with the tangent to the flight path.

By May 1943, Felix demonstrated promise and the NDRC chose to issue contracts to develop and build 240 preproduction bomb bodies by mid-May 1944, with forty to be experimental models to be used in field tests in mid-May 1944. The NDRC awarded prime contracts to the Remington Rand Company of Bridgeport, Connecticut, for 100 complete shroud units; to the Norton Company of Worchester, Massachusetts for 100 cruciform tail units; to the Fairchild Camera and Instrument Company of New York for 140 more assemblies of which 100 would be used in Norton's tail assemblies and forty with tail assemblies made by Gulf Research; and to General Instrument of Elizabeth, New Jersey, for 100 amplifiers for use only with the Remington units. Fairchild and Remington were responsible for final assembly of the units manufactured by them. Gulf Research, which had previous experience in developing the RAZON bomb and the Heat Research Laboratory of MIT, were to serve as advisors during manufacture and organize testing.

In preparation for testing, Gulf configured their octagonal-tail bomb and confirmed that it had adequate stability and maneuverability to transport a homing device such as their homing device, which had undergone extensive flight tests over Boston and its harbor area. After much effort but on schedule, the Gulf bombs were equipped with automatic controls and servo systems to utilize the commands from the head, six complete Felix units were approved for drop tests.

During early January 1944, the six completed Gulf VB-6 photoelectric target-seeking bombs were sent to Eglin for flight tests. After the first drop indicated that the normal range target was an inadequate heat radiator, another target was constructed by clearing an 800 by 800-foot-square area surrounded by scrub undergrowth. Of the six bombs dropped from 15,000 feet, two failed to stabilize in roll and went out of control into serious spins, one narrowly missing Wright Field Representative, Lt. Col. A. Nyman. Three homed or tried to home on the target but went off track. One made a successful homing flight landing about 60 feet from the target center.

However, filmed records showed that these results were not as dismal as first indicated as the three bombs, which did not home on the intended targets only homed on other targets because, at launching, the human controller allowed other targets to come into the eye of the seeker, which was unable to distinguish the specific desired target. The two spin failures were easily correctable as they were due to a gyro malfunction that caused the bombs to oscillate and spin. The B-23 control bomber was limited in space and during the bombing run a crew member inadvertently stepped on the rubber tubing connecting the bomber's air supply to Felix's gyros causing them not to spin.

When these revised results were reported to Washington, they were sufficiently encouraging to solicit the persuasive support of the Air Forces communication's officer, who had been assigned the additional responsibilities of acting as senior liaison officer for the division. These revised test results were brought to the attention of Brig. Gen. H. M. McClelland, director of Technical Services, H.Q. AAF, who proposed a high-priority target that seemed suitable for Felix. At this time, Allied intelligence had discovered the fixed, well-camouflaged launching ramps for the German V-1 buzz bomb in northern France. These ramps used diesel engines and air compressors, which, it was anticipated, could be a sufficient source of heat to make Felix an effective weapon against them. McClelland ordered a crash procurement program to be completed in early May, only four months away. McClelland granted the NDRC funding and personnel for 240 VB-6 prototypes for continued testing and let contracts to Fairchild Camera and Instrument for bomb head manufacture, General Instrument for electrical component manufacture, and Remington-Rand and Norton for tail production. The NDRC accepted the project, although it undoubtedly understood that these targets might be marginal and that the chances of proving a combat design, even within a year were improbable. By the summer of 1944, the Felix's V-1 buzz bomb offensive was no longer viable, as the ramp sites had been overrun by the Allied armies. However, McClelland's order to accelerate production had begun, but the bomb's oscillation problem had been causing some concern, and Gulf continued to be undecided about the relative merits of the cruciform VB-1 AZON tail that permitted better stowage inside bombardment aircraft *versus* the VB-3 octagonal tail for the RAZON bomb.

In a series of tests at Tonopah during October 1944 using forty of the first Felix prototype bombs equipped with both tail types, cruciform and octagonal, results showed that the Felix bombs with the cruciform-type tail dropped from between 10,000 and 25,000 feet went into a severe spin and were less controllable, forcing Gulf to grudgingly decided that there was no expectation of the cruciform tail functioning. As a result, the 100 cruciform tails ordered from Norton were canceled while Remington-Rand's 100 octagonal units continued to be scheduled for combat use. Gulf's accelerated efforts on aerodynamics determined Felix's external structure and the production model was basically similar to the Eglin model, but its size had to be increased to allow room for the standard 1,000-pound GP bomb placed between its head and tail.

The initial test target consisted of aluminum foil nailed to panels as a cross displayed on the desert floor. The arms of the cross were 40 feet by 100 feet, the total circumscribing square being 240 feet by 240 feet. The intent was to have the bombs home on the sun's reflection from this foil target, which proved to be completely insufficient. While the signal from the sun's reflection was very large, tests could only be flown in the middle of the day, when the elevation of the sun was about the same as the bomb after falling to an altitude of 10,000 feet from a release point of 15,000 feet. The aircraft had to fly directly into the sun for the scanner to receive an effective reflection. The greatest disadvantage, however, was that in mid-day, the hot desert air was so turbulent that the bombardier was unable to get a good approach run and eight drops against this target had to be aborted.

A second target was constructed, consisting of 100 rectangular 30-square-foot steel plates. These plates were mounted so that they inclined 30 degrees from the vertical and were heated to a very dull red heat with three oil burners (orchard heaters) per plate. Eleven Felix bombs were dropped at this target with seven having electrical malfunctions, but four made successful homing flights, scoring misses of 100 to 300 feet. The design then underwent an engineering analysis. Longer rudders and elevators were installed, producing a larger angle of attack and permitting the elimination of a problematic lift shroud. The control relays were redesigned and contained in a hermetically sealed case. The rudder deflection speed was reduced about 30 percent to remove the range of forced oscillation; the feedback coupling mechanism was simplified; and the bias device to provide parabolic thinking was introduced.

The Tonopah test results continued to be unsatisfactory, principally due to lack of manufacturing quality control on Felix components, which was the natural outcome of any accelerated, high-priority developmental program. Frederick Jennings had been engaged to perform a comprehensive reanalysis of all the details of the records of the drop tests and survey flights of first Eglin tests. He found that much of the effort that had been made attempting to increase the speed of response of the controls to a target signal had been misdirected. Instead, to eliminate large-amplitude bomb oscillations, it would be essential to institute some time lag. Many factors would have to be reconsidered to establish the optimum adjustments for many interrelated factors. These issues made it clear that the Felix crash program had been an imprudent decision and that the Felix project should be restored to laboratory status, giving it an opportunity to refine a design whose basic fundamentals were sound and whose specifics required extensive modifications to create an operational Felix. Staging field tests would require hundreds of bombs with the unknown prospect that satisfactory results could be achieved, so, instead, the Felix testers instituted a test table on which all control factors could be simulated without the destruction of a bomb drop. An intricate assembly of gears, pulleys, wires, etc., activated a succession of pens that drew an accurate record on charts of the operation of relays, elevators, rudders, bomb body, and velocity vector, as the target was moved. This systematic examination of all the variables revealed the necessary changes that were incorporated into the production model.

Meanwhile, the homing devices continued to encounter successive problems, which further delayed the Felix project. The target discriminator was still incomplete, although MIT had individually built the seekers used in testing; their facility was limited in capacity and standardization was necessary. Also, a redesign of the unreliable vacuum tubes was necessary. During a conference sponsored by the Vacuum Tube Development Committee, Saul Dushman, head of the General Electric Research Laboratory, offered to make these facilities available for an analysis of the problem. With the assistance of A. J. Kling, Dushman quickly redesigned the necessary vacuum tubes. Russian-American Dushman's textbook *Scientific Foundations of Vacuum Technique* is a classic embracing vacuum design principles and its later editions are still in use today. By the end of October, the VB-6 design had been standardized so that aircraft installation testing was begun to determine how many could be carried and what modifications to each bomber would be required. These tests determined the B-24 could carry a maximum of four VB-6s and four standard 1,000-pound bombs, the B-29 eight but no standard bombs, the B-17 two and two 1,000-pound bombs, the B-25 one and one 1,000-pound bomb, and the A-26 none. Finally, tactical testing was ordered by the Army at Eglin Field and Remington-Rand was contracted to produce 1,000 units.

Meanwhile, MIT and Wright Field studied target suitability for assorted Felix-seekers and the Navy BuOrd also conducted an elaborate study of the sensitivity of various seeking devices towards land and marine targets. Additional target analysis was also carried out in October 1944 using the improved Bemis infrared-seeker. These tests demonstrated this IR seeker could be best used at night against landlocked, heat-emitting targets, such as steel mills and factories, as at night the heat of the sun would not be radiating off the surrounding land and adjacent buildings that would interfere with target acquisition. Targets located in coastal areas, particularly navy vessels and docks, could be attacked during daytime because the cooler surrounding water usually caused these targets to be obvious.

By late 1944, development of a seemingly reliable redesigned weapon had progressed once more to the pre-production testing stage and tests at Tonopah had twelve of sixteen test VB-6s fall within 200 feet of the target. These successes relieved many of the previous anxieties and the Felix supporters moved ahead with renewed motivation. The NDRC anticipated placing the first 125 prototype VB-6s into their first production run by early January 1945 at an estimated average per unit cost of

$2,500, which would actually increase to $4,000 per unit due to cost overruns and delays before the first production run. In order to keep the VB-6 Project viable, the NDRC requested that an additional $200,000 be provided to pay for the design costs. To begin production, the AAF had to complete VB-6 tactical testing and obtain approval. The NDRC recommended that the VB-6 to be sent to Eglin for tactical evaluation as soon as possible and that an initial production run of at least 1,000 units be begun. This production run recommendation needed to be completed by December 15 to avoid a five- or six-month delay and to prevent Fairchild, Offner, Remington, and other subcontractors from moving on to other projects and releasing trained workers.

It was not until the last week of December 1944 that the AAF Tactical Center at Eglin received twenty-seven upgraded VB-6 prototypes for tactical evaluation testing. Each of their components was thoroughly examined by NDRC engineers and AAF technicians before testing. These tests, which would encompass several months, began with demonstration for the Air Force Board that would later completely control the VB-6 Project. There were initial problems concerning the move from desert Tonopah to semitropical Florida, such as the effect of the increased humidity on instrumentation and target identification. Due to the high humidity, the thermal guidance varied so much at a range of altitudes and on different days that it was almost impossible for the testers to determine whether the Felix homed on the intended target. At Eglin, because, unlike Tonopah, where a target was set out in the middle of the desert, the intended Eglin target was surrounded by vegetation, which tempted the homing eye of the seeker to stray from its target. A search for a unique target for the Felix to head unerringly toward was necessary and finally Channel Key, an isolated small island in the Florida Keys, provided a good contrast to the surrounding water and would provide a unique target. While this target identification was relatively weak in comparison with recently surveyed industrial targets, it was believed that its contrast with the surrounding water would make it a satisfactory target. Permission for its use was obtained, but not without difficulty, as the Key was located only about a mile from the Key West Overseas Highway. From December 27 to January 13, 1945, twenty-three sand-filled dummy bombs were dropped from a B-17 at 20,000 feet and four more from 15,000 feet. Standard 1,000- or 100-pound bombs, to act as spotters for each Felix, were also dropped (in trail to prevent them from getting in front of the Felix and becoming a target for the Felix's seeker). But after testing, only nine of these twenty-seven handmade bombs were considered to have passed the testing standards. The failures were attributed to seeker head guidance, flare non-igniting, and battery charge problems. The Felix batteries had to power the seeker-head, the stabilizing gyroscopes, and the servomotor flight-control apparatus. Battery charge had been a problem with the two batteries during the VB-1 tests and now had occurred with some of the ten batteries in the VB-6, which held only a low charges or were completely dead. The low batteries caused the Bemis seeker-head to malfunction, caused poor aileron and rudder responses to seeker-head inputs, and underpowered the stabilizing gyros. The Felix's automatic-guidance system was unable to recognize and compensate for weak control inputs from the drained batteries. The excessive Florida humidity seriously affected the bomb's instruments but, relocating testing to Florida was beneficial in that these moisture problems were discovered then rather than in operational use in the damp tropical Pacific combat theaters.

Before the next trials in February 1945, the erratic original handmade Felix tail assemblies were replaced by the more accurate bombs manufactured by Remington and better results were obtained. Thirty-one individual Felix releases were made with twenty successful homing flights landing on the target after making evident corrections. Of the eleven failures, five were due to failure of the bomb shackles to release or to the bombardier's neglect to energize the warmup circuit to bring the amplifier tubes up to temperature before the release. One impressive test occurred when eighteen Felix bombs were released simultaneously from a formation of nine B-17s flying in loose line abreast in elements of three. Fourteen bombs homed well, their impacts forming three distinct clusters corresponding to three observed heat centers on the target. During the Eglin tests, ninety bombs were dropped on the island from altitudes varying from 8,000 to 28,000 feet. Corrections by the Felix homing mechanisms produced hits on the island by bombs whose free fall points varied as far as 9,000 feet from the straight-line course to the center of the Key.

By April 1945, the production VB-6s continued to deliver acceptable results causing both the NDRC and the AAF Board to proclaim the Felix ready for acceptance trials, with the NDRC recommending that the VB-6 be slowly introduced into combat. The first VB-6 shipments were ready from Remington in May, and by June, an agenda for the first 1,000 units was scheduled: 875 to the AAF for storage at the 829th Specialized Depot, Gadsden, Alabama; 100 to the Navy; fifteen to the AAF Board; and ten for training.

The Navy Bureau of Ordnance had also been interested in Felix and obtained bombs and conducted a few tests with moderate success against a ship anchored near Cape Cod. Then, for better tactical evaluation, with more bombs, the Navy had instituted a more elaborate program under Cdr. S. S. Ballard of the Bureau of Ordnance to measure the signals obtained by various devices from both land and ship targets, in Lake Michigan, off Traverse City, Michigan. The end of the war and the Navy's involvement with the Bikini A-bomb tests prevented completion of this project.

On August 9, 1945, the day of the Nagasaki A-Bomb mission, the 20AF requested that 300 VB-6s of the 1,000 on order be shipped to Guam for experimental combat testing. By late August, the Felix VB-6 contract was 95 percent completed, but the war ended with the weapon continuing to be officially considered an experimental prototype, despite the project's teething problems having been eliminated. At the end of October 1945, the Engineering Division requested that the 739 completed stored Felix units and the eighty-two spare tail units be reserved for experimental purposes. The NDRC assigned any records, test results, and equipment to the Special Weapons Units, but today there are no records of any testing. Post-war interest soon diminished as the U.S. military became preoccupied with the atomic bomb tests at Bikini and other potentially more destructive projects. The engineering characteristics and specifications of the equipment were (only) reviewed in 1948 by the recently independent USAF, which was seeking more effective methods to guide air-to-surface missiles carried by strategic bombers.

In conclusion, the Felix VB-6 was America's first homing bomb to be tested, with the testing finally eliminating problems until Felix was affirmed as acceptable and reliable to become the only homing bomb to attain the status of a theater request. An elaborate target survey had shown that there were many areas in Japanese-held islands that well-suited to Felix attacks. The war ended too soon for combat verification of Felix proficiency and to vindicate the aspirations of its supporters.

VB-7 and VB-8

The VB-7, with a 1,000-pound warhead, and VB-8, with a 2,000-pound warhead, were early TV-seekers with windstream-operated vanes or ears to aim the TV camera into the direction the bomb was aimed. The project experienced major technical problems in the experimental stage and was discontinued by the NDRC on June 1, 1944. The main problem was that, unlike GBs, these VBs dove very steeply on the target at near transonic speeds, which greatly reduced the time the bombardier had to make the necessary course corrections. The orthicon television transmitter and camera system provided a poor-quality image that made it difficult for the bombardier to distinguish the fast-moving target against its background, especially when transmitted at the steep closing angle.

VB-9 ROC I

The VB ROCs were purportedly named after the large mythical bird that destroyed Sinbad's ship in *The Arabian Nights* by dropping boulders on it. The Douglas VB-9, the first of the ROC series, was a radar-directed, specialized 1,100-pound armor-piercing or 1,000-pound general-purpose bomb mounted on four symmetrical cruciform wings and a tail with four fins spaced midway between the wings in a cruciform array. The wings were for guidance, not lift, as the ROC I fell on a mostly ballistic course rather than gliding to the target. In other ROC series models, this original wing design was replaced by a more compact circular airfoil

The ROC I's radar guidance was selected over TV due to its all-weather capability. The radar transmitter was installed in a controlling aircraft; the receiver was located in the bomb's nose; and the radar image would be sent to the control aircraft, where the bombardier would view the image and send radio commands back to the bomb to guide it to its target. The VB-9 was a medium angle bomb of 30 degrees to 60 degrees glide angle from horizontal but even a minimal 30-degree angle was found to be too great for the radar to acquire the target. The radar energy from this active homing (SRB) type system could not discern the target from the surrounding ground clutter, making it impossible to discriminate the target against the background interference called noise. This low-priority project was canceled in early 1945, after the radar-seeker was found to be unusable in experimental testing.

The body of the original ROC had four large wings set in a cruciform pattern, with the four smaller tail fins also forming a cross and set to bisect the angle formed by the two wings in that quadrant. (*AAF*)

VB-10 ROC

Initially, a paltry $30,000 was granted to the Douglas Aircraft Company to begin the VB-10 project, which was would eventually consume $2.5 million distributed to all contractors from late 1941 and on through the next four years. During the preliminary design stage, five different means of guidance were considered: direct-sighting, radar, heat-seeking, light-seeking, and television (MIMO).

During November 1941, E. L. Bowles, then secretary and member of Section D-5, proposed that radar could be used in guiding a bomb and that the MIT Radiation Laboratory's AGL beam-following radar system developed under Louis Ridenour and David Griggs could be modified to be made to fly down the radar beam. Physicist Ridenour was instrumental in the American development of radar, particularly the development of airborne Mickey microwave radar, which permitted bombing through clouds (BTO). The NDRC commissioned Douglas Aircraft, Los Angeles, to conduct the research and development of the airframe under the direction of Frank Collbohm and thus ROC was initially designated as the Los Angeles Project and then the Douglas Project. Wolfgang Klemperer of the Douglas Santa Monica Engineering Laboratory designed and developed the airframe, which was designated as the X-ROC. Klemperer, a 1924 German *émigré* to America, was recruited by Douglas in 1936, which recognized his special talent for instrument design. During World

War II, he was engaged in the development of optical and other instrumentation as the head of Douglas Instrumentation Research Group, which developed into the company's guided missile division. After the war, Klemperer became one of America's preeminent missile scientists overseeing the Nike, Sparrow, Honest John, and Thor missile programs.

Once the reorganization of NDRC occurred in December 1942, Section 5.4 assumed the supervision of the ROC project. The new ROC NDRC team consisted of missile wizards Jerome Hunsaker and Hugh Dryden, with H. H. Spencer, as technical aide. As members of the division, Louis Ridenour and, later, Alfred Loomis provided liaison with the radar factions. Hunsaker, like Dryden, was a major force in American aeronautical engineering as Chief of Design in the Navy's BuAer from 1916 to 1926. He returned to Alma Mater, MIT, in 1936, chairing the departments of Aeronautical and Mechanical Engineering until he retired in 1951. He was a member of the National Advisory Committee for Aeronautics from 1938 to 1958, serving as chairman from 1941 to 1957.

The ROC VB-10's body was similar to the VB-9, having four large wings set in a cruciform pattern with the four smaller interdigitated tail fins also forming a cross (X) set to bisect the angle formed by the two wings in that quadrant. The first ROCs were designed to carry a 500-pound warhead in a streamlined shell. For the ROC to be controlled at the required glide angle of approximately 45 degrees, it was necessary for it to have wings that provided adequate lift. A series of wind-tunnel tests determined the feasibility of an X-wing model, in which lift could be created in any direction normal to the bomb axis without having to bank and would fly at zero angle of attack (e.g. the missile always pointed at the target). The success of this design required precise consideration to aerodynamic forces but, ultimately, the zero angle of attack would be a goal rather than an actuality. Gyroscopically operated wing flaps functioned as ailerons that were activated by individual servo motors to maintain the bomb's rate of roll within acceptable low limits and to control flight. Initially ROC was to fly down a radar beam, but due to several reasons—mainly to allow a greater freedom of action for the controlling aircraft—this was quickly altered to radar-homing.

When the first air frame models were available for drop tests, the radar equipment was not available in expendable quantities. Consequently, alternative plans were made to substitute a photoelectric homing eye as an interim device for the airframe testing as the photoelectric cell used at night with a flare as a target was a very dependable method. A four-quadrant photoelectric cell was used for locating the target direction, which had required further development effort to produce a high-quality cell. To create a satisfactory cell required expert glass blowing, which was beyond the ability of the first contractor selected. The Farnsworth Television and Radio Corporation, Fort Wayne, Indiana, with its experience in building television receiver tubes, agreed to accept the project despite its very busy production schedule. O. S. Duffendack, Chief of Section 16.4 and electron microscope pioneer, obtained the release of Farnsworth shop time to complete photocells for first nine light-seeking Douglas ROCs.

Above left: Jerome Hunsaker: A major force in American aeronautical engineering, he served as chairman of the National Advisory Committee for Aeronautics from 1941 to 1956. (*USN*)

Above right: ROC 00 had the cruciform wings and tail of the original ROC replaced by a set of ingenious circular lifting shrouds. The payload of the 00 was a 1,100-pound or 1,600-pound armor-piercing bomb. The forward compartment contained the homing device and the aft for the power supply. (*AAF*)

After undergoing comprehensive laboratory, wind-tunnel, ground, and airborne tests, these nine X-ROCs were tested in June 1943, with four homing satisfactorily but five suffered the malfunction of some component, exposing the necessity for additional information to be collected by further test drops. Farnsworth, however, objected that it could not continue to overload their research shop with the fabrication of additional photo cells. To remedy this predicament, Section 5.5 sought a new establishment to develop a new and easier method to build and use photoelectric scanner and contacted Henry Blackstone and Curtis Hillyer, who had been occupied for the past three years on a photoelectric control for various missiles. Originally, their photocell had been devised to control anti-aircraft projectiles but later, with the backing of Fairchild Camera and Instrument Company, it was applied to GBs for Wright Field. Fairchild found it to be relatively simple to transform its device into a control for ROC. Fairchild designed, built, and assisted in installing six photoelectric eyes for ROC that used a light-interrupter in front of a standard photoelectric cell. By using these photocells, further valuable information was obtained for refining ROC operation.

During the entire Douglas ROC series, there was a need for an intermediate amplifier and decoder to collect data from the target-seeking eye and decode it into commands to the control surface. This undertaking necessitated substantial electronic development, and Section 5.5 coordinated a contract with the Bendix Aviation's Pacific Division. Models of the Bendix equipment were to be made and delivered in time for each of the different ROC versions: two for photocell eyes, one for the radar-homing, and one for the radio-controlled type. During the model development, Bendix had been in continuous liaison with Douglas engineers. For the radio-controlled type, W. S. Leitch developed two different systems to allow transmission over the radio link of signals to indicate the amount of rudder motion desired.

By December 1943, most of the design problems had apparently been resolved and Douglas was instructed to develop an X-ROC (X=crossed wings) design, suitable to carry the 1,000-pound GP bomb and the Zenith RHB radar receiver. The MIT Field

During late 1944, there were continual tests to resolve ROC 00 problems, particularly in the various seeking systems. The television tests were progressing slowly and concurrent tests were made using the direct-sight/radio-link while MIMO testing continued into the summer of 1945. The photo shows a B-17 conducting load tests with a ROC mounted on the fuselage centerline aft of the chin turret and another under the starboard wing between the inboard engine nacelle and fuselage. (*AAF*)

Experiment Station in Washington, D.C., was assigned to modify the radar set, if necessary, to make it operate for ROC. However, this change to radar homing initiated new problems for Griggs and his assistants at the Radiation Laboratory. Since the RHB radar receiver had been designed for GBs, with a lower angle of approach, two concerns arose: first, it was necessary to decide whether to keep the eye blind or to bias it during the initial curved portion of the trajectory; secondly, it remained as an unknown whether sufficient echo contrast could be developed between the target and its background at ROC's high-angle of approach. Despite the fact that these very fundamental questions remained unresolved, ROC development continued.

During April 1944, the Navy stated that it would have no interest in ROC unless it could be transported on aircraft carrier-based aircraft. Since the X-ROC could only be suspended on larger bombers, and not on any carrier-based aircraft, this would necessitate a complete redesign.

ROC X-1000

In December 1943, Douglas Aircraft was delegated to redesign the X-ROC to carry a 1,000-pound GP bomb or 1,100-pound SAP bomb and a Zenith RHS radar receiver. The missile, code named X-1000, was 11.42 feet long and had wings measuring 6.83 feet, which could be carried only by large bombers. The X-1000 was to fly with a zero angle of attack suitable for control either in line of sight or by the installation of television equipment, or by a suitable homing device. Bendix Aviation, North Hollywood, California, was given a contract to develop the radio control equipment. Polaroid, Cambridge, Massachusetts, was to develop and build a heat scanner for of the ROC heat-seeker. The Radio Corporation of America, Princeton, New Jersey, was to develop the MIMO television equipment. MIT was to modify the Zenith RHS, which had been developed for GBs using a lower angle of approach than the X-1000's 45-degree angle. In April 1944, the Navy decided it would terminate its interest in the ROC project unless its relatively small carrier-based aircraft could carry it.

ROC 00-1000

Once ROC expanded from a small research and development project into an engineering and production undertaking, Douglas formed a special project group in their Santa Monica Engineering Laboratory. Klemperer remained as head of research while Kingdon Kerr was appointed project engineer. Elmer Wheaton became project coordinator, alternating between the MIT Radiation Laboratory and Douglas Santa Monica. This organization remained in effect through 1944, until the Douglas Applied Physics Laboratory assumed control. Under Klemperer's competent direction, design and preliminary production proceeded rapidly to develop the new model, ROC 00-1000, called the 00. For this model, the previous ROC crossed wings were replaced by a ring type of shroud with the fixed tail also built as a ring shroud, giving the new ROC version its nickname, the "Double Cookie Cutter."

The smaller, perforated, fixed tail shroud had no control surfaces and was used to decelerate the ROC to make guidance easier for the remote control operator. The larger mid-fuselage mounted shroud was movable being installed on a universal joint to create lift in any direction. Aerodynamic deflection in range and azimuth was controlled by two electrically-operated actuators whose servo motors were energized by remotely controlled radio link equipment. One actuator in the fuselage moved the shroud in yaw (azimuth) while the other located in the shroud itself moved the shroud in pitch (range). The power to drive the actuators was obtained from an electronically-controlled amplifier developed by Bendix. This amplifier received its signals from the radio link receiver mounted in the tail shroud. The 00 was roll stabilized by gyros, which controlled the four ailerons in the empennage. At maximum aileron movement, a 7,500-foot turning radius could be achieved. Like the X-ROC, this 00 configuration also flew at a zero angle of attack and did not have to bank to turn. Since the shroud was mounted on gimbals, the 00 was steered by tilting the shroud in two orientations at right angles to each other, corresponding to azimuth and elevation. The design permitted symmetrical and interchangeable function of azimuth and range control allowing a minimum of time delay in response.

The fuselage and wings were both of hollow cast magnesium and the structure was designed to contain either a 12-inch, 1,100-pound or a 14-inch, 1,600-pound armor-piercing bomb. The forward compartment contained the homing device and the aft for the power supply. Servo motors actuated by the homing device were mounted in the wings and moved the controlling surfaces. The tail had no elevators or rudders, but flaps attached to the fins acted as a brake to keep the maximum velocity to 800 feet per second (545 mph).

Weight:	1,593 pounds
Payload:	1,000 pounds
Wing (shroud) areas:	8.9 feet
Length:	12.3 feet
Fuselage diameter:	1.5 feet
Control shroud diameter:	2.5 feet
Braking shroud diameter:	4.0 Feet

The ROC was a hybrid between the large GB structure and the much smaller VB tail assembly. While it was smaller than a GB, only the B-29 could actually carry the weapon internally; when employed by any other AAF bomber, the ROC displayed all of the negative qualities of externally mounted weapons—aerodynamic drag, small numbers carried per bomber per sortie, and the exposure of the weapon to the weather while on the way to the target.

Unlike the other VBs of the VB series, the ROC was a medium-angle bomb of 30 degrees to 60 degrees glide angle from horizontal. Although bombs equipped with the ROC system could approach the target at an angle as shallow as 30 degrees, this was still too steep to effectively use television, except under the most ideal lighting conditions. The problems encountered were the same as those encountered with the VB-7 and VB-8. Efforts to enable the VB-10 to sail at shallower angles began to succeed in the summer of 1945, allowing the ROC television-guidance system to continue testing throughout the war. Testing revealed that the ROC's maximum speed to allow maneuvering turns was 400 mph and that the target could speed up to 60 mph, which made the ROC a suitable anti-shipping missile.

The initial small-scale production lot of twenty ROC 00-1000 models was built by Douglas, with the final three being expended by April 25, 1945. A second lot of 100 ROC 00-1000 models was contracted, of which the first thirty-five were completed by June. The cost breakdowns for the ROC 00-1000 were $20,000 each for the first batch of twenty, while the next 100 were to cost $13,000 ($7,500 for the airframe, $5,000 for the TV guidance, and $500 for the radio equipment) with an estimated cost of $8,000 per unit projected for the mass-produced version.

Douglas had designed ROC 00-1000 as a missile, possessing stability, homing ability, and remarkable aerobatic maneuverability. Soon after it was ready for tests, the MIT radar group finally announced in a negative report that after prolonged analyses on target contrast at the desired glide angle that reliable homing signals could not be acquired at that angle. Thus, the once promising ROC, whose perpetuation existed on the supposition that its perfected radar control was impending, was no longer feasible. Other ROC applications were then considered: the far infrared receiver (FIR), a direct-sight radio-controlled version, and a TV-guided homing ROC.

The FIR was developed by Swiss-born Dr. Marcel Golay, chief scientist of the Signal Corps Engineering Laboratory, Fort Monmouth, New Jersey. The Golay Detector/SCR-268T detected targets by their emitted infrared radiation. However, the 268T was only used in the Pacific and was abandoned before the end of the war as its sensitivity was limited.

The direct-sight radio-controlled version was proposed by Division 7 for use against difficult targets where there was lengthy flight path correction available. This ROC was to be built by Schwien Engineering and some version of the Crab bombsight attachment was to provide the preliminary control according to a pre-calculated program. After launching, the ROC, under Crab control, was initially sailed toward the target and then was placed into a collinear (along a single line) dive with the line of sight to the target, which permitted the eclipse method of control to be used during the last several seconds of flight. If the bomb was controlled so that it continuously eclipsed the target from the bombardier's viewpoint, it had to hit the target regardless of any errors in the dropping technique. This procedure had been considered for RAZON but was abandoned due to its inadequate maneuverability. The ROC, because it was carried externally and not in confining bomb bays had much larger control surfaces and therefore greater mobility. However, during a series of tests, the complicated additional sighting mechanism combined with the very maneuverable ROC was more than controllers could manage. The direct-sight radio-controlled project was terminated after bombardiers persistently lost control of the ROC.

After the immediate plans for use of television on AAF and USN GB were delayed or abandoned, Section 5.3 continued to investigate the use of TV control, partially to assist these two services in association with Army GB and Navy drone projects, but primarily for use in ROC as an installation of a television camera in the ROC nose and then controlling the missile from a mother aircraft or a ground station. As D-5's television undertaking became more involved, it became necessary to coordinate their effort under one director, Oliver Buckley of the Bell Telephone Laboratories became head of Section 5.3 and was assisted by Pierre Mertz, D. B. Hansen, and D. E. Harnett. Electrical engineer Buckley was president of the Bell Telephone Laboratories from 1940 to 1951 and had previously been recognized for his contributions to the field of submarine telephony.

By late 1943, TV systems were available from four manufacturers, each having individual advantages and disadvantages. RCA and to a lesser extent Hazeltine, Farnsworth, and Remington-Rand—all of which had received numerous contracts from Section D-3 requiring picture improvement and the reduction of equipment size. The Columbia Broadcasting System's Engineering Research Laboratory was requested to conduct comparative tests on the three units under controlled conditions. The BLOCK III TV unit with a Hammond radio control was tested first as at the time this unit was being installed in the GB-4 series. This TV unit intended to be installed in the ROC 00-1000, required the nose of the missile to be lengthened, rendering the system as unsuitable for the proposed internal stowage in a B-29 and the increased length also affected ROC inflight stability.

Through various contracts, RCA was able to assign many engineers to work on all aspects of television control development, concentrating on the improvement of equipment sensitivity; reliability and selectivity; picture quality; antenna design; and reduction of equipment size and weight. The result was the development of the RCA MIMO Orthicon that was selected by the CBS Laboratory as the control unit for ROC. The laboratory deemed the RCA MIMO superior for military requirements because of its simplicity and reliability under the extremes of combat, which differed widely from civilian requirements. The MIMO unit weighed only 59 pounds and used electro-magnetic deflection and focusing. The TV receiver in the mother aircraft had 350 lines and flashed forty frames per second.

The simple radio link used in the AZON/RAZON series was tested to control ROC. These tests demonstrated that while the ON/OFF control was satisfactory, the ROC, with its larger, more responsive control surfaces, required a proportional control system in which the setting of the missile's control surfaces was to correspond to the position of the remote operator's control stick. Bendix Aviation embarked on the modification of existing standardized units and Proportional Modulation (PM) was developed. It was not until March 1945, that the first MIMO-equipped ROCs were ready for testing. Scientists supposed now that control and a good TV picture were available that flying the ROC would be much the same as flying an airplane. Tests proved this to be mistaken as many remote operators reported that they lacked the seat-of-the-pants response associated with flying an aircraft. Even with the minimum miss being 70 feet, the initial results were considered unsatisfactory. It was obvious that the necessary in-the-field training could not be completed using the scarce and very expensive ROCs (only ten MIMO control sets were available by the time the project terminated) and consequently Columbia University and Douglas Aircraft began to develop simulators to train operators.

Preliminary laboratory studies were conducted to develop a MIMO ROC simulator by Loebe Julie, a NDRC Division 7 civilian engineer at Columbia University's Division of War Research. In 1943, Julie was credited with inventing a faster, more powerful differential input circuit, which allowed much greater versatility in applications circuits and remains in wide use today. With the ROC simulator operating in one co-ordinate, it was evident that control could be achieved, but to obtain good results would require a trained operator. Specialties Inc. was awarded a contract for the manufacture of an electronic simulator based upon the Columbia design but operating in two co-ordinates. Due to the end of the war, the device was not used for training AAF bombardiers for the ROC tests but was sent to Langley, where NACA engineers used it for their research programs.

Meanwhile, Douglas had constructed their own, much more unsophisticated one-co-ordinate mechanical simulator. It was a three-wheeled cart on which the operator rode while looking into a mock television screen and scaled control mechanisms of an actual ROC. A shipping target moving along a cable simulated evasive action or crosswind. The reduced scale condensed 15,000 feet of trajectory on to a 150-foot floor space, while reproducing the fall time correctly. Numerous test runs on the Douglas cart proved the value of this system.

Although a proportional control system had originally been believed necessary for AZON and RAZON and used in their early tests, they were controlled with a simple radio link with adequate ON-OFF control. ROC, however, responded much more actively to only small control movements and the setting of ROC's control surface needed to correspond to the position of the operator's control stick. A proportional control system would be necessary for ROC and two systems were tested.

The first system, known as DAM (differential amplitude modulation), was found to be unsatisfactory in field tests. Four standard audio-control tones from a standard RC-186 Bendix transmitter were used simultaneously, with rigid automatic volume control on the output. The control stick when moving from full right to full left varied the amplitude modulation of the right-left tones from 100 percent right through 50 percent right, 50 percent left at the neutral point to 100 percent left. In intermediate positions, the relative degree of modulation of the two tones, always equaling 100 percent, determined the position of the rudder in relation with the stick position. While this system functioned satisfactorily in the laboratory, it exhibited some instability at the neutral point in field tests. A modification, proportional modulation (PM), was implemented and demonstrated good performance. PM was similar to DAM, but only used one tone at a time for each co-ordinate, with the percentage modulation varying from zero at the neutral point to 100 at the extreme position of control stick and rudder. The Bendix proportional-control system allowed a minimum of alteration of existing standardized equipment and was accepted.

Since the MIMO television/ROC phase was progressing so slowly in late 1944, concurrent tests were made using the direct-sight/radio link method with twenty direct sight tests conducted with encouraging results. However, MIMO testing continued into the summer of 1945 without simulator training and the next six MIMO tests were regarded as promising failures and extensive tests were scheduled by the AAF at Wendover. By the early summer of 1945, the VB-10, which had been developed under 2A priority, had achieved results in tests extending from September 21, 1944 to May

24, 1945 that did not justify its cost and complicated system and further development, and on November 30, 1945, Douglas closed out the ROC project. The unused ROCs and equipment was divided into laboratory equipment to be transferred to Wright Field and field test equipment to Wendover Field.

VB-11 Dove and Dove Eye

In early 1944, the Navy Bureau of Ordnance urgently requested that the NDRC Division 7 join with the Polaroid Corporation for the development of a quantitative heat-homing scanner for the Navy's version of AAF's VB-6 Felix, which was approved and named Bomb Mk. 64 Dove.

At the time, the Division concluded that the war had shifted too much in the Allies' favor to begin the development of a totally new missile system. BuOrd, however, did support two projects with Polaroid physicist David Grey as the designer, to be conducted cooperatively, with the BuOrd administering work at Polaroid on the missile's structure, aerodynamic control surfaces, and servo links, and the division administering the development of a quantitative heat-homing scanner, known as Dove Eye. The AAF had originally intended the VB-6 to be used against hot targets with a definite IR signature, such as coal or oil-burning electric power plants, coke ovens, blast furnaces, etc. The Navy chose to adapt the VB-6 to be launched from a high altitude, to have its infrared (IR) sensor lock-on to a ship's hot engine exhaust stacks, which would then operate the bomb's control surfaces to automatically pilot the bomb.

The Polaroid Corporation, Project Dove's prime contractor, built test bombs at the company's Boston facility. The Dove was basically a standard 1,000-pound AN-M65 GP bomb, which was equipped with a heat-seeking infrared homing device, an optical system, a scanning system, and an amplifier in the special nose and control fins in the tail. The distinct box kite-shaped Bomb Fin Mk. 1 was 8 inches longer than the standard M-65 bomb tail fin and made normal internal suspension difficult. The Dove was 8.25 feet long, 1.7 feet in diameter, and weighed 1,185 pounds (heat-homing equipment and special tail weighed 185 pounds and 1,000-pound bomb).

Aerodynamic range and azimuth control was achieved by four movable nose deflectors independently controlled, which formed quadrants of a cylindrical surface whose axis was parallel to that of the bomb. The deflectors could be extended a maximum distance of 4.5 inches. The movement of the deflectors was determined by the control unit (called the "Intelligence Unit" in technical manuals), which consisted of the heat-detecting eye, gyro system, auxiliary electronic relays, servo motors, and battery. It was to be capable of being dropped from unusually high (for a free-fall bomb) altitudes of up to 30,000 feet because the seeker could correct aiming errors of up to 1,500 feet. The bomb, traveling at Mach .98 was to be used against targets with a clear IR signature, such as ships in the open sea or isolated industrial plants.

The Polaroid lock-on scanner-detector, using vacuum tube circuitry, responded to the angular velocity of the optical axis relative to the direction of the heat target area

The VB-11 Dove was basically a standard 1,000-pound AN-M65 GP bomb equipped with a heat-seeking infrared homing device, an optical system, a scanning system, and an amplifier in the special nose and control fins in the tail. (*From AAF microfilm document*)

until the signal from the target was maximized. Since it was mounted on a gyroscope, the sensor would stay pointed at the target if the bomb was on a collision course. If the bomb was not on the proper trajectory, the target's image on the sensor would drift, and the sensor would need to be moved to re-center the image. The same movements would be amplified and applied to the steering fins of the bomb, correcting its path in a feedback loop. When the bomb was on target, the target's image would not move on the infrared sensor, and there would be no further adjustment of the bomb's fins. Steering was by yawing the bomb by the action of seeker-directed lift spoilers protruding from the nose. The nose was roll-stabilized by an internal reaction against the remainder of the bomb.

Special Project Unit (SPU) Dove was established at NAS Squantum Quincy, Massachusetts, during April 1944 to provide flight-testing services in support of Project Dove. SPU Dove was associated with the Naval Air Modification Unit (NAMU) based at the Naval Air Development Center (NADC) in Johnsville, Pennsylvania. SPU Dove was administratively headquartered at NAS Squantum, but its aircraft operated from the Bedford AAF (now Laurence G. Hanscom AAF). Beginning during the late fall of 1944, SPU Dove Curtiss SB2C Helldivers and/or Eastern TBM Avengers stationed at Bedford AAF initially test-dropped Project Dove bombs on ground targets at the bombing ranges at Camp Wellfleet on Cape Cod and on Monomoy Island, Nantucket Sound. Later, during April 1945, the Liberty Ship SS *James Longstreet* was scuttled in shallow water on New Found Shoal in Cape Cod Bay so that guided bombs could be drop-tested on a tangible vessel. Previously, the *Longstreet* had been the target of Pelican and SWOD Bat tests off New York, by Navy aircraft out of Floyd Bennett Field.

Oil-burning smudge pots were ignited on either ground or sea targets to provide a heat source for the guided bomb's infrared sensor to home. On each test, SPU Dove aircraft dropped a pair of bombs simultaneously, one an IR guided bomb and the other a conventional 1,000-pound bomb to provide a baseline comparison of both methods. The trajectories of both bombs were measured by triangulation and direct observation from the shore, surface craft, and aircraft.

From its beginning during February 1944, the Dove Eye homing device was planned as an infrared detector and the first derivative-taking *Eye* was assembled and tested during the first three months of the project. It reported the angular velocity of a line from the bomb to the target relative to any stabilized line in space, which would use this derivative to generate the minimum aerodynamic acceleration necessary to convert a miss into a hit. However, because of its poor target discrimination and loss in threshold sensitivity, the derivative-taking *Eye* was canceled after successful laboratory tests demonstrated the superiority of the lock-on *Eye*.

By the end of the war, Dove development remained incomplete, and by June 1946, more than 30 percent of the Dove Eye units dropped from an altitude of 20,000 feet hit within 50 feet of a target. SPU Dove continued to operate in the Boston area through the summer of 1946, after which the project relocated to NADC Johnsville. During July 1946, development was transferred from Polaroid to Eastman Kodak and the Dove was subsequently designated as air-to-surface missile XASM-4 in September 1947. Due to the slow development of the Dove's IR guidance system, it was not until a year later that a contract for twenty XASM-N-4 prototypes was let. Testing of the XASM-N-4 prototypes by the Bureau of Ordnance was completed as only moderately satisfactory in October 1952 and would develop into the ASM-N-4 and remain active through the early 1950s, with production orders let. The infrared sensor aspect of Project Dove, however, influenced the development of the successful AIM-9 Sidewinder heat-seeking air-to-air guided missile.

VB-13/ASM-A-1 TARZON

During January 1945, the Air Force proposed the development of remote-controlled very high tonnage bombs to be designed and manufactured by Gulf Research and Development. The project was entitled "Development of a Control for the British 12,000 pound Tallboy Bomb" with the code name TARZON (TAllboy, Range and aZimuth ONly). At this time in the war, there were very few targets available for the smaller remote-controlled 1,000-pound VB-3 or 2,000-pound VB-4 RAZON bombs, and those available targets could be destroyed with a full load of the less costly and more easily deployed conventional M-65 1,000-pound bombs. However, it was considered that the RAZON guidance system could be combined with substantially heavier bombs for use against targets requiring destruction by deep penetration and very heavy explosives. Due to their high cost, Tallboys were to be used expressly against high-value strategic targets that could not be destroyed by any other means, such as large warships (Kriegsmarine battleship *Tirpitz* by RAF Lancasters on November 12, 1944); concrete and steel fortifications and structures (RAF attacks on German U-boat pens and V-2 weapon bunkers); caves, tunnels, storage depots, and other underground installations; dams, canals, and dikes; and to trigger landslides. However, TARZON operations were restricted to daytime use with excellent visibility and the launching/controlling bomber had to remain on a vulnerable course to guide the TARZON to the target.

The American World War II T-10 Tallboys were a version of the 12,000-pound Barnes Wallace-developed British Tallboy Earthquake bomb modified to use standard

American components. The American Tallboy/TARZON weighed 13,000 pounds overall, was 21 feet long, 38 inches in diameter, had a 4.5-foot wingspan, and carried a 5,200-pound Torpex D-1 warhead. Basically, the TARZONs were Tallboys with a new tail assembly that provided limited azimuth and range control via an AN/ARW-38 command radio transmitter in the launching/mother aircraft and an AN/URW-2 radio guidance receiver radio link with the mother aircraft installed in the TARZON bomb. The Norden M-series bombsight was modified for the controller to view a superimposed image of both the bomb's tail-mounted flare and the target. The TARZON's tail contained ailerons for roll stabilization and set of elevators to control range and azimuth. The elevators and ailerons were actuated by an electrical servo system in response to radio signals from the launch aircraft.

The TARZON's projected impact velocity was to be 1,000 feet per second (682 mph) compared to the supersonic 1,250–1,300 feet per second (852–886 mph) impact of the British uncontrolled Tallboy. Because of its large size, the controllability of the RAZON Tallboy was to be about only one-third of the VB-1. NACA was delegated to provide the TARZON with increased controllability to +/- 1,000 feet from 15,000 feet after a fall of fifteen seconds with no control and to increase impact speed.

Several modifications were made on the carrying B-29s to accommodate the TARZON bomb. The fuselage section between the bomb bay doors was removed, and the bomb bay doors were cut to conform to the cross section of the bomb. Modifications were made to the bomb racks to support the weight at the individual shackles. In June 1945, it was projected that only one B-29 squadron, fifteen aircraft, was scheduled to carry the TARZON as its developmental time for combat was to be late in the war, which, at the time, was projected to end in September 1946.

Although, it was recommended that funds and personnel could be better used to deploy the standard RAZON to the Pacific, the TARZON project was initiated on February 26, 1945. Soon the Air Force, NDRC, and Gulf Research and Development obtained several standard 12,000-pound Tallboy bombs for development into the guided TARZON. NACA was to aid in solving the supersonic aerodynamic problems with entirely new bomb shapes with new control surfaces. A fixed shroud of 20-inch chord and 5-inch diameter was placed about the center of gravity. A RAZON octagonal tail unit also of 20-inch chord but of 54-inch diameter was placed 11.58 inches from the center of gravity. Tests demonstrated the control forces and speed were too great for RAZON-type controls and, consequently, none were ready for use in the war; only thirteen prototypes were completed by January 1946.

The VB-13, redesignated as ASM-A-1 in 1948, was developed under the project MX-674. Although the VB-13 project had not reached the testing stage by the end of the war, it avoided cancellation, continuing as a low-priority project with limited testing conducted during 1948 and 1949.

During 1950, the RAZON bomb was resurrected for several months testing but the 1,000-pound RAZON was determined to be too small for effective use against bridges and other hardened targets. The TARZON was then also resurrected with additional testing at Alamogordo, New Mexico, during 1950, which resulted to the TARZON being approved for operational service in the Korean War. The 19th Bomb Group, which had

American World War II Tallboys were converted to TARZONs, which were basically a Tallboy with a new tail assembly that provided limited azimuth and range control. (*USAF*)

The TARZONs were so large that modifications had to be made to the carrying B-29's bomb bay and the bomb had to be placed into a loading pit (pictured) to hoist it toward the bomber. (*AAF*)

previously conducted the RAZON's testing was to be the sole TARZON user, switching to developing the TARZON for combat in December 1950 as the redesignated M-121.

Three B-29s, similar to those modified to carry Tallboys in World War II, flew thirty TARZON missions against North Korean bridges and other hardened targets between December 1950 and March 1951. During the early tests, of the first ten bombs dropped, only one recorded a hit. As the 19BG became reasonably proficient, it confirmed the destruction of six high-priority targets, including bridges and a hydroelectric plant. Despite continual technical problems, the weapon's tentative success led to a contract for the production of 1,000 additional ASM-A-1 missiles.

However, the TARZON's twenty-ninth mission, against the Sinuiju bridges on March 29, 1951, was to lead to the TARZON project's undoing. One aircraft returned to base with mechanical problems, a second aircraft flown by Col. Payne Jennings, 19BG CO, exploded due to the premature detonation of the bomb, and the third aircraft continued on to the target only to have its TARZON miss its objective. Three weeks later, another B-29 also experienced an unintentional detonation of a jettisoned, supposedly safe bomb, although without the loss of the aircraft. An inquiry confirmed that the fault was in the construction of the bomb's tail and while modifications were being completed, the TARZON project was doomed. The TARZON's poor reliability (only six of twenty-eight bombs dropped successfully destroyed their targets), the safety issues, increased maintenance outlays compared to conventional bombs, the drawback of the bomb's guidance system requiring only clear weather use, which rendered the bombers vulnerable to enemy interceptors, and the required TARZON release altitude that placed the bomber in danger from enemy AA all combined to result in the production order being canceled by the USAF; the entire TARZON program terminated in August 1951.

During the Vietnam War, before the lethal 15,000-pound parachute BLU-82 Daisy Cutter bomb was introduced, some of the remaining M-121s, minus their rear streamlined shrouds and tail fin assemblies, were shipped to Vietnam for use in clearing helicopter landing zones in the jungle. The TARZON warheads were incorporated into the BLU-82 bombs to be dropped by Lockheed C-130 Hercules turbo-prop transports using radar control as part of the Commando Vault missions, which were considered to be more accurate in bomb delivery than the more contemporary B-52 bombers. The warheads were mounted on a platform and pulled by parachutes from the rear of the C-130s loading ramp. After clearing the aircraft, the large extraction chutes and pallets were released and small triangular chutes stabilized the large warhead until the 3-foot nose probe detonated the bomb at the precise standoff distance. One of the last of the World War II Tallboys was dropped accurately from 10,000 feet during a Commando Vault mission to clear a landing zone for helicopters on a ridge during the well-known 1969 Battle of Hamburger Hill.

Conclusions: Vertical Bomb Series

Between 1941 and 1945, all AAF guided-missile projects experienced the lack of dedicated leadership, coordination, and direction, and the VB series was no exception.

These advanced controlled bombs clearly did not meet their potential during the war, despite an occasional exceptional success during testing. Except for the VB-1 AZON's successful albeit limited use, none of the other VBs became operational before the end of the war.

Although the development of VBs faced continuing challenging technical problems, they were not the only basis for the weapons failure. The AAF leadership and the high operational echelons had little understanding of these weapons and how they were envisaged to be used operationally. Again, as seen in the GB series, established AAF doctrine was a very important issue in the development of the VB series. Any advanced guided weapons that began to demonstrate exceptional potential during testing against worthwhile isolated maritime and hard targets received little consideration or support from important operational commanders who continued to be influenced by AWPD-1 (the use of heavy bombers to conduct strategic daylight precision bombing attacks as the primary scheme of defeating Germany). While the GB-1 had been disregarded almost entirely based upon its being was an area weapon, the more advanced accurate VB systems were considered as unfavorable because they were unable to be manufactured and then delivered operationally in large numbers. Operationally, only one VB could be delivered by one bomber at one time whereas many conventional bombs could dumped on enemy targets, more quickly by the same bomber.

The VB's slow development and eventual failure was a consequence of allocating available R&D resources too broadly and not establishing and then applying effective priorities. Although limited, the America did possess sufficient scientific and R&D personnel and facilities during 1941–42 to warrant that any promising, high-priority guided bomb could be satisfactorily designed and developed. Without any specific requisite and feasibility of the concept established for a VB weapon, its research and design consequently progressed slowly. The AAF High Command prioritized weapons that would be available for this war and these weapons were awarded most of the funds and materials without considering the VB's operational promise if granted higher priorities.

Guided Air-to-Air Fragmentation Bomb

In November 1944, after preliminary wind tunnel tests, the NDRC issued specifications on Project MX-570, which was for a special fragmentation bomb to be used against flying aircraft. The weapon was to have a maximum weight of 150 pounds and dimensions of 15 inches in diameter and 15 inches in length so that the most efficient fragmentation could be employed against aircraft structures within a 25-foot radius. A guidance system for the bomb was to be investigated. It was to have a proximity fuse, an electric detonator with a safety switch operated by an external electric circuit, and an air travel safety device. The AMC Development Engineering Branch was assigned to furnish the Air Service Technical Command with a prototype by January 1, 1945 and ten inert units by March 1 for flight tests. This project seems to have had very low priority and very little is known about it.

3

Guided Missiles

Dragon: Visual Tracking and Radio Control

The first of these visual tracking and radio control gliders was the Dragon (also known as the Dryden bomb), which was 14 feet long, had a 12-foot wingspan, and could carry a 2,000-pound bomb against shipping. Only a few were built or tested as the project was terminated as the controlling aircraft had to follow too closely to the Dragon to guide it accurately and was thus vulnerable to enemy AA fire. Nothing more is known of the Dragon as it was an early low-priority secret project.

EMR Homing Device

Electro-Mechanical Research (EMR) of Houston, Texas, was a small nonprofit Schlumberger (Oil) Well Surveying Corp subsidiary established to develop and build military devices. EMR President H. G. Doll, an officer in the French Army until the fall of France, had proposed several ideas for new military devices during his previous military career. At EMR, Doll and Charles Aiken began work to bring into fruition the idea of a homing bomb. Despite rather large limitations, such as having no priorities and accordingly no materials and the lack of support from the Army and Navy, the pair was able to make some advances. However, there were also the suspicions of why aliens, Frenchman Doll and one of his engineers, wanted to spend their time and own money helping America.

By the end of 1942, Doll had spent the then large amount of about $80,000 of personal funds on his innovations that included a spiral scanning system for locating and locking on to the target, aerodynamic design and trajectory calculations showing the feasibility of the homing scheme, a successful anti-roll stabilizer, and a course-predicting apparatus that provided the interception course. It became obvious to Doll that EMR would be unable to continue his expenditure without receiving some

Dragon: radio-controlled Dryden glide bomb. (*From USN microfilm document*)

promise that funds would be available from some another source or if the project were successful that the Army or Navy would accept it.

At Assistant Secretary of War Robert Lovett's impetus, Aiken obtained an interview with Lt. Col. A. Nyman of Wright Field and Harold Richmond and J. C. Boyce of Division 5. Definite interest was shown by all three men, and an NDRC contract followed. EMR's first project was a semi-GB that resembled the Douglas X-ROC. It became apparent to Division 5 that most of EMR's projects duplicated the efforts of other Division 5 contracts, particularly Felix, RAZON, and ROC programs. Division 5 then decided that EMR should best concentrate on developing a different type of scanner for operation on its semi-GB or on one of the AAF's GBs. Division 5 allowed EMR to continue with its homing device as insurance if other devices failed. This homing device was given no official designation or nickname and was simply known as the EMR after the company.

After receiving this new contract, EMR directed its research and development to a back-and-forth scanner for right-left indication. Little previous investigation had been done on this type of scanner, which was intended to avoid some of the difficulties inherent in rotary scanning near the horizon. EMR's first demonstration of its preliminary scanner model was considered satisfactory, as it gave good target indication at usable distances when directed at ships in harbors. However, the scanner required refinement and was much too large and heavy to be carried as an airborne weapon. In their R&D, EMR conducted an extensive study of the relationships between the details of construction of receivers and their sensitivity and speed of response, which was considered as a major contribution to basic scanner theory. Field work to finalize the scanner was conducted on the shore of Galveston Bay using shipping entering or leaving Houston harbor. The completed scanner provided very good performance during its demonstrations at a station overlooking Boston Harbor and later at Wright Field. The AAF granted EMR a contract for the development of the scanner for a GB control, but work continued slowly onward, until finally the end of the war negated the contract.

U.S. Navy Development of Television-Controlled Missiles

On October 27, 1937, R/Adml. Arthur Cook, Chief of the Bureau of Aeronautics, directed Walter Webster, manager of the Naval Aircraft Factory, Philadelphia, to conduct a comprehensive analysis of the possible use of radio control for testing new aircraft. Webster would serve as the NAF manager from June 1936 until his death in a plane crash on March 16, 1943. The Naval Aircraft Factory analysis delineated the following as necessary for the development of such a project:

1. A method of radio transmission of the information indicated on the missiles flight instruments.
2. A method by which the synchronized records of the control positions could be obtained.
3. A method of obtaining records of the structural test instruments by radio and of recording them.

Upon receiving the analysis, numerous Bureau Divisions became involved in protracted deliberations before finally directing the Naval Aircraft Factory to develop the project with the emphasis to be on a television repeat-back system.

During early 1938, the BuOrd discussed the possibility of using television equipment in a repeat-back system with RCA engineers. Soon, the Naval Aircraft Factory recommended that television equipment be purchased for tests but this was not approved until October 1939 and was not delivered until late February 1940 for tests that were conducted over the remainder of that year.

In January 1941, negotiations were finalized with RCA for the installation and testing of one set of their latest type of television equipment in an experimental twin-engined observation and utility tricycle landing aircraft. On January 17, 1941, BuAer Chief, R/Adml. John Towers, delineated the required tests, placing great emphasis on the televising of instruments to permit control of a drone beyond visual range, on the transmission of structural test data to a ground station, and the televising of the view ahead of a projected assault drone headed toward a target.

Adml. John Towers was a major USN personality, beginning as a pioneer naval aviator, making significant contributions to the technical and organizational development of American naval aviation from its early stages, eventually acting as Chief of the Bureau of Aeronautics from 1939–1942. He was then named Commander, Air Force, Pacific Fleet, during which time he administered the fleet's aviation development, organization, training, and supply and helped develop the strategy, which led to the ultimate defeat of the Japanese fleet.

By February 17, 1941, tests of this equipment gave promise of usable TV picture information from an aircraft in flight at distances of 20 to 30 miles from a ground receiving station. By June, the tests had progressed to where the television transmitter was providing pictures of adequate quality on the receiver in another aircraft that the pilot in the latter could direct the pilot of the transmitting aircraft to alter course to fly directly over a selected target. Meanwhile, the Radio Corporation developed a

Capt. Walter Webster, manager of the Naval Aircraft Factory. (*USN*)

Admiral John Towers was a leading USN personality, pioneer naval aviator, chief of the Bureau of Aeronautics from 1939–1942, and commander, Air Force, Pacific Fleet. (*USN*)

small television camera and transmitter that, with its power supply, weighed only 70 pounds. This equipment proved successful in supplying satisfactory information for telemetering purposes.

Robin: The First Television-Guided and Radar Homing System Test Project

The summer of 1942 saw the nadir of German U-Boat successes with reports of ships sunk just off the American East Coast being a daily occurrence. In the previous year, the NDRC and NBS with BuOrd sponsorship were contracted to develop a GB for use against enemy shipping and submarines using television guidance.

The first television-guided Dryden GB test project, designated as Robin, was underway in January 1941 as RCA collaborated with Dr. Hugh Dryden at the Aerodynamics Section of the National Bureau of Standards. Preliminary tests of both 7:10 scale and full-scale models of the Robin were conducted, but Dryden and the NDRC were underfunded and the development of the final airframe segment of the project proceeded very slowly. Meanwhile, because of Dryden's slow progress, RCA proceeded to contract an outside manufacturer to complete the airframe which subsequently was a failure. The Bureau of Standards took offense at RCA's snub and because it was providing project funding took complete control of the project and contracted Vidal Research to build the airframes.

Although the RCA television system functioned properly, it did have an average error of 600 feet with some of this error due to the method of attack. At the 11-degree glide attack angle the target appeared to be foreshortened to the TV operator and a small compensating steering error in range caused a larger error at the target. RCA was able to produce a smaller iconoscope using electron multiplication which gave an eight-fold increase in sensitivity, but this set did not meet RCA's goals and standards and further development would be needed. The MIT Radiation Laboratory's radar homing system (RHS) had shown it was more proficient than the Robin's RCA TV/manual guidance system, so the TV research for the Robin was suspended and

Robin television-controlled Dryden glide bomb. (*From USN microfilm document*)

transferred to the more promising ROC guided vertical bomb series. Meanwhile, the Robin's airframe was used to continue testing radar homing system (RHS) systems.

After the reorganization of the NDRC in December 1942, radar development continued at the MIT Radiation Laboratory and a closer coordination with the Navy was established. The BuOrd formed an Experimental Unit at the Bureau of Standards and a Field Test Unit at Warren Grove, New Jersey. The experimental design and testing role of the RHS radar was assigned to Dr. Dryden's group and their Robin airframe while assembly and mechanical support were furnished by the Navy.

Following the Robin's initial tests and the transfer of the RCA television unit to the ROC project, Capt. Dundas Tucker and Lt. Cdr. Dan Jurias of BuOrd proposed using the Robin glider equipped with a RHS being developed by MIT and carrying a payload of a 325-pound depth charge to be used against vulnerable surfaced U-Boats at night. The RHS weapon had three possible methods of operation: a transmitter located on a mother aircraft could guide the weapon (e.g. Pelican), an enemy radar transmitter could be the target (e.g. Moth), or it could carry its own transmitter (e.g. Bat).

The Navy SWOD Project

The first six missiles of the secret USN SWOD (Special Weapons Ordnance Device) series, Mk. 1 through Mk. 6, are unidentified, however, some of the radar homing guided weapon projects described elsewhere, Robin, Moth, and Falcon, have no known designations and possibly could have been given one of the first six SWOD numbers. During World War II two, SWOD missiles, the Mk. 7 Pelican and the Mk. 9 Bat were developed and tested with the Mk. 7 becoming the first successful guided weapon developed by the Navy, and the world's first operational guided missile that did not require operator input after launch.

A major player in the SWOD program would be new NACA Chairman Dr. Vannevar Bush, who directed NACA's Executive Secretary John Victory to draft Congressional legislation for the formation of the National Defense Research Committee (NDRC) during 1940. The NDRC, of which Bush would become chief in June 1940, was to enlist the best and brightest civilian scientists. Afterward, the Office of Scientific Research and Development (OSRD), was spun off from the NDRC for which Bush then left the NDRC to head during June 1941. Bush, the engineer, inventor and science administrator, and the OSRD was responsible for virtually all wartime military R&D, embracing important developments in radar, the proximity fuse, and the initiation and early administration of the Manhattan Project.

An exploration of the feasibility of guided missile was one of the first subjects on the OSRD agenda. At this time, the Navy's BuOrd also became interested in guided missiles and enlisted several MIT scientists to review the project. The OSRD then requested aerodynamics expert Dr. Hugh Dryden at the National Bureau of Standards (NBS) to accept a leading role in this group, to be known as the Bureau of Ordnance Experimental Unit, headquartered at the Dryden's NBS where it

Dr. Vannevar Bush, chairman of the NDRC, OSRD, and NACA is awarded the Presidential Certificate of Merit for his work on the SWOD project by President Truman in 1948. (*NA*)

would also incorporate Dryden's own staff. Dryden was to be the future director of NACA, NASA's predecessor, from 1947 until October 1958 and then served as the NASA deputy administrator (1958–1965). He would be awarded a Presidential Certificate of Merit for his work on the SWOD project by President Truman in 1948. Ultimately, the development of the SWOD Mk. 7 Pelicans and Mk. 9 Bats to BuOrd specifications would be credited to the NDRC Division 5 (radar guidance) and NBS.

During March 1942, BuOrd formed a unit, directed by Navy Lt. Cdr. Dundas Tucker, to monitor the Rad Lab's experiments in radar homing technology as part of the subject of bombing through overcast (BTO) conditions and the crucial immediate concern of developing anti-submarine weapons to target Nazi U-boats that were successfully operating along the American East Coast. The Navy considered radar to be the most favorable technological solution to both the BTO and submarine targeting issues. The Pelican GB seemed to resolve the issue of overcast bombing and nighttime and beyond-visual targeting and the project's overseers believed that any technical issues could be quickly resolved. A 1925 Naval Academy graduate, Dundas Tucker, was fleet communications officer and also in charge of Navy electronic research from 1934–1939. During World War II, he was program director of Electronics and Guided Missiles for the BuOrd, and from 1950–1953 R/Adml. Tucker was director of the Navy's Electronics Laboratory.

SWOD Mk. 7 Pelican

In 1942, the NDRC, assisted by the National Bureau of Standards, the Navy BuOrd, and the MIT Radiation Laboratory, developed the semi-active radar-seeker Pelican (originally designated as the Bomb Mk. 55) concurrently with the active radar-guided SWOD Mk. 9 Bat. The Pelican was intended as the development of radar-guided anti-shipping GB carrying a 325-pound depth charge payload for the Navy to be used against submarines and small surface vessels carried by Navy TBF, PBY, or PBM aircraft or with a 600-pound depth charge to be carried by the larger PBY or PBM aircraft. The Pelican consisted of an airframe developed by the NBS to carry a semi-active RHS radar-seeker that homed on radar reflections from the target, which was illuminated by the AN/APS-2 radar. Two versions of Pelican were developed: the Pelican Mk. II used a 1,000-pound bomb as its basis, while the Pelican Mk. III used a 1,500-pound bomb. The Pelican Mk. III received the designation SWOD Mk. 7 late in its development.

The Pelican GB had a 10-foot wingspan carrying a 325- or 600-pound depth charge or 500-pound bomb. The Pelican used elevon controls, which were merely ailerons operating as flaps or spoilers as well as conventional ailerons. It had a proportional control system that allowed high rates of turn correction with large course deviation and conversely low rates with small course deviations. The glide ratio was 3.5 to 5.5 to 1. The nose housing covered a panel of signal lamps indicating the application of radar controls.

SWOD Mk. 7 Pelican radar-guided missile. (*USN*)

Pelican components included:

Airframe:	SWOD (air stabilized) Mk. 12
RHS:	SWOD (radio receiver) Mk. 1 carried on board
Gyros:	SWOD (gyro panel) Mk. 6
Demolition Unit:	Mk. 117
Fuses:	Mk. 235–236
Bomb:	500-pound GP or 325- or 600-pound depth charge

For field tests, the Pelican mounted a 16-mm Bell and Howell Type M-4A gunsight aiming point camera and, slightly forward and lower to it, a 16-mm Cine Kodak Model E camera was mounted. These cameras simultaneously photographed the panel and the ground ahead of the glider.

Good results were obtained through twenty-five radar test flights during early 1943, initially against a target beacon and later against a reflector hung from a barrage balloon. By establishing the optimal radar and servo settings and using improved techniques and refined instrumentation, thirty-five more tests were conducted by that autumn, with increasingly improved results, establishing that the radar-homing Pelican was significantly more accurate than bombs using television guidance. Although the Navy had ordered that several squadrons were to use the weapon in combat, it found that it did not have enough confidence that the Pelican was yet an operational weapon. On October 18, 1943, the NDRC tested an early Pelican carried by an AAF B-17 against a barge anchored in Chesapeake Bay. The B-17's radar search set illuminated the target and the Pelican was released at about 5,000 feet at 3.5 to 4 miles' range. The missile passed 15 to 20 feet over the barge and crashed into the Bay about 100 yards beyond. The near miss was attributed to the Pelican being too close to the target for the search radar to illuminate it properly during the end of the attack run as the set could only be depressed 50 degrees to 60 degrees. Despite this failure, the Radiation Laboratory was confident that the development of its radar homing equipment had been optimized and concentrated on other projects.

Meanwhile, by late 1943, the Kriegsmarine submarine threat had diminished and the basic Pelican premise had lost its purpose. BuOrd decided to extend the Pelican's use against surface vessels of all sizes by increasing the warhead size to 1,000 pounds using the AN M-65 bomb and a larger glider body. In early 1944, the Radiation Laboratory transferred five men to the MIT Field Experimental Station at the Bureau of Standards with Ralph Lamm as project engineer, assisted by Perry Stout. Under a NDRC Division 5 contract, Lamm's group was to continue pure research and conduct the project engineering phase to build standardized enlarged production models. As with any design change, associated teething problems arose, which were finally resolved, and the airframe, radar system, and controls were all placed into production. The NDRC engaged Timm Aircraft, Van Nuys, California, for tooling, and twenty enlarged Pelican glider bodies to be completed by the end of January 1944 at a cost of $800 to $1,000 per unit. During this time, Timm was engaged in building 434 wooden Waco CG-4A Gliders for the AAF.

On October 18, 1943, the NDRC tested an early Pelican carried by an AAF B-17 against a barge on Chesapeake Bay. The Pelican (arrow) in the movie film still overflew the barge and crashed into the Bay. (*From AAF microfilm document*)

Early Pelican ground tests (Dr. Hugh Dryden standing on left). (*USN*)

The enlarged Pelican was to be air-launched at 205 to 230 mph by a Lockheed PV-1P (also known as the B-34 or Lockheed Ventura with the "1P" for Pelican) and later by a North American PBJ (Navy version of the B-25) each equipped with search radar, mounting shackles, and control equipment as the carrier aircraft. These carrying aircraft were to be ready for tests beginning in April or May 1944. PV-1Ps of VP 152 and 153 were assigned to carry either two 1,000-pound Pelican Mk. IIs or a single 1,500-pound Pelican Mk. III. The Pelican Mk. II was originally designated as the Bomb Mk. 55, but the 1,500-pound Mk. III version was later redesignated as SWOD Mk. 7. This is the only known SWOD designation for Pelican but possibly the 1,000-pound Mk. II type received one of the earlier SWOD numbers.

The first tests of the Mk. II and III Pelicans in June 1944, using the old Liberty ship *James Longstreet* as a target, were dismal failures, as all six production models failed to home on the target. Lamm and Stout were able to determine and correct the relatively minor problems and the first successful Pelican tests were conducted at the end of July. Two of four missiles hit the *Longstreet* and subsequent tests over the next months demonstrated a 30–40 percent success ratio.

The Navy had planned to send two PV-1Ps Squadrons to the Pacific during mid-1944. Crews were trained and the PV-1s modified to carry three Pelicans, but work was stopped when it was found that the PV-1 had insufficient range to reach its target when loaded with two or three externally mounted Pelicans. Meanwhile, the Navy Brass decided that the SWOD Mk. 9 Bat project, which was believed to

Two 1,000-pound Pelican Mk. IIs carried under outboard the engine nacelles of a PV-1 Lockheed Ventura (B-34) with its ventral radome extended aft of the third Pelican. (*USN*)

be nearing an early completion, was more promising. The Navy judged the Pelican Program to have no operational potential and it was returned to developmental status.

Both the Bat and Pelican used the same type airframe, controls, and radar receiver. The Bat's advantages were that it carried a 1,000-pound warhead and contained its RHS on board requiring no maneuvering of the controlling aircraft after release to radar illuminate the target for precise control by the radar operator. During this time, radar development had quickly accelerated to a point at which MIT engineers soon found they could install a small transmitter into the nose of a guided weapon, to make it completely self-guiding.

The advantages of the Pelican over the Bat were that it had twice the effective range, was lighter, carried less expensive expendable equipment, and was not hindered by increased signal strength as it approached the target. The major factor in the Navy's decision to use the Bat instead was its inflexible requirement that targets were to be positively identified before attack, which was an important limitation in European waters where many Allied vessels were present but not so much in the waters near the Japanese Home Islands. Thus, the two advantages of the Pelican, its ability to attack from 20 miles out and through cloud or overcast, were voided by this restriction. Although the defects in the Pelican project were minor and it was near operational status, BuOrd decided to concentrate on the Bat project. Additionally, the Rad Lab had been scheming for months to escape from its Pelican guidance efforts, considering that it was pointless to continue completing a less advantageous system. Pelicans were stripped of their classified electronics for reuse in the Bat program. Many Pelican program staff considered that if equivalent time and effort were expended on the Pelican project it could have been a better weapon than the favored Bat project. Furthermore, the Bat's combat readiness would later be delayed by its untried, self-contained, radar transmitter.

On September 18, 1944, the Pelican production program (3,000 at 300 per month) specified in October 1943 was terminated. The project was returned to developmental status and sent to the Special Weapons Test and Tactical Evaluation Unit at Traverse City, Michigan, where it was utilized as a test vehicle, but this phase was also soon terminated. Once the Pelican program was canceled, a number of airframes remained and a few were used in the Moth missile program and several hundred others were converted to anti-aircraft targets, designated as Vultures in late 1944. These sand-filled targets were dropped in a high-angle dive from patrol bombers which orbited above the fleet and provided a simulation of Kamikaze attacks for shipboard gunnery practice. An interesting aside to Pelican project is that, in early 1942, renowned behavioral scientist B. F. Skinner studied the use of trained pigeons to guide the Pelican, which is described elsewhere.

Falcon

The Falcon was a Bat or Pelican airframe powered by jet rocket motors to increase its range, but little else is known about this weapon, which probably did not progress beyond the drawing board or scale model stage.

Moth

The Moth was 650-pound bomb with a 10.2-foot wingspan developed from leftover Pelican airframes when that program was canceled. The airframe was equipped with radar receivers and antennae that could be tuned to home on enemy radar frequencies and crash into the radar site—much like a moth drawn to a flame, hence the name. The first test flights of the radar homing glider were conducted against a beacon target. Although operational reasons precluded the Moth from reaching combat status, development continued utilizing the beacon homing apparatus as a testing device. The Navy canceled its Moth program but the AAF did successfully develop its own version as the GB-15.

PMB

The so-called PMB, "Poor Man's Bat," was a 325-pound depth bomb with an 8-foot, 4-inch wingspan. It was a very inexpensive and practical modification of the Pelican radar system as it contained its own radar sender located in a tube under nose cone and was dependent on the accuracy of the initial approach on to the target by the mother aircraft. This radar system was both earlier and superior to the Bat's system but the fixated Navy top echelons continued to consider the Bat system to be more desirable and quietly allowed the *PMB* fade into oblivion.

Above: Moth radar homing test glider. (*USN*)

Below: PMB, "Poor Man's Bat." (*USN*)

SWOD Mk. 9 Bat

General Description

The November 1941 RCA test model demonstrations at Muroc Dry Lake Bed for the NDRC were intended to collect flight characteristic data on a proposed television-guided GB. Although the results of these tests were disappointing, the NDRC found the missile's potential persuasive enough to continue the project as a radar-directed missile. Dr. Hugh Dryden was named as director of the project and was joined by other eminent scientists and designers, such as Hunter Boyd, Ralph Lamm, Ortho McCrackin, and Dundas Tucker. The Bureau of Standards was to design the weapon and Vidal Research Corporation, Bendix, New Jersey, was given a contract to produce the prototypes. Vidal Research was headed by Eugene Vidal (the father of author Gore Vidal) who experimented wood-resin composites from 1937 to 1940 using a thermosetting polymer process similar to Duramold. NBS designer Hunter Boyd, who had previously created several early aircraft designs, was responsible to the new missile's distinctive airframe design. Originally designed to carry a Mk. 34 2,000-pound bomb with 160 pounds of guidance equipment, early prototype test models had a 12-foot swept wing and twin vertical tail surfaces at the ends of a horizontal stabilizer.

The Rudolph Wurlitzer Organ Company, renowned for making jukeboxes and organs, constructed the SWOD Mk. 9's plywood airframe and O-shaped body frames using their expertise in bending plywood. The Mk. 9 measured 11 feet, 6 inches in length, had a 10-foot wingspan, and was 2 feet, 6 inches in diameter at the thickest point. The weapon presented such a small cross-section that it was nearly impossible for enemy AA fire to destroy it before impact. Its weight, including the 1,000-pound bomb, was 1,660 pounds. All the missile's working components, except the two spinners that armed the special side-arming fuses, were located inside the airframe. Most of the radar systems components were mounted on a circular bulkhead in the forward end of the airframe with the radar spinner located in the nose. The three 14-volt storage batteries and the inverter were placed amidships.

The equipment was designed to operate at temperatures between -40F degrees and 131F degrees (-40C degrees and 55C degrees) and to withstand relative humidity as much as 95 percent, and any atmospheric pressure from sea level to 30,000 feet. A silica-gel dehydrating unit was installed to remove excess moisture from air entering the radar compartment. While this unit was suitable during good weather, its operation was problematical for the very rainy conditions encountered in the proposed tropical Pacific operating areas.

Warhead

The Bat warhead was a 1,000-pound GP bomb that was attached to the airframe by steel straps from the wings and was entirely enclosed by aerodynamically clean removable plywood sections. Two special fuses were used, which were armed from the side by connections with spinners under the airframe while the arming wires were attached to the rack. A Mk. 122 self-destruct system was installed to prevent the secret RHS unit from falling into Japanese hands.

SWOD Development Team (left to right) R. C. Newhouse (Bell), H. K. Skramstead (NBS), O. McCracken (BuAer), D. P. Tucker (BuOrd), L. P. Tabor (BuOrd), and H. L. Dryden (NBS). (*USN*)

NBS designer Hunter Boyd, who had previously created several early aircraft designs, was responsible to the new missile's distinctive airframe design, which pictured in the NACA wind tunnel. (*USN*)

The SWOD Mk. 9 consisted of a plywood airframe fabricated by the Rudolph Wurlitzer Organ Company, famous for making jukeboxes and organs, using their expertise in bending plywood. (*USN*)

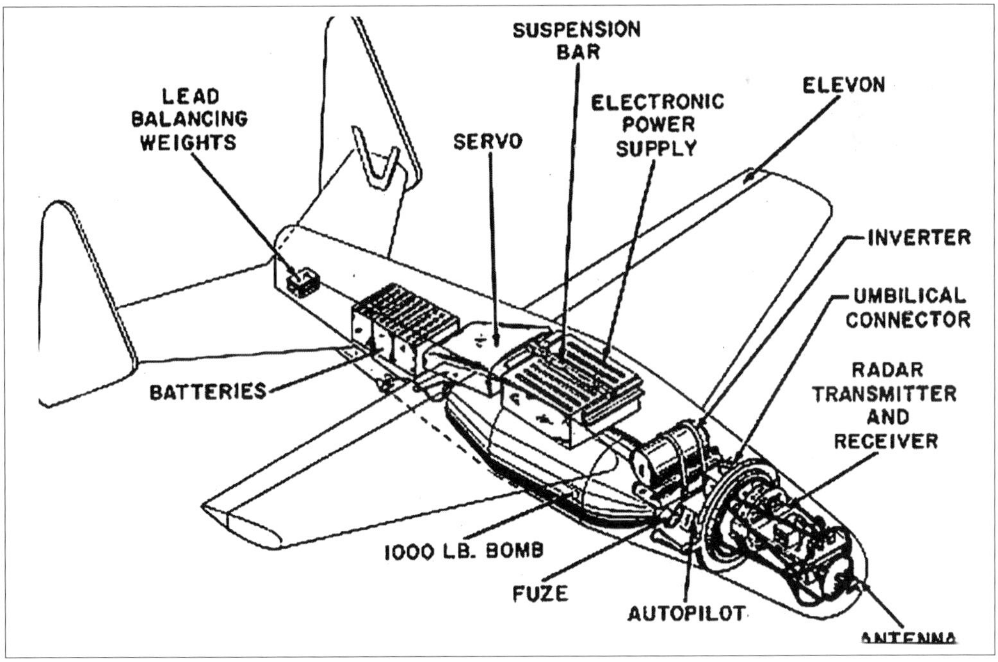

Gyroscopic Autopilot

Smaller Bat models were developed for testing at Eglin to resolve stabilization issues. During later tests conducted at Lakehurst, New Jersey, in order to eliminate control problems during a mission that did not require maneuverability (fixed targets), a simple Bendix Aviation gyroscopic autopilot was installed to provide to a smooth stabilized flight that could be corrected on to the target by input from the radar in the nose cone. The gyros provided automatic stabilization as the Bat only needed controllable surfaces, which initially used radio signals from a police-type transmitter. This automatic stabilization achieved by using gyros was considered a technical milestone at the time.

Electrical Power System

After its electrical release by an electrical switch, the Bat operated via its own storage battery system, to home on the target. Three 14-volt batteries supplied power—two for the radar and one that operated the control servos. Although the duration of its flight was only a few minutes, the Bat's batteries were rated to operate the equipment continuously for fifteen to thirty minutes, depending upon battery condition and ambient temperature.

Bat body rear section containing the servo (center) and three 14-volt storage batteries (rear). (*USN*)

Mk. 2 Radar Homing System: Description and Operation

The SWOD Mk. 2 Radar-Homing System (RHS), developed by Bell Telephone Laboratory and manufactured by Western Electric, was functionally complete with its own transmitter and receiver. The Mk. 2 radar-seeking components were mounted in a circular faired bulkhead in the forward end of the airframe. The Mk. 2 was to automatically track the pre-selected target and to furnish directional control signals to the Bat to home it on the target.

The RHS was a self-sufficient complete S-Band system. It transmitted a strong 3,000-mc pulse of radio frequency energy with a duration of 0.75 microsecond, every 500 microseconds from a rapidly revolving paraboloidal reflector (spinner) and a fixed dipole antenna located in the Bat's nose. Any target within this area reflected a small portion of the original radiated energy back to the spinner and antenna, which directed it into the radar receiver circuits. The resulting video signals illuminated the target area on a Type A "Bat Scope" oscilloscope located at the Bat operator's position with horizontal sweeps of 10 and 25 miles.

In combat, the target was first selected by the AN/APS-2 search radar in the controlling aircraft. The search radar operator helped the Bat operator identify the target on his Type A oscilloscope. Once the target was identified, the SWOD Mk. 2 radar was adjusted to automatic tracking. The gated video signal was used to actuate

The SWOD Mk. 2 radar-homing system (RHS), developed by Bell Telephone Laboratory and manufactured by Western Electric, was functionally complete with its own transmitter and receiver. The Mk. 2 radar-seeking components were mounted in a circular faired bulkhead in the forward end of the airframe. (*USN*)

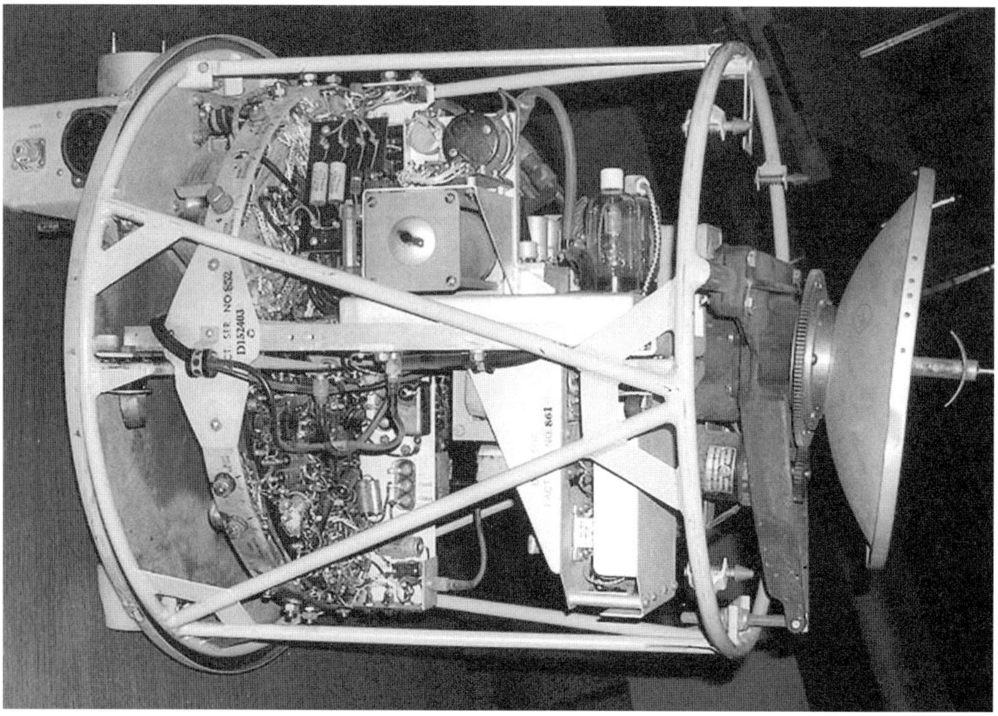

Starboard view of the RHS equipment. (*USN*)

Ground check of the Mk. 2 RHS system. (*USN*)

the directional control units and also to energize a directional indicator, which revealed whether the target was above, below, right, or left of the axis of the radar antenna system. This indicator, one for the SWOD operator and one on the pilot's instrument panel, was the same as that used in blind landings to establish course and glide angle. The Bat operator and controlling aircraft pilot each used this indicator so that the Bat could be carried into target range, which had a theoretical maximum distance of 25 miles; however, under test and operational conditions, this was found to be closer to 12 to 13 miles.

After a suitable target was selected by observing the scope and by coordination with the search radar operator, the control switches and knobs were manipulated to cause the radar equipment to track the selected target. A movable 0.75-microsecond time gate was adjusted until it coincided (in terms of time delay after the transmitter pulse) with the target echo. The circuit was then switched to a status that caused it to track the target automatically.

The Bat was not released until specific range, glide ratio, altitude, and release speed limits were established along with the positive locking of the target into the radar system. The optimal release speed was about 185 mph (160 knots). The missile design dictated that the glide ratio (slant range to altitude) had to be between 3.5 and 5.5 to 1 (i.e. on a mission flown at one-mile altitude, the missile release had to be between 3.5 and 5.5 miles' slant range). The control scope was provided with a basic computer, which enabled the operator to determine when the glide ratio was within allowable limits. The maximum range when searching was 25 miles and 15 miles with the automatic tracking system. Locking on a target was attained at about 15 miles under ideal conditions but usually was at not more than 12 or 13 miles. Small targets did not reflect a signal of adequate strength for locking at long range.

After release, the Bat's two 14-volt batteries powered the radar, while a third 14-volt battery operated the servo motors. The Mk. 2 radar then completely controlled the Bat, causing it to home on the target. Upon tracking a target, early Bats hunted by moving back and forth through a true straight-line course to the target. The reduction of hunting oscillations had previously been studied at MIT's Servomechanisms Laboratory as part of the Pelican project and was continued for the Bat under the direction of Dr. A. C. Hill. When the missile moved off its proper heading in one direction, the course was altered by the radar in the other direction along the true heading. Accuracy then depended on what stage in the hunting cycle the Bat happened to be when it reached the target. Because of the time and expense of manufacturing, such intricate and sophisticated (for 1945) equipment all idiosyncrasies needed to be eliminated before operational use. A gyroscopic automatic pilot was adapted to stabilize the weapon, while an intricate system of servo motors controlling external steering surfaces (elevons) were developed to reduce deviations in the hunting cycle. Dryden's team had developed the elevon approach using simple, low-cost elevons on the wings for control, with the elevons moving up or down in synchronism for pitch and opposite of each other for roll-to-turn smaller.

An automatic volume control (AVC) system controlled the receiver sensitivity of the target echo pip on the Bat's locked in radar. As the missile closed on the target, the pip echo strength increased. To prevent these ever stronger pips from saturating the receiver, the receiver sensitivity was automatically decreased. The AVC, therefore, concentrated the receiver on the target pip on which the Bat locked and was prevented from changing targets.

Throughout Bat's development, the Bat Scope operator had difficulties in identifying a target on which the Bat's RHS could lock. A range coordinator was developed to help the Bat operator to choose the correct target pip on his Bat Scope. By pressing a button, a downward moving pip on the scope indicated the target pip by moving adjacent to it. Only one range coordinator was ever used in combat, which was installed in an aircraft of VOB-124 that was lost on its first mission.

Carrying Rack and Hoists

A Mk. 51 Model 7 missile-carrying rack was mounted outboard of each outboard engine of the carrying aircraft. After trying various hoisting methods, the Mk. 9 bomb hoist was selected as the type to be used for operations. The Bat was lifted on to the rack by two standard Mk. 9 bomb hoists operated from the top of the wing with their lifting cables extending down through holes in the wing. The Bat hoisting equipment was stored on the flight deck behind the pilot.

The Bat was shipped in a special crate with its wing, tail, and nose cone detached from the body. The body with its fragile radar and electrical and other components were shipped separately. (*USN*)

Hand-cranked Bat hoist. (*USN*)

Electric Bat hoist. (*USN*)

The Bat was lifted on to the rack by two standard Mk. 9 bomb hoists operated from the top of the wing with their lifting cables extending down through holes in the wing. (*USN*)

A Bat in position after being hoisted from a special platform built on a Jeep. (*USN*)

Testing and Operational Training

During November and December 1944, forty-five test drops were made against reflectors on land and sea targets and ten drops against target ships; the 416-foot-long ex-Liberty ship *James Longstreet* (one test drop) and the 189-foot target ship *Carisee* (nine drops). After test drops of 30–40 percent accuracy, the Bat was ordered to become operational. The Consolidated PB4Y-2B ("B" for Bat) Privateer was modified for Bat operations with a simple kit that allowed modification to be completed in less than two days (300 man hours).

During testing, the Bat was also test-mounted on the SB2C Helldiver, F4U Corsair, and F6F Hellcat, but little is known about the results of these tests.

On February 6, 1945, Chief of Naval Operations Adml. Ernest King ordered VPB Squadrons 109, 123, and 124 of Fleet Air Wing Two to be equipped to employ the SWOD Mk. 9 Bat guided missile in combat and begin operational training at the Kaneohe Naval Air Station, Hawaii. On March 17, Lt. Cdr. Ortho McCrackin was assigned to head the Bat operational training program. McCrackin and one ground officer, sixty-five enlisted personnel, and the Bat equipment departed NAS Alameda, California, on board the escort carrier *Altamaha* (CVE-18) and arrived at Kaneohe on April 2. Beforehand, on March 17, 1945, twelve crews and squadron aircraft departed NAAF Crow's Landing, California, arriving at Kaneohe on March 20, 1945. Later, one officer and twenty-one enlisted personnel were added to the squadron to maintain equipment. Upon the squadron's arrival, the first three PB4Y-2Bs of VBP-109 were equipped to transport and launch the Bat, and their crews were briefly instructed in its use before practice drops were made. Lt. Col. Richard Craig, representing the AAF, served temporary duty with the Navy as the AAF liaison officer of Bat operations in the Pacific and made periodic reports on the Bat project. Training in deployment of the Bat continued at NAS Kaneohe into April 1945.

Operational Bats were to be employed by VPB-109 PB4Y-2B Squadron based in Palawan for a month, and this squadron and the two other PB4Y-2B squadrons, VPB-123 and VPB-124, were to be based on Okinawa for three months. These three patrol bombing squadrons would be the only squadrons equipped with SWOD Mk. 9.

Balikpapan Bat Missions

April 23, 1945 Mission

On April 23, 1945, two VPB-109 PB4Y-2Bs left Puerto Princessa on the first Bat combat mission, flying 700 miles to attack Japanese shipping in Balikpapan Harbor, Borneo. Squadron CO Lt. Cdr. (later rear admiral, USNR-Ret.) George Hicks in the lead aircraft and Lt. Leo Kennedy in the second aircraft, approached the harbor containing a large transport, a freighter, and five smaller merchant vessels. Each launched its Bat from 6 miles at 10,000 feet, but they performed erratically, each falling short of their intended target. Thus, the first employment of World War II's only automatic homing missile was a failure.

A Bat is pictured hitting the target ship *Carisee* during testing. (*From USN movie still*)

OTHER BAT-CARRYING AIRCRAFT

Grumman TBF Avenger. (*USN*)

Above: Curtiss SB2C Helldiver. (*USN*)

Below: Vought F4U Corsair. (*USN*)

On April 23, 1945, two PB4Y-2Bs (B for Bat) of VPB-109 based at Palawan launched the first Bats in combat against Japanese shipping 700 miles away in Balikpapan Harbor, Borneo. (*USN*)

April 28, 1945 Mission

On April 28, two Privateers, each carrying two Bats, flown by Lt. Cdr. Hicks and Lt. Chay, again attacked Balikpapan Harbor. Hicks released his first Bat from 9 miles and 10,500 feet at a large transport, but, instead, the Bat locked on a small nearby freighter and destroyed it and a wharf at the Pandanseri Oil Refinery. Hicks attempted to release his second Bat, but its electronics malfunctioned and it was not released. Lt. Chay aimed at the same large transport, but his Bat's radar again locked on another small freighter that happened to lie in line with the intended target, causing the ill-fated vessel to be sunk instead. Chay released his second Bat from 7 miles, but it veered off target at 45 degrees, flying inland, and only by luck destroyed a large oil storage tank of the refinery—3 miles short of the transport. So chance, rather than technology, made the raid a great success.

After only a short stay at Palawan, it became apparent that meaningful enemy shipping targets had either been sunk or driven into areas beyond the range of squadron aircraft, while those remaining in range were mostly small fleets of small wooden hulled coastal vessels (70 to 100 tons) that hugged the Malay and Borneo coasts. It was discovered during Palawan operations that these vessels posed problems because of the Bat's target selectivity. Bat tactics were often unsuccessful because of the weapon's difficulty in detecting the exact target from long range, or when there were multiple radar targets at the same range as the Bat's radar would automatically shift its homing to the best target at the set range. Nonetheless, Borneo, which had supplied Japan's military with 40 percent of its oil, was rapidly being cut off by Allied air and naval forces, and on May 1, the invasion of Borneo began with landings by Australian units. Consequently, further operational use of the Bat was suspended and the squadron would have to wait until it reached its new base at Yontan, Okinawa, on May 10 to see further combat using the Bat. This move to Okinawa would position the Bat-equipped aircraft within closer range of larger enemy vessels plying the Japanese Homeland waters.

Okinawa Bat Operations

VP-109 Bat Operations

May 13, 1945, VPB-109 Mission: The initial VPB-109 Bat missions were sweeps along the Chinese and Korean coasts. The first VPB-109 Bat mission flown from Okinawa was an encouraging failure. Two PB4Y-2Bs carrying only one Bat apiece attacked two 2,000-ton-plus merchantmen with one Bat exploding 20 feet ahead of the ship, lifting its bow out of the water, probably causing damage. The Bat launched from the second aircraft passed through the enemy's superstructure before it exploded in the water 1,500 feet beyond. These results were encouraging but the encouragement would be short-lived.

May 14, 1945, VPB-109 Mission: Two Privateers launched one Bat each with one exploding after flying 75 feet over the target, while the second Bat exploded over a mile away.

May 16, 1945, VPB-109 Mission: One Bat was released which exploded about 1,500 feet from the target.

May 24, 1945, VPB-109 Mission: The squadron continued sweeps along the coasts of China and Korea throughout the last week of May 1945, with several patrols attempting to use the Mk. 9 Bat. On May 24, Lieutenants Joseph Jobe and George Serbin, piloting a pair of Privateers carrying a mixed load of one Bat and general-purpose bombs, attacked shipping in the Korean Strait. Two hours after sinking three small freighters with a combination of strafing and bombing attacks, a large 7,000-ton troop transport was identified and Lt. Serbin launched his Bat from 10 miles out from 4,000-foot altitude. The missile traveled nose high, and dove vertically into the sea, approximately 2 miles short of the intended target. Moments later, Lt. Jobe released his Bat from 8 miles out at an altitude of 5,000 feet, and the missile appeared to function normally, but it struck the water about a quarter mile short of the transport.

May 27, 1945, VPB-109 Mission: The potential of the Bat was finally demonstrated on May 27, 1945, when two Privateers piloted by Lt. Cdr. George Hicks and Lt. Leo Kennedy took off from Yontan Airfield each carrying a Bat under one wing and a load of conventional bombs in the bomb bay. On the way to the target, a large 2,000-ton Japanese coastal freighter was encountered in the Korea Strait and strafed and then sunk by conventional bombs. A quarter hour later, four small vessels were sighted along the southeast tip of Korea a strafed and sunk by gunfire alone. About an hour later, on their homeward leg, Hicks and Kennedy spotted two single-stack destroyer escorts of approximately 970 tons on their radar from 20 miles, cruising at 15 knots and were identified visually at 15 miles from 2,000 feet. Range was closed to 6 miles and the Bats were readied for an attack as both warships began firing heavy but inaccurate AA. The Privateers turned 180 degrees, with Kennedy climbing to 8,500 feet, while Hicks, followed 2 miles behind at 6,000 feet. The AA fire, which had been intense and increasingly accurate as the Privateers approached, ceased as Kennedy began his head on attack on the destroyer from the optimum launch distance of 3 miles so that the targeted destroyer could not make evasive turns once the Bat was launched from 6,000 feet. The Privateer's radar was locked on the target but was not transferred to the Bat's homing device until just before launch. Nonetheless, the Bat's 1,000-pound warhead exploded off starboard bow above the water line, demolishing the whole foredeck area ahead of the bridge and killing thirty-three Japanese sailors. As soon as the Bat detonated, the undamaged escort, originally a mile away, moved to a position 100 yards from the damaged sister ship, turned broadside, and began firing accurate anti-aircraft fire. Hicks and Kennedy circled at 5,000 feet to assess the damage before the enemy fire forced their withdrawal to Okinawa. The mission was a success, the Bat sinking the destroyer escort, and conventional means, bombing and strafing, sinking a 2,000-ton freighter, four small freighters, and damaging two smaller vessels for which Kennedy was awarded the Navy Cross. However, the award was posthumous as Kennedy was killed in action by AA fire three days later during a conventional attack off the mouth of China's Yangtze River. Post-war records indicate that the DE *Aguni* was not sunk by a Bat but successfully returned to base severely damaged.

A combat movie still of a Bat about to strike a Japanese warship in the Korean Strait off Okinawa on May 27, 1945 for the first successful attack by a fully automated and operational guided missile. (*From USN movie still*)

May 29, 1945, VPB-109 Mission: On the squadron's last Bat Mission on May 29, Lts. May and Warren, investigating intelligence reports, searched for large concentrations of shipping in the mouth of the Yangtze River off Shanghai. A 2-ton and a 3-ton freighter were spotted, which were attacked, but the Bats were defective and did not track the target.

May 31, 1945, VPB-109 Relieved and VP-124 Deployed: After their frustrating May Bat combat experience, VPB-109 was relocated to West Field, Tinian, Marianas Islands. Meanwhile, VP-124 deployed to the Marianas, arriving at NAS Tinian on May 25, 1945, and on May 31, 1945, the squadron arrived at Yontan, under the operational control of FAW-l to relieve the previous Bat-equipped VPB-109.

VP-124 Bat Operations

June 7, 1945, VPB-124 Mission: Two destroyer escorts were sighted off the southern Korean coast, and a VPB-124 PB4Y-2B, armed with one Bat, climbed to just above a solid overcast at 7,000 feet while the other aircraft remained low to observe results. The Bat operator locked on what he thought was the correct target and dropped the Bat to about 6.5 miles' range and at 167 mph, almost at the Bat's minimum launching air speed. When the controlling Privateer descended below the overcast, the two DEs remained afloat and appeared undamaged. The observing aircraft did not identify the inflight Bat or any explosion; however, a vestige of smoke was reported near a prominent rock protruding from the sea about three-quarters of a mile from the targeted ships. Squadron records show no indication of whether the miss was due to mechanism failure or because it was locked on the wrong target as there were numerous blips were reported on the Bat scope and the operator could not be certain that the Bat was tracking the correct target.

June 14, 1945, VPB-124 Mission: Two VPB-124 bombers carried two Bats each on an anti-shipping search patrol along the Korean coast. A large enemy convoy consisting of three large merchant vessels, five or six destroyer escorts, and numerous other smaller merchant vessels, was located in a bay roughly surrounded on three sides by islands. Although most of the enemy ships were at least a half mile from any of these islands, the Bat scope screens were muddled by the numerous nearby small islands and rocks. One Privateer attempted three Bat attacks at about 8,000 feet and 200–210 mph. The first attack was abandoned when the operator/pilot's interphone malfunctioned. The second attack was attempted without interphone communication, but the pilot/radar/Bat coordination was so difficult, that the Bat operator was unable to determine which pip to use as target. On the third run, the Bat's power shutdown. After this frustrating experience, the Privateer pilot flew out to sea and jettisoned both Bats. Subsequently, it was discovered that the loss of power to the Bats was caused by some crewman inadvertently bumping the Bat's power switch and turning it to off.

The other Privateer also flew three attack runs. On the first attack, the scope operator had difficulty in deciding which pip to lock on. On the second run, the starboard Bat malfunctioned immediately before it was to be released. On the third run, the port Bat was released at 8,000 feet, 207 mph, and 6 miles' range, in increasing, but inaccurate AA from the enemy DEs that had formed a screen between the convoy and its attackers. During this run, the pilot did not fly smoothly during the release of the Bat, which exploded between two ships, a half mile apart. The starboard Bat was ordered to be jettisoned by the pilot on the diving getaway turn after release of the port Bat.

June 15, 1945, VPB-124 Mission: A VPB-124 PB4Y-2B patrol bomber, carrying one Bat, patrolling 15 miles off the southern Korean coast, intercepted a convoy composed of two large merchant vessels and one DE spaced 30 yards apart. The bomber flew its attack run from over land toward the open sea, releasing the Bat at 6,000 feet, 207 mph at a range of six miles. It exploded in the middle of the convoy and again it was supposed it could have homed on the average of the signals from the three enemy ships. The pips were so close together on the screen that the Bat operator could not determine on which ship the Bat's automatic tracking system had locked in on.

June 25, 1945, VPB-124 Mission: A VBP-124 Privateer patrolling the southern Formosan coast released one Bat at an unidentified enemy vessel from 6,000 feet, but it exploded on the shore a mile away from the target. The cause of the poor result was undetermined but possibly the Bat was locked on the wrong pip, or failed mechanically despite comprehensive pre-flight checks.

July 1, 1945, VPB-124 Mission: Two Bats were carried on one VPB-124 patrol bomber that was assigned to attack a radar station on the shore of a relatively large island. This first Bat missed, hitting the sea about 1,000 feet short of the island for undetermined reasons (but considering the second release report, it probably was released outside its design limits). The second Bat was released at an enemy merchantman from about 2,500 feet and 4 miles but hit about a mile and a half short and did not explode. Later enquiry determined this Bat was to have been definitely released too low and too close, outside its design limits, and thus, definitely had no possibility of hitting the target.

July 10, 1945, VPB-124 Mission: A VPB-124 Privateer sighted three DEs off southern Korea and launched two Bats. The first attack run from 6,000 feet became a dry run because the operator could not lock on to the target. The next run was also made at 6,000 feet, 184 mph, and released at 6.5 miles' range. The DE evaded in a tight circle and the Bat exploded within in this circle, causing no apparent damage. On the third run, the second Bat was released at 7,200 feet, 184 mph, and 6 miles' range. Clouds prevented reliable observation, but it was reported to also to have hit close to its target.

June 23 and 25, 1945, VPB-124 Missions: On June 23 and 25, 1945, VBP-124, Bat-armed Privateers were patrolling over the Tsushima Straits between Japan and Korea. There is no record of the June 23 mission except it was apparently unsuccessful. On the June 25 mission, pilots, Lts. Preis and Griffin, were on patrol at 2,000 feet above the Tsushima Strait, when three patrol boats were spotted by radar from 10 miles away, Preis remained at 2,000 feet while Griffin made a climbing turn to 8,000 feet and 8 miles out from the three Japanese patrol boats. Griffin's Bat was released and although the missile flew true, its homing radar became come confused by the multiple targets and exploded between the enemy vessels. Preis and Griffin returned to base, thus ending VPB-124s Bat experience.

VP-123 Bat Operations

June 1 to August 15, 1945, VPB-123 Bat Deployment: During its comparatively short combat tour, VPB-123 flew 230 combat missions, sinking sixty-seven enemy ships. However, VPB-123 records mention no results from its Bat deployment as by the time the squadron arrived, few suitable targets for the missile were left. The squadron's history states that the pilots had "minimal enthusiasm" for the missile and "preferred established bombing techniques" to using the "new and relatively untried device." Many Bats seemed to have been jettisoned by their crews rather than carrying them when no targets were to be engaged.

During July, all VPB-109, VPB-123, and VPB-124s SWOD-specific "Batmen" were transferred to combat Air Service Unit Seven (CASU-7), at Yontan, where use of the Bat was consolidated, and was to be test-carried by TBM Avengers and Curtiss SB2C Helldivers.

Apparently, the Navy tried using several Bats equipped with modified radar systems (SWOD Mk. 9 Model 1) and late in the war were reportedly dropped on Japanese-held bridges in Burma, the same targets that the VB-1 AZON was designed to attack.

Bat Operational Results and Summary

Of the thirty-three Bats used in combat between April 23 and July 15, 1945, the following results were recorded: hits, four (12.1 percent); near misses, four; misses, seven; mechanical failure, three; jettisoned by mothership, fourteen; and unobserved, one. Only fifteen Bats were successfully launched, recording four hits, but three of four of these hits were deemed as dubious successes due to chance. Three suffered mechanical failure but fourteen were jettisoned, supposedly due to carrying aircraft reporting "engine trouble" or "fuel shortage." However, often it was the failure to identify the target initially on search radar or later on the Bat Scope that caused the cumbersome drag-inducing Bats to be jettisoned by the mother aircraft rather than be carried back to base for a hair-raising landing with an over-sized 1,000-pound bomb slung under the wing. Tropical temperatures, humidity, mud, dust, and fungus did not agree with the Bat's sophisticated and sensitive instrumentation. Some Bats were damaged while being flown to forward areas for combat (if not flown, they would not have been available before the war ended). Rough ground handling and lack of spare parts affected the Bat's performance in combat. Dundas Tucker, the Bat's program manager for BuOrd, was present to supervise and urge the Bat's use by the three Navy Privateer squadrons. Four civilian scientists from the NBS were dispatched to maintain the weapon's functionality. However, the Bat's major problem was that its pioneering radar guidance system was unable to identify targets amid the surrounding clutter, particularly against targets close to shore.

Almost 3,500 Bats were produced under the program and many government patents were issued. The Bat consumed 8 million man hours of research and cost nearly $850 million in 1945 dollars ($12.3 billion in 2020), which was exceeded by the Manhattan Project (almost $29 billion in 2020) to develop the atomic bomb during the World

War II period. If it had been available earlier in the war, more technological concerns could have been identified and addressed, and the Bat could have had a major impact on Japanese shipping attempting to transport vital raw materials, especially oil to Japan, and then to transport arms and vital supplies from the home islands to its beleaguered far-flung armies. While the Bat did not achieve any impressive successes during World War II, post-war evaluations were mixed, but almost all concurred on its prospects in any future conflict as the Bat laid the foundation for guided standoff weapons that were to be so lethal and effective in modern warfare.

Bats in the Post-War USN Missile Program

Post-war analysis attributed the Bat's mediocre combat success to inadequate flight crew training and insufficient technical support, maintenance, and repair facilities in the field, which more or less exonerated the Bat, especially when post-war tests demonstrated its greatly increased accuracy. While the Air Force never adopted the Bat, the Navy continued to employ the weapon (redesignated as the ASM-N-2) for several years after the end of the war with post-war Privateer crews maintaining their Bat proficiency by attacking icebergs in the North Atlantic.

The Navy's post-war guided missile progress profited substantially from the evaluation of the more-advanced German missile projects of the late war. On March 12, 1946, the CNO directed the continuance of the Bat and Gorgon II-A and III-A testing programs (discussed later), which began in the final years of World War II. During May 1946, Navy VPB-104 and 115 Squadrons were designated as the lead squadrons for the operational continuance of the Bat SWOD 9. On August 14, 1946, the CNO directed that the terminology SWOD and pilotless aircraft (P/A) be discontinued for the standardized term guided missiles. The first Naval Air Missile Test Center, established in 1946 at Point Mugu, just west of Los Angeles, was established as the Navy's first instrumented missile test sea range to conduct tests and the evaluation of guided missiles and components on its 36,000-square-mile sea range.

The proliferation of post-war missile types under development prompted the Army and Navy to adopt a standard system of designating guided missiles on April 30, 1947. The designations "A" (Air), "S" (Surface), and "U" (Underwater) were combined to indicate their function followed by the letter "M" (Missile). Thus, a surface-to-air missile was designated SAM. A following letter denoted the service: "A" (Air Force), "G" (Army), "N" (Navy), such as SAM-N with an added letter for multiple service use. An optional prefix, "X" (Experimental) and "Y" (Service Test), could be added. Names assigned to the designations were as follows: ASMs would be named for birds of prey, AAMs for other winged animals, SAMs for mythological terms, and SSMs for astronomical terms or bodies. The current designation system for U.S. military missiles, rockets, and target drones was introduced by the Department of Defense and became official on June 27, 1963. It was not based on any previous U.S. missile designation system and, consequently, all missiles then in service were allocated new designations as per the new system.

There were two post-war Bat versions, designated SWOD Mk. 9 MOD 0 (Bat-0) and SWOD Mk. 9 MOD 1 (Bat-1), In September 1947 and early 1948, the Bat was redesignated as a guided missile:

Previous Designation	September 1947	February 1948
SWOD Mk. 9 MOD 0	ASM-2	ASM-N-2
SWOD Mk. 9 MOD 1	ASM-2a	ASM-N-2a

Project TED and the Bat-0

By V-J Day, 3,000 Bats had been manufactured and combat ready, and after the war, the Navy remained enthusiastic about their potential. The Bat experience in the South Pacific had indicated that with a dedicated technological analysis, improvements could make the Bat a more viable weapon. The Pilotless Aircraft Unit (PAU), Naval Air Station Mojave, California, initiated Project TED on September 27, 1946, with the intention of further evaluating the Bat for fleet use. However, only four days later, this unit was officially transferred to the new Naval Air Missile Test Center (NAMTC) at Point Mugu, which was directed by Navy missile veteran Capt. Delmar Fahrney.

Project TED's mission was to evaluate the missile's performance and its radar homing system. Some 300 Bat missiles were modified and shipped to the Pacific Fleet Patrol Squadron in two versions, with 150 of each type to be evaluated, the Bat-0 and the somewhat more advanced Bat-1. At the project's conclusion in March 1949, nine modifications were incorporated to improve the Bat's accuracy. The most interesting change involved its tail as positioning the Bat on the PB4Y-2B had required that 4 inches be removed from the top of its tail to clear the bomber's wing flaps. These modified tails were conjectured to be a possible cause of several failures at the end of the Bat's flight. Investigation determined that drag had changed, causing the radar to provide an up command correction as the last usable guidance signal, which caused the Bat to overshoot the target just before impact. This problem was resolved by reducing the bottom portion of the tail an equivalent 4 inches.

The Bat's feasibility was restored by the final February 1948 NAMTC report that stated that seventeen of the twenty drops had been successful, with typical ranges extended to more than 9 miles with launch altitudes of more than 11,000 feet. The following year, all existing Bat missiles were to be retrofitted with the nine recommended modifications and a large supply of spare parts was to be available because of expected damage in transit. Some electronic components required continued development.

Grounding the Bat

Bat demonstrations against an obsolete battleship during the late 1948 Hawaiian War Games were unimpressive, with four successive failures that were to some extent attributed to radar interference from other ships and aircraft. Also, the post-war was a time of rapidly developing technology and the wooden Bat quickly became an obsolete weapon as it could be easily deceived by very simple radar countermeasures. The contemporary rocket-propelled Sparrow and Sidewinder homing missiles were the forerunners of the more sophisticated weapons in the Navy missile pipeline.

By 1953, the Bat program was terminated, with most of the remaining airframes stripped down to become aerial targets. A few remained as test vehicles for new ASM-seekers, which became the Corvus (Raven) program and were dubbed Battus (Bat test units). A few years after the war, the USAF requested the Radioplane jet-powered drone for target practice, and in 1950, they first flew the YQ-1, which was powered by a pulse jet. However, this drone only had a flight time of about sixty minutes, which did not fulfil USAF specifications. (Both to be discussed later.)

With only a few years of development, a last-minute introduction into the war, and a short life in the operational inventory, today the Bat remains in relative obscurity despite its milestone status as the world's first self-guided missile and the first true smart weapon. The Bat remained classified until after the war and was not made public until the early 1960s; even today, there are only a few particulars available.

Seven Bats are currently on display:

Planes of Fame Museum (Bat-1), Chino, California
NAWCWD China Lake, (Bat-1), California
USN Museum at the Naval Yard (Bat-1), Washington, D.C.
NAS Point Mugu (Bat-1, California
National Bureau of Standards & Technology (Bat-1), Washington, D.C.
Admiral Nimitz State Historic Site (Bat-0), Fredericksburg, Texas
NASM Udvar-Hazy Center (Bat-0), Washington, D.C., Dulles International Airport

SWOD Mk. 10

The SWOD Mk. 10 was a guided bomb originally designated as Bomb Mk. 69 but no further information can be found in the literature.

Kingfisher

The Kingfisher was intended to produce standoff delivery systems to allow for the release of torpedoes "from outside of the range of enemy defences, specifically calling for radar-controlled, subsonic, self-homing, air-borne missiles … to deliver explosive charge below water line of floating targets." The Kingfisher Type E was an exception as it was proposed for submarine targets and was to be released from shipboard.

Project Kingfisher was initiated in August 1944, as a response to the increasing vulnerability of torpedo bomber aircraft to successfully complete attacks in the face of the increasing defensive firepower of Japanese warships during late war. The program was an extension of the Pelican and Bat guided-bomb projects, which were conducted at the NBS under the direction of Hugh Dryden and Edward Conden, under the sponsorship of the NDRC and the BuOrd. The Kingfisher's subsidiary radar development was under the auspices of the MIT Rad Lab. The first design consideration given to Kingfisher was during September 1944, but active project development did not begin until after the end of the war. The BuOrd originally conducted the project, but in early 1947, the Navy BuAer joined BuOrd in control; meanwhile, technical direction remained the responsibility of the NBS.

Initially, the Kingfisher was a low-priority portion of the Bat program, and thus it was considered practical to adapt as many component parts of the Bat airframe as feasible. Utilizing this idea would expedite any future production by using existing Bat forms and jigs and also facilitate parts interchangeability in service. To implement this consideration, the existing 2,000-pound Bat airframe (SWOD Mk. 14) was to be modified by redesigning the body to accommodate a releasable torpedo payload.

The first Kingfisher airframe design was intended for a glide missile capable of carrying a standard Mk. 13 aircraft torpedo, but the use of this payload complicated the design of an airframe with radar homing intelligence. The Mk. 13 torpedo was more than twice as long as a standard GP bomb (called a plunge bomb in Kingfisher literature) and of comparable weight, thus creating an airframe for it with suitable rigidity and adequate stability needed to be addressed. However, even more complicated design problems arose from this payload having to be released from the airframe before water entry, which made it necessary to incorporate the aerodynamic control system that was currently in use on the Bat.

However, an evaluation established that to achieve structural strength and stability, the Kingfisher body would become overly large and heavy, causing handling problems in service. As a remedy, the main supporting wings and the stabilizing empennage were to be attached directly to the torpedo by using the existing Mk 14 Bat wings with simple pin attachments to a central frame that, in turn, was strapped to the torpedo near its center of gravity. This central frame formed a superstructure in which the batteries, the servo, and some of the electronic equipment were housed. The straps that held this assembly to the torpedo terminated at a standard 14-inch bomb shackle, thus allowing release of the wings by some electrical initiator prior to water entry. At the same time, the nose and tail assemblies could be detached by a cable release latch.

An 1:6 scale model of this design was fabricated and tested in a NBS wind tunnel. The results of these tests revealed satisfactory performance qualities and five full-scale Kingfisher airframes were then ordered from the Vidal Research Corporation, which had available the Bat molds and jigs for the airframes. Two of these airframes were assembled on mock Mk. 13 torpedoes and prepared for flight testing. These units contained no homing equipment but were roll-stabilized, using the standard control gyro SWOD Mk. 6 and servo SWOD Mk. 6 Mod 0. The decalage (angle between the chord of the wing and the horizontal tail surfaces) was set at 2.5 degrees, which was deemed the best adjustment from wind tunnel model tests. A release mechanism for detaching the nose, wing, and tail assemblies after fifty seconds of flight was included.

On June 11, 1946, two were tested, the first, Flight K-9, was launched at 207 mph from an altitude of 4,000 feet, descending at an glide angle of about 34 degrees to the horizontal with roll stabilization obtained. However, the missile hit the ground before the release mechanism had time to activate. The second, Flight K-10, was launched at 230 mph from 6,000 feet, descending at a glide angle of 25 degrees to the horizontal in a steady flight. This release mechanism operated successfully at thirty seconds at an altitude of about 1,000 feet. The results of these tests were considered satisfactory to allow use of this airframe, designated as SWOD Mk. 15, as an interim test vehicle for future development of new radar homing equipment.

Consequently, a contract was let to Camden Eastern Marine Company, Camden, Maine, to build nineteen additional plywood airframes using the Mk 14 Bat wings then on hand. Later, another contract was let to the Goodyear Aircraft Company, Phoenix, Arizona, to reproduce the wooden Bat airframes as metal airframes, which facilitated quantity production. This wood-to-metal conversion was based on service experience using the Bat airframe, which disclosed that adverse warping occurred when the plywood structures were subjected to unfavorable climatic conditions.

During November, two additional flight tests were made using the Mk. 15 airframe. Since the first two tested, Test Flights K-9 and K-10, descended too steeply, the decalage was increased to 3 degrees on one unit and 3.5 degrees on the second. Each missile was equipped with Mk. 1 (Pelican) radar equipment for homing against a stationary beacon. The first unit, Flight K-23, was released at 230 mph, but exhibited a large roll amplitude that affected the operation of the pitch gyro and it crashed about one mile short of the target. The second unit, Flight K-24, dropped away normally, but after about three seconds, the radar equipment failed, and it descended into a steep angle, spiraling into a landing nearly below the release point. Changes were made on the elevons and stabilization; during the next Test Flights, K-25 and K-26, the problems were shown to be corrected

With the prospect of more compact radar homing equipment, the airframe was simplified by eliminating the body portion. It was initially proposed to attach the wings directly to the torpedo by latches incorporated in the torpedo structure but examination disclosed that the latches could not be placed at appropriate positions because of interference with the torpedo's air flask. Further inquiry developed a method to strap the wings directly to the torpedo, which required additional aerodynamic testing, during which the wing could be repositioned longitudinally to compensate for any change in the position of the center of gravity. The flexibility of this design significantly contributed to conversion into a Kingfisher C powered missile, in the attachment of a turbo-jet motor to the rear of the shroud ring assembly of the torpedo tail.

Experience with the Bat, along with many mathematical analyses, had determined the pursuit-course type of homing to be unsuccessful against fast-moving targets and that some method of course navigation would be necessary for the Kingfisher. Any method of automatic navigation, which caused the missile to fly a course differing from a pursuit course, caused the missile to fly at an angle to the line of sight path. Undesirable cross effects occurring in the homing signals, especially in the case of a rolling motion that could critically affect either the stability or the accuracy of the missile but with adequate computers for both azimuth and elevation, difficulties from cross effects were resolved.

By VJ-Day, many surplus missiles and missile components became readily available from the Pelican and Bat development programs. A series of preliminary tests were outlined to demonstrate the practicability of using course computers in homing missiles. For these tests against moving targets, an 8,000-foot railroad had been constructed at the Warren Grove, New Jersey, test field. The target was a radar beacon, mounted on a railroad section car with its speed preset. It moved down the track unattended while track switches along the way automatically recorded the target position at various time intervals and operated mechanisms to stop the car at the end of the track.

During the first three months of 1946, nine of the available Pelicans (SWOD Mk. 7 Mod 0) were dropped on the moving target at Warren Grove (Test Flights K-1 to K-8). The antennas of two of these units were offset in azimuth by fixed lead angles of 12 degrees and 6 degrees, respectively, and were estimated to give true collision course compensation for the particular flight conditions. On two other Pelicans where the target moved at 46 mph, the antennas were offset by an amount less than that required to produce a true collision course. The antenna of one of these was offset by one-half the total value, or 6 degrees and that of the other, by three-quarters of the total amount, or 9 degrees. For comparison, the other four were dropped with zero lead angle compensation.

In all these tests, the azimuth flight path was as expected. In the two with full lead angle compensation, the flight path was very straight throughout the major portion of the flight, however, since the line of flight passed the target path slightly ahead of the target, it was decided that the lead angle was slightly too large. The two missiles with one-half and three-quarters of full collision course lead angle flew a modified collision course path with a slight curvature in the direction of target motion, with their line of flight passing the target path slightly behind the target. The four with zero lead angle all flew typical pursuit paths, with their line of flight passing the target path behind the target. Analysis of the flight charts of these tests revealed no adverse effect on the stability of the glider when the antenna was offset in azimuth. However, the accuracy in range was considerably influenced by the squint angle (the angle between the effective zero axis of the antenna and the axis of the missile). A fairly large dispersion in range occurred when the antenna assembly was offset in azimuth but fixed in pitch as, during this condition, a pitch error was introduced whenever the glider banked to correct for an azimuth error.

A study was conducted to investigate the feasibility of using servo tabs to control the Kingfisher. A servo tab is a small hinged device installed on an aircraft control surface to assist the movement of the control surfaces. Introduced by the German firm Flettner, servo tabs were formerly known as Flettner tabs. For the tests, two Mk. 13 airframes were provided with auxiliary control surfaces attached to the elevons and operated by standard White-Rodgers servo motors in each elevon.

Mk. 1 (Pelican) homing equipment was installed in the missiles for homing on a fixed beacon. These units were dropped at the Warren Grove Test Area in June (Flights K-11 and K-12), but while neither of the units homed, they showed successful roll

The Kingfisher program, developed from surplus Pelican and Bat airframes, would lead to a series of six different missile designs, designated A–F, employing a variety of payload and guidance options. (*USN*)

stabilization. The rates of roll developed in the roll hunting motion were very large and the failure to home was explained by the effect of these high rates of roll on the action of the gyros.

During July 1946, to examine the performance of a simplified lead computer system in azimuth, four SWOD Mk. 8 Mod 0 units, containing these computers, were dropped against a beacon carried on a moving target car at the test field at Warren Grove. Each contained Mk. 1 (Pelican) radar homing equipment with all the antennas put in order installed so that they could be rotated in azimuth by White-Rodgers reversible motor servos. The test result reported that the computers were found to be adequate.

Kingfisher Series A through F

The Kingfisher program developed a series of six different missile designs, designated A through F, employing a variety of payload and guidance options: Types A and B, which were gravity-powered (glider); Types C, D, and E, which ware jet-powered missiles; and the new Type F, essentially a powered version of the former Type B, was added in early 1947. Of these designs, four (C–F), were determined to be suitable for full development; however, due to the end of the war, the priority of the project was reduced and development was slowed. Flight testing of the early Type A and B glider models occurred in late 1946 and was abandoned in early 1947 at the direction of the

CNO because of the lack of an operational demand. Full development of the selected (C–F) operational versions began during 1947.

Kingfisher A

Kingfisher A, also known as SWOD Mk. 11 and later as SWOD Mk. 15 was an unpowered, gravity-driven GB design, launched from an aircraft at high altitude, having a 20-mile range. It was intended to carry a passive, acoustic-homing Mk. 21 Mod 2 torpedo for use against surface vessels in low-threat situations, where the attacking aircraft did not require defensive cover from fighter escorts. Considered to be an interim design before fully-powered missiles were available, the Kingfisher A design was used as a basis for glide tests to verify the aerodynamic properties of the Kingfisher series. Tests occurred during late 1946 using the PB4Y-2 Privateer as the launching aircraft. The Kingfisher A was canceled in early 1947 as being no longer being required by the Navy; however, the SWOD Mk. 15 airframe design was used as a basis for the Kingfisher series.

Kingfisher B

Kingfisher B, or SWOD Mk. 21, was designed to be lightweight Kingfisher A, weighing 1,000 pounds, including the payload—only two-thirds the weight of the Bat guided bomb. Its payload, a 360-pound non-homing, non-powered gravity bomb, was to have a 20-mile range when launched from an aircraft at high altitude. After launching, it was to glide along a ballistic trajectory for a short time before sinking alongside a target and detonating underwater. This Kingfisher was also canceled in 1947 as no longer meeting BuOrd requirements.

Kingfisher C Petrel

Kingfisher C was developed from the SWOD Mk. 15 airframe and given the designation AUM-2 initially, and then AUM-N-2 Petrel, (AUM for air-to-underwater missile). The 3,800-pound, 24-foot-long Petrel, manufactured by the Fairchild Guided Missiles Division, Wyandanch, Long Island, New York, was essentially a Mk. 21 Mod 2 torpedo equipped with wooden fins, 13-foot 2-inch wingspan, and a nose fairing housing guidance equipment. It was powered by Fairchild J44 turbojet (rather than the simpler rockets used by the British on their early missiles). The Fairchild Engine Division had begun its study project for a small, inexpensive turbojet during 1946. During June 1947, Fairchild was awarded a Navy contract for a low-power turbojet, designed to equip an anti-submarine missile. This J44 was the first U.S. consumable turbojet, for which a maximum lifetime of ten hours was required. During August 1948, the XJ44 made its first run up and made its first flight in mid-1950 when it powered the Petrel.

The Type C *Kingfisher* was designed to be released from currently available aircraft, primarily the Lockheed P2V Neptune, and to use currently available torpedoes, the Mk. 21 Mod 2 torpedo, in particular. When launched from an aircraft at low altitude, the missile dropped to 200 feet above the water and cruised up to 23 miles at Mach 0.5 towards the target, using semi-active radar-homing. Once the missile had reached a range of just under 4,900 feet from its target, the Fairchild turbojet would be shut down and the wings and fins were jettisoned. The torpedo (by 1951, the Mk. 41 torpedo had replaced the Mk. 21 Mod 2) dropped on a free trajectory into the water and began to home in on the target. The weapon was suitable for use against surface targets only, principally ships and surfaced submarines, moving at up to 38 mph.

The National Bureau of Standards authorized AUM-2 tests in 1951, after which further AUM-N-2 development was transferred to Fairchild Aircraft's Guided Missiles Division in 1954. During 1956, the Type C became the only Kingfisher to be declared operational, as one East Coast patrol squadron, VP(HM)-13, and one West Coast patrol squadron, VP(HM)-10, both flying P2V-6M Neptune carrier aircraft, were equipped with the Petrel. The Navy never granted the Petrel a very high priority, because at the time it was much more anxious about the threat from enemy nuclear submarines than from surface ships, since nuclear submarines, armed with atomic weapons, could remain submerged for very long periods. The phase out of the Petrel began in the late 1950s once it was no longer being considered necessary in the quickly evolving strategic environment. On January 29, 1959, the program was canceled entirely and the remaining Petrels were converted to serve as air-launched target drones.

Kingfisher D Diver

The Kingfisher D missile, proposed in 1946 by Navy's Bureau of Ordnance, was similar in concept to Kingfisher C except it was intended to carry a new, lightweight, yet-to-be-developed, solid-propellant rocket-propelled torpedo. This torpedo had a 200- to 400-pound warhead charge that used a single innovative dual-purpose rocket propulsion system that would provide thrust both during the flight of the missile launched at a 20-mile range from an aircraft at low altitude and, then following the release of the torpedo, propelling it underwater during its terminal run. The total weight of the unit was to be about 3,000 pounds, including the torpedo payload. Under contract to the NBS, work on Kingfisher D, given the designation AUM-4 Diver in September 1947 and the definitive designation AUM-N-4 in 1948 that continued until its cancellation. However, technical issues encountered in the development of the new torpedo meant that a viable weapon could not be produced. Without its intended torpedo warhead, the Diver missile was no longer required, and the program was canceled prior to 1950, without any being built.

Kingfisher E Grebe

Constructed by the Arizona Goodyear Aircraft Company Plant, under subcontract to the NBS, the Kingfisher E, the only surface-launched Kingfisher variant, was redesignated as the SUM-2 in September 1947 and SUM-N-2 Grebe in 1948. It was a large, 16-foot, 5-inch long, 21-inch-diameter, 2,500-pound (at launch) conventionally-configured missile resembling a small unmanned aircraft, with a high-mounted, straight 14-foot-span wing, and a twin tail empennage configuration. Power was initially delivered by a solid-propellant rocket, providing a range of 5,000 yards at Mach 0.5; later in the designs, the development of a variant with a pulse jet sustainer engine was conceived, weighing 3,000 pounds including the deep-diving homing torpedo that was then in the research stage and was to increase the missile's range to 23 miles at a cruising speed of Mach 0.26. The original specification for the missile mandated the Mk. 35 torpedo as the SUM-N-2's payload, but later, to reduce weight, the design was changed to use the Mk. 41 torpedo. Several forms of guidance were evaluated, although none had been definitively selected by the end of the program. Assigned the cover designation of AA Target Mk. 52 Mod 2, testing of twenty XSUM-N-2 prototype missiles began in early 1950, but by 1953, however, the program had been canceled. The specified motivation for the cancellation was that the missile outranged the sonar equipment that was required to find targets for it, thus making it impossible to use at its maximum range. The Navy would later develop the RUR-5 ASROC, a rocket-delivered torpedo (or a pure missile in the nuclear version), for attacking submarines at long range. In 1972, one Grebe was refurbished for evaluation as part of studies into cruise missile development.

Kingfisher F Puffin

On February 5, 1947, McDonnell Aircraft, St. Louis, began work on Kingfisher F as the AUM-6, which was redesignated as the AUM-N-6 Puffin in 1948. Weighing 1,300 pounds, the missile was of conventional small-aircraft design with a high-mounted wing and V-tail. A pulse jet engine was mounted in the rear of a streamlined fuselage. Guidance was by onboard active radar homing unit housed in the missile's nose. After release from the launching aircraft, the radar selected a target and navigated the missile into position to release its 500-pound gravity bomb payload, carried in the mid-fuselage. The bomb was intended to be dropped alongside the target ship and detonate underwater, holing the target vessel below the waterline, causing flooding. The XAUM-N-6 Puffin began flight testing in 1948, and was considered for carriage by USAF bombers, the B-47 Stratojet and B-50 Superfortress, as well as USN aircraft, the AD Skyraider, PB4Y Privateer, and P5M Marlin. Tests did not demonstrate that the weapon was suitable for service, and on October 1, 1949, the AUM-N-6 program was canceled.

Aftermath

Although Project Kingfisher largely failed to produce the intended operational weapons, with only Kingfisher C, as the AUM-N-2 Petrel, seeing operational service, much was learned about the issues of aerodynamics and control of guided weapons from them. Meanwhile, the Navy chose to use fully ballistic rocket-powered weapons for antisubmarine use, developing the RUR-5 ASROC as its standard anti-submarine missile. The concept of an unpiloted torpedo-carrying aircraft-type missile was developed by other nations, with the French *Malafon* and Australian *Ikara* being markedly similar in concept to the Kingfisher E.

Gorgon Series

During May 1943, Delmar Fahrney and Ivan Driggs, a civilian scientist working at BuAer, submitted a plan for the development of a guided weapon that could be used against either aircraft or small ships. It was to be powered not by a rocket but by a small turbojet, the 9.5A, which Westinghouse was already developing under a Navy contract. BuAer approved the proposal on July 19, 1943 and established the project at the Naval Aircraft Factory, which became part of the new Naval Air Material Center (NAMC), Philadelphia, on the next day. NAMC was to participate in the quantity conversion and modification of newly produced aircraft prior to delivery to the fleet for combat use. The project and the missile were named Gorgon from Greek mythology, which were ugly dragon-like monsters with huge wings, writhing snakes for hair, sharp fangs and claws, and bodies covered with scales. The gaze from their staring eyes was so terrifying that anyone who looked upon them immediately turned to stone.

In August 1943, Driggs completed Gorgon's specifications and general arrangement drawings. Its 760-pound design and configuration were conventional except for a cast magnesium airframe. Powered by the Westinghouse 9.5A turbojet, it could attain an estimated top speed of between 475 and 510 mph and could deliver a 50- to 100-pound warhead.

NAMC assigned the Gorgon program to a relatively low priority until October 19, 1943, when BuAer raised the project's priority and requested estimates for the manufacture of fifty Gorgons, half to be turbojet-powered and half rocket-powered. The engine change was due to delays in Westinghouse's development of its 9.5A turbojet. BuAer directed the NAMC to finalize designs for a liquid-fuel rocket-powered Gorgon that was currently under development by Lt. Robert Truax of the Naval Engineering Experiment Station at Annapolis.

During an October 1943 Washington, D.C., conference, the present status and future of the Gorgon project was discussed by NAMC and BuAer representatives. At the conference, there was agreement that the NAMC would proceed with the concurrent development of two Gorgon airframe designs: one of conventional arrangement, and the other of the canard-type, with its control surfaces forward of, rather than behind, the wing. Each would be equipped with RCA BLOCK I television equipment and would be powered by either the Westinghouse turbojet or the rocket under development. By November, the NAMC had completed a conventional layout mockup and had two canard-type mockups of the under construction.

The Gorgon program received an important personnel addition at this time when the notably experienced Lt. Moulton "Molt" Taylor was named as Gorgon project engineer for which he would be awarded the Legion of Merit. After the war, Taylor was known for his design of the Aerocar, a viable automobile/aircraft combination of which only six prototypes were built.

An important BuAer study determined that the Gorgon should be as uncomplicated as possible, even if that simplicity experienced weight consequences. BuAer's Structures Branch considered Drigg's original magnesium fuselage proposal and

The Gorgon program began with a relatively low priority, but when the particularly experienced Lt. Moulton "Molt" Taylor was named as Gorgon project engineer, the program made significant progress; for which, Taylor would be awarded the Legion of Merit. After the war, Taylor was known for his design of the Aerocar, a viable automobile/aircraft combination (both are pictured). (*Aerocar*)

supposed that there would be significant production advantages if the Gorgons were built with monocoque magnesium fuselages. In February 1944, the NAMC and NAF formed a relationship with Dow Chemical to investigate the potential of magnesium in the Gorgon program. At the time, Dow was America's major magnesium producer (Freeport, Texas, plant) and researcher. Meanwhile, the fuselage was to be fabricated of molded plywood, similar to the material used in the NAF's Assault Drones. The Singer Manufacturing Company, South Bend, Indiana, became the major supplier to the NAF of wooden structures for the missiles.

The Gorgon program made heartening progress early in 1944, as NAMC had completed the Gorgon canard-configured mockup by the end of February. On March 17, the Mockup Board arrived in Philadelphia to inspect it and found the Gorgon design fundamentally sound but did suggest changes, particularly concerning the weight of the missile's warhead. Originally, the Gorgon was to carry 100 pounds of Torpex, an explosive approximately twice as powerful as TNT, but the Mockup Board thought the weapon's structure should be strengthened to accommodate a heavier Torpex payload. NAMC's Capt. Ralph Barnaby admonished that the Gorgon was a "highly experimental article" and that armament studies would be best deferred until the aerodynamic, guidance, and propulsion issues were resolved in flight testing. Utilizing the Mockup Board's recommendations, BuAer instructed the NAMC to proceed with the construction of Gorgons for flight and structural tests.

Nonetheless, time and events would impose changes in the Gorgon itself and the test program at the NAMC. The magnesium Gorgon airframe was finally rejected and the molded plywood monocoque fuselage was continued, with only the missile's control surfaces metal—albeit cast aluminum not magnesium. The Westinghouse 9.5A Turbojet engine planned for some of the early Gorgons encountered problems and its development became stalled, causing the Gorgon program to reallocate its orientation toward the Annapolis Rocket Motor and other power plants, including pulse jets. NAMC did not possess the necessary aerodynamic equipment to test the Gorgon at Philadelphia and used that at NACA's Langley, Virginia Laboratory. In June, Langley tested the aerodynamics of the canard configuration missile powered by the rocket motor and the Westinghouse turbojet. The test results did specify some longitudinal stability problems but no inherent design defects or intractable aerodynamic defects and the Gorgon program would settle into a testing, redesign/development, and testing regime that would continue through the end of the war with ongoing airframe/power plant configuration determinations.

The Naval Aircraft Factory had the primary responsibility for the design, engineering, and construction of the Gorgon. The Naval Aircraft Modification Unit (NAMU)—first at Philadelphia and, after early July 1944, at the former Brewster Aeronautical plant at Johnsville, Pennsylvania—conducted Gorgon testing and subsequent development. Both the NAF and the NAMU were subordinate commands within the Naval Air Material Center (NAMC). To determine the best airframe/power plant combination, four missile designs were to be tested: the Gorgon II-A, which was of the canard configuration with rocket propulsion; the Gorgon II-B, of identical configuration but with the Westinghouse 9.5A Turbojet; the Gorgon III-A, which had a conventional wing and tail configuration and an Annapolis Rocket Motor; and the Gorgon III-B, with the conventional layout and the Westinghouse 9.5A Turbojet. The NAF began deliveries of Gorgon IIs to the NAMU on September 1, 1944 and completed eighteen Gorgon IIs before the first week of December. By the spring of 1944, the NAF had made advances with the design phase of the Gorgon III, and engineers projected deliveries of the first five in October. As it had with the Assault Drones, the NAF subcontracted many of the Gorgon components.

In early 1945, the NAMU was ready to flight test the Gorgon, using a venerable PBY-5A Catalina that had been previously active in towing tests of gliders and GLOMBs. The initial test was with a Gorgon II-A equipped with radio control apparatus but without the Annapolis Rocket Motor. On January 17, the PBY released the II-A at 10,000 feet over Warren Grove, New Jersey, with an FM-2 Wildcat fighter as the chase plane. Only seconds after its launch, the Gorgon went into a series of rolls that the control operator was unable to stabilize and that eventually led to a spiraling destructive crash dive into the ground. Before the second test flight on February 3, the radio control unit was adjusted to prevent the roll and stabilization problems and a parachute was installed for emergency recovery. Soon after launch, the Gorgon's new parachute deployed, flowing back over the missile's tail but, nevertheless, the Gorgon performed perfectly and was safely glided to a landing.

The powered flights of the rocket-propelled Gorgon II-A were transferred by NAMU from inland Warren Grove to the Atlantic Ocean off Cape May because of concerns about the toxicity of the acid aniline oxidizer and fuel combination. On March 8, the Catalina carried the Gorgon II-A, with a FM-2 Wildcat acting as the control aircraft, a Martin JM-1 (the Navy B-26 version) as the chase plane, and two SB2Cs composing a photographic record of the test. As scheduled the rocket fired ten seconds after launch and accelerated rapidly away at an estimated 550 mph; when its fuel was spent, the Gorgon was more than 5 miles ahead of the JM-1. Later that month, NAMU conducted the second flight test with a television camera on board the Gorgon and a TV monitor on the control aircraft *to* record airspeed readings. After attaining 400 mph, the missile inexplicably completed a right-hand turn and dove vertically into the Atlantic.

Taylor was concerned about the rocket-powered Gorgon's speed, the controller's capacity to control, and chase aircraft's ability to remain within sight of the speeding missile. Taylor considered whether the turbojet-powered Gorgon would be more easily controlled. Nonetheless, Taylor remained enthusiastic as the rocket-powered Gorgon tests were considered beneficial for resolving various stability, control, and launching technique questions.

Some advocates thought the Gorgon could become a good high-speed test vehicle for NACA, but throughout the early Navy testing, NACA exhibited no interest. However, NACA's awareness was aroused by Gorgon II-A's flight tests and high speeds. During March 1945, two NACA Langley Laboratory engineers conferred with NAMU about the Gorgon, and less than a month later, on April 2, R/Adml. Lawrence Richardson, BuAer's Assistant Chief, directed NAMU to develop a new Gorgon variant, designated as the III-C. The III-C employed the same airframe as the III-A but was equipped with a more powerful rocket motor. In the spring of 1945, the NAF manufactured twenty III-Cs for NACA, which were delivered to NACA's new flight station at Wallops Island, Virginia.

Gorgon production for NACA coincided with early deliveries of Westinghouse 9.5A Turbojets for the Gorgon II-B and III-B. During the middle of January, Westinghouse delivered two 9.5A units to the NAF, but these engines' performance at high altitudes was mediocre and the company was struggling to develop an improved 9.5B model and was unable to make delivery before July. Meanwhile, the NAF, had been assigned the development of a modified Gorgon III-B designated as the TD2N, to be used as a high-speed target drone.

By April 1945, as the Gorgon program was accelerating, problems occurred with turbojet deliveries, and the weapon's requirements were changing, causing BuAer's Chief, R/Adml. Ramsey, to reevaluate the Gorgon program. Currently there were orders for 130 Gorgons: twenty-one II-As, four II-Bs, thirty-four III-As, sixteen III-Bs, twenty III-Cs, and thirty-five TD2Ns. Ramsey's reassessment revised the Gorgon's original concept and the project's guidance. Rather than developing an operational air-to-surface or air-to-air missile, the Gorgon program was to become an experimental engineering project for the NAMC to develop and test propulsion systems, and control, guidance, and homing methods (especially television) for high-speed missiles. The NAMC was directed to complete the assorted Gorgon test programs and to conclude the TD2N target drone program.

However, Germany's impending collapse and surrender would impact Ramsey's directive. Strategists predicted that the Pacific War would continue into 1946 with the Navy responsible for pre-invasion shore bombardment of Japan. Continued delays in deliveries of Westinghouse turbojets, impeded any speedy reworking of II-B or III-B Gorgons as long-range shore bombardment missiles, but a new Gorgon II-C model offered some encouragement. The II-C was propelled by a 14-inch pulse jet being developed by the Naval Engineering Experiment Station, Annapolis. The so-called "Junior Buzz Bomb," which was thought to become operational relatively quickly, was to be catapulted from escort carriers or other ships and directed to its target by radio and television control. Even though Ramsey had directed that the NAMC consider the Gorgon program as a research and development project, BuAer delineated an II-C production program that projected the delivery of 200 of the missiles by December 1.

However, NAMC's CO, R/Adml. Donald Royce, was not optimistic about the II-Cs prospects as that program would use many of his center's resources and divert it from research and development. Royce was aware that there could be problems and delays in the development of the pulse jet engine and the catapult launch method. The Gorgon II-C would probably have to be redesigned to integrate a metal rather than a molded plywood airframe. Nonetheless, these potential technical difficulties were thought to be easily surmounted and that the Gorgon II-C would be a potent new weapon that would capable of delivering a 1,000-pound warhead with imposing accuracy at ranges of up to 130 miles.

As Royce predicted, the Gorgon II-C would consume much of the NAMC's time and assets, as BuAer began the program by directing the center to manufacture thirty-six Gorgon II-Cs and in August ordered the procurement of sixty-four more. The bureau expected the NAMC to deliver 200 before the end of the year, then increase production to 200 per month; by April 1946, output was to increase to 500 monthly. By late June 1945, the consequences of the Gorgon II-C program became apparent: the Gorgon II-A, II-B, and III-C projects were essentially halted while the center concentrated on pulse jet-powered II-C engineering studies. Just as the II-C program began to gain momentum, two atomic bombs suddenly ended the Pacific War, causing the cancellation of the chief production orders and a significant reduction in the project's magnitude. The first Gorgon II-C (redesignated KGN-1 in October 1945) did not fly until September 1946.

Gorgon II Models

The Gorgon project would lead to numerous diverse types with a confusing roll of designations with some Gorgon variants being redesignated four times in about two years.

Gorgon II-A

The Gorgon II-A, considered the baseline design of the Gorgon series, was a 14-foot, 6-inch-long, 970-pound, laminated wood missile of canard configuration, with a conventional high-mounted monoplane wing (span: 11 feet). Propulsion was provided by a Reaction Motors CML2N liquid-fuel rocket, fueled with monoethylamine (ethanolamine or MEA) and nitric acid, which gave the Gorgon II-A a speed of 500 mph and a range of 25 miles. In 1945, Reaction Motors, Pompton Plains, New Jersey, was granted a contract from the Army to develop a rocket engine for the first of the X series of experimental airplanes, designed to break the sound barrier. On October 14, 1947, test pilot Chuck Yeager would be the first to break the sound barrier, piloting the X-1 engined with the four Reaction Motors engines.

Production of the Gorgon II-A, to be designated as the KA2N-1 anti-aircraft missile in October 1945, was ordered from the sewing machine manufacturer, Singer Manufacturing Company, Elizabethport, New Jersey. A mockup of the missile's configuration was approved in March 1944, and by April 1945, orders for twenty-one Gorgon II-A missiles had been confirmed—all of which would be built. Initial flight tests of the system, beginning as unpowered glides early in 1945, proceeded to fully-powered guided trials in March 1945, which showed the launching and aerodynamic characteristics to be generally satisfactory, but the guidance system was unacceptable. A live air-to-air test of the Gorgon II-As radio command guidance system with a TV camera in the nose, failed badly, because the closing speeds of the missile and its target (approaching 800 mph) were too excessive for the Gorgon II-As rather limited maneuverability to allow the missile's controller to correctly steer the weapon. Nonetheless, the Gorgon II-A was the first American jet- or rocket-powered radio-controlled aircraft to fly successfully.

The control problems, along with the general undeveloped state of missile technology, caused the realignment of the Gorgon program as a testing program; the Gorgon II-A

Gorgon IIA (KA2N-1) anti-aircraft missile. (*USN*)

being redesignated in 1946 as KU2N-1 control test vehicle, then as CTV-4 in 1947, and finally as CTV-N-4 in 1948. The CTV designation reflected its status as a Control Test Vehicle, although the program was then largely completed. Despite the difficulties with its guidance system, the Gorgon II-A was considered aerodynamically satisfactory. A Gorgon II-A is currently on display at the Steven F. Udvar-Hazy Center. Washington, D.C.

Gorgon II-B and III-B

These missiles were turbojet propelled with the II-B being an unconventional canard design and the III-B of conventional design. Five II-Bs (no III-Bs) were contracted and none were built because no suitable flight-rated turbojet engine was available at that time. These models were considered to be obsolete by the end of the war.

Gorgon II-C

Late in the war, the Navy initiated development of the Gorgon II-C, a pulse jet-powered bombardment missile, proposed to be launched ship-to-shore round-the-clock area bombardment for use against onshore targets for the invasion of Japan with an expected dispersion of one mile at maximum range. The warhead was a 1,000-pound GP AN-M65 or 500-lb. GP Bomb AN-M64 bomb. Initially, twenty prototypes were to be produced by the Naval Aircraft Modification Unit in Pennsylvania, while an order for 100 was placed with the Singer Manufacturing Company in August 1945.

The 1,950-pound, 19-foot, 7-inch-long Gorgon II-C was very similar in design to the Gorgon II-A air-to-air missile, being of canard configuration with a high-mounted, 11-foot, 6-inch span monoplane wing, and vertical and ventral stabilizing fins. The 9-foot-long pulse jet mounted above the rear fuselage, developed at the Naval Engineering Experiment Station, was 14 by 10 inches in diameter and provided 200 pounds thrust for ten to twenty minutes on 174 pounds of gasoline. Launch was from the ground used a 150-foot, multiple-charge type, level catapult or sled with a rocket booster, giving the missile an initial velocity of 240 mph. Launch from a carrying aircraft was also considered. The Gorgon II-C had a rate of climb of 600 feet per minute with a radius of turn of 10,000 feet and reached an impact speed of 450 mph.

In its original, bombardment configuration, the Gorgon II-C was intended to use active radar-homing, similar to that used on the SWOD Bat guided bomb. Control to the target area was provided by AN/APN-33 radar with a 70-mile range. Radio control of the missile was via the AN/ARW-17 receiver, which had a range of 70 to 100 miles. Radio signals from the receiver actuated servo controls, which maneuvered the missile while a gyro system furnished stability.

However, like the other early Gorgon vehicles, in late 1946, it became a pure test vehicle known as the KUN-1 to reflect its non-combat role, being used to test homing devices, control systems, and a variety of other equipment related to guided missile development. In September 1947, it was redesignated as CTV-2, and then as its definitive designation of CTV-N-2 in early 1948, which was used to test guidance and control devices for guided missile development. During 1950, an active radar guidance system was tested using a CTV-N-2, successfully homing from 10 miles.

Gorgon IIC (TD3N-1) test vehicle. (*USN*)

Gorgon IIC (KD2N-1) target drone. (*USN*)

There were eight target drone versions of the Gorgon II-C, originally designated TD3N-1, but in March 1946, they were redesignated KD2N-1, which was used in parachute-recovery trials around 1950.

The RTV-N-15 *Pollux* was the last and largest of all the Gorgon series of post-war experimental Navy missiles. It was derived from the Gorgon II-C airframe with its pulse jet engine being relocated internally, attempting to increase the normally slow operating speed of a pulse jet vehicle by streamlining to give the design a range of 75 to 100 nautical miles. *Pollux* was a research vehicle for missile development and testing piloted aircraft components and was intended to use a mixture of active radar and infrared heat-seeking homing guidance. *Pollux* was first flown in 1948, however, by 1951, it had been flown only three times, and the program was canceled.

Gorgon III Models

The Gorgon III, a conventional aircraft-type design, with a high-mounted wing and twin tail fins, was proposed as an air-to-air missile to be employed by patrol aircraft. The Gorgon III-A, III-B, and III-C designations were based on their prolusion systems. Originally, three different propulsion systems were to be tested: the Gorgon III-A was to be rocket-powered; the Gorgon III-B to be powered by a turbojet engine, and Gorgon III-C was to employ pulse jet propulsion; however, Gorgon III-C was later changed to a rocket-powered configuration. Both Gorgon III-A and, in its as-built configuration, Gorgon III-C were to be powered by the Reaction Motors CLM2N with a single motor in the III-A and twin motors in the III-C. In April 1945, orders had been placed for thirty-four Gorgon III-A missiles, with sixteen Gorgon III-Bs and twenty Gorgon III-Cs also on contract.

Gorgon III-A

All thirty-four of the Gorgon III-As ordered were built and were designated as the KA3N-1 when testing began in late 1945. With the change of the program to research status in 1946 the missile was redesignated KU3N-1, with the designation later becoming CTV-6 and then as the definitive CTV-N-6. The 16-foot, 2-inch-long, 1,280-pound Gorgon III-A/KA3N-1 air-to-air missile was of conventional design, powered by a liquid-fueled rocket-powered engine that was the same Reaction Motors CML2N type as in the Gorgon II-A. It was guided by visual radio direction and used radar homing with a range of 12 miles. The warhead was a 257-pound fragmentation bomb armed by a radio proximity fuse. Gorgon III-A was used to test components and control systems for guided missiles.

Gorgon III-B

The Gorgon III-B was canceled before any had been built as its turbojet engine was not available. However, nine of the spin off TD2N target drones were manufactured and tested.

Gorgon IIIA/KA3N-1 air-to-air missile. (*USN*)

Gorgon III-C

The Gorgon III-C was initially intended to be pulse jet-powered but was developed as very similarly to the Gorgon III-A, and was powered by two CML2N liquid-fueled rocket engines instead of only one as in the III-A. The Gorgon III-C, designated as the KA3N-2, had a limited production of twelve airframes. At the end of the war, it was redesignated as the KU3N-2 with the Navy employing six in trials of missile stability, control, and performance. NACA used the other six for research of flight conditions at high subsonic speeds. These missiles were launched from the Pilotless Aircraft Research Station at Wallops Island, Virginia, using a 400-foot launch ramp. The Gorgon III-C was redesignated RTV-4, then RTV-N-4, before being canceled with several consumed as target drones.

Gorgon IV

During May 1945, BuAer, in conjunction with Project Gorgon, contracted the Glenn L. Martin Company, Baltimore, Maryland, to develop the Gorgon IV as the KUM-1 air-to-surface missile, powered by a ramjet engine and using active radar homing for guidance. The 21-foot, 8-inch, 1,600-pound PTV-N-2 was of relatively conventional design, with slightly swept, 10-foot span, wings and a conventional empennage. Roll control was achieved through spoilerons, also known as spoiler ailerons. Spoilerons are flight control surfaces that assist rolling an aircraft by reducing the lift of one wing, but, unlike ailerons, not by increasing the lift of the other wing. Flight control was through a combination of a preset course via autopilot and radio command guidance; the vehicle was equipped with radio telemetry to transmit data. The Marquardt XRJ30 20-inch ramjet, mounted below the aft fuselage, was developed

Gorgon IIIC (KA3N-2/KU3N-2) test vehicle. (*USN*)

and built by the Marquardt Aircraft, Venice, California. Roy Marquardt had worked at Northrop during the war on the YB-35 flying wing bomber project. While occupied with its engine cooling/heating problems, which were caused by the engines being enclosed in the wings, Marquardt found that the heat generated by the engines could also produce a useful thrust that led to his interest in the ramjet principle. During November 1944, he opened the Marquardt Aircraft Company to develop and sell ramjet engines. The ramjet gave the Gorgon a speed of Mach 0.7 (519 mph) and a range of 70 miles. The later PTV-N-2 was equipped with drag brakes to prevent exceeding the engines design limits.

Originally intended as an air-to-surface weapon, the KUM-1 emerged as a propulsion test vehicle, but the end of the war reduced this role. However, the contract was continued in 1946 as a propulsion test vehicle as the PTV-2 before finally being redesignated as the PTV-N-2 and finally as the KDM target drone. Nineteen PTV-N-2s were produced, with flight tests beginning during July 1947, and it became the first ramjet-powered winged aircraft to successfully fly in America. In November, with a Northrop P-61 Black Widow night-fighter as the launching aircraft, the PTV-N-2 first achieved high-speed flight, reaching approximately Mach 0.85 (630 mph) with testers claiming that the missile's speed was intentionally limited to keep it below the speed of sound. The flight time of eleven minutes, fifteen seconds, achieved on the second flight test was an endurance record at the time for ramjets. Following the end of each test flight, a parachute would be deployed for recovery in the ocean. In 1948, the installation of a newer Marquardt ramjet increased the speeds to Mach 0.9 (667 mph).

During March 1948, the heavy seaplane tender *Norton Sound* (AV-11, later AVN-1) was modified over seven months in Philadelphia Naval Shipyard for the installation of equipment for handling, stowing, launching, and controlling guided missiles. The *Norton Sound* was scheduled to be refitted to test the feasibility of launching the Gorgon/PTV-N-2 from an ocean-going platform; however, the project was canceled as the *Norton Sound* relocated to the West Coast for Loon and Aerobee testing.

The Gorgon test program continued through December 1949, originally at the Naval Air Missile Test Center test range at Point Mugu, but to be closer to the Martin Baltimore factory, testing was later transferred to the Naval Aviation Ordnance Test Station in Chincoteague, Virginia.

Following the end of the program, Martin was awarded a contract to convert the remaining PTV-N-2s into KDM-1 *Plover* target drones and contracting Marquardt for 600 more ramjet engines. The *Plover* made aeronautical headlines in 1951 when it flew on a 125-mile flight to set the world's longest ramjet powered flight record. The Gorgon IV airframe was also used as the basis of the ASM-N-5 Gorgon *V* chemical weapon's dispenser. A recovered Gorgon IV was donated by the Navy to the National Air and Space Museum in 1966, and it is on display at the Steven F. Udvar-Hazy Center.

Gorgon V

The last of the Gorgon series was the ASM-N-5 Gorgon V, an unpowered air-to-surface missile developed by the Glenn L. Martin Company during the early 1950s for use by the Navy, capable to disperse chemical warfare agents over a combat area. Developed from the earlier PTV-N-2/Gorgon IV ramjet test vehicle, the program was canceled in late 1955 without any Gorgon Vs being built.

Other Gorgon Versions

TD2N-1

Although the Gorgon III-B tactical missile was canceled very early (during 1945) in the Gorgon program, except for the II-C, the only Gorgon project that continued with any commitment was the TD2N (later designated as the KDN-1). It was a high-speed target drone similar to the Westinghouse turbojet-powered Gorgon III-B. In June 1945, the NAMU performed a drop test of an engineless TD2N released from the PBY-5A at 6,000 feet over Cape May. The TD2N descended in a radio-controlled glide to about 500 feet when its parachute deployed and the drone was recovered intact. The first powered TD2N test flight occurred on June 27, 1945 and was not a success, as although the turbojet engine operated throughout the flight, the radio control system malfunctioned and the drone crashed into the Atlantic off Cape May. The August 17 test was successful, as the TD2N, with its engine already running, was launched from the Catalina, then flying for twenty-one minutes at about 219 mph (190 knots) while executing various maneuvers under radio control. Unfortunately, the missile was not recovered intact as about 100 feet over the Cape May runway, the parachute deployed, but the inflatable bag intended to cushion the landing impact caused the drone to somersault over on its back, badly damaging the fuselage and causing minor damage to the wings and tail surfaces. Nevertheless, this was considered the first successful test of the Gorgon series with the Westinghouse turbojet and was an encouraging step forward in this long-delayed program.

TD2N test flights continued through the end of 1945 with the NAMU delivering nine drones to Experimental Utility Squadron 25 (XVJ-25), a singular squadron established on June 15, 1945 at NAS Brunswick, Maine. The XVJ-25 used the high-performance TD2N target aircraft to develop tactics, procedure, and equipment for use in special defense against Kamikazes. During a familiarization exercise in November at the Naval Air Station, Wildwood, New Jersey, the drone stalled before the parachute deployed, and was destroyed as it crashed on to the runway. During December, a demonstration for the press at the Naval Air Station, Atlantic City, New Jersey, was successful. The radio-controlled TD2N made several high-speed passes over the reporters and completed a series of maneuvers before being recovered in a successful parachute landing. The Atlantic City flight demonstrated the TD2N's capability but the continued difficulties with the Westinghouse 9.5-inch turbojet engine and the program's high cost led to its cancellation on March 12, 1946 after only the nine drones had been delivered.

TD3N-1 Gorgon Target Drone

Eight Gorgon target drones, very similar to the Gorgon II-C were designated as TD3N-1 and, after March 1946, as the KD2N-1.

JB: Jet Bomb Series

In 1939, Gen. H. H. Arnold, an avowed advocate of advanced technology, failed to appreciate the potential of jet and rocket engine technology, and by 1944, America was not close to matching that of the Luftwaffe's newly operational Me 262 jet and Me 163 rocket fighters. American Intelligence had been aware of another new German secret weapon since August 22, 1942 when a Danish naval officer found an early V-1 test version that had crashed on Bornholm Island in the Baltic Sea, about 75 miles northeast of the Peenemunde Army Research Center. As more intelligence was obtained through aerial reconnaissance and German sources, Gen. Arnold decided in 1943 to develop an American jet-powered bomb that foreshadowed the future American cruise missile/unmanned aerial vehicle (UAV). However, again American jet engine technology lagged, and it would not be until mid-June 1944 when the first German V-1s crashed into London that Arnold was became obsessed with an American "buzz bomb."

The AAF Re-engineers the German V-1 and its Pulse Jet Engine

By mid-June, once the Germans launched their first 100 V-1s over London, Allied Intelligence provided Ford with a five-page report that vaguely described the construction and specifications to recreate the Nazi robot's engine. On July 13, engineers at Wright Field received the remains of over a ton of V-1 undamaged salvaged parts from crashed V-1s. Because Paul Schmidt's Argus As 014 pulse jet was a masterwork of simplicity, within three weeks, Ford engineers were able to reverse-engineer a copy using both German and American derivative components, and successfully test fired it on August 1, which was followed by contracts for the design, development, and fabrication of twenty-five experimental engines signed with Ford, Dearborn, Michigan. Republic Aviation Corporation, Farmingdale, Long Island, New York, was contracted to build the airframe. On September 8, the first of thirteen complete JB-2s, reverse-engineered by the Air Technical Service Command, were assembled at Republic Aviation. The AAF then initiated Project MX-544 as the JB-2 (jet bomb) program under the AAF designation "Power Bomb" but nicknamed the ThunderBug.

In its redesign effort, the AAF followed the same improvisational techniques and a lack of direction in research, design, and procurement as it had for many of the other AAF guided bomb programs. Consequently, the AAF attempt at redesigning and improving the entire weapon airframe and controls were so mediocre that the final JB-2 version was directly copied from the captured German V-1 buzz bomb.

Northrop JB-1 Bat

The AAF's most highly developed jet bomb project (MX-543) in 1944 was the large delta-winged JB-1 developed by Northrop Aircraft of Hawthorne, California, which was contracted to produce thirteen. The JB-1 was a singular, innovative new design and not a V-1 copy. The JB-1 weighed 7,084 pounds fully loaded, measured 10.5 feet long, 4.5 feet high, and had a 28.25-foot wingspan and a 155-square-foot wing area.

Northrop found that German pulse jet design to be particularly impressive and decided to adapt it to their JB-1. Their new streamlined and lighter JB-1 design was equipped with a single centerline pulse jet that was hypothetically capable of producing 500 pounds of thrust to a maximum speed of 400 mph over 220 miles. The redesign would reduce the bomb load from 4,000 to 3,400 pounds, which was carried in enclosed bomb containers located in the wing roots.

The center section of the wing was constructed of welded magnesium alloy, stressed skin construction while the outer wings were of a combined riveted and spot-welded aluminum alloy, stressed skin, and multi-cellular construction incorporating integral fuel tanks and magnesium wing tips. The wing access panel covers were to be held in place by (too) many self-threading screws that were difficult to remove. Also, the integral fuel tanks leaked and needed to be sealed. The elevons were constructed of welded magnesium alloy and measured 5.5 square feet. Their angular movement as an elevator was 13 degrees up and 8 degrees down, and as an aileron 10 degrees up

AAF Northrop JB-1 Bat Jet Bomb

and 10 degrees down. The tail fin was constructed of magnesium alloy and measured 3.7 square feet.

The all-electric automatic control equipment, manufactured by the Hammond Instrument Company, Chicago, was mounted in the outer wing panels and consisted of a roll gyro servo, a pitch gyro and servo, and an aneroid altitude control device, all powered by Delco-Remy 14-volt AC batteries. The JB-1 carried an early version of the black box, which contained a movie camera set to record air speed, elevon position, jet velocity, and altitude; however, this unit did not function properly during the only test of the JB-1.

The launching sled was designed to launch both the JB-1 and JB-2 within a 1,000-foot run and a provision was made to stop the sled's movement in an additional 1,000 feet. The sled engaged the double rail (56.5-inch gauge) track on two pairs of "slippers" (one pair fore and the other aft), which had rail-shaped grooves that fit over the rail. The sled was driven by two Monsanto Mk. I, 11.75-inch rocket motors, used in the Tiny Tim rockets, which were incorporated into the rear of the sled. There was an alternative provision to use five 10-inch Monsanto Rocket motors. The airframe was mounted on sled at 9 degrees from horizontal and both elevons were carefully adjusted to 9 degrees up from their streamlined position.

While Northrop was actively pursuing the single pulse jet design, the company also decided to continue with its original twin-engined project using redesigned General Electric turbo-supercharged Type B-1 200-hp turbojet engines capable of producing the required 400 pounds of thrust, which were to propel the missile over 670 miles at 452 mph while carrying two 2,000-pound GP bombs internally. While the proposed 800-pound combined thrust of the two GE B1 400-hp turbojet engines was 300 pounds more than produced by the single pulse jet engine of the German V-1 buzz bomb, they had to propel the JB-1, which weighed nearly 2,000 pounds more. However, the June 1944 static tests showed that each JB-1 engine was only capable of producing 200 of the anticipated 400 pounds of thrust, which meant that combined they produced 100 pounds less thrust than a single V-1 engine. This reduction of power was supposed to be compensated by the lighter weight aluminum and magnesium construction of the body and wings.

The September 1944 manned aerodynamic glide trials using a towed unpowered glider proved the airframe to be aerodynamically stable but somewhat difficult to land. Northrop decided to test its only prototype, not with the single pulse jet engine, which was still unavailable, but with the original two 200-pound thrust GE engines. Northrop had to postpone the tests while the airframe was modified to reduce its weight to slightly over 3,000 pounds so that these less powerful engines could maintain the missile airborne. This model encountered numerous integral fuel tank leaks and the engines and the control equipment were found to be not easily accessible as they required the removal of 270 screws in each wing panel for maintenance. The engine was started by turning the turbines with compressed air and at the same time applying a spark via spark plugs charged by a high-voltage transformer. This difficult starting procedure would postpone the first powered test at Eglin on December 6, 1944 until the next day. This first test was conducted with the JB-1 propelled by two Monsanto Rockets mounted on a modified JB-2 sled set at 0 degrees (level) and

JB-1 prototype (foreground) and JB-2s in the Range 64 Missile Barn, Florida, during December 1944. (*AAF*)

The sled was powered by two Monsanto Mk. I, 11.75-inch rocket motors incorporated into the rear of the sled, which rode on "slippers" that had rail shaped grooves that fit over the 56-gauge rails. (*From AAF movie still*)

launched along a 500-foot ramp that was similar in construction (not elevation) to the German V-1 "Ski Ramps." Thirty seconds before launching, with both engines running at full power, substantial sparking was observed in the right engine tail pipe. The JB-1's underpowered jet engines did get it airborne but only for 400 yards of flight from the end of the launch ramp, after which the continued thrust of the engines was insufficient and the JB-1 went into a stall and crashed. An investigation of the salvaged remains disclosed that the elevons were incorrectly set and that the GE engines were not suitable power plants for the JB-1 as half the buckets of the right turbo were damaged and missing at speeds only sufficient to provide half the required thrust.

The mid-January 1945 delivery date would be met and the reworked GE jet engines were tested that month in a JB-1 airframe. However, the improvement in performance was so minimal that the twin-engined design was abandoned for a single pulse-engined airframe that varied enough to be designated as the JB-10 (to be described in detail later). But even before the final JB-1 twin-engined tests were completed, the AAF had tentatively decided that the JB-2 would be its primary jet bomb project.

The JB-2: America's Buzz Bomb

Despite the rapid development of the Ford/Argus pulse jet engine, as early as October 1944, the AMC Engineering Division had not been provided with the military requirements or been informed as to the purpose of the JB-2 so it could establish its final configuration. Also, at that date there was no official authorization for developmental work on the JB-2, and consequently, the AMC Engineering Division was unable to coordinate with industry or to request personnel or other resources

A movie still of the December 7, 1944 JB-1A test showing the steep 45-degree liftoff angle that was too steep to be compensated for by the JB-1's 9-degree elevon setting and the insufficient thrust of the GE jet engines. (*From AAF movie still*)

from other sectors of the AAF to begin work, which was typical of the AAF's attitude toward its guided missile program. However, Gen. Arnold boosted the JB-2's production priority to 1-A and the JB-2 project was definitely underway.

During October 1944, Bell Aircraft, Buffalo, New York, and Republic Aviation were the manufacturers considered for the first quantity production of the JB-2, but Bell soon withdrew, leaving Republic with the contract for the first 1,000. Republic's Farmingdale, New York, Plant floor space was limited and much of the work was subcontracted to Willys-Overland, Toledo, Ohio. Ford Motor, Detroit, was contracted for the manufacture of the initial contract for twenty-five experimental production Argus pulse jet motor copies. RCA was contracted for remote guidance and Jack and Heintz, Cleveland, for the automatic controls. Alloy Products, Waukesha, Wisconsin, was to supply the pressure vessels and Air Reduction Sales, Jersey City, New Jersey, the pressure regulators. The AN/ART-19 radio transmitters were contracted to Jack Mack, Plymouth, Indiana.

Initially, a German V-1 site had not been captured in France, so the AAF was uncertain as to what a launch system would require but soon a rocket-propelled launch cart on a ramp to accelerate the JB-2s to speeds above 150 mph was designed and approved. This system boosted the pulsejet engine, which was too weak unaided to power and sustain sufficient airspeed for lift and forward thrust for take-off. Northrop Aviation, Hawthorne, California, was awarded the contract for the carts and Monsanto Chemical, Dayton, Ohio, for the launching rockets, known as RATOs for Rocket Assisted Take-Off (later more commonly known as JATOs for Jet Assisted Take-Off, even though none of the secondary power sources consisted of jet engines). Later, the concrete launching ramps for testing were to be constructed by the Army Corps of Engineers.

Wind tunnel tests of scale models helped in the quick reverse engineering of the JB-2. (*AAF*)

Opposite page: Only weeks after the first German V-1 Buzz Bombs were launched against England on June 12, 1944, Wright Field engineers were able to examine captured or crashed examples and then reverse engineer a copy. The photo shows a 393rd Fighter Squadron Bomb Service crewman examining a captured V-1. (*AAF*)

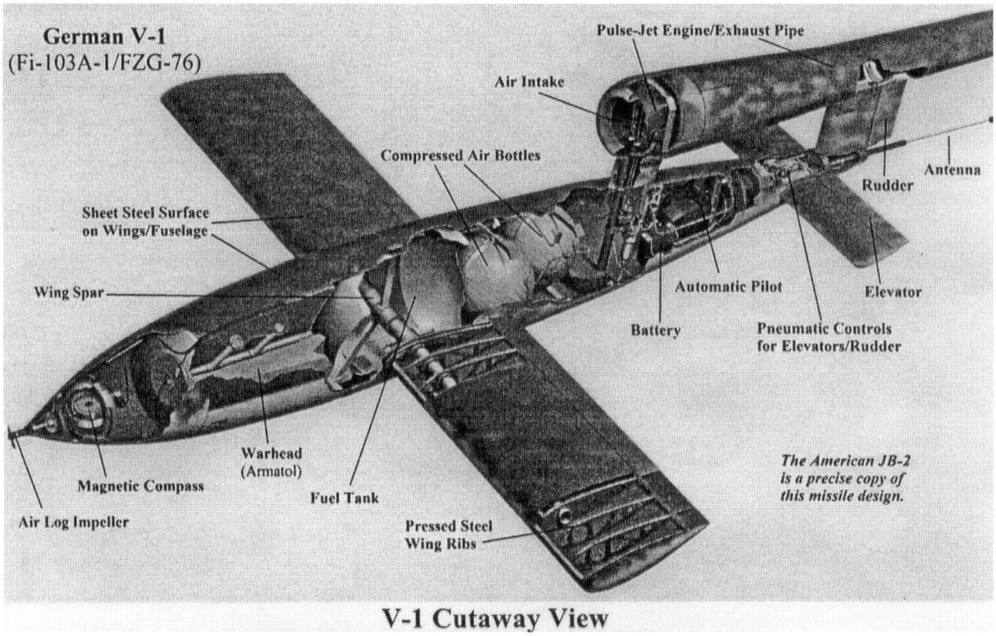

V-1 (Fi 103A) Cutaway adapted from captured German specimens. (*AAF*)

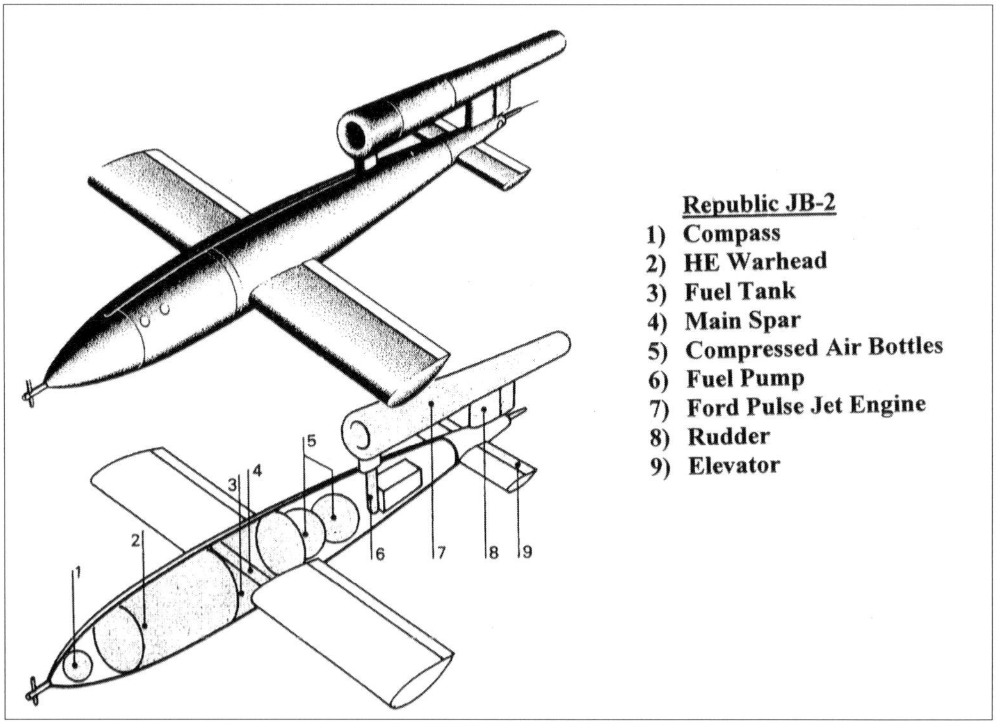

JB-2 Described

As illustrated by the accompanying chart below, the AAF JB-2 differed from the German V-1 in only the smallest of dimensions and launching method, but in later missiles, the guidance system was modified. The simple impulse duct Ford jet engine on top of the main body was a copy of the German Argus version.

	V-1/Fi-103	JB-2/LTV-N-2
Wing Span	17.52 feet	17.67 feet
Length	27.25 feet	27.09 feet
Height	4.67 feet	4.67 feet
Max. Fuselage Diameter	3.75 feet	3.81 feet
Engine	Argus 109	Ford PJ-31
Engine Length	12.13 feet	11.63 feet
Max. Engine Diameter	1.89 feet	1.89 feet
Engine Orifice Diameter	1.28 feet	1.28 feet
Thrust	807 pounds	900 pounds
Fuel	176 gallons	180 gallons
Engine wt.	337l pounds	
Empty wt.	1,864 pounds	
Warhead wt.	1,830 pounds	2,100 pounds
Warhead	Amatol	T-8 LC Bomb
Launch wt.	4,796 pounds	5,025 pounds
Optimum Range	150 miles	150 miles
Service Ceiling	8,840 feet	6,000 feet
Optimum Cruise Speed	360 mph	400 mph
Maximum Speed	400 mph	440 mph
Speed at Launch	250 mph	220 mph
Launch Time	1 second	1 second
Duration of Flight	25 minutes	25 minutes

A poor-quality 1944 AAF movie demonstrated the JB-2 components:

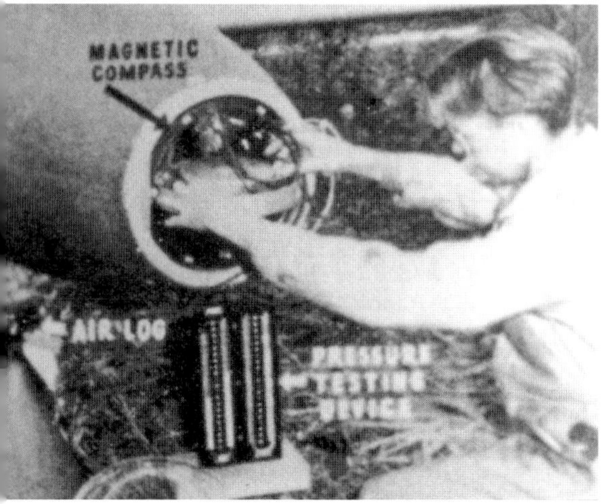

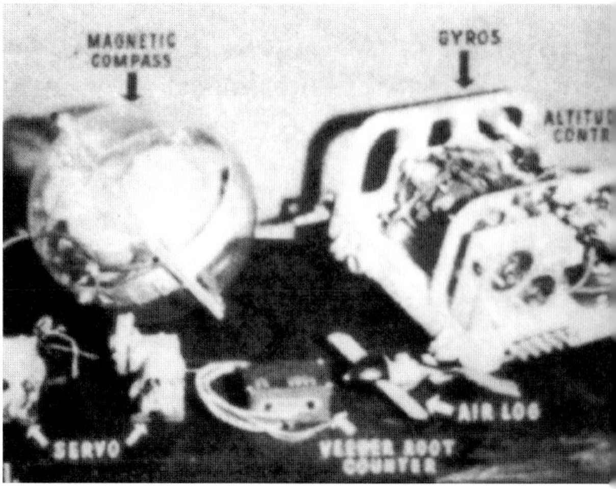

Above and below: Movie still sequence show Ford reverse-engineered components into nose of the "American" V-1. (*From AAF/Ford movie still*)

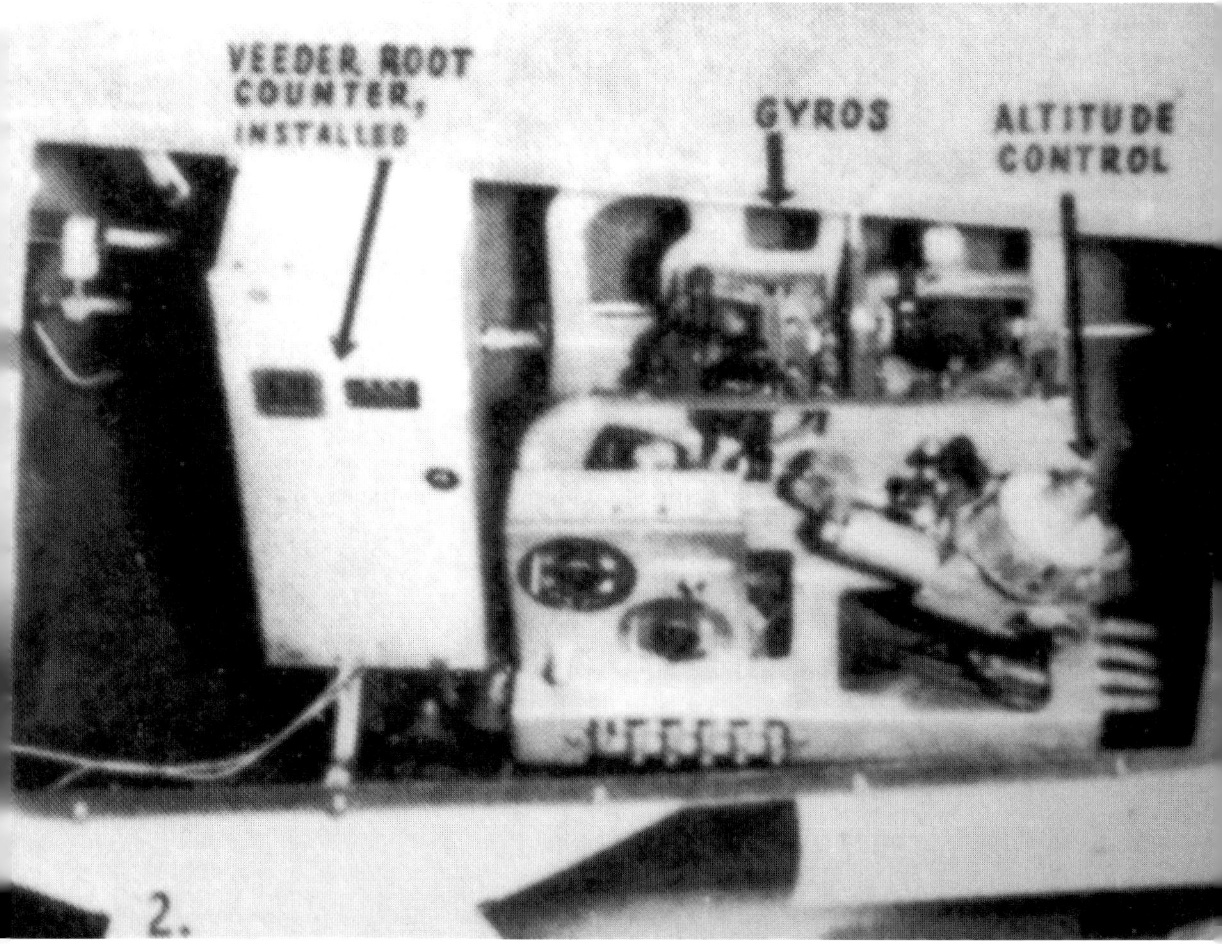

Pulse Jet Engine

All pulse jet engines operated by alternately accelerating a contained supply of air rearward and then taking in a fresh mass of air to replace it. The energy to accelerate the air mass was provided by the burning at a very high heat (deflagration) of fuel mixed thoroughly into the newly acquired fresh air supply with this cycle repeated many times per second. There were two basic types of pulse jets: the valve and valveless designs. The valve-type was the traditional pulse jet combustion chamber and an acoustically resonant exhaust pipe. Starting the engine usually required forcing air through the spring-loaded flapper valves and an ignition method in which the fuel was either mixed with the air in the intake or injected into the combustion chamber plug for the fuel-air mixture, which had a set of one-way reed-type valves through which the incoming air passed. When the fuel-air mixture was ignited, these valves slammed shut so that the hot gases could only exit through the engine's tailpipe causing a forward thrust. Part of the exhaust gases flowed back up the discharge pipe and met the new air coming through the valves, compressing the new air slightly. This compression, plus residual burning fuel, plus the heat of the walls of the combustion chamber, ignited the new fuel-air mixture at about 250 pulses per second. The frequency of the cycle was mainly dependent on the length of the engine. A small engine would have a low frequency of about forty to fifty pulses per second.

The advantages of the pulse jet were that it was inexpensive and easy to manufacture, used common, low-grade aviation fuels and atmospheric oxygen, and did not need an oxidizer. Its disadvantages were its low subsonic speed (450 mph) and low operating altitude, which made it vulnerable to AA fire and interception by aircraft. Ram jets could reach supersonic speeds, which led to the pulse jet's post-war demise. The engine had high fuel consumption and low fuel efficiency that reduced its range. Because the pulse jet produced limited thrust when at rest, it needed to be launched into the air. It required heat-resistant materials and vibration-resistant construction. The engine's loud intermittent pulsing/stuttering noise did not make the buzz bomb a stealth weapon, but once the engine cut out, there was no longer any noise and the V-1 became a terror weapon as the human targets below feared for their lives until the bomb exploded elsewhere.

Due to the American pulse jet project's urgent and secret nature, separate facilities at the government-owned Ford Rouge Plant, Dearborn, Michigan, were utilized for the production of parts that, when they became available, were directed to a central assembly area. After only three weeks, the first Ford jet engine was successfully operated at the Rouge plant and a 300-mph wind tunnel was erected. This wind tunnel caused such intense and unbearable noise and vibrations that the productivity of employees in a nearby main building was lowered. Initially, Ford erected sandbag barricades to dampen the engine noise but the intensive vibrations and pressure impulses of the engine disintegrated them and special silencers were ultimately designed. By October 1944, an assembly line had been set up in the Rouge aluminum foundry and the first three PJ-31-1 engines were built, tested, and accepted by the

AAF, eliminating the necessity of building the other twenty-two engines on order but led to an initial production order for 3,000 engines. Once Ford's licensed GE B-2 turbo-supercharger manufacture contract was completed, nearly all its supervisory and Engineering Department personnel were transferred to the pulse jet engine project. During pulse jet production, numerous improvements were instituted. Air valves were improved providing increased durability, as the V-1's valves endured for only seven minutes, while Ford's design continued for two hours under greater power output. Grid bars were die cast instead of being milled, which increased power and engine life while reducing cost. The redesigned fuel metering unit provided more accurate controls. Stainless steel valves replaced steel valves, increasing engine performance while reducing costs. After the first month of full production, efficiency quickly reduced assembly to 104 man-hours per engine from 161 man-hours and with later increased production this performance was expected to improve significantly. To test and measure the actual performance of the engine in flight, a TB-26 (AT-23 tow target version of the twin-engined B-26 bomber) was modified into a flying laboratory by the AMC and Ford. Ford also conducted one- and three-week courses for AAF personnel in the operation and maintenance of the engine.

Within weeks after receiving the first captured German example of the V-1's 900-pound thrust Argus-Schmidt pulse-jet engine, Wright engineers reverse engineered a copy and Republic Aircraft conducted a static test of a Ford pulse jet copy at Farmingdale, New York. (*AAF/Ford*)

Soon after the static tests, contracts for twenty-five experimental pulse-jet engines were signed with Ford at the government-owned Rouge Aluminum Foundry Plant. (*AAF/Ford*)

By October 1944, an assembly line completed the first three PJ-31-1 engines were built three weeks later and then tested and accepted by the AAF, eliminating the necessity of building the other twenty-two contracted engines. (*AAF/Ford*)

Launching

Throughout JB-2 testing and beyond, assessing and developing launch procedure was a continual problem. Because the pulse jet engine only functioned efficiently in forward flight, the missile had to be boosted into the air to a flying speed of about 250 mph. The Germans achieved this speed by using a 155-foot ramp with rails having a long, hollow, slotted tube with a piston inside running between. A slot on top of the tube allowed the piston to be attached to a dolly to which the V-1 was attached and the dolly would slide up on rails to the top of the tube. The launching explosive charge had to give a fast but steady rise in pressure inside the tube to move the buzz bomb smoothly along the ramp but have enough power to push the bomb to flying speed at the end of the ramp after one second. Analysis of the German launching propellants found that a high concentration (89 percent) of hydrogen peroxide and potassium permanganate was required for launching. That high peroxide concentration could not easily be duplicated by American facilities, which generally produced 30 percent concentrations, and production of that percentage was already fully utilized and new facilities would have to be built. Also, at the time there were no facilities to store hydrogen peroxide concentrations of over 50 percent in America.

By early January 1945, a captured German V-1 launch ramp was shipped to Range 64 for the comparative test launches. The German launching technique required 2 tons of hydrogen peroxide and 400 pounds of calcium permanganate. So while the German peroxide launching method was not feasible, several alternative methods of launching the JB-2 were suggested:

1. Air turbine.
2. Large motor operated flywheel connected to a cable that would pull the bomb along a ramp.
3. A cart with either tricycle wheels or operating on a rail, pulled by a cable winding around a motor-operated windlass along a runway or long track.
4. A launching cart operating along a long rail (2,000 to 5,000 feet) powered by enough aircraft engines to attain the required launching speed and then braked to a halt.
5. A flash boiler system to generate the steam for the German-type ramp instead of using peroxide or explosives.
6. The Technical Service Command prepared a preliminary design for the inflight launching of two underwing JB-2s from a B-17.

Impact, the official AAF publication, issued this propaganda statement in its January 1945 issue about the very successful, but dangerous, German peroxide/permanganate launching propellant:

> Since we felt that this was not as good as some others, we have been experimenting with steam and have found this to be a satisfactory substitute for use with the German-type ramp. But this requires a steam generator and much equipment.

Steam propulsion would not be the solution because it did require a steam generator and much complex equipment that was unavailable and would require a long developmental time.

The ramp take-off solution was to drive the JB-2 along a 500-foot, 6-degree ramp aided by solid fuel rocket boosters to thrust the JB off the ramp. This complicated and hazardous rocket-assisted take-off method, called RATO, had been successfully used to assist overloaded aircraft in taking off from short airfields. However, during the first five months of JB-1 testing, the reliability and stability of RATO rockets used to propel the missile up to ramp launch speed was the programs most persistent and vexing problem. The Monsanto RATO boosters were propelled by solid rocket fuel consisting of ammonium picrate and potassium nitrate in a resin binder. It was determined that 100 operational launches per day would require approximately 2.5 million pounds of propellant powder per month, which would hamper conventional weapon production. The hydrogen peroxide-potassium permanganate mixture used to propel the German launch piston was considered to be very dangerous, but subsequently was proven to more stable than the JB-2 RATO fuel. Test firing revealed that when used for JB-2 launching, four small solid-fuel RATO rockets were needed for each two-second launching, which was one second more than the German system. The August 1945, *Impact* later cryptically stated that the extra one-second launch time with rocket launching system had "important advantages, now secret." The RATO rockets had to be jettisoned promptly after the jet bomb had reached flying speed, or their drag would cause it to go into a stall and crash. To assist in the jettisoning of the RATO rockets, they were attached to a sled, to which the jet bomb was fastened. The rocket sled was intended to fall away when the jet bomb left the end of the ramp, but on several occasions, JB-2s were destroyed when they collided with bouncing rocket sleds during or immediately after the sled-release sequence. Other JB-2s were lost when the RATO rockets exploded during the ignition cycle, causing sympathetic detonations of the jet bombs fuel. Four ramps using rocket launch were completed by September 1945 and the JB-2 was ready for flight testing.

JB-2 Test Launching

Above: Initial JB-2 test flights began at Eglin Field on October 12, 1944 using a 400-foot, 6-degree concrete and steel launching ramp facing the Gulf of Mexico. (*AAF*)

Below: The jet bomb was attached to a sled carrying RATO rockets that was intended to fall away when it left the end of the ski ramp after reaching flying speed in about two seconds. (*AAF*)

The JB-2 was propelled by four small solid-fuel RATO rockets for launching. (*AAF*)

Initial JB-2 Testing

During the late summer and early fall of 1944, private land was leased on the Gulf of Mexico between Fort Walton and Destin, on Florida's Panhandle, after which the construction of Range 64, the JB-2's first test facility, quickly proceeded. Range 64 consisted of 2½ miles by 1 mile of uninhabited Gulf shoreline and would be used for JB-1, JB-2, and JB-10 testing operations between October 1944 and November 1945. Range 64 was a self-contained facility with barracks, a mess hall, assembly shop, engine shop, rocket shop, ordnance/explosive storage building, and two bomb-proof range equipment shelters. In addition to the water range stretching outward from the beach 150 miles to the south, JB-2 tests also utilized a 4-square-mile land range where wingless missiles could be dropped from a B-17 bomber.

The initial JB-2 test flight was scheduled at Range 64 on October 12, 1944. For the test, the partially dismantled test missile arrived in a custom wooden shipping crate at the maintenance shops for final attachment of the engine and wings. Before launching, the missile was towed to a special concrete semi-circular compass swing base located in an area designed with no ferrous metal. Here the JB-2's magnetic compass and gyro guidance mechanism was preset without any magnetic interference. After the range and bearing was set, the missile was towed to the ramp base where a crane lifted it onto the launch cart, which was positioned on the 400-foot, 6-degree concrete and steel launching ramp. While launch personnel took shelter in the nearby concrete bunker or behind temporary sand bag revetments, the Ford pulse jet engine was started when atomized gasoline was injected by an air compressor and was ignited by the single spark plug in the

The photo shows a JB-2 in a cradle ready to be transported to the test ramp. (*AAF*)

top of the engine casing. The missile was fired from the control bunker by electronically engaging a switch on the control panel that ignited the four RATO boosters at the rear of the launch cart. During the first launch on October 12, the JB-2 rapidly accelerated down the launch ramp and climbed away as the launch cart fell toward the sand below. The missile soon began a shallow descent over 2 miles before it crashed into the Gulf. Nonetheless, the forty-second flight was considered a success as the missile launched correctly, separated safely from the launch cart, and briefly flew on course.

With much work to be accomplished to improve range, accuracy, and reliability, tests continued and between October 18 and November 11, with eight more test launches conducted to establish a feasible launching system. The first two launches were failures with one JB-2 crashing off the ramp and the other several miles away. Photographic studies determined that the take-off speed was too low and future launches were to be made with five or six rockets instead of four and with an 8.5-degree ramp incline instead of 6 degrees. The next two JB-2s also launched unsatisfactorily and crashed as different combinations of five or six launching rockets and ramp inclines were tried. Investigation of the wrecks showed that the elevator control surfaces had been burned off causing the JB-2s to crash just offshore. When the JB-2 was placed on the launching cart at 8 degrees or more the tail dropped 4 inches and the rocket blast from the six rockets burned the elevators. The fifth test was a disaster as the gasoline shutoff valve malfunctioned and gasoline flowed on to the ground and began to burn as two rockets exploded and the remaining three ignited and launched the burning wreck into the Gulf. Finally, during the sixth test, the JB-2 was launched by five rockets from a 6-degree ramp incline and became airborne successfully and flew out over the Gulf. The surveillance pilot lost visual contact with the 400-mph JB-2 before it crashed after flying 9 miles over the Gulf.

The seventh JB was launched and reached its preset 6,500-foot altitude and finally had to be shot down as it surpassed its allotted 50-mile distance. During the eighth and last test on November 11, the JB-2 left the launch ramp successfully and leveled off at the preset 3,500-foot altitude at 400 mph but outran and lost its tracking fighters and disappeared over the Gulf.

In his book *Into the Teeth of the Tiger* (Bantam, NY, 1986), Capt. Donald Lopez, five-victory CBI fighter ace, described JB-2 surveillance and destruction by fast, low-level P-63 or P-51 fighters in case the buzz bomb turned back towards Florida:

> The first two fighters circled at about 5,000 feet just north of the launch site until the countdown began. They then dived south toward the site at full throttle, timing it so as to be just behind and to the side of the buzz bomb as it was launched. The pilots climbed with the bomb and chased it until the momentum of the dive was lost and they fell too far behind to shoot the JB-2s down if necessary. The second team of fighters that had been following along at about 15,000 feet then dived into position behind the bombs and followed them until they dived into the sea. The first team followed at a distance too, since they could cut off the bombs and shoot them down if they headed for shore. Of course, all the pilots hoped that the bombs they were following would malfunction so they could score an easy victory. The bombs were quite cooperative, and most of us were able to shoot down at least one. 1 was fortunate enough to get two while flying a P-51, and the next year I got two more while flying a P-80, which could easily outrun the bombs.

Tests continued between November 17 and December 21, 1944. The success of test eight on November 11 fostered optimism for test nine on November 17. When

A sequence of stills from a test film showing a JB-2 launch. The last two photos show the rocket sled separating from the JB-2. (*From AAF microfilm*)

launched from a 6-degree, 400-foot inclined ramp, two of the five RATO boosters exploded during the take-off roll, causing the attachment lug connecting the missile to its launch cart to fail. The cart disconnected from under the JB and, unable to attain flying speed, the missile crashed just off the ramp. After the November 21 test also failed to launch successfully, test eleven and twelve on December 6 and 9 were successes validating new launch techniques. The December 6 test made a successful launch from a 500-foot level track ramp and achieved a 300-mph take-off speed, climbed into the overcast at 1,500 feet, and flew 22.5 miles, tracked by radar. The December 9 launch demonstrated that four RATO boosters could be used successfully rather than five. Launched from the 400-foot, 6-degree inclined ramp, this JB-2 reached a speed of 225 mph, losing altitude briefly on leaving the ramp before it recovered and climbed to its preset altitude of 2,000 feet on course. At its preset range termination of 50 miles, the robot bomb dived to the water and JB-2 testing took a three-week hiatus.

JB-2 Air-Launching

As JB-2 testing was about to continue through the first months of 1945, the scheme to air-launch the missiles from B-17 bombers began the trial phase. These tests were motivated by the Luftwaffe's 1,176 V-1s successfully air-launched from He 111H-22s from July 1944 to January 1945 after their French and Dutch land-based launch sites were overrun by the Allies. The JB-2's 17-foot, 8-inch wingspan and 5,000-pound weight required it to be carried externally under the B-17s wing, instead of internally. A second JB-2 had to be carried under the opposite wing for balance and symmetry to prevent the mother from going into a stall. Launching in flight eliminated the need for the sometimes unreliable RATO units to accelerate the buzz bombs to a speed that allowed the missile to attain lift, as the B-17 simply had to maintain an indicated airspeed between 180 and 220 mph prior to the missile's release. The bomber's airspeed also eliminated the need for the air compressor required during ground launches to provide forced air into the pulse jet engine to allow ignition, which was from controls inside the bomber just before release. December 1944 tests determined that a B-17 could carry two JB-2s over a combat radius of 1,000 miles, but it was not until March 2, 1945 that the first successful air launch of JB-2s from a B-17 took place. Bomber crews launched a total of ten JB-2s during March and April, however, five of the missiles launched from the bomber experienced engine starting malfunctions, resulting in unsuccessful flights. Of the remaining air launches, four proved successful and one experienced a control malfunction, causing it to nose-dive into the Gulf. The test report concluded that JB-2s could be launched successfully from a B-17, and that the engine failures could be eliminated by the installation of a motorized fuel valve. The JB-2's air-launch capability increased its limited range to over 1,000 miles. Once Germany surrendered in May 1945, the JB-2's range was far too short for deployment in the Pacific. Using the B-29 to air-launch the JB-2 was considered but was not possible as the bomber would require extensive modification, and besides, it was unavailable because the XXI Bomber Command was unwilling to divert any from its bombing of Japan.

JB-2 Air-Launched Tests

Above: During 1944, the Luftwaffe air-launched 1,176 V-1s from twin-engined He 111H-22 bombers over England. (*Author*)

Below: The JB-2's 17.67-foot wingspan and 5,000-pound weight and consequent aerodynamic drag required it to be carried externally under the wing of the B-17. A second JB-2 needed to be carried under the opposite wing for balance and symmetry to prevent the mother from going into a stall. (*AAF*)

Close up of the wing rack carrying the loaded JB-2. (*AAF*)

On March 2, 1945, the first successful air launch of JB-2s from a B-17 took place. The JBs were launched one at a time in quick succession so as not to cause aerodynamic balance problems. (*AAF*)

JB-2 Testing Continues

After a three-week hiatus, JB-2 testing at Range 64 resumed with tests on January 10 and 12 seeing both missiles burn on the launch ramp when their RATO rockets exploded, causing the fuel to combust. A week later, the crash percentage of JB-2 tests rose to 62.5 percent as fifteen of the first twenty-four test launches ended in failure either during the launch sequence or shortly thereafter. In the face of these failures, during January 1945, the NDRC investigated alternatives to the real and potential problems of rocket-propelled ramp launches. A flywheel inertial system, in particular, was thought to have merit, and was tested as a scale model but never developed any further. Also, at the time, there was doubt that American launching rocket propellant production would not be sufficient if the JB-2 did become operational, and if it did, it would be at the expense of other vital ammunition production.

After the January 1945 launching failures, further testing confirmed the most successful method for ground-launch utilized four RATO units and the Zero Launch Ramp that required only a 40-foot ramp to achieve flight speed with the RATO nozzles turned downward and to the side. This RATO configuration allowed for a vertical thrust component strong enough to maintain a positive rate of climb for the JB-2 using only one-tenth the length of the longer ramps. The Zero ramp launch method provided substantial mobility, defense, and stealth advantages, particularly when used with truck and trailer launch units. Test missiles flew between 350 and 430 mph, usually at altitudes between 1,500 feet and 2,500 feet, with one JB-2 functioning successfully at 10,500 feet. Maximum range increased to approximately 130 miles. The AAF took delivery of 437 JB-2s by the first week of April 1945 and forty-seven successful test launches had occurred after seventy-one attempts, raising the overall success rate to 66 percent. During May 1945, with the introduction of a zero-length launch system, ninety-seven consecutive launches were successful but accuracy did not improve as the JB-1's guidance system was basically the same as used by the 1918 Kettering Bug and by the Nazi V-1, which the Allies had disparaged as an indiscriminate terror weapon. So, as successful launches increased, JB-2 technology concentrated on guidance and accuracy.

By 1945, the JB-2 still did not have a guidance system except, like the V-1, for a fixed compass heading flown for a predetermined time, after which the engine was shut off, utilizing the German impeller timing system that locked the control linkage to the elevator into full rapid descent position at the correct moment in flight, optimistically over the intended target that was necessarily a large city. The JB-2s required large, 8-mile or more radius, target area that limited its use to terrifying large enemy metropolitan areas. During testing, none of the Eglin JB-2s was armed with explosive because of its inaccurate guidance system, but instead carried a sand and aggregate concrete ballast to provide the correct aerodynamic weight and balance.

Again, this guidance problem and its attempted resolution was caused by the indifferent research, design, and procurement methods that the AAF and ultimately, countenanced by Gen. Arnold. The Technical Service Command responded to the guidance problem by developing an electronic scheme to detonate small explosive charges that would detach the JB-2's wings in flight at supposedly a precisely timed instant, which presumably would result in more predictable, controlled, and therefore more accurate trajectory toward a target. Finally, during April 1945, Wright Field Aircraft Radio Laboratory Engineers developed a practicable radio/radar control system utilizing a modified version of the very accurate and combat-proven SCR-584 microwave radar unit to track an AN/APW-1 radar transceiver installed in the JB-2. This system allowed the missile to transmit a locator beacon and receive multiple radio control signals from the ground, to continuously identify the exact location of the missile relative to the target. This system was similar to the Orphan/Cottongrass phase of the Abusive Project (discussed elsewhere). For the preliminary trials, the AN/APW-1 was installed in a Beech C-45 Expeditor transport and the controller inside was supposedly able to track and guide the JB-2 anywhere within the range of the radar with a theoretical accuracy of 15 yards in range and 250 yards in azimuth out to 60 miles. With the installation of a low-frequency radio transponder on the JB-1, it was believed that the range and same accuracy could be increased to 200 miles. However, tests showed that with the transponder the maximum range was only 85 miles with a very large average error of 6 miles.

JB-2 Tracking and Flight Control

The AN/APW-l Radar Set was a radio control receiver specifically designed for installation and use in the tracking and flight control of the JB-2. This unit combined the functions of an airborne beacon transponder (an adaptation of AN/APN-19) with that of target-control receiving equipment. A SCR-584-M Radio Set, modified for longer range and variable Pulse Repetition Frequency (PRF), was the control station that could be used to track and control the missile's flight at a maximum range of 95 miles at 7,000 feet. The PRF of the radar system is the number of pulses that are transmitted per second. Control of the missile was by changing the PRF of the ground station.

Remote control of the missile could be attained from the SCR-584-M by positioning the control mechanism to the various control positions. This resulted in the modulation of the SCR-584-M interrogation signal and transmission to the missile one of four tones (PRF) for each movement or function that could be chosen (up, down, etc.). Fifteen control functions resulted from application of the four tones: one tone could be used to actuate the step switch to set up one of three pairs of flight functions; another tone could be used to actuate the transponder; and the other two tones could be used to select and control one of the flight functions (up, down, etc.) set up by the step switch.

The Receiver Transmitter Unit RT-86/APW-1 functioned as both a receiver and transponder, and included an audio-filter-selector circuit for discrimination between the various tones received. The output of the selector circuit was relayed to servos that actuated the JB's control surface mechanisms, or to relays that actuated the transponder. Actuation of the transponder resulted in the transmission to the SCR-584-M of coded signals that made possible the tracking of the missile.

Gen. Arnold Authorizes JB-2 Manufacture and Deployment

On January 14, apparently unaffected by the problematic JB-2 test program, General Arnold, in an obvious digression from AAFs precision bombing doctrine, increased the previous proposed order for 1,000 JB-2s to a staggering 75,000 missiles to be produced with a delivery schedule of 100 per day not later than September 1, 1945 and then increasing by 100 more per day for each month until 500 per day were produced in January 1946. Arnold also ordered that "remote control be added as soon as practicable but ... not delay the delivery or launching programs." The following day, Arnold gave the JB-2 project the highest AA-1 priority, which was equal to the production priority of the B-29 Superfortress.

Ironically, the German RLM and High Command had echoed the identical benefits of their weapon as Arnold had in support of the JB-2. The JB-2 would not risk a pilot or crew, its small size, high-speed, and low-altitude approach made it difficult to destroy, and it could be launched at any time in any weather. Since it was fabricated mostly of sheet steel, such critical war materials, as aircraft aluminum, were not consumed. Inexpensive to manufacture, the American flying bomb could readily be deployed and expended in mass quantities without depleting valuable materials and human resources.

Arnold's decision to multiply the JB-2 production order by seventy-five times came immediately following the Battle of the Bulge, the major late December 1944, German offensive that shocked the Allies by causing massive casualties, materiel loss, and delaying the end of the European war. Afterward, Generals Marshall and Eisenhower demanded that Arnold send large numbers of JB-2s to the ETO as this large all-weather weapon could have been used when the Germans attacked under cover of poor weather and low cloud ceiling, preventing Allied airpower from interdicting. In order to prevent a repetition of the Bulge experience, Eisenhower, also a JB-2 advocate, pushed to deliver as many JB-2s to the ETO as possible. Arnold, faced with the possibility of losing control of the JB-2 program to Marshall and Eisenhower and the Army Ground Forces (AGF), persevered in controlling the JB-2 program.

Even at this late date in the war, the Nazi Wonder V-weapon assault on London and the Wehrmacht Battle of the Bulge attack had shaken the public's confidence, causing the Office of War Information (OWI) to begin a 1945 JB-2 publicity blitz through radio broadcasts, newspapers, and films. Their propaganda featured such headlines as "US Rockets Mean Trouble for Foes" and "Yankee Doodle Robot Bomb; Undergoing Tests, Assures Precision Attacks on Tokyo, Nazis." These ringing praises of the American Wonder Weapon and the resultant public support further buoyed Arnold's big-ticket request.

An important consideration in Arnold's decision to grossly increase JB-2 production was that the small-scale deployment of the bomb would largely have it considered to be an immoral terror weapon but that launching at it at a rate of between 500 and 1,000 per day against a target such as the industrial Ruhr could realize substantial over riding strategic results.

The Billion-Dollar American Buzz Bomb

At the end of 1944, the War Production Board (WPB) placed the cost of a completed JB-2 at $7,925 plus $1,888 per each launching cart and RATOs for a total cost of $9,813 per launch. A then colossal total of $950 million ($13.7 billion in 2020 second only to the Manhattan A-bomb Project at $29 billion) was to be expended to produce an eventual 150,000 JB-2s:

Airframe Prime Contactors*	$390 million at $2,600 each
GFC Contractors	
Control Units	$300 million at $2,000 each
Pressure Regulators	$15 million at $100 each
Air Containers (2 per unit)	$25.5 Million at $170 per set
Shutoff Valves (2 per unit)	$7.5 million at $50 per set
Jet Engine and Metering Units	$150 million at $1,000 each
Warheads	$90 million at $600 each
Radio Sets (1,500/1 for each 10 airframes)	$2.25 million at $150 each

Launching Requirements for 150,000 JB-2s would add $458,500 million for a staggering total of $1,408,750,000 billion**:

Propellant Fuel***	$36 million for 75 million pounds at $45 per 100 pounds
New Propellant Facilities	$130 million
Rocket Motor Cases	$125 million (750,000 at 5 rockets per Launch) at $250 each or $1,250 per launch
Launching Carts****	$75 million at $500 each

*Airframe prime contractors were Willys producing 3,275 and Higgins, Murray, Budd, Firestone, and Nash Kelvinator each contracted for 30,260 by July 1946. The monthly total production was to reach 15,200 by December 1945 and the grand total by July 1946 was to be 154,575.

** The cost to develop and produce 3,943 B-29s was $3.7 billion, the 9,817 B-25s cost just over $1 billion, while the Atomic Bomb cost over $2 billion so the $1.4 billion for JB-2 project would not have been insignificant if the war had continued.

*** The amount of explosive propellant and presses to grain the explosive into rocket propellant to launch 100 JB-2s per day was worrisome but to launch 500 per day was an exorbitant demand on America's munitions production. The Ordnance Department was to contract for one million pounds of rocket fuel per month which was to be sufficient for 1,500 launchings at 500 pounds of fuel per launch. A new $5 million plant to produce propellant for 1,000 launchings per month was recommended to be built at the New York Ordnance Works by Monsanto, which was then to be in charge of production beginning in April 1945. To provide for 15,000 launchings per month (500 per day) was estimated to require a facility ten times as large.

****Launching ramps were an unnoted expense as Arnold ordered 100 ramps to be constructed by the Corps of Engineers; twenty immediately for training and eighty ramps at sixteen per month beginning July 1945.

While feedback to the new weapon was generally positive, there were significant concerns. To manufacture 75,000 JB-2s would require the priority transfer of 5 million square feet of production floor space, machinery, the use of some critical materials, along with the diversion of over 13,000 skilled airframe and instrument personnel from conventional warplane production. These requirements would not only jeopardize AAF conventional aircraft production and guided bomb programs but more importantly conventional bomb production and production of medium and heavy artillery ammunition for the Army Ground Forces. An early estimate indicated a reduction in the production of artillery shells by 25 percent and bombs by 17 percent. The filling of JB-2 warheads would reduce the amount of TNT available for artillery ammunition by over 4 percent and aircraft bombs would be similarly affected. Also, ten cargo ships (25 percent of Allied shipping ETO capacity) would have to arrive safely at European ports each month to maintain the required JB-2 daily firing rate. For the projected use in the Pacific, once the JB-2 was in full production it would require seven to nine months to transfer units operating in the ETO back to the U.S. to train them and afterward deploy them to the Pacific. An interesting suggestion to meet the JB-2 production quota was to manufacture the propulsion units, gyros, and other components in the U.S. and then ship these components to France where the airframe would be fabricated and the final assembly completed. The Germans had several V-1 assembly and manufacturing plants in France one of which (at Thil) was captured intact and there were adequate French laborers available in the area. Also, there was factory floor space and labor available in the Paris area that could be converted to JB-2 manufacture and assembly.

In addition to the production issues, the American JB-2 exhibited the many of the same disadvantages as the Nazi V-1:

1. Once launched, it could not be terminated which became very important during Elgin and Wendover testing, in case of an errant missile heading for populated areas.
2. Its flight path could not be changed, making it predictable and an easy target for an enemy with VT proximity AA shells and with fast fighter aircraft able to chase the JB-2 down.
3. Ground-launched JB-2s required booster rockets and a ramp which revealed not only the missile's predictable and unchanged flight path, but were choice, easily identifiable targets for enemy attack.
4. The JB-2's small size limited its explosive warhead to just less than a ton, reducing its destructive potency.
5. The weapon's poor accuracy of being able of hitting within an 8-mile radius, relegated the weapon to large cities as their only feasible target.

Thus, like the Nazis V-1/V-2 assaults, appallingly, the Americans were willing to unleash thousands of these bombs haphazardly on already heavily-damaged Japanese cities as psychological weapons intended to only terrorize their inhabitants.

Instead of the standard procurement system that was used to research, design, and acquire conventional aircraft; the JB-2 and other AAF guided missile programs suffered from the haphazard way they were handled. The JB-2, specifically, being a ground-launched missile that threatened to compete with manned aircraft, had many more detractors than advocates. In October 1943, Brig. Gen. H. M. McClelland, ACO, had been assigned inclusive responsibility for guided aerial weapons research and development. As discussed earlier, McClelland, as ACO, had little expertise and no authority within the AAF and was ineffectual in promoting or defending any missile matters, and in December 1944, he was relieved, and no replacement was named. So by the early spring of 1945, only Gen. Arnold remained as the JB-2's major supporter. Arnold, who had suffered multiple heart attacks due the stress of commanding the entire AAF for seven years, named himself the CG of the new 20th Air Force and had little time to vigorously defend the JB-2 against influential factions in the AAF.

It was not until February 6, 1945 that Lt. Gen. Barney Giles finally released a memorandum to validate not only the control of guided aerial weapons by the AAF, but particularly the JB-2 ground-launched missile, which was being touted by the AAF based upon strategic as well as tactical requirements. Giles objective was to continue and assure future control over ground launched missiles of any type, range, or capability for the AAF. The Joint New Weapons Guided Missile Committee was established on January 16, 1945 with its authorized purpose being to study the influence of guided missiles on future trends in warfare and to recommend a national program for their development. In response to Giles' memorandum, the committee concluded that ground-launched missiles would be controlled by the AAF when they supported tactical aerial bombardment or had a strategic target and that control of ground launched missiles would be granted to the Army Ground Forces (AGF) when they complemented artillery fire and the AAF. The bottom line was that the JB-2 was considered both an air and a ground weapon and the service, either AGF or AAF, that would be the most effective in utilizing it in combat would probably gain possession of it.

The competition between the Army's Air Forces and Army Ground Forces for control of the JB-2 had begun with the salvage of a damaged German V-1 by the AGF in July 1944. The V-1 engine was soon duplicated and tested and the completed JB-2 began its troubled testing phase. Once the JB-2 appeared to become a viable weapon, the Army Ground Forces decided that the JB-2 could be launched from the beach during an amphibious operation and that they could be used as very long-range artillery to strike an area rather than a precise target and consequently would not require complicated guidance and control equipment.

This AAF/AGF skirmish for JB-2 control led to the McNarney Directive of October 2, 1944; formulated by Lt.Gen. Joseph McNarney, Army Deputy Chief of Staff, who approved a War Department General Staff policy statement giving guided missile development responsibilities to the Army Air Forces, the Army Service Forces (ASF), and the Army Ground Forces. The directive gave the AAF responsibility for all guided missiles launched from aircraft as well as ground-launched guided missiles that "flew using aerodynamic forces." Both the AAF and the AFS would be responsible for the development of their own integral missile components such as propulsion and control subsystems. The ASF's technical services, would be used by both parties to develop warheads, non-integral launching devices, and ground portions of the control system. The AGF was to convey its guided missile requirements to either the AAF or ASF, which would then develop the missile. It gave the AGF responsibility for missiles that "flew by way of momentum" (e.g. ballistic missiles such as the V-2). Arnold and the AAF did not realize the potential of the German V-2 rocket and that in the post-war, the V-2 would be under AGF control. Note: The Army Service Forces (ASF) were one of the three autonomous components of the Army during World War II, the others being the AAF and AGF. The ASF was created on February 28, 1942 in a comprehensive reorganization of the Army. This was the result of dissatisfaction with the existing structure, as the AAF, in particular, was seeking greater autonomy as its role and importance increased. The ASF was comprised of the Technical Services, the Corps of Engineers, Signal Corps, Ordnance Department, Quartermaster Corps, Chemical Corps, Medical Corps, and the Transportation Division.

The AGF wished to deploy the JB-2 in large numbers as early as September 1, 1945 as part of Operation Olympic, the projected invasion of Kyushu, Japan, and requested 25,000. Not to be outdone, Gen. Arnold counteracted with his request for an eventual 75,000 to be launched at a rate of 100 per day by October 1945.

Meanwhile, to gain the initiative on the AGF, the AAF authorized the formation of the first operational JB-2 unit, which was to be able to launch four missiles per hour, twenty-four hours a day, seven days a week, which would be only four missiles less than the 100 per day Arnold had set as his goal. When the war in Europe ended in May 1945, this squadron was to be sent to the Pacific where it was to be deployed from captured territory during the invasion of the Japanese Home Islands to bombard Japanese cities. However, by June 1945, with AAF conventional bombing utterly decimating Japanese cities, interest in combat testing the JB-2 diminished and production requirements were reduced from the 10,000 that were then on order to 7,000, which included the JB-2s already delivered.

The inter-service rivalry between the AAF and the AGF for the control of guided missiles and the combat testing the JB-2 ended with the Hiroshima and Nagasaki Atomic bombs that not only ended the war but also questioned the need for any other weapon systems, including the JB guided bomb series. JB-2 production continued until September 15, 1945, when all contracts were canceled after the AAF had taken delivery of only 1,391, which was less than half the number Arnold had wanted to be available for operations by September 1. Each JB-2 had required about 400 man hours to manufacture and cost approximately twenty times as much as each German V-1, which was partially due to the JB's currently much smaller production run, which still amounted to $30 million.

Post-War JB-2 Testing and Successors

Concurrent with JB-2 testing ongoing at Eglin, on June 22, 1945, the AAF selected the sprawling and desolate Wendover Army Air Field Range, Utah, as the next JB-2 testing site, to conduct testing and the initial use of live warheads. Six weeks later, after the atomic bombs destroyed Hiroshima and Nagasaki, the necessity for unique weapons such as the JB-2 and even conventional weapons were called into question. Testing continued at Eglin and Wendover, through the Japanese surrender on September 2, 1945, but on September 15, the contracts with all manufacturers of JB-2 components were canceled. Although facing an ambiguous future, both the Army and Navy continued their commitment to their missile programs during the enormous post-war military demobilization. Both services recognized the value of weapons like the JB-2 in the dawn of a new era of air bombardment where large-scale air attacks could be remotely instigated by the mere push of a button. Thus, the JB-2 began its transition from a weapon, albeit never used in combat, to a research vehicle for the development of future missiles. After launching 233 of the 1,382 JB-2s received by the AAF, Range 64, as per lease agreement, was returned to its civilian owner at the end of hostilities. Eglin began construction on a new 4,700-acre ground missile launching site near Eglin, to be located 22 miles west along the Gulf Coast on Santa Rosa Island. These two launching areas included two concrete pads for 50-foot-long mobile ramps, mounted on flat-bed trailers, and a 400-foot-long inclined steel ramp on concrete piers. Each missile site contained launch controls in a concrete bunker, and exclusively used RATO propellant cylinders to accelerate the JB-2s to flight speed. Previous testing at Range 64 during 1944 and 1945, where experimentation with nine different ramp configurations occurred, resulted in more efficient methodology for Santa Rosa.

Meanwhile, the Air Technical Service Command at Wendover conducted tests from September 1945 through January 1946 to determine the accuracy, reliability, and limitations of JB-2s guided by remote radar/radio ground control. These tests resulted in much improved accuracy, with the missiles impacting within one-half to one and one-half miles of the target marker with a maximum range of 85 miles. A Proving Ground Command Memo of March 1, 1946, recapped the JB-2's development, concluding that the preset mechanically controlled JB-2 could deliver a warhead 150 miles at 400 mph with 50 percent accuracy within a 5-mile radius of the target center "which rendered it, suitable for area bombing of cities or other large areas." A remotely controlled JB-2 was able to deliver that warhead only 100 miles, hitting a half square target "consistently."

The AAF conducted its final JB-2 tests at Eglin in 1945 and at Wendover in 1946, and with these final tests the initial JB-2 development phase had been completed as per the original expenditure order and the JB-2 program *per se* was officially closed. Meanwhile, the AAF had previously begun the construction of two new missile launch sites, at Santa Rosa Island, Florida, and Alamogordo Army Airfield, New Mexico, for the continuation of the JB-2 program. On February 6, 1946, the AAF activated the First Experimental Guided Missiles Group, and assigned personnel to the JB-2 program, to test new launching technics.

On June 22, 1945, along with the ongoing JB-2 testing at Eglin, the AAF selected Wendover Army Air Field Range, Utah, as the next JB-2 testing site, for the testing and the initial use of live warheads. (*AAF*)

After the AAF conducted its last JB-2 tests at Eglin in 1945 and at Wendover in 1946, two sites, nearby Eglin, were located on Santa Rosa Island, off the Florida Panhandle and were initiated during 1947. (*AAF*)

A B-17 heads toward the Florida Panhandle carrying two JB-2. (*AAF*)

During 1947, BuAer and the Navy Department's Office of Naval Research conducted Project Squid, a program of fundamental research on liquid rocket and pulse jet propulsion in conjunction with New York University, Polytechnic Institute of Brooklyn, Purdue University, Cornell Aeronautical Laboratory, and Princeton University (the administrative center). This very analytical program produced extensive technical research on the performance analysis of the ducted pulse jet and computational flow dynamics.

JB-2 testing continued through the remainder of 1947 and onward. During June 1947, with the Iron Curtain closing, the Pentagon directed the First Experimental Guided Missiles Group to launch 179 JB-2s from Zero Mobile Ramps and 107 from aircraft to compare the accuracy of missiles with the preset, fire and forget, mechanical guidance system against those under radio/radar control. The JB-2, as the only operational U.S. cruise missile, served as the lone test platform for the new radar guidance systems that improved range and accuracy for the next generation of missiles. Air Proving Ground CO Brig. Gen. Grandison Gardner deemed the JB-2 test program as "Invaluable to its application to future projects of similar scope now in the research and development stage." The advanced, radio/radar-controlled JB-2s demonstrated improvements in range, control precision, and accuracy compared to the preset mechanical missiles as they transformed guidance from relative mechanical simplicity to electronic complexity.

In 1947, the JB-2 test program at Wendover, dormant since January 1946, moved to Alamogordo Army Airfield (renamed Holloman AFB in January 1948), New Mexico, and the adjacent White Sands Proving Ground (renamed White Sands Missile Range in 1958). Personnel at these installations, concurrently tested captured German V-2 ballistic missiles and began a brief eight-month evaluation at Holloman/White Sands on April 23, 1948, wherein eleven radio-controlled JB-2s were launched until testing concluded on January 10, 1949.

Although it was never used in combat, the JB-2 played a significant role in the development of more advanced surface-to-surface missile systems after the war. Most of the remaining 1,391 JB-2s were expended in testing as the development of the JB-2 was continued as the redesignated as the LTV-1 in late 1947 and then as the LTV-A-1 in early 1948, which was canceled in early 1949. There were two versions: one with preset internal guidance and another with radar control. Several launch platforms were developed, including permanent and portable ramps, and airborne launching from under the wings of the B-17 and B-29 bombers. The designers of new missiles then in the research and development stage, utilized the Santa Rosa Island data to aid in the development of the Martin MGM-1 Matador and the KUW-1 Loon, the Navy's JB-2.

Martin MGM-1 Matador

During August 1945, the AAF established a requirement for a 175- to 500-mile range, 600-mph surface-to-surface missile. Martin received a one-year contract in March 1946 to investigate both a subsonic and supersonic version, but the latter was canceled in December. The Martin MGM-1 Matador (Project MX-771) was America's first operational surface-to-surface cruise missile, which was similar in concept to the V-1/JB-2. It was 39 feet, 7 inches long, 4 feet, 6 inches in diameter, and had a wingspan

Martin MGM-1 Matador. (*AAF*)

of 28 feet, 7 inches. It was boosted by an Aerojet General solid-fuel rocket and powered by a small Allison J33-A-37 turbojet engine in place of the JB-2's much less efficient pulse jet and could operate at Mach 0.9 (666 mph) and 43,000 feet. It was guided by a radio command that allowed in-flight course corrections and accuracy to be maintained over greatly extended ranges of just under 600 miles. Despite its subsonic speed, the Martin missile survived the 1947 Guided Missile Committee of the Research and Development Board funding cut. In March 1949, however, the board recommended its elimination, but the Matador continued, although USAF cut its priority back in August 1949. That decision was rescinded by the USAF in December 1949 but then in September 1950 gave the missile top priority, no doubt because of the Korean War. It was not until 1954 that the 1st Pilotless Bomber Squadron deployed it, armed with a 20-kiloton W5 nuclear warhead (by the late 1950s, all Matadors carried the nuclear warhead). After 1,200 Matadors were produced, the last Matadors were removed from active service in 1962 as the Matador's flight profile was very simple and predictable, which no doubt contributed to its cancellation.

KUW-1 Loon: The Navy Initiates the Cruise Missile Age

After the AAF commenced its JB-2 flight tests during October 1944, the Navy soon indicated an interest, intending to launch the missile from escort carriers with guidance from either shipboard or airborne radar. The Navy's buzz bomb project was then initiated by the BuAer in April 1945 and designated the KGW-1 Loon. The end of the European War in May 1945 presented the opportunity to deploy an operational American cruise missile on targets in the Japanese Home Islands. The Navy wanted their own JB-2s, wishing to execute a plan that had been under development since the previous September to launch the missiles from an aircraft carrier. The JB-1 Loon would be America's only operational-ready cruise missile between 1944 and 1953, providing the only opportunity to test and evaluate new and improved systems and train personnel in their use. By 1953, the Navy's Loon had progressed from a V-1 copy to a sophisticated submarine-launched, computer-controlled cruise missile, albeit one that would soon reach the end of its development potential and never operate as a cruise missile.

The Loon was 27 feet, 1 inch long, had a diameter of 34 inches, and a wingspan of 17 feet, 8 inches. It weighed 5,020 pounds with its 2,100-pound warhead and a fully-fueled 180-gallon tank. The missile was powered by a Ford PJ 31-1 Pulse Jet that could use any gasoline-type fuel to develop a gross thrust of 850 to 900 pounds at a specific impulse of about 1,100 pounds per second. The Loon was launched at a minimum speed of 220 mph, climbing at a rate of 500 to 1,000 feet per minute to the altitude set on its altimeter. Its optimum altitude was between 2,000 and 4,000 feet, and its optimum speed in flight was 400 mph with a maximum range of 150 miles. The Loon was tracked by radar to the target and was controlled by radio. Stabilization was provided by three air-driven position and rate gyros and its control surfaces consisted of a rudder and elevators. An aneroid unit and magnetic compass-controlled altitude and course through the gyro system.

Initially, BuAer received a few JB-2s from the AAF as LTV-N-2s, but in June 1945 it contracted with Republic Aviation for 151 missiles, fifty-one at once and 100 later. In late 1945, tests of the XM-1 launching system (a slotted tube powder catapult) using dummy Loons were conducted at the newly opened Point Mugu Naval Base Naval Air Missile Test Center. During January 1946, the USN completed several operational test launches of a Loon, now redesignated as the KUW-1. Proposals for a joint Army/Navy program to launch JB-2s from LST (Landing Ship Tank) vessels benefitted from unusually amicable inter-service cooperation. As plans progressed for the invasion of Japan, Army planners planned to deploy JB-2s from the beachheads once they had been secured.

In September 1947, directives were issued to develop a launching capability from submarines with the designation of LTV-2 and finally as LTV-N-2 in early 1948. The Loon's first successful submarine launch was from the *Cusk* (SSG-348) on February 12, 1947. The missile was carried behind the conning tower in a large, water-tight cylinder. Once the submarine surfaced, the tank was opened and the Loon was moved to the rear of the boat and positioned on its aft-facing ramp where it was assembled, the wings attached, and a guidance check was run. The Loon was then placed on a launching sled on rails and a booster rocket launched it. The entire operation required nearly an hour to assemble, launch, and for the sub to then submerge. During August 1947, based on the successful results of these tests, the Navy directed that submarine launchings continue through 1949 to develop terminal guidance procedures and tactical concepts for the Regulus, a submarine-launched guided missile with a range of 500 miles that was then under development. Several months after the first Loon/*Cusk* launch, a second *Balao*-class submarine, the *Carbonero* (SSG-337), joined the tests to launch the Loon and act as the control and tracking station.

In late 1948, BuAer issued directives to develop a Loon launching capability from surface vessels as well. Late that autumn, the Navy's first guided missile ship, heavy seaplane tender *Norton Sound* (AV-11, later AVN-1) cruised off the coast of Southern California for missile training. After four successful Loon launchings during 1949, Aerobee rockets were installed on the *Norton Sound* but then the surface ship Loon Project was canceled.

The outbreak of the Korean War, amid the escalation of the Cold War and the Communist Menace, gave the obsolete Loon new life as a test vehicle and, if necessary, an operational submarine and air-launched (from B-29s and B-36s) weapon. The Navy CNO ordered twenty-five Loons to be armed with fuses and warheads for possible operational use.

Meanwhile, the USAF had continued its JB-2 tests but the Korean War redirected the Air Force priorities and its JB-2 program was soon terminated and only the Navy would receive R&D funding for America's only viable cruise missile program. The remaining USAF JB-2s were launched from B-29s to be sacrificed to P-80 jet fighters to test their new A-10 Infrared gunsight. The last USAF Eglin JB-2 launch occurred on August 11, 1950.

Navy modified its 399 JB-2s obtained from the AAF in a series of guidance, tracking, and target acquisition upgrades. The Navy pioneered radar guidance to replace radio control guidance. The Navy's crowning achievement during this time was the development

Navy KUW-1 Loon. (*SNASM*)

Spectacular test launch of a Loon from the *Carbonero*. (*USN*)

of the Marine Guidance Computer (MGC) which, in conjunction with radar tracking, set the standard for modern missile guidance. The Loon Program had advanced the cruise missile from the mechanical to computer and trained America's first true missileers. Arguably, the Loon can be credited with bringing a comprehensive reexamination of future strategy and tactics. On September 11, 1953, the last Loon was launched and the LTV-N-2 submarine program was terminated in favor of the Regulus, which was under development. Knowledge gained from Loon testing onboard submarines and surface ships led to the subsequent development of more advanced guided missiles, and eventually as the sea-launched cruise missiles as deployed by today's USN fleet.

Regulus, the Loon Successor

During October 1943, Chance Vought Aircraft Company, Stratford, Connecticut, was awarded a study contract for a 300-mile-range missile to carry a 4,000-pound warhead. The project remained in Limbo until May 1947, when the AAF awarded Martin the Matador contract to replace the JB-2. The Navy considered the Matador as a threat to its future in guided missiles and during August 1947 began a development program for a missile that could be launched from a submarine and use the same Allison J33 turbojet engine as the Matador. The Navy missile, the Regulus, carried a 3,000-pound warhead over 500 nautical miles at Mach 0.85 (630 mph). The first Regulus launch from a submarine occurred in July 1953 from the deck of the *Tunny*, which carried two missiles armed with the W2 nuclear warhead, making the *Tunny* America's first nuclear deterrent patrol submarine.

Hughes JB-3 Tiamat

The JB-3 Tiamat subsonic air-to-air, anti-bomber, missile program commenced in January 1944 as Project MX-570. Tiamat was the Babylonian primordial goddess of the salt sea. Hughes Aircraft Company, Electronics Division, Los Angeles, the prime contractor, was committed to develop twenty-five Tiamats in conjunction with NACA, four of which were to be ready for testing by July 3, 1945. The 14.33-foot-long, 600-pound JB-3 was propelled by a Monsanto dual-thrust (7,200-pound boost/200-pound sustain) solid-fueled rocket motor and had three comparatively large wings with control surfaces for stability and control. The initial ten were to be auto-pilot controlled by modified Jack & Heintz* units that were used on the JB-2. The Tiamat used a semi-active radar-seeker mounted on gimbals that acted as a gyro. Control was a pendulous gyroscopic radar-seeker that operated pneumatic servos to the three wings. It was to carry a 500-pound HE warhead triggered by a proximity fuse. The projected cost was to be $363 million at $13,721, each with an additional $56 million allocated for a wind tunnel test model.

(*Cleveland natives Bill Jack and Ralph Heintz formed Jack & Heintz in 1940 in Palo Alto, California, but soon moved their company to the Cleveland, and with fifty employees began to manufacture airplane starters. The company then received

Hughes JB-3 Tiamat. (*AAF*)

an order for the production of autopilot devices; by 1944, they employed over 8,700 and expanded to several other new local plants. In 1946, the company merged with Precision Products and both Jack and Heintz sold all their stock after the acquisition.)

Wind tunnel tests were conducted in the Wright Field and were followed by tests in the Free Flight Tunnel at NACA, Langley Field. The first prototype test launch of a series of tests was ground-launched with the aid of a booster on August 6, 1945 at Wendover. These free flight tests generally produced poor results due to difficulties in the development of the radar-seeker and when the launching booster left the missile. Later air-dropped launching was tested with a company, Northrop P-61 Black Widow scheduled to be the control aircraft but was later replaced by A-26 Invader aircraft. JB-3 testing and development continued until after the war, but the program was eventually terminated in September 1946 because of its continuing problems and due to Government Fiscal 1947 R&D cutbacks, which maintained the more advanced air-to-air missile projects, particularly the AAM-A-1 Firebird and AAM-A-2/F-98/GAR-1 Falcon.

JB-4

The air- and ground-launched 3,000-pound, 12-foot wingspan, primarily plywood JB-4 was developed by Wright Field under Project MX-607. It was essentially a GB-1 guided glide bomb powered by a Ford PJ31 Pulse Jet engine, which gave the JB-4 a standoff range to 75 miles at 445 mph. Because the pulse jet required fuel, the size of the JB-4's warhead was limited to 750 pounds compared to the 2,000-pound bomb carried by the GB-4. Like the GB-4, it was equipped with an AN/AXT-2 television transmitter broadcasting a television signal from a camera in the missile's nose to a remote operator viewing the transmitted picture in the launching aircraft, who could

JB-4. (*AAF*)

then send radio commands to change the course of the missile to ensure hitting the target. The JB-4 began flight testing during January 1945, but experienced reliability problems and the television-guidance system was of the limited contemporary technology broadcasting inadequate images, except in perfectly clear weather. These issues along with the war ending resulted in the project's termination before any of the JB-4s saw combat.

JB-5

The planned-only JB-5 (Project MX-595) was to be a wingless, unguided, air-to-surface rocket with a 3.7-mile range,

JB-6

The JB-6 (Project MX-600) was planned-only as a spin-stabilized supersonic air-to-surface guided missile.

JB-7

The JB-7 (Project MX-605) was planned-only to be a 9,700-pound turbojet-powered surface-to-surface cruise missile with a range of 400 miles but was canceled when no suitable design was tendered.

Boeing JB-8/XSAM-A-1 GAPA. (*AAF*)

Boeing JB-8/XSAM-A-1 GAPA

In June 1946, the AAF began Project MX-606, and awarded Boeing a three-month contract to study the general problems involved in the development of a surface-to-air guided missile, which was briefly designated as the JB-8. The missile was categorized as a ground-to-air pilotless aircraft (GAPA), and in late 1945, MX-606 requirements were extended to include the development of a tactical supersonic surface-to-air missile with remote control that could intercept enemy aircraft flying at speeds up to 700 mph at altitudes between 8,000 and 60,000 feet. In 1947, the designation SAM-A-1 was assigned to the GAPA, and between 1946 and August 1950, more than 100 XSAM-A-1 GAPA test missiles were launched.

The XSAM-A-1 vehicles were of several significantly different configurations to test various aspects of the projected operational missile. The first missiles, the Boeing Model 600 series, were all two-stage solid-propellant rockets of various configurations and were used for preliminary aerodynamic research and development. The first Model 600 launch occurred in January 1946, but the first stable flight test occurred during mid-summer 1946. Forty were launched by the newly independent USAF at Wendover before the program was moved to Holloman AAF, New Mexico, during March 1947.

The Model 601 Series, first launched in March 1948, was 19 feet, 4 inches long, had a finspan of 4 feet, a diameter of 19 inches, and weighed 640 pounds with its solid-fueled booster weighing 1,625 pounds more. The 601 Series was propelled by an Aerojet 30AL-1000 liquid-fueled rocket sustainer and a solid-fueled rocket booster that gave it speed of Mach 1.8 (1,370 mph) and a range of 6.3 miles. They were used to test the GAPA's guidance system consisting of radar beam-riding mid-course guidance, but in some variants, a target-seeker was employed for terminal homing.

The Model 601A Series was also boosted by a solid-fueled rocket and tested ramjets as cruise propulsion system. The 601As were similar in size to the 601s but weighed more at almost 3,000 pounds (1,000 pounds plus 2,000 more, including the various boosters). The maximum speed in tests was Mach 2.5 (1,900 mph) with a range of 16.5 miles.

The 602 Series was a slender, 5,000-pound missile that consisted of a rocket-booster ramjet that powered it to Mach 2.5. More than 100 were tested to investigate the launching and boosting of these missiles to supersonic speeds and its control along a radar-tracking beam.

The Model 603 Series comprised many different larger configurations that were studied for the tactical missile, but none were built. Ordinarily, the operational SAM-A-1 would have used a ramjet sustainer, beam-riding guidance, and some type of terminal homing system. The GAPA tactical missile program was terminated in 1949 when the USAF's surface-to-air missile development had moved toward the much larger and more advanced IM-99/CIM-10 Bomarc.

JB-9

The designation JB-9 was earmarked for an unfinished short-range surface-to-surface missile, probably identical to Project MX-626, which was described as a jet-propelled short-range surface-to-surface guided missile.

Northrop JB-10

The final successor to the JB Project was the JB-10 using an airframe that was 12 feet long, 4 feet, 9 inches high, had a wingspan of 29 feet, 2 inches, and weighed 7,210 pounds. A single Ford PJ31 pulse jet engine (thrust rated at 900 pounds) was mounted in a centerline shroud, which was of a larger diameter than the pulse jet to allow the flow of cooling air around the engine. The pulse jet was to drive the JB-10 at 425 mph over a range of 200 miles at an operating altitude of 2,500 feet. The prominent cast magnesium bomb containers of the JB-1 were also removed and replaced by two integral 1,825-pound HE warhead sections in the wing roots. The Hammond control equipment was the same as used on the JB-1 with slight modification in the rigging of the control surfaces for elevon control in both pitch and roll. The JB-10 was equipped with a new, very successful telemetering transmitter that sent data in flight to the test center for six minutes from the firing of the rockets.

The JB-10 testing program was delayed for long periods due to problems in loading of the inert warheads. During weight and balance measurements, it was found that the

Northrop JB-10. (*AAF*)

weight of plaster and lead added to the warhead at the factory was 750 pounds too heavy. The correct weight and balance for each bomb had to achieved by the removal of a portion of the warhead and adding approximately 100 pounds of lead to the airframe rear section.

Like the original JB-2 the JB-10 was to be a low-precision standoff weapon intended for the planned invasion of Japan. The missile used a simple preset guidance system, which would fly a predetermined distance into the direction of launch and then dive into the ground. Eleven JB-10s were built and ten were expended in testing. The first flight of a JB-10 occurred in April 1945 at Range 64, Eglin Field, using a level ramp with 370 feet of track using modified launching sleds equipped with five Monsanto Rockets having a burning time of 1.8 seconds. This first launch was unsuccessful as were the next seven due to mechanical malfunctions at launching or just after take-off. Test JB-10 No. 9 climbed to 1,300 feet and then flew level for ninety seconds at 225 mph and then began a pitch oscillation flying for another three minutes and ten seconds and 16 miles before crashing into the Gulf. For the next test, JB-10 No. 10 had slight modifications to its altitude control to improve pitch control. When this JB separated from the sled, it climbed sharply and went into a spin to the right apparently due to another malfunction of the control equipment. JB-10 No. 11 was prepared for testing but since this was the last available bomb it was decided to save it as a museum piece and sent to Freeman Field, Indiana. So, because of system component developmental problems, its expensive construction, non-disposable standards, and, finally, because the post-war demand for such a weapon had disappeared, the JB-10 program was terminated in March 1946 and the JB Project along with it.

Project Bumblebee: The First SAM Missiles

Mostly unknown today, the Project Bumblebee research and development program was to become one of Americas largest and most comprehensive early post-war missile projects. Activated in 1944, it eventually led to large series of surface-to-air missiles (SAMs), which would shield USN and Allied warships against air attack for the next thirty years. As early as mid-summer 1944, the Navy appreciated that the research and development effort regarding SAMs was going to be too huge to be self-supported. The Navy's options were to grant large contracts to private industry or to engage prominent technical leaders from the academic world's leading institutions and laboratories. On December 1, 1944, the Navy BuOrd contracted the celebrated Applied Physics Laboratory of the Johns Hopkins University (APL/JHU), Baltimore. APL/JHU's Dr. Merle Tuve, developer the noteworthy radio proximity VT (variable time) fuse for anti-aircraft shells, was designated as the project manager. Tuve named the Bumblebee project after a bumblebee insect, which he described as "although aerodynamically unable to fly, does not know this and flies anyway." Tuve's original APL/JHUs Central Laboratory staff of eleven was restructured as Section T (Tuve's initial) as an entity directly under contract to the BuOrd, but to operate independently as the Applied Physics Laboratory under which the Tuve's Johns Hopkins administration and its subcontractors were quickly funded to get the program underway. Funds were channeled through the Bureau of Ordnance to the Applied Physics Laboratory. Dr. Tuve's team was given priority and the secret program's funding bypassed prerequisite Congressional approval. Task F was created to develop a prototype interceptor missile or to determine that it could not be accomplished.

During World War II, America indicated almost no interest in developing SAMs as the need was not for defensive missiles but offensive ones. This changed when the German *Fritz-X* and HS 293 guided missiles sank Allied warships in the Mediterranean and USN invasion fleets closing in on Japan found themselves under terrorizing and effective attack from Kamikaze suicide aircraft. Development began immediately of two guided missiles to protect USN ships: the subsonic KAN Little Joe and KAY/KAO Lark missiles, both directed by radio command.

Instrumental in the development of these missiles was 1930 Naval Academy graduate Grayson Merrill. During 1941, he was attending the electrical engineering course at the Naval Postgraduate School when Cdr. Delmar Fahrney, director of BuAer's Pilotless Aircraft, selected him to be his deputy in the BuOrd's Special Design

Cdr. Grayson Merrill, deputy, BuOrd's Special Design Branch. (*USN*)

Branch, which was developing the Navy's first guided missiles. These two officers devised and directed much of the Navy's World War II early postwar guided missile efforts. During 1943, Lt. Cdr. Merrill succeeded Fahrney as head of the Special Design Branch, where he directed the engineering and production program for the Assault Drone (AD) Program. After working on the STAG-3 TDR Drone Project, Merrill initiated and directed the development of the Lark surface-to-air missile, the Little Joe ship-to-air missile, and the Gargoyle air-to-surface-to-air surface missile. In March 1945, Merrill left BuOrd to become the technical director of the Naval Air Missile Test Center at Point Mugu. During the 1996 fiftieth anniversary of Point Mugu's commissioning, Merrill was named Father of Point Mugu. Between 1950 and 1960, Capt. Merrill co-authored and edited a multi-volume series of influential textbooks entitled *Principles of Guided Missile Design.*

KAN-1/2 Little Joe

After the NAMU submitted its design proposal for the short-range surface-to-air missile Lark on May 10, 1945, it realized that a more quickly developed alternative was necessary as an immediate answer to the increased Japanese Kamikaze threat as the Navy neared the Japanese Home Islands. The Little Joe project, a ship-based, short-range surface-to-air missile, was authorized, and subsequently, the NAMU withdrew from the Lark project to focus on KAN-1 Little Joe with the NAMC.

As a crash program, Little Joe made use of readily obtainable materials and as many existing components as possible. The Little Joe's fuselage was virtually identical to the standard Aerojet jet-assisted take-off (JATO) solid-fuel rocket, which was generally used to provide additional take-off thrust for heavily loaded aircraft. Little Joe's mild steel sheet fuselage was 8 feet, 6 inches long and 22.7 inches in diameter. Its simple cruciform wings spanned 4 feet, 9 inches and presented canard control surfaces. It weighed 591 pounds with four JATO rockets (including the 100-pound AN M30 warhead) and 769 pounds with six. Each JATO rocket weighed 139 pounds and contained 75 pounds of Galcit propellant, which delivered 1,000 pounds of thrust in eight seconds.

Four or six 3.25-inch Aircraft Rocket Motors Mk. 7 auxiliary rockets assisted in launching Little Joe from a 20-foot launching rail fixed to a modified 40-mm anti-aircraft gun mount, after which a 1,000-pound thrust JATO unit provided for the rapid launch (300–400 mph in two seconds) reaction needed to contend with rapidly incoming Kamikaze aircraft. This propulsion system would give Little Joe a speed of 400 mph, a range of 2.5 miles, and a ceiling of 7,900 feet. After launch, Little Joe was gyro-stabilized and was guided by radio control by an operator who visually tracked the missile by the line-of-sight system via a flare in the tail. The warhead was a standard 100-pound GP aerial bomb, which was to be detonated within lethal distance of the target by a proximity fuse (VT M166).

On June 21, 1945, the first of the fifteen Little Joe's authorized by BuAer were available for initial flight tests at the Applied Physics Laboratory, Johns Hopkins

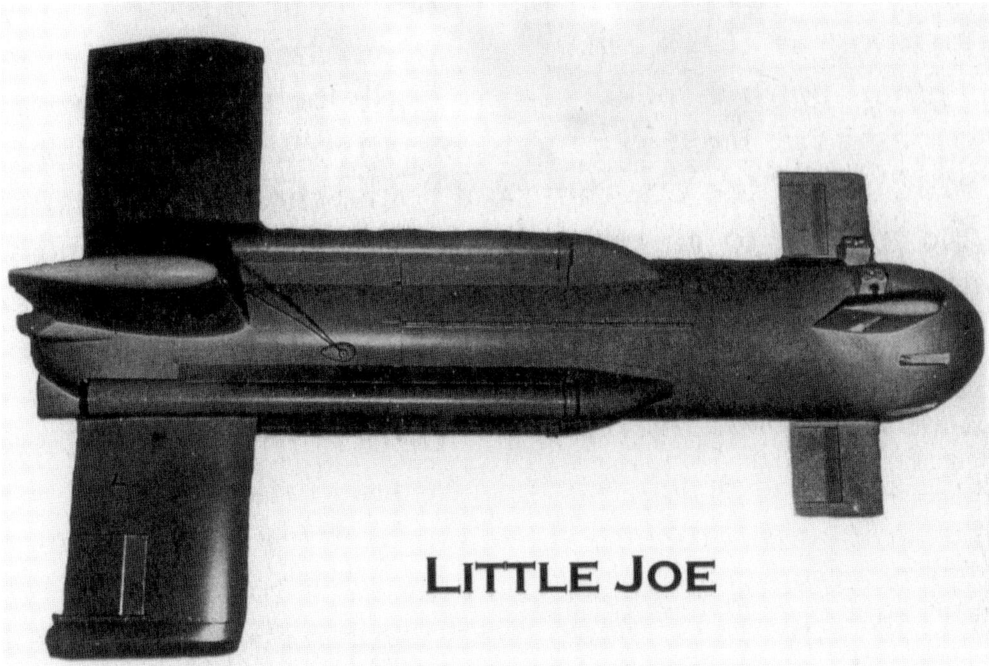

Little Joe (KAN-1/2). (*USN*)

University, test range at Island Beach, New Jersey. The first two launches on July 20, 1945 were completely successful and represented the first successful American flights of a surface-to-air missile in combat configuration. After these encouraging initial flight tests, Little Joe then met a succession of vexing difficulties. The two subsequent Little Joe flights failed: one when the launching rockets malfunctioned and another, at Patuxent River NAS on the Chesapeake Bay, Maryland, in August, when the JATO unit did not ignite. The missile's performance was considered to be less than had been anticipated and also, the smoke from the boosters and the sustainer made it difficult for the missile's controller to follow the weapon. To overcome KAN-1's issues, an improved version, designated KAN-2, was developed using a new, less smoky propellant for the sustainer; in addition, flares were installed on the missile's tail to assist in visual tracking, and two additional boosters, for a total of six, were added to boost performance. It would not be until October 25, 1945 that another successful Little Joe test would occur, but two months after Japan's formal surrender. Despite the war's ending, NAMU continued the Little Joe program into 1946, with most of the test launches taking place at the Navy's test range at the Marine Corps Air Station, Mojave, California. Since Little Joe was an emergency project, with the war's end and testing program ended, there was no requirement for the continuation of Little Joe and, accordingly, BuAer concentrated on the development of Lark, which was more promising as a surface-to-air weapon than Little Joe. On March 12, 1946, BuAer terminated Little Joe.

Fairchild KAQ/SAM-N-2/CTV-N-9 and Convair KAY/SAM-N-4/ CTV-N-10 Lark

The Lark project was a high-priority, high-performance, radar-directed, solid-fuel boosted, liquid-fueled rocket propelled, surface-to-air anti-aircraft missile that had been under development by BuAer since fall 1944. By January 1945, BuAer established a Lark configuration to include requirements for ship defense against aircraft attack, approaching enemy reconnaissance aircraft, and enemy aircraft launching standoff weapons.

BuAer granted Lark high priority in February 1945 and directed the NAMC to submit a design, development, and manufacture proposal for fifteen Larks. However, NAMC soon realized that the Lark would not become operationally ready anytime soon, and in the meantime, the Kamikaze threat increased in intensity. R/Adml. Ramsey conferred with NAMC's Capt. Ralph Barnaby to discuss getting Lark completed and operational ASAP. The BuAer quickly established the Lark configuration in March 1945.

During March, a contract was awarded to Fairchild Aircraft, Farmingdale, New York, for the production of 100 Lark test missiles using radio command guidance with a semi-active radar homing AN/DPN-7. Due to Fairchild's slow progress, a backup contract for another 100 Larks was awarded to Consolidated-Vultee, San Diego, in June 1945. The Convair Lark used beam riding guidance with AN/APN-23 active radar homing. In October 1945, the Fairchild and Convair Larks were designated as KAQ and KAY, respectively, and the flight testing of KAQ-1 and KAY-1 Larks began in June 1946.

The 1,820-pound, 18-foot, 6-inch, 18-inch diameter KAQ-1/KAY-1 Larks had 6-foot, 3-inch span cruciform wings and tail surfaces with the tails being offset 45 degrees from the wings for stability and control, while the booster assembly used an unusual square fin configuration. The KAQs wings had flaps, while the KAY used variable-incidence wings. The Lark was armed with a 100-pound HE fragmentation type anti-aircraft type warhead that was detonated by a radar proximity fuse to be fired electrically or on impact.

The missile was propelled by two Reaction Motors two-chamber acid-aniline liquid-propellant rocket engines. One 200-pound thrust continuous rocket was augmented by a 400-pound thrust intermittent motor. The latter was governed by a Mach number meter so that a relatively constant speed was maintained. Both rockets weighed about 75 pounds and had 490 pounds of fuel. Lark was launched at 150 mph from a multiple--charge shipboard catapult by two 410-pound, 4-foot, 7-inch solid-fueled JATO boosters that were jettisoned after exhaustion. It had a range of 45 miles, an optimum ceiling of 30,000 feet, a rate of climb of 8,200 feet per minute, and could develop a maximum speed of 650 mph (Mach .85). Later, KAQ-2 and KAY-2 Larks used an upgraded LR2-RM-6 engine that only slightly improved performance. The early test flights used a simple manual radio command guidance system, but by 1947, guidance systems requiring no human operator were available. Both the Fairchild and Convair test versions were considered only moderately successful.

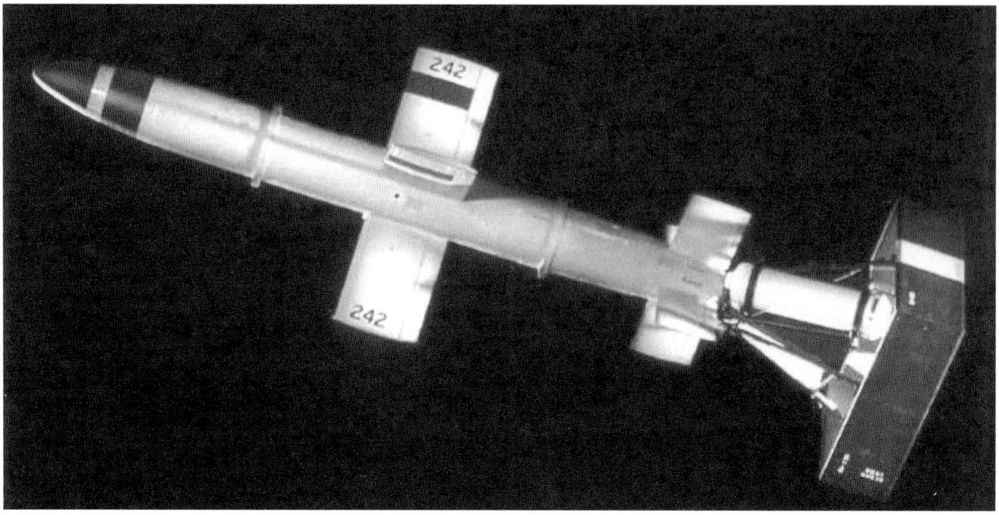

Lark (KAQ/KAY). (*USN*)

During September 1947 and then in early 1948, the Lark models were redesignated as follows:

Old Designation	September 1947	*c*. February 1948
KAQ-1	XSAM-2	XSAM-N-2
KAQ-2	XSAM-2a	XSAM-N-2a
KAY-1	XSAM-4	XSAM-N-4
KAY-2	XSAM-4a	XSAM-N-4a

Six Convair airframes were allotted to the Raytheon Company, Cambridge, Massachusetts, to investigate the use of velocity-gated continuous wave Doppler radar for guided missile target-seekers, in a time when most other investigators used range-gated pulse radar. A Raytheon guidance system installed in a Convair airframe recorded the first successful American surface-to-air missile interception of an airborne target during January 1950, followed by two others. Modified Larks were used for guidance system development testing by all three U.S. services through the early 1950s. However, by this time, the subsonic Lark missile was of doubtful use against anticipated supersonic targets, and BuOrd ceased further Lark development in the late 1950 in favor of the XSAM-N-6 Talos and RIM-2 Terrier missiles, which incorporated a supersonic ramjet-powered sustainer, boosted by a separable solid rocket that were being developed by Operation Bumblebee.

Project Bumblebee Ramjet Development

On every occasion after the expansion of the Naval Ordnance Test Station at Inyokern, California, the AAF opposed the Navy's large, new, and aggressive *entrée* into the missile realm. However, in November 1945, when General Arnold learned of the Navy's planned $50 million missile test range at Point Mugu, he described it as a "definite danger signal," as was the Navy's cornering of the academia talent market. The war-long inter-service rivalry continued and the American intramural missile race was on!

Meanwhile, Dr. Tuve's basic problem was that the BuOrd required SAMs that were superior to the rather unsophisticated, subsonic Little Joe and Lark. The original USN requirements were for a 2,000-pound missile to have an effective horizontal range of 20 miles at 1,800 mph at 30,000 feet armed with a 300–600-pound warhead, with an accuracy of 2 feet per 100 feet target range. These requirements were shown to be impossible unless a new means of propulsion was developed. After Bumblebee had been established in 1944, the project's initial research effort, in conjunction with the John Hopkins University Applied Physics Lab, was to develop a ramjet-powered surface-to-air missile at a time when no useful data on supersonic ramjets was available. By the spring of 1945, contracts had been let with M. W. Kellogg Company, New Jersey, and Allegany Ballistics, West Virginia, for large solid rocket motors, and with Bendix for the fuel metering system for an advanced supersonic ramjet.

A ramjet engine test facility was constructed at Silver Spring, Maryland, using three large air compressors that had been used to drive pneumatic hammers during the Shasta, California, dam's construction. These compressors generated airflow for a new supersonic wind tunnel. By July 1945, experiments were underway to test ramjet engine models and fuels.

The Navy's new experimental Ordnance Aerophysics Laboratory, Daingerfield, Texas, facility opened in November 1945, as part of an up-to-date government-funded Lone Star Steel plant built during World War II. It was the steel plant's air compressor systems associated with blast furnaces that led Project Bumblebee there. The

Ordnance Aerophysics Laboratory Wind Tunnel. (*USN*)

100,000-cubic-foot-per-minute blower for a blast furnace was converted to drive a 10-foot-diameter, 125-foot-long high-altitude wind tunnel, generating airflow at supersonic speeds and compressing air released through nozzles to generate thrust large enough to test prototype missile designs. It operated at wind speeds between Mach 1.75 (1,332 mph) and Mach 2.75 (2,093 mph) and could simulate sea-level flight at 2,000 mph. It initially tested 19- and 21-inch ramjet models that thrust flight beyond the speed of sound and then collected data that contributed development of missile guidance systems and to the Mercury space flights. The wind tunnel, which was for years the largest in the world, closed in November 1957.

In the fall of 1944, BuOrd had requested a study to explore defensive weapons for ships. Johns Hopkins APL furnished an analysis of the problem that revealed that the missile would have to be supersonic to be able to reach a target before it would be close enough to launch an anti-ship missile, and that, at the time, the ramjet was the most efficient propulsion mode available. The ramjet, sometimes referred to as a flying stovepipe or an athodyd (an abridgement of aero thermodynamic duct), is a type of air-breathing jet engine that uses the engine's forward motion to compress incoming air without an axial compressor or a centrifugal compressor. Ramjets are unable to produce thrust at zero airspeed and thus they cannot move a vehicle from a standstill and required an assisted take-off to accelerate it to a speed where it begins to produce its own thrust. The post-war ramjet burned kerosene or a naphtha/kerosene mixture that required only on-sixth to one-eighth the fuel that a comparable rocket motor of the time would require to attain the same speed and thrust duration. It flew at Mach 2.5 (1,900 mph) and a nose-mounted Pitot tube that in combination with a temperature probe modulated the fuel flow regulated speed. Early versions had a maximum range of approximately 75 miles and flew below 30,000 feet. Performance enhancements occurred due to continued improvements of the guidance system in making mid-course guidance more efficient. Ramjets were thought to be theoretically capable of meeting the BuOrd requirements, but previously a practical ramjet had never been tested. APL proposed a supersonic ramjet-propelled missile with a range of 11 miles that would carry a 600-pound warhead. It would use radar guidance and some form of homing system to navigate it to the target. The APL estimated that a prototype could be built in two years, with limited use in the later stages of the war (at the time, it was assumed that the war would continue into 1946 or 1947).

Cobra: Ramjet Engine and Vehicle

In early 1945, Bendix-Westinghouse, Elyria, Ohio, was contracted to develop a ramjet engine and vehicle, code named Cobra. Within three months, the company flew a working model, 6 inches in diameter, fabricated from a section of P-47 exhaust pipe, to a distance of 6.25 miles while producing more power than the P-47's 2,600-hp Pratt & Whitney R-2800-59B twin-row radial engine. The initial Cobra missile used only dummy ramjets and evaluated launching and flight stability issues. Later that year, development had progressed to larger vehicles using live ramjets, and during

A P-61 Black Widow carries a test ram-jet under its fuselage during Project Cobra. (*AAF*)

October 1945, a 10-inch-diameter model reached a speed of 1,400 mph at an altitude of about 20,000 feet. To initiate their ramjets, the Cobra missiles were generally launched aided by clusters of solid-fueled rocket motors. Cobra was a failure because it was unable to withstand the stresses during flight. In late 1945, an 18-inch-diameter Ramjet Test Vehicle (RTV) was built designed to carry guidance equipment and a warhead. It was a scaled-up Cobra that used kerosene fuel and cruised at Mach 2.4 (1,827 mph) at 30,000 feet. It demonstrated throttle ability, an ability to accelerate from Mach 2.0 (1,522 mph) to 2.4 (1,827 mph) after boost, and had a cruise range of 10 miles. Originally referred to as a burner test vehicle (BTV) or "Burner" during September 1945, the Cobra/BTV was officially designated as the PTV-4 propulsion test vehicle that was amended to the PTV-N-4 in early 1948.

In January 1945, no facilities existed for Bumblebee to field test its supersonic ramjets. An abandoned Coast Guard Station at Island Beach, New Jersey, was hastily developed into a field test site. By April, Bumblebee personnel were firing test vehicles off the New Jersey shore with truck-mounted SCR-584 radar tracking them. However, these tests were complicated by shipping passing off shore and fishing boat traffic that often required tests to be delayed until the coast range was clear. In 1946, about 200 Operation Bumblebee Navy personnel, John Hopkins scientists, civilian contractors, and employees were relocated to Topsail Island, a 26-mile barrier island on the North Carolina coast. Topsail was an ideal location for a secret missile testing site as there were few residents and the only access to the island was by a pontoon bridge. Within the first year, an assembly building, a control tower, eight separated observation and data-collecting towers, a launching platform, bomb-proof room, mess hall, dorms, roads were built on the island, along with an improved access bridge. During 1947–1948, 200 experimental rockets were fired but as the test missiles became larger and flew longer distances, the Bumblebee test flight program was relocated to the Naval Ordnance Test Station (China Lake) at Inyokern, California. Further tests of long-range intercepts were also conducted at White Sands, New Mexico.

The PTV-N-4 could achieve a speed of Mach 2.4 (1,827 mph) and an altitude of about 30,000 feet and was used to evaluate acceleration characteristics, throttle ability, and powered range of the ramjet propulsion system. When the BTV flight tests were successfully completed, Bumblebee continued to develop even larger 24-inch ramjets using the RTV-N-6 Bumblebee Experimental Prototype Missile (XPM), which, in 1951, was the immediate predecessor of the XSAM-N-6 Talos tactical surface-to-air missile prototype that would finally lead to the development of the first tactical Talos SAM-N-6b in 1955.

Talos and Terrier: Bumblebee End Products

The Bendix Talos and Terrier were the end result of the Navy's sixteen-year surface-to-air missile development program for protection against guided anti-ship missiles. Talos was a long-range naval shipboard surface-to-air missile that was the first (1958) production missile to incorporate ramjet propulsion. The initial thrust was provided

Talos (RIM-8) surface-to-air missile (SAM). (*AAF*)

by a solid rocket booster for launching and a Bendix ramjet for flight to the target with the warhead acting as the ramjet's compressor. Talos used radar beam riding for guidance to the vicinity of its target, and then Semi-Active Radar Homing (SARH) for terminal guidance where a proximity fuse detonating the warhead. The Talos was originally designated as the SAM-N-6, which was redesignated RIM-8 in 1963. The Talos saw relatively limited use due to its large size and dual radar antenna system as there were few warships that could accommodate these large missiles.

The second and more significant result of Project Bumblebee was the Terrier series of surface-to-air missiles, which were the first operational shipborne medium-range surface-to-air missiles to enter service. During 1948, supersonic beam-riding was demonstrated with the CTV-N-8 STV (supersonic test vehicle). These tests were very encouraging, and STV would be developed into a tactical missile of its own, the medium-range SAM-N-7/RIM-2 Terrier. It was test launched from the old (1917) battleship (BB-41) *Mississippi* on January 28, 1953, and first deployed operationally on the *Boston*-class cruisers with the *Canberra* being the first to achieve operational status (June 15, 1956) as the SAM-N-7 (re-designated in 1963 as the RIM-2).

Terrier (RIM-2) surface-to-air missile (SAM). (*USMC*)

4

Drones Before Drones

Today, when people think of the drone, it is first, as one of the millions sold to civilians who use them several times, take a few videos, and ultimately lose interest or wreck them. However, it is the USAF release of amazing videos transmitted from aboard a military drone, showing the remarkably accurate destruction of terrorist leaders in the Middle East, that mesmerizes the public.

As previously described, the British Royal Navy acquired the early lead in the development of radio-controlled unmanned aircraft during the post-World War I era, using the Fairey Queen series mainly as target drones. These early UAVs were programmed to imitate the maneuvers of enemy aircraft during anti-aircraft training, and, so in the original meaning of the word, a drone is simply a remote-controlled aircraft designed to be shot at.

GL-1/2/3: Early American Target Drone

Jean Roche joined the Army Air Service as an aeronautical engineer at McCook Field, Dayton, Ohio, during the summer of 1922 where he was assigned the design and development of a small, maneuverable, unmanned target glider, the GL-1, for the Army Coast Artillery. The GL-1, ready by December for testing, was a mid-wing monoplane glider with a 12-foot wingspan and a linen-covered wooden frame fuselage supported by a metal tubular structure. The GL-1 was transported atop the wing of an AAS DH-4 biplane to the target range where it was released from approximately 10,000 feet and then would begin a circling descent at 330 fpm (a rather leisurely 3.75 mph) toward the gunners below. Before its destruction or crash landing, it could fly for approximately thirty minutes, giving ample time for the gunners to practice. Soon afterward, Roche developed a larger and improved glider, the GL-2, which was a high-winged using the Curtiss JN-4 Jenny's upper wing structure. Unlike the GL-1, the GL-2 was flown by an Army pilot who was actually fired upon by live ammunition!

GL-1/2/3. Early target drone. (*AFSHRC*)

In response for the need for a gunnery target for air-to-air gunnery practice, the GL-3 (also called the G-3) was developed. Like the GL-1, it was small and was carried aloft on top of the wing of the training biplane. The pilot would release the GL-3 and then turn away and then circle back to engage the GL-3 as a target and repeatedly set up firing passes, practicing his interception procedures, deflection shooting, and air combat maneuvering. The GL-3 was designed to considerably vary practice intercepts and could be set to fly straight, to orbit, or to change directions on seemingly random programmed pattern. Roche's claim to fame came during February 1930 when he introduced the affordable Aeronca C-2 monoplane, which was the first lightweight aircraft to be type certificated for production and would soon set many official and unofficial records.

Reginald Denny and the Radioplane

The first remotely-piloted scaled aircraft can be traced back to 1930s and flying model hobbyists, and, surprisingly, to Reginald Denny, an eminent stage and screen actor who appeared in nearly 200 movies during a career extending over more than half a century into the 1950s and 1960s television era. The British-born Denny (November 20, 1891), the son of a stock company actor, began acting professionally at six years old and appeared in his first motion picture in 1912 and also along the way was a British amateur boxing champion. During World War I, Denny interrupted his acting career to join the Royal Flying Corps, as an observer/air gunner in Bristol F.2B Fighters with

Reginald Denny, actor and drone pioneer. (*Radioplane*)

a home defense night fighter squadron. During a night interception training mission, he was wounded, evidently by friendly anti-aircraft fire, and recovered to complete his pilot training, but the war ended before he could fly in combat.

After the war, Denny immigrated to America and resumed his acting career, starring in numerous Hollywood silent dramas and comedies. But once the talkies prevailed, his English accent and age relegated him to steady employment as a character actor in a wide assortment of supporting roles, usually playing an impeccable English gentleman or military officer. During the 1920s, Denny also continued to fly for sport and joined an elite group of Hollywood stunt pilots known as the "Thirteen Black Cats." Despite earning a very good income, he nearly became bankrupt during the Stock Market Crash, by speculating in oil and mining stocks.

Between acting roles, Denny pursued his interest in radio-controlled (RC) model aircraft, opening a model-airplane shop during 1934 with a partner on Hollywood Boulevard, through which he marketed his line of Dennyplane flying models and miniature gasoline engines for model planes. Denny had wanted a miniature engine he could sell under his name and created a contest for such an engine. Walter Righter, a 1928 California Institute of Technology (CIT) graduate, designed and built Denny's Dennymite engine, which was the first reliable model airplane engine available. From 1928, Righter had served as Kinner Airplane & Motor Company's first graduate engineer but had been laid off in 1933 due the Depression. While employed by Jerry Vultee in 1934 as the Chief Engineer for the Vultee V1-A, a single-engined airliner, Righter had finalized his engine.

Denny selected the engine after Righter demonstrated its reliability by running ten prototypes flat-out for fifty hours. The demonstration bonded the two men in a productive relationship that would continue for many years with Righter forming the Righter Manufacturing Co. in 1936, eventually manufacturing over 10,000 engines for Reginald Denny Industries.

In 1935, Denny associated with Nelson Whittier to form Reginald Denny Industries to develop a new radio-controlled model. With Whittier as Chief Engineer, they were joined by electronics engineer and another model airplane and amateur radio enthusiast, Kenneth Case, who had developed an effective miniature radio control system and demonstrated it for Denny who was very impressed and later would use it for RP series drones.

RP-1

Over the next three years, the trio attempted to develop Denny Industries' first remote-controlled aerial target known as the Radioplane One, or RP-1. The aircraft was essentially a much-enlarged 42-pound high-wing model Dennyplane monoplane with a 12-foot wingspan, complete with a fuselage area that included the step where a windscreen was in a real aircraft. It was powered by a 3-hp, two-stroke, two-cylinder engine built by Walter Righter. The ground equipment consisted of a short-wave unit and rotary telephone type control box based on a rotary telephone dial with contact points that modulated the radio impulse wavelengths. The RP-1 had a three-tube

Reginald Denny (left), engine designer, Walter Righter, and the RP-1. (*Radioplane*)

radio receiver that relayed impulses to two electric train motors, each on its own frequency. This rotary dial system and receiver is described later.

During 1936, Denny, realizing the military potential of employing remotely controlled model airplanes as aerial targets, met with Gen. W. S. Thiele of the Coast Artillery at Fort MacArthur in Los Angeles. Thiele informed Denny that anti-aircraft gunnery crews target practice was currently limited to firing at towed target sleeves that had numerous disadvantages: they flew only in straight lines; they did not look like airplanes; during a target run, the crews could not verify whether the sleeve had been hit; and there was always the risk of hitting the towing aircraft. Denny suggested that a radio-controlled model aircraft could be a viable, more cost-effective solution and he persuaded the Army to allow him to proceed with its development as his small radio-controlled aircraft were targets that looked like aircraft, sounded like aircraft, flew like full-size aircraft, and even simulated attack maneuvers.

In an effort to interest the Army in his design, Denny and Righter demonstrated the RP-1 at Dale Dry Lake, near Twenty-Nine Palms, California, on February 21, 1938, with the *Los Angeles Times* promoting the event as "Army to Test Model Robot Plane as Artillery Target." However, during the demonstration the radio failed (it had a range of only 400 feet) and the little drone performed a number of unintentional but remarkable, out of control aerobatics. On landing, it hit hard, somersaulting and tearing the engine out of the airframe. After this unfortunate flight demonstration, Denny and Righter waited anxiously for about two and a half months for a response. Finally, on May 5, 1938, Denny Industries received a message from the Air Corps at Wright Field that their representatives were to be in Dayton on May 10 to negotiate a contract for radio-controlled aerial targets. Unknown to Denny and Righter, the ACC's decision had been based on the RP-1's final unintentional aerobatics. After a hurried cross-country railway trip, Denny and Righter met with Capt. George Holloman, second in command at the Materiel Command and head of the Special Weapons Unit. Also present were at least ten other representatives from each materiel branch that might be interested in the Denny project in any way.

RP-2

Denny began the presentation using his considerable acting skills to eloquently explain his company's proposal. Righter answered the many technical questions relative to launching, control, and landing, and after the meeting, the two drafted a formal proposal for Wright Field to present to Washington. Lt. Col. Volant, who oversaw AAC contracts, requested that they then proceed with bid preparations and change all their proposal figures to conform to Air Corps practice. The following day, Denny Industries was authorized an experimental contract for $18,000 to build three target drones that looked like aircraft to be delivered within a year. The contract stipulated maneuverability and performance and that they had to be able to be ground-launched, radio-controlled in the air, and be landed within a quarter-mile of the launching spot.

For Denny Industries to develop and manufacture these three experimental drones, it would be necessary not only to design a drone that would be inherently stable, but to design and develop an entirely new type of engine and a radio control mechanism. After a year of experimental building and testing at Muroc Dry Lake, the first of the three drones was completed under Righter's direction as a new design by Fred Hardy, with a new radio designed and built by Kenneth Case.

The glue-and-screwed balsa wood RP-2 had a length of 8 feet, 8 inches, a wingspan of 12 feet, 3 inches, and a gross weight of 104 pounds. It was powered by a two-cylinder, two-cycle, 6-hp Righter 0-15-1 piston engine, which gave it a maximum speed of 85 mph and an endurance of one hour. Kenneth Case's RC control system was built by Bendix. No ailerons were used as control was by rudder and stabilizer. The landing gear was placed to cushion the landing by parachute. The RP-2 was demonstrated to the Army during March 1939 and was much more successful than the RP-1 and led to a series of similar but improved variants beginning with the RP-3.

RP-3

By November 1939, the RP-3 was ready. It was built of welded steel tubing instead of the RP-2 wood framework and added a new parachute recovery system designed and built by Case that could be activated when the flight was over, making landings a simple push-button task. Continued testing was carried out at March Field, east of Los Angeles. These early tests were not very successful, but a series of improvements were quickly worked into the design. However, at this point, the Whittier estate withdrew further funding. Denny and Whittier went looking for bankers to provide bridge financing, and one of these put them in contact with Whitney Collins, a vice president at Menasco Motors Company and a budding entrepreneur. Collins and Denny estimated it would require somewhere between $50,000 and $75,000 to bring the RP-3 up to the performance demanded by the original $18,000 contract, but Collins was willing to take a chance that this would lead to future business. Collins and his partner, Harold Powell, split the drone program off from Reginald Denny Hobby Shops and formed the Radioplane Company with Denny and Whittier, who was later bought out.

RP-4 (OQ-1?)

The RP-3 was discontinued, and the RP-4 was to be developed into the design to meet required performance standards. The RP-4 is referred to as OQ-1 by some sources, but this designation was never officially allocated by the AAC as OQ-1 in the OQ-series had remained unassigned. The RP-4's mistaken OQ-1 designation was caused by its immediate predecessor, the RP-5 being officially designated as the OQ-2.

The new RP-4 design required another year of extensive redesign, by Ferris Smith, a well-known aeronautical engineer, and then development before it was considered as completed. For aerodynamic testing, models were mounted on the front of a Packard automobile and then were tested by racing up and down Muroc Dry Lake at

Walter Righter (left), radio-control designer, Kenneth Case, and the RP-3. (*Radioplane*)

RP-4/OQ-1. (*Radioplane*)

speeds up to 120 mph. In addition to the significant aerodynamics changes, the new design introduced a tricycle landing gear and side-by-side contra-rotating propellers to eliminate engine torque from its new Sidewinder engine. The fuselage was built from steel tubing and the wings of wood. The aircraft was fabric covered and usually launched from a crude rail launcher. The RP-4 also used a new joystick-based control system that operators found far easier to use. Three were delivered to the AAC, which then placed an order for an additional fifty of the company's first totally successful target drone, which began delivery in June 1941. With the success of the RP-4, orders multiplied, causing the company to expand into the former Timm Aircraft factories on the northeast corner of the Van Nuys Metropolitan Airport. The production models were further modified, known to Radioplane as the RP-5, and to the Army as the Radioplane RP-5/OQ-2.

RP-5/OQ-2 and TDD-1

Following the success of the RP-4, the prototype RP-5 was completed in June 1941, and tested by the AAC as the A-2 powered aerial target. During 1940, the AAF had introduced an "A" for aerial targets category in its aircraft designation scheme. This evidently duplicated the "A" for attack designator and was replaced in June 1941 by the following categories, with existing "A" models being redesignated: OQ—Model Airplane Target; PQ—Full-Scale Target (with provision for a pilot).

During that month, the RP-5's A-2 designation was changed to OQ-2. The RP-5A production model was initially designated as A-2A but was changed to OQ-2A before completion. The USN designated the RP-5 as the TDD-1 (first Target Drone, Denny). When the Air Force became a separate organization during 1947, the OQ and PQ categories were discontinued and replaced by the "Q" category.

The OQ-2 was a simple, 104-pound aircraft of steel-tube construction, measuring 8 feet, 8 inches long, with a wingspan of 12 feet, 3 inches. It was of the conventional aircraft arrangement with a high-mounted, straight monoplane wing riding on a boxy, slab-sided fuselage. The empennage incorporated a single vertical fin with low-set horizontal stabilizers.

The early fixed, tail-dragger landing gear featured short legs and small wheels. Although equipped with a wheeled landing gear, launching was by catapult only. If drone should survive target practice, it was to be recovered by a deployed 24-foot-diameter parachute stowed inside the fuselage. The conventional landing gear was used as it cushioned the landing impact. None of the later OQs, including the improved variants shipped to the Navy had landing gear, which would be useless on water.

RP-5/OQ-2. (*Radioplane*)

RP-5A/OQ-2A/2B and TDD-1

Primarily, the Denny drones were used to train AA ground defense units, which were firing automatic weapons up to and including 40-mm cannons. Flying at a maximum speed of 88 mph, the small radio-controlled drone was relatively equal in size and speed at a range of 200 yards as a standard fighter aircraft at 500 yards. The rugged little drone was able to duplicate actual attack situations and was easily maneuvered through almost all flight attitudes over any type of terrain.

The updated RP-5A/OQ-2A was a small tail-dragger aircraft with fabric-covered fuselage and wings, the latter having a wooden structure. The 6-hp Righter O-15-1 two-cylinder piston engine drove two contra-rotating propellers. The OQ-2A was launched by a catapult and intact target drones could be retrieved by parachute, which, on loss of signal, would be automatically deployed. For remote control, the operator, who tracked the drone visually, used an RC-56A radio transmitter to transmit a signal to the drone's RC-57A receiver. The OQ-2B was identical to the OQ-2A, except that the wing ribs had lightening holes drilled into the wing ribs for a slightly lighter structure. The Army purchased the RP-5A as the OQ-2A, while the Navy's TDD-1 was also an OQ-2 without the landing gear.

Generally, the Target-Control Receiving Equipment AN/AKW-26, RC-56-A, and RC-57-B operating with Target Control Transmitting Equipment RC-56-A and-B was installed in a target aircraft to control the elementary movements of that aircraft for gunnery practice. The Target-Control Receiving Equipment consisted of a radio receiver/selector and battery box that supplied all the required power for one hour and thirty minutes of continuous operation.

The operating frequency of the receiver could be set to any one of four or five preset frequencies within the band of 67 to 74 mc, with the frequency used depending on the number of similar systems in operation at one location. Although the target control receiving equipment could be controlled from a distance beyond normal vision, the equipment was intended only for use in the normal visual range of the control operator. Its range was normally 3–4 miles and 10 miles maximum.

Manual operation of the control joystick at the RC-56 transmitting station resulted in transmission to the target aircraft of a different tone for each of the five control movements or functions desired (i.e. up, down, etc.). Receiver-Selector BC-464 included a five-channel audio filter selector circuit for discrimination between the various tones received and a complex relay circuit for passing resulting control voltages to the control surfaces mechanism of the target.

The OQ-2/TDD-1 was mass produced in 1943/44 by Radioplane and the Frankfort Sailplane Company, Frankfort, Michigan, with a total of 3,865 targets built. Some sources cite that only 980 delivered to the AAF, which indicates that, apparently, the bulk of the production were TDD-1s. Stan Corcoran's Frankfort TG-1A Glider was the first aircraft selected to train Army glider pilots to fly the Waco CG-4A combat assault glider, but the Frankfort lacked the resources to quickly produce large numbers of these gliders and the Schweizer Aircraft Corporation, Horseheads, New York, easily built many more TG-2 gliders, a design similar to the TG-1A. Consequently, Frankfort did have the resources to subcontract the OQ-TDD-1.

RP-5A/OQ-2A. (*Radioplane*)

OQ-2 Specifications

First Production	June 1941
Total Produced	3,865 units
Fuselage	Fabric-covered, welded steel tubing
Length	8 feet, 8 inches
Height	2 feet, 8 inches
Gross Weight	104 pounds
Wing	Interchangeable, fabric-covered spruce
Air Foil	NACA 23012
Span:	12 feet, 3 inches
Area	19.24 square feet
Chord	21 inches
Dihedral	7 degrees
Loading	6.12 pounds/square foot
Empennage	Fabric-covered, welded steel tubing
Vertical Stabilizer	1.5 square feet
Rudder	0.9 square feet
Horizontal Stabilizer	3.0 square feet
Elevator	1.12 square feet
Fuel Tank	1.8 U.S. gallons
Fuel Consumption	1.6 gallons/hour
Flight Duration	1:10 hours
Engine	Righter Type O-15-1, air-cooled, two-cylinder, two-cycle
Weight	26.5 pounds
Dimensions (inches)	16.5L × 19.5W × 11H
Horsepower	6 hp at 3,800 rpm
Displacement	16.9 cubic inches
Power Loading	17.3 pounds/hp
Propellers	Two, two-bladed, 26-inch wood, counter-rotating

Radioplane Factory. In order to meet the large influx of new orders, the company expanded into the former Timm Aircraft factories on the northeast corner of the Van Nuys Airport in 1942, when Timm moved to the western side. (*Radioplane*)

Navy TDDs

In a letter dated February 26, 1943, Capt. Delmar Fahrney, head of the USN Special Design Branch, praised Denny:

> You are entirely right, the initials TDD stand for Target Drone Denny and is named in your honor in keeping with your long association and pioneering on this radio control project. I feel that you should be given great credit for this work because it is the early pitfalls and headaches of the development program which deserves the commendation and not the smooth flow that is involved in production.... I believe that the Denny target will be of great service in training gunnery crews and we are eager to get some into the Service to prove the point.
>
> Fahrney, D. S., *History of Radio-controlled Aircraft and Guided Missiles* (Naval History Division, Wash., D.C., 1950)

There were three Navy TDD units—Nos. 36–38—that typically consisted of eight men with a lieutenant (jg) acting as the commanding officer and the drone pilot; the chief or first-class petty officer as the alternate pilot; two motor mechanics; two electronic technicians; and two seamen as parachute packers and general repairmen. Toward the end of the war, TDD Unit 37 was assigned to train gunners on the battleship *Mississippi* (BB 41) where its launching ramp was placed on top of the No. 3 14-inch aft main battery turret. The turret had to be rotated sufficiently for the TDD to clear the ship's observation aircraft's retrieval crane boom on the fantail. After the war, TDD Unit No. 37 was assigned to the fleet carrier *Bunker Hill* (CV 17) and the carrier *Tripoli* (CVE 64), while TDD Unit 38 was assigned to the battleship *Colorado* (BB 45). Other USN vessels known to use TDDs during 1945 were the *Wyoming* (BB 32), *Miami* (CL 89), *Makin Island* (CVE 93), *Wisconsin* (BB 64), and *Cape Gloucester* (CVE 109).

A very short catapult was used by the Navy for launching their TDDs from 63-foot aircraft rescue vessels (AVR). Being rescue boats, these boats could achieve speeds as much as 40 mph and running into the wind at this speed required only a moderate catapult launch assist. Drones were usually retrieved from the ocean by another AVR or sometimes smaller pick up boats. Catapult launch and parachute landing systems made the use of these drones practical because no large smooth area was necessary for their operation. The drones were trucked to Newport Harbor, California, and loaded aboard the AVR boats from which they were launched for naval target practice from ships off of San Clemente Island. Later, the Navy relocated the drone base to Point Mugu, or Port Hueneme, California.

In 1942, the Navy introduced the TD designation for target drones into its aircraft designation system: TDD Radioplane (as the AAF OQ-2/3), TD4D Radioplane Quail (as the AAF OQ-17), and KDR. In March 1946, the Navy included missiles and drones in its aircraft designation scheme and introduced the K class with the type designation KD for drones. Existing TD drones were redesignated. Drone conversions of manned aircraft received normal aircraft designations with a K suffix. The latter designations are not listed below. A single TD drone was redesignated in the short-lived "U" for unmanned category.

Navy TDD. Target Drone, Denny, is pictured flying off USS *New York*, September 1943. (*USN*)

Marilyn Monroe and the OQ-2

During June 1945, Sgt. David Conover of 1st Motion Picture Unit was sent by his commanding officer, Capt. Ronald Reagan (an actor friend of Reginald Denny), to photograph the classified operations and products at the Radioplanes factory in Van Nuys. During his tour of the plant's RP-5 assembly line, Conover was drawn to an especially attractive young women, Norma Jeane Dougherty. Though her main job was spraying the RP-5s with fire retardant, she was photographed assembling one. Conover seems to have an eye for beautiful women and arranged a modeling audition that led to a modeling contract and eventually a screen test. Norma Jeane subsequently changed her hair color and her name to Marilyn Monroe.

Norma Jeane—not your average Radioplane factory girl. (*Radioplane*)

OQ-3/TDD-2

By 1943, there was a demand for an improved and faster OQ-2 version, which led to the December introduction of the OQ-3, or TDD-2. This was essentially a strengthened version of the OQ-2 with a larger 8-hp, two-cylinder, two-cycle, Righter O-15-3 engine that allowed it to reach 103 mph. As the torque effects were no longer concerned controllers, it used a single propeller in place of the OQ-2s counter-rotating type. Its fuselage was fabricated of sturdier steel-tube construction, it no longer had a wheeled landing gear, and relied solely on the parachute for recovery.

The OQ-3/TDD-2 was the most-produced Radioplane drone of the war era, with over 9,000 produced (probably including the TDD-2 versions for the Navy)—5,822 built by Radioplane and 3,581 by Frankfort. The serials were: 44-54708/44-56107 (Frankfort); 44-56108/44-59707 (Radioplane); 44-65660/44-66659 (Frankfort); 44-66660/44-67699 (Radioplane); and 45-46725/45-49087 (Radioplane).

OQ-4

OQ-4, built by Brunswick-Balke-Collender, Chicago, was an experimental aerial target aircraft of which a few were reportedly built. Development and production were halted because other was a sufficient availability of other aerial target aircraft. Brunswick-Balke-Collender manufactured wartime products, including mortar shells, flares, assault boats, fuel cells, floating mines, aircraft instrument panels, and aluminum litters, and post-war would become well-known to bowlers and pool sharks.

OQ-3/TDD-2. (*Radioplane*)

OQ-5

The OQ-5 was an experimental aerial target aircraft designation that may have been canceled because sufficient other aerial targets were available and no contractor may have been selected.

OQ-6 (Radioplane RP-14, RP-15, and RP-16)

Radioplanes RP-14, RP-15, and RP-16 were all to be designated as OQ-6 versions.

OQ-7

In November 1943, the company produced the OQ-7, essentially an OQ-3 derivative with some modifications for increased performance and a new mid-mounted, slightly swept wing. Its Righter O-15 engine gave it a maximum speed of 112 mph. The OQ-7 was not placed into production apparently because the considerably much improved and higher-performing OQ-14 was available.

OQ-8 (RP-8)

The RP-8 was introduced as a totally new design in April 1944. It was powered by a new 22-hp Righter/Kiekhaefer O-45-1 air-cooled, four-cylinder, two-stroke aircraft engine of flat-twin engine that drove it to 141 mph. This was taken into service as the OQ-14 and TDD-3, and a larger 35-hp O-45-35 engine (same as AAF O-45-3) was used by the Navy's TDD-4. This new engine provided speeds of 195 mph on two experimental RP-15s (OQ-6A) in November 1944. Later, OQ-17/TDD-4 used the more powerful O-45-35 engine and then by combining this engine with a totally new metal-skinned fuselage and wings resulted in the RP-19, which reached 140 mph.

OQ-9/10 (RP-10)

The RP-10 tested a new low-mounted wing on an otherwise unmodified OQ-7. It was powered by a 60-hp O-60 four-cylinder engine designed by Robert Paxton McCulloch and built by McCulloch Motors Corporation Milwaukee, Wisconsin, in 1943. McCulloch Motors was a manufacturer of small two-stroke gasoline engines and, after the war, became famous for its first chainsaw in 1948, after moving its operations to California in 1946.

OQ-7. (*Radioplane*)

OQ-9/10 (RP-10). (*Radioplane*)

OQ-11

During 1941, Simmonds Aerocessories built a small (9-foot-long, 12-foot wingspan), low-performance radio-controlled target drone, which was tested by the AAF as the OQ-11 as a single experimental aerial target prototype and was not produced in quantity. Simmonds was a British-based supplier of aircraft parts and equipment that had enterprises in the U.S. (Cleveland and New York), Canada, and Australia. The most famous Simmonds accessory is the elastic stop-nut license purchased in from the Elastic Stop Nut Corporation of Cleveland in 1933. The OQ-11 was powered by a single Herkimer Tool & Model Works (Herkimer, New York) four-cylinder piston engine that gave it a maximum speed of 60 mph.

OQ-12

The OQ-12 may have been a model redesignated to differentiate between Radioplane and another manufacturer, probably Simmonds Aerocessories. Like the OQ-11, the OQ-12 was a single experimental aerial target aircraft, test-flown in October 1941, and not produced in quantity.

OQ-13

In the dearth of information on these secret OQ Projects, the OQ-13 was only described as an OQ-3 modification for use over water, apparently using a flotation gear. The OQ-13 probably was a design and was never produced.

OQ-14 (RP-8A)

First flown in July 1944, Radioplanes' RP-8A model was a significantly improved OQ-3/TDD-2. It was of heavier construction and was engined by the more powerful 22-hp Righter O-45-1 built by the Kiekhaefer Corporation, Cedarburg, Wisconsin, which drove it to a maximum 140 mph. Compared to the OQ-3, the RP-8A also had a longer fuselage, a shorter wingspan, and wings set flush with the fuselage to improve streamlining. The improvements increased the maximum speed to 140 mph. The RP-8 was designated OQ-14 by the AAF and TDD-3 by the USN. The designation TDD-4 referred to a TDD-3 variant with a more powerful O-45-35 engine. Designated as the OQ-14, 3,550 RP-15s were built by Radioplane and 1,464 by Frankfurt Sailplane Company. These orders included the TDD-3 version for the U.S. Navy. First flown in April 1945, the serials were Radioplane 45-22796/25435 and 45-56375/57286 and Frankfort 45-24380/45-25435. A number of OQ-3 and OQ-14 targets remained in USAF service after 1948. Although no new OQ-series designations were allocated after 1948, existing OQ drones were not redesignated.

OQ-14 (RP-8A). (*Radioplane*)

OQ-15

Again the lack of sources only reveals that the OQ-15 was known to be powered by one Kiekhaefer O-45. Five test versions were believed to be built but the aircraft was not produced in quantity.

OQ-16

The OQ-16 was designed and developed under a contract let to the Frankfort Sailplane Company for a radio-controlled target drone in early 1945. Fifteen aircraft were ordered by the AAF; later in the year, the contract was transferred to the USN, which assigned the designation TD3D-1 to the type. However, the contract was canceled before any of the aircraft were built. The 135-pound Frankfort OQ-16 was to have a 9-foot length and a 12-foot wingspan. It was to be powered by a 35-hp Righter O-45-35, which was to provide a maximum speed of 150 mph for sixty minutes.

OQ-17 (Radioplane RP-18)

As the end of the war neared, the AAF issued a requirement to Radioplane for a new target drone to replace the company's OQ drone series with a higher performance

OQ-17 (RP-18). (*Radioplane*)

to better simulate the improved capabilities of combat aircraft. The new drone was designed and produced by the Radioplane for the AAF as the OQ-17 and, as the TD4D/KDR Quail, for the USN.

The all-metal, 8.5-foot-long OQ-17 had a high-mounted wing with a 10-foot, 2-inch span and a conventional empennage. One Kiekhaefer four-cylinder horizontally-opposed O-45 engine gave it a 190-mph maximum speed. The OQ-17 had a 5-gallon fuel tank that provided flight duration of one hour. It was launched via catapult, but at 143 pounds gross take-off weight, the OQ-17 was at the mechanical limit for the bungee-powered A-2 catapults used for the previous target drone aircraft. Control was maintained through conventional radio control, which Radioplane claimed could perform any maneuver of an ordinary fighter aircraft. If the drone survived the gunner's fire in training, it could be recovered via an onboard parachute.

Evaluation of the XOQ-17 as an aerial target began in March 1945, and following trials, on February 16, 1946, the AAF ordered the production of 400 of these drones they designated as OQ-17s followed by another batch of thirty at a later date. The USN evaluated and then also ordered the drone as the XTD4D-1, but before entering service, the production TD4D-1 was given the new designation of KDR-1 Quail. After continuing reliability problems with the O-45 engine, OQ-17 and KDR production was terminated after 430 had been completed and the Radioplane OQ-19 was ordered as a replacement.

OQ-18

The OQ-18 was an experimental aerial target aircraft developed by Radioplane and built by an unknown contractor and tested in 1945. The 143-pound OQ-18 measured 8 feet, 5 inches long, and had a wingspan of 10 feet, 2 inches. It was powered by one 35-hp Righter O-45-35 engine that gave a maximum speed of 190 mph and an endurance of an hour.

OQ-19

As a development of the OQ-17, the OQ-19 (also associated with the MX-721 Project) was designed by Radioplane and built by Radioplane and the Helio Company. The OQ-19 had wingspan of 11 feet, 6 inches, a length of 12 feet, 4 inches, and was driven by a McCullough O-90-1 engine that propelled it to a maximum speed of 200 mph. The designation XOQ-19 was assigned to prototypes that were similar to the Navy's KD2R-1. After testing in July 1945, the design was eventually assumed by Northrop and became known as the Ventura. Radioplane was purchased by Northrop in 1952, becoming the Radioplane Division of Northrop. Although the OQ designation series was canceled in 1948 and those aircraft remaining were being redesignated in the Q series, the OQ-19 designation remained in use until September 18, 1962 when it was replaced by designations in the M-33 series.

BTT/Shelduck/RP-71

Late in the war, the company began development of an entirely new drone design known as the basic training target (BTT). Unlike the previous models, which retained some semblance of their original model airplane origins, the metal-skinned BTT series were much more streamlined. The first BTTs mounted a 72-hp McCullough O-100-1 engine that drove it to 220 mph and was designed so that at a range of 700 feet, it appeared and flew like a jet fighter flying at 700 mph at a range of 300 yards. It was accepted into service in 1950 with some in use as late as the 1980s. The improved OQ-19/KD2R-5, designated as the MQM-36 Shelduck, ultimately became the company's greatest success, with just 60,000 manufactured in a production run that continued into the 1980s.

Post-War Radioplanes

By the end of the war, the company's factory floor had expanded from 979 square feet in 1940 to 69,500 spread over five buildings and was delivering fifty drones a day. The company, along with production partner Frankfort Sailplane Company, produced nearly 15,000 drones during the war. The engine plant remained in Burbank and was eventually purchased from the government by Radioplane in May 1945.

After the war, Radioplane was contracted to modify four Grumman F6F Hellcat pilotless fighter drones to fly radio-controlled recon sorties through the 1946 Operation Crossroads, Bikini A-bomb test blast zones. During these tests, Denny was personally aboard the carrier *Shangri-La* to assist in the F6F drones set up and control. Along with the very successful BTT series, the company also produced several radio-controlled and

OQ-19 (KDR-1) Quail. (*Radioplane*)

BTT/Shelduck/RP-71. (*Radioplane*)

self-guided missiles, the largest being the GAM-67 Crossbow, which did not enter service. Denny sold his 25 percent interest in Radioplane in 1948 to Radioplane President Whitney Collins and continued to play character parts in film and TV until his death in 1967 from a stroke while visiting his native England. One of the last projects carried out at the original Van Nuys Radioplane factory was the construction of the Gemini Paraglider. The company was purchased by Northrop Corporation in 1952, becoming the Radioplane Division of Northrop. The factory later moved to a Northrop plant at Newbury Park, California, and the name was changed to the Ventura Division, Northrop Corporation.

Radioplane Designations

Navy: 1942–1946

During 1942, the Navy instituted the TD designation for target drones into its aircraft designation system: TDD Radioplane (as USAAF OQ-2/3) and TD4D Radioplane Quail (as USAAF OQ-17) KDR.

Navy: 1946–1963

During March 1946, the Navy included missiles and drones in its aircraft designation system and instituted the K class with the type designation KD for drones. Existing TD drones were redesignated. Drone conversions of manned aircraft received normal aircraft designations with a K suffix. The latter designations are not listed below. A single TD drone was redesignated in the transitory U (unmanned) category: KDR Radioplane Quail; KD2R Radioplane/Northrop Quail/Shelduck MQM-36A; KD3R (no information); and KD4R Radioplane (Model RP-70).

Army Air Force: 1940–1947

In 1940, the Army Air Force introduced an A for aerial targets classification in its aircraft designation system, which apparently duplicated the A for attack category and was replaced in June 1941 by the resulting categories, with existing A models being redesignated: OQ Model Airplane Target and PQ Full-Scale Target (with pilot provision).

When the Army Air Force became a separate organization, USAF, via the National Security Act of 1947, effective September 18, the OQ and PQ categories were discontinued and replaced by the Q category: OQ-1 (not assigned); OQ-2 Radioplane; OQ-3 Radioplane; OQ-6 Radioplane; OQ-7 Radioplane; OQ-8/9/10 (no information available); OQ-12 Radioplane; OQ-13 Radioplane; OQ-14 Radioplane; OQ-17 Radioplane; OQ-18 Radioplane; and OQ-19 Radioplane/Northrop Shelduck.

Air Force: 1947–1963

The new Air Force introduced the Q category for drones in 1947. Existing PQ models were redesignated. While no new OQ-numbers were assigned, existing OQ drones retained their designations (but see notes below): Q-1 Radioplane (jet-powered target similar to GAM-67); Q-3 Radioplane (identical to the OQ-3); Q-7 Radioplane*; Q-10 Radioplane (OQ-19 version); and Q-11 Radioplane*.

*It is unknown if OQ-7 and OQ-11 were actually redesignated as Q-7 and Q-11, or if the Q-7 and Q-11 numbers were omitted, because OQ-7 and OQ-11 were in use.

The Radioplane: Its Structure, Equipment, and Systems

Contractors and Sub-Contractors

The target drone was designed, developed, and manufactured by Radioplane Company (later Northrop-Ventura) and Frankfort Sailplane. Its radio transmitting equipment was manufactured by Doolittle Radio (Chicago), the radio receiving equipment by Bendix Aviation (North Hollywood, California), and the servo unit by Hansen Manufacturing (Princeton, Indiana) and the catapult by Montpelier Manufacturing (Montpelier, Ohio).

Structure

The fuselage, triangular in cross section, was constructed of strong welded steel tubing, entirely covered by eighty-thread muslin cloth fabric, dope treated in two colors. The tops of the wings were white and the rest of the drone was red, which provided a visible method of differentiating the top and bottom of the plane during flight. There were two openings along the fuselage top surface; the larger providing the parachute installation while the rear hatch gave access to the servo control unit and stabilizer mounts.

The strong welded steel tubing, entirely covered by eighty-thread muslin cloth fabric, can be seen on this burning TDD shot down during Navy target practice in 1945. (*From USN movie still*)

The airfoil utilized spruce NACA 23012 section wings that were interchangeable and could be used for either right- or left-hand installation. Each wing was supported by a single streamlined steel tubing strut and used two full-depth spars, with the ribs in three sections. Each wing contained twelve ribs with the two end ones solid but the ten inside ribs had lightening holes cut, giving a slight weight reduction. Thin plywood covered the top and bottom leading edges back to the front spar. The muslin wing fabric was manufactured as a sock, which was later slipped on to the wing structure and doped.

The muslin fabric-covered tail surfaces also were fabricated of steel tubing framework. These surfaces were flat, since no airfoil section was required for good flight characteristics. The horizontal and vertical stabilizers were identical and interchangeable. The conventional elevator and rudder were the only method used for control in flight.

The landing gear, when installed, was of the conventional three-point type had two front shock-mounted landing wheels and a leaf-spring tail skid. Two tubular front landing struts were provided with rubber shock cord to withstand landing impact. The shock travel was 5 inches in the strut, plus approximately 2 inches in tire deflation.

Engine

General Configuration of the Righter-Designed World War II Drone Engines

Walter Righter's technical evolution of the O-15 and O-45 series of his little-known, efficient power plants would ultimately propel the nearly 15,000 Radioplane drones produced during World War II. With contra-rotating propellers, the first production engine drove the sub-scale RP-4 drone to 70 mph in 1939, culminating with 35-pound, 35-hp single-prop units driving prototypes to 190 mph by March 1945.

The Righter engines were horizontally-opposed, two-cylinder, simultaneously-firing, loop scavenged, two-stroke engines with rotary valve induction. The alloy casting crankcase had a strong ball bearing in its forward face to support the crankshaft and to lessen the thrust loads of the tractor propeller. The cylinders were 180 degrees opposed with a two-throw, unsupported steel crankshaft in the middle. The engine's power section was an alloy casting that contained the intake trunk for the carburetor and bearing(s) for the rear of the crankshaft. The forward face of the rear crankcase cover was machined smooth to mate with the cast iron rotary induction valve driven by the crankshaft. The ignition system was bolted to the aft end of the rear cover, and the rear of the crankshaft performed as a cam to open the ignition points.

The engine incorporated a two-throw type crankcase supported on three bearings. The rear main bearing was a bronze sleeve. The forward main, a ball-bearing type, was of sufficient size to carry both radial loads and front propeller thrust. The extreme front end of the shaft was supported by a pair of ball bearings that were inside the aft propeller hub. The bearings, piston, and cylinder walls were lubricated by mixing the lubrication oil with the fuel (eight parts fuel to one part lube oil). The engines were equipped with a centrifugally-operated spark advance mechanism, while earlier models had a manually-operated spark advance control timer.

The sand or die-cast aluminum cylinders were fitted with shrink fit cast iron cylinder liners, each fastened to the crankcase by four studs. The intake transfer and exhaust ports were opposed by 180 degrees and the single spark plug was seated in the center of the head. The aluminum alloy pistons were shaped for loop scavenging. The piston rings, connecting rods, and bearings varied between the four drone engines types.

The fuel system was operated by pressure developed in the engine crankcase. The 2-psi pressure required to operate the system was provided by a small check valve while the pressure was transmitted from the crankcase to the fuel tank by a neoprene hose. Total fuel carried by the drone was 1.8 gallons, which provided an hour of flight.

The ignition system was a battery-coil-condenser type, while the 6-volt ignition battery was sufficient to start the engine and typically had a one-hour useful life.

The engine suffered common operation problems. There were no throttle control so the carburetor needle had to be set for maximum rpm immediately before launching, which was very demanding on the engines and few endured for more than a few hours before burning out. While waiting to launch on the catapult and not receiving enough cooling air, the engine was not to run for more than a minute. A recurrent stalling problem occurred in a steep dive with the wings level but could often be resolved by rocking the wings.

Basic Radioplane Engines

Righter Sidewinder: The power plant for the first fifty-three drones purchased by the AAC was the excellent twin-cylinder, dual-output, dual counter-rotating propeller Sidewinder engine. Due to the slow response time electronics available at the time, two dual-rotation propellers were the solution to engine torque, which rotated the drone toward the ground at the relatively low take-off airspeeds. The Sidewinder displaced 10.2 cubic inches, produced 4–6.5 hp, and used 24–36-inch-diameter wooden propellers. The propellers were supplied by either Story, Glendale, California, or U.S. Propellers, Los Angeles. There were two Sidewinders versions: propellers rotating outwards at the top or propellers rotating inwards at the top with the latter the final version.

Righter O-15-3 and O-15-3 Engines: To circumvent purchasing, stocking, and restocking two propellers for each OQ-2, the AAF test flew an O-15-1-powered OQ-2 installing a single, larger diameter propeller on the forward hub. The resurgent propeller torque at low airspeed continued to be an issue. Walter Righter simplified his O-15-1 engine design, which yielded a significant impact on overall drone performance. It raised its horsepower, producing the improved performance: higher speed, higher horsepower, and lower fuel consumption. Righter O-15-3 engine would power the modified, without landing gear, Radioplane OQ-3 (USN TDD-2) aerial gunnery target. At least 5,822 Radioplane OQ-3 drones were produced during the war, which exceeded Righter production capacity. McCulloch Motors of Milwaukee, Wisconsin, was subcontracted to build its version of the O-15-3.

2-GS-17 (O-15-1) Engine: The original Sidewinder configuration was unacceptable to the AAF, and it directed Radioplane/Righter to design an engine that utilized coaxial propeller shafts. The result was the 2-GS-17 (O-15-1) of which 3,869 were manufactured by Righter Manufacturing Company, Burbank, California, or Herkimer

Left: Walter Righter displaying his Sidewinder GS-15 engine that powered the RP-4 drones that garnered Radioplane its first contract in May 1939. (*Radioplane*)

Below: Righter 2-GS-17 (O-15-1) engine of which 3,869 were manufactured. (*Radioplane*)

Tool and Model Works, Herkimer, New York. The designation 2-GS-17 denoted: two-cylinder, geared, simultaneously-firing, and 17-cubic-inch displacement. The military designation O-15-1 signified opposed: 15-cubic-inch displacement, version 1. These two designations were used interchangeably in the various company and military documents.

Righter/Kiekhaefer O-45: The AAF required a faster drone to better reproduce a maneuvering enemy aircraft and Walter Righter designed the larger, more powerful O-45-1 engine, to power the OQ-14/TDD-3 gunnery target aircraft that first flew in July 1944. The 34-pound Righter/Kiekhaefer O-45 was produced in three versions: -1 (20-hp), -2 (35-hp), and -3 (35-hp Navy version) series, which were air-cooled, two-stroke, horizontally-opposed engines of flat-twin configuration. The O-45 differed from the O-15-1/O-15-3 engine series in physical size and the location of the carburetor on the top of the engine and cast aluminum crankcase. The O-45 engine powered 5,204 OQ-14/TDD-3s, the majority by Kiekhaefer. Menasco and Righter O-45-1 engines appear to have been assigned to the AAF while the Kiekhaefer O-45-1 engines were assigned to the USN.

Kiekhaefer O-45-35: In the continual pursuit for higher speed and better performance from the greatly improved OQ-17 gunnery target airframes, the final opposed twin-engine powering production Radioplane drones was the 35-pound, 35-hp Kiekhaefer O-45-35 that spun a 42-inch Kroehler propeller. The OQ-17 displayed a graceful aluminum monocoque fuselage, cantilevered wings with slots, and a fully-cowled engine with spinner giving it a maximum 190-mph speed. The OQ-17/KDR-1 first flew in March 1945, but the 430 did not go into production until 1946, as the engine was unreliable.

Radio Control

Controllers

The early RP-1 had a ground control visual range of only 400 feet, but later OQs could be controlled at altitudes of 12,000 feet through visual contact using binoculars and later OQs could also be operated from control aircraft. After launch, gunnery target missions were flown by a ground controller, during which a skilled operator could duplicate fighter attack tactics for training gunners using all anti-aircraft artillery weapons in calibers up to 40 mm.

Rotary Dial Control

The original hand controllers were based on a short-wave unit and a standard rotary telephone dial sending pulses via the transmitter to the flight surface control systems onboard the drone. On the rotary dial, the digits were arranged in a circular fashion so that a finger wheel could be rotated with one finger from the position of each digit to a fixed finger stop position to prevent further rotation. When released at the finger stop, the wheel returned to its home position by spring action at a speed regulated by a governor device. During this return rotation, the dial interrupted the direct electrical current a definite number of times for each digit and generated electrical pulses, which the drone's receiver decoded into each dialed digit. The drone controller was the standard telephone ten finger hole type with only six of the ten holes used:

Hole 1: Stop Control
Hole 2: Neutral
Hole 3: Up
Hole 4: Down
Hole 5: Right
Hole 6: Left.

On the control box, below the rotary dial was a light that indicated "Parachute Normal."

The RP-1 had a three-tube radio receiver that relayed impulses to two electric train motors each on its own frequency. One for elevator control and the other for rudder control, so that when current was applied to one motor this would be up elevator. The next signal would be stop or neutral elevator and the next down. The sequence was the same for rudder control. Due to the latencies in the system, these aircraft were found to be almost uncontrollable and development continued.

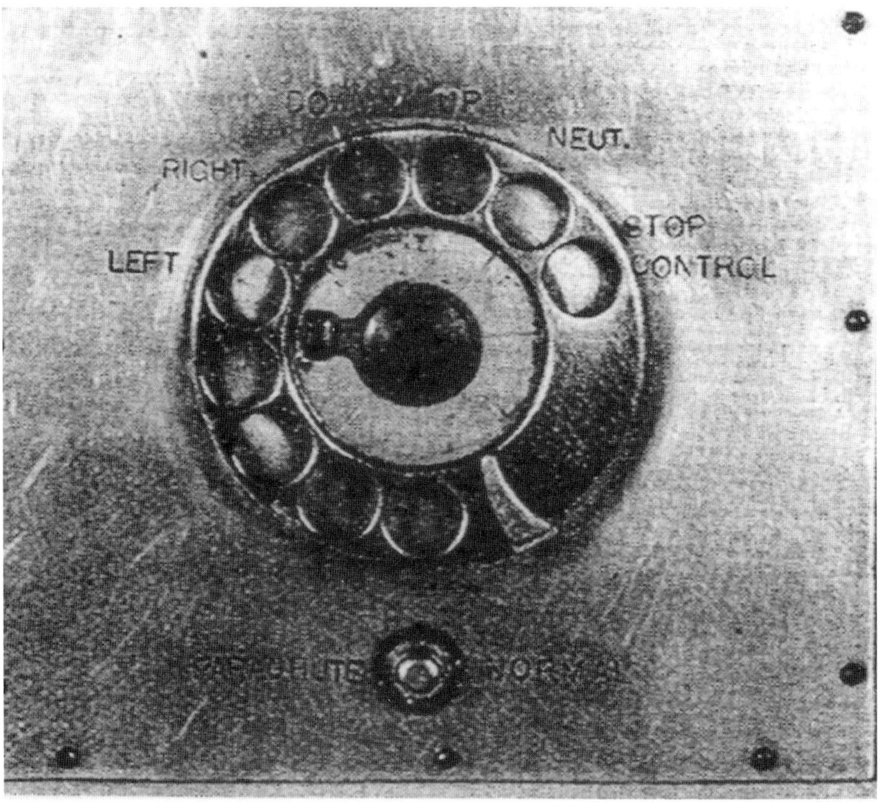

Rotary dial control. The original hand controllers were based around a short-wave unit and a rotary telephone dial that sent pulses via the transmitter to the drone's flight surface control systems. (*Radioplane*)

Ground controller using rotary dial to control a RP-3. (*AAF*)

Joy Stick Control

The target drone was controlled by an ultra-high-frequency carrier that generated and modulated five different audio frequencies, but only one of these audio frequencies could be in use at any one time. A joystick-type control box simulating an aircraft control stick selected four frequencies that were used to direct the target aircraft, while the fifth held the parachute in place until it was released to land the drone. By moving the control stick right, left, up, or down, a different audio frequency was applied as carrier modulation for each of these desired motions, and reception of the modulated carrier by the receiver-selector in the drone, due to frequency-selective circuits, closed a different relay for each motion. These relays then applied voltage to electric servo motors that moved the drone's control surfaces to adjust its course as mandated by the stick. When the four other controls were not in operation, the fifth or parachute tone was switched on automatically to hold the parachute in place. When the flight was to be terminated, a button was pushed to interrupt all the tones, releasing the parachute and cutting the drone's ignition switch on the airplane target to stop the engine.

Transmitter

The large and heavy transmitter was usually located on the nearest convenient flat surface and connected to the joystick control box by a cable long enough to give the controller some freedom of movement. The output carrier frequency was in the 73-MHz band, with plug-in crystals allowing several transmitters to operate simultaneously in the same area. The transmitter received its power from a dynamotor unit, which in turn was powered by a gasoline generator.

Joystick and receiver. (*Radioplane*)

Testing the RP-6's control surfaces before take-off using the joystick. (*AAF*)

The transmitter superimposed were five audio signals on the carrier as follows:

Command	Frequency	Action
Right	300 Hz	Rudder
Left	650 HZ	Rudder
Up	1,390 HZ	Elevator
Down	3,000 HZ	Elevator
Parachute	955 HZ	Release*

*Absence of a continuous tone caused the release of the parachute after a one-second delay.

There was no proportional control. Both the rudder and elevator moved at a constant rate when the appropriate signal was received. The rudder returned to neutral when the signal ceased so the pilot had to learn by experience how long to signal and when to stop. The elevator, unlike the rudder, had no automatic neutral, so it locked in position when the signal stopped and so it was imperative that the controller set the elevator properly before launching and then avoid it use as much as possible. Over time, several drones had left the catapult, climbed into a stall, and then crashed immediately into the ground because the controller overlooked checking and setting the position of the elevator.

Receiver

The shock-mounted, high-gain, super-regenerative receiver consisted of nine vacuum tubes, crowded into an 8-inch-square aluminum box along with connecting cords to the dynamotor antenna, battery box, servo unit, and parachute sockets. The unit was powered by starter button or pull rope gasoline-oil engine that ran continually throughout the flight. Power was provided by the 6-volt battery box unit mounted in the fuselage in a channel-type tray that could be adjusted both fore and aft, to balance the drone for correct flight attitude. High humidity and salt water, in particular, greatly affected the receiver, which was a detriment during Florida testing and in the tropical Pacific combat theaters.

Servo Unit

The servo unit, manufactured by the Hansen Manufacturing Company, Princeton, Indiana, was located just forward of the horizontal stabilizer and was accessible through the fuselage top. The single package servo was activated by the receiver, which connected two 6-volt motors with reversible fields providing action to the gear trains; these operated the rudder and elevator control levers, which, in turn, by mechanical linkage, operated the target aircrafts surface controls.

Catapult

The OQ-2 was equipped with a landing gear, while the OQ-3, OQ-14, and all the Navy's late TDDs had none and were launched from a 37-foot catapult by electric shock cords powering a carriage with 700 pounds of thrust that propelled the drone off the catapult at about 65 mph. The Army catapult was portable to benefit from the wind direction while the ship deck-mounted Navy type had to have the ship turn to take advantage of wind direction. Later a 30-foot catapult version arrived with the

Portable AAF catapult launching an OQ-2A. The ramp could be positioned to take advantage of the wind. (*Radioplane*)

Fixed Navy catapult aboard USS *New York* launching a TDD-1. The ship had to be turned to take advantage of the wind. (*USN*)

new Navy TDD-3s, which was powered by coiled steel springs in place of the shock cords, increasing the thrust to 900 pounds.

Recovery System

Stronger, more resilient, welded tubular steel construction replaced the drone's early plywood construction, resulting in an increased proportion of drones that were hit during AA training surviving to be returned for repair to fly again. Improvements in maintenance and repair procedures along with the maximum of interchangeable parts and accessibility of radio, engine, and servo installations minimized the lost time in the field repair of damaged target drones.

The drones were recovered by parachute that could be released either by the transmitter operator or automatically when hits were scored on the airborne radio unit. The target drone also could be, and frequently was, landed by dead stick remote control when ample landing area was available. The parachute had a standard 24-foot-diameter circular canopy but used an 18-inch circular vent rather than the standard puckered vent. The main parachute was provided with a standard pilot chute with twenty-four suspension lines, which were shackled to the apex of four riser cables fastened to four points on fuselage. The parachute was packed in a metal tray with canvas flaps and was fixed in the welded hinged steel tube parachute hatch located in the upper top fuselage between the wing and empennage. This hatch was closed by a spring tension yoke and was held shut by an electromagnetic relay armature providing that a continuous signal was received on the parachute channel. The rip cord, attached to the fuselage, released the parachute when the opening of the hatch pulled the cord. An engine ignition switch was activated to the OFF position when the parachute hatch opened.

A-Series 1-8 Target Drones

The Air Corp's A Series (A for aerial target) originally classified all radio-controlled target drones, irrespective of size. In June 1941, the use of the designation A for attack aircraft caused confusion and the AAC to redesignate the existing A model drones with OQ (Model Airplane Target (Radioplane) and PQ (Full-Scale Target Aircraft (with provision for pilot)).

Fleetwings A-1

The medium-size (20-foot wingspan) Fleetwings A-1, manufactured in 1939 by Fleetwings Incorporated of Bristol, Pennsylvania, was the first aircraft designated under the original A series. The A-1 was powered by an 80-hp engine that yielded a maximum speed of 180 mph with a ceiling of 10,000 feet. The A-1's control unit was developed by Radio Frequency Laboratories (RFL) of Boonton Township, New Jersey, headed by Richard Seabury. The Model H-26 35-watt crystal-controlled ground station transmitter operated at a carrier frequency of 73 MHz, modulated by nine separate audio tones signifying the various command functions. The ground controller used a traditional throttle and joystick configuration, supplemented by an

The parachute was packed in a metal tray with canvas flaps and was fixed in the welded hinged steel tube parachute hatch located in the upper top fuselage between the wing and empennage. (*Radioplane*)

The 24-foot-diameter canopy could be released either by the transmitter operator or automatically when hits were scored on the airborne radio unit. (*Radioplane*)

optional aircraft control yoke mounted to a breastplate support worn by the operator. The ground station equipment was driven by a 1,200-volt DC gasoline generator and a 12-volt storage battery. The drone was controlled via the audio output of the Model H-26-R receiver that was fed to the Model H-26-S selector unit, which decoded the various tones to operate the various flight control surfaces and other functions. Several unofficial test flights were conducted at Boonton Township Airfield, after which the system was taken to the Aberdeen Proving Ground, Maryland, for official acceptance trials sometime during 1939. During its first flight trial, the Fleetwings A-1 was under the ill-fated remote control of an influential, but inexperienced AAC officer and pilot. After the first take-off run (which was too slow) was aborted, the second take-off attempt was successful but the A-1 then banked, turned back toward the control station, and then disappeared overhead and eventually crashed.

A-2 Radioplane (see Radioplanes)

The AAF designated the Radioplane RP-5/RP-5A as the A-2 and A-2A followed by the PQ-2 designation. The RP-5A production model, initially designated A-2A but was changed to OQ-2A before completion. The USN designated it as the TDD-l Target Drone, Denny.

A-3 Curtiss Fledgling

During the 1930s, the U.S. Navy converted some obsolete N2C-2 Fledgling biplanes, modified with tricycle landing gear and equipped for radio control, to be used as anti-aircraft artillery targets. In 1940, one of these was tested by the AAC as A-3. (See “The USN Begins its Radio-Controlled Aircraft Program” in Chapter 5.)

A-4 Douglas BT-2B

Douglas BT-2 was a basic trainer with excellent flight characteristics, originally produced by converting O-32 observation aircraft but was later manufactured as the BT-2B. During 1940, fifteen Douglas BT-2Bs and two BT-2BIs were furnished with tricycle gears (later a steerable nosewheel was added and main gear moved aft), faired-over rear cockpit, remote control equipment, and single controls, allowing the aircraft to be test-flown. They were initially redesignated as BT-2BR and BT-2BG but were eventually simply designated as A-4 aerial targets. The seven remaining BT-2Cs were converted into drone control aircraft to operate with the A-4s and given the designation BT-2CR. By June 1941, they were no longer in the inventory. The fifteen radio-controlled BT-2Bs were 31-36/39/49/56/58/60/72/76/91/99/101/114/116/12 7/135.

A-5 Boeing P-12/F4B-4A

After Pearl Harbor, twenty-three miscellaneous P-12s were delivered to the USN for use as radio-controlled A-5 target aircraft. The Navy assigned them serial numbers 2489/2511 and designated them as the F4B-4A, the A designating their former Army status. Most were shot down during training exercises. The radio-controlled P-12s were P-12C (31-151, - 154, -209, -210); P-12D (31-245, -258); P-12E (31-561, -564,

-576, 32-010, - 013, -025, -033, -040, -041, -044, -046,-048, -057, -066, -069, -074); and P-12F (32-85).

A-6 Douglas O-38

The Douglas O-38 single-engined two-seat observation aircraft was numerically the most important in the family of biplane observation aircraft that began with the Douglas O-2. During 1940, it was proposed to convert O-38 airframes as A-6 aerial targets, but the development was canceled.

A-7 Bell Airacobra

In 1940, there was a proposal that all the YP-39s or P-39Cs, which were not considered combat worthy (lacking self-sealing fuel cells and adequate armor protection) be converted as A-7 aerial targets, but the conversion proposal was never acted upon. During the late war, the Navy acquired a single P-39Q from the AAF and converted it to a radio-controlled target drone, designated as the XTDL-1. In 1946, the Navy operated two other P-39Q drone conversions, later redesignated F2L-1K, to be tested as target drones at NAS Cape May.

A-8 through -16 Series

Because PQ-8 was the first allocation in the A series, numbers PQ-1 through PQ-7 remained unassigned but were known by their A designations.

A-8 Culver PQ-8 and PQ-8A

Culver Cadet/PQ-8 Predecessors

While at Lambert Aircraft, Albert Mooney designed the Monoprep G, one of the company's Monocoupe series. It was a low-wing monoplane with an open cockpit, seating two side-by-side, which became the Monosport G with the installation of a cabin enclosure. During October 1935, financial problems prevented the aircraft from reaching production and subsequently Mooney left Lambert and purchased the Monosport design and production rights. Mooney joined with Knight Culver (wealthy son of the founder of Culver Military Academy) to form the Dart Aircraft Co. at Port Columbus, Ohio, and was joined by his brother, Arthur, who became the company's production manager. Several uncompleted Monosport airframes were modified to produce an improved version named the Dart. The basic layout of the Dart and generally all Culver aircraft was relatively similar. The Dart's fuselage and tail surfaces were constructed of welded steel tubing, faired with wooden formers. Its elliptical cantilever wing was constructed with laminated spruce spar beams, and spruce and plywood ribs. Double drag bracing was provided above and below the spar to increase torsional stiffness. The airframe was fabric covered except for metal leading edges. The Dart's undercarriage was fixed, although there were future contingencies to make it retractable. The aircraft was powered by one of three engines, the 90-hp Lambert R-266 in the model G, the 90-hp Ken-Royce in the model GK, and the 90-hp Warner Scarab Junior in the model GW. Ninety-five of the light, aerodynamic Darts were

Albert Mooney, a self-taught aircraft designer, developed the Culver Cadet model and later with his brother, Arthur, established the Mooney Aircraft Company. (*AFHSRC*)

delivered and were popular as a highly-maneuverable sport aircraft. In 1939, Knight Culver renamed the company Culver Aircraft after himself.

Culver Cadet

During February 1939, Mooney developed the Culver Model L prototype, a Dart version with improved performance using a smaller Continental engine. The Model L first flew on December 2, 1939 and was renamed the Culver Cadet in March 1940. The 17-foot, 8-inch-long, 5-foot, 6-inch-high, 806-pound Cadet was a side-by-side two-seater with dual controls, with access to the cabin via large metal doors hinged at their forward edge. The cockpit included a metal frame with transparent cellulose acetate windows. Although similar to the previous Dart, instead of the Dart's welded-steel-tube fuselage, the Cadet fuselage was constructed of wooded semi-monocoque construction and used a stressed skin, plastic-bonded plywood reinforced with wood longerons and bulkheads. The 27-foot-span, 120-square-foot area wings were constructed of laminated spruce and mahogany plywood with an I-beam main spar. The leading edge was made of plywood that covered back to the spar and the whole wing was fabric-covered. The leading edge had slots built into it for improved low speed control response. The undercarriage retracted inwards into the wings, by winding it up and down manually while the tailwheel was fixed. The fixed tail surfaces were of wood, covered in plywood, but the moving surfaces were of welded steel tube and fabric covered. As was the typical circumstance with tail-draggers, the rudder was masked by the wing while taxiing, and steering was by use of the hydraulic brakes. The first variant, the two-seat Cadet LCA, was powered by a 75-hp Continental

Culver Cadet LCA (restored civilian 1960s version). (*Author*)

A75-8 four-cylinder horizontally-opposed piston engine and later with the 80-hp Continental A-80-8. In 1941, the LCA successor, the model LFA, was available powered by the 80-hp flat-four piston Franklin 4AC-176-F3, which gave the LFA a 142-mph maximum speed, 500-mile range, and 17,000-foot service ceiling. A further development was the LFA-90 with the 90-hp Franklin 4AC-199-E3. The Cadet was considered one of the most efficient aircraft ever built, and as a sport plane, it was advertised as a "high-speed bargain for sportsman pilots who demand extra speed and performance." Knight Culver decided that he no longer wished to continue with the stresses of the aircraft manufacturing business and a company faced with an Ohio factory that was too small to meet anticipated wartime orders. Consequently, Culver and Mooney were induced by Wichita aviation investors Charles "Pappy" Yankey and W. L. McMahon to move to Wichita. After Pearl Harbor, with a new military role, civilian Cadet production ended at about 360 units including some export orders, many to Uruguay.

The Cadet Drone

In August 1940, the AAC issued a requirement for a small radio-controlled aircraft for use as a target drone to aid in the training of the expected influx of pilots as war loomed. The AAC's proposed drone was to be radio-controlled for use as a target, but also had to be piloted for ferry, delivery, and training purposes. The AAC considered the Culver Cadet as a prime drone candidate and approached Al Mooney about the possibility of Culver manufacturing the drone. The supply of suitable engines was a problem for Culver and after being rejected by Continental and Lycoming, the

Franklin engine company was contracted, and Culver opted to produce the drone. Mooney selected the Franklin O-200, which after the war would also be used to power the Tucker automobile. Mooney submitted a drone variant of their Cadet LFA sports model, which, after successful tests, was subsequently ordered in two versions, 200 drones for the A-8 powered by a 90-hp air-cooled, four-cylinder opposed Franklin O-200-1, and later 200 drones for the A-8A with a more powerful 125-hp air-cooled, four-cylinder, opposed Lycoming O-290-1. After AAC approval of the drone, Mooney immediately began the installation of the radio control apparatus to the Cadet to produce a prototype.

In June 1941, the A for aerial target category was abandoned, and because PQ-8 was the first allocation in the series, numbers PQ-1 through -7 remained unassigned but were known by their A designations. The prototype of the Cadet target was designated as XPQ-8 while the A-8 and A-8A became the PQ-8 and PQ-8A, respectively.

The Navy designated the PQ-8 Franklin 0-200 model as the XTDC-1 while the PQ-8A Lycoming 0290-1 model was designated as the XTDC-2 at the end of 1941 to train anti-aircraft gunners. After a positive Navy evaluation, a production order for 200 TDC-1 (for Target Drone Culver) drones followed. During late 1941, the Navy acquired a PQ-8A for evaluation and afterward ordered 200 as the TDC-2. The Oklahoma City Air Depot at Tinker Field conducted the routine checks of the PQ-8 and later the PQ-14, as part of the AAF's delivery and acceptance review.

The PQ-8s were equipped for radio control with provisions for a ferry or a safety pilot. The ferry pilots who flew the fast, maneuverable little drones from the Wichita factory to Texas for installation of the radio control equipment could not resist the

Culver PQ-8. (*AAF*)

temptation to engage in simulated dogfights over the factory before heading off in formation. Conventional stick and rudder pedal flight controls were provided for the safety pilot. The servo flight controls were connected in unison with the safety pilot's controls and were provided with overpowering devices permitting the safety pilot to take over quickly without disengaging the servo control in the event of a servo failure. The radio equipment was mounted on a frame located to the right of the pilot's seat. As an unmanned drone, a radio operator controlled the drone usually in a twin-engined advanced trainer Cessna UC-78 Bobcat mother ship.

The AAF PQ-8A (Army Contract No. W 535 ac-32100) and USN (Navy contract No. NOa(s)242) TDC-2 Target Aircraft were 1,820-pound, low-wing, single-engined, monoplanes constructed of wood, metal, and fabric. The variances between these two military models being in their servo control systems and location and particulars of equipment. The fabric-covered, 26-foot, 11-inch span, 120-square-foot wing was of the full-cantilever type, constructed of wood and tubular torque trusses. The ailerons consisted of a metal frame covered with fabric. The all-wood, stressed-skin, 9-foot span horizontal and vertical stabilizers (17.66 square feet) were attached in fixed alignment to the fuselage. The rudder and elevator were fabric-covered metal frames. The rudder (5.8 square feet) was statically balanced. The elevator (5.5 square feet) was equipped with a trim tab controllable by the pilot, while the rudder and right aileron were equipped with ground-adjustable trim tabs.

The fixed tricycle landing gear (then called "alighting gear") was independently mounted. The main gear was installed in the inboard torque truss of each wing panel. Each wheel was mounted on a spring-oil type shock-absorbing strut. Goodyear single

Navy TDC-2. (*USN*)

disc hydraulic brakes were installed on each main gear wheel and were controlled by toe pedals. No brakes were installed on the nose gear. The nose gear swiveled in a support tube that was integral with the engine mount and was mounted on a spring-oil type shock-absorber strut. The nose wheel could rotate 35 degrees for the TDC-2 and 20 degrees for steering via a linkage with the rudder pedals. A mud wiper was installed for propeller protection.

The aircraft was powered by one Lycoming 0-290-1 engine turning a wooden Sensenich fixed pitch prop that gave it a maximum speed of 142 mph over a range of 500 miles. The fuel system consisted of one 25-gallon fuel tank mounted in the fuselage to provide a gravity feed system. The oil system was a wet-sump type with a 2-gallon capacity. The electrical system was a single-circuit 12-volt ground system with one battery installed in the fuselage and one generator installed on the engine.

Once radar-equipped anti-aircraft guns were introduced, unexpectedly, fewer PQ-8 were shot down. Investigation revealed because the drone had been designed to use non-strategic wood for its construction, it did not return a good radar reflection. To remedy this early form of stealth, wires were connected to the wings and radar reflective paint was coated on the bottom.

Culver PQ-8s awaiting fate at Wheeler Field, Oahu, Hawaii, April 1944. (*AAF*)

Testing the PQ-8's controls. (*AAF*)

Cadet Variants

Cadet LCA:	Initial production version powered by a 75-hp Continental A75-8.
Cadet LFA:	Improved variant with an 80-hp Franklin 4AC-176-F3, Franklin 4AC-176-D2, or Franklin 4AC-176-D3 engine, and a full electrical system and engine starter.
Cadet LFA-90:	Limited edition variant with a 90-hp Franklin 4AC-199-E3 engine.
LAR (AAF A-8):	Initial designation of military radio-controlled drone version, later redesignated PQ-8.
LAR-90 (AAF PQ-8):	Initial production military drone version, 200 built.
PQ-8A:	PQ-8 powered by a 125-hp Lycoming O-290 engine, redesignated Q-8A in 1948, 200 built.
TDC-1:	One PQ-8 for evaluation by the USN.
TDC-2:	Production version of the PQ-8A for the Navy, 201 built.

Production

Culver produced one XPQ-8 and 200 PQ-8s (from August 1941 to July 1942) and 200 PQ-8As (from March to October 1943) for the AAF and 201 PQ-8/TDC-2 for the USN (from June to December 1943). The production run of the PQ-8 Cadet was relatively limited (601) because its success led to the development of the factory designated NRD—a single PQ-8 that was converted to the new configuration and tested by the AAF as the XPQ-14 prototype. In 1943, Al Mooney designed a strengthened drone with retractable landing gear, which was officially accepted on

July 4, which terminated PQ-8 production and was then continued as the preeminent Culver drone, the PQ-14.

AAF Culver PQ-8 Serials

Culver XPQ-8-CL Cadet (originally designated A-8): 41-18889.

Culver PQ-8-CL Cadet Serials (Survivors redesignated Q-8A in 1948): 41-19513 through 41-19587, 42-38538 through 42-38662.

Culver PQ-8A-CL Cadet Serials (Survivors redesignated Q-8A-CL in 1948): 42-96833 through 42-97032, 43-30762 through 43-30762.

USN Culver TDC Serials: TDC-1, 46449; XTDC-2, 32386; TDC-2, 44355 through 44554.

Culver PQ-9

In 1941, Culver designed the factory model NR-B as an improved PQ-8 Cadet with a more powerful Franklin O-300-3 engine. The AAC planned to evaluate the NR-B target drone as the PQ-9, however, the XPQ-9 prototype and the PQ-9 production versions were canceled, apparently because the PQ-14 (Culver model NR-D) was more promising.

Culver PQ-9. (*AAF*)

Culver XPQ-10

The prototype XPQ-10 was ordered by the AAC in 1941. Derived from the civilian Culver Model MR, the XPQ-10 was a high-wing (30-foot span) monoplane equipped with twin 175-hp Franklin O-300 opposed piston engines and a fixed tricycle landing gear. It was 30 feet long and 4 feet, 6 inches high. Production plans were made for the PQ-10 series; however, before the XPQ-10 was completed, the project was canceled.

Fletcher XPQ-11 (FBT-2)

Fletcher Aviation Corporation, Pasadena, California, entered the aircraft manufacturing market in 1941 with the FBT-2, a low-wing cantilever monoplane military training aircraft that seated the pilot and instructor in tandem in an enclosed cockpit. Construction was of plywood throughout, incorporating symmetrical wings and control surfaces to provide complete interchange-ability of wings, flaps, ailerons and tail-surfaces. The aircraft was 23 feet, 3 inches long, 10 feet, 5 inches high, with a 30-foot wingspan and a fixed tailwheel and undercarriage. A single FBT-2 prototype with a Wright R-760 engine, which gave it a maximum speed of 175 mph and a range of 540 miles, was evaluated for military use but generated no interest as Fletcher lost the contract to Vultee's BT-13. However, the AAF purchased this FBT-2 prototype and converted it for use as a CQ drone controller as the YCQ-1A with tricycle undercarriage and Wright R-760 Whirlwind engine. The YCQ-1A (41-38984), one of only three CQ designations, with Stinson CQ-2 and Beech CQ-3 (UC-45F Expeditor). During late 1941, the AAF then ordered the type as a radio-controlled target drone under the designation XPQ-11 with a tricycle undercarriage and 400-hp Pratt & Whitney R-985 Wasp Junior engine. Two lots of fifty were ordered, but before any were delivered, the type was canceled in favor of the PQ-8 Cadet and PQ-14 drones. However, the ten PQ-11As under construction at Fletcher were completed and were delivered in May 1942 as XBG-1 bomb gliders. See Chapter 6.

PQ-11. Fletcher FBT-2. (*AAF*)

Fleetwings PQ-12

The PQ-12 design was a radio-controlled target drone with a fixed tricycle landing gear and an open cockpit for an optional on-board pilot. It was powered by a single 225-hp Lycoming O-435-5 piston engine. A single XPQ-12 (41-39057) ordered in 1941 was canceled, but one XPQ-12A (41-39098) and eight YPQ-12s (41-39049/39056) of an order for fifty aircraft were delivered. A production batch of forty YPQ-12s, with serials 41-39058/39097, were to be completed as YPQ-12As but were canceled. The YPQ-12A had provision to carry a 500-pound bomb as a payload in place of the pilot.

During October 1943, one of the eight Fleetwings PQ-12A radio target aircraft was equipped with a television camera transmitter mounted on a wing and a 500-pound bomb in the fuselage to become a power-driven controllable bomb. A television receiver was installed in a mothership in which the radio control operator controlled the PQ-12A using the TV picture as a reference for the attitude of the PQ-12A to the target. On October 10, 1943, the Materiel Command conducted a test at Muroc to demonstrate an air-to-air explosion. Using different radio frequencies, a radio-controlled PQ-9 was intended as the target and the PQ-12A as the controlled missile. A Cessna UC-78 control aircraft controlled the PQ-9 visually and the PQ-12A by reference on a TV screen toward the PQ-9. The control aircraft flew about a mile off the right wing of the two PQs. The bomb on the PQ-12A was armed remotely while in the air. After twenty-five minutes, the PQ-9 was centered on the TV screen of the control aircraft and appeared to be of a size to indicate a reasonably close range and the detonator circuit was remotely actuated (later this range was estimated to be 75 feet). The PQ-12A completely disintegrated and the PQ-9 spiraled steeply into the ground.

The second demonstration had a PQ-12A fly into a target by using a TV camera that transmitted a picture to a screen in the control aircraft flying 3–5 miles away. The take-off and climb to 1,000 feet were controlled visually after which control was established using the TV screen as reference. Once the target was located on the screen, the PQ-12A was put into a shallow dive at full throttle with the target being held on the screen for a minute appearing to grow larger and larger as the distance decreased between the target and the incoming PQ-12A. At the last instance, the target filled the whole screen but off to the left center as the increasing speed of the dive caused a deviation in the directional trim. These tests were considered as moderately successful and would be part of the development effort for the Fleetwings BQ-1/BQ-2 radio-controlled assault drones.

PQ-12A/14 RC-64/65 Target Control Receiving and Transmitting Equipment

Target Control Receiving Equipment RC-64 and RC-65 consisted of a FM radio receiver and auxiliary equipment designed for installation in target aircraft to control the elementary movements of the remote flight control of a target aircraft such as the PQ-12/14 during gunnery practice. It operated in conjunction with Target Control Transmitting Equipment RC-64 and RC-65. The operating frequency of the receiver could be set between the limits of 30 to 40 mc; however, the normal setting was 38.54

Fleetwings YPQ-12. (*AAF*)

Fleetwings PQ -12. (*AAF*)

mc with an alternate frequency of 35.3 mc. Its range was 10 miles in the air and one mile from the ground. Manual operation of the control stick at the transmitter resulted in transmission of selected tones to the target for each control movement or function desired (up, down, etc.). Receiver-Selector BC-617 included a ten-channel (five for the RC-65) audio filter selector circuit for discrimination between the various tones received. Relay Unit BC-622 passed control voltages to the target aircraft control surfaces mechanism from the receiver output. Thus, by moving the control stick right, left, up, or down, a different audio frequency was applied as carrier modulation for each of these desired motions, and reception of the modulated carrier by the receiver-selector in the target, due to frequent-selective circuits, closed a different relay for each motion. These relays then applied voltage to electric servo motors, which moved the targets control surfaces to alter its course as mandated by the stick.

For the RC-65 Transmitter to obtain radio control of the target aircraft, an ultra-high-frequency carrier was generated and modulated by five different audio frequencies, four of which were selected by a control box simulating an aircraft control stick with only one of these audio frequencies available for use at any one time. The four frequencies selected by the stick on the control box were used to influence the gliding of the target, while the fifth held the parachute in place until it was released to land the target. When the other controls were not in operation, the fifth or parachute tone was automatically switched on to hold the parachute in position. Thus, the parachute relay remained energized through the receiver-selector circuit, when any of the 5 tones were modulating the carrier. When the targets flight was to be ended a button was pushed to cut off all the tones, releasing the parachute and cutting the targets ignition switch to stop the engine.

The audio frequency tones (cycles per second) used were as follows:

Right	300 cps	Controls rudder
Left	650 cps	Controls rudder
Parachute	955 cps	Controls parachute
Up	1,390 cps	Controls elevators
Down	3,000 cps	Controls elevators

The receiver-selector circuit prevented the parachute relay contacts from opening for approximately one second after pushing the parachute release button. This delay prevented momentary open circuits from releasing the parachute.

ERCO XPQ-13 Ercoupe

In 1941, the AAC purchased two low-wing, monoplane Ercoupe 415-C aircraft from the Engineering and Researching Corporation (ERCO) of Riverdale, Maryland, to convert them into radio-controlled drones with the designation XPQ-13. The Ercoupe was 20 feet, 2 inches long, had a 30-foot wingspan, and weighed 749 pounds empty and 1,260 pounds loaded. It was powered by a 65 hp Continental engine that gave it maximum speed of 110 mph, a cruising speed of 95 mph, and a range of 300 miles.

ERCO XPQ-13 Ercoupe. (*AAF*)

The first XPQ-13 (ERCO No. 110) was purchased on August 19, 1941 by the AAC and delivered to Wright Field; it officially entered into inventory on August 12, 1941 as 41-25196 to be one of the two aircraft entered in the Aerial Target Competition, which eventually was won by the Culver PQ-14, a superior design for that purpose. No. 110 was the last model produced before the war, while Nos. 111 and 112 were built from spare parts during 1942. The second ERCO (No. 111) was built in December 1940 and was purchased by the AAC on January 4, 1941 for $10 and delivered as 41-39099 to the AAC Material Division, Wright Field. This XPQ-13 was used during July 1941 for the AAF's first tests of JATO (jet-assisted take-off) rockets intended to significantly improve an aircraft's take-off performance. These tests were very successful and led the way for standard application of JATO on many operational aircraft. In August 1945, production of the Ercoupe 415C was resumed for civilian sales.

Culver PQ-14 (USN TD2C-1)

The success of the factory designated NRD, a PQ-8 transformed to the new configuration, was developed and tested by the AAF as the larger and faster XPQ-14 prototype with a retractable landing gear. The XPQ-14's fuselage, wings, and tail components were constructed of wood with stressed plywood skin gear. The XPQ-14 was followed by YPQ-14A service test model and then by 1,348 PQ-14A production models. Of the latter, 1,198 were transferred to the USN, which designated them as TD2C-1 with the particularly unappealing name Turkey. The YPQ-14B was a slightly heavier variant; a total of twenty-five were produced before production transferred to the PQ-14B. A total of 594 PQ-14Bs served as target drones for the AAF. A single PQ-14B was converted to use a Franklin O-300-9 engine and designated XPQ-14C, but the engine change offered no advantage.

YPQ-14A service test model. (*AAF*)

XPQ-14 prototype. (*AAF*)

AAF Culver PQ-14B. (*AAF*)

USN Culver TD2C-1. (*USN*)

Description

The Army Models YPQ-14A, PQ-14A, YPQ-14B, PQ-14B, and Navy Model TD2C-1 target aircraft were single-engined, low-wing, wood, metal, and fabric monoplanes weighing 1,830 pounds. All models were equipped for radio control with provisions for a ferry pilot or a safety pilot. Conventional flight was controlled by a standard stick in the cockpit, which operated the ailerons and elevator. Pedals were normally located for controlling the rudder, for steering the nose wheel, and for operating the wheel brakes.

The 19-foot, 6-inch-long, 8-foot, 4.5-inch-high fuselage was constructed of wood longerons and wood bulkheads with stressed plywood skin. The cockpit included a molded acrylic windshield and a sliding hatch made of cellulose acetate with metal framework. Cockpit ventilation was furnished by sliding the hatch to the desired position.

The 30-foot span wooden wing was a full-cantilever type with two laminated wood spars running the full length of the wing from tip to tip. A stressed plywood skin completely covered the wing with wooden ribs forming the airfoil. The ailerons were constructed of wood ribs and stressed plywood skin. The electrically operated wing flaps extended from the fuselage to the ailerons. Fixed slots were located near each wing tip. Alighting gear wells were incorporated in the wing to accommodate the retracted gears.

The horizontal and vertical stabilizers and the elevator trim tab were all of wood stressed plywood skin construction. The horizontal and vertical stabilizers were attached to the fuselage in a fixed position. The rudder and elevator were constructed of metal framework covered with fabric. The rudder was statically balanced and had a tab adjustable from the ground while the elevator trim tab was controllable by the pilot.

The fully-retractable tricycle type alighting (landing) gear had each unit mounted independently. Shock absorbing was accomplished by an air-oil type strut, which incorporated oil and compressed air in the strut. The main gear retracted into wells in the wing while the nose gear retracted into a well in the fuselage nose. All gears simultaneously retracted electrically and locked automatically. Each main gear was equipped with a Goodyear hydraulic brake unit that was controllable by toe action brake pedals. The nose gear was steerable 6.5 degrees to the right and 5.5 degrees to the left through the action of the rudder pedals.

All models were equipped with a 150-hp, six-cylinder, air-cooled (by direct air blast from full pressure type baffles), horizontally-opposed, Franklin piston engine built by Franklin Motors Corporation, Syracuse, New York. The carburetor air system was designed to furnish hot or cold air to both carburetors when required. The Franklin engine and the two-blade Sensenich fixed pitch propeller gave the aircraft a maximum speed of 185 mph, a cruising speed of 150 mph, a range of 512 miles, and a service ceiling of 17,000 feet.

Fuel was contained in six aluminum cells in the wing: three cells holding 13 gallons in each wing. The three left cells operated as the left tank while the three right cells operated as the right tank, or the left and right tanks could operate as one tank. A selector fuel valve located in the center of the floorboard determined how these tanks operated. Fuel was supplied to the carburetor by an engine-driven fuel pump with a hand-operated fuel pump intended to build up pressure for emergency use. The 2-gallon oil supply was contained in the crankcase since the engine was of the wet sump type. The oil radiator was installed on the top of the engine and air was directed through it from a baffled opening in the cowl. The air flow through the oil radiator could not be controlled manually. Oil temperature was controlled by an automatic valve which was an integral part of the oil radiator.

After the war, most PQ Cadet Targets that survived AAF and USN gunners were sold as surplus and flown as small sporty civil recreational aircraft. Several PQ-8As were alleged to have remained in USAF inventory in 1948, when they were redesignated as Q-8A. A number of the 1,198 Navy TD2C drones continued in service into the early 1950s.

CULVER CONTROL AIRCRAFT GALLERY

Above: Beech CQ-3 (UC-45F Expeditor) mother ship controlling a PQ-14B and a Curtiss Helldiver. (*USN*)

Below: Controller in a CQ-3 mother ship guiding a PQ-14. (*AAF*)

Consolidated B-24 Liberator test controlling two PQ-14s over Hawaii. (*AAF*)

Douglas C-47 Dakota testing the controls of a manned PQ-14. (*AAF*)

AAF PQ-14 Series Serials

Culver YPQ-14B-CL: 44-22510, 44-22520, and 44-22586 through 44-22608.

Culver PQ-14A: 43-44214 through 43-44363, 44-21758 through 44-21907, 44-22509, 44-22511 through 44-22519, and 45-58760 through 45-59119.

Culver PQ-14A to USN as TD2C-1: 43-44514 through 43-44713, 44-22521 through 44-22585, 44-22584 through 22585, and 44-68499 through 44-68738.

Culver PQ-14B-CL: 43-44364 through 43-44513, 44-68255 through 44-68498, 44-68739 through 44-69256, and 44-68789 through 44-69256 canceled.

USN Culver TD2C-1

Nos. 69539 through 69739:	201
Nos. 75739 through 76138:	400
Nos. 83752 through 83991:	240
Nos. 119979 through 20338:	360

Culver XPQ-15 (USN TD3C)

In anticipation of the booming (hopefully) civilian market, Albert Mooney designed the sleek Model V (V for Victory), which borrowed from the LCA and the LAR but differed significantly in fuselage layout, which had a forward open canopy and the cockpit was level with the leading edge of the wing, giving the aircraft its characteristic appearance. It was powered by the 85-hp, four-cylinder, air-cooled, opposed Continental C85 engine that gave the Mk. V a speed of 125 mph and a range of 700 miles. A Simpli-Fly control system was installed to make flying as "easy as driving a car." However, the aircraft was overweight and the control system was susceptible to failure and the Model V was unable to compete in the post-war market and only 378 were built. A final model, the V-2, was designed to overcome some of the failings of the V, but it also failed. However, undeterred, Culver developed a completely new design as the XPQ-15 as a potential third generation target drone. The AAF bought two as the XPQ-15 with 200-hp Franklin O-405, six-cylinder, opposed, air-cooled engines. The USN also bought two as the XTD4C-1. After these four drones were delivered, the Culver Company declared bankruptcy in 1946, as its wooden airframes could not compete with the all-metal Cessna 120 in the civilian market.

The Superior Aircraft Company, division of the Priestly Hunt Aircraft Corporation, was formed in mid-1956 at Culver City, in an attempt to revive the Mk. V as the Superior Satellite, a two-seat, low-wing cabin monoplane derived from the Culver Model V with the 90-hp (up from 85-hp) Continental C90 engine. However, after forty had been built, Superior also went bankrupt.

After the Culver bankruptcy, Mooney, his brother, Art, Charles Yankey, and W. L. McMahon formed the new Mooney Aircraft Company in 1946, located at Wichita.

Culver XPQ-15 (USN TD3C). (*AAF*)

The first aircraft Mooney produced was the successful small single-seat Mooney Mite M-18 featuring a 25-hp Crossley auto engine and the now famous "backward" Mooney tail. It was the smallest, most inexpensive (in today's dollars), and considered the most efficient civilian aircraft ever built in quantity. After several reorganizations, Mooney International exists today as a Chinese-owned light aircraft manufacturing company located in Kerrsville, Texas.

McDonnell TD2D Katydid

During March 1941, McDonnell Aircraft, St. Louis, was awarded a contract for an unmanned radio-controlled target drone, designated as the XTD2D-1 for anti-aircraft and aerial gunnery practice. The 11-foot, 2-inch drone weighed 320 pounds and its mid-mounted wing spanned 12 feet. A unique feature was that its empennage consisted of two stabilizers joined at the tail to form a V and two movable surfaces called ruddvators (rudder and elevators) that performed both functions of lateral and vertical control by moving co-directionally, up and down for elevator control and left and right for rudder control. It was powered by a McDonnell XPJ40-MD-2 pulse jet mounted on top of the rear fuselage, which was similar to that pulse jet mounting on the German V-1. Its 8-inch pulse jet was capable of developing 115 pounds of thrust at sea level, giving it a maximum speed of 250 mph and an endurance of forty minutes. It could be either launched from the ground by a catapult or from underwing racks on Consolidated PBY Catalina flying boats. It was gyro-stabilized and controlled by radio command. At the end of its mission, the drone could be recovered by parachute.

McDonnell TD2D Katydid. (*USN*)

Testing at the Naval Air Missile Test Center, Point Mugu, was invaluable as it provided much information for future jet-propelled missiles. The Katydid entered service in 1942 where its ultimate use was for gunnery practice for AA crews and pilots and air crewmen. Production models were originally designated TD2D-1; however, when the Navy changed its designation system in 1946, the XTD2D-1 and TD2D-1 were redesignated as XKDD-1 and KDD-1, respectively. Later that year, the Navy changed McDonnell's manufacturer code letter from D, which had been shared with Douglas Aircraft, to H, and the KDD-1 was again redesignated, as KDH-1. A KDH-1 is displayed in the Steven F. Udvar-Hazy Center of the National Air and Space Museum, having been donated by the Navy in 1966.

Assault Drones (AD): War-Weary Drones

The AAF pursued a series of aerial torpedoes, under the general designation of Controllable Bomb, Ground Launched, ambiguously abbreviated as BQ. The BQ series included several fascinating configurations, including purpose-designed weapons and conversions, such as the Fairchild AT-21 twin-engined gunnery trainer and the single TDR-1 loaned from the Navy and evaluated as the XBQ-4. However, the most ambitious and best known of the BQ weapons were radio-controlled conversions of war-weary BQ-7 Boeing B-17 (mostly F models) and the BQ-8 Consolidated B-24 (mostly D models) bombers, packed with explosives.

USAAF Aphrodite Program

In its search for a powered bomb, the AAF considered using unmanned, remote-controlled training aircraft as a relatively inexpensive delivery vehicle, but these aircraft had a limited range and were too small to carry an effective bomb load. During January 1944, the Development Engineering Branch recommended the modification of the obsolete twin-engined Douglas B-18 bomber, its B-23 variant, and Douglas C-47 transports into powered bombs. These aircraft not only could carry a heavy bomb load under remote control but could accommodate the extra radio and ordnance specialists who would be necessary to arm the bombs and check that the radio control equipment was working properly before baling out and relinquishing control to operators in the monitoring controlling aircraft. However, the B-18 and B-23 were no longer being manufactured by Douglas and their limited numbers could jeopardize the continuation of the program if it were successful. The C-47 transport remained in production, but in 1944, the Skytrain was the workhorse transport in every combat theater and thus was in short supply so the AAF was reluctant to expend them as bombs.

A March 1944 Development Engineering Branch study had determined that battle-damaged B-17s or B-24s, so-called "war-weary" combat aircraft, were an alternative and constant source of large aircraft that could be used as powered bombs. War-weary or Category E aircraft were classified as BER (beyond economical repair) and were to be salvaged for parts only. However, while emphasis was placed on the basis that the aircraft were worn out, their engines, landing gear, and AFCE had to be judged in at least very good condition for their new purpose. These war-weary aircraft were soon being dubbed as Weary Willies, and by the summer of 1944, any program involving war-weary aircraft, such as Aphrodite or Castor, was called a Willie project. In the spring of 1944, the largest concentration of war-weary bombers meeting these requirements were battle-damaged B-17s and B-24s parked in 8th Air Force maintenance and repair depots throughout the U.K. While these aircraft would serve as the guided powered bombs, new and undamaged bombers were required for conversion into control mother aircraft. On June 24, 1944, the Special Weapons Branch began modifying six B-17Fs and six B-24Hs at an Air Service Command Maintenance Depot at Woodbridge, England. On June 1, Lt. Gen. James Doolittle, 8AF CG, informed Brig. Gen. Carl Spaatz, CO of the Strategic Air Forces, that he had two B-17 and two B-24 War Wearies, and two Droopsnoot P-38s available to be converted into control aircraft in time to participate in the TV guidance Castor program tests at the Proving Ground Command scheduled for later in the month.

Shortly after D-Day, the V-1 buzz bomb, the first of Germany's secret V-weapons, struck London. It was apparent to Gen. Eisenhower that for both military and political reasons, these weapons had to be quickly neutralized, and on June 18, Eisenhower met with British Prime Minister Winston Churchill and directed that the V-1 targets are to take first priority over everything except urgent requirements of the ground battle. Eisenhower's urgent V-1 target directive to his staff would include the June 19 authorization to the AAF Engineering Division at Wright Field to expedite development of all Castor aircraft and equipment. This authorization was provided through Technical Instruction No. CTI-1747, which stated that the project "was to have highest priority in order that shipments of the equipment for the control plane to combat theaters would be possible prior to 1 August 1944." CTI-1747 was to provide preliminary military requirements, which included the following:

1. The range of drone aircraft, after pilot bail out, was to be 600 miles.
2. The drone aircraft were to be able to operate at 25,000 feet altitude.
3. The drone aircraft were to have necessary servo mechanism to dive it from a 15–45-degree angle.
4. Each drone aircraft was to be equipped with BLOCK III television equipment.
5. The controls were to be designed to permit radio-controlled direction of drone aircraft to point targets.
6. The drone aircraft combat load was to be about 20,000 pounds.

By March 1944, air recon had taken an astonishing 1,250,000 aerial photos of nearly 100 suspected V-1 sites under construction in northern France and the Low Countries. So, targeting these V-1 launch sites, code named Noball, was not the problem, but destroying them was. With hundreds of buzz bombs being launched against England, even the most concerted efforts to accelerate the Castor program would take too long to provide operational powered bombs. If V-1 launching sites were to be neutralized quickly, more immediate action was necessary and Operation Aphrodite was born. Had the Germans not started launching their V-1 guided missiles against London on June 13, 1944, the Aphrodite program would certainly have required the usual three to six months to complete technical testing and another month or more for acceptance and tactical trials at the AAFTAC at Eglin.

Project A or Aphrodite, the Air Force's use of war-weary B-17s, was initiated on June 23, 1944 with the following message from Brig. Gen. Carl Spaatz to Gen. H. H. Arnold:

> Aphrodite is the code name which this headquarters will use to refer to the overall project of attacking targets by special techniques. Our first flight test with modified AZON units in war-weary airplanes demonstrated the practicability of this makeshift and we are going ahead immediately with four more war-wearies.
>
> USAAF, *Case History of Castor*
> Maxwell AFB, MF Reel A2082, A2083, and A2051

Unlike Castor, which was tested at the Eglin Proving Ground Command test facilities and received technical support from the Air Materiel Command, Aphrodite was an improvised program that utilized any available equipment and technical support available to the 8AF in England.

On June 20, 1944, Spaatz sent a priority report to Arnold stating that he considered that success was possible against V-1 sites if large enough loads of explosives could be placed with "extreme precision, namely within 10 to 20 feet of the aiming point."

Spaatz informed Arnold that he had directed that surplus VB-1 AZON guidance equipment be used to convert war-weary B-17s into powered bombs. Spaatz further stated that he had directed that the "urgency of this project is paramount and therefore only those equipment and crews which are immediately, repeat, immediately available should be selected." On June 24, Lt. Gen. Doolittle responded by directing the Third Bombardment Division to initiate a project to prove the tactical soundness of remotely controlled B-17 robot aircraft as weapons, to develop methods for their employment, and to test them in actual combat operations. Of course, Arnold, long a proponent of guided weapons, supported Spaatz and the resurgence of Aphrodite program.

As early as May 8, Doolittle had requested that twelve sets of equipment, including BLOCK III television apparatus for the drones, five sets of equipment for the controlling aircraft, and technical support personnel be dispatched to the 8AF as soon as practicable. On June 1, nearly two weeks before the start of the V-1 attacks, Doolittle had informed Spaatz that he had two B-17s, two B-24s, and two Droopsnoot P-38s available to be converted into Castor control aircraft and had designated six B-17G and six B-24J war-wearies to be used as powered bombs. Consequently, when Spaatz directed Doolittle to expedite the Aphrodite *Program*, much of the Castor equipment and personnel were already available.

The BLOCK III television equipment used was identical to that used in the GB, except that power was derived from the electrical system of the airplane, and a selsyn compass indicator was added to the camera. This compass projected a course-reading directly on the upper left-hand corner of the receiving monitor, superimposed on the picture information.

War-weary B-17s (designated as BQ-7s) and B-24s (designated as BQ-8s) were withdrawn from combat and stripped of all unnecessary equipment, armament, and armor plate and had the special Double AZON equipment installed. The first motherships were to be B-34 (ex-RAF Lockheed Ventura) bombers but were replaced before trials by B-17s designated as CQ-17s and later a B-24 (CQB-5) was also used. In operational sorties another B-17 was used for navigation and observation. Because of the vulnerability of the drone and mother, a fighter escort was required for each drone with one fighter assigned to shoot down any errant drone.

Two B-17-G Aphrodite Mothers: Boeing B-17G-65-BO (43-37637) (ex-332BS/94BG) Rotate U-Uncle and Boeing B-17G-70-BO (43-37793). Ten Aphrodite B-17 Double AZON Babies: Boeing B-17F-27-BO (41-24639) (ex-323BS/91BG) Careful Virgin transferred to the AFSC for the Aphrodite project. Send to V-1 installation sites in Pas-de-Calais, France, but exploded before reaching the target; Douglas-Long Beach B-17F-60-DL (42-3440) (ex-544BS-B/384BG Broadway Pink); Douglas-Long Beach B-17F-65-DL (42-346) (ex-407BS/92BG); Douglas-Long Beach B-17F-70-DL (42-3493) (ex-325BS/92 BG); Lockheed/Vega B-17F-45-VE (42-6080); Boeing B-17F-100-BO (42-30342); Boeing B-17F-110-BO (42-30595) (ex-560BS/388BG) OLINS 69ERS then Gremlin Gus II; Boeing B-17G-15-BO (42-31394); Douglas-Long Beach B-17G-10-DL (42-37760) (ex-532BS/381BG) Avenger; and Lockheed/Vega B-17G-1-VE (42-39835) (ex-351BG transferred to 388BG) Lost on mission Aphrodite August 4, 1944.

The tests were to be conducted by the Third Bomb Division with the 388th Bomb Group stationed at Khettishall to staff the operation and to provide base facilities at remote RAF Fersfield, an airfield specially selected for security reasons as it was located in a sparsely populated area of Norfolk. Initially, RAF Woodbridge had been selected because of its long runway, but damaged conventional aircraft returning from combat were to be diverted to Woodbridge for emergency landings and colliding with a drone loaded with 20,000 pounds of explosive caused some anxiety for planners. Aphrodite was under the overall command of Maj. Gen. Earle Partridge with Lt. Col. Roy Forrest acting as CO and Maj. James Henry Rand III, son of the president of Remington-Rand, heading the developmental team.

Maj. Rand was able to prepare the first Aphrodite powered bomb for testing in less than two days, and by July 1, both aircrew and technical personnel began training. Four controller aircrews received twenty-five hours of training on controlling the drones along with comprehensive training in target study and route navigation. Ten volunteer safety pilots and ten C-1 autopilot technicians received training on setting automatic flight controls in the drones and arming the explosives.

To control the B-17s and B-24s, Rand's team had modified the same control system used to control AZON free-falling guided bombs. The Aphrodite system used two AZON units, one to control azimuth and one to control range. This RAZON, range and azimuth system, was called Double AZON. The first test of this control system occurred in late June, when Rand in the controlling mother B-17 climbed to 20,000 feet while the drone circled at 2,000 feet waiting to be taken under control. However, the unpredictable English weather closed in and Rand lost the drone. After several anxious minutes, Rand's mother B-17 descended to 6,000 feet to make visual contact with the drone and was able to take control. Despite this initial setback, the succeeding tests were generally successful, with Rand controlling the test drones for two hours or more—executing various maneuvers. However, Rand did find that the mother aircraft tended to overrun the drone but determined the solution was to have mothership use of flaps, prop pitch, and S-ing maneuvers, etc. to remain behind the drone.

Two major concerns were that the Germans could jam the AZON radio frequencies and that Allied FM radio signals could possibility cause interference with control frequencies. Intelligence verified that AZON radio frequencies did not fall into the bands normally jammed by the Germans but required that great care would have to be exercised to ensure no friendly (Allied) spurious radio signals interrupted control over the unmanned guided aircraft, especially when loaded with explosives and still over friendly territory.

Initially, it was decided that the mother and drone should cross the Channel at a high altitude to remain out of friendly AA range. However, tests with sandbag-loaded B-l7s demonstrated that the bomber could not be put into a 30,000-foot dive as the faster the bomber descended, the more marked was its natural predisposition to level off due to the anti-dive tendency that Boeing had incorporated into its B-17s design. The Double AZON's servo-motors were not powerful enough to overcome this tendency. Low-level tests were conducted using an ACE (automatic control equipment) radio altimeter, which maintained the drone at 300 feet while the mother aircraft transmitted left or right steering signals to the automatic pilot. Once over the target, a radio signal was transmitted to overpower the ACE unit sending the drone diving into the target.

To aid in the visual tracking of the drone from the mothership, its upper wing surfaces were painted white or yellow. Smoke tanks, activated by the mothership, were installed on the wing tips or under the rear fuselage of the drone. The smoke tank was a modified 75-gallon fighter aircraft auxiliary fuel tank equipped with twin nozzled smoke generators attached underneath with a dispersion of 1.5 gallons per minute, remote-controlled via a solenoid that activated a radio valve controlled by the operator.

BQ-7/8 Radio Control Receiving and Transmitting Equipment

AN/ARW-1 and AN/ARW-18 Radio Control Receivers were selected as the FM receiving equipment of a system designed for remote control of BQ-7 (B-17) and BQ-8 (B-24) war-weary bombers. When used in conjunction with Radio Transmitting Set AN/ARW-18 and AN/ARW-1, 1A, or 1B, remote control could be operated from ground to air, or air to air, up to a normal range of 18 miles. The effective control range could be extended to 75 miles through use of an AM-33/ART RF Amplifier unit at the transmitter. Manual operation at the transmitter of the BC-756 Control Box resulted in the transmission to the aircraft of certain tones for each of the (ten) control movements or functions that may be desired (up, down, etc.). Receiver-Selector BC-617-T2 included an eight-channel audio filter selector circuit for discrimination between the various tones received. Relay Unit BC-622 passed control voltages to the automatic pilot from the receiver output. Although the altitude of the aircraft was normally controlled by the altimeter equipment in the aircraft, the altimeter setting could be overridden when necessary through Relay Box RE-20/ARW-1. Because of a shortage of equipment, only one drone was equipped with BLOCK III television while the remainder would be guided by the radio-controlled GB-8 glide bomb method.

Aphrodite/Castor Babies, Mothers, and Equipment

Above: This "Baby" (drone), formerly of the 95BG, has undergone Castor modification at Fersfield. It had its nose armament removed, the forward crew hatch door removed and an anterior wind spoiler installed, a TV antenna installed under the nose, and an egg-shaped smoke tank installed on the centerline under the wings. (*AAF*)

Below: The drone smoke tank was a modified 75-gallon auxiliary fighter fuel tank equipped with a smoke generator attached below the smoke tank. The tank was activated from the mother ship. (*AAF*)

Double AZON servo motor linkage to the throttle of the drone controlled to increase or decrease engine power settings. (*AAF*)

Ventral receiving antenna on drone. (*From AAF microfilm document*)

Dorsal receiving antenna on drone. (*From AAF microfilm document*)

Eureka AN/TPN-1 airborne radio beacon transponder installed in drone. (*From AAF microfilm document*)

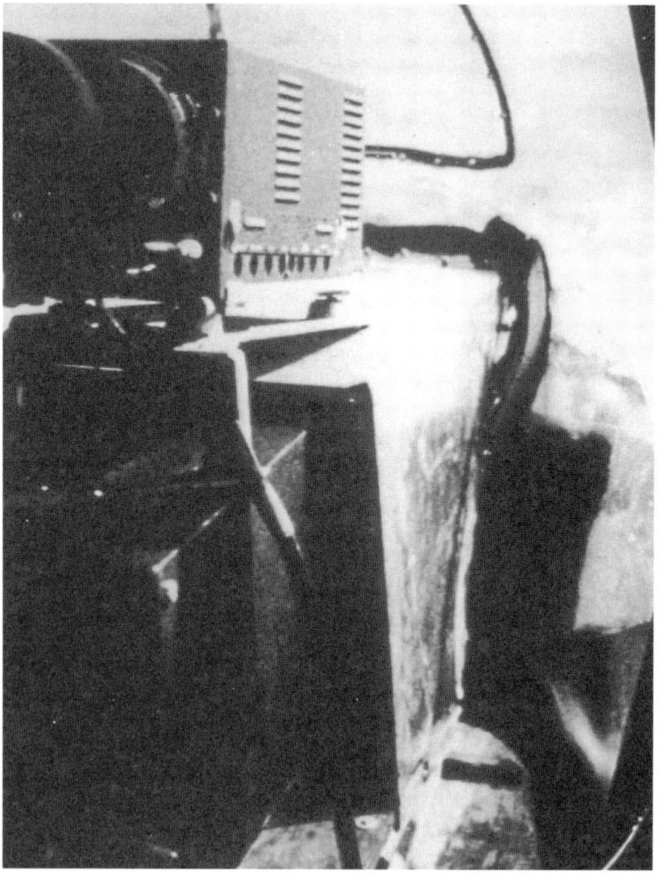

Left: Drone's BLOCK 1 CRV-59 TV camera installed on starboard side of the nose. (*From AAF microfilm document*)

Below: View on mother ship's TV monitor of drone TV camera transmission of the target. The photo has "SECRET" stamped on it, of which "ECR" can be seen superimposed on white building. (*From AAF microfilm document*)

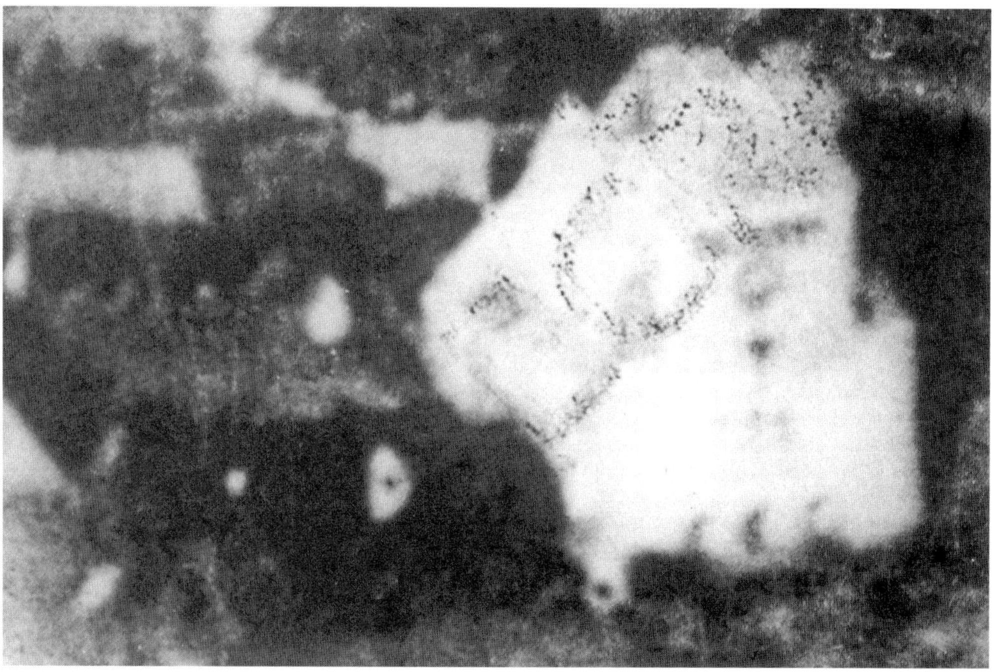

Above: Mother ship with modified nose to accommodate Baby controller and Rebecca AN/TPN-2 airborne interrogator antenna installed on the side of the fuselage to track the Eureka AN/TPN-1 airborne radio beacon transmissions. (*AAF*)

Below left: Exterior view of controller seated in the nose looking at 7-inch TV monitor. (*AAF*)

Below right: TV monitor with control box below. (*AAF*)

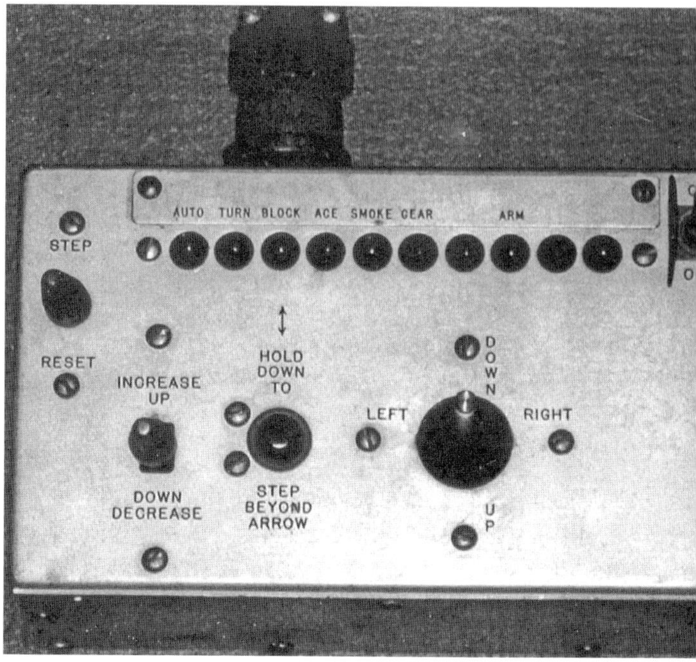

Above left: Control box with small joystick (center). (*AAF*)

Above right: Rebecca AN/TPN-2 airborne interrogator was a precursor of identification friend or foe (IFF) designed to keep track of the drone. (*AAF*)

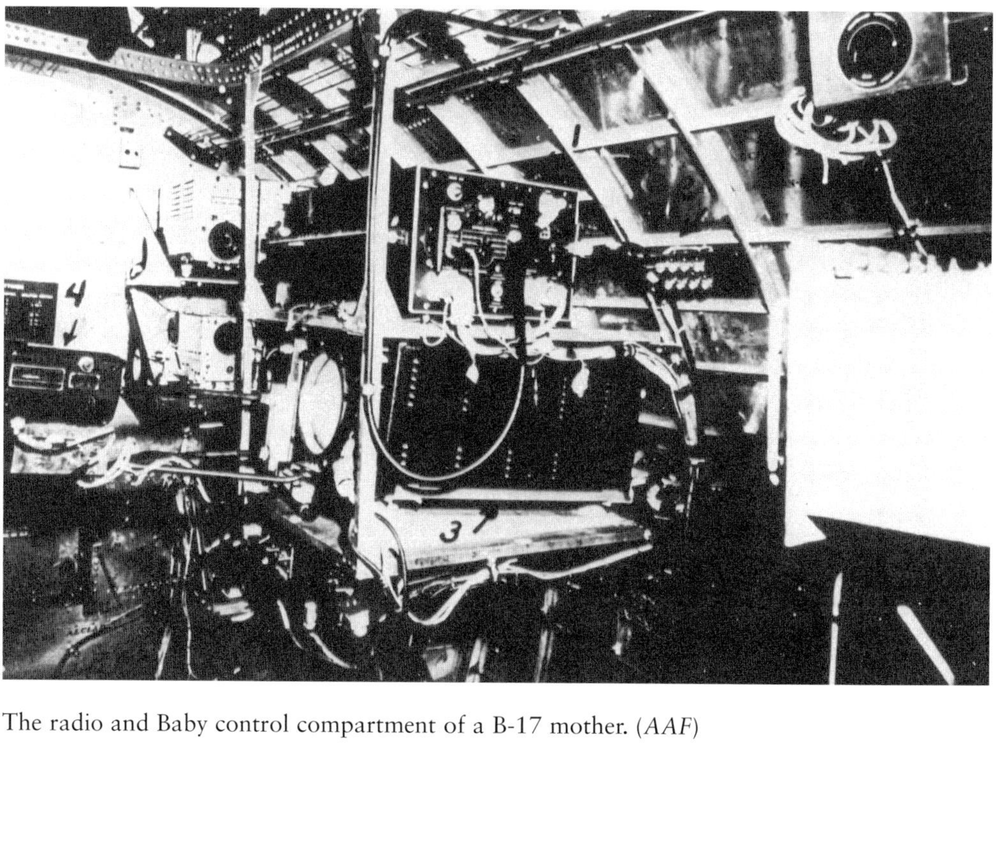

The radio and Baby control compartment of a B-17 mother. (*AAF*)

Aphrodite Mother and Baby Combat Technique

The AAF crew vernacular for the controlling aircraft was "Mother," while the drones were referred to as "Babies." The B-17 Babies selected for the project were stripped of about 9,000 pounds of their normal military equipment and equipped with the Double AZON radio-controlled flight system. In early trials, the two crewmen exited at 175 mph (paratroops in C-47s baled out at 90 mph) through the 2 by 2-foot navigator's hatch, which resulted in the loss of several pilots when they collided with a radio antenna (relocated later) upon baling out of the drone. Later, this hatch was increased in size, its door removed, and a wind deflector added. For safety, a static line was rigged to the main backpack parachute and a reserve chest pack was also worn.

The combat technique evolved for Aphrodite missions was to have a pilot assisted by an autopilot technician, to take the drone off the ground and climb up to an operational altitude of 2,000 feet. Observation and navigational B-17s with escorting fighters accompanied the mission along with photo-recon P-38s to take movies and stills. Mosquitoes were to photograph the parachuting drone pilots and several light liaison aircraft were to track the parachuting pilots. The drone was flown on

Above left: Two flanking B-17 motherships take control of the war-weary B-17 drone heading for its target. The drone pilot had gone through his check list and armed 20,000 pounds of explosives crammed throughout the bomber and can be seen in his parachute (lower right/ arrows) after baling out. (*From AAF movie still*)

Above right: After his responsibilities were completed, the drone pilot strapped on his parachute and dropped through the navigator's hatch. A static line was rigged to the main backpack parachute and a reserve chest pack was also worn. (*AAF*)

a rectangular course so that the autopilot could be tuned after which the autopilot technician would bale out. The pilot would decrease the drone's speed to 175 mph and place it into a gentle dive, which would eventually reach 300 feet where the ACE would take control as it crossed the English Channel. As the drone was descending, the pilot set a ten-minute clock on the instrument panel, checked the safety lights on the electrical fusing device, and then completed the fusing circuit by plugging in two jacks. The pilot pulled a lanyard to arm the fourteen impact fuses leading to 370 50-pound boxes containing 18,500 pounds (well over manufacturer's maximum gross weight) of explosive stowed in every available space in the bomber: twenty-five boxes on the flight deck; 245 in the bomb bay; and 100 in the radio compartment.

On July 8, 1944, Gen. Spaatz had estimated that a total of sixty-five drones would be required to eliminate all the V-weapon sites in a series of attacks. Twenty-one were to be fully loaded with jellied gasoline (napalm) whose oxygen-consuming fires would suffocate the occupants of the underground sites, while the other forty-four were to be loaded with Nitrostarch, an explosive closely related to nitrocellulose. Nitrostarch was similar to dynamite but did not include the highly sensitive nitroglycerin as a component. However, later, Torpex was used as it was less sensitive and, pound for pound, gave a 50 percent increase in explosive power over TNT. The crews of drones scheduled to carry a cargo of loosely-packed jerry cans filled with jell-gas (napalm) were very unenthusiastic and further development of carrying methods were required. After his responsibilities were completed, the pilot donned his parachute and exited over the south coast of Britain with the remote control operator in the mothership at 20,000 feet assuming control of the BQ-7. Mother would then guide it to the target area over the Continent and lock its controls into a crash course into the target before returning to return to its U.K. base.

First Aphrodite Mission: August 4, 1944

On August 27, 1943, 8AF B-17s, armed with 2,000-pound conventional bombs, attacked a large underground concrete V-weapon facility under construction at Watten, a few miles inland from the Pas-de-Calais. Most of the bombs missed, but those that did hit the target did not penetrate the thick reinforced concrete structure. The second 8AF mission against this site on September 7 was just as futile. By March 1944, three more large concrete underground V-weapon sites in northern France were completed or near completion at Mimoyecques, Siracourt, and Wizernes. The possible, but unknown, use of these four giant sites caused great consternation among the AAF high command.

The operational plan for the first Aphrodite mission allocated 250 RAF bombers to conduct a diversionary raid north of Paris just before the Aphrodite raid, which was scheduled for 3 p.m. The four drone Babies were each to have a primary and backup Mother aircraft with sixteen P-38s scheduled to fly cover for the Mothers. There were to be observation and navigational B-17s with escorting fighters for each. Also accompanying the mission were four photo-recon P-38s to take movies and stills, two Mosquitoes to photograph the drone pilots parachuting, and several light liaison aircraft to follow the parachuting pilots to their landing. The entire operation was to be covered by two Spitfire squadrons. British AA defenses, which had become trigger happy since the buzz bomb siege on England, were alerted. All Mother aircraft were instructed to crash any malfunctioning drones into the North Sea and to call in fighters to destroy drones that could not be controlled.

On August 4, the first Aphrodite mission commenced when four drones took off from Fersfield toward northern France to attack the giant sites at Mimoyecques, Siracourt, Watten, and Wizernes. Lt. Gen. Jimmy Doolittle and Maj. Gen. Earl Partridge followed the progress of the mission while flying in P-38s. The first drone, No. 835, carrying the only BLOCK III television equipment available to the Aphrodite program, flew its specified rectangular course after take-off to allow the autopilot technician to check out instrumentation and prepare the autopilot and ACE before baling out. The pilot, Lt. John Fisher, finished his assignments and sent the code word "taxi-soldier" for James Rand in the mother aircraft to take control. As Fisher tried to leave the drone, there was a malfunction and it went into a steep climb, stalled, and spun to earth carrying Fisher to his death along with it. The drone crashed into a wooded area near Suffolk in an enormous explosion marked by a large 25 by 35-foot crater, which was 5 feet deep, demolishing the trunks of large, grown oaks for 200 feet around.

The second drone, No. 342, was assigned to attack the giant site near Watten, which was protected by its massive ferro-concrete dome. The autopilot technician and the pilot vacated the drone by parachute without incident and it was guided by experienced AZON bomb controller Glen Hargis. Upon descending to 300 feet, the drone encountered an Allied balloon barrage over the coast, which had been forgotten to be removed. Somehow Hargis guided the drone through the maze of cables and chains without mishap using only the slowly-responding servo-control for left or right maneuvers. The drone continued to respond to Hargis' signals *en route* to the target, but when he toggled the switch to overpower ACE to apply full down elevator, there was no response to dive the drone into the target. Despite the loss of surprise and the resulting heavy flak, Hargis turned No. 342 drone around for another run at the target again with the same no response by the elevators to the dive command. The alternate mother was summoned to try a different set of controls, but these also did not activate the defective elevators. Hargis was instructed to destroy the faulty drone so he flew it over a particularly harassing German flak battery. On the first fly past, the drone escaped unscathed and Hargis again flew it directly over the flak battery whose accuracy was much improved this time. There was a great ball of fire and explosion that pommeled the surprised flak battery.

The third drone, No. 461, took-off piloted by 2Lt. Frank Houston, and at the co-pilot's autopilot control was Tech. Willard Smith who parachuted to safety after completing his duties as did Houston. The mothership, with Rand aboard as controller, headed toward the Wizernes V-Rocket site, which was misreported to be protected by 400 flak guns. On the unhindered approach to the target just at the moment for the full down elevator dive on the target, No. 461 passed into a small cloud causing Rand to lose sight of the target. Nonetheless, he toggled the dive switch by guesstimate, but the drone had over flown and it exploded about a quarter-mile away without causing any damage to the target.

Photo stills from movie photographed by recon Mosquito of B-17 Baby exploding about a quarter mile away from its Wizernes V-Rocket site target without causing any damage to the target during the first Aphrodite mission on August 4, 1944. (*From AAF movie stills*)

After its capture, it was found that the persistent air attacks with heavy conventional and super-heavy Tallboy bombs so hammered the Wizernes site area that by the spring of 1944 craters and landslides made further work on the project impossible. (*AAF*)

The fourth drone, piloted by 1Lt. Cornelius Engles with Tech./Sgt. Clifford Parsons, took off at 4 p.m. for Mimoyecques, and both parachuted from the drone without incident, though both were injured during their parachute landings—Engles seriously. Control of the drone was passed to the B-24 mother with Hargis on board, and it was guided and lined up perfectly on the target. The drone instead of remaining at 300 feet climbed to 600 feet and Hargis tried to dive the drone back to the preset ACE 300-foot altitude. The B-17 descended to 300 feet but would not level out and crashed about 500 yards short of the aiming point in a spectacular, but ineffective explosion.

The first Aphrodite mission was, at best, inauspicious, with three drones missing their V-site targets and one blowing a huge crater into the English Suffolk countryside, Lt. Fisher was killed, five parachutists were injured, two hospitalized, and, to add insult to injury, Hargis mothership was nearly shot down by British anti-aircraft gunners. The rendezvous, control handoff, and arming procedures functioned reliably, but several changes in the drone crew bale-out procedures were needed. The use of two motherships for each drone was a safeguard against losing control over the drone in case of malfunction of the motherships' control equipment. It also provided a second aircraft to visually keep track of the drone, especially if the lead mothership, flying at 20,000 feet, was separated by clouds from the lower-flying drone. The second mother could then descend and monitor the drone until the lead mothership regained visual contact. The Aphrodite missions required large amounts of intelligence on each of its targets, which further overloaded Allied intelligence resources, and it was recommended that future Aphrodite missions have only one assigned target. Aphrodite's major advantage was that conventional bombing missions included many bombers striking one target, while an Aphrodite mission had one or two drones strike one target with a large explosive load, expectantly with great (but future) accuracy.

Second Aphrodite Mission: August 6, 1944

On August 6, after forty-eight hours of round-the-clock adjustments, two drones were readied to attack Watten on the second Aphrodite mission. At 10:50 a.m., the first drone, *Franklin Yellow*, was to take-off followed ten minutes later by *Franklin White*. Each was to be controlled by its own mother and alternate mother. The first drone, well over manufacturer's maximum gross weight, carrying 18,000 pounds of Torpex, rather than the standard 20,000 pounds of nitrostarch, was to crash into the Watten's dome causing the cement casement to crack and fissure and then *Franklin White* carrying combustibles would follow it to crash into the site pushing burning jelled gasoline and incendiaries through the newly created fissures.

A diversionary raid of 100 RAF bombers was sent over the target to occupy the heavy German AA defenses. Almost immediately after take-off, *Franklin Yellow* encountered an unexpected assemblage of B-24 Liberators, which were rendezvousing for an unrelated bombing mission. Pilot 1Lt. Joseph Andrecheck aided by Tech./Sgt. Raymond Healy managed to bank their heavily overloaded B-17, piled high with boxes of Torpex, through the B-24 rendezvous area and then miraculously got it back to level flight. Although it was not uncommon for B-17s to carry a few pounds over max gross, that weight was positioned in the bomb bays therefore at the bottom of the fuselage where this weight acted to stabilize the aircraft much like a sailboat's keel. But the explosives in the drone were piled 4–5 feet above the center of gravity and a tight turn could throw the aircraft out of control.

During the hectic maneuvering, *Franklin Yellow*'s motherships lost sight of it, but after a few anxious minutes, it was spotted again with the crew still onboard not wanting to bale out, thus leaving the drone without control. Mother found the Baby circling and once positive control had been established, the crew baled out without incident. The drone was successfully controlled over the North Sea as briefed but then abruptly began a sharp turn to its port and rolled over, with neither mother able to correct drone's course before it crashed into the sea

Franklin White, piloted by 2Lt. Frank Houston, carried nine incendiary bombs in the nose, thirty-five in the pilot's compartment, 116 in the radio operator's compartment, and twenty in the ball turret. All these pyrotechnics were augmented by 830 gallons of inflammable jellied gasoline in the bomb bay tanks. Tests conducted at Eglin Field disclosed that occupants of the target site would suffocate if the exits were blocked by flames. After an uneventful take-off and mother rendezvous, the crew baled out ahead of schedule, and the drone came under Hargis' control. Hargis discovered that the drone drifted toward the right because the autopilot apparently had been incorrectly set, possibly because the pilot and tech. sergeant had baled out prematurely. Hargis passed control to the alternate mother and the drone made a 360-degree turn, causing

Hargis to think the new controller was trying a different heading to try to unlock the autopilot. But the drone then turned again and headed toward London! Hargis tried to contact the alternate mother but received no answer indicating that control had not been passed. Meanwhile, *Franklin White* disappeared into the haze and the escorting fighters were quickly radioed to find and destroy the missing bomber. Finally, the tail gunner in the observer B-24 spotted the drone circling the suburbs of Ipswich, and Hargis again attempted hard left controlling maneuvers, which were only marginally successful—on each circuit, the drone moved slightly farther away from Ipswich. A cloud bank moved in from the North Sea and again *Franklin White* disappeared, and another frantic search began. Hargis briefly spotted the errant drone over the sea and decided to risk diving the drone to its destruction and, fortunately, the tail gunner was able to report a huge flaming explosion in the sea below him.

During these two missions, very heavy interference was encountered in the control aircraft, virtually rendering the picture was useless, although the controller had occasional glimpses of the target. The observation aircraft, however, trailing behind received an excellent picture during the entire flight. It was determined that a phenomena called multipath reflection caused the loss of synchronism between the picture in the drone and the control aircraft. These reflections were finally reduced to a minimum by relocating the position of the television receiving antenna on the control aircraft and underscored the need for a wide ratio between the strengths of direct and reflected signals.

In a turbulent post-mission debriefing, Gen. Doolittle angrily returned the Aphrodite to training status. Also, a few hours later, Third Bomb Division H.Q. ordered the group to abandon the Double AZON system as it was considered too dangerous, especially since it was not designed for this use. Thus, the Air Force's drone project was canceled and the fate of America's first drone program, Aphrodite, was passed to the Navy's Special Attack Unit No. 1 (SAU1), under the code name Anvil, which was a parallel project.

U.S. Navy Anvil Drone Project

Doolittle's grounding order for the AAF Aphrodite program did not pertain to the USN Anvil component attached to Aphrodite. On July 6, 1944, eleven officers and sixteen enlisted men had commenced an expedited drone program at the Naval Aircraft Factory (NAF) as the Navy Special Attack Unit (SAU-1) under the Commander Air Force, Atlantic (ComAirLant), with Cdr. James Smith as the CO. They were to adapt the results of the Navy's previous experimental drone programs, to use the PB4Y-1 Privateer (the Navy's version of the B-24) as the assault drone. Within a week, a factory-fresh PB4Y was divested of all non-essentials and a control and arming panel was installed to attack German V-1 and V-2 launching sites.

The PB4Y and a R4D transport (Navy version of the C-47) were ferried from the U.S. to the AAF Aphrodite drone base at Fersfield, U.K., without incident, but the two PV Ventura motherships became stranded by storms in Greenland for three weeks. Meanwhile, Cdr. Smith and AAF base CO Lt. Col. Roy Forrest were trying to resolve Army-Navy differences and jealousies at various levels at Fersfield. The Navy's control system used television control and was much more sophisticated than the AAF's Double AZON system. A RC-487 television transmitter and a Eureka AN/TPN-1 airborne radio beacon were installed in the drones. A Rebecca AN/TPN-2 airborne interrogator was installed on the motherships to track the Eureka transmissions. In addition to being controllable on the vertical and horizontal axes like the Double AZON, Anvil also controlled an increase or decrease in engine power settings. The Anvil drones could automatically assume straight and level flight when control contact was interrupted or on the controller's command. They could transmit a radio beacon signal, code named Rebecca, which provided controllers a relative bearing to the drone from the mother. The control equipment was able to direct ten drone functions including steering, diving and climbing, varying speed, and activating the ACE from the PB4Y. The controller not only had a televised image from the nose of the drone but also a second televised image was provided of the compass in the drone, which allowed the controller to quickly determine the exact heading of the drone; this was essential during final guidance to the target. The drones also could trail colored smoke on command to help the controller in visually acquiring them in hazy conditions.

The arming of the explosives would be completed remotely from the mothership after the crew baled out. A FM radio signal would cause a solenoid to release the safety pins from the inertial switches to arm the system. The chance of a stray FM signal activating the system had been considered as a possibility, though a remote one. In tests at the NAF back in Philadelphia, this remote possibility had occurred and subsequently a safety pin had been installed, which was to be removed by the pilot prior to baling out. Also, for another check against accidental arming, frequency searching recon aircraft flew over both English and Nazi-occupied territory in search of FM signals on the drone's intended FM channel but none were found. Also, unlike the Air Force drones, the Navy pilots flew their drones fully-loaded in test flights, enabling the pilots to become accustomed to the heavy flying characteristics of the loaded drone. The test loading of the Anvil drone was equal to 20,000 pounds of Torpex loaded into 335 boxes: 210 in the bomb bay, 100 in the radio room, and twenty-five next to the pilot in the co-pilot's seat position.

First Navy Anvil Mission: August 12, 1944

The first Navy mission was scheduled for August 11, 1944 but was scrubbed due to bad weather and reset for the next day when the PB4Y drone No. 32271, dubbed *Zootsuit Black*, was loaded with Torpex while technicians checked the two PV-1 Ventura motherships: *Zootsuit Pink* and *Zootsuit Red*. The mission was to include a B-17 radio relay ship, four P-51 Mustangs to fly cover, two P-38s, and two Mosquito weather and observer aircraft along with several liaison aircraft to identify the parachutists jumping from *Zootsuit Black*. An AAF B-17 navigation ship would lead the drone to the rendezvous point where it would be acquired by lead mother.

The mission plan was uncomplicated with the PV-1s scheduled to take-off after learning that the weather over the target was clear. Upon reaching the rendezvous point at 2,000 feet, the mothers were to clear the drone for take-off from Fersfield. *Zootsuit*

Black, piloted by Joseph Kennedy, the future president's older brother, and crewed by Lt. Bud Willy, the executive technical officer, was to fly a check out course under the control of Lt. John Anderson in Lt. Hugh Lyon's mothership *Zootsuit Red*. The drone crew was to bale out and drone control was then given to Lt. Harry Wherry's mother, *Zootsuit Pink*, whose controller, Lt. John Demlein, was to guide the drone over the Channel to an area 6 miles from the French Coast. To avoid anti-aircraft fire, Wherry was to return control to Lyons/Anderson flying 10 miles behind. Controller Anderson was then to guide the drone into the Mimoyecques site via TV control.

Due to morning fog and haze over the target, the mission was postponed until early evening. The take-off and initial control went well, but as Anderson was to relinquish control to Demlein in preparation for the bale out leg of the mission, a huge double explosion disintegrated the drone, Kennedy, Willy, and seven years of Navy experimentation. The final irony in the mission's failure was when Allied troops overran these four hard V-sites soon afterward, making their destruction by the Anvil drones unnecessary.

A comprehensive post-mission investigation suggested thirteen possible causes for the explosion, and some, such as the possibility of friendly fire from British AA batteries or friction caused by the shifting of the explosive load, were quickly and easily discounted, while others, such as the possibility of an onboard fire or static electricity, required more time to eliminate as a cause. Finally, three possibilities were culled out: radio jamming or interference, a possible short circuit in the arming panel, and the inherent instability of the Torpex explosive, which also were all discounted. The investigation concluded that the most likely cause was the overheating of the arming circuit holding relay, which was designed to prevent the accidental tripping of the detonators. The holding relays had been hastily developed by the NAF and designed to be activated as the mother transmitted the arming signal to the drone. In this way, the relays would permit the electronic detonators to arm but protected them from being accidentally fired by spurious FM radio signals. Once the holding relays were activated, only the physical G-forces caused by impact with the target or the ground would cause the detonators to fire and explode the 20,000 pounds of Torpex.

Second Anvil Mission: September 3, 1944

By September, after the breakout from the Normandy beachhead beginning on July 25, ground forces had overrun V-weapon Noball launching sites in northern France and the four hard sites previously targeted by Aphrodite. With these targets no longer available, the Anvil detachment believed they could justify their agenda in future missions against dams, canals, locks, viaducts, marshaling yards, and submarine pens. The next attack was scheduled for early September against the U-Boat pens carved into the cliffs of Heligoland, two small islands located 30 miles off the German coast, 300 miles across the North Sea.

The replacement PB4Y drone arrived, not factory-fresh like the first, but war-weary and in need of immediate renovation. The first step was to replace the disastrous defective electronic arming panel that doomed the first Anvil mission. It was replaced by the manual lanyard system used in the Air Forces early Aphrodite B-17s and, accordingly, the drone pilot's last act before baling out would be to physically pull a bundle of lanyards to arm the firing mechanism. The PB4Y was also thoroughly inspected, engines changed, all control surface cables replaced, new tires installed, and the arming wires sheathed in aluminum conduit.

The mission was postponed several times due to poor weather, but in the morning of September 3, the drone, piloted by Lt. Ralph Spalding, flying alone with no technician, completed a flawless take-off. Sixteen P-51 escorts, a photo recon Mosquito, a weather Mosquito, two P-38 photo ships, a P-38 radio signal search aircraft, and three B-17s to be used for observation, radio message relay, and navigation joined the mother, which was flying 200 feet over the drone flying at 2,000 feet. There was to be no diversionary bombing raid. The usual hour of instrument checking had been canceled to eliminate the flying time of the explosive-laden drone over heavily populated eastern England and to minimize the radio signals that could be picked up by Nazi jamming stations. Spalding handed over control to the mother PV piloted by Wherry and controlled by Demlein and then successfully baled out over England. The 300-mile flight across the North Sea to Heligoland encountered a squall that caused the second mothership, piloted

The Anvil mission of September 3 was aimed at the U-Boat pens cut into the cliffs of Heligoland 300 miles away across the North Sea. The mission's TV system went dead and the drone was dumped and exploded on a coal pile. (*From USN movie still*)

by Lyon and crewed by controller Anderson, to lose their VHF radio, which was to be used to transfer control of the drone from Demlein to Anderson 5 miles from the target. Unable to warn Demlein of the circumstances, Anderson blinked an Aldis Lamp message N-O/V-H-F at the Wherry/Demlein mother aircraft, but the message was not understood. As the Heligoland cliffs came into view, Demlein tried to contact Anderson on the VHF to transfer control but was unsuccessful. Demlein instructed pilot Wherry to stay on course as he watched through his TV monitor to observe the drone fly through flak puffs. When the U-boat pens came into view, the drone was off course to the right, probably due to flak damage, and did not respond to Demlein's correction. Unfortunately, due to poor TV picture quality, the controller misidentified the breakwater on nearby Dune Island for the breakwater on Heligoland, but within seconds, the television picture went blank, probably due to a hit by anti-aircraft fire and Demlein toggled the dump control and ordered Wherry to climb away. Simultaneously, Anderson, not knowing Demlein was controlling the drone, also continued to follow the drone's course through his TV monitor, controlling it also. As the picture faded from his screen, Anderson also toggled the dump control. Both mothers turned from the target, Wherry/Demlein climbing through flak a few hundred feet above the Heligoland cliffs and Lyon/Anderson fleeing 20 miles behind. A large mushroom cloud was observed, but the outcome of the attack would have to wait for the P-38 Droopsnoot photo recon aircraft to bring back photos. The next morning, SAU1 found that its second Anvil mission had destroyed a large coal pile, scattering coal dust over the island and had added a 60-foot-wide, 12-foot-deep crater to the much-attacked island's collection of bomb craters.

The first Navy Anvil mission on August 11, 1944 to attack the Mimoyecques V-weapon site via TV control was piloted by Lt. Joseph Kennedy. There was a malfunction that caused a huge explosion of the drone's 10 tons of explosive and the future president's older brother and son of the influential U.S. Ambassador to England was killed. (*USN*)

The expense of the Anvil program and the resulting failures gave the anti-drone contingent in the Navy Department reason to cancel the program. Another compelling reason for cancellation was if the true circumstances of Joseph Kennedy Junior's death were revealed, his father, the very influential and irascible Joseph Kennedy, Sr., would raise holy hell and heads would roll throughout the Navy Department. To placate old man Kennedy, a Medal of Honor was requested for Joe Junior's heroic exploit of being blown up; however, a Navy Cross for him and Willy were approved instead. A destroyer (DD 850) that later stopped Russian ships during the Cuban Missile Crisis was also named after Joe Jr. Future President John F. Kennedy was also recommended for the Medal of Honor for his more heroic PT-109 exploits, but he also was awarded the Navy Cross instead.

The AAF Castor Drone Contingent

After the Navy left Fersfield, the five mothership crews of the departed James Rand remained behind along with a new group of technicians from Wright Field. This group used a TV guidance system designated as Castor, which was virtually identical to the Navy's system. Lt. Col. Dale Anderson was the brilliant new technical head of the Castor contingent and was aided by Peter Murray, a civilian electronics genius. To improve Castor's chances for success, using the lessons learned from the previous Anvil failures, they added several innovative concepts. The controller was now able to view the drones compass through his TV monitor to determine its exact bearing. The drones were equipped with all-weather electronic navigation equipment to prevent the loss of control. Also, a P-47 fighter drop tank was again converted into a smoke-emitting apparatus with radio-controlled on/off switches to allow the drone to be followed more easily by the controller.

Lt. Col Roy Forrest, Fersfield CO, had expected the Air Force program to be canceled after its failures and especially after the Navy's failures and cancellation. But scuttlebutt had it that Aphrodite was Hap Arnold's pet project and no one was going to take his toy away from him. Arnold had approved 500 Castor M (missile) and 100 Castor C (control) B-17s and B-24s and modification kits all to be ready by November 1, 1944. The Castor M B-17G's code was BQ7 and the B-24J's was BQ8 while the Castor C B-17 code was CQB4, the B-24 was CQB5, and the P-38 was CQB6. The Castor C aircraft, fifty B-17Gs and fifty B-24Js, were to be modified in America at the Birmingham, Alabama, Modification Center, requiring 200 man-hours for the first several aircraft and then decreasing with subsequent modifications.

A block of twenty B-17s were modified to Castor drone specifications, but only eleven were deployed and operational: Boeing B-17F-90-BO (42-30180); Boeing B-17F-100-BO (42-30363) (Ex 803BS (P)); Lockheed/Vega B-17G-1-VE (42-39827); Boeing B-17F-85-BO (42-30039) (Ex 803BS (P)); Douglas-Long Beach B-17G-10-DL (42-37743) (Ex 803BS (P)); Boeing B-17F-85-BO (42-30066) (Ex 803BS (P)); Douglas-Long Beach B-17F-60-DL (42-3438); Lockheed/Vega B-17G-1-VE (42-39824); Boeing B-17F-100-BO (42-30353) (Ex 803BS (P)); Boeing B-17F-90-BO (42-30178); and Boeing B-17F-95-BO (42-30237).

Five Castor Motherships: Boeing B-17G-75-BO (43-37946); Boeing B-17G-75-BO (43-37953); Boeing B-17G-75-BO (43-37962); Boeing B-17G-75-BO (43-38006); and Boeing B-17G-80-BO (43-38081).

Forrest was intrigued by the prospect of attacking the German battleship *Tirpitz* that had taken refuge in Norway's Alten Fjord. To placate Arnold, Forrest had concocted a plan using British hydrostatic bombs packed in a B-17 drone, which was to crash land and settle next to the battleship. The Hydrobombs were to be set to explode simultaneously underwater from the sunken B-17 and rupture the battleship's hull. However, the Hydrobombs were too large to fit into a B-17's bomb bay, even if there was equipment available to load them. After consulting Boeing Company representatives, the top of the B-17 fuselage was removed and the bombs were lifted by a cherry picker-type crane that gingerly lowered 26,000 pounds of Hydrobombs into the aircraft. An open cockpit was also created so that the two-man crew could exit the plane with minimum delay once they had completed their tasks. As the cockpit top was also removed, Forrest dubbed the chopped-top B-17 as the *Roadster*. However, when the British learned of this huge and lethal load, they refused permission for the aircraft to take-off from populated British soil. At least this was the official explanation as, shortly afterward, the British announced that on November 12, 1944, thirty Lancasters from No. 9 Squadron, loaded with huge 12,000-pound Tallboy bombs, had sunk not only the *Tirpitz* but also this Aphrodite scheme.

First Castor Mission: September 11, 1944

Castor's immediate problem was the lack of suitable targets. On September 11, the Castor group was briefed to repeat the previous three September Anvil attacks on the submarine pens at Heligoland. The B-17F (42-30180) drone, piloted by Richard Lindahl and co-piloted by Donald Sells, took-off at 6 p.m., but the mission began badly after Lindahl completed his responsibilities but was killed when his parachute failed to open. A *post-mortem* determined he had broken his back when the parachute static line wrapped around him as he fell through the escape hatch. Sells then baled out and landed without mishap. The primary mothership, this time a B-17, had Wilfred Tooman piloting and John Anderson controlling. Both drone and the primary mother flew at 2,500 feet with the second mother 2 miles astern. Sudden, heavy AA fire caused Tooman to violently dive his mother aircraft to wave top level but lost the drone in the process. Anderson activated the smoke release on the drone and was able to pick up it up, flying 5 miles ahead. However, by then it was the time for the drone to turn on its course toward the U-boat pens, but Anderson was too far behind to execute the turn visually. He turned the TV monitor on and the drone's compass appeared. The experienced Anderson deftly maneuvered the drone to the desired heading via the TV monitor and control box. The ACE was activated and held the drone at a steady 250 feet. After 320 miles, the drone's TV cameras focused on Heligoland's cliffs and soon Anderson was able to view the target's various identifying landmarks on his monitor. As the U-Boat pens came into view, he turned ACE off and readied the dive controls, which would crash the Torpex-laden B-17 into the pens. Tooman

Above and below: "Roadster" was a one-of-a-kind B-17 that had the cockpit and upper fuselage removed to have 26,000 pounds of hydrobombs were lowered into the aircraft to attack on the German battleship *Tirpitz*. The aircraft was never used as the British refused permission for it to take-off with huge and lethal load that could endanger surrounding English countryside. (*USN*)

then viewed the drone's right wing hit by flak setting it on fire, causing the U-Boat pens began to disappear out of the side of his TV screen, veering off course only a quarter-mile from the target. When he tried to correct, the pens disappeared from the screen altogether and then the picture went dark. The drone crashed putting a large indentation in the cliffs about 200 yards to the right of pen's doors. Post-mission examination suggested that had the drone continued on course for only fifteen seconds longer, it would have hit the doors directly. So, the result of this mission was that, at least, it did hit Heligoland Island and duplicated the September 3 Anvil mission, destroying some barracks and yet another large pile of coal. The frustrated Roy Forrest had had enough and transferred back to America.

Second Castor Mission: September 14, 1944

In mid-September, the Castor targets were amended to attack vital German oil production and storage facilities that had become an 8AF priority. It was considered that drone could be controlled to crash its 20,000 pounds of Torpex close enough to oil storage tanks to rupture them, causing enormous fires. On September 14, two mothers controlling one drone each, B-17F (230363) and B-17G (239627), attacked a large oil refinery near Hemmingstedt, Germany, 376 miles distant. Both mothers rendezvoused with and were able to gain control of their drones after the safety pilot and technical sergeant baled out. Approaching the target, one mothership controller lost the drone's television image and tried to guide the drone to the target visually, but, having little experience with this method, the controller released the drone at the target too late and it overflew it by over a mile. It was later determined that the erratic television picture was caused by improper tuning of the television receiver by the radio operator. The second drone was guided by the lower mothership to the coast and was passed to the control of the high mothership at 16,000 feet. The drone's Rebecca radio beacon system malfunctioned and the drone was unable to transmit a radio direction signal, making it necessary to keep the drone in visual contact to guide it to the target. The high mother's pilot was about to overfly the drone and made a 360-degree turn, during which the controller lost sight of the drone in his television monitor due haze and sun. The drones smoke generator failed to ignite and the escorting fighters were ordered to begin a search, concerned that drone loaded with fuel could deviate back over friendly territory, leaving the controller with no choice but to dive the drone into the North Sea.

Third Castor Mission: October 15, 1944

With two abject failures, the Castor operations were postponed for a month to make necessary equipment and technique adjustments and modifications, particularly given the impending fall and winter bad weather. The danger of bale out by the drone crews was a problem that needed addressing. The solution was to pad and increase the size of the escape hatch and to use a static line to automatically pull the parachute from the pack as the drone crew jumped. A bizarre suggestion to have the drone crew slide down a rope from the drone to board the mothership in midair was quickly rejected. A television image of not only the drone's compass but also of the airspeed and altimeter was recommended as was the installation of the new Black Maria radar beacon on the drone that would allow it to be controlled in any weather.

The Heligoland U-boat pens were attacked again on October 15. Since the island was heavily defended by German AA batteries, twenty 452nd Bomb Group B-17s were directed to bomb the area fifteen minutes before the first drone arrived. The B-17s and two drones, B-17F (42-30039/former 384BG)) and B-17G (42-37743/ former 94BG), took-off in quickly deteriorating weather. The 452nd diversionary B-17s had to bomb through a solid undercast cloud using radar. As the first drone approached the target below the cloud deck, the weather there began to worsen even more. Without warning, this drone began to lose airspeed and altitude and drifted to port and the controller was unable to correct the problem remotely. Just as the drone turned on its final descent toward the U-boat pens, the television monitors went blank and the controller had to guide the drone visually. About a half-mile from the target the flak batteries, undamaged in the 452BG's pre-bombardment, hit the drone causing it to veer and crash and explode about 500 yards from the aiming point, leaving the target intact. The second drone was also hit by flak, exploding it at 500 feet altitude and a mile and half from the target but destroyed 2½ acres of buildings in the target area.

Fourth Castor Mission: October 30, 1944

On October 30, another mission to Heligoland was undertaken with even worse results. The target's flak batteries were again pre-bombed by B-17s, but their effectiveness would remain unknown as both drones, B-17F (42-3438/former 96BG)) and B-17F (42-30066/former 388BG), were lost before reaching the target. One drone was dispatched on a compass heading for Berlin but managed to fly to Sweden putting a large hole into that country's southern region and neutral Sweden, which had also been subjected to the attack of errant German V-2 rockets issued a protest. The second drone could not be made to turn or dive and headed along the Danish coast at 10 feet and crashed into the sea with an enormous explosion.

Fifth Castor Mission: December 5, 1944

The next Castor mission was flown on December 5 by two drones, B-17G (42-39824) and B-17F (42-30353/former 95BG), against railroad marshalling yards at Herford, Germany, 336 miles away. The intended target could not be found due to cloud cover and the drones were diverted to Haldorf. The first drone was destroyed by AA fire while turning on the target run. Meanwhile, both wings and carburetors of the second drone were believed to have iced up, causing the drone to descend into a protracted, uncontrollable dive over Holland through thick clouds. Incredibly, the fully loaded drone made a perfect belly landing in soft, wet ground, and failed to explode. To ensure that the undamaged Aphrodite's secrets would not be compromised, the Air Force sent sorties to find and destroy the drone on the ground but their extensive search failed to find it. After the war, it was found that German soldiers investigating the crash shot at the aircraft getting a very, very momentary surprise as the huge bomb load detonated.

Sixth and Last Castor Mission: January 1, 1944

On January 1, 1945, a Castor mission was sent to attack the thermal power station in Oldenburg, Germany. Both drones, B-17G (42-30178/former 95BG) and B-17F (42-30237/former 379BG), escaped AA fire but missed target due control malfunctions.

Conclusion of the Aphrodite/Castor Programs

With the onset of winter weather and with only one fully-equipped Castor drone available, the Castor program was canceled. The scorecard for Aphrodite/Castor tallied a perfect record of nineteen B-17 drone sorties and nineteen failures. Since the drones could not hit strategic targets, Gen. Arnold, its major booster, instructed Gen. Spaatz to send twenty-five war-wearies a month over Germany as an irritant and possibly a means of breaking down the morale of the people of interior Germany. The British Chiefs of Staff refused approval of this proposed mass use of war-wearies as they felt the Nazis could also retaliate and London certainly presented a large target that could not be missed. (Willie Orphans are discussed in detail next.) Roosevelt consulted Churchill at Yalta in early February 1945 on the subject, and Churchill indicated he would reconsider. After Roosevelt died on April 12, Churchill wrote new President Harry Truman that he again reluctantly approved Aphrodite's new use, hopeful that it would not boomerang, endangering beleaguered London, which had suffered V-1 and V-2 terror weapon attacks. However, Truman, secretly informed that the atomic bomb was a reality and would render schemes such as Aphrodite obsolete, canceled the project.

The reason that Aphrodite was not transferred to the Pacific was mainly one of geography. The longest distance from England to the most distant Aphrodite German target was less than 400 miles, but it was 1,600 miles one way from the Marianas' airbases to strategic targets in Japan. The Aphrodite drone's maximum bomb load over these long Pacific distances would have to be greatly reduced to meet the fuel requirements to fly one way. Also, these long distances required that the B-29 be used as the controlling mothership since neither the B-17 nor B-24 had the range to guide a drone to Japan and then return. If the two mother configuration for controlling one B-17/B-24 drone was to be retained in the Pacific, then two B-29s would be delivering perhaps as much as 10,000 pounds of explosive via the one drone, which was 20,000–30,000 pounds less than both B-29s could carry individually (15,000–20,000 pounds at medium altitudes as a bomb load in a conventional mission over the same distance). Also, the difference between the most efficient cruising speeds for the B-29 and a fully loaded B-17 drone was as much as 200 mph, meaning the B-29 had to fly slower, which required lengthening an already very long mission. Using a B-29 as a drone was considered as it could carry up to 40,000 pounds of explosive, but the Superfortress was a too valuable commodity. However, once the airbases on Okinawa were operational in late June 1945, their relative proximity to Japan changed the Aphrodite drone circumstance but so would the use of the atomic bomb less than two months later.

A summary of the Final Report on the Aphrodite *Project* (and Anvil/Castor) from Maj. Gen. Carl Spaatz, CO, USSTAF, appeared in a memorandum to the Assistant Chief of Air Staff dated February 7, 1945. The basic conclusions were as follows:

> The results of the missions flown were not satisfactory as far as damage to enemy installations. However, these missions were in the nature of experimental missions and have proved the value and serviceability of the weapon and equipment. The failures can be chiefly attributed to weather, with personnel failure, and in the possibility of equipment failure. Since the equipment was designed for a limited number of flying hours and since none of the equipment had had nearly 100 hours of actual flying time on training missions, any equipment failure does not reflect on the serviceability of these installations....
>
> This weapon is not satisfactory as a strategic weapon in this theater due to extremely adverse weather conditions and very concentrated flak defenses on all important targets....
>
> This weapon does not constitute a worthwhile striking force when limited to only two missiles per mission, as with this project, due to limited radio frequencies....
>
> It is felt that his weapon is of less value against small installations as against heavily built up areas, since its effectiveness is due to blast alone....
>
> The equipment has been dangerously compromised in the theater, due to the fact that on the mission of 5 December 1944, one Robot aircraft, flying through severe icing conditions, landed in an open field in enemy territory from a power stall without exploding. This means that a full set of equipment has fallen into enemy hands ...

The Report recommended:

> If this weapon is to be continued in use in this theater, it should be used as a tactical rather than a strategic weapon with its launching base well forward ... because of the extremely adverse weather conditions greatly limit the frequency with which long range flights can be carried out under visual conditions. It is further suggested that this weapon would prove of more value in a different theater where weather conditions are more favorable....
>
> It is strongly recommended that sufficient radio frequencies be assigned for both control equipment and television to allow a minimum of ten missiles to be dispatched simultaneously without interference from each other....
>
> Targets should be selected which are susceptible to blast effect and should not have too concentrated an anti-aircraft defense....

> Steps should be taken to obtain new frequency ranges and make necessary changes in the equipment to minimize the danger arising from the compromise of the equipment on the 5 December 1944 mission.... A radio detonator should be installed enabling the load to be detonated at the will of the controller ...
>
> USAAF, *Case History of Castor*
> Maxwell AFB, MF Reel A2082, A2083, and A2051

War-Weary Willie/Abusive Project

Even though the major emphasis was being placed on Aphrodite and Castor guided aircraft/drone/bombs by the AAF, in September 1944, Brig. Gen. Grandison Gardner, Commander of Eglin Proving Ground, suggested to Gen. Arnold that unmanned, powered, ground-launched, and ground-controlled bombers could be used for area bombing deep inside Germany in the winter months, which limited normal bombing operations. Once the Aphrodite/Castor program began to fail, Arnold decided that the Castor technology could be employed to convert hundreds of readily available war-weary bombers into very potent ground-launched and ground-controlled cruise missiles designated as Willie Orphans to bombard industrial and other strategic targets located deep inside Germany and, eventually, bomb the Japanese home islands. By the summer of 1944, any program relating to war-weary aircraft became a Weary Willie project, which was frequently abridged in most official communication to simply a Willie project with the controlling aircraft remaining as Mothers, the missiles air controlled by mothers were again called Babies and ground-controlled missiles were called Orphans. These rather obvious code names were later, November 28, 1944, radically changed as Willie became Abusive, Mother became Bluefish, the Baby became Corticated, and Orphan became Cottongrass.

Types of Control

There were three control systems comprised of eight types or phases of control that could be employed, depending upon the desired type of attack. These control systems were divided into three phases of the ground control system called Orphan/Cottongrass, three phases of the air control system called Baby/Corticated, and two phases of close support visual control.

Orphan/Cottongrass System

Phase 1 of the Orphan/Cottongrass system provided for the use of a B-17 or B-24 placed on a preset course and at the end of a pre-determined time interval, the time control cut the ignition switches and armed the explosive load while the aircraft glided into the target. The originally installed C-1 automatic pilot controlled the drone and maintained it on a pre-determined heading. Altitude was maintained at a preset value by a barometric altimeter operating in conjunction with the C-1 pilot. An electric time clock armed the fuses and cut the ignition switches at a pre-determined time. However, during the war, the automatic equipment was not developed enough so that the drone could be taken-off under preset control and the drone's size and weight prevented catapult launching. The drone was taken-off by remote control or by a pilot with its required heading set and the automatic timing device started. If the drone was taken-off by remote control, the remote control receiver was automatically turned off when the timing device was started. If the drone was taken-off by a pilot, he was to bale out afterward. Neither take-off system could be jammed by the enemy.

Phase 2 of the Orphan/Cottongrass system improved the drone's accuracy by tracking it with radar throughout its flight, by making any necessary course corrections, and by controlling the dumping of the missile via a FM radio link. This system upgraded the drone's accuracy, where, at a range of 85 miles, it was estimated that a 3–4-mile-square target could be reliably hit. In addition to the equipment employed in Phase 1, this system required, a ground control station with an AN/ARW-18 FM transmitter and an SRC-584 radar set with a plotting board. The drone was also taken-off either by a pilot who baled out or by remote control. The radio equipment used for control was susceptible to enemy jamming that could deflect it from its set course. However, the maximum course change that enemy jamming could make was limited by adjustable switches in the steering motor to prevent any possibility of the enemy returning the drone to friendly territory. As an added precaution, the time clock was again employed and was set to dump the drone five minutes after the calculated time of arrival over the target.

Phase 3 of the Orphan/Cottongrass system engaged radar for controlling as well as tracking the drone. The accuracy of the system and all other elements remained the same as Phase 2 except that the possibility of enemy jamming was much reduced.

Baby/Corticated System

While all three phases of the Orphan/Cottongrass ground control system employed the drone against a rather large area objective, the air control or Baby/Corticated system included a television camera in the drone's nose, which was the equivalent of providing the remote control operator with an eye looking at the area toward which the drone was heading, allowing the drone to be used against pinpoint objectives.

Phase 1 of Baby/Corticated System was as an air-controlled guided missile, controlled by a FM radio link. The drone was navigated visually to within 10 miles of the target and the Block III television was then used during the final run. The requirements for weather depended upon the type of mission planned, which was determined by the distance at which the Mother/Bluefish control aircraft was to remain from the drone but, generally, the visual navigation employed in this system required good weather throughout the mission. During October 1943, the possible accuracy of the Baby/Corticated system was demonstrated when a YPQ-12A aircraft, equipped with inferior BLOCK I television equipment, was expended against a 30-foot-square target with the point of impact only 30 feet from the target.

The Mother/Bluefish control aircraft used in the Baby/Corticated system was a B-17 equipped with the required FM and television equipment. The drone was controlled by an FM radio link similar to that employed in Orphan/Cottongrass Phase 2. The FM radio equipment could be susceptible to enemy jamming, which was considered unlikely other than to deflect the drone momentarily, as the control aircraft transmitting station provided the strongest signal to the Baby and was the one having control. If the BC-617 monitor in the control aircraft indicated enemy interference, the amplifier could be used to increase the power output in order to maintain control by supplying the stronger signal than the enemy's jamming signals.

The main disadvantage in the Phase 1 Baby/Corticated system were navigation difficulties caused by unfavorable weather. Phases 2 and 3 of this system showed continuous improvements in equipment to provide more accurate navigation during poor weather. If television was to be used, the weather minimums at the target, remained the same for all phases.

In Phase 2, a H2X radar search set was installed control aircraft to track the reply from an AN/APX-14 Black Maria radar beacon in the drone. An alternate system for locating the drone was provided by the SCR-729 navigation equipment that, when used with an AN/TPM-1 beacon in the drone, indicated the range of the drone from the control aircraft. The bearing of the drone could be determined by the radio compass in the control aircraft when tuned to the BC-375 liaison transmitter, which could be remotely turned on in the drone.

Phase 3 of the Baby/Corticated system was designed for long-range missions, during which varied weather conditions could be encountered and blind flying would be required, including changes in altitude. It was identical to Phase 2, with the exception that telemetering was installed in the drone. By using his instruments, the remote pilot could fly the drone in instrument weather.

Close Support Visual Control System

In Phase 1 of the Close Support Visual Control System, the drone was provided with a FM radio control system and a smoke tank. Two ground control stations were located within visual contact with the target. The drone was flown by a Bluefish Control aircraft or by the bale out pilots to within sight of the ground control stations. Smoke was used as an aid in locating and identifying the drone from the ground stations. The Baby was flown directly over the ground station, which controlled it in azimuth while the ground station controlling the pitch angle or range was positioned as far as possible to one side of the line of flight.

Phase 2 of the Close Support Visual Control was identical to Phase 1 with the exception that a television transmitter was installed in the drone and a television receiver was added to the master ground control station. With this system, the drone was flown toward the target just as in Phase 1 and as soon as the target was seen on the television receiver screen, the control operator monitoring the screen assumed control of the drone from the visual control operators.

Target Suitability and Accuracy

Orphan/Cottongrass systems were suitable for attack against area targets. Phase 1 was limited in accuracy by its preset nature, its accuracy decreasing directly with range while Phases 2 and 3, were limited to approximately 85 miles by the range of the control equipment. The Baby/Corticated systems and Close Support Visual Control systems were only limited by the requirement for good visibility within 2–3 miles of the target. Baby/Corticated systems were suitable for any easily recognizable pinpoint targets while Close Support Visual Control systems were suitable for camouflaged targets which could be located from the ground.

Warhead and Fusing

The Abusive drone carried an explosive load of Torpex, TNT, or gel gas/white phosphorous, which is usually packed in boxes or other suitable containers. The weight of explosive depended upon the particular target being attacked, however, approximately 18,500 pounds were usually employed in either the B-17 or the B-24 drone. The arming relay could be actuated either by the electric time clock in the Orphan/Cottongrass Phase 1 or by the appropriate control signal in any of the other phases. This arming relay in turn then operated an electric motor, which armed the T-83 fuses. Even when armed, these fuses required an acceleration of 9Gs before detonation could occur.

Launching Systems

Two launching systems were available: by remote control or by pilots who baled out. If the aircraft was taken-off by pilots, they remained in the aircraft until they had adjusted the automatic pilot and turned on the remote control equipment. Launching by remote control required approximately 30 percent longer runways than were required for pilot take-off and were only reluctantly performed if there were obstructions or populated installations near the end of the runway.

Autopilots

A plan was created to develop A-5 Autopilots for remote use in Willie Orphans in B-17s and B-24s already equipped with A-5s and to install obsolete A-4s and A-5s in A-20s, B-25s, and B-26s for use as drones. B-17 and B-24 Willie Orphans with C-1 autopilots were considered for use with radar tracking and plotting of approach resulting in dead reckoning course with preset flight after the pilot had baled out or tracking and plotting the entire flight after the pilot had baled out or tracking and plotting the entire flight with remote radar after the pilot had bailed out. The operational plans for Mother and Baby were visual tracking of Baby by remote radio control, altitude control, TV and smoke dispenser (i.e. the same as Castor); continual determination of relative position of Baby and Mother by visual control and radar; long-range operation by visual control, radar, telemetering of Baby instruments; and remote control of other Baby instruments. The Air Technical Service Command directed the procurement of 550 drones and 110 control kits for Willie and to cancel the installation of control equipment for all Castor aircraft, which were then to be used for Willie Orphans. The cost for automatic pilots for remote control was C-1, $4,700 without or $6,000 with a bomb stabilizer; A-5, $5,000; and A-4, $800. Only a few of the 550 Willies available in the U.S. were required for testing at Eglin, so there was no need to store them in the U.S. and they were scheduled to join the about 100 were available in the U.K. and MTO. Gen. Spaatz planned to use twenty-five per month in operations, but the lack of targets in the MTO made their use in that theater unlikely. Fifty of the 550 were scheduled to be sent to the ETO by January 15, 1945, but the Germans had captured a Baby intact and their mass deployment could possibly be reduced until radar control development was ready in about four months. The 20AF also had expressed interest in the Orphan program for use in the final air campaigns against the Japanese Home Islands.

A major factor in the failure of the Aphrodite/Castor project had been their susceptibility to enemy AA fire. To circumvent this, the Orphans were to be deployed at night or in poor weather by dead reckoning, making the Orphan a terror weapon or by ground-based radar control without the need for visual ground references to guide the weapon. Even veteran navigators had problems using dead reckoning and often experienced navigation errors of about seven miles in every 100 miles flown. The Orphan's location in the air was to be provided by a Black Maria radar beacon signal transmitting from the Orphan. In early October 1944, the ground-controlled radar stage of the project was given a top priority in the American guided missile program, while the NDRC was to adapt the SCR 584 radar unit for control. The ground-based controllers would control the Orphan by directing its beacon over the target and, when it was in the correct location, give it a final command, causing the heavily loaded bomber to dive onto the objective.

Willie Orphans controlled by a ground radar control station did not have nearly the range or the accuracy of their air-controlled counterparts. Initially, the Willie Orphans were anticipated only to be able to hit a 1,200 by 200-foot rectangle and only from 100 miles from the ground control station, but later, even this unfavorable estimate was found to be too optimistic. Once the Orphans flew beyond 100 miles, they were out of range of the ground controllers and became unguided and flew to their targets by dead reckoning, a method that used in 1918 by the Kettering Bug. The dead reckoning procedure was to be as follows.

The drone was to be flown by a pilot in a direct line towards the target 50 or 60 miles away. The drone was tracked over friendly territory by a tracking station several miles inside friendly territory using modified SCR-584 radar, an automatic plotting board, and a UPN-2 beacon in the drone. The drone pilot was then informed of his corrected course and time from the target, and would then make the necessary corrections and set the air log or time mechanism after which he bailed out over friendly territory. The drone was then flown by preset automatic pilot and altitude control equipment to the target where the air log or time mechanism flew it onto the target.

The ground control of the drone was through continual control using a modulator added to the SCR-584 ground radar equipment and a CRN-3 selector added to the UPN-2 equipment in the drone. Ground control could also be accomplished by the

FM radio control link with a 250-watt amplifier in conjunction with the previous equipment described above.

Despite their rather lackluster promised performance, on October 12, 1944, Gen. Arnold gave the Willie program the highest priority of all the AAF guided weapon programs and within the Willie program the Orphans received the highest priority.

With the poor weather of the 1944 fall and winter approaching, it appears that Arnold would rather continue his attacks on targets in Germany with the inaccurate Orphans than not attacking at all. In a remarkable letter to Maj. Gen. Spaatz in November 1944, Arnold reveals he would willingly sacrifice his precision daylight bombing policy to activate an indiscriminate policy of area terror bombing, reminiscent of RAF Bomber Command CG Bomber Harris!

> ... to break the will of the enemy population to continue to fight by turning the Willie Orphans loose to land all over Germany so that the Germans would be just as much afraid of our war-weary planes on account of not knowing just where they were going to hit, as are the people in England from buzz bombs and rockets. I think the psychological effect on the morale of the German people would be much greater this way, not knowing where they were going to fall, and they would have to be constantly on the alert with fighters and anti-aircraft to knock them down.
>
> USAAF, *Case History of the GB-1*
> Maxwell AFB, MF Reel A2082, A2083, and A2051

The evidently dismayed Spaatz answered Arnold:

> We are making a study as to the requirements for an organization to launch war-weary airplanes at a maximum rate of 25 per month. The rate of operation will be limited by the extensive amount of training and technical preparation, and the supply of war-weary airplanes. For this reason, I do not believe that we will achieve significant effect if we turn them lose to land all over Germany. We must perfect our equipment and control technique so that we can be reasonably sure of hitting the target. The Germans V-2 lands all over eastern England, but only those which land where they cause damage and casualties have any significant effect on morale. Even that effect is localized.
>
> USAAF, *Case History of the GB-1*
> Maxwell AFB, MF Reel A2082, A2083, and A2051

The British Chiefs of Staff refused approval of this proposed mass use of Willie Orphans from U.K. bases as they believed the Nazis would retaliate, with London offering a large easily hit target. On January 31, 1945, Gen. Marshall sent a priority, top secret message to Gen. Eisenhower, informing him the British had withdrawn their agreement to use the U.S. Willie Orphan project and that all launching of aircraft in connection with this project be suspended.

Nonetheless, Arnold continued the Willie Orphan's 1-A priority and its extensive testing at Eglin because it was the most promising, numerous, and otherwise expendable AAF missile. By March 1945, the Eglin tests reestablished that the Orphans could only be ground radio-controlled out to 96 miles and only if the drone was above 7,000 feet and if the Orphan descended below that altitude, all its radar contact and radio control was lost. Tests continued but confirmed that the Orphans were not precision weapons, being unable to hit a target the size of an average size industrial factory. To position the radio control station with the 96-mile limit near a major strategic enemy target in the ETO was difficult and was impossible against the Japanese homeland. Orphan's accuracy against a tactical target was significantly less than that regularly achieved by medium or fighter bomber attacks.

Further tests concentrated on deploying Orphans against targets on the Japanese Home Islands, but due to the long distances, the idea of using a modified Aphrodite system was resurrected. The safety pilot would fly the Orphan from a distant base to a predetermined point where he would bale out to be picked up by a submarine or ASR picket ship used for B-29 raids. The Orphan would continue to fly itself to a point off the Japanese coast where a B-29 mother would rendezvous with it and gain radio control. The Orphan would then be guided to the target, not by the mother following the drone as with the Aphrodite system, but by using the B-29's H2X radar to locate the target and an onboard receiver to track emissions from the Orphan's Black Maria radar beacon. When the Orphan's beacon signal appeared to be at the correct distance from the target, it would be given the final command to dive into the target. Tests disclosed the greatest accuracy achievable using this method was a circular error of 1–2 miles, which was about the same as if the Orphan had been controlled by a ground station. The time and effort in training and employing specially trained aircrew and ground technicians then precluded XXI Bomber Command's interest in the project. Another suggestion was to use Babies controlled by B-24s or B-29s as decoys to draw Japanese fighters from targets areas attacked by B-29 formations; however, B-29s dispensing Rope/Window could be an effective alternative.

In May 1945, tests to determine if the Offner Infrared heat-seeker, which had been used with moderate success in the GB-6, could be employed to provide terminal guidance in the Orphan B-17. This B-17 with its large nose allowed the Offner-seeker to pivot 10 degrees vertically or horizontally to keep the target in its sight as the aircraft banked and turned. However, in practice, it was much more difficult to remotely control a multi-engined bomber carrying 20,000 pounds of explosive than a 1,000-pound GB-6. As the Orphan approached the target, the Offner-seeker was unable to anticipate or make the rapid fine adjustments a human controller was able to make and would attempt to force the nose of the bomber on to the target with increasingly large corrections. These corrections would ultimately cause increasing oscillations in the Orphan's final approach to the target and often resulted in the loss of the control of the drone. In sixty-two test dives using the Offner, there was an 80 percent miss rate of between one-quarter to 4 miles, but the 20 percent hit rate was considered to have been able to cause some damage to a large industrial site. These tests did not actually expend an Orphan on each test, but the test drone had a safety pilot on board who would intercede just before the Orphan was to hit the target and fly it back to base. Engineers onboard the Orphan would evaluate where the drone would have hit if it was allowed to proceed to the target. The Offner's continued poor showing resulted in its cancellation in May 1945.

Due to the inaccuracy, guidance, and control problems encountered during testing, the Willie Orphan was never deployed in combat. By September 1945, with the war over and the number of available war-weary aircraft quickly decreasing, the Air Force Board suggested the cancellation of the Willie project.

Fighter Baby Project

In late April 1945, Col. V. R. Haugen, Chief of the Aircraft Project Section, issued a directive to the Special Weapons Branch for the modification and testing of P-38, P-39, P-40, P-47, and P-51 fighters for use as Babies/drones. The Special Weapons Branch was to estimate the suitability and the amount of modifications required for each fighter with a possible range of 130 miles from either a control aircraft or from a ground station (launched from a ramp) and to incorporate controls to permit low-level operations (minimum 25 feet) over land or water targets. The instruments and controls were to be designed for all-weather operation and maximum security against jamming. Investigation showed that the P-38 and P-39 were most suitable as Babies, but the war ended in the ETO where these fighters would be most useful and the Fighter Baby Project was canceled.

Shipboard Cottongrass

Cottongrass later became another scheme using fighter and bomber Babies under shipboard control stations located at close range to bombard targets on the Japanese mainland. The close proximity to the target made the controlling vessels vulnerable, and also only five or six sorties could be flown per day and therefore would harass the Japanese less than conventional multi-aircraft bombing methods and investigation into this Cottongrass scheme was discontinued.

Hermit

Hermit was a Cottongrass ground-controlled, rather than shipboard-controlled, scheme flying drone aircraft into Japanese cave entrenchments in order to minimize American infantry casualties. Because of their unimpressive ETO operations, aircraft in better condition than war-weary was a requirement, and thus, their procurement only reached a point necessary to complete the development program and the master kits for the Cottongrass phase of the project. The project was initiated by the Air Technical Service Command while NDRC was to develop a ground-control system not utilizing radar due to a prolonged development time. Testing, using ground-controlled B-l7s was generally successful, but prolonged, as the war ended before operational use could be effected.

XBQ-1/2/3/4 Series

Kaiser-Fleetwings XBQ-1/XBQ-2

XBQ-1

During March 1942, the AAF initiated a program to develop radio-controlled assault drones, frequently called aerial torpedoes at that time. These aerial torpedoes were to be unmanned expendable aircraft, either purpose-built or converted from existing types, armed with a large payload of high explosive, remote-control equipment, and a forward-looking TV camera. The drones were to be directed to the target by radio commands from a control aircraft, where the operator would control the drone by watching the image transmitted by the camera.

On July 10, 1942, Fleetwings of Garden City, New York (Henry Kaiser purchased Fleetwings in 1943 to become Kaiser-Fleetwings), was awarded a large contract for $1.34 million to develop the XBQ-1 assault drone with a scheduled delivery date of February 1944. The aerodynamic aircraft, with a fixed tricycle landing gear covered by sleek, faired wheel spats, was powered by two 225-hp Franklin O-405-7 piston engines that gave it a speed of 225 mph and a range of 1,700 miles. The XBQ-1 had a high wing with a span of 48.6 feet and weighed 7,700 pounds without the proposed 2,000-pound HE warhead. The XBQ-1 was provided with a cockpit so that it could be flown by a pilot during test and ferry flights while for unmanned flights the cockpit was to be covered by a flush fairing. It was not until October 1943 that Fleetwings was able to successfully develop a television-based command guidance system in an YPQ-12A Target Drone and adapt to the radio-controlled XBQ-1 with a TV camera. The XBQ-1 flew in May 1944; however, the aircraft crashed on its maiden flight. And the Kaiser-Fleetwings BQ-1 program was canceled in July 1944.

XBQ-2 and -2A

Along with the XBQ-1, the AAF also ordered one XBQ-2, which was to be identical to the XBQ-1 except for using Lycoming XO-435-3 engines and a jettisonable landing gear. The XBQ-2 had a scheduled delivery date of December 1943 but was not built and was replaced by a contract for a single XBQ-2A. The XBQ-2A design replaced the XO-435-3 engines with two Lycoming R-680-13s. After the -2A was built, the project was terminated in December 1943 because of high costs; the aircraft was subsequently redesignated as ZXBQ-2A to denote its obsolescence.

Fairchild XBQ-3

On October 1, 1942, AAF awarded a $1.4 million contract to the Fairchild Aircraft Company, Hagerstown, Maryland, to develop two XBQ-3 guided bombs (Fairchild Model 79) based on the company's AT-21 Gunner, developed from the AT-14 Bombardier. This aircraft was a specialized bomber crew trainer, intended to train crews in the use of power gun turrets or a gun on a flexible mount. Built at the Fairchild Field Plant in Burlington, North Carolina, the twin-engined AT-21 was mainly constructed of a plastic-bonded laminated plywood called Duramold because

Fleetwings XBQ-1. (*AAF*)

Fleetwings XBQ-2A. (*AAF*)

Fleetwings XBQ-2A-1. (*AAF*)

of the concern over an aluminum shortage. The AT-21 encountered production problems and with American production of medium and heavy bombers at such a high level, an adequate number could be set aside for training purposes. After 175 AT-21s had been delivered, the contracts were canceled, with some being used as target tugs; two were committed to be modified into XBQ-3 prototype unmanned assault drones procured with a delivery date of February 1944. These drones were to be equipped with a large payload of HE and were directed to the target by radio commands from a control aircraft. The modified XBQ-3 remained very similar in size and appearance to the AT-21 at 15,300 pounds, 31 feet long, 13 feet, 2 inches high, with a 52-foot, 8-inch wingspan, twin rudders, and retractable tricycle landing gear. However, the XBQ-3 had the top of its fuselage abridged with a small rudimentary cockpit added to accommodate the pilots during testing (if the XBQ-3 would have gone into production this cockpit would have been faired over). It had all training paraphernalia removed and the nose-mounted machine gun and dorsal turret were deleted. It was powered by two twelve-cylinder, 450-hp Ranger V-770 engines that provided a maximum speed of 220 mph, over a range of 1,500 miles, and ceiling of 17,000 feet. This engine was the only American inverted V12-type inline air-cooled engine to reach production and was used almost exclusively by the AT-21. As an assault drone, it carried a 4,000-pound explosive load (two 2,000-pound bombs or two torpedoes) to be transported within the fuselage, which was twice the load as the purpose-designed, but smaller, Fleetwings XBQ-1/XBQ-2 drones. For test flights, the onboard pilots were trained in the AT-21. Like the other XBQ-series drones, the XBQ-3 was equipped with a TV camera, whose image would be used by the remote control operator to control the drone. During its first flight test on July 19, 1944, both its notoriously unreliable Ranger engines lost power and the aircraft was badly damaged on landing. Despite the accident, flight testing continued; however, there are no other records concerning this XBQ-3 or the other prototype except that, after a $1.4 million was expended on the program, it was canceled later that year as the progress of guided missiles rendered the assault drone swiftly obsolete.

Fairchild XBQ-3. (*AAF*)

XBQ-4 and XBQ-5

The Interstate XQB-4 was designated as the Navy Assault Drone XTDR-1 and the Interstate XQB-5 was designated as the Navy Assault Drone XTD2R-1 and will be described as TDR drones.

XBQ-7 and XBQ-8

The XBQ-7 was a Boeing B-17 associated with the operational Aphrodite and Castor programs. The XBQ-8 was a Consolidated B-24 D/J that was not used operationally by the AAF while the other XBQ-8 was a Consolidated PB4Y-1 that was used operationally by the USN in the Anvil program. The XBQ-7 and -8 are discussed elsewhere in detail.

As discussed previously, the BQ program was canceled because it was slow in developing and expensive, requiring almost as much time and money as would the development of a full-fledged combat aircraft without sufficient tactical return. The power-driven XBQs required clear visibility, extensive fighter protection, and highly trained crews.

Post-War Surplus Aircraft Drones

B-17 Post-War Drones

After the war, thousands of war-weary combat aircraft returned from the overseas and were scheduled for scrapping and metal reclamation. A few B-17s were sold to the civil marketplace, but most ended their days as the victims of aluminum recycling smelters. However, the AAF retained several hundred new B-17s as personnel and VIP transports (CBA/B-17), for trainers (TB-17), for mapping (FB-17), for air-sea rescue (SB-17), for weather reconnaissance (WB-17), were loaned to defense contractors for various research purposes (EB-17 and JB-17), and as drone/drone controllers (QB-17). Most B-17s slated for conversion to drone directors and ongoing depot-level maintenance were received from storage depots and the modifications were completed at the Middletown Air Depot at Olmsted AFB, Pennsylvania.

B-17 and F6F Drones at Operation Crossroads

Operation Crossroads was a pair of atomic bomb tests at the Bikini Atoll in the Marshall Islands during mid-1946. The first test was *Able*, during which the atomic bomb *Gilda* was dropped from the 509th Bombardment Group B-29 Superfortress *Dave's Dream* on July 1, 1946. The second test was *Baker*, in which the bomb, *Helen of Bikini*, was detonated 90 feet underwater on July 25, 1946.

B-17 Drones Prepare for Crossroads

The post-war development of the control technology was significantly enhanced by the drone requirements of Operation *Crossroads that* required the use of unmanned aircraft equipped with research instruments to be flown through and near the radiation-contaminated mushroom clouds of the two planned atomic detonations. During the initial *Crossroads* planning conferences, the AAF committed to providing B-17 drones to the project under the direction of Brig. Gen. Roger Ramey, Commander of Air Task Group 1.5. The 509th Composite Group had dropped the atomic bombs on Hiroshima and Nagasaki during August 1945. On January 10, 1946, Col. Paul Cullen was assigned to organize the 509CG for Operation Crossroads coordinated by V/Adml. William "Spike" Blandy's Task Force 1.

During May 1946, sixteen new B-17s were drawn from storage at South Plains Army Air Field, Lubbock, Texas, and were flown to the San Antonio Air Depot, Kelly Field, Texas. While at Kelly Field, ten (six primary, four backup) B-17s were developed into drones by removing all defensive armament and turrets, and sealing the bomb bay doors and the waist gunner openings. These B-17s were then equipped with the refined remote control system radio, radar, television, and other equipment, which the Air Materiel Command had developed in about six weeks, rapidly advancing World War II technology to meet the new requirements. This equipment was demonstrated on February 19, 1946, when a war-weary B-17 drone was controlled through all requirements of a test flight conducted at Clovis Field, New Mexico. Also, six director B-17s (four mother ships, one super mother ship with the capability to control any drone, and one back-up mother ship) were equipped with drone director equipment to control one drone aircraft and the capability to back up one other director aircraft. By April 15, 1946, four B-17 drones and five B-17 drone controllers were attached to the 509CG at Roswell AAF, New Mexico, manned, equipped, trained, and ready to be tested at Clovis AAF. During June 1946, the director and drone B-17s were operationally ready to be deployed to

During the summer of 1946, U.S. postwar A-Bomb tests at the Bikini Atoll, Operation Crossroads, five motherships were to control four B-17 drones into the atomic explosions. Pictured are three of the four Drones, distinguished by No. 1 Drone with one fuselage band and one horizontal tail stripe, etc. (*AAF*)

the Eniwetok Atoll in the Marshall Islands, about 200 miles west of Bikini Atoll where the Crossroads tests were to take place.

The Four B-17 Drones and Five B-17 Drone Controllers

Task Unit 1.5.3 of Air Task Group 1.5

Drones: B-17G-85-DL 44-83560; B-17G-85-DL 44-83553; B-17G-90-DL 44-83603; and B-17G-85-DL 4-83519.

Drone Control Aircraft: B-17G-110-VE44-85818; B-17G-110-VE 44-85815; B-17G-105-VE 44-85752; B-17G-105-VE 44-85738; and B-17G-100-VE 44-85690.

Modifications to the B-17 Drones and B-17 Drone Controllers

B-17 Drone Aircraft

AN/ARW-1 (Control): Opened and closed air sampler bag equipment in addition to normal use.
SCR-718 (Altimeter): Normal use
SCR-522 (VHF): Transmitted Geiger counter-warning.
SCR-274-N (Command): Was auto-keyed for propagation tests on two drones and remained silent on the other two drones
BC-375 (Liaison): Auto-keyed on all drones to aid location by control aircraft.
AN/APT-5 (Jamming): Transmitted for propagation tests on only one drone.

B-17 Drone Control Aircraft

AN/ARW-18 (Control): Opened and closed air sampler bag on drones in addition to normal use.
AN/AXR-1 (Television): Camera recorded transmission from drone.
AN/APN-9 (Loran): Normal use
SCR-718 (Altimeter): Normal use
AN/ARN-7 (Compass): Homed on BC-375 (liaison) in drones.
Beacons: Navigation by means of two beacons on 260 kc and 300 kc.
SCR-522 (VHF): Normal use
VHF Receiver (1st Extra): Guarded 140.58 mc at all times
VHF Receiver (2nd Extra): Received Geiger counter-warning from drones. Normal.
SCR-274-N (Command): Normal use
BC-375 (Liaison Transmitter): Used by radiological observer
AN/APR-4 RCM/AN/ARR-5 Search/AN/ARR-7 Receiver: Two aircraft were equipped to monitor communications frequencies and two aircraft were equipped to monitor radar frequencies with specific attention paid to emissions from the drone aircraft.

B-17 and F6F Drones at Operation Crossroads

In the months leading up to the July 1946 Operation Crossroads, the first post-war U.S. nuclear tests, which were to be conducted at the Bikini Atoll in the Marshall Islands, the AAF ballyhooed the participation of their drones in the test. In February 1946, V/Adml. William Blandy, the Crossroads Commander, stated in *The New York*

Times: "Robot aircraft will dive into the atomic blast to gather scientific data ... to uncover facts of the radioactive phenomena as well as supply data on blast effects on airborne aircraft." During a April 17 press conference, Maj. Gen. William Kepner, the Deputy Commander of Aviation for Crossroads, enlightened reporters on the "unpiloted but mothered drone planes into the sky, reaching irradiated cloud. Where men cannot go," and added, "the drone will take electronic and other recording instruments ... controlled by mother planes from miles outside the target area." Other *New York Times* articles described how Navy F6F Hellcats would be remotely launched from aircraft carrier *Shangri-La* to fly into the atomic cloud to collect data.

B-17 *Radio Control Technique at Crossroads*

Radio control technique was mastered and improved upon during the postwar years. Drones were entirely pilotless throughout the flight and take-off and landing, which was performed by technicians stationed in two jeeps equipped with radio control boxes stationed near the runway. Jeep 1 was located at the very end of the runway and controlled direction through rudder control and also applied the brakes on landing. Jeep 2 positioned to one side of the runway controlled the throttles and elevators on take-offs and landings. The control boxes were small weighing four pounds and had ten radio channels. Once the Jeep controllers flew the B-17 into the air, control was transferred to a mother aircraft circling above and equipped with an identical control box in the nose that guided the drone to the target at a long distance. On the landing approach, the mother switched control of the drone back to the Jeep controllers at about 400 feet of altitude.

Ground controllers checking Jeep-borne portable control equipment at Sticknell Field, Eniwetok. (*From AAF Microfilm document*)

Above left: The controller in the mother banks the No. 2 B-17 drone toward the atomic blast after a radio-controlled take-off. (*From AAF Microfilm document*)

Above right: The drone flew into the atomic blast area to collect air samples for radiation in this air filter. (*From AAF Microfilm document*)

Below: A drone in a return landing at Eniwetok after collecting A-Bomb blast samples. (*From AAF Microfilm document*)

Crossroads B-17 and F6F Markings

Particular markings were specified for the task force B-17s. All carried the 58BW insignia on both sides of the nose, and black Roman numerals were carried on the yellow tails of the five drone control aircraft. A set of black horizontal tail stripes and broad 24-inch-wide black fuselage waist bands were carried on the four drone aircraft, with the number of stripes corresponding to the number of bands (i.e. No. 1 Drone had one fuselage band and one tail stripe; No. 2 had two. Etc.). In addition, insignia yellow paint was applied to the outboard wing panels, tail section, and between the waist bands on the drone aircraft. F6F-3K Hellcat drones were painted bright red, each with different color empennages apparently to denote radio frequency. The national insignia lacked the red bar.

Drones at Crossroads Tests Able and Baker

The first test on July 1, called *Able*, was an air drop explosion from a B-29 Superfortress, *Dave's Dream*, on a ninety-ship target fleet comprised of obsolete USN ships and captured enemy warships. Only eight minutes after the *Mike Hour* explosion, the first B-17 control aircraft directed its drone *Fox* into the mushroom cloud at 24,000 feet. *Fox* was then switched to its automatic pilot, while the control aircraft (called *Beeper*) raced around the cloud and resumed control when the drone emerged through the other side. *Fox* was followed by *George* at 30,000 feet, *How* at 18,000 feet, and *Love* at 12,000 feet. All four B-17 drones were directed back to Eniwetok Atoll where they were transferred back to the Jeeps' ground controllers parked at the end of the runway, who would taxi them to the radiological safe area where the filters and bags were removed and flown to Los Alamos Laboratory for analysis. The Navy launched four F6F-3K Hellcat drones from the carrier *Shangri-La* but only three emerged as one lost control and crashed. Hellcats *Yellow*, *White*, and *Blue* sampled the cloud at 5,000, 10,000 and 15,000 feet before being directed back to Roi Island, off Kwajalein, for a ground landing and sample recovery. No manned aircraft flew directly over the Zero point until four hours after *Mike Hour*. The B-17 drones entering the mushroom cloud emerged mostly unharmed, however, a B-17 drone was damaged when it overshot the runway during a landing and one control aircraft erroneously flew too close to the billowing mushroom cloud and almost lost control.

Drones were also flown after the second test, *Baker*, on July 25, which was an underwater explosion suspended from a target ship in Bikini's lagoon. One B-17 drone, which flew directly over Zero point at detonation, had its brakes damaged in the blast and overran the runway at Eniwetok, but suffered only minor damage. A third atomic test, Charlie, was canceled.

Overall, Operation Crossroads was considered a significant success for drone aircraft. In *Bombs at Bikini, The Official Report of Operation Crossroads*, (W.H. Wise, NY, 1947), author W. A. Shurcliff, considered that the remote-controlled flights advanced the science of drone-plane operations by a year or more. The media coverage of Operation Crossroads gave the public a new perception of a groundbreaking and fearsome age of nuclear warfare. Hanson Baldwin, long-time military editor of

Above: Shangri-La (CV-38) passing through the Panama Canal with its load of F6F drones and other support aircraft, including some helicopters then development. (*USN*)

Left: Former F6F pilot, now a controller, launching a F6F5-K Hellcat drone off the carrier deck. (*USN*)

Grumman F6F5-K Drones wait on Roi Island for Crossroads deployment. Each had a different tail color to differentiate their radio frequency. (*USN*)

Ex-Hellcat pilot, now controller, landing a F6F5-K drone at Roi. (*USN*)

The New York Times, proclaimed the drone as a "portent of push-button war that would soon be a familiar sight in the skyways of the world."

The *Bombs at Bikini* report emphasized that the scientific drone flights were a notable first as at Hiroshima and Nagasaki, a few photographs and pressure measurements were made of the explosions, but physicists learned almost nothing of value. At Crossroads, for the first time, samples had been taken from an atomic cloud. The AAF drones had not only advanced the aerial sampling program but had also greatly advanced the development of remote operations as well. Shurcliff stated in *Bombs at Bikini*:

> For the first time, four-motored drone aircraft had been flown without a safety pilot aboard.... With no one aboard, these great planes were radio guided through their prescribed flights across the target area, a unique and impressive feat.... A number of Army Air Forces officials believe that the drone-plane program undertaken for Crossroads advanced the science of drone-plane operations by a year or more.... Operation Crossroads was the first operation in which take-off, flight, and landing were accomplished with no one aboard. The feat was an impressive one; many experts had thought it could never be accomplished with planes of this size.

The success of the B-17G drone/controllers triggered the development of other types B-17 drone use and the formation of other units for a wide assortment of programs. During September 1947, the B-17G drones were redesignated as QB-17 for drones and the DB-17 for the controller aircraft.

Post-War QB-17 Drones

Drone Directors and Drones

During early 1946, the Engineering Division of the Air Materiel Command at Wright-Patterson activated the 1st Experimental Guided Missiles Group at Eglin Air Force Auxiliary Field 3. One of its first undertakings was developing the DB-17 drone director/QB-17 drone combination for operations considered to be too hazardous for manned aircraft. Task Unit 7.4.2 consisting of 460 men from the Experimental Guided Missiles Group was created to operate the drones and retrieve the sampling material.

During May 1946, sixteen B-17s were withdrawn from storage for conversion into drones followed by six other B-17s that were converted into drone controllers for the Crossroads Atomic Tests. The development of the drone director and drone occurred simultaneously as two components of the same system. In the early to mid-1940s, the designator BQ-7 was allocated to this B-17 drone version, with the director version becoming the CQ-4. After 1947, the designation QB-17 was used. The two aircraft in this category were the QB-17L target drone and QB-17N target drone director. The QB-17s were transferred to the Air Proving Ground Command for changes to the airframe group compartments to accommodate the equipment specific to the QB-17 mission.

BQ-17: Drone aircraft that would fly near or even through atomic mushroom clouds during postwar atomic tests. Equipped with air sampling equipment and other technologies for monitoring the test.

DB-17: B-17s converted as drone director aircraft used to guide QB-17 target drones during the missile tests.

MB-17: Aircraft used as airborne launchers for experiments with the VB-6 Felix, VB-3 RAZON, VB-13 TORZON guided bombs and first-generation Republic-Ford JB-2 aerodynamic winged guided missiles with one VB bomb or JB-2 missile mounted under each wing of the MB-17. They were also used to launch small drones for airborne gunnery targets. One MB-17 survives, 44-83624, at the AMC Museum, Dover AFB, Delaware, as *SLEEPY TIME GAL*.

QB-17L: A target drone conversion of the B-17G having TV cameras in addition to remote control equipment. They were usually painted in red-orange Day-Glo paint with black diagonal stripes for increased visibility. Guidance Equipment: AN/ARW-40 and AN/ARW-1C. Television Equipment: AXT-3B with PH-563/AXT. Telemetering Equipment: None.

QB-17N: Drone conversion was similar to the QB-17L but with a different guidance system and not equipped with television cameras. The optical tracking equipment was installed in detachable wingtip pods equipped with explosive bolts and parachutes for recovery of test data if the drone was lost. Guidance Equipment: AN/ARW-64. Television Equipment: None. Telemetering Equipment: AN/AKT-7.

The QB-17N was the main drone modification with the addition of the Drone Stabilization Control System (DSCSE), which controlled the surface controls (aileron, rudder, elevator, elevator trim tab, flap extension, and retraction); landing gear retraction and extension and braking; throttle, mixture, propeller pitch, turbo-supercharger, and auxiliary power plant control.

Among the other changes included the replacement of the Type C-1 automatic pilot system with an E-4 system, and autopilot control units were added. Flight path

DB-17P (44-83684) drone director. (*USAF*)

stabilization was achieved by signals transmitted from the ground or airborne radio stations. An auxiliary instrument panel was added to the QB- 17L for the TV system.

DB-17P: B-17Gs converted as drone directors that would often be utilized to guide QB-17L and N target drones during the missile tests. Once they became worn out or their need was reduced, the DB-17Ps would frequently be converted to the QB drone configuration and then become themselves.

The Typical DB-17/QB-17 Mission

The Air Proving Ground Command DB-17/QB-17 Mission procedure: QB-17 runway alignment, engine start, and pre-flight checks carried out normally by ground crewmen. A ground control pilot, utilizing a mobile ground unit, would then assume control of the drone and fly it from the runway at which point the airborne DB-17 would assume control. The QB-17 would often be the subject of intentional near-misses during missile tests to preserve the drone for as many missions as possible. If the QB-17 survived the test, the DB-17 would fly it back to the airfield for landing by the remote ground controller

QB-17: Further Post-War Deployment

Operation Remote

On August 6, 1946, two remote-controlled B-17 drone prototypes, veterans of the Crossroads Atomic Bomb Tests, took-off from Hilo NAS Hawaii to begin Operation Remote and flew 2,600 pilotless overwater miles before landing at Muroc AAF, California. The flight was under the direction of Brig. Gen. William Richardson, Chief of the AAF Guided Missile Division. The drones were accompanied by mother aircraft, which directed all their flight operations from distances varying from 200 feet to 3 miles by radio, throughout the fourteen hours and fifty-five minutes of the record-breaking flight. Before landing at Muroc, one of the drones dropped a practice smoke bomb off Santa Rosa Island, of the Channel Islands, off Ventura, California, remotely opening the bomb bays, releasing the bomb, and then closing the bomb bays.

Post-War Deployment

After the Operation Crossroads tests, administration of the B-17 drone program was transferred from the Material Command to the Army Air Forces Proving Ground Command. The 1st Experimental Guided Missiles Group (1 EGMG) was assigned to supervise the development of drone aircraft to support Atomic Energy Commission nuclear tests. On January 13, 1947, the 1 EGMG received national hype by flying a successful drone flight from Eglin AFB to Washington, D.C., in a simulated bombing mission. In April 1948, the group deployed the QB/DB drones to Eniwetok for the Operation Sandstone nuclear tests by which time most DB-17s and QB-17s had been assigned to the 3205th Drone Group. Sandstone consisted of three separate A-bomb tests carried out during April and May 1948 by Joint Task Force 7, at the Pacific Proving Grounds, although at the Eniwetok Atoll rather than Bikini Atoll. The timing of the scheduled A-bomb detonations caused a problem

Above: During Operation Remote, a B-17 Drone begins its record-breaking 2,600-mile pilotless flight from Hilo Naval Air Station, Hawaii, to Muroc Army Air Field, California, August 6, 1946. (*AAF*)

Right: Movie still of Bendix RIM 8 Talos surface-to-air missile intercepting a B-17 target drone during 1957. (*From USAF movie still*)

as the gamma ray measurement experiments required darkness, but the QB-17 drones that were to sample the clouds required daylight to visually control them. As a compromise, all three Sandstone detonations occurred just after daybreak.

Squadrons from the 3205th Drone Group were deployed to provide drones at the Missile Test Center at Patrick AFB, Florida; the Holloman Air Development Center at Holloman AFB, New Mexico; and the Pacific Missile Test Range at Naval Air Station, Point Mugu. Pt. Mugu drones were also utilized at the Air Force Flight Test Center at Edwards AFB and the U.S. Naval Ordinance Test Station at Inyokern, both located in California's nearby Mojave Desert. At Holloman Air Force Base, the group established a detachment to support the 2754th Experimental Wing, and testing for the Bell ASM-A-2 RASCAL (RAdar SCAnning Link) missile supplying QB-17 drones as aerial targets for the missile. The QB-17 drones were also used as targets for the testing and development of the AIM-4 Falcon air-to-air missile.

During 1949, the 550th Guided Missiles Wing was activated at Eglin as an expansion of the 1st Experimental Guided Missiles Group. Its 2nd Guided Missiles Squadron operated QB/DB-17 drone/director aircraft as flying targets for the early Bell Nike Ajax surface-to-air missile, Hughes Falcon air-to-air missile, and the Bendix RIM 8 Talos surface-to-air missile. The squadron also supplied B-17 drones to support the Atomic Energy Commission Nuclear Testing program.

A derivative of the DB-17G was the DB-17P, which utilized different control systems as developed in 1955; however, many directors remained as DB-17Gs, until retirement in 1959. Additional derivatives of the QB-17G were also developed, becoming the QB-17L and the QB-17N. Sources for QB-17 conversion were new B-17s in storage, B-17s retired from other duties such as VB-17 staff transport, and DB-17s excess to requirements. The later series utilized sophisticated optical tracking equipment in detachable wing tip pods equipped with explosive bolts and parachutes for recovery of test data in the event of loss of the drone. Other modifications, beyond the installation of the Drone Stabilization Control System (DSCSE), included exterior lighting to assist external operators in determining the drone's attitude, heavier electrical system capacity, additional radio equipment, and numerous minor internal changes. Differences between the QB-17L and QB-17N lay in specific control and television transmitting equipment installed.

The utility of the DB-17/QB-17 combination ensured their use until the late 1950s. However, the supply of QB-17s was dwindling in the late 1950s, as during World War II, new combat bombers were not designed or built for long-term use (of the 12,731 four-engined bombers built, 4,735 were lost during the war) and thus the supply of replacement parts was extremely limited, causing these aircraft to be very expensive to maintain. Regardless, the 1930s-designed, piston-engined B-17 could not realistically represent late 1950s Soviet jet aircraft as simulated targets, but by then, jet and rocket-powered drones had become available in sufficient numbers and could more approximate the type of targets realistically envisioned for the equipment being tested. The first of these jet drones were two renovated RB-47E Stratojets (53-4245 and 53-4246) that were being phased out of the inventory to the QB-47E drone configuration.

The last active USAF B-17, was a Douglas B-17G-90-DL (44-83684), which flew

Mother ship Douglas B-17G-90-DL (44-83684). Last operational USAF B-17 on August 6, 1959. *(AAF)*

the last operational mission by a B-17 on August 6, 1959 when it directed QB-17L (44-83717) from Holloman AFB as a target for an AIM-4 Falcon air-to-air missile fired by a McDonnell F-101 Voodoo supersonic fighter. A few days later, it was flown to storage at Davis-Monthan. It is currently under restoration at the Planes of Fame Museum, Chino, California. The last QB-17G was destroyed in a missile test in the summer of 1960 at the test range off Patrick AFB, Florida. By then, the remaining QB-17s had been gradually removed from service and retired to the 2704th Air Force Aircraft Storage and Disposition Group at Davis-Monthan AFB, Arizona, sold to private owners, or delegated to air museums; thus the B-17 era that bridged three decades quietly ended.

Post-War F6F Hellcat Drones

By the end of the war, the USN had a surplus of carrier-based piston-engined fighters, and the fabled F6F Hellcat was deemed to be less suitable for air group operations than its wartime rival, the F4U Corsair that saw combat over Korea, and was relegated mainly to training squadrons and drone operations. On March 2, 1946, CNO, Adml. Chester Nimitz, ordered 360 Hellcats be set aside from scrapping for use as target drones under the designation F6F-3K and -5K and painted bright yellow, blood red, or deep orange. The Hellcat drones were initially developed at the Naval Air Development Unit at Johnsville, Pennsylvania, to contribute in three major roles: for target drone operations, as a rudimentary surface-to-surface guided missile, and to sample airborne radioactivity during nuclear tests.

After their use as aerial radiation samplers during the Bikini and Sandstone nuclear tests, F6F drones were assigned to VU-7(a), based at NAS Santa Ana, California, for the continuation of pilotless aircraft evaluation. The squadron was allocated Culver TD2Cs and F6Fs as target aircraft for surface-to-air gunnery training with Beech SNB Expeditors as the drone controllers. On-board pilots ferried them to and from

Santa Ana. The squadron was relocated at MCAS El Toro, Irvine, California, in 1948 and target drone operations were subsequently established at China Lake and Point Mugu for missile-test purposes and at other locations, again using utility squadrons, as targets for training. Some aircraft were modified with wing tip tanks and large wing tip fairings containing flares to simulate a jet exhaust, and therefore approximating targets of the various seeking missile types under development.

Six F6F-5K Hellcat drone variants were part of Guided Missile Unit 90, formed at Naval Air Development Unit at Johnsville. While aboard the carrier *Boxer* (CVA-21/LHD-4) during the Korean War, Hellcat drones with VC-35 AD-2Q Skyraiders as controllers, participated in six individual missions against bridges, tunnels, and power plants in North Korea between August 28 and September 2, 1952. The F6F drones carried a 2,000-pound or two 1,000-pound bombs and a TV camera in a pod under the right wing for targeting. Because of the starboard TV pod, only the port wing could be folded for storage. An antenna for transmission of the TV image from the drone to the controller was mounted on the upper surface of the right wing above the pod. The six attack drone F6Fs were painted an overall glossy sea blue and were differentiated with V1 through V6 markings on the cowling. On August 28, the first pilotless, radio-controlled F6F-5K off the *Boxer* was launched against a bridge at Hungnam, North Korea. The aircraft, loaded with two 1,000-pound bombs, was guided by a controlling Skyraider to become the first guided missiles to be launched from a USN carrier in combat. Of the six missions, only the second scored a hit, badly damaging a bridge. The fate of the other five F6Fs was four misses due to either equipment or controller error and a mechanical error abort.

Beginning in 1947, pilotless aircraft evaluation was continued for Target Drone Operations by VU-7(a), based at NAS Santa Ana. The squadron was assigned Culver TD2C/PQ-8 Cadet and F6F Hellcats as target aircraft for surface-to-air gunnery training using Beech SNB Expeditors as the drone controllers. Outlying Landing Field (OLF) Palisades, Newport Beach, California, was used to launch the unmanned drones and fly them out to the over water target area for ship-to-air target practice. If they survived target practice they were flown under control back to Palisades, repaired, if necessary, and then controlled back to home base. The squadron was relocated at MCAS El Toro in 1948 and target drone operations were subsequently established at China Lake and Point Mugu for missile-test purposes and also at other locations, again using utility squadrons, as targets for missile tests.

The Hellcat drones continued in use as missile tracking target throughout the 1950s. On January 13, 1950, the first successful automatic homing flight of a SAM missile occurred when a Lark flew 17,300 yards to intentionally pass within lethal range of a Hellcat drone flying at 7,500 feet. During December 1952, AAM-N-2 Sparrow medium-range semi-active radar homing air-to-air missile was used to intercept and destroy an F6F flying from Point Mugu, for purportedly the first successful U.S. air-to-air guided missile kill. On September 11, 1953, at the China Lake Naval Ordinance Test Station, the experimental XAAM-N-7 Sidewinder heat-seeking air-to-air missile of Guided Missile Unit 61 (GMU-61) scored its first hit when it passed within two feet of a radio-controlled florescent red F6F-5K Hellcat

F6F-5K Hellcat drones launched from the port catapult of carrier USS *Boxer* (CV-21) during the Korean War in August 1952. The F6F-5K drones were guided into the target by Douglas AD-2D Skyraider controllers. (*USN*)

which was to be preserved. The Sidewinder was equipped with an infrared-seeker to track the heat signature of the Hellcat drone that had flares mounted on the wingtips to give the experimental missile a target for its first success in a sixty-year-long career during which it was oldest, least expensive, and most successful and widely used missiles in the U.S. weapons inventory. The F6F target drones continued to be slowly expended and faded into history to be remembered as the Navy's premier top-scoring fighter in the Pacific War.

5
U.S. Navy Drone Program Development

History

To reiterate, the Navy successfully launched its first NOLO (NO Live Operator) aircraft as radio-controlled target drones in 1924 under the auspices of the Navy's BuOrd and BuEng at the Naval Proving Ground at Dahlgren, Virginia. A Curtiss N-9 was tested thirty-three times during 1924 with a control (safety) pilot, and on September 15, 1924, the N-9, equipped with a Norden automatic pilot and a keyboard teletype controller, maneuvered successfully for forty minutes through a long series of fifty maneuvering radio signals. Tests continued through December but further development was curtailed in the low budget interwar years.

Navy interest in radio-controlled aircraft was revived in 1935 when directives establishing a new radio-controlled aircraft project resulted from the necessity to supply more realistic aerial targets for the training of fleet anti-aircraft gunners and to improve AA fire control equipment. Previously, anti-aircraft gunners fired on practice sleeves towed by aircraft at set altitudes and speeds, which were found to be stereotyped and artificial and did not duplicate actual maneuvering in ever-changing combat situations.

In early 1935, V/Adml. Harris Laning, CO Aircraft, Battle Force, requested that Chief of Naval Operations Adml. William Standley provide high-speed, radio-controlled, armored target aircraft. While on an official trip to England to attend the Second Naval Conference (December 1935 to March 1936), Standley observed a demonstration of Britain's Queen Bee target drone and became involved in consultations with prominent Royal Navy and Royal Air Force officers regarding the indispensable gunnery training that the Queen Bee aerial targets provided. Standley was so impressed with the Queen Bee test results that on his return to Washington, D.C., he was determined to immediately acquire a similar target aircraft for the U.S. Navy.

On March 23, 1936, CNO Standley, in a memorandum on the subject to the BuOrd, BuAer, and BuEng, called attention to the demand for radio-controlled aircraft targets to simulate the conditions of aerial warfare for realistic training of shipboard gunners and the need to collect data, so the Navy could examine methods on how to defend against aerial attacks. In the memorandum, he also delineated the characteristics and anticipated performance of the target aircraft. Standley received prompt and enthusiastic replies from both BuAer and BuEng, but the BuOrd replied that it regretted that the services of radio-controlled flight guru Carl Norden and his staff would not be available as they were totally absorbed in the development of the Norden Bomb Sight and furthermore, the crowded conditions at the Dahlgren Naval Proving Ground precluded work there on such a project as radio control of aircraft. The BuOrd reply also observed that Standley's project would severely impede and set back other critical ordnance programs and that the cost of its development and operation for the routine training of AA units would far exceed the benefits.

Standley then conferred directly with Chief of BuAer R/Adml. Ernest King, who he learned was in full agreement with his view that it was necessary to develop a realistic target for anti-aircraft firing practice. On May 1, 1936, Standley authorized BuAer and BuEng to engage in the development of radio-controlled aircraft targets and gave BuAer primary control over the project, which was granted high priority. On July 20, 1936, Capt. Delmer Fahrney was named the Officer-in-Charge (OIC) of the project and was given three to five years to fulfill its objectives. Fahrney, a class of 1920 U.S. Naval Academy graduate with a master's degree in mechanical engineering and a

Adml. William Standley, Chief of Naval Operations (CNO). (*USN*)

Capt. Delmer Fahrney, Officer-in-Charge (OIC) of Navy's first missile program. (*USN*)

Navy veteran aviator, was to review all previous work in the field of radio control and then was to submit a plan for the implementation of the project to develop a similar system for U.S. Navy gunnery training.

Name Confusion: Drone, UAV, UAS, RPA, RPV

Fahrney is often credited by various sources with coining the term drones for unmanned aircraft. During November 1936, Fahrney discussed the selection of a code name with Dr. A. Hoyt Taylor, which would best describe the Navy's radio-controlled aircraft. Their discussion centered on the British Queen Bee, which had instigated the Navy project and allegedly, in tribute, the name "drone" was selected. Drone was an appropriate name as the singular purpose of honeybee drones is to do the bidding of a Queen Bee mother. In his final semiannual report of 1936, Fahrney first officially used the term drone as indicative of the radio-controlled aerial targets. In the Navy's 1922 aircraft designation system, drone first makes an appearance in 1936, but only as TD (target drone), as an aircraft designed to be shot at for target practice. During the World War II, the Army and Navy utilized TDs for gunnery practice and assault drones (ADs) for offensive combat operations. Thus, drone became the official U.S. Navy designation for controlled, unmanned aircraft for many decades until the end of the Vietnam War, when the Air Force began using the term remotely piloted vehicles (RPV), which were piloted, albeit remotely, while performing missions, such as reconnaissance and surgical strikes, that were typically flown by piloted aircraft but without risk to the pilot. However, from this point, the American Media began the confusing interchangeable use of drone, RPV, RPA, UAV, and UAS. During the 1990s, the word drone was widely interchanged with unmanned aerial vehicle (UAV), and a few years later, remotely piloted aircraft (RPA) was introduced. Then, in 2005, the DOD and FAA began the use of unmanned aerial system (UAS) with system denoting the entire flight scheme: the ground-based controller, the connecting communications (computers, satellites), and the vehicle. Cruise missiles, which perform similarly as UAVs, are single use weapons, as once a cruise missile hits its target, it is destroyed; whereas, the drone, etc. are intended to be recoverable. The quadcopter is a type of drone that is an extremely popular style of consumer-use drones, which the human operator typically uses to shoot videos or photos.

The USN Begins its Radio-Controlled Aircraft Program

On August 6, 1936, Fahrney submitted his proposal for the development of unmanned remotely-controlled aircraft. Fahrney's plan projected budget of $77,500 was include the purchase of two, old, slow, Stearman Hammond Y-1s (Navy JH-1); the development of special mechanical apparatus for the target aircraft; installation of radio control equipment in the target aircraft and in the control stations (two field control carts and two control aircraft); and the salaries of an engineer and a draftsman. This budget would be exceeded by $11,625 because the delivery of the

Stearman Hammonds was delayed, requiring the modification of two Curtiss N2C-2s training aircraft by adding a tricycle landing gear.

On September 9, 1936, Adml. King, Adml. Standley, and the Chiefs of the Bureaus of Aeronautics and Engineering approved Fahrney's plans and selected the Naval Aircraft Factory (NAF), Philadelphia, as the hub of the project, and the Radio Division, Naval Research Laboratory (NRL) at Anacostia NAS, Washington, D.C., as the center of guidance development. In addition to Fahrney heading the center of operations at the NAF, he was assigned a position at the BuAer designated as the Special Designs Desk. Fahrney's dual commission was largely responsible for assigning the project its high priority.

Naval Aircraft Factory (NAF) was established by the Navy in 1918 in Philadelphia, Pennsylvania. During World War I, the Army required large quantities of aircraft and civilian aircraft manufacturers showed little interest in supplying the Navy's relatively small aircraft requirements. The Navy decided that it needed its own aircraft factory to ensure a portion of its aircraft source and to have control of a factory that was able to develop and fabricate its experimental designs. Over the years, the Naval Aircraft Factory provided the Navy with its own manufacturing and test establishment, and also built aircraft designed by other manufacturers to evaluate the cost of aircraft submitted by industry. The Naval Aircraft Factory was controversial, as it placed a federally-funded aircraft industry in direct competition with civilian aircraft industry, which was one of the causes for it being disestablished in early 1945 and the formation of the new Naval Air Test Center at Naval Air Station Patuxent River, Maryland.

Naval Aircraft Factory (NAF), Philadelphia, Pennsylvania. (*USN*)

At the NAF, Fahrney was assisted by civilians, William Wait as aero engineer and George Spangenberg as assistant aero engineer. Wait had worked for Curtiss during the 1920s and had been credited as one of the primary designers of a series of Navy Curtiss CR and Army R-6 racing aircraft that won a number of speed competitions. The thirty-year-old Spangenberg would later serve as Evaluation Division Director, Naval Air Systems Command, where he was responsible for the design requirements/procurement of the F-14 Tomcat and the F/A-18 Hornet. The NRL allocated two radio engineers, E. L. Luke and J. C. Link, to the project and the NAF assigned Petty Officers C. E. Herzog, L. B. McKeon, H. D. Schultz, and H. E. Foster. Lt. Cdr. Frederick Wallace was assigned as the chief pilot. At the NRL, Dr. Albert Hoyt Taylor was assigned as the developer of the radio equipment with Carlos Mirick as a consultant. Previously, Taylor had done award-winning research on short waves, and at the time, Taylor and his NRL team were perfecting America's first practical shipboard radar (CXAM) system. Mirick was Hoyt's long-time associate and is credited with the development of the joystick controller.

Fahrney immediately began project research and development by ordering four Stearman Hammonds with tricycle landing gears and one old training aircraft built by the defunct New Standard Aircraft Corporation. The BuEng recommended that the automatic pilot not be used unless it was later found to be required. Since the original mid-1920s unmanned aircraft projects, radio communications had improved immensely with the availability of high-frequency equipment and very dependable improved standard equipment such as the GP-2 transmitter and its allied RV-3 receiver, which Fahrney designated for use. The NRL oversaw the design of the new circuits, selection of components, fabrication, and tests under the direction of Matthew Schrenk. The development of the radio equipment mainly involved the establishment of an oscillating circuit that, when activated, would send out a note or tone of modulated frequency over the selected carrier wave via the transmitter. The equipment provided twelve distinct oscillating radio channels: two circuits for up and down aileron movement, two for up and down elevator movement, two for on and off throttle, two for on and off control of any desired instrument or control device (as flap controls or steering control on the ground), and a circuit to instantly disengage the radio control gear by the safety pilot. The rudder and ailerons were operated mutually, so there was no direct rudder control. With this circuit assignment, four circuits were available for future control applications. Conventional stick or wheel control and foot rudder controls were used to activate electrical contacts, which caused the radio control signals to be sent out. The necessary hydraulic servos with control valves and electric solenoids were developed by the Radio Control Unit at NAF and installed in various test aircraft—first in an NT plane and later in two Curtiss N2C-2 trainers and two JH-1 Stearman-Hammond Y-1 aircraft equipped with tricycle landing gear.

The Naval Research Laboratory constructed a laboratory drone to test the design of the systems and the selection of components while on the ground. This drone was equipped with a working model of the radio control system with a control station located several hundred yards away. The NRL controller transmitted signals that activated movements of the laboratory drone's simulated control surfaces. Numerous

On October 7, 1937, the Navy began tests on radio newly developed radio control equipment using an N2C-2 drone under radio-control with a safety pilot. The nose wheel added to aid take-offs and landings can be seen in the photo. (*USN*)

tests were subsequently conducted, which perfected both the radio and mechanical components. On February 17, 1937, during a demonstration attended by Assistant Secretary of the Navy Charles Edison and many other leading naval officers, a TG-2 control aircraft successfully controlled the laboratory drone from 25 miles.

By mid-March 1937, one complete control unit was ready for installation in the TG-2 control aircraft and the NT drone. The NAF TGs, originally designed for gunnery training, were a series of prototype equal-span biplane seaplanes (one each: TG-1 to TG-5) with tandem open cockpits that were and built by the New Standard Aircraft Corporation and modified by the Naval Aircraft Factory. The TG-2 was modified with the installation of the hydraulic and radio control apparatus; after installation, tests were conducted with both the NT drone and TG-2 control on the ground and then with the control TG-2 in the air and the drone on the ground. Finally, both aircraft were ready for aerial testing, each taking-off in the early afternoon with the NAF's test pilot, Frederick Wallace, in the NT drone as the safety pilot and Fahrney as the controlling pilot seated in the TG-2's forward cockpit. The circuits were tested at 3,000 feet and found functioning, and Wallace was directed to engage the control equipment. The drone immediately went into a series chaotic twists, climbs, turns, and dives, during which the rather anxious Wallace verified that the climb and dive controls were functioning, but the aileron controls were crossed, left and right. After Wallace disengaged the control, the drone again functioned normally. Subsequently, the malfunctioning aileron controls were corrected and the two aircraft flew another test, which found the radio control satisfactory for all standard maneuvers.

No pilotless drone flights had been made as the delay in the Stearman Hammond's delivery prevented any unmanned attempt as it was considered unsafe to attempt a landing under radio control except by drones equipped a with tricycle landing gear. By early August 1937, when the Stearman Hammonds still had not been delivered, a Curtiss N2C-2 Fledgling was reconfigured to carry the radio control equipment and was reequipped with a makeshift nose gear to complete the required tricycle landing gear configuration. The Curtiss N2C was a training aircraft developed for the Navy in the late 1920s. It was a conventional biplane with the pilot and instructor in tandem, open cockpits. On October 7, after this aircraft was equipped as a pilotless drone, it was tested repeatedly under all possible situations. A second TG-2 was also assigned for use as a second aerial control station.

The development and fabrication of the essential equipment progressed so well at the NAF and the NRL that tests of an N2C-2 drone under radio control with a safety pilot were underway by October 7, 1937. Fahrney controlled the first take-off and landing using a field radio unit cart and three others followed. The next drone flight tests used a radio control pilot in a TG-2. The first tests were ground tests in which the grounded drone's throttles and control surfaces were controlled by an airborne TG-2 from as far as 25 miles away. For the next series of tests, the field control pilot would take the drone off and turn over control at around 200 feet to the control pilot in the front seat of the TG-2 plane. After maneuvering the drone, the TG-2 control pilot would line the drone up for the landing approach and turn control over to the field cart control pilot, who would make the landing.

During early November 1937, testing was relocated to the Coast Guard Air Station at Cape May, New Jersey, which had better overall facilities, weather conditions, was not near a highly populated area, and had no commercial or military air operations conducted in the area. By November 13, many tests simulating a flight of the drone without a safety pilot were conducted. Each of the four pilots (Fahrney, S. E. Herbst, Fred Wallace, and W. M. Bowlin) had rotated and become proficient as drone safety pilots, TG-2 control pilots, and field cart control pilots.

After the first NOLO radio-controlled N2C-2 drone had been completed, Fahrney scheduled the drone's first flight for November 15. During that morning, all equipment was completely tested and four seamless take-offs and landings were completed under radio control but with a safety pilot present in the drone. During the afternoon, the TG-2 control aircraft took-off with Wallace in the radio control cockpit, and once on station, Fahrney, at the ground control cart, opened the pilotless drone's throttle by radio and it made a routine take-off. Once at 200 feet, the control was transferred to Wallace in the TG-2 who then controlled the drone through basic maneuvers for about ten minutes before he lined it up for the landing approach. At about 100 feet, drone control was transferred back to Fahrney at the field cart control. The drone made a hard landing that tore off the nose wheel, causing the plane to skid along on its nose for about 40 feet while the main wheels slowly collapsed. However, only slight damage occurred, which put the aircraft out of service only briefly. Insignificant accident aside, this was the first successful flight of a full-scale American aircraft under radio control and without a safety pilot.

Meanwhile, the long-awaited two Stearman Hammond JH-1 drones (BuNo. 0908 and 0909) arrived and an additional N2C-2 was also allocated. Designed by Dean Hammond in 1934, the unusual appearing Hammond Model Y was a low-wing, aluminum and fabric covered, twin-boom pusher monoplane, powered by a 150-hp Menasco C-4S engine. Only fourteen were built, and although it was designed to be very easy to fly, its high price made it an unaffordable civilian aircraft during the Depression.

The TG-2 was a tandem, open cockpit torpedo plane/seaplane built by the New Standard Aircraft Corporation and modified by the Naval Aircraft Factory used as a control plane for the N2C-2. (*USN*)

The JH-1 Stearman-1 drone was successfully tested during the November 1937 NOLO test flights. (*USN*)

Once the JH-1s arrived, Fahrney focused on equipping them in their drone configuration. After numerous tests with a safety pilot onboard the JH-1, a NOLO attempt was conducted on December 23, 1937. For the test, Fahrney employed the same method as used on the November 15 NOLO flight, except the troublesome hard landing was rectified by using a slightly stalled landing technique that was to be controlled closer to the field control cart. Also, a Sperry directional gyro had been modified so that it could be connected by radio to hold the drone on an accurate heading. For the test, the TG-2 control aircraft took-off first and flew to 300 feet and downwind from the drone. The Stearman-Hammond drone then began its take-off run under control from the field cart, and when it reached about 200 feet, control was transferred to the control aircraft. The control pilot placed the drone into simple maneuvers for about ten minutes and then manipulated the drone down into a landing approach. When the drone had descended to about 50 feet on its glide approach, control was transferred to the field cart to end the first wholly successful flight, after which flight testing was suspended for the winter. The winter hiatus was employed in improving current equipment, designing and testing new components, and equipping four drones for operation with the fleet. Although, personal observation and the experience acquired in controlling the drones was found to be adequate, an important installation was the NAF-designed and manufactured automatic pilot. This device provided greater input that would be used as a radio-controlled wing-leveling instrument bringing the drone into level flight under any flight condition.

Flight testing recommenced on April 18, 1938, and nine days later, after sufficient test and practice flights, three pilotless tests with an N2C-2 drone were completed under the control of various pilots from both ground and air control stations. On June 1, 1938, after several demonstration NOLO flights at Cape May for BuAer Chief R/Adml. John Towers and other high-ranking officers, the project began its move to the West Coast for anti-aircraft tests by the fleet.

Fahrney's continued success led to the official establishment of a dedicated Navy experimental drone unit to provide aerial targets for the fleet, which was to be transferred to Naval Air Station (NAS) San Diego and assigned to the Fleet Utility Wing for duty with Utility Squadron VJ-1. The transfer was completed by early June 1938 after two TG-2 control aircraft were ferried across the country and the four drones (two N2C-2s and two JH-1s) were shipped by rail along with two field control trucks and necessary equipment and spare parts. Fahrney selected a section of flat land on the Otay Mesa south of San Diego, which offered the requirements of safety and remoteness from a populated area and from other aircraft operations.

On August 10, Fahrney reported to C-in-C Adml. Ernest King that his unit was ready to be part of the first AA/drone target firing tests. The aircraft carrier *Ranger* was selected to conduct two firing runs, which were to simulate the firing by a screening vessel on a bomber passing over the ship. Firing was to commence when the slant range (line of sight) was 4,000 yards and to cease when the slant range reached 6,000 yards. On August 15 and 16, the radio control aircraft flew practice passes over the *Ranger* using a safety pilot in the drone. The procedure was for the No. 1 control aircraft to take station at 10,000 feet, one mile abeam of the drone. The No.

2 standby control aircraft trailed the drone at a 2-mile interval. All control for the run was placed in the No. 1 control plane while No. 2 would take over control if there were a malfunction in No. 1.

On August 24, 1938, after the preparations for employing drones as aerial targets were completed, the first ever American drone was used by the Navy as an aerial target for the aircraft carrier *Ranger*. The *Ranger*'s starboard AA battery fired on the drone on the first run and its port battery on the second run. The *Ranger*'s anti-aircraft battery crews were considered to be extremely well-trained but did not register a single hit on either of two drone's passes on the first run over the ship while firing between 4,000 and 6,200 yards range. Unfortunately, for the second run the *Ranger* requested that the No.1 control aircraft increase its distance from one to two miles abeam of the drone. The increased distance and the smoke from the exploding AA shells obscured the drone from the controlling aircraft whose pilot was unable to determine the drone's altitude. During its climb to 10,000 feet, the drone's wing-leveling device failed causing the control pilot to lose control. The control pilot then decided to fly closer to the drone and placed it in a tight 180-degree turn, from which it went into a dive. Control was transferred to Fahrney in the standby controlling aircraft, which was above the diving drone. Fahrney transmitted an up-elevator signal and the drone made a full loop and then went into a steep spiraling dive from which it did not recover and crashed into the sea. On this second run, the *Ranger*'s gunners had again achieved similar dismal results after which *Ranger* Captain John McCain (the father of Arizona senator, Presidential candidate, and USAF Vietnam war hero) complained that the results would have been better if the drone had maintained a steady course and speed while passing over the carrier. The poor effectiveness of the fleet's AA defenses during the drone tests caused more demanding tests to be conducted at Guantanamo Bay, Cuba, during the following winter.

On September 14, 1938, Fahrney's unit would deploy the world's first attack by a guided missile in that the drone was a full-scale powered aircraft capable of carrying a bomb, was controlled remotely by radio, and was visually guided to the target by a control pilot at a safe altitude. The first German guided missile, the SD 1400 Fritz X, was successfully tested on December 18, 1940. This missile, developed by Prof. Herbert Wagner, was an unpowered GB, remotely controlled by radio and visually guided from an altitude of 7,000 feet.

In preparation for the to-be-historic test, the unit completed a series of dive tests on selected land targets on Otay Mesa from 10,000 feet. It was observed that at that altitude the control pilot was able, with visual guidance, to direct the drone with a safety pilot aboard accurately into near impact with the target before the safety pilot gained control. The September sea test was scheduled to be a dive bombing attack on the old battleship *Utah* (BB-31), which was launched in 1909 and during 1932 was converted into a target ship (AG-16) that could be completely radio-controlled from another ship. The *Utah* would serve for the next nine years as mobile target and gunnery training ship until she was sunk at Pearl Harbor. For the test, a pilotless Curtiss N2C-2 drone was taken-off under radio control and flown to the *Utah*'s firing area. A field control cart was placed on the deck of the *Utah* to control the last segment of the dive to keep the drone from actually crashing into the ship. The control pilot in the TG-2 control aircraft placed the drone into a dive from 8,700 feet into a position angle of about 38 degrees, after which the drone settled into the dive toward the ship at a final dive angle of 45 degrees. The *Utah* had a newly installed battery of 75-caliber guns operating in a single mount, which fired two bursts and during the second burst, the drone was hit and went out of control and crashed into the sea. This hit apparently was by chance because in later identical tests at Guantanamo Bay, Cuba, many dives were made on the *Utah* by the target drone and no hits were made by the poor-shooting Navy deck gunners.

After the completion of the *Utah* tests, Fahrney and his drone target unit returned to the Naval Aircraft Factory and relinquished the equipment to the Commander of the Utility Wing U.S. Fleet at San Diego, which placed it under Utility Squadron VJ-1 under Lt. (jg) Robert Jones. While he was in command of the NAF Instrument Laboratory, Jones was a prominent factor in the modification of instruments for radio control projects. Meanwhile, the NAF installed radio control equipment in twelve more N2C-2s to convert them to drones.

After Fahrney's experimental drone unit was transferred to a U.S. Fleet Service Unit, Jones' VJ-1 was given the new designation of Project Dog and returned to Guantanamo Bay, Cuba, to support a series of additional anti-aircraft drills during early 1939. Five N2C-2 drones were transported aboard the *Ranger* and operated from Leeward Point Field, Guantanamo, with the destroyer *Patterson* (DD-392), battleships *Maryland* (BB-46) and *California* (BB-44), plus the target ship *Utah* (AG-16). From February

In 1932, the old battleship USS *Utah* was converted into a target ship that could be radio-controlled from another ship without onboard human intervention. The *Utah* was used during the September 1938 radio-controlled diving attack tests by Curtiss N2C-2 drone controlled by a TG-2. (*USN*)

1 through March 30, 1939, VJ-1 drones successfully flew over the AA positions on seventeen fleet warships off Guantanamo Bay with no equipment failures or control difficulties. Fleet gunnery reports stated that the N2C-2 drones received no hits in about half their sorties and only two of the five were ultimately shot down with a few flying on with hits in their wings or fuselages. The *Utah*, which in 1938 had brought down an N2C-2 drone off San Diego on the second drone pass, now expended 1,500 rounds against an identical drone at Guantanamo Bay scoring no hits. Subsequent to these early drills, fleet use of radio-controlled target drones increased substantially and eventually became standard. During the seventeen-month period from August 1938 to December 1939, thirty-eight drone firing drills occurred, with only seven drones lost to ships' gunfire during the one to six runs being made per drill. During 1940, sixty-one practices were conducted with single ships or several ships firing together with only ten drones lost to gunfire, which was either a testament to drone toughness or, most probably, poor Navy marksmanship.

This second round of poor shooting by Navy warships against the target drones caused a reappraisal of fleet anti-aircraft defenses and the redesign of both fire control and gun systems against bombing aircraft. However, besides revealing the shortcomings of fleet anti-aircraft defense against a maneuvered target, it was Fahrney's intention to introduce and advance the notion of the target drones radio-controlled offensive capability during the 1938 August *Ranger* and the September *Utah* exercises, during which numerous, potentially bomb-carrying drones, passed over warships with impunity.

During this time, the AAC showed an interest in the Navy's target drone projects. AAC Captains George Holloman and Gilbert Hayden and a Mr. Hendricks of Wright Field observed and participated in radio-controlled flights at the NAF on February 4, 1938. As the control pilot in a TG-2, Holloman easily controlled the Stearman Hammond drone (with a safety pilot). Holloman reported positively on the sensitive and instantaneous responsiveness of the drone to his control signals. His also commented the drone's excellent response when the lateral stabilizing instrument (a modified Sperry Horizon) leveled its wings when activated by a radio signal.

AAC Chief Hap Arnold directed Capt. Holloman and Lt. Rudolph Fink to observe the spring 1939 Navy firing tests at Guantanamo Bay and inform him as to the adaptability of the radio control gear for AAC service. These two officers witnessed the ground control operations for the *Idaho* practices on March 16, 1939 and personally flew the control aircraft during the *Patterson* practices the next day. Holloman and Finks persuasive post-exercise report recommended that Gen. Arnold request immediate assistance from the Navy, which R/Adml. Arthur Cook quickly approved, allowing VJ-1s Project Dog personnel to train Holloman's Air Corps Target Project personnel at the Naval Aircraft Factory. During the summer of 1939, the Navy provided the AAC with one TG-2 control aircraft, one N2C-2 drone, and one field control cart, complete with all necessary radio control equipment, and living accommodations for the fifteen Army personnel involved during this training. In reciprocation, when Adml. Cook was prevented from obtaining or fabricating essential components or resolving critical problems, due to Great Depression budget restraints, Fahrney would reach out and inform Holloman as to his needs. Holloman who had some certain influence over Gen. Arnold was most often able to either purchase or fabricate the needed equipment without the usual red tape.

Two earmarked Navy pilotless aircraft squadrons were established, VJ-3 on August 9, 1939 to serve the Pacific Fleet at NAS San Diego, followed by VJ-5 on July 15, 1941 to be stationed at Cape May, New Jersey, for the Atlantic Fleet. The Pacific Coast squadron operated from the previous NOLO field at Otay Mesa until relocated to Puunene, Maui, Hawaii, in 1940. Lt. (jg) Robert Jones served as CO of VJ-3 until his 1941 transfer to command the newly established VJ-5. Jones would eventually command VG-6 and play an important part in transitioning Fahrney's assault drone perception (future Project Fox) into an operational reality.

The success of the Project Dog drones led Fahrney and the NAF to consider the concept of a flying missile that could be guided to its target beyond visual ranges. With their drones, the NAF already possessed a vehicle that could be controlled by radio and only needed a guidance system. In November 1935, RCA's Dr. Vladimir Zworykin submitted a 50-pound "electric eye" to the BuOrd, which had no interest in his proposal at the time. In 1937, Zworykin again presented the Navy Department with the possibilities of television-guided missiles, and after some deliberation, CNO Adml. William Standley concluded that he was satisfied with the status quo for the present and did not wish to fund experimental work on guided missiles. Meanwhile, RCA continued to develop its television system; in 1939, the NAF approached that company to determine the possibility of developing a small TV transmitter to be carried on a drone and a small TV receiver to be carried in a control aircraft. On October 14, 1939, the BuAer authorized the purchase and test of a small TV set, which was contracted on February 24, 1940 and was shop tested by the NAF with good results during 1940. During January 1941, the TV equipment was satisfactorily tested in a two-seat, twin-float Berliner-Joyce XOJ observation aircraft. Throughout the June 4, 1941 tests, the TV transmitter mounted in an aircraft was delivering pictures of such good quality on the TV receiver in a second aircraft that the operator in this aircraft could direct the first plane to pass directly over a designated target. The 325-line picture at forty frames transmitter weighed 35 pounds with dimensions of 7.5 by 7.5 by 23 inches and the power supply also weighed 35 pounds.

During February 1940, CNO Adml. Harold Stark directed Fahrney's team to begin development of a radio-controlled bomber that could be employed for low-altitude bombing exercises without risking an aircrew. In response, Fahrney proposed development of an assault drone that could deliver either bombs or torpedoes by remote control. Stark approved Fahrney's proposal and designated the program Project Fox. During March 1940, R/Adml. John Towers, the BuAer Chief, directed that one of the TG-2 drone control aircraft be furnished with radio control equipment and a radio altimeter as a radio-controlled drone that would enable the aircraft to fly at a selected low altitude above the water for torpedo release.

The radio altimeter was indispensable for a successful drone aircraft torpedo attack as it maintained the drone at a set low-altitude for the torpedo release. RCA made great advances in greatly improving radar-control, target-seeking, and target-homing equipment. The development of a sensitive radio reflection altimeter, Sniffer, was assigned to eminent RCA radar pioneer Dr. Irving Wolff, with electronic engineer R. C. Sanders as his project engineer. Once they perfected the altimeter, they proposed its use to determine the presence of a target directly ahead by operating in the horizontal instead of the vertical plane. In addition to determining the presence of a target ahead, it could be adapted to launch a torpedo or drop a bomb at a selected distance from a target.

During 1934, Dr. Wolff and his RCA research staff demonstrated prototype radar equipment to the Army Signal Corps. By using reflected 9-cm radio waves, they located a ship entering New York Harbor and followed it for the first successful American demonstration of microwave radar. In 1938, Dr. Wolff and his RCA colleagues were instrumental the first installation of radar equipment in Navy combat ships. His research resulted in the design of an altimeter that utilized radar principles that was used in military aircraft and assault drones during World War II and in automatic homing equipment for guided missiles.

On January 29, 1941, the RL 101 Sniffer radio altimeter was successfully demonstrated for USN officials who then determined that this radio altimeter would fulfill the exacting specifications required by the assault drone. Lt. (jg) Moulton Taylor, suggested that right and left switching be included to make it a target-seeking device that, in the summer of 1942, was integrated in the Sniffer and was tested and functioned successfully for ranges up to 4,000 yards. Following these tests, RCA fabricated ten that would, after detecting a target, lock on it and launch a torpedo or drop a bomb automatically at a preset distance from it. By April 1943, the RL 101 satisfactorily released bombs at speeds between 130 and 180 knots, and by May, the minimum speed was decreased to 90 knots.

Simultaneously, RCA launched an analogous project, developing the RL 102 Supersniffer that had all the qualities of the RL 101 but had the additional capability of searching in an arc and then locking upon a target. In November 1942, specifications were drafted for RL 102, requiring a range of two miles (later increased to 6 miles), which were approved by BuAer.

Testing of the RL 102 showed it could potentially crash ships and lighthouses at ranges of 4–5 miles when released at an altitude of 50 feet and hit a target at ranges of 6–8 miles when released at 200 to 300 feet. However, the Supersniffer equipment's power and frequency needed to be altered to have it operate at the longer range from the shorter range. During tests a drone was directed into a target area and searched for and locked upon a moving tanker at two miles for the first successful radar homing test on a moving target. During a late spring 1943 conference, Wolff reported the RL 102's success and Fahrney emphasized that it could be used not only as an air-to-ground GB but also as a surface air-to-air missile. After the television guidance equipment, the radio-controlled automatic pilot, and the radio altimeter had been persuasively demonstrated, the next phase was to incorporate them in an assault drone (AD).

In August 1940, Lt. Robert Jones, CO of VJ-3 Squadron, conducted tests at Cape May to demonstrate the practicality of a controller in a control aircraft following at

Dr. Irving Wolff, eminent RCA radar pioneer. (*RCA*)

a safe distance visually directing a drone emitting small puffs of smoke. C-in-C Adml. James Richardson's report to the CNO on these tests stated that the radio-controlled attack "offers promise." Adml. John Towers stated in a letter to the NAF:

> BuAer is particularly desirous that the technique of operating offensive torpedo-carrying, radio-controlled aircraft in quantity be pushed on to a conclusion and that sufficient flight tests of aircraft television be carried out to permit recommendations of useful application for naval purposes.
>
> USAAF, *Navy and Ordnance Guided Missile Projects*
> Maxwell AFB, MF Reel A2050

In the early summer of 1940, Fahrney was designated as CO of the Naval Air Modification Unit (NAMU), which had control over all target drone and guided missile design and development as well as all modifications to combat aircraft. At the time, there were several projects under way that held promise in the development of a guided missile: interference-free radio control system (Naval Research Laboratory); radio altimeter (Naval Aircraft Factory and Western Electric); radio-controlled automatic pilot (Naval Aircraft Factory); and television guidance (RCA and Naval Aircraft Factory).

By early 1941, shortages of equipment and experienced personnel were causing delays in the Navy's drone program due. On January 17, 1941, in order to advance the program, R/Adml. John Towers upgraded Project Fox priority for both the development of the guided missile and a television guidance system. Almost word-for-word, Towers reiterated his 1940 NAF statement:

> The Bureau is particularly desirous that the technique of operating offensive torpedo carrying radio-controlled aircraft be pushed to a conclusion and that sufficient flight tests of aircraft television be carried out to permit recommendations for useful application for naval work.
>
> USAAF, *Navy and Ordnance Guided Missile Projects*
> Maxwell AFB, MF Reel A2050

Soon afterward, several other advocates also recommended the development of the assault drone. In an April 15, 1941 letter to CNO Adml. Harold Stark, R/Adml. William Blandy, BuOrd Chief, provided that bureau's first indication of support of the program when he sanctioned that all efforts for the development of radio-controlled offensive weapons be concentrated on the development of a torpedo plane drone. Contained in an April 18, 1941 BuAer report, Adml. John Towers notified the CNO that progress in the program was satisfactory and that radar was being developed to replace television as a guidance system in order to allow operations under all conditions of visibility.

Vice Admiral William Blandy, commander of the U.S. Navy forces in the Crossroads operation, along with his wife and Rear Admiral Frank Lowry ceremoniously, cut the atomic mushroom cloud cake. This photo led to the first anti-nuclear protests. (*USN*)

William "Spike" Blandy graduated first in his class from the Naval Academy in 1913 and served in World War I aboard the battleship USS *Florida*. He became the captain of the USS *Utah* (AG-16) from 1938–1940; served as a captain in the Bureau of Ordnance 1940–1941; and became its chief from 1941 to 1943 as a rear admiral. Here, he promoted the Navy's guided weapons' programs but had a controversial role in the infamous Mk. 14 Torpedo scandal and in December 1943 was reassigned as the Commander, Group 1, Amphibious Force, Pacific Fleet. After the war, he commanded Joint Task Force 1 during the Crossroads atomic bomb tests as a three-star admiral and was promoted to a four-star admiral before his retirement in 1950.

Lt. Robert Jones had become interested in guided missiles following the radio-controlled torpedo tests he had conducted at the direction of the C-in-C U.S. Fleet. As soon as his VJ-3 squadron became established at Cape May, he began pursuing a developmental assignment in this field. On July 9, 1941, he submitted a plan for the development of a radio-controlled fighter to be used as an aerial ram, which could be aimed into a large enemy bomber formation and exploded. He maintained that this ram could be developed, tested, and personnel trained in its operation in four months. Jones proposal met keen opposition by some subordinate BuAer officers who felt that VJ-3, an operational unit, should not be utilized for research and development. However, R/Adml. Towers, BuAer Chief, was very much interested in the remote control of the latest type of fighter aircraft and Jones' plan was accepted as the low-priority Project Ram, which continued with the ill-starred and deservedly much-maligned Brewster F2A Buffalo fighter chosen as the controlled drone, which crashed during testing. When a second F2A was assigned to testing, the BuOrd rejected it as unsafe to fly and Project Ram was terminated, although later it was briefly utilized for the Gorgon missile project.

During 1941, tests, supervised by NAF Manager Walter Webster, were conducted guiding a converted TG-2 using RCA television equipment. On August 7, 1941, approximately forty-seven successful (three were unsatisfactory) simulated attacks were conducted where depth charges and torpedoes were dropped from a TG-2 radio-controlled drone, using television equipment to sight and nearly crash) the target (to preserve the drone). Television guidance permitted a larger and safer distance between the control aircraft and the drone than using radio control alone. At a distance of 6 miles (the maximum distance for a clear TV picture), the drone was no longer in the controller's vision and was operated through a television screen onboard the control aircraft. During these trials, the drone was under continuous radio control/television guidance, usually for forty minutes, during which time the control pilot was unable to see the drone itself. Watching the television monitor in the control aircraft, the control pilot made a run on the target, then returned the drone to the initial point, and repeated the runs.

Although only the altimeter control was unavailable but was in development at RCA, on October 8, 1941, Webster reported that the radio-controlled assault drone was nearly ready for service testing and inclusion in naval warfare planning. Webster noted that a drone aircraft could be visually directed by a control aircraft from 4 miles away to crash into a target or get into position for torpedo launching but with television guidance, the control aircraft could guide the drone at a much greater distance. Webster also revealed that a very promising all-weather radar guidance system was being developed by the Naval Research Laboratory and the National Defense Research Council. Webster passed his report on to CNO Adml. Stark, who stated: "Progress in the Assault Drone program is of great interest to the Chief of Naval Operations and to the service at large. It is considered that exploration are being conducted along lines dictated by possible practical service applications."

Subsequently, Adml. Stark immediately issued a broad directive to VJ-5 to develop, test, and operate radio-controlled offensive weapons and to train personnel in their use and also approved the squadrons request for aircraft, personnel, and electronic equipment to do so. This directive created a duplication of effort by the Naval Aircraft Factory and VJ-5, which was a problem for VJ-5 as it was too involved as an operating unit and in supplying services to the fleet and lacked adequate laboratory, shop, and test equipment facilities to conduct such a complicated experimental program. The project was then separated with VJ-5 then to manage Project Dog and the NAF Project Fox.

Not before long, discord arose between the personnel of the two projects over the type of control to be employed. VJ-5 Project Dog personnel recommended the utilization of all electric photocell (television) control while NAF Project Fox personnel maintained that the established radio control was superior. On April 30, 1942, Jones was requested by Adml. Ernest King, the recently appointed as the First

Chief of Naval Operations*, to issue a progress report. Jones submitted the report on May 20, 1942, listing the following successes in the development of new equipment or improvement of existing equipment: the directional stabilizer, the automatic band control and control box, the pulse control, and automatic altitude control. He stated that, in his opinion, the equipment was satisfactory for guided missile controls. Jones concluded his report by stating that the drone requirements had become challenging, and that operational obligations and the lack of shop facilities, test equipment, and laboratory facilities had caused unforeseen delays.

(*Note: On March 12, 1942, President Roosevelt issued Executive Order 9096, which unified the titles of Commander in Chief, U.S. Fleet (COMINCH) and Chief of Naval Operations (CNO). King as COMINCH exercised ultimate command over the Navy operating forces while the order also established the Vice Chief of Naval Operations (VCNO), who would head the CNO and was responsible for all Navy logistics and training during the war.)

The result of Jones report was that Project Dog was separated from VJ-5 and transferred to VG-6, which had been especially formed for this purpose. Nevertheless, the CNO's next monthly report recommended the transfer of Project Dog to the Naval Aircraft Factory, which was fulfilled. However, after Pearl Harbor, Project Dog's termination was responsible for accelerating Project Fox.

Under the direction of Cdr. W. P. Cogswell, Officer-in-Chief of radio-controlled aircraft, the NAF's development and tests using the TG-2 torpedo aircraft had advanced so satisfactorily that by October 8, 1941, the NAF believed that service trials could be initiated. BuOrd Chief Adml. Blandy agreed to torpedo dropping tests to be carried out in the Atlantic, off Newport-Quonset, when the drone was ready. On October 24, 1941, a conference was convened between BuOrd and BuAer representatives to plan future tests for proving the feasibility of the drones as a new weapon and to initiate an investigation into the potential of large-scale production using obsolete aircraft as well as inexpensively-constructed wooden aircraft as possible mounts for the remotely guided weapons. Following this conference, BuAer Chief Towers sent a letter to CNO Stark delineating the proposed tests. In this letter, he suggested that 100 obsolete TBD Devastator dive bombers be assigned the program and that as SB2D and SB2C Helldiver torpedo bombers became obsolete that they also be allocated. Additionally, he stated that investigations were being conducted to determine the design of both new low- and high-performance special expendable assault aircraft. Towers made it a priority that these unproven aircraft be designed so that they could be manufactured in quantities by industries not associated with the conventional aircraft industry that was fully occupied in producing aircraft, engines, and aircraft equipment for Great Britain as well as manufacturing that equipment for the Army and Navy.

On November 4, 1941, Towers issued a confidential correspondence listing the general specifications for an assault missile project "considered of great potential importance, and both its early completion and its extremely confidential nature should be given special consideration." The specification included that the carrying drone was to be a low-cost, expendable using molded plywood or other plastic materials in the construction of the aircraft and that its design was to be manufactured outside the aircraft industry and provide for a maximum of subcontracting. It was to be powered by two 300 hp Franklin engines, be able to withstand catapult launching so it would use jettisonable landing gear. After flying overwater under control for two hours and thirty minutes, the unmanned drone was then to be capable of evasive action using television guidance and then release a 1-ton Mk. XIII torpedo within 500 yards of the target. Also, a 100-pound explosive charge was to detonate when the carrying drone struck either a moving or stationary target. On November 29, 1941, BuAer completed the preliminary design and specifications of a special assault drone, which was suggested offered to the NAF.

After Pearl Harbor, the plans to use obsolete aircraft for assault drones were canceled, as every available aircraft was then needed for combat and the specially-designed assault drone was consequently given high priority for earliest development with tentative plans to build 5,000 for deployment in eighteen squadrons. During mid-December 1941, Capt. Oscar Smith proposed that a simple type of radio control be placed on a robot plane that would be flown to a distance of not less than 50 miles from the target where the pilots in the robot planes would put them under radio control and parachute to the sea for a prearranged pickup. The robot plane would then be directed by a controlling aircraft to fly within 100 yards of the enemy ship before dropping a torpedo. NAF Manager Webster appeared to have a clearer understanding of the complexity and problems facing development of the assault drone project than suggested by Capt. Smith's proposal.

Webster and his NAF engineering staff, in close conjunction with Fahrney's staff, quickly drafted a $354,000 proposal for BuAer in January 1942 in which the NAF agreed to supply complete drawings and design data, one aircraft for static tests, and four prototypes for flight testing. The molded plywood, twin-engined monoplanes were to be television-equipped. The BuAer reviewed the NAF proposal, and on February 14, 1942, directed the NAF to proceed immediately with the design and production of the prototype aircraft, designated as the XTDN-1. BuAer substituted the 220-hp Lycoming 0-435 engines that were more readily available and made several other minor changes to the factory's proposal.

It was not be until mid-February 1942, that Smith was assigned as director of the Plans Division in the Office of the CNO. Immediately Smith investigated the status of ongoing development of Projects Dog and Fox and determined that Cdr. Fahrney's efforts under Project Fox at the Naval Aircraft Factory, using a drone equipped with TV guidance showed the greatest promise for operational use. On March 9, Smith wrote the CNO enthusiastically recommending that the assault drone initiative be expedited: "... the possibilities of this weapon are such as to make it essential that regular peacetime developments be shortened and the TV guided drone be hurried along for combat use." After reading Smith's impressive report, V/Adml. Frederick Horne (the new and First Vice Chief of Naval Operations) directed Smith to arrange for operational testing to determine such a drone's ability to accurately hit a moving target. On March 14, on the advice of his Vice Chief, Adml. King signed off on assault drone attack tests.

On March 4, 1942, Fahrney's television-equipped TG-2s conducted simulated torpedo attacks, low-altitude bomb runs, and mock collisions with targets and also

Above left: As the Director of the Plans Division in the office of the CNO, Capt. Oscar Smith, was instrumental in developing the Navy's drone equipped TV guidance programs. (*USN*)

Above right: V/Adml. Frederick Horne. The new and first Vice Chief of Naval Operations (VCNO). (*USN*)

included radio control take-offs and landings, approach runs to water targets, and evasive maneuvers. These test results were indecisive with only 32 percent of the torpedo runs and 12 percent of the low-altitude bombing attacks successful, although 80 percent of the collision attacks were hits. The television guidance system was satisfactory with optical ranges up to 6 miles. These problematic results caused the assault drone to be considered as unrealistic as an operational weapon and that conventional weapons were as effective due to their uncomplicated mobilization and employment. At this time, television had a maximum 4–6-mile visual range and signals could be received at a 30-mile maximum range but considerable time intensive research and development would be required to achieve higher performance. The current television guidance system was regarded by many as an interim step toward the development of a lightweight, completely radar-directed system for terminal guidance that was necessary in the often prevalent less than ideal visual conditions. However, the development of an effective radar system was even more of a time and developmental challenge than the TV system.

A production contract for 100 TDN-1 drones capable of employing either television or radar guidance were ordered by the Bureau of Aeronautics on March 23, 1942. However, the TDN-1 design (Target Drone with N = Naval Aircraft Factory manufacturer's code), a full-size, twin-engined aircraft, was expensive and not well-suited for mass production and after flight testing, its combat capabilities raised doubts. Before the first TDN had even flown, Fahrney had anticipated its design deficiencies and had wisely implemented a back-up plan. When his intuitions were confirmed, the Navy contacted the El Segundo, California, based Interstate Aircraft and Engineering Company regarding the design and manufacture the improved TDR drone. (Target Drone with R = Interstate manufacturer's code).

On April 1, 1942, NAF Project Fox was transferred to Naval Air Station Quonset Point, Rhode Island, to conduct ten tests of a torpedo attack during the month by a radio altimeter and television-guided TG-2 torpedo drone. During these tests some Mk. XIII aerial torpedoes failed to function, which was a frequent occurrence during 1942; during other tests, the drone did not take the required evasive maneuvers. However, on April 9, the Project Fox unit performed its most important trial to date. Lt. (jg) Moulton Taylor operated the drone control station located in the Beech JRB (AAF/AT-11 Kansan) control aircraft of VJ-5, piloted by Ens. S. E. Herbst. The newly commissioned destroyer *Aaron Ward* (DD-483) was the target vessel that navigated parallel to the torpedo range off Narragansett Bay, Rhode Island. The unmanned, television-equipped assault drone TG-2 torpedo bomber took-off by radio control at 11:13 a.m. with its dummy torpedo set to depth of 38 feet so it would pass under the destroyer. The drone was flying at 85 knots at 130 feet when its TV camera picked up the target at 4 miles. As the drone approached, the destroyer began evasive maneuvers, turning north from an easterly course and increasing its speed to 15 knots. The Beech JRB control aircraft was 8 miles from the target when Taylor, the drone control pilot, directed the drone to the torpedo release point about 300 yards astern of the *Aaron Ward*. Taylor released the torpedo by radio and it passed directly under the full length of the target for the historic first successful American air-to-surface guided missile attack. (On August 25, 1943, the German Henschel Hs 293, a rocket-propelled, radio-controlled GB made the first successful air-to-surface combat attack by a guided missile, striking the sloop HMS *Bideford*; however, the damage was minimal as the warhead did not detonate.)

On April 19, 1942, the NAF Project Fox VJ-5 unit conducted additional tests over Chesapeake Bay, which confirmed the viability of crashing an assault drone into a moving target. For the first test of the day, a TG-2 drone equipped with a sensitive radio altimeter, radio control, and television guidance took-off by radio control from Liveley, Virginia, via a field cart control pilot and was handed over to the control pilot, Lt. (jg) Taylor, in the JRB. Taylor successfully crashed a drone into the water just beyond its battle raft target using outside-in visual control. Later that day, Taylor,

German Henschel Hs 293 rocket-propelled, radio-controlled glide bomb. (*Author*)

using inside-out control*, remotely piloted a television-equipped drone toward the battle raft being towed at 8 knots. At 5 miles, the drone acquired and relayed a good television picture of the target to the control Beechcraft JRB that then turned away. Taylor was able to maneuver the drone by watching only the television screen and directing it into a collision course by radio. Taylor was 11 miles away when the drone crashed the target raft. (*The terms inside-out and outside-in denote the operator's viewpoint relative to the vehicle being controlled: outside-in pertains to when the operator is observing from the outside, looking in toward the vehicle, while inside-out indicates a camera inside the vehicle, allowing the controller to look out as though he was onboard.)

During early May 1942, Captains Smith and Fahrney introduced films and oral presentations regarding the notable April 9 and 19 tests to CNO Adml. King and other Navy department bureau chiefs. Immediately after their presentation, the impressed Adml. King ordered Towers' BuAer to direct the design, development, and procurement of an unmanned guided missile.

After the TDR-1 had demonstrated its encouraging preliminary combat possibilities, Project Option was established within BuAer on May 22, 1942 and Project Dog was incorporated into Project Option, which was responsible for the development of a service weapon and the preparation of plans for its employment in combat within the shortest possible period of time. King had appointed Capt. Oscar Smith as Officer-in-Charge (OIC) of Option, which was under the control of King's Aide for Readiness R/Adml. Willis Lee. Smith was an appropriate choice as he was a strong advocate for the assault drone project. Essentially, Smith was delegated to develop an operational weapon from the experimental guided assault drone and to prepare the weapon for quantity combat deployment ASAP. However, responsibility for research and development of guided missiles remained with Fahrney's Project Fox, which meanwhile was initiating an investigation of the potential of radar homing devices. BuAer retained authority over the missile's design and production, which was an odd and contentious division of responsibility that, although it reflected the prevailing balance of interests in Washington, did nothing to expedite current guided weapons programs.

By late May 1942, partially due to Smith's lobbying, the Navy's first attempt to mass produce a remotely-controlled weapon was approved by Adml. King, who had nurtured the project that he had overseen since 1936. King delineated two requirements: first to develop an operational weapon from the experimental AD guided missile and secondly to prepare the weapon for combat employment at the earliest workable date. King's proposal requested that BuAer provide and train personnel for eighteen assault drone squadrons and supply 162 control aircraft and 5,000 assault drones, as smaller quantities would lose the advantage of surprise inherent in these new weapons. However, the assault drone proposal required a large investment of BuAer's budget and personnel and the new BuAer Chief John Towers, a former Navy pilot and proponent of naval aviation since World War I, was uncertain about King's proposal he now inherited. Differences soon developed between Smith and Towers due to the large scale of the program outlined by Smith and his staff and from the CNO's orders to carry them out. Towers was very opposed to a plan that would put a new weapon into mass production before it had been proven even on a small scale in combat to demonstrate its effectiveness as well as to determine its performance and logistic requirements. More traditional high-ranking naval officers backed Towers, arguing that the program was a waste of essential material and manpower resources at a time when U.S. production and manpower capacity were already overextended. BuAer planners had projected that a program of this magnitude would require 1,300 aviators and 8,700 men, and to realize a production rate of 300 to 500 drones per month, an initial contract for 5,000 would be at a cost of $235 million (nearly $19 billion in 2020). Towers noted: "This Bureau is considerably concerned over premature commitments of funds, materials, and personnel to this project which otherwise would be available for current needs."

During 1942, the NAF's TDN-1 program was gaining increased impetus. In early May, Webster presented revised cost estimates and a proposed production schedule for the initial 100 aircraft lot plus 10 percent spares at $2,750,000 and 444 radio control units costing $1,320,000. Webster believed the November 1 completion date "while very difficult of accomplishment, is believed possible by resorting to every conceivable means at the Factory's disposal and considering cost to be of minor importance but would also delay the NAFs PBN-1 Nomad Flying Boat program (an improved version of the PBY Consolidated Catalina) by about two months." TDN deliveries were scheduled to commence in August with six and then increase to ten weekly through the end of October. The bulk of the large molded plywood assemblies were to be subcontracted, with final assembly and testing in Philadelphia.

Upon being informed of the NAF's TDN-1 high cost estimates and the possibility of delays in the PBN-1 program, Towers wanted clarifications from Webster. In justification, Webster countered that the TDN-1 project's size, the necessity for research and development, and the stringent completion deadline predestined some unavoidable interference with the large PBN-1 project but would only affect the first two or three of these flying boats. Webster also defended the high TDN-1 costs by countering that they would eventually be decreased to $21,000 each.

On April 3, 1942, the CNO authorized an additional 100 assault drones, but understood that conventional aircraft manufacturers, already contracted to manufacture established warplanes, would be unable to undertake the large-scale production of drones. The Navy awarded the new AD contract to the Interstate Aircraft and Engineering Company, with plants at El Segundo, California, and DeKalb, Illinois. The Interstate aircraft, designated TDR-1, was virtually identical to the NAF's TDN. From 200 drones, the program had increased to 1,000 on May 22 with the creation of Project Option. The rationality behind this rapid, enormous increase in production was stated to be that it would be a miscalculation to launch the new weapon into combat piecemeal, which would allow the enemy an interval to develop effective countermeasures. However, the BuAer suggested that this degree of production would be demanding to sustain, but Vice CNO Adml. Horne, a guided missile stalwart, maintained that the weapon's requirement was so urgent that every effort should be made to meet the production goals. Towers, no advocate, was incensed by CNO's declaration and reason for a fivefold increase in production. Towers and BuAer had previously estimated that the projected program would require 10,000 people, including 1,300 naval aviators, and would cost $235 million, which would critically stress current resources.

In early June, to consider Towers' misgivings, a meeting, headed by Fahrney and Jones, deliberated the new assault drone production program. The conferees agreed that Interstate was capable of manufacturing thirty airframes per month in its present plants and that it could increase output to 300 to 500 per month utilizing extensive subcontracting. Meanwhile, RCA was expanding its BLOCK I (to be followed by BLOCK III) production facilities to supply television equipment for the assault drones. Notwithstanding this promising progress, at the time, neither the NAF nor Interstate had delivered prototypes; it was concluded that it was impossible to make rational estimates of productive capacity. On June 29, 1942, Towers subsequently endorsed reducing the program to an initial production order of 500 under Project Option. In August, CNO Adml. King approved this request and proposed that the 500-drone program be comprised of the following: four preliminary XTDN-1s followed by 100 TDNs designed and manufactured by the NAF and two XTDR-1 prototypes. 200 TDRs, 100 TD2Rs, 100 TD3Rs designed and manufactured by Interstate Aircraft Co.

XTDN-1, TDN, and TDR

XTDN-1

During March 1942, Fahrney had delivered the NAF XTDN-1 model to the Washington Navy Yard for wind tunnel tests to verify the basic reliability of the wooden structure. In order to reduce costs, the NAF initially proposed using engines that rotated the props clockwise, which could cause directional control problems; so, instead, counter-rotating engines were specified. On June 1, Fahrney assembled the fourteen-member mockup board in Philadelphia to review the XTDN-1's general layout and the arrangement of instruments and guidance equipment. In their report a month later, the board determined that the mockup was generally satisfactory but recommended:

1. Improvements to the jettisonable landing gear.
2. Provisions for moving the airplane about and storing it on shipboard.
3. No provision for folding wings, which were thought to be an unnecessary complication and expense.
4. The relocation of the gyro-stabilizers and inspection hatches.
5. Several minor cockpit changes for the safety pilot.

Initially, BuAer had difficulties deciding XTDN-1 engine and propeller requirements with the Lycoming O-435s selected on the assumption that they would be available before the Franklin XO-300s. However, Lycoming was unable to supply their engines until November and the NAF then was compelled to revert to the non-counter-rotating Franklin engines for the first aircraft and to consider the Lycoming R-680 radials in later versions. The world's largest wooden prop producer, Sensenich, was selected to supply the fixed-pitch wooden propellers built at their new factory in Lititz, Pennsylvania. Although NAF engineers were to test the propellers installed on the first XTDN-1 before letting a production order, NAF Manager, Webster, decided to risk awarding the contract before all tests were completed, in order to begin production and prevent delivery date delays.

The first XTDN-1 (No. 27873), which was not equipped with complete radio control and television guidance systems, flew three test flights at Philadelphia on November 15, 1942, which were described by now-Captain Fahrney in a May 6 memo to BuAer, as having excellent ground handling and that the aircraft was expected to perform according to plan. The first XTDN-1 was delivered to the BuAer's Board of Inspection and Survey in December, which tested it at Mustin Field at Philadelphia's Municipal Airport until March 1943. In its report at the end of March, the board stated that the XTDN-1 was found to be satisfactory in all respects. In the final test, at Patuxent River, Maryland, the 100-pound bomb in the first XTDN-1 was purposely detonated, destroying the drone in flight. The second XTDN-1 (No. 27874), equipped with all the necessary control and guidance equipment (as were the remaining two prototypes) was tested during early in 1943.

Naval Air Factory XTDN-1. (*USN*)

TDN-1

As discussed previously, the development of television and the radar altimeter during the late 1930s and early 1940s made remotely guided bomb- or torpedo-carrying aircraft practical. Diverging from its past utilization obsolete biplanes, the Navy opted to develop a smaller and faster aircraft, which would more difficult for enemy gunners to hit. Despite the TDN drones being designed as assault drones, the TD signified target drone, with the N identifying the Naval Aircraft Factory as its manufacturer while the R in TDR denoted Interstate Aircraft and Engineering Corporation.

The original November 1, 1942 TDN-1 completion date passed, but despite the many problems encountered the NAF did a commendable job, completing the first twelve TDN-1s before the end of 1942. Webster's assistant, Capt. Lloyd Harrison, who managed most of the program's detail work, was responsible for the belated success, especially manufacturing many parts in-house and scavenging virtually all the materials available in the Philadelphia area. These shortcomings were resolved as later aircraft production involved substantial subcontracting, with the Singer Manufacturing Company, South Bend, Indiana, and the Brunswick-Balke-Collender Company, Muskegon, Michigan, providing many mechanical and structural components. Once TDN-1 deliveries resumed in mid-March, they averaged between four and five aircraft daily through May. Brunswick-Balke-Collender, however, assembled the last thirty TDN-ls, the first of which arrived at the NAF early in August 1943 for final inspection and flight testing.

In January 1942, the Naval Aircraft Factory had been contracted by the Navy to initiate the development of an assault drone, followed a month later by an order for two

XTDN-1 prototypes. A production contract for 100 TDN-1 drones capable of employing either television or radar guidance was issued in March with John Kean named as project manager. The shortage of materials ordinarily used in aircraft manufacture forced the new aircraft to be built almost entirely of plywood. Nevertheless, it had a 2,000-pound payload capability, a lesson perhaps learned from the manufacture of the superb wooden RAF Mosquito. The 36-foot-long TDN-1 was similar to the XTDN-1 except for its high wing layout that spanned 50 feet. The drone had conventional vertical and horizontal stabilizers but had a fixed tricycle landing gear that facilitated the carrying of a 2,000-pound bomb or torpedo beneath its belly. It was a relatively simple, low-performance twin-engined aircraft with a TV camera, radio control equipment. The XTDN-1 originally was powered by two 150-hp Franklin O-300 air-cooled, six-cylinder, horizontally-opposed engines but they were changed to two-220-hp Lycoming O-435 horizontally-opposed six-cylinder piston engines, on the production aircraft and would power the TDN at a cruising speed of 175 mph. In addition to the TV control system a standard removable conventional cockpit in place of its guidance equipment so that it could be ferried from the factory for test flights and to operational air bases.

Delivery of the TDNs, which would only total 114, began in December 1942 and continued on through 1943. Most were built at the Naval Aircraft Factory, the last thirty, however, were built under Navy license granted to the Illinois-based Brunswick-Balke-Collender Company, which would later be better-known for such peacetime commercial products such as bowling balls and billiard tables. TDN-1 flight testing commenced in late 1942 and soon its capabilities raised doubts. However, during August 1943, TDNs demonstrated their ability to fly off the flight deck of the *Sable*, a Great Lakes paddle wheel steamship that had been converted for use as a training carrier, which will be discussed later.

Naval Aircraft Factory TDN-1. (*USN*)

TDN STAG-1 Training

Only STAG-1 was be trained for and to see combat in the TDN/TDR Program. It was trained at Clinton, Oklahoma, where an USN airfield with thick, 10,000-foot concrete runways was constructed in 1942 to handle the converted PB4-Y (B-24) drones that STAG-2 was expected to operate. Significant testing began in Clinton, where training missions were flown, designed to become acclimated to launching, landing, and controlling the drone in the air.

After training at Clinton, the TDN pilots required training over open water. STAG-1 was transferred to Traverse City, Michigan, on Lake Michigan, where all men and equipment arrived during the night to maintain the top-secret project's security. Grand Traverse West Bay served as a training site for deck and catapult launchings of TDNs from the training carrier *Sable* and also from the nearby Naval Air Station to conduct missions over Michigan's northern Lower Peninsula. Traverse City citizens never suspected that of the two aircraft flying overhead the front aircraft had no pilot, although there was a reported incident, during which civilian onlookers were dismayed when no attempt was made to rescue the occupants of a TDN that crashed into the Bay.

USS *Sable* (IX-81) was originally built as the coal-burning, sidewheel paddle, passenger steamer the *Greater Buffalo*. It was purchased by the Navy in 1942 and converted to a training aircraft carrier (along with the similar carrier USS *Wolverine*) to be used on the Great Lakes beginning during May 1943. While having no hangar deck, elevators, or armament, the *Sable* provided advanced training of naval aviators in carrier takeoffs and landings. A trainee aviator who carrier-qualified upon the *Sable* was future President George H. W. Bush.

On August 10, 1943, STAG-1 executed the first aircraft carrier catapult launch of a radio-controlled TDN-1 drone. STAG-1's subsequent training catapult launches included fully loaded drones carrying 2,000-pound bombs. Training missions included bombing a target or just crashing the drone directly into it. Long-range practice runs over Lake Michigan were made on a lighthouse with a 50-mile separation between drone and control plane. The TDN-1 is often credited as the first U.S. drone to freely take-off from an aircraft carrier (USS *Sable*). An Airspeed Queen Wasp drone had previously been catapulted, not flown, from HMS *Pegasus* in 1937.

Sable/TDN Gallery

During December 1943, twelve plywood, pilotless TDN assault drones had been delivered to the Board of Inspection and Survey for tests. On January 19, 1944, the board submitted its preliminary report concerning these initial tests with the recommendation that a suitable control system should be developed and be available for future drone development without delay. However, the dozen drones were found to be slow and low-performing, with their cost far surpassing the available budget. Consequently, the Interstate Aircraft and Engineering Company was contracted to build the next model, the TDR, which was ready to be flown in late 1943 and became the Navy's choice as its AD.

With the TDN never to see combat, the hundred or so completed airframes were obliged to serve as anti-aircraft training targets. Most TDN-1s were delivered to

USS Sable/TDN Gallery

The Navy wished to deploy the TDN-1 drone off carriers and conducted tests from the training carrier USS *Sable*, a converted Great Lakes paddle-wheel steamship in 1943. (*USN*)

The TDN-1 is often credited as the first drone to freely take-off from an aircraft carrier (USS *Sable*). A RAF Airspeed Queen Wasp drone had previously been catapulted from HMS *Pegasus* in 1937. (*USN*)

J2F amphibian drone control aircraft flying off the TDR's starboard as the drone attacks a floating target. (*USN*)

TDN-1 drone test from the decks of USS *Sable* while steaming in reverse in Grand Traverse Bay, Michigan, on August 10, 1943. This particular drone is about to stall and would crash into the sea. (*USN*)

training unit, Utility Squadron 6, based at Cape May, New Jersey, which was nearby Philadelphia, allowing the NAF personnel to continue evaluation in reference to the TDR aircraft and to directly become involved with any problems as they occurred. The jettisonable tricycle landing gear was designed and constructed to cleanly break away but also needed to be strong enough to carry the projected bomb and torpedo loads and the acceleration forces of catapult launches from aircraft carriers. The release mechanisms were found to be inadequate, and during June 1943, the NAF redesigned and began production of a new hydraulically actuated release mechanism.

TDR-1

Before the first TDN had flown, Fahrney and Smith had anticipated its design difficulties and wisely implemented a back-up plan. When these forebodings were confirmed, the Navy contracted the Interstate Aircraft and Engineering Company, to design and manufacture two improved XTDR-1 drone prototypes. Interstate was a small but experienced manufacturer of civilian aircraft, including the two-seat Cadet, monoplane (the L-6A Grasshopper was the military version), which was a competitor of the celebrated Piper Cub with over 600 built.

The XTDR-1 prototypes quickly proved the design to be functional and the TDR-1's use of low-performance engines and relatively few strategic materials did not interfere with other wartime aircraft production. Within six months, Interstate had

One of two XTDR-1 drone prototypes that led to the 189 production versions built by Interstate. (*USN*)

Piloted TDR-1. For testing and ferrying, several TDR-1s had very simple standard open cockpits. The pilot would only assume the controls when the remote-control equipment failed or when the aircraft was to be landed. (*USN*)

Unmanned TDR-1. For unmanned operational missions, the pilot's cockpit canopy was replaced by a flush fairing and the landing gear was jettisoned after take-off. The TDR-1 was to carry a 2,000-pound bomb or a torpedo. (*USN*)

completely converted their tooling, an adjoining furniture factory was renovated as an assembly line, and a runway was constructed nearby. The Brunswick-Balke-Collender Company and the American Aviation Corporation were associate contractors in the assembly. The TDR was practical to manufacture with a steel tubing frame built by the Schwinn Bicycle Company, Chicago, covered by molded wood supplied by musical instrument manufacturer, the Rudolph Wurlitzer Co., North Tonawanda, New York, which had several patents on distinctive assembly processes. The 5,900-pound (not including an explosive payload of up to 2,000 additional pounds) TDR-1 closely resembled the TDN as, like its predecessor, it featured twin flat, air-cooled Lycoming 0-435-2 220-hp piston engines (or two horizontal six-cylinder, 150-hp Franklin engines), a tricycle landing gear, and a removable cockpit. Its low-mounted wingspan measured slightly less at 48 feet. The drone cruised at about 150 knots (173 mph) with a payload of a 2,000-pound bomb or torpedo over a range of 425 miles.

For testing and ferrying, some TDR-1s had very simple standard open cockpits that included an instrument panel with an air speed indicator, a simple ball and turn indicator, an altimeter, and a compass. However, to cut costs, the engine gauges (oil pressure, cylinder head temperature, etc.) were located on the engine cowling, causing the ferry/safety pilot to look out four feet forward to read them. The safety pilot would only take over the controls if the remote control equipment failed or when the aircraft was to be landed. For unmanned operational missions, the cockpit canopy was replaced by an easily-installed flush fairing. After testing and becoming operational, its tricycle landing gear was modified so it could be remotely jettisoned after take-off, after which the unmanned assault drone completed a one-way trip, increasing its terminal velocity (175 mph) to crash and explode into the target from as far away as 425 miles. During testing in the latter half of 1943, before the guidance system was tested, several TDRs with temporary cockpits with minimal controls and instruments were tested and were found to be exceptionally stable and maneuverable. But the TDR-1 had some shortcomings, such as the landing gear having no brakes. To hold the drone in place when it was being prepared for take-off, the tail skid had to be fastened to a stationary object—often the bumper of a truck parked on a runway. After engine run up, a ground crewman cut the line, permitting the drone to start down the runway.

The TDR's most outstanding innovation was its improved guidance system, particularly the RCA BLOCK I Cyclops-like television camera mounted in its nose, which was considered a marvel of miniaturization for the time, long before vacuum tubes were replaced by transistors. Zworykin's guidance consisted of the BLOCK I TV camera and the transmitter in a box that measured only 8 by 8 by 26 inches and the entire system weighed only 97 pounds, including a battery power supply. Paired with an onboard radar altimeter, the TDR-1's guidance system could be controlled remotely from a relatively long distance.

USN TDR Variants

XTDR-1: Two prototypes built.

TDR-1: XTDR-1 production version, 189 aircraft built by Interstate.

TDR-3: Last of the TDR variants and was powered by two 450-hp Wright R-975-13 radial engines.

XTD2R-1: Powered by two Franklin O-805-2 engines, two prototypes ordered, canceled by the Navy and completed as the XTD3R-1.

XTD2R-1: Two prototypes canceled.

XTD3R-1: Powered by Wright R-975 radial engines, three prototypes built.

XTD3R-2: XTD3R-1 Variant, one prototype built.

TD2R: Proposed TDR variant mounting two 450-hp Franklin 0-805-2 engines.

TD3R-1: Production version of XTD3R-1, forty ordered but canceled

AAF XBQ TDR Versions

XBQ-4: AAF designation for TDR-1. One aircraft converted from TDR-1 in April 1943 but discontinued after initial tests in December.

XBQ-5: AAF designation for XTD2R-1. Designation reserved but no aircraft ordered.

XBQ-6: AAF designation for XTD3R prototype. None built.

BQ-6A: AAF designation for TD3R-1 for production models. But none built before the program was canceled in 1944.

XTD3R-1. (*USN*)

XBQ-4. AAF designation for the TDR-1. One aircraft was converted from the TDR-1 during April 1943, but was discontinued by the AAF after initial tests in December. (*USN*)

TDR Tribulations

On September 22, 1943, Adml. King instructed his vice CNO, V/Adml. Horne, to coordinate and accelerate all guided missile development and research projects and put them into operations as soon as practicable. Adml. Horne directed Smith to visit Pacific Fleet H.Q. to discuss the Pacific combat deployment of the assault drone at a time when the Pacific War was beginning to gain the initiative with the use conventional weapons. Adml. Chester Nimitz, C-in-C U.S. Fleet, in a November 25, 1943 report, not wanting to earmark vital personnel, materiel, or equipment, particularly aircraft carriers, to the assault drone project, "warned against the experimental use of an unproven weapon that could interfere with normal operations." Nimitz continued: "While deeply interested in the development of new weapons of this type, we lack carriers, landing fields, and other facilities to try out unproven weapons." Moreover, Nimitz noted the low-speed and maneuverability of the assault drones and specifically recommended that SBD Dauntless dive bombers, if suitable and available, be converted into drone missiles.

Additionally, Adml. Towers also admonished that it would be irresponsible to provide any shipping space or support for the operational testing of the unproven TDR-1, which would be deleterious to the delivery and use of conventional weapons. Despite Smith's vigorous backing of their use during low-visibility or in association with conventional bombing and torpedo attacks, the reproaches from Nimitz and Towers seemingly stymied the deployment of the TDR-1s in combat. Smith continually and actively emphasized that enemy targets could be attacked with greater accuracy and with less exposure to the attacking force and at a lesser cost than any other weapon currently available.

The Naval Aircraft Factory continued its involvement in the assault drone program during 1943, as NAF representatives assisted Interstate with the design and development of the TDR-1, particularly with the installation and testing of the guidance equipment and also tested the XTDR-1, the first Interstate drone.

Smith presented a progress report to Adml. King concerning the TDR developmental and service testing, together with specifics regarding their guidance and control system. Smith specified that "the drone was superior to a gun, bomb, or torpedo in accuracy and could make an accurate horizontal approach against targets that were out of the range of other conventional weapons." He concluded his report by advocating that this airborne remote-control bomb "be brought into action by trained crews and that it be used during periods of low visibility, boldly, and in sufficient force to gain full benefit of its power and surprise characteristics."

On March 23, 1944, King approved Smith's request but first required information relative to its operational organizational scheme and added the caution that secrecy was to be maintained and information provided on a need to know basis. Smith responded that an assault drone force was organized into Special Task Air Groups called STAGs, with each STAG comprised of two to three squadrons. Three STAGs were initially established under the command of Cdr. Oscar Smith. STAG-1 was organized under Cdr. Thomas South for carrier-based missions. STAGs -2 and -3 were intended for service in the ETO, using the next generation 225-mph TD2R-1s that were to be guided by controllers in medium bombers. This intended use was never realized as on March 10, 1944, two months before the Normandy invasion, STAGs -2 and -3 were disbanded, but there was no decrease in the orders for electronic equipment that could be installed in obsolete aircraft to be used as drones.

Also, on March 23, 1944, VCNO Horne ordered the AD program to be increased to 3,000 assault drones at a delivery rate of 250 per month by June 1944. However, Adml. Towers was concerned about the program's capability to deliver the 3,000 drones, the necessary pilots, and other personnel, without substantially hampering the production of conventional aircraft. The subsequent debate reduced the requirement to 1,500 drones in addition to the 500 already under contract. For deployment in combat, these 2,000 drones were to be designed for and equipped with radio control apparatus, a radio altimeter, television, an automatic bomb release device, a radar beacon, and radar equipment. Contracts were let to the F. M. Fink, New York, to fabricate the frequency modulated radio control equipment and to RCA for the altimeter, television, automatic bomb release, and homing equipment.

Towers, now Commander of the Pacific Fleet, continued his opposition to any effort to include television guided drones into his battle plans. Towers maintained that the TDRs were untried and that the current conventional Navy efforts in the South Pacific were shown to be increasingly effective against the flagging Japanese war machine. Between 1942 and 1944, disagreements continued between the two AD advocates, Fahrney and BuOrdman Smith, *versus* the conventional pioneering Navy aviator Towers over their objectives concerning the revolutionary, unproven assault drone program. Initially, during its developmental stage, Towers and BuAer were inclined to fund the pilotless, television-guided assault drone program. However, aviator Towers would develop reservations about non-aviator Smith's assertions concerning the potential of radio and television control technology's ability to replace a human pilot in a targeted attack.

Fahrney departed BuAer in June 1943, leaving leadership of guided weapons to Lt. Cdr. Grayson Merrill. Fahrney was then assigned to command the Naval Aircraft Modification Unit (NAMU) in Johnsville/Philadelphia, a branch of the Naval Air Material Center (NAMC) formed on July 14, 1943 that also included the NAF. During 1944, the Fahrney/Smith *versus* Towers dispute continued and climaxed in June 1944 when Fahrney was relieved at NAMU by Capt. Ralph Barnaby. Fahrney was reassigned as head of the Logistics Section of the Aircraft Command between 1944 and 1945, his only post not associated with drone or guided missile development between 1936 and his 1950 retirement. This forced reassignment resulted from a Towers' 1943 ineffectual directive that Fahrney have no further unofficial or official personal contacts with Adml. King, concerning the assault drone program. On February 15, 1944, a crony of Towers, Capt. Harry Temple, was assigned Fahrney's old position as the head of the Navy's guided missile program as part of the Office of the Chief of Naval Operations. Temple immediately appraised the AD program and in a memorandum to Adml. King, he recommended that, because of the increasing time and (shipping) space requirements of the Pacific War, declining target availability, and because of the fast movement of U.S. forces, a declining requirement for a weapon such as the assault drone was indicated. Temple (via Towers) then significantly reduced the scale of the assault drone program, diminishing its status to a combat test and reassigning many of its personnel that had been specifically-trained for television guidance. Fortunately, Smith continued to have a certain influence within King's chain of command and maintained that the television-guided assault drone should be tested in combat. King acquiesced and granted the deployment of the one remaining STAG-1 unit to the Russell Islands in June 1944.

During 1943, new orders had trimmed Smith's Project Option originally-sought-after 5,000 drones to 2,500 drones, and then to only 500, plus 162 control aircraft. On November 10, 1943, a conference had been convened at the H.Q. of C-in-C U.S. Fleet, Adml. Chester Nimitz, in Hawaii to discuss the future deployment of assault drones in the Pacific. Attending were Adml. Nimitz, V/Adml. Towers (newly appointed as the Commander Air Forces Pacific), V/Adml. John Newton, R/Adml. Charles McMorris, Capt. Forrest Sherman, and AD advocate Lt. Cdr. Oscar Smith. During the discussions, Smith fervently outlined and defended his drone program and openly clashed with Towers, who again questioned the worth of consigning indispensable resources to Smith's unproven project. This meeting, probably influenced by the vexed Towers, determined that before drones entered combat the following recommendations were to be fulfilled:

1. The drone had to demonstrate advantages over other conventional weapons in use.
2. The method of deployment had to be established.
3. Develop high speed and maneuverable combat drones as the speed and maneuverability of the drones had to be increased as slow speeds reduced its effectiveness and vulnerability.
4. SBD dive bombers, if suitable and available, were to be converted to drones.

STAG-1, including a headquarters squadron and two combat squadrons, had been transferred to Monterey, California, in November 1943 for training in anticipation of being deployed to the Pacific. During February 1944, Adml. King (CNO) and Adml. Horne (VCNO) reviewed the deployment of STAG-1 to the Pacific, and on February 24, King directed C-in-C Pac Nimitz that experience using the STAG-1 drones must be gained methodically but without delay so that when Germany was defeated, this experience could be utilized when the large numbers of long-range B-17s and

B-24s that would become available in the Pacific for use as drones, using B-29s as control aircraft. King ordered STAG-1 to provide tests of the TDR-1 in the Central or South Pacific ASAP. Cdr. Smith as the CO of the newly organized Special Air Task Force (SATFOR) was ordered to report to Nimitz and organize a combat trial of the STAG-1 using TDR drones and TBM control aircraft. Since Admirals King and Horne had recommended the deployment of assault drones, Nimitz had no choice but to reluctantly agree. However, BuAer Chief Towers was opposed to any further prototyping of the SBD Dauntless as a drone until the TDR-1 operational assault drone experience was successful and confirmed that there was a justification for it.

V/Adml. Raymond Spruance, Commander of the 5th Fleet, was in Pearl Harbor planning the attack on the Marshall Islands and became acquainted with SATFOR and the TDR drone project. Spruance specifically requested that the drones be deployed during the planned invasion on Eniwetok and his suggestion was approved by Nimitz and King. STAG-1 with the SATFOR staff was to be transferred from Monterey to one of the airfields in the Gilbert Islands and then was to be staged forward to recently-captured Majuro Atoll to assist in the attack on Eniwetok in late May 1944. Unfortunately, for STAG-1, the initial Marshall Island's campaign was so successful that the date of the attack on Eniwetok was moved forward making it impossible to transfer STAG-1 in time to join in that campaign.

For the next five months, STAG-1 remained in Monterey while their future deployment was continually being deliberated. Adml. King supported their immediate and extensive use while Adml. Towers maintained that they should be further tested under controlled conditions and then utilized on a limited basis. To make the situation even more difficult for Smith, Towers again recommended that the SATFOR project be disbanded.

STAG-1 Deployment to the Pacific

Cdr. Oscar Smith went to Pearl Harbor to personally request the transfer of an escort carrier for STAG-1 use. Smith's request for a valuable carrier was denied and he was ordered to report to Adml. William Halsey, CO of the South Pacific Area. Halsey then referred Smith to R/Adml. E. L. Gunther, CO of the Air Forces, South Pacific, to discuss the fate of STAG-1. On March 18, Gunther approved the Russell Islands as a SATFOR base for STAG-1 operations. By mid-May 1944, most of STAG-1's personnel and materiel, plus personnel of two squadrons from the disbanded STAG-2 and STAG-3 left Alameda, California, ferried aboard the newly-launched carrier *Marcus Island* (CVE 77) on her first Pacific cruise. Several days later, the remainder of the unit's personnel, materiel, and a dozen crated TDRs followed on two transport ships.

For the voyage, a drone and its components were packed in several crates and on arrival were unpacked and reassembled, after which the electronics were installed, calibrated, and checked. The drone was first ground checked as an aircraft only and then its radio control and other electronics were checked by equipment in a command car. The command car was a panel truck that could communicate with the control aircraft in the air and also was outfitted to control the drone for ground check out or prior to handing off the airborne drone. After the ground checks, the drone was flight checked by the check pilot as a conventional aircraft. Then the check pilot served as passenger while the mothership controlled it as a drone. The check pilot had to be constantly alert to take over control as the new electronics and control mechanisms were unreliable. An important part of the electronics check was of the automatic control equipment (ACE/ radio altimeter), which was essential in controlling the drone's dive toward the target. The ACE was a shoe box-sized container mounted inside the fuselage that contained the altimeter scaled from 0 to 1,000 feet and worked off two antennas (one forward-facing and the other aft on the aircrafts ventral centerline). The altimeter control box allowed the check pilot testing the drone to set his altitude in 100-foot intervals from 600 down to 100 feet to check the accuracy of a drone being radio-controlled into a target.

TBM/TDR Control: STAG-1 Control Aircraft

Initially, Twin Beech SNB-1 Kansans (AAF: AT-7 and AT-11) were allocated as the control aircraft and a Vultee SNV (AAF: BT-13) training aircraft as the radio-controlled drone stand-in until the TDRs began to leave Interstates' assembly line and were ferried to Clinton. Also, during the training period, the SNBs were replaced by several Navy TBM Avenger torpedo bombers that were modified by General Motors for this purpose and redesignated TBM-1Cs. These TBMs carried four crew: a pilot, a radioman, a 50-caliber turret gunner, and a drone control pilot. Radio controls for the drone were provided for the Avenger's pilots in the forward cockpit while duplicate controls, plus a BLOCK TV screen and a radar altimeter were installed in the rear of the crew compartment of the mother ships. A retractable dome was installed below the Avenger fuselage to house the necessary transmitters and receivers. The drone and control pilots originally were assigned to STAG-1 on a top secret basis and were primarily fully-trained TBM torpedo bomber pilots and most were disappointed when they learned of the true nature of the new assignment.

TDR Control Aircraft Gallery

Preliminary tests on the Russell Islands were conducted using Douglas SBD Dauntless dive bombers as the mother ships with an ungainly control box suspended under the port wing. Soon, STAG-1's mother ships were modified Grumman and General Motors (built under license) TBM Avenger C-1 torpedo bombers. A large radome, installed in the Avenger's radio position, protruded about a foot from the lower fuselage when retracted and extended several feet in flight. The radome contained the radio and TV receiver/transmitter and did not appreciably affect the Avenger's speed or performance. The radio controls were carried in both the forward and rear cockpit, but the rear cockpit also had the BLOCK television receiver (scope) and radar installed. Besides the radioman and gunner, the TBM crew included two carrier qualified pilots: the normal or Control Plane Pilot (CPP) who sat in the front cockpit and the drone control pilot (DCP) who sat next to the radioman cramped in the rear cockpit with the TV control equipment. After the command car guided the drone into the air on take-off, the CPP gained control of the drone. The CPP jettisoned the drone's landing (actually a take-off) gear and then guided it until it was within

Control Aircraft Gallery

The Douglas SBD was used as an early control aircraft. The crude box installed on the Devastator's port wing contained a TV camera and a radio transmitter. (*USN*)

In addition to the standard pilot, radioman, and gunner crew, for TDR missions, the Grumman TBM-1C carried a drone controller who shared the rear cockpit with the radioman. The photo shows the radio and TV receiver/transmitter deployed in a retractable radar dome from the rear fuselage. (*USN*)

The cockpit of the TBM contained the "state-of-the-art" control equipment, which included the BLOCK TV monitor (mid-right) and a central joystick controller located on the so-called "telephone box." (*USN*)

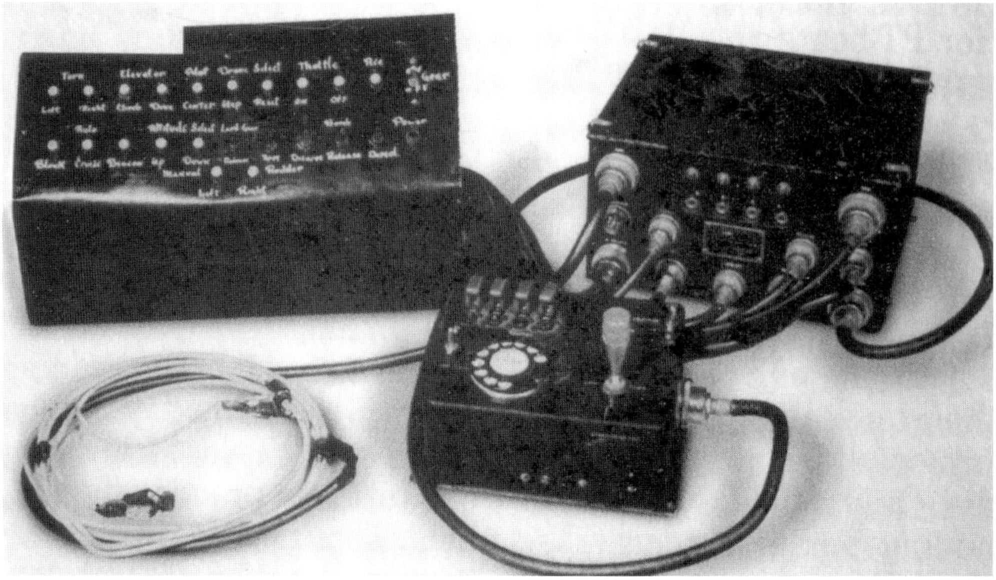

Control apparatus in the TBM cockpit. The joystick/telephone box (center), the telephone box command control box (left), and radio-control box (right). (*USN*)

television range of the target where the DCP would take control. Once the DCP gained control the CPP Avenger pilot could turn away to a safe distance from the target area while the DCP continued to guide the drone's attack via television. The DCP was entirely dependent upon the picture on his 7-inch CPV-59 television screen that was transmitted by the TV camera and transmitter located in the drone's nose. To operate his TV and radar set, the DCP would lower his head under a black drape to block out the sun and turn the sets on. The only input on the target the DCP had were the TV image, the position indicated on the radar scope, and the instrument repeaters on the control panel. Once the DCP acquired control of the drone using a joy stick, he was able to control its attitude. This control was supplemented by the automatic control system based in the electronic telephone box that was distinguished by a telephone dial, which controlled a number of pre-programmed commands. These commands included left and right rudder, up and down elevator, left and right bank, increase and decrease throttle, ACE on and off, BLOCK on and off, step altitude (e.g. if the operator dialed 1 the drone would fly at 50 feet, 2 at 100 feet, etc.), and four irreversible functions—jettison landing gear, arm bomb, drop bomb, and detonation. Each TV transmitter and receiver operated on one fixed channel and the transmitter had only four pre-channels that allowed only four drones to be operated at once without interference. Several types of smoke tanks and generators were tried to more easily follow the TDR drone to the target.

TDR Drone Gallery

Above: STAG-1TDR Drone Edna III being prepared for operations. A fairing was placed over the cockpit, a small CVR television camera was installed in the nose, while a 2,000-pound bomb was loaded under the fuselage. (*USN*)

Below left: CVR television camera. (*USN*)

Below right: Block TV equipment. APN-7 beacon. Beacon antenna, KY-3 coder. (*USN*)

Since the 2,000-pound bomb was not dropped it was strapped to a special cradle under the TDR's fuselage. (*USN*)

Several types of smoke dispensers were tried to more easily follow the TDR drone to the target. (*USN*)

STAG-1 TDR Testing and Operations in the South Pacific

STAG-1, divided into two squadrons, VK-11 and VK-12 (VK was the Special Air Task Force Squadron, STAGRON, designation), was based at Sunlight Field, a 4,400 by 150-foot coral strip, on Banika Island, which was a small island in the Russell Island's group in the Solomons, 25 nautical miles off the northwest tip of Guadalcanal. Though STAG-1 had been designated and trained for carrier operations, it was now land-based. By mid-1944, the Pacific War was being fought far to the north, but STAG-1 needed to demonstrate that their drones could be tactically effective. Drone test flights began on June 20, and six days later, the technical staff successfully achieved the first radio-controlled TDR-1 take-off from the airfield. Through the last few days of June and much of July, numerous test and practice flights were flown under the code name Affirm. After four weeks of training, eight TBMs were ready as control aircraft and twelve TDRs as drones. Eighty three of the ninety-two controlled take-offs had been successful while on the others the safety pilot had to assume control. During testing, two Avenger control aircraft were lost as were several TDRs. Weather occasionally was a factor in canceling flights as tropical rain squalls would suddenly appear while winds of over 16 knots made unmanned take-offs very hazardous. On the ninety-two total test flights 72.3 percent were judged to be successful after take-off, 77.3 percent of the altimeter-controlled flights were successful; followed closely by 76.3 percent of the radio-controlled flights; and then by 63.9 percent of the television-controlled flights. Cdr. Oscar Smith reported that the radio control equipment, although successful due to the constant efforts of STAG-1 engineers, was fragile, substandard, and should be entirely redesigned in order to make them more rugged, more reliable, and less liable to interference with and from other equipment. Smith concluded that the TDR had basically proven itself to be reliable despite its limited specifications. Smith continued on to praise manufacturer, Interstate, saying it had done an "excellent job" considering the obstacles of building the TDR with parts (e.g. wooden fuselage and wings, the Franklin engines) that would not interfere with other aircraft programs.

A TBM control aircraft follows the TDR drone just after take-off. Soon the CCP would jettison the drone's landing gear and guide it until it was within television range of the target. (*USN*)

In the unit's log, July 30 was officially termed "STAG-1's D-Day," as it was the date of a scheduled demonstration for Adml. Gunther and USMC Maj. Gen. Ralph Mitchell, CO Solomon Island Air Forces. Four control Avengers and a standby for each and four drones carrying 2,000-pound bombs with a standby for each were scheduled to attack the hulk of the Japanese merchant ship *Yamazuki Maru* 34 miles away. The Japanese vessel had been beached on November 15, 1942 off Cape Esperance near Guadalcanal's northwestern tip, while running the Slot, to supply Guadalcanal's beleaguered Japanese garrison.

Five drones were controlled in their take-off in early afternoon but the nose wheel of one drone collapsed on take-off. The four drones arrived over the target area with their control TBMs following 6–8 miles behind. At 1:59 p.m., the first TDR-1 dove toward the target vessel and hit the port side ripping open an 8 by 25-foot hole. Three minutes later, the second drone just missed the ship's superstructure by 5 feet and crashed into a coconut grove beyond. At 2:05 p.m., the third drone dove and hit the ship a glancing blow but its demolition bomb did not explode. Ten minutes later, the fourth drone, which was the standby, slammed into the port side and exploded at the deck line causing another large hole that was similar to the first.

STAG-1's "D-Day"

The Japanese freighter *Yamazuki Maru* beached off Cape Esperance, Guadalcanal, was used for the July 30, 1944 TDR demonstration during which two of four drones hit the target tearing open large holes in the hull. (*USN*)

Movie still shows drone approaching the target. (*From USN movie still*)

Controller television monitor view of approaching target. (*USN*)

Movie still of TDR drone exploding the target. (*From USN movie still*)

Encouraged by the success of the July 30 test, Smith left for Pearl Harbor with film footage of the test and the endorsement of Adml. Gunther to promote the SATFOR project. He wished to expand the project and to propose the carrier flight deck testing of a SBD scout bomber modified into a drone. Once back at Pearl Harbor, Smith not only met strong resistance to his proposals but was transferred back to America when he objected, perhaps too strongly! Cdr. Robert Jones became SATFOR's Acting Commander on September 5, 1944 and was determined to use STAG-1's assault drones in combat operations. Films and reports of the July 30 test had impressed USMC Brig. Gen. Claude Larkin, Commander of Air Forces in the Northern Solomons, and Jones gained approval for a thirty-day combat trial.

On September 19, STAG-1 left Banika to mount combat operations from Stirling Island, located 300 miles to the northeast and only 50 miles south of Bougainville. On September 27, STAG-1 launched the first TDR-1 attack on an active enemy target, which was a Japanese anti-aircraft battery located onboard a 460-foot merchant vessel beached in the shallows off the southern tip of Bougainville near Kahili. Each of the four TDR-1s carried a 2,000-pound GP bomb. One drone was lost on the way, but the remaining three reached the target. One crashed into the ship's port quarter and detonated; one hit the water 30 yards astern but its bomb failed to detonate; and the last made a direct hit amidships at the main deck and destroyed the AA battery.

Four days later, STAG-1's control planes successfully guided four TDRs to AA installations on Ballale and Poporang Islands off the southern Bougainville coast. The first drone dove through heavy AA fire and exploded among the three heavy AA positions. The second exploded within 100 feet of heavy and automatic gun positions

Cdr. Robert Jones, SATFOR's acting commander. (*USN*)

at the southwest end of Ballale's runway. The third and fourth exploded amid heavy gun positions located on a ridge on the northern portion of Poporang Island.

That afternoon STAG-1 launched four additional TDR-ls into Japanese AA positions on Kanga Hill on South Bougainville, but this attack was not nearly as successful as the morning's. In the midst of AA fire, the first drone exploded below the Kanga Hill gun emplacements. The second drone hit within 50 feet of the guns but failed to detonate. The third struck near a town but failed to detonate while the fourth exploded 4 miles north of the hill.

STAG-1 moved to Green Island, about 100 miles north of Bougainville, which placed the unit within range of the major Japanese base at Rabaul on the eastern end of New Britain. On October 5, STAG-1 launched four drones against the Karavia supply caves overlooking Rabaul Harbor. Because of radio frequency control problems, two drones were lost on route to the island fortress. The third drone flew through anti-aircraft fire and exploded in the area of the cave entrances. The final drone overflew the target area and hit near Japanese barge dockage.

Four days later, four TDR-1s were launched against the Matupi Island Bridge that connected the island in Rabaul Harbor to the mainland. Two drones were shot down by heavy anti-aircraft fire; one exploding 1,000 feet from the bridge; and the other exploding near a cluster of AA emplacements. The third was thought to have been shot down while the fourth crashed in St. George Channel between Rabaul and neighboring New Ireland Island.

On October 15, four more TDR-1s were guided to Rabaul for another attack on the unscathed Matupi Bridge. One crashed *en route* due to equipment failure. Another went down on land south of the target when the television signal to its control aircraft failed. The two remaining drones crashed off-target, due to problems that were traced to TV signal failures.

Two days later, four STAG-1 drones attacked a target area near East Rabaul Town. *En route*, equipment failure caused one drone to crash off Cape St. George on the southern tip of New Ireland. A second hit its target, a building in East Rabaul Town. The third blew up in the junction of Rabaul Town's two main thoroughfares, setting off a huge secondary explosion. The final TDR-1 crashed into buildings on a ridge west of town.

The next day, three control plane/drone elements attacked the lighthouse on New Ireland's Cape St. George that was 30 feet high and about 10 feet wide at its base. One drone crashed *en route* and the other two hit the target area but only one of their bombs exploded, leaving the lighthouse still standing,

On October 19, STAG-1 again attacked the gun positions on Ballale, using a variation in the usual method of attack. A single TDR-1 drone was dispatched, armed with two 500-pound bombs in the fuselage and four 100-pound bombs under each wing for a total payload of 1,800 pounds. But before reaching its target, the drone was lost because of mechanical problems. An identically loaded TDR-1 made a more successful solo attack that same afternoon. The drone control pilot remotely dropped the two 500-pound bombs that landed just short of the gun positions and then hit them directly with eight 100-pound bombs, dropped in two clusters. The drone's left engine was hit by AA fire and twenty minutes later it crashed. For the first time, the drone was used not as a self-destroying guided bomb, but as a pilotless bomber.

The following day, STAG-1 further refined their attack method with an ambitious plan by using three TDR-1s, which would act as guided bombers dropping their two 500-pound bombs on the Ballale Island gun positions but then would fly on to crash into the derelict Japanese cargo ship *Kahili Maru*. One drone crashed *en route*. The second made an accurate bomb run over the gun emplacements but before it could be directed to attack the ship, its remote control was lost and the drone crashed on South Bougainville. The third TDR-1's bombs straddled the gun positions and then accurately struck the cargo ship at the deck line amidships.

On October 23, three drones carrying 2,000-pound bombs again attacked the beached *Kahili Maru*. Control of one drone failed on the way and it exploded immediately west of the Shortland Islands just south of Bougainville. The second drone hit the target at its deck line while the third overshot and detonated in the sea beyond. That afternoon, three more drones attacked beached ships in the area. Two made direct hits while the third overshot its target.

Four more drones were expended on October 26. One crashed into the lighthouse at Cape St. George on New Ireland and destroyed it. Two of the other three hit their targets in Rabaul Town. When the fourth TDR-1 had signal trouble over Rabaul Harbor, it was redirected to its secondary target, AA positions on Duke of York Island outside Rabaul Harbor.

Despite the encouraging results and the best efforts of Robert Jones and Oscar Smith, on October 27, 1944, the Navy suddenly and unexpectedly canceled the SATFOR Project. Segments of the Stirling Island and Green Island detachments were returned to the main base at Banika to complete their temporary duty. On the next day, two TDR-1s from Stirling were guided along Bougainville's southwest coast as target drones for Army AA gunners on the shore. The Army gunners were finally able to shoot down the first TDR-1 on its fifth run and managed to destroy the second drone on its third pass.

STAG-1 was fully decommissioned by the end of 1944. Plans to produce a new version of the TDR featuring radial engines and a better TV system never progressed beyond the prototype stage. By the end of 1944, STAG-1 became a footnote in history. Many of their TDR-1 drones and accompanying TBM-1C control aircraft were unceremoniously dumped into the sea. Most STAG-1/SATFOR personnel were sent to Pearl Harbor for reassignment to Fleet units and squadrons. However, a number of STAG-1 pilots were returned to Clinton, Oklahoma, to ferry TBF control planes and the remaining TDR drones to the Naval Ordnance Test Station at China Lake. Once there, they were based at Harvey Field, an auxiliary field in Inyokern, and were designated as the Drone Utility Unit under Cdr. Frederick Wallace, a radio control pioneer. The TDR assault drones were delegated to be target drones, and ignominiously to be depleted as targets for anti-aircraft shell proximity fuses and air-to-air rockets. Some were sold, post-war, as civilian sport aircraft without their TV guidance systems.

Summary of STAG-1s Operations

During operations, all controlled take-offs were successful. Of the forty-six drones launched, nine were lost *en route* to the target. Two of these were lost due to interference believed to be from friendly communications in the area whose frequencies overlapped with those employed by the drones while seven were lost on the way to the target due to equipment failure. The remaining thirty-seven drones arrived at the target area and were launched into attacks, many meeting medium to intense AA fire. Despite their low speed, the drones were not easy targets for AA fire as only three were shot down before reaching their targets. Five suffered TV failures and could not locate their targets. The remaining thirty-two completed their attacks with 46 percent of the drones launched by STAG-1 making hits or damaging near-hits. It appears by most conventional weapon criteria, the SATFOR program had been a success as not a single American operator is known to have been killed or even injured on any of the drone attacks, many of them against heavily defended areas.

In a report to Adml. Halsey on October 30, 1944, Brig. Gen. Claude Larkin, Commander of Air Forces in the Northern Solomons, concluded:

> During the period of concentrated operations against enemy targets, the STAG-1 Detachment was confronted with many difficult technical and operational problems.

> Operating from forward fields from which heavy routine combat missions were being flown involved a high degree of coordination with other units. Due to the uncertainty of weather, availability of diversion aircraft, limited periods of radio silence on control frequencies and similar features directly involving these operations, it was often necessary to plan attacks hastily and to change pre-arranged details at the last minute. The STAG-1 Detachment, with no previous actual combat experience with drones, carried out its difficult operational and highly technical missions in an admiral manner. It is considered that valuable practical experience was gained during the one-month period of combat operations and that the knowledge gained by this unit may well serve to advance the development of this specialty.
>
> HQ of the Commander, Aircraft, Northern Solomons
> *Report on the Operations of STAG-1 in the Northern Solomons Area, 30 October 1944*

By the end of 1944, King terminated SATFOR and the AD program, offering to transfer the remaining radio and television technologies to the AAF, ostensibly trying to reduce expenditures and redeploy Navy research and development toward more cutting edge advances in propulsion, aerodynamics, and electronics and the Navy's attention became fixated on the SWOD Mk. 9 Bat radio-controlled GB. King's disbanding of the AD television-guided systems would doom the promising concept before it had even been deployed in combat. All the valuable technology SATFOR had gathered was allocated a top-secret classification that essentially consigned it to be buried, but later it would have large effect on U.S. postwar guided missile development. The SATFOR Project was not publicly revealed until 1952 and was not officially declassified until 1966. On July 5, 1990, SATFOR was finally officially recognized by Secretary of the Navy Henry Garrett who stated: "The vision, determination, and dedication with which you performed your secret duties during World War II laid the groundwork for today's modern cruise missile." The SATFOR Project's only remaining TDR-1 was found in Oklahoma long after the end of the war and is on display at the National Museum of Naval Aviation in Pensacola, Florida.

Fahrney/TDR Postscript

After his decade-long struggle to advance the Navy's unmanned aircraft and missile programs, the beleaguered Fahrney continued to pursue their development. His efforts included plans for an improved version of the TDR-1, which employed more powerful radial engines and a much-improved BLOCK III TV system. Four prototypes were built and flown, but by that time, the war had ended, and the Navy abandoned that effort, as well. Interstate Aircraft, with Fahrney's input and influence, designed the XBDR-1, a jet-powered flying wing drone (see next). Fahrney's next endeavor was to assist in the development of the nuclear-capable Regulus missile. Ironically, the Regulus did not have a TV guidance system as the military establishment believed that in the next war a precision weapon would be unnecessary, since whole cities would be annihilated by nuclear warheads. Fahrney eventually attained the rank of rear admiral and served for a few years was the Navy's Chief of Guided Missile Research. After thirty-two years of active service, Fahrney retired from the Navy in 1950. Later, he became interested in the possibility that UFOs were extraterrestrial. In 1957, at the height of the flying saucer fervor, this comment he made became widely publicized: "Reliable reports indicate there are objects coming into our atmosphere at very high speeds and controlled by thinking intelligences." Delmar Fahrney, the man mainly responsible for the excess of drones in use today, passed away in 1984 at the age of eighty-six. Fittingly, in June 2000, the new headquarters building at the Naval Air Missile Test Center, Point Mugu, was named in his honor.

Interstate XBDR-1

In its effort to upgrade the performance of its TDR-1 assault drone, on October 29, 1943, the Interstate Aircraft and Engineering Corporation filed a design patent application for an aircraft, to be designated by the Navy as the XBDR-1. At the time, it was referred to as an assault drone, and was the only aircraft ever designated in the BD series. The squat, tailless bat-shaped airframe was very similar to Northrop's N-9M prototype of its B-35 Flying Wing, except it was powered by a pair of jet engines, rather than by twin pusher propellers. The aircraft did not have a conventional empennage, as the rudder was integrated into the rear of the fuselage, with elevons (i.e. combined elevator and aileron flight control surfaces) on the trailing edges of the wings providing roll and pitch control. The aircraft's planned for but never installed jet engines were to be the Westinghouse 19B axial-flow (later to become the successful Westinghouse J34), developed for the U.S. Navy under a May 26, 1943 contract, and was first flown on September 28, 1944 powering a Martin JM-1 Marauder testbed. The twin turbojet engines were to be buried in the XBDR-1's wing near the wing roots with the horizontal air intakes located along the wing's leading edge of the on both sides of the cockpit. These engines were to propel the aircraft to 182 mph. The television-guided XBDR-1 was to weigh 10,800 pounds, have a wingspan of 51.66 feet, wing area of 362 square feet, and a wing loading of 29.8 pounds per square foot.

Because of this innovative design, the Navy ordered two prototypes (BuNos. 337635 and 37636) and tests of a 1/17-scale model of the XBDR to be conducted in the NACA Pilot Gust (Wind) Tunnel at Langley Field in 1944. The pilot gust-tunnel testing technique consisted of launching dynamically scaled, free-flight, 2.2-pound 1/17-scale XBDR model with a 3.04 wingspan through gusts of known shapes and intensities. The gust tunnel was capable of testing scaled models with wings of about 3-foot span at speeds up to about 50 mph (XBDR 44.3 mph). During the flight, measurements were made of the accelerations and reactions of the model due to the gusts. The test gust tunnel consisted of a gust generator, a catapult for launching the model, and two screens used to decelerate and catch the model at the end of the flight. The propelling catapult was operated by dropping a weight, and the maximum model flight speed was regulated by altering the amount of weight. The gust generator was

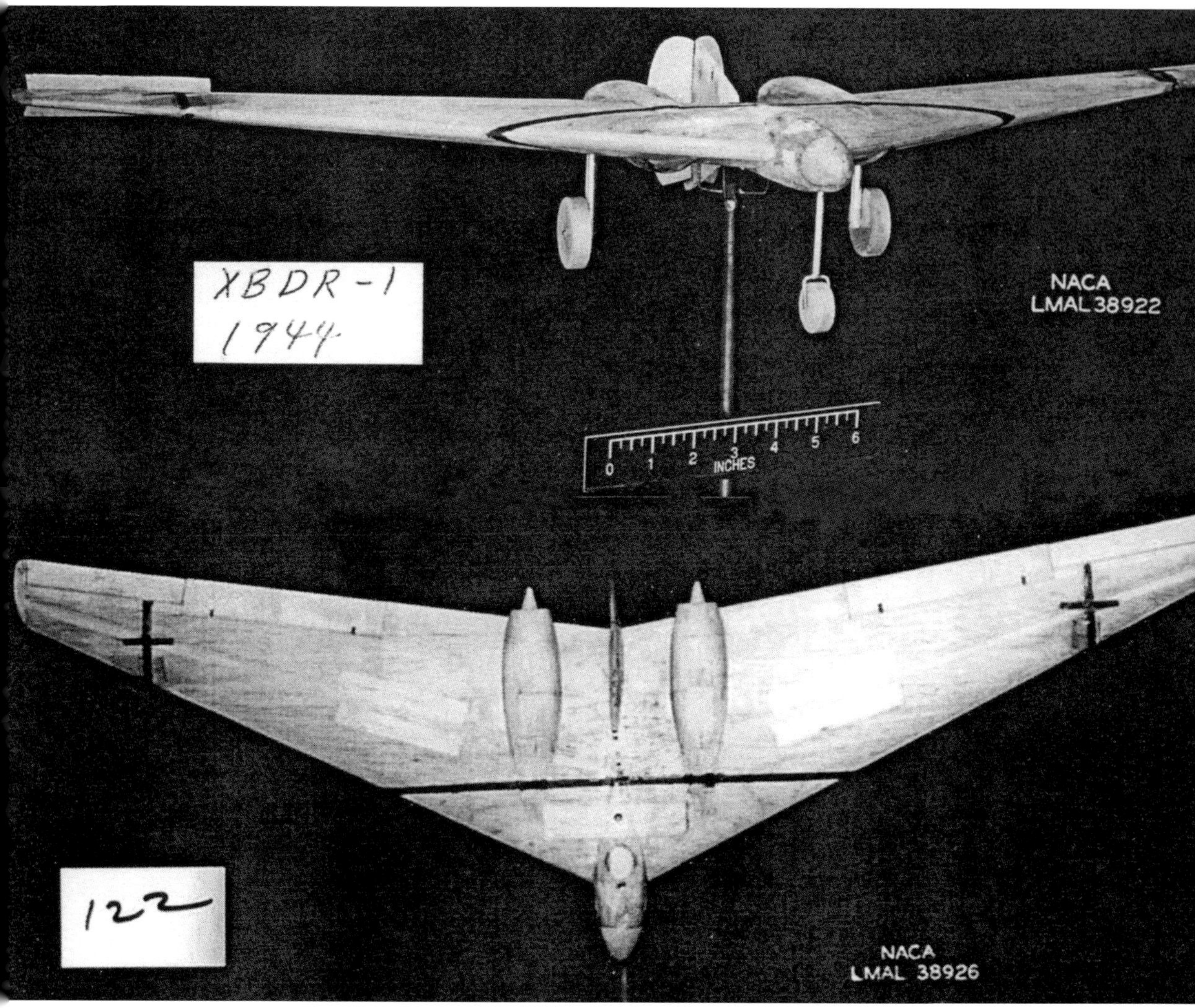

Interstate XBDR. (*AAF*)

Piloted Interstate XBDR. (*AAF*)

a large squirrel-cage blower, which provided air to an expanding rectangular channel expelling a stream of air upward. The vertical jet of air was 6 feet wide and 8 feet long and its air speed shape was formed by a combination of screen meshes designed to produce the chosen gust shape. After the catapulted model completed its flight through the vertical-gust field, it impacted a barrier of vertical rubber strands, which decelerated the model. After deceleration, the model's barbed hook-shaped nose was caught in a burlap screen, which stopped the model and held it until the model was removed by the tunnel operator.

One XBDR prototype was apparently built, based on Northrop's N-9 flying wing and since its proposed twin Westinghouse 19B jet engines were never installed; it flew as an unpowered glider to test control surfaces. Further XBDR development probably terminated as collateral victim of the Navy's TDR Assault Drone program (Project Option) being canceled on October 27, 1944.

6

GLOMB (Glider Bomb) Series

U.S. Navy GLOMBs

During December 1940, Lt. Cdr. Delmar Fahrney, head of the Special Designs Branch at BuAer, who had been working on the Navy's powered drone project since 1936 suggested the use of an unmanned explosive-filled remotely controlled glider, towed, self-stabilize behind a tug, and released to attack high-value, well-protected, pinpoint targets reducing the risk to aircrew. Fahrney's glider would weigh up to 15,000 pounds and was to be towed under automatic stabilization to within its glide range to a target by a fighter or transport aircraft. If towed by a fighter, the pilot could escape the area quickly and defend himself successfully. A television camera in the nose of the glider would provide a picture of the target to the remote control pilot located in a nearby mother ship that would guide the glider by radio control. The gliders were inexpensive airframes that could be towed by an aircraft that also contained the remote controller. Plans were also made for the glider to provide supplemental fuel to its towing aircraft. In March 1941, Fahrney was appointed to direct the glider bomb project at the Naval Aircraft Factory, under the direction of Cdr. Ralph Barnaby, Assistant Chief Engineer at the NAF. Barnaby was a skillful glider pilot who supervised the Navy's entire transport glider developmental program. Later Barnaby replaced Fahrney. On April 19, 1941, the Navy ordered the start of the program under the official designation of Project George but Barnaby originated the term GLOMBs (GLider bOMBS) for the project.

Early USN GLOMBs

Schweizer LNS-1

Automatically stabilizing the glider on take-off and tow was a critical problem and the NAF attempted to develop an auto-tow system using its previous experience using drone autopilots. The Schweizer Company (Horseheads, New York) created the

Right: Cdr. Ralph Barnaby originated the term GLOMBS. During June 1944, he relieved Fahrney at NAMU. (*USN*)

Below: Schweizer LNS-1 (Army TG-2) at USMC Page Field, SC, 1942. (*USMC*)

popular, easy-to-fly civilian two-place pre-war SGS 2-8 glider, which was contracted by the USN and USMC as the LNS-1 and as the TG-2 for the AAC for glider training. In early 1942, the NAF obtained two Schweizer LNS-1s to develop and test auto-tow. Although the tests were successful, a heavier, more representative testbed was required and the Great Lakes BG-1 was chosen.

Great Lakes BG-1

After achieving limited success using the LNS-1 glider for auto-tow tests, the NAF obtained an obsolete Great Lakes BG-1 biplane (9512) during the spring and summer of 1942. This BG-1 was used for initial radio control and TV transmission trials, which also encompassed simulated tow, remote radio release from the tug, and glide to targets. To test a prospective guidance system, a Douglas TBD-1 Devastator torpedo bomber towed the BG-1 using the auto-tow system. The BG-1 tests were satisfactory with releases from 3–9 miles from the target, scoring five hits during seven runs. This success of the BG-1 and the disastrous torpedo aircraft losses at Midway caused the Navy to modify this BG-1 (9508) as an improvised glider drone with a safety pilot in June 1942. Its engine was removed (and lead ballast added), and tow and TV equipment installed. A Grumman J2F Duck amphibian was used as the tow plane but the performance of the combination was unsatisfactory and even dangerous.

Taylorcraft XLNT-1

Initially, the British Hotspur and Horsa transport gliders were evaluated under auto-tow, as were the Waco LRW-1, and the LNR-1 and LNP-1 three-place trainers. While GLOMB tests using these gliders showed encouraging progress, all the GLOMB equipment was experimental and none had been tested as a single integrated unit. It became obvious to concentrate on a single type for development and training and, consequently, future tests originally scheduled for the Hotspur and LRW-1 were now to be conducted using the Taylorcraft LNT-1 (Army TG-6), which were considered as the most applicable for further GLOMB development.

Three 7,320-pound LNT-1 three-place, high-wing, training gliders, based on light aircraft designs were obtained from the Army in September 1942. Changes were completed at NAMU including a modified main landing gear, a new nose gear, and electronics gear with external antennae installed in the cockpit. The conventional landing gear was replaced as it proved to be too unstable for towing off the ground under automatic control and made radio-controlled landings too difficult.

The resulting drone was designated as the XLNT-1, but its progress was slowed by continued parallel auto-tow work on other gliders. Although a safety pilot was in the glider until a final successful test on April 4, 1943, the XLNT-1 appeared to be most suitable for conversion to a GLOMB. Some thirty-one additional XLNT-1s and LNT-1s were obtained in the last half of 1943 from a canceled USMC training program and from the AAF, which held them in storage. These LNT-1s were to be used in more thorough testing while the production design was completed. The auto-tow system was ultimately finalized, allowing the glider to take-off and follow behind its tug.

Great Lakes BG-1. (*AAF*)

Taylorcraft XLNT-1 (Army TG-6). (*AAF*)

The XLNT-1 had a maximum weight of 5,000 pounds, could be towed up to 240 mph, and descended at 2,400 fpm (27.3 mph) with dive tests up to 260 mph and with 5G pull-outs performed. The RCA radio remote control and TV transmit/receive systems for targeting finally developed into a BLOCK I design that fit into both the XLNT-1 and a control aircraft as small as a trainer. The system permitted controlled flight the entire way to the target by reference to the TV image or locked into a stabilized flight path. The TV image was only available after release. By the fall of 1943, further alterations were made to the XLNT-1s and three were selected for expenditure in destructive trials of the experimental GLOMB design.

The first GLOMB test was conducted at Pax (NAS Patuxent River) on September 17, 1943. The XLNT-1 (36429) carried a live 325-pound depth charge armed by remote signal and was towed by a Vultee SNV-1 Valiant (12963) whose pilot also controlled the XLNT-1 after release. The take-off of the first unmanned GLOMB auto-tow was faultless, and while the 20-mile flight met turbulence, there were no problems on the way to the target located off Bloodsworth Island in the Chesapeake Bay. Release was at 3,000 feet and 3 miles from the target, but disappointingly, there was no TV image and the target could not be located. The control pilot was obligated to put the GLOMB into a spiral descent into the Bay, well short of the target, where the depth charge exploded on impact. It was determined that the GLOMB's magnetic field disrupted the delicate TV equipment, which could have been corrected if the final system adjustments had been made in the final flight configuration. Soon, a second XLNT-1 destructive test was also unsuccessful due to an auxiliary power supply failure near the release point causing the glider to crash. Nonetheless, BuAer continued to believe in the GLOMB as a feasible and effective weapon.

On February 25, 1944, the third and final destruction test was conducted at NAS Lakehurst, New Jersey, with a 30 by 50-foot sand pit acting as the target. The weight of the XLNT-1 (67803) and the radio and television equipment left only 228 pounds of sand bags to represent the explosives. After a practice run, release was at 4,500 feet and 4 miles upwind of the target. After a three-minute flight, the GLOMB was released at 5 miles from the control aircraft and struck within 23 feet of the center of the target and with enough force to trip an arming circuit. The test was termed an "expeditionary operation," with the aircraft and all equipment and personnel flown to Lakehurst, the mission completed, and departing after only six hours. Despite the limitations of the early TV systems, the tests were promising and demonstrated that a tow pilot could direct the GLOMB after release. However, XLNT-1 GLOMB applications were never realized as the glider was plainly unsuitable for operations as it could only carry a small explosive payload in its congested cockpit and aft fuselage area.

Carrier-Based XLNT-1 GLOMBs

On August 10, 1943, before the final XLNT tests, the NAF proposed a production GLOMB with a 3,000-pound glider carrying a 4,000-pound bomb, towed by a Grumman F6F-3 Hellcat or F4F-3 Wildcat fighter mothership over a 350-mile combat

The RCA radio remote control and TV transmit/receive systems for targeting used on the XLNT-1 was finally developed into the BLOCK I. The photo shows the unit on the ground powered by a generator used on ground-directed tests. (*AAF*)

The February 25, 1944 second and final XLNT-1 test was conducted at NAS Lakehurst, New Jersey, with a 30 by 50-foot sand pit acting as the target. After a three-minute flight, the GLOMB struck within 23 feet of the center of the target as seen in the photo. (*From AAF movie still*)

range. Launch from an aircraft carrier was obvious, and on March 25, 1944, BuAer stated that GLOMBs should be operated from carriers, and directed NAF to perform catapult trials of a glider and tow plane combination. The tests included towing by a land-based F4F-3 (3990), which was catapulted with the glider in tow at NAS Patuxent River. Since the XLNT-1 (TQ-6 42-58561) did not have the nose gear modification, its tail was placed on a ramp and the tail wheel held back with a breakable restraint. To bear the large launching loads, some reinforce of the glider's structure was required while the 100-foot, 0.44-inch steel cable towline release mechanism also required modification. Although, catapulting a fighter with glider in tow was wholly feasible, the concept seems to have lost impetus and was abandoned.

August 1943 Navy GLOMB Requirements

Originally, the Navy desired to have GLOMBs function as amphibious Marine cargo gliders in addition to serving as guided bombs. During August 1943, the requirements for a production GLOMB were issued specifying a 3,000-pound empty weight glider with a 4,000-pound explosive payload and a 350-mile radius of action when towed by a Grumman F4F. These gliders could be towed at 150 mph under auto-tow while remote control, and television systems were to be installed along with a warhead. Six companies submitted proposals in September 1943 and contracts were negotiated with three companies: Pratt-Read, Piper, and Taylorcraft.

Pratt-Read XLBE/LBE

Under a September 1943 contract, the Gould Aeronautical Division (Sycamore, Illinois) of the Pratt-Read Company (Deep River, Connecticut), a former piano parts maker, was to produce 100 LBE-1s with the first three as XLBE-1s (USN s/n 85290/291/292). These 29-foot, 1.5-inch, 7,138-pound conventional low-wing (32-foot, 6-inch span) aircraft resembled a modified Culver TD2C-1 Target Drone with split dive flaps of the type used by dive-bombers, fixed tricycle landing gear, and with the engine compartment replaced by an enclosed nose. Electrical power was generated by a ram air turbine with variable speed fan placed under the nose. The three prototypes had a cockpit for a safety pilot for training and evaluation but in the combat configuration the pilot's compartment would be replaced with mounts for a 4,000-pound bomb case without fins. A mockup of the glider was inspected on June 5–6, 1944, and the first LBE was delivered in May 1944 and was towed by a Lockheed PV-1 Ventura on its first flight that required 6,800 feet of runway. Later, assistance from six 1,000-pound JATO bottles would reduce this to 3,800 feet. During continuing testing, the XLBE revealed that its low performance and technical issues with the intended television guidance system made the concept operationally impracticable; consequently, the contract was reduced to only thirty-five aircraft in early 1945. The Pratt-Read contract was finally terminated on August 14, 1945 with only the three XLBE-1s delivered and being used only for evaluation. A fourth was 90 percent complete at cancellation but was finished in Johnsville. However, in light of the promising radar-homing SWOD Bat missile

Pratt Read Company XLBE-1. (*AAF*)

The forward fuselage of the XLBE-1 was low set for ease of loading a 4,000-pound bomb into the nose. (*AAF*)

program, the C-in-C of the U.S. Fleet decided that that canceling GLOMB program was premature and maintained that the system be adapted to gliders. On May 29, 1945, he directed that three LBE-1s be modified but the proposed schedule as not met and this program faded away at the end of the war.

Piper XLBP

During November 1943, Piper Aircraft Corporation, Lock Haven, Pennsylvania, was awarded an USN contract for 100 LBP-1 GLOMBs (USN s/n 85165–85264) with the first three being prototypes and designated XLBP-1. Previously, Piper had submitted an unsuccessful pilotless GB proposal for the AAF's MX-108 GB project and had previous experience building 253 AAF TG-8 (Navy LNP-1) gliders.

The XLPB was an expendable bomb-carrying, 2,800-pound towed glider, capable of operation by a pilot or by remote control as a guided missile with a 4,000-pound bomb. It resembled a light tricycle gear aircraft with all surfaces fully cantilevered and its lines aerodynamic configured for high speed tow. The 28-foot, 9-inch semi-monocoque fuselage was constructed of wooden circular transverse frames and stringers, covered by plywood skin. The forward fuselage was low set for ease of loading a 4,000-pound bomb into the bottom of the fuselage through the bomb bay that was also used for pilot escape if being flown manned. The safety pilot entered the glider through a hatch in the upper fuselage, which was opened by pressing a push button located on the left-side just forward of the wing leading edge and then ascending steps on both sides of the fuselage. The fixed tricycle gear included main gear posts under the wing with Firestone-designed spring shock absorbers. The cantilevered wing and empennage were fabricated of wood, sheeted with plywood covered with fabric. The 33-foot-span, 173-square-foot wooden wing, manufactured by furniture-maker, Grand Rapids Industries, Michigan, was straight tapered, high-mounted, cantilevered with slightly rounded tips. The perforated flaps also acted as dive brakes. The wooden vertical tail was tapered with a ground adjustable trim tab inset into the rudder. The horizontal tail was tapered with a one-piece elevator

The nose cone had nose hook in its center, a clear panel for the TV camera above the hook, and a wind-driven power provision. The XLBP-1 was capable of either towed or snatch take-off from an airfield or from an aircraft carrier deck or by catapulting from land or aircraft carrier with a towline attached to it. The ideal cruising speed to achieve the maximum range would vary with different tow aircraft. There were three separate flight control systems in the XBP-1: manual system for manned test, check, and ferry flights; automatic control by the auto-tow mechanism while the glider was being towed; and a remote control system for the time when the aircraft was manipulated from a control aircraft. The remote control system allowed the glider to be controlled from a directing aircraft using a radio control system connected into the glider's autopilot system. The LBP-1 was to be equipped with a RCA BLOCK III television camera mounted in the nose that transmitted a pilot's eye picture to the controlling aircraft. The complete LBP-1 BLOCK III system television system consisted of a camera, transmitter, antenna, battery, dynamotor power supply, and filter junction box.

Piper XLBP-1. (*AAF*)

The LBP-1 mockup was inspected on April 3, 1944 and the first XLBP-1 (USN 85165/Piper s/n 1) was trucked from the Piper factory to the airfield at Fort Dix, New Jersey, for testing. Meanwhile, Piper began production of the USN 85166/Piper s/n 2. However, the original order for 100 aircraft was reduced to eighty-five in November 1944 and then would be further reduced to thirty-five in February 1945. In January 1945, the first flight was conducted at Fort Dix with the XLBP-1 being towed behind a Grumman F4F Wildcat with Piper test pilot, Curt Wetzel, as the safety pilot. Testing continued until April 18, 1945, when the first prototype was damaged during tests at Fort Dix. The second prototype (85166) was trucked to Fort Dix on April 25 to continue testing. The contract was canceled on June 8, 1945 partially due to problems landing the fully loaded aircraft. Later, both prototypes were trucked back to Lock Haven and scrapped along with the completed third prototype (85167) and all production parts for the next twelve LBP-1s.

Taylorcraft XLBT

Taylorcraft, Alliance, Ohio, was contracted to build twenty-five LBT-1s (with the first to be a XLBT-1), then expanded to fifty in June 1944 and then to 100. Designed to carry a 2,000-pound bomb, the 25-foot, 2-inch LBT-1 resembled the company's LNT-1 training glider except for a stronger structure, cleaner aerodynamics for a smooth tow and an abridged canopy and cockpit in lieu of its TV-and-radio remote guidance system for a safety pilot to fly the aircraft on training and evaluation flights. Two LNT-1s had been previously been converted to remote control and had been tested as part of initial GLOMB trials as XLNT-1. The LBT-1 had a high, strut-braced wing (35-foot span) without flaps but retained spoilers like the LNT-1. The aircraft had a tricycle landing gear, perforated dive brakes located on the aft fuselage, a wind turbine mounted off the port side, and a nose that ended in a port for the TV camera.

Taylorcraft XLBT. (*AAF*)

Take-off weight was increased to 5,000 pounds, tow speed to 240 mph, and landing speed 120 mph.

The first XLBT-1 was available for evaluation and testing during April 1944 to be towed and controlled by a Grumman F4F Wildcat or a Lockheed PV-1 Ventura. A second, fully equipped with auto-tow, remote control, and TV systems, was available in October. The third, without any electronics, was delivered to the Test and Evaluation Unit, Traverse City. Michigan. XLBTs Nos. 4–9 arrived at Traverse City without electronics while Nos. 10–25 were equipped with the special equipment at the Taylorcraft, Ohio, plant before following sent to Michigan in March 1945. However, by October 1944, flight trials disclosed a lower than anticipated performance and the Piper LBP-1 and LBE-1 were considered superior and so the LBT contract was canceled in October 1944 with only twenty-five constructed—none of which would see any operational service. The LBT-1 was also subjected to catapult trails which were suspended with the contract cancellation.

Gargoyle LBD-1

During November 1943, the LBD-1 Gargoyle (RTV-N-2), the last of the LB series, was developed by the Navy as part of their glider bomb series as an answer to the successful Fritz-X and German HS-293 guided anti-shipping GBs to which the Gargoyle seems to be similar in conception. Operationally, it was to be used by aircraft carrier dive and torpedo bombers in good conditions against maneuvering enemy shipping. The speed of the parent aircraft was reduced about 10 mph and the take-off distance was increased 15 to 80 feet, but maneuverability was not significantly affected. The 1,650-pound, low-wing monoplane missile, ready by March 1944, was characterized by a thick, short (9-foot, 10-inch) fuselage, stubby (8-foot, 6-inch) wings, and a broad V-shaped butterfly tail assembly. Launching was to be by carrying aircraft, but during March 1944, an Aerojet 8AS100 solid-fuel, 150-pound JATO rocket booster was installed in the tail to give it a higher diving speed. A launch speed of 200 mph was required so that the short, low-wing design would not stall. The speed was projected to be 600 mph over a range of 4–5 miles when released from 15,000 feet at a 30-degree dive.

The Gargoyle was remotely radio-controlled using a bright flare in the V-tail. Pitch control was via ruddavators working together, while control to left and right was by the ruddavators working individually. These control surfaces were positioned by servo motors, which received their signal from the 20-pound AN/ARW-17 radio receiver. The Gargoyle's maximum range was limited by the controller's ability to visually follow the flare. It was to carry a 1,000-pound M65 general purpose or M59 semi-armor piercing anti-shipping warhead.

In September 1944, McDonnell Aircraft, St. Louis, was awarded a contract for five Gargoyle prototypes. Successful glide tests began in March 1945, after which McDonnell was awarded a full production contract for 395 missiles. The first powered tests in began in July with only five of fourteen tests considered successful. It was redesignated as the KSD-1 anti-shipping missile just as the war ended and then was again redesignated as the KUD-1 test and research vehicle, which first flew in July 1946. McDonnell produced 250 Gargoyles before ending production in mid-1947. The remaining missiles were again redesignated as the RTV-2 in September 1947 and the RTV-N-2 in early 1948 and were used to test components for other missile programs. The Gargoyle program was officially terminated in December 1950 and the remaining missiles were scrapped.

McDonnell Gargoyle LBD-1 (RTV-N-2). (*USN*)

USN Cargo-Carrying Glider GLOMB Development

AGA XLRG-1, Snead XLRH-1, Allied Aviation XLRA-1, Bristol XLRQ-1

During the late summer of 1941, the BuAer requested a GLOMB cargo glider that could transport fuel and freight, or explosives, while supporting Pacific amphibious operations. On September 29, the request was expanded to three types of different sizes.

The smallest GLOMB gliders were the Allied Aviation Corporation's (Cockeysville, Maryland) XLRA-1s and Bristol Aeronautical Corporation's (New Haven, Connecticut) XLRQ-1s. Both were to be U.S. Marine Corps' twelve-seat flying boat amphibious transport gliders intended to be used for landing troops or as remote-controlled bombs during island hopping campaigns in the Pacific. Allied built two aircraft as XLRA-1 (BuNos. 11647/11648) with the first flight occurring during early 1943. Manufacture of 100 production aircraft as LRA-1s (BuNos. 31403/31502) was canceled after Allied management had continually battled with the Navy over cost overruns and design disagreements. Meanwhile, the financially and management troubled Bristol Aeronautical Corporation also produced two overly-costly XLRQ-1s (BuNos. 11561/11562). The first flight was in January 1943. Although initial ultimate production was estimated at 12,000, only 100 production LRQ-1s were ordered (BuNos. 33715/33814) but these too were eventually canceled.

Both the Allied and Bristol projects lagged, and although technically successful designs, the project was canceled on September 27, 1943, as the Navy decided it no longer had a requirement for these gliders as transports and transferred the four X gliders and incomplete units to the AAF for further final preparation and evaluation at the NAF as GLOMBs. The project continued to stagnant through lack of interest and the wooden airframes were scrapped.

To fulfill the intermediate glider requirement, on September 17, 1942, BuAer requested Bristol to produce an enlarged version of their twelve-place XLRQ-1 to carry twenty-four to thirty troops, or 2,000 gallons of fuel, or 7 tons of explosives. BuAer had hoped that this project could save the failing company, but prudently decided to wait on this request until the NAF had tested its XLRQ-1. However, by May 1943, the internal circumstances at Bristol had deteriorated to the extent that by June 1943 that the company had no chance for procurement.

The largest glider was to be developed into a GLOMB from one of two twenty-four-place transport gliders then being developed for the USMC: G&A Aircraft's (Willow Grove, Pennsylvania) XLRG-1 and Snead & Company's (Jersey City, New Jersey) XLRH-1 twin-hulled amphibious gliders, which were to be among America's largest gliders with 108-foot wingspans. Prototypes for both were ordered, but none were built as both companies encountered management, financial, and workmanship problems.

Bristol Aeronautical Corporation XLRQ-1. (*USN*)

Allied Aviation XLRA-1. (*USN*)

Naval Aircraft Factory XLRN-1

On June 29, 1942, the CNO directed the Naval Aircraft Factory to construct a large wooden glider following one of two designs recommended by BuAer: the first for a high-wing monoplane capable of carrying 6 tons of fuel to a forward battle position or delivering alternatively, 6 tons of fuel, or 5 tons of explosives against a land or naval target, and the second for a similar aircraft with a capacity of 9 tons of fuel or an identical weight of explosives. The NAF opted for the larger of the two designs and the bureau issued a project order for the construction of three gliders, designated XLRN-1, the first of which would be used for static tests and the other two for flight tests. The impressive XLRN-1 would become America's largest glider of the war and one of its largest wooden aircraft.

The NAF was to construct a mock up and static test unit, while the two flight test airframes were to be built at Naval Air Modification Unit where Capt. Fahrney was CO. The auto-tow, remote pilot, and television systems from the current GLOMB project were scheduled to be incorporated for testing. As work on the XLRN-1 slowly progressed into 1943, the Navy's requirements for the aircraft changed considerably. The NAF's mockup, including room for the installation of radio control and television guidance systems, was ready for inspection by Lt. Cdr. Grayson Merrill by October 1, 1943. Merrill's report on October 25 discussed problems with the NAF's design and questioned the glider's anticipated mission. The XLRN-1's design and wooden construction was not amenable to quantity production, and its large size limited its use in most operational zones. Also, there were few Navy aircraft that could tow the big glider; the PBY-5A was satisfactory for hauling it when lightly loaded, but only the R5D-1 (Navy four-engined Douglas DC-4 Skymaster) could tow the glider at its full gross weight. The glider's original planned use as an aerial tanker was eliminated when it was found that fuel could not be safely transferred from the craft while it was under radio control. Although there was some demand in the BuAer for canceling the XLRN-1 project, at this time expectation continued that the XLN-1 still had some potential considering the funds already expended on it. When completed, the XLRN-1s (BuOrd 36431) measured 67.5 feet in length and had a wingspan of 110 feet. The second XLRN-2 (36432) was not completed. The maximum take-off weight of 37,764 pounds (18,000 pounds of cargo) was almost 5 tons more than a fully loaded DC-3 could carry. While the second XLN-1 was under construction at Philadelphia, flight tests on the first began in October 1944 at NAS Patuxent River, using a PBY-5A as a tow plane at speeds up to 180 mph. The XLRN-1 displayed adverse handling features, particularly a lack of longitudinal stability, which were believed to be sufficiently critical to effectively necessitate a total redesign of the tail surfaces, causing the BuAer to cancel the project; the two XLRN-1s were scrapped in February 1945.

NAF XLRN-1. (*USN*)

Demise of the Navy GLOMB Program

As was usual with many wartime projects, production orders were placed for all three GLOMB designs before the control and auto-tow systems had passed testing. However, on September 23, 1944, due to the manufacturer's sluggish progress and the Navy's diminishing interest, CNO Adml. King was obliged to order cancellation of all GLOMB production beyond a total of 100, causing all GLOMB contracts to be reduced to eighty-five each in November 1944 and thirty-five each in February 1945. The order for 100 Taylorcraft LBT-1s was canceled in October 1944 after twenty-five were eventually produced (85265–85289). One hundred Pratt Reed LBE-1s were ordered initially (ninety-six were given series 85293–85389), with the contract finally terminated in August 1945, with only four delivered of which the CNO requested that three be modified for homing radar, but time constraints prevented this. An order for 100 LBP-1 GLOMBs (85165–85264) was canceled in June 1945. Continuing problems, particularly with auto-tow system delayed GLOMB system and an LBT-1 accident at Traverse City in July 1945 caused a review the following month, resulting in the cancellation of the entire Navy GLOMB project before testing.

The once-promising Navy GLOMB program was ultimately doomed by its early slow development when compared the Navy's drones, which fielded operational weapons, albeit with mediocre success. By 1944, the Navy large glider as a weapon was without a mission in the Pacific War as it became obvious that the assault glider was not tactically practicable against the small, heavily-defended Japanese-held Pacific islands. GLOMBs also experienced technical problems that had no easy solutions, which delayed their development, causing Cdr. Barnaby to lose enthusiasm for the costly project. Nevertheless, the Navy's GLOMB and glider programs had some enduring benefits as they had continued the Naval Aircraft Factory's participation in America's guided weapons programs and boosted the NAF's position in the new technology. Simply, with more practical guided weapons in the future, GLOMBs obviously were not going to be required.

AAF GLOMBs

After the disastrous August 17, 1943 Schweinfurt mission, the USAAF investigated a guided weapons program intended to reduce the losses that mass bomber raids were sustaining while attacking individual German targets. The AAF had fixated on manually or automatically guided free-fall VB vertical or GB glide bomb, which allowed the releasing aircraft to remain outside AA range of a heavily defended target. Analogous to the Navy's development of an unmanned towed GLOMB glider, the AAF also confronted and developed an auto-tow system while actively contracting GLOMB designs.

Fletcher XBG-1 and XBG-2

The AAF's towed GB series was similar in design to the GB series but not of the GB series designation; however, it was designated as the XBG (BG=bomb glider). After being towed to the vicinity of the target, the XBG-1 was to be released to glide toward the target, being radio-controlled from the towing aircraft. The XBG-2 was a standard troop glider filled with explosives. It was equipped with radio controls and was guided after release by the towing aircraft.

As described earlier, Fletcher's failed FBT-2 prototype trainer was converted for use as a drone controller as the YCQ-1A and then ordered the type as a radio-controlled target drone under the designation XPQ-11. After the AAF had canceled the order for the Fletcher PQ-11A radio-controlled target drone, it contracted Fletcher for ten XBG-1s (42-46892–42-46901) for $87,250 on March 5, 1942. The ten PQ-11As under construction at Fletcher were completed and were delivered in May 1942 as fixed landing gear XBG-1 bomb gliders by removing the P&W R-985 engine and adding an aerodynamic nose. A television camera and radio remote control systems and a 2,000-pound bomb were installed in its 23-foot, 4-inch-long, 3-foot, 10-inch-wide wooden fuselage. Electrical power was supplied by the wind-driven turbine beneath the fuselage. Piloting equipment and a windscreen could be installed in place of the bomb for ferry missions.

The first XBG-1 was completed during April 1942, although in a manned configuration for flight testing and probably without remote control equipment. Three satisfactory piloted tow (a Douglas B-23) and free-flights tests were conducted at Muroc AAB on April 26–27. During stall tests at Mines Field, Burbank, California, on August 23, 1942, a CQ-1A drone control aircraft (41-38930) was equipped with a television guidance system mockup, faired under the port wing. By June 1942, conversion of the PQ-11s was progressing, with five accepted that month and the remainder delivered by the end of the month. Additional manned flight testing at

Muroc was planned along with remote flights at Biggs Field, El Paso, Texas. The XBG-1 was to be towed to the target area by a larger aircraft and upon release was to be guided to target impact by radio commands using imagery transmitted from a TV camera in the glider's nose. The XBG-1 was to be released as far as 11 miles from the target; the operator aboard the towing bomber guiding the glider into the target by using TV. No information on the XBG-1 test program is available, but the model was never used operationally. Despite extensive revisions on the basic PQ-11A and XBG-1, a June 9, 1943 Engineering Division memorandum stated that, ultimately, the XBG-1s flight characteristics were unsatisfactory.

On April 1, 1942, the AAF also contracted Fletcher for $83,000 for the development of three XBG-2s (42-46902/3/4). The XBG-2 was converted from Fletcher's CQ-1A drone control aircraft. After flight testing the contract was terminated in September 1942 with no XBG-2s delivered. There were two alternate designs for the XBG-2. When the Frankfort eight-seat XCG-1 troop-carrying glider was canceled in 1941, the three XCG-1s under construction were completed by Fletcher as XBG-2 bomb gliders. The other configuration was two Frankfort XCG-2 (a larger fifteen-seat derivative of the XCG-1) fuselages joined by common center wing and tail sections and could carry two 2,000-pound bombs. There is no information available whether either configuration was built before the XBG-2 program was canceled with none completed and Fletcher paid $16,546. The AAF recommended canceling both the XBG- 1 and XBG-2 programs on September 8, 1942.

Fletcher XBG-1. (*AAF*)

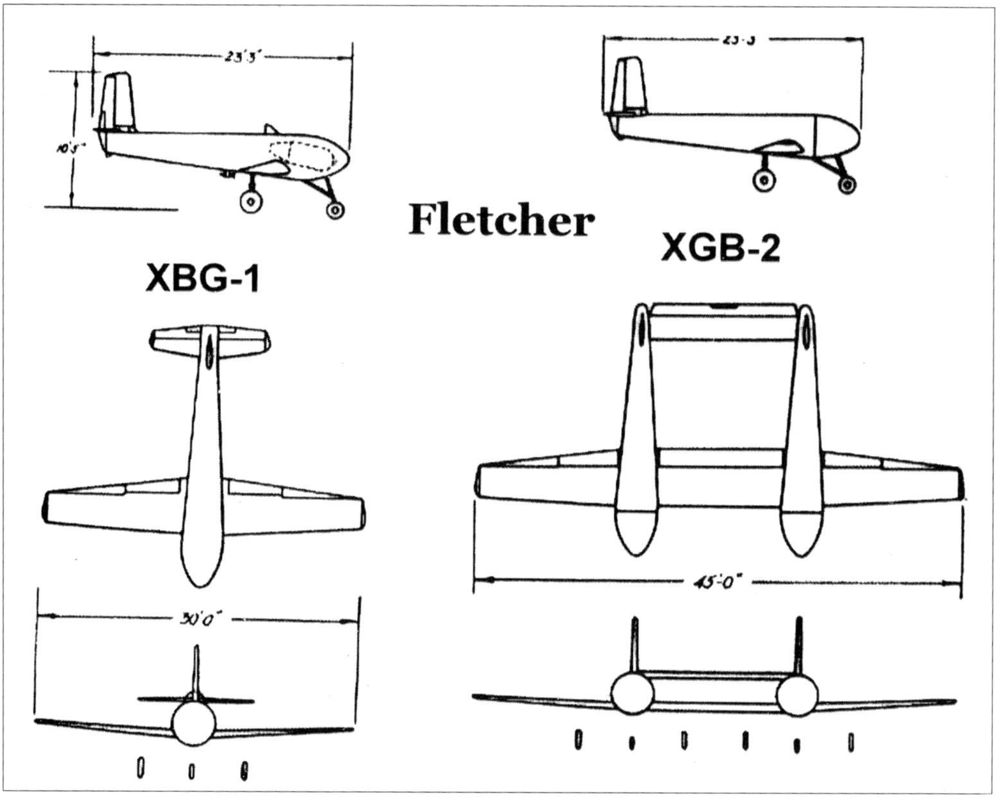

Fletcher XBG-1. (*AAF*)

Cornelius XBG-3

In 1930, George Cornelius established the Cornelius Aircraft Company at Glendale, California; during 1935, the company moved to Van Nuys, California; and in 1940, the company, renamed the Cornelius-Hoepli Company, moved to Dayton, Ohio. Over the years, George Cornelius and his company designed unconventional aircraft that featured forward-swept wings (FreWing, LW-1, Mallard, XFG-3, and XFG-1). The Cornelius Mallard, designed in 1943, had a 38-foot wings that were sharply swept forward and had no tail. Like other Cornelius designs, the sole Mallard was built by the Spartan Aircraft Company, Tulsa, Oklahoma. Concurrently, on January 28, 1943, George Cornelius submitted a proposal for an unconventional glider capable of carrying a 4,000-pound bomb. The proposal was accepted on May 8 with a recommended cost of $92,959 for a one XBG-3 (42-46911) to be delivered six months after agreement. The tailless XBG-3 was to be a 28-foot, 9-inch-long design that featured a tail-first configuration, with canard foreplanes, nose-mounted horizontal stabilizers, and a 53-foot, dramatically forward-swept wing. The leading edge of wing swept abruptly forward while the trailing edge extended into a broad V to within one foot of the tail. The necessity for a separate elevator was eliminated as the elevator surfaces were incorporated into the wing itself on the inboard side of the trailing edge. Because there was no vertical tail, the stabilizer and rudder were very

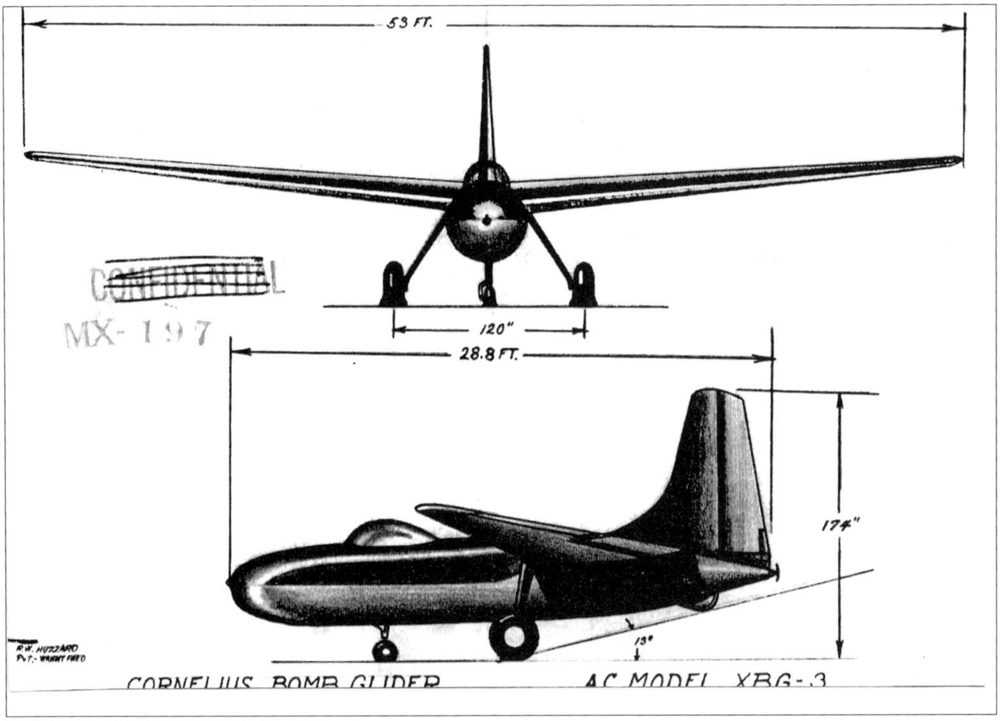

Cornelius XBG-3. (*AAF*)

large to ensure directional control and stability. The wing roots were attached well aft on the fuselage, but because of the forward sweep of the wings, the center of lift was the opposite of the center of gravity. Its tricycle landing gear would be jettisoned after tow-off. The towline attachment to the nose was a bridle to leave the proposed TV camera port exposed. However, the project was canceled in late 1942 before delivery, when the GLOMB concept was abandoned by the AAF. Since the aircraft could fly while almost 700 pounds overweight, an enlarged, tailless, forward-swept wing glider would be built by Cornelius later in the war as the XFG-1, acting as a flying fuel tank, carrying 764 gallons of fuel to transfer to long-range B-29s flying to Japan.

War-Weary Bombers and Fighters as Towed Gliders

The Air Materiel Command also investigated the possibility of stripping down worn out aircraft removing their engines and armament and using them as remotely controlled towed gliders. An onboard pilot would aid the take-off and then soon bale out while the glider was towed toward the target. Once approaching the target the war-weary/glider was released and then remotely controlled into the target by the towing aircraft. The initial test studies singled out the B-24D, less engines, fuel, and armament, which could carry a 25,000-pound payload and the C-66 (Lockheed Lodestar), less engines and fuel, which could carry 10,000 pounds. There are brief mentions of a study that was made to determine the performance characteristics of war-weary and/or obsolete P-39 fighters when towed as a glider by a P-38 or B-25.

The Demise of the AAF GLOMB Program

The original premise of the AAF GLOMB program—to save mass bomber formations from alarming losses from enemy AA and interceptors—was negated by American industry's remarkable increase in bomber production and the bombing of and continual diminution of enemy fighter and fuel production. Thus, by the time operational AAF GLOMBs would be available, there already was no reason for them.

7

Conclusions on the American Guided Missile Program: 1917–1950

During its twelve short years in power, the Nazi government encouraged scientific research with little consideration for its monetary or moral cost. Its research scientists were indulged and basic research was encouraged for the sake of science without the immediate assurance of possible practical or technological application. But had Nazi Germany advanced in technological development and manufacture as she had in fundamental research, had she waited a few more years to begin the war, or had she not made initial and costly mistakes in conducting it, the Allies could possibly have lost the war, or certainly not have won it as soon as they did. Had Germany not committed these miscalculations and had been able to develop and manufacture these possibly decisive advanced weapons in mass quantities, the prewar American military machine would have had nothing on its drawing boards to counter them. At the end of the war, new adversaries, America and Russia, both discovered how far they lagged behind the Germans in guided missile research, development, and production and made it a priority to capture German scientists and equipment to rapidly advance their postwar missile agenda.

Before 1939, only a few innovative men in American industry and military were engaging in missile design and systems research albeit with limited funds and authority. It would not be until September 1939—only weeks after Germany invaded Poland to start World War II—that the AAC received the then very sizeable Congressional allocation of $300 million to begin a program to expand its insufficient forces. But of this amount, only $3.5 million was allotted for research and development, which was then pursued with limited and undirected vigor.

America was fortunate that, at the beginning of the war, it had under development and manufacture, or at least on the drawing boards, virtually every combat aircraft that it had in operational service at the end of the war. Throughout the war, America, despite its superior resources, production capacity, and production proficiency, continued to neglect technological research with an indifference to its vast potential. During the war, Gen. Arnold's conservative theater operations staff had resisted guided weapons, mainly because from 1939 to 1945, with vast funding, conventional air weapons were supplied in enormous numbers and performed well within expectations. America was winning the air war without resorting to exotic, unproven, so-called "Buck Rogers" technological weapons that were thought to be too tenuous for operational use. These guided bombs were generally less effective than their standard gravity bomb counterparts as they needed to be delivered one 1,000-pound warhead at a time whereas a heavy bomber could deliver its full 4,000–6,000-pound payload in a single bomb run over the target. Although it was a secret project, it was well-known among 8AF theater commanders that the GB-1 glide bomb was an utter failure in its only combat use with some landing many miles from the target. The GB and VB weapon's marginal effectiveness, lack of reliability, one-at-a-time straight on delivery method exposing the mother bomber and its aircrew to greater risk to enemy AA and interceptors, justifiably caused theater commanders to be less than enthusiastic and confident in their combat use.

General Arnold's successful pragmatic scheme of translating prewar airpower theory into developing a palpable and effective Air Force is incontestable, as is his resolute quest and use for the most advanced available technology for his Air Force. However, Arnold's leadership methods also effectively delayed some of the most promising guided bombs developed during the war. Inflexible and demanding, Arnold was too inclined to undertake far too much personal responsibility and then coordinated poorly with his own staff. This lack of coordination was somewhat less of a problem regarding standard weapon systems such as conventional aircraft and bombs, which Arnold's staff and operational commanders already mostly understood. However, Maj. Gen. Barney Giles, Arnold's Chief of the Office of Commitments and Requirement (OC&R); Brig. Gen. Benjamin Chidlaw, his Chief of Materiel, Maintenance, and Distribution (MM&D); and many in the Air Material Command never really correctly understood Arnold's priorities with his guided bomb programs and were left in guided bomb limbo.

American guided weapon development was also adversely affected by the inadequate organization of and coordination between military and civilian Research & Development factions. The civilian R&D became organized relatively quickly immediate prewar period with establishment of the NDRC and the OSRD. These organizations were sanctioned to justify and prioritize various R&D programs and then allocate meager R&D funds on the most essential schemes that would probably succeed during set time limits. Meanwhile, the AAF's R&D organization remained in disorder throughout the war, particularly concerning the choice of the inept Brig. Gen. H. M. McClelland as ACO to restore order to the AAF's R&D program. McClelland was then not replaced when dismissed, causing continued AAF R&D chaos, which led to the withdrawal of the support of civilian R&D factions, particularly Dr. Vannevar Bush's OSRD. Before the withdrawal of OSRD support, Chief of Staff Gen. George Marshall had attempted to resolve the R&D issues relating to all guided-weapons development, particularly those designed by and for the AAF. During October 1944, he named Lt. Gen. Joseph McNarney, Marshall's deputy, to direct this project. However, the resulting McNarney Directive failed to resolve the R&D organizational problems because it only divided the responsibility for specific guided missiles between the Army Air and Army Ground Forces and because it gave control over a particular missile system based on the technicalities of how it was to fly rather than on how it was to be used in combat. Thus, Army Ground Forces were granted control over long-range surface-to-surface ballistic missiles (i.e. V-2s), whereas the Army Air Force was to control the much shorter-range, ground-launched cruise missiles (V-1s). The McNarney Directive also failed to address the failure of the AAF's guided-bomb R&D program, as did the previously described Joint New Weapons Committee.

By the spring of 1945, with the war against Germany coming to a close and the Pacific air campaign devastating Japanese cities, any guided weapons could not hope to compete against well-established and successful conventional bombardment weapons, which were also mostly incompatible with guided-bomb employment. Thus, the above described issues were factors in the most prolific and successful war machine in history finding itself far behind its badly defeated Nazi rival in guided weapon development.

Bibliography

Magazine and Internet Articles and Press Releases

Air Classics, *Bat Victory* (Letters to the Editor) (*Air Classics*, April 2007)
American Psychological Association, *Pigeon in a Pelican* (*American Psychologist*, January 1960)
Associated Press, *WW-II Bat Bombs Went Bust for US* (*Dispatch,* March 22, 1995)
Early Television Museum, *Early Broadcast Equipment: RCA's Television Activity During WWII* (www. early television.org)
Fahrney, D. S., *The Birth of Guided Missiles,* (*US Naval Institute Proceedings*, Vol. 106, No. 12 December 1980); *The Genesis of the Cruise Missile* (*Astronautics and Aeronautics,* January 1982); *Guided Missile: US Navy, the Pioneer* (*AAHS Journal*, spring 1982)
Gault, O., *Dive bombers: The Warplanes That Shaped Aircraft Evolution* (*Sea Classics,* July 2007)
Gemelli, G. (editor), *The Pigeon and the Predictor* (*American Foundations and Large Scale Research*, 2001)
Glines, C. V., *Top Secret World War II Bat and Bird Bomber Program* (*Aviation History*, May 2005)
Gradidge, J. M. G., *American Classics: The Culvers*, (*FlyPast,* August 1999)
Gray, E., *Operation Aphrodite's B-17 Smart Bomb* (*Aviation History*, May 1996)
Hallstead, W., *The US Navy's Kamikazes* (*Aviation History*, January 2004)
Helmick, F. F., *Our Search for Guided Missiles* (*Air Force*, October 1945)
IEEE, *Milestones: MIT Radiation Laboratory 1940-45* (www.ieeeghn.org)
Impact, *American Buzz Bomb Now Gets Launched from 50 Foot Ramp* (*Impact*, August, 1945)
Keane, J., and Carr, S., *A Brief History of Early Unmanned Aircraft* (John Hopkins APL Technical Digest, V32 N3 2013)
Lethbridge, C., *History of Rocketry World War II* (www.spaceline.org/history
Marshall, C., *Television Equipment for Guided Missiles* (*Inter Avia*, January 1947)
Mets, D., *The Quest for a Surgical Strike: The Air Force and the Laser-guided Bombs* (*Air and Space Case Study*, 1987)
Mormillo, F., Defenseless Warrior: Culver's PQ-14 Drone (www.airenthusiast.com)
Naval Aviation News, *Pilotless Aircraft* (*Naval Aviation News*, January 1946)
Norton, B., *Sideshow Curiosities: American Military Glider Experiments of World War II* (AAHS, Summer 2008)
Pearson, L., *Developing the Flying Bomb* (*Naval Aviation News*, May 1968)
Spark, N., *Classified: The Secret Weapons of World War II*, (*Wings*, October, 2004); *Secret Arsenal: Advanced American Weapons of WWII*, (*Wings*, December 2004)
Victor Amateur Radio Association, *Military Television Equipment Built by RCA: 1940-1945* (www.qsi.net)

Vintage Wings of Canada, *Mother of All Drones*, (www.vintage wings.ca)
Wainwright, M., *Mr. Stout's Torpedo-Bomber*, (*Air Classics* November, 2008)
Wells, W., *Top Secret Mission: Project Anvil* (*Kings Cliffe Remembered*, January, 1984)
Werrell, K., *The Forgotten Missile: The Kettering-General Motors A-1* (*AAHS Journal*, Spring 1985)
Wolf, W., *American Glide Bomb of WW-2: The GB Series* (unpublished article); *Glider Borne Pattern Torpedo (GT-1)* (unpublished article); *V for Vengeance* (*Airpower*, March, 1978)
Impact, *Around the World with the Rocketeers* (*Impact*, October 1944)
Kopp, C., *The Dawn of the Smart Bomb* (*Airpower Australia* July 2006)
Impact, *US Buzz Bombs* (*Impact*, January 1945)
Fuller, C., *Rockets and Aircraft* (*Flying*, February 1945)
Impact, *AZON* (*Impact*, March 1945)
Neufeld, J., *Development of Ballistic Missiles in the USAF 1945-60* (Office of History, Wash, DC, 1990)
Baumann, P., *Lethal Sky Rockets*, (*Air Force*, November 1945)
Air Force, Guided Missiles, (*Air Force*, March-April, 1946)
Peck, J., *Man-Made Meteors* (*Air Force*, July 1946)
Army Ordnance, *Homing Missiles*, (*Army Ordnance*, May-June 1947)
FlyPast, *The Flying Bombs of Rabaul* (*FlyPast*, September 1982)
Carter, H., *You want Me to Fly What?* (*Air Classics*, March 2017)
Knight, C., *Dress Rehearsal for Drones* (*Air Force*, March/April 1946)

Books

Abramson, A., *History of Television, 1942-2000* (McFarland & Co, NC, 2003)
Banks, H., *379th Bombardment Group (H) Anthology, Volume 1* (Turner, KY, 2000)
Bowman, M., *The B-24 Liberator: 1939-1945* (Wensum, UK, 1979)
Baxter, J., *Scientists Against Time* (MIT Press, MA, 1946)
Botzum, R., *50 Years of Target Drone Aircraft* (Hawthorne, CA, Northrop, 1985)
Bowen, E. G., *Radar Days* (Institute of Physic, NY, 1987)
Boyce, J., *New Weapons for Air Warfare* (Little Brown, Boston. 1947)
Burckhardt, J., *QED: MIT in World War II* (John Wiley, NY, 1966)
Carpenter, D. M., and D'Alessandro, P. V., *Thunder Bug: WWII Flying Wing Bomb* (Jet Pioneers, MA, n.d.)
Christman, A., *Sailors, Scientists, and Rockets* (Naval History Division, Wash, DC, 1971)
Couffer, J., *Bat Bomb: World War IIs Other Secret Weapon* (U. of Texas, TX, 1992)
Craven, W., and Cate, J., *Army Air Forces in World War II: Men and Planes, Volume VI* (University of Chicago, IL, 1955)
Fahrney, D. S., *History of Radio-controlled Aircraft and Guided Missiles*, (Naval History Division, Wash., D.C., 1950)
Freeman, R., *Mighty Eighth* (Janes, UK, 1978); *Mighty Eighth War Diary* (Janes, UK, 1981)
Friedman, N., *US Naval Weapons: Every Gun, Missile, Mine, and Torpedo Used by the US Navy: 1883 to Present* (Naval Institute Press, MD, 1983)
Gerrard-Gough, J. D., and Christman, A., *Grand Experiment at Inyokern Vol. 2* (Naval History Division, Wash. DC, 1978)
Gunston, B., *The Illustrated Encyclopedia of the World's Rockets and Missiles* (Salamander, London, 1979)
Hall, J., *American Kamikaze* (Pvt. Printing, 1984, FL)
Hanle, D., *Near Miss: The Army Air Force's Guided Bomb Program in World War II* (Scarecrow, MD, 2007)
Howeth, L. S., *History of Electronics-Communications in the United States Navy* (Bureau of Ships and Naval History, Washington, DC, 1963)
Kay, A., *Buzz Bomb: Close Up* (Monogram, MA, 1977)

Lloyd, A., *B-17 Flying Fortress in Scale & Detail, Part 1* (Aero, PA, 1985); *B-17 Flying Fortress in Scale & Detail, Part 2* (Aero, PA, 1986)
Lopez, D., *Into the Teeth of the Tiger* (Bantam, NY, 1986)
O'Callaghan, T., *Ford in the Service of America* (McFarland, NC, 2009)
Neufeld, J., *Development of Ballistic Missiles in the USAF: 1945-60* (Office of History, Wash. DC, 1990)
Newcome, L., *Unmanned Aviation: A Brief History of Unmanned Aerial Vehicles* (American Institute of Aeronautics and Astronautics, Inc., Reston, VA 2004)
Norton, B., *American Military Glider of World War II*, Schiffer, PA, 2012
Ross, F., *Guided Missiles: Rockets, & Torpedoes* (Lothrop, N, 1951)
Rowland, B., and Boyd, W., *US Navy Bureau of Ordnance in World War II* (BuOrd, Wash, DC, 1948)
Schmitt, V., *Controlled Bombs and Missiles of the World War II and Cold War Eras* (SAE, PA, 2002)
Shachtman, T., *Terrors and Marvel* (Morrow, NY, 2002)
Shurcliff, W. A., *Bombs At Bikini,* The Official Report of Operation Crossroads, (W.H. Wise, NY, 1947)
Theismeyer, L., and Burch, J., *Combat Scientists* (Little Brown, Boston, 1947)
Trimble, W., *Wings for the Navy* (Naval Institute Press, MD, 1990)
von Karman, T., and Edson, L., *Wind and Beyond: Theodore von Karman* (Little, Brown, Boston, 1967)
Werrell, K., *The Evolution of the Cruise Missile,* (Air University Press, AL, 1985)
Wolf, W., *German Guided Missiles: Henschel Hs 293 and Ruhrstahl SD 1400X Fritz* (Merriam, VT, 1999); *North American B-25 Mitchell: The Ultimate Look from Drawing Board to Flying Arsenal* (Schiffer, PA, 2008); *Rockets and Guided Missiles of World War II* (Unpublished Manuscript)
Young, R., *The Flying Bomb,* (Ky Books, NY, 1977)
Aviation Unit, *Naval Aviation News,* March-April, 2003.

Technical Manuals and Reports

38th Tactical Missile Wing, *Early History and Evolution of Cruise Missiles, JB-2 Loon Development and Testing* (38th Tactical Missile Wing n.d.)
388th Bomb Group, *388th Bomb Group: Fortress for Freedom* (Newsfoto, TX, 1946)
397th Bombardment Group (M) Headquarters Detachment, Historical Report, (from 20 April 1943 to 5 May 1945)
458 Bomb Group History, *753rd Bombardment Squadron History: June-July-August 1944* (Private printing, n.d.)
Air Materiel Command, *Case History of Controlled Guided Missiles: Vertical Bombs* (Assistant Chief of Air Staff, AMC, February 1945)
Air Materiel Command, *Case History of Controlled Guided Missiles: Aircraft* (Assistant Chief of Air Staff, AMC, February 1945)
Air Materiel Command, *Case History of Controlled Missiles* (National Archives, MD, ATSC, Historical Office, OH, 1945)
Air Materiel Command, *Development of Guided Missiles, Case Histories, 1941-1946* (Historical Division Intelligence, AMC, June 1946)
Air Materiel Command, *Graphic Survey Remote Control and Television Equipment* (AMC 1 April 1946)
Anthony, Alistair; Walker, Norman; *Accuracy of the AZON Guided Bomb as Affected by Battle Conditions in World War II* (US Army Human Engineering Laboratories, MD, May 1964)
Figley, R., *XLNT-1 GLOMBs, Expendable Tests,* (Memo Report, No.1-44, 26 February 1944)
Gordon, G., *A Case Study of AZON: An Azimuth Guided Bomb* (Air University, AL, July 1989)

HQ of the Commander, Aircraft, Northern Solomons, *Report on the Operations of STAG-1 in the Northern Solomons Area, 30 October 1944*, Gen. Claude Larkin.

Malina, F. J., *Essays on the History of Rocketry and Astronautics* (NASA, 1977)

NACA, *Wartime Report: Tests of the 1/17th Scale Model XBDR-1* (Langley Laboratory, VA, February 1944)

NDRC, *Glide Bomb: Guided Missiles and Techniques, Summary Report* (Division 5: NDRC, Wash. DC 1944)

NDRC, *Radio Control Systems: Guided Missiles and Techniques, Summary Report* (Division 5: NDRC, Wash. DC 1944)

NDRC, *Television: Guided Missiles and Techniques, Summary Report* (Division 5: NDRC, Wash. DC 1944)

Northrop Aircraft, *Model Specification & Model Description: JB-1 (Report N8-16)*, (Northrop Aircraft, CA, 6 July 1944)

Patent Office, Carlos B. Mirick, *Electrical Distance-Control System, Patent # 1,597,416*, August 24, 1926.

RCA Victor Division, *RCA's Contribution to the War Effort through Television: 1937-1946* (Confidential Report: Radio Corporation of America, 1947)

STAG-1, *War Diary: 5 June 1944 to 30 October 1944, Aircraft South Pacific Force*, 30 October 1944.

USAAF Proving Ground Command, Eglin Field, FL, to Gen. George Kenney, CG 5th Air Force, 13 October 1943, *Final Report Glider Borne Pattern Torpedo.*

USAAF, *12,000 Lb. High Angle RAZON Controlled Bomb (Tallboy)*, Maxwell AFB, MF Reel A2051.

USAAF, *AAF Missile Documents*, Maxwell AFB, MF Reel A2050.

USAAF, *Case History of Castor*, Maxwell AFB, MF Reel A2082, A2083, and A2051.

USAAF, *Case History of the GB-1*, Maxwell AFB, MF Reel A2082, A2083, and A2051.

USAAF, *Case History of the GMA-1*, Maxwell AFB, MF Reel A2082, A2083, and A2051.

USAAF, *Case History of Vertical Bombs: AZON, SPAZON, RAZON, Felix, ROC*, Maxwell AFB, MF Reel A2082, A2083, and A2051.

USAAF, *Erection & Maintenance Instructions for the PQ-8 and TDC-2 Airplanes* (AN 09-FB-2, 20 October 1943)

USAAF, *Guided Missile Policy Documents*, Maxwell AFB, MF Reel A2050.

USAAF, *JB-1 through JB-10 Series*, Maxwell AFB, MF Reel A2051.

USAAF, *Navy and Ordnance Guided Missile Projects*, Maxwell AFB, MF Reel A2050.

USAAF, *Operating and Flight Instructions for the Model PQ-8 Target Airplane* (Chief of the AAC 3 March 1942)

USAAF, *Pilot's Flight Operating Instructions for YPQ-14A, PQ-14A, YPQ-14B, PQ-14B Airplane Targets*, (AN 09-5FC-1, 20 May 1944)

USAAF, *Power-Driven Weapons Developed by the Special Weapons Branch Equipment Laboratory*, Maxwell AFB, MF Reel A2051.

USAAF, *Report: Operations of STAG-1 Detachment in Northern Solomons Area*, Commander of Air Forces in the Northern Solomons, Brig.-Gen. Claude Larkin to Adml Halsey, 30 October 1944.

USAAF, *SWOD-7 Bat*, Maxwell AFB, MF Reel A2051.

USAF, *Bombs for Aircraft*, TM9-1980. Wash., D.C., 1950.

USN, *Aircraft Bombs, Fuses, and Associated Components*, Bureau of Naval Weapons, Wash, DC, 1 August 1960.

War Department, *History of Launchers and Rockets*, Bureau of Public Relations, Press Release, n.d.

War Department, OSRD, *US Rocket Ordnance Development and Use in World War II*, n.d.

War Department, *Rockets, Launchers, and Propellants*, Bureau of Public Relations, Press Release, 24 September 1944.

XXI Bomber Command, *Combat Crew Manual*, May 1945.

Index